From Harappa to Hastinapura

A Study of the Earliest South Asian City and Civilization

AMERICAN SCHOOL OF PREHISTORIC RESEARCH MONOGRAPH SERIES

Series Editors

C. C. LAMBERG-KARLOVSKY, Harvard University
DAVID PILBEAM, Harvard University
OFER BAR-YOSEF, Harvard University

Editorial Board

STEVEN L. KUHN, University of Arizona, Tucson
DANIEL E. LIEBERMAN, Harvard University
RICHARD H. MEADOW, Harvard University
MARY M. VOIGT, The College of William and Mary
HENRY T. WRIGHT, University of Michigan, Ann Arbor

Publications Coordinator

WREN FOURNIER, Harvard University

The American School of Prehistoric Research (ASPR) Monographs in Archaeology and Paleoanthropology present a series of documents covering a variety of subjects in the archaeology of the Old World (Eurasia, Africa, Australia, and Oceania). This series encompasses a broad range of subjects—from the early prehistory to the Neolithic Revolution in the Old World, and beyond including: hunter-gatherers to complex societies; the rise of agriculture; the emergence of urban societies; human physical morphology, evolution and adaptation, as well as; various technologies such as metallurgy, pottery production, tool making, and shelter construction. Additionally, the subjects of symbolism, religion, and art will be presented within the context of archaeological studies including mortuary practices and rock art. Volumes may be authored by one investigator, a team of investigators, or may be an edited collection of shorter articles by a number of different specialists working on related topics.

From Harappa to Hastinapura

A Study of the Earliest South Asian City and Civilization

Piotr Andreevich Eltsov

TUTA SUB AEGIDE PALLAS · 1683 ·

BRILL

BOSTON • LEIDEN
2008

Cover and interior image of two-sided terracotta molded "tablet" or "token" from Harappa Mound ET by Richard Meadow, Harvard University. Image used by permission and copyright reserved by the Harappa Archaeological Research Project.

Figure 4.13, artist's reconstruction of the southern gateway at Harappa, mound ET. Drawing by Chris Sloan, courtesy of J. M. Kenoyer, HARP. Image used by permission and copyright reserved by the Harappa Archaeological Research Project (HARP).

Library of Congress Cataloging-in-Publication Data

Eltsov, Piotr Andreevich, 1970–

From Harappa to Hastinapura : a study of the earliest South Asian city and civilization / Piotr Andreevich Eltsov.
p. cm. -- (American School of Prehistoric Research monograph series)
Includes bibliographical references and index.
ISBN 978-90-04-16060-6

1. South Asia--Civilization. 2. Extinct cities--South Asia. 3. South Asia--Antiquities. 4. Sanskrit literature--History and criticism. 5. Pali literature--History and criticism. 6. South Asia--Historiography. I. Title. II. Series.

DS339.E58 2008
934--dc22

2007018450

ISSN 1543-0529
ISBN 978-90-04-16060-6

Koninklijke Brill NV incorporates the imprints Brill, Hotei Publishing, IDC Publishers, Martinus Nijhoff Publishers and VSP.

PRINTED IN THE UNITED STATES OF AMERICA

In memory of my parents, Andrey Vassilievich Eltsov and Irina Nestorovna Surina

Civilization is a thing of a mind; an inquiry into the nature of civilization, then, is to ask what persons have used the word "civilization" and what they have meant by it.

—R. G. Collingwood, 1942
The New Leviathan; or, Man, Society, Civilization, and Barbarism, p. 280
The Clarendon Press, Oxford

Contents

Figure List xi
Table List xiii
Abbreviation List xv
Foreword xvii
Preface xxv
Acknowledgments xxix

1 From Historical Agents to Structure: A New Method for the Study of Ancient South Asia 1
Between Archaeology, Anthropology, and History 2
Subjective Humanism 4
The Historicity of Ancient Indian Literature 7
The Ideas of the City and Civilization in the Study of Ancient South Asia 10
Conclusion: Three Groups of Data 15

2 The Chimera of the City: From Saint Augustine to Doxiades and to Ancient Indian Literature 17
Torn Between the Two Cities 17
The Idea of the City in Ancient Indian Literature 22
Conclusion: From Texts to Material Culture 29

3 The Idea of the City in the Ganges Civilization 31
Ahicchatra 33
Atranjikhera 35
Bhita 38
Hastinapura 43
Kausambi 47
Mathura 57
Pataliputra 60
Rajghat 62
Rajgir 68
Sonkh 73
Sonpur 75
Sravasti / Saheth-Maheth 77
Vaisali 81
Conclusion: The Idea of the Gangetic City 87

4 **The Idea of the City in the Harappan/ Indus Civilization** 95
Allahdino 96
Banawali 98
Chanhu-Daro 101
Dholavira 106
Harappa 111
Kalibangan 117
Kot Diji 121
Lothal 123
Mohenjo-Daro 128
Nausharo 132
Surkotada 136
Sutkagen-Dor 140
Conclusion: The Idea of the Harappan City 144

5 **The Idea of Civilization: From Voltaire to Braudel and to the Sanskrit Puranas** 153
The Idea of Civilization in Theory 153
World History in the Yuga Story 156
The Yuga Story and the Idea of Civilization 160
Conclusion: From the Paurāṇicas to V. Gordon Childe 164

6 **The Idea of the Ancient Indian Civilization: A Framework of Enquiry** 167
Agricultural Economy and Rural Lifestyle 168
Orality and Mnemonic Devices 170
Social Organization 173
Religious Practices 177
Conclusion: The Ideas of Civilization and the City in Ancient South Asia 180

Postscript: On Theory and Politics 183
Endnotes 187
Critical Editions of the Quoted Sanskrit and Pāli Texts 197
References 199
Index 239

Figure List

1.1 Archaeology and texts in ancient South Asia: Directionality of a conjunctive analysis 6
1.2 Archaeology and texts in ancient South Asia: Chronological correlations 6
1.3 Ancient texts as historical sources 8

3.1 Contour plan of Ahicchatra 32
3.2 Rampart of Ahicchatra 33
3.3 Contour plan of Atranjikhera 36
3.4 Atranjikhera: The main mound 37
3.5 Bhita 39
3.6 Bhita: Plan of main excavations 40
3.7 Bhita today: Remains of John Marshall's trench 41
3.8 Contour plan of Hastinapura 43
3.9 Cultural sequence of Hastinapura 44
3.10 Hastinapura: Trench HST 1 45
3.11 Hastinapura today: Remains of the main trench 46
3.12 Sketch plan of Kausambi 48
3.13 Kausambi today: Rampart and bastion 48
3.14 Kausambi: Section across the guardrooms of EF 49
3.15 Cultural sequence of Kausambi 50
3.16 Kausambi: Section across defenses 51
3.17 Kausambi: Plan of defenses 52
3.18 One of the minor ramparts of Kausambi today 53
3.19 Kausambi: Ghoshitarama Monastery 55
3.20 Mathura 58
3.21 Pataliputra 61
3.22 Pataliputra: Kumrahar 63
3.23 Pillared hall at Kumrahar, Pataliputra 64
3.24 Contour plan of Rajghat 65
3.25 Rajghat: Trench RGT II 67
3.26 Rajghat: Section of Trench RGT II 68
3.27 Rajgir/Rajagriha 70
3.28 Fortifications of Rajgir 71
3.29 Rajgir today: Remains of outer fortifications 72
3.30 Sonkh 74
3.31 Sonkh: Level 27 76
3.32 Sonpur: Period III 78
3.33 Sravasti 79
3.34 Sravasti today: Rampart with a gap 80
3.35 Sketch plan of Vaisali 82
3.36 Mound of Raja-Visala-ka-Garh 84
3.37 Mound of Raja-Visala-ka-Garh 85

3.38 Mound of Raja-Visala-ka-Garh at Vaisali today 86
3.39 Fortifications of the Ganges civilization: Approximate dates of construction 92
3.40 Authorities in the Ganges civilization: Approximate time of emergence 92

4.1 Allahdino 97
4.2 Banawali 99
4.3 Chanhu-Daro: Contour plan 102
4.4 Chanhu-Daro: Mounds II and III 103
4.5 Chanhu-Daro: Mound II, Harappa II level 104
4.6 Dholavira 105
4.7 Dholavira: North gate of the castle 107
4.8 Dholavira: Section across southern defenses of the castle 108
4.9 Dholavira: East gate of the castle 109
4.10 Plan of Harappa 112
4.11 Harappa: Mound AB, section across the defenses 113
4.12 Harappa: Sections of defenses 114
4.13 Artist's reconstruction of the southern gateway at Harappa, Mound ET 116
4.14 Kalibangan: Period II 118
4.15 Kalibangan: Period I 119
4.16 Kot Diji: Contour plan 120
4.17 Kot Diji: Excavated areas 120
4.18 Lothal 125
4.19 Lothal Acropolis 126
4.20 Mohenjo-Daro 129
4.21 Mohenjo-Daro: Remains of the eastern retaining wall of the Stupa Mound 131
4.22 Nausharo 134
4.23 Nausharo: Dividing wall and the circular structure 135
4.24 Surkotada: Contour plan 137
4.25 Surkotada: Cultural sequence 137
4.26 Fort of Surkotada 138
4.27 Sutkagen-Dor: Plans of excavations 141
4.28 Sutkagen-Dor: Sections 142–143
4.29 Fortifications of the Harappan civilization: Approximate dates of construction 151
4.30 Authorities in the Harappan civilization: Approximate time of emergence 151

Table List

2.1 What is the City? 21
2.2 Definition of the city in the *Anguttara-Nikāya* 24
2.3 City of Righteousness in the *Milindapañha* 25
2.4 Traits of the city from the selected Sanskrit and Pāli texts 28

3.1 Ahicchatra: Periodization 34
3.2 Ahicchatra: Periodization 34
3.3 Atranjikhera: Periodization 37
3.4 Atranjikhera: Phases of period IV and sub-phases of the rampart 37
3.5 Atranjikhera: Weapons 37
3.6 Bhita: Cultural sequence of buildings 12–13 41
3.7 Hastinapura: Periodization 44
3.8 Kausambi: Periodization 50
3.9 Mathura: Periodization 59
3.10 Kumrahar, Pataliputra: Periodization 61
3.11 Pataliputra: Periodization 61
3.12 Rajghat: Periodization 66
3.13 Rajgir: Periodization 69
3.14 Rajgir: Periodization 69
3.15 Sonkh: Periodization 73
3.16 Sonpur: Periodization 75
3.17 Sravasti: Periodization 77
3.18 Sravasti: Periodization 77
3.19 Vaisali: Periodization 83
3.20 Vaisali: Periodization 83

4.1 Banawali: Periodization 98
4.2 Chanhu-Daro: Periodizations 100
4.3 Dholavira: Periodization 106
4.4 Dholavira: Fortification system 110
4.5 Harappa: Periodization 111
4.6 Major cultural transformations at Kot-Diji 123
4.7 Alternative periodization of Kot-Diji 123
4.8 Periodization of Lothal 124
4.9 Nausharo: Periodization 135

5.1 Sociocultural traits of the Yugas and transitional periods 161
5.2 Two models of a complex society based on the Yuga story 164

6.1 Ancient Indian city and civilization 181

Abbreviation List

AN	*Aṅguttara-Nikāya*
ARASI	*Annual Review of the Archaeological Survey of India*
ASI	Archaeological Survey of India
BaP	*BrahmāṇḍaPurāṇa*
BRW	Black and Red Ware
BSW	Black Slipped Ware
HARP	Harappa Archaeological Project
IAR	*Indian Archaeology: A Review*
KA	*Kauṭilīya Arthaśāstra*
LM	*Lalitāmāhātmya of the Brahmāṇḍa Purāṇa*
MASI	*Memoirs of the Archaeological Survey of India*
MBH	*Mahābhārata*
MiP	*Milindapañha*
MP	*MatsyaPurāṇa*
NBPW	Northern Black Polished Ware
PBW	Polished Black Ware
PGW	Painted Grey Ware
RV	*Ṛgveda*
RM	*Vālmīki Rāmāyaṇa*
SP	Structural Period
VP	*VāyuPurāṇa*

Foreword

A Different Path: Piotr Eltsov's Journey "From Harappa to Hastinapura'"

In recent years a reconsideration, a redefinition, even a challenge to the historical reality of the neo-evolutionary paradigm, from band to tribe and state, has been unfolding. The nineteenth century version was best articulated by E. B. Tyler (1881) who argued for a series of cultural stages characterized by "Savagery–Barbarism" and "Civilization". "Savagery" and "barbarism" were terms comfortably used in the first half of the twentieth century. V. G. Childe assigned particular archaeological cultures to these evolutionary stages in his classic *Man Makes Himself* (1936). In the first half of the twentieth century cultural anthropologists studied the ethnographic presence of "savages" and "barbarians", and, following E. B. Tyler, referred to theses cultures as "survivals", living fossils that had not evolved to a higher stage of evolutionary development. The mid-twentieth century experienced an increasing critique of colonial, racist, and imperialist attitudes, and an intellectual fashion of revived Marxist thinking. In such an intellectual climate such terms as savagery and barbarism, to characterize living ethnographic polities, became unacceptable. The writings of Morton Fried (1967), Elman Service (1974) and Marshall Sahlins and Elman Service (1960) offered us a new vocabulary while insisting on the survival of evolutionary stages. The tripartite stages of savagery, barbarism and civilization, were morphed into the more acceptable terminology of "bands", "tribes" and "states". The theoretical arguments of the above authors (and others) are well reviewed by Norman Yoffee (2005).

In our own day some continue to support the utility of neo-evolutionary stages (Flannery 1999; Earle 1991); others simply avoid massaging their evidence to fit the neo-evolutionary paradigm (Adams 1966; Kemp 1989; Renfrew 1973; Chang 1986), while an increasing number fail to find it applicable to the evidence (Yoffee 2005; Trigger 2003; Wengrow 2006).

In this book Piotr Eltsov offers an original perspective on the emergence and nature of social complexity in both the Indus (Harappan) and Gangetic civilizations. His approach is comparative and informed by the ancient Sanskrit texts, that explicitly discuss the manner by which cultural complexity emerged in South Asia, as well as the material evidence recovered by archaeologists.

Eltsov's approach abjures the neo-evolutionary model of bands-tribes and states preferring an "emic" approach, one that attempts to understand how the indigenous cultures perceived the emergence of their own cultural complexity. He neither debates nor confronts the issue as to whether the Harappan was a Chiefdom, a State, or an Empire; a subject of debate with a considerable literature (Fairservis 1989; Kenoyer 1998).

Eltsov uses textual evidence, derived from ancient Indian literature, to contextualize the written word with the evidence derived from the archaeology of the Harappan and later Gangetic Civilizations. His comparative approach, wedding these distinctive lines of evidence, is original, informative, and controversial. One is left with a richer understanding of the complexity, similarities, and differences within both civilizations. The texts indicate aspects of ideological significance that confound informed archaeological wisdom, i.e., the paramount significance of villages rather than the conventional emphasis placed on cities.

Within the past few decades methodological concerns within archaeology emphasized settlement pattern hierarchies and wed them to theories concerning the origin of the state. Settlement patterns and state origins are seen as inextricably interwoven. The application of the former, settlement patterns, are used to identify the presence of the later, the state. Thus, the discovery of a settlement hierarchy of three or four levels, that is villages, towns, and cities of increasing size, is said to signify the emergence of the state. Such a simple correlation has been used to exemplify the origins of the state in Mesopotamia (Wright 1977, 1984; Wright and Johnson 1974), Mesoamerica (Culbert and Rice 1990), the Indus Valley (Mughal 1997), Egypt (Church and Bell 1988) and China (Chang 2000). A model, inspired by a modern perspective, whereby a settlement distribution of cities, towns and villages, representing an urban process as well as a political hierarchy, and suggests the presence of a state, is adopting an "etic" approach. This approach adopts a model derived from our world and imposes it upon a set of data derived from the past. In this instance a 3–4 settlement pattern hierarchy, if detected in archaeological survey, is said to represent a state level of political organization.

Addressing the origin of the state on the basis of a hierarchy of settlement, or on the assumed functions of a particular suite of artifacts, however, tells us absolutely nothing about the nature of that state. What form and structure did the assumed state take? Was it presided over by kings? Were they benignly autocratic or tyrannical? What other institutional forms existed within the State? How was the bureaucracy articulated and by what means was justice adjudicated? Was the state a secular institution or presided over by a divine king? These are but a few significant questions that simply cannot be informed by settlement pattern analysis. Fundamental problems such as the chronology of a given site, the size of the sites at different periods of time, and demographic questions can be addressed only in the most general terms by settlement survey. If a similar settlement pattern in China and Mesopotamia signify the presence of a State does that tell us anything of the nature of that State? Certainly not! Settlement hierarchies assume that smaller communities are politically subordinate to larger settlements. This is not true today and need not be in the past. New York City is larger than Albany and Washington, D.C. respectively capitals of a State and a Nation. Pella, the Macedonian capital of Alexander's empire was small even by the measure of classical Greek cities.

Settlement hierarchies are said to mirror political hierarchies. Thus, the city dominates the town, the town the village, etc. In this manner settlement pattern studies stand as proxy evidence for political systems and the origin of the state. Such evidence, however, tells us little of the specific social, economic or political structure of the settlements. Settlement surveys may indeed suggest, through the presence of particular artifact types, the *presence* of bureaucratic administration and/or decision making processes but they tell us very little of the manner in which that bureaucracy functioned. In discussing the issue of the origin of the state, so inextricably interwoven with settlement pattern analysis, it is worth reviewing the Mesopotamian narrative and comparing it to Eltsov's approach.

The archaeologist who pioneered settlement pattern analyses in the Near East is Robert McC. Adams (1981).[1] His surveys in southern Mesopotamia had as their principal focus a concern "with certain major features of the infrastructure of Mesopotamian civilization, principally its patterns of agricultural land use and the hierarchical array of communities in which people lived"

(Adams 1981:xvii). Adams focuses upon regularities of spatial patterning, shifting demographic patterns, ecological constraints and opportunities, all within an initial context of urban origins and a subsequent concern for shifts in settlement regime. Adams admits that "While this is in no sense a theoretical treatise...." (1981:76). He is one of the few scholars to directly confront, and take issue with the two architects who have linked settlement pattern analysis with state origins in Mesopotamia: Henry Wright and Gregory Johnson.

Henry Wright (1977:383), strongly influenced by Elman Service's (1974) *The Origins of the State and Civilization*, suggests that "...a state can be recognized as a cultural development with a centralized decision making process which is both externally specialized with regard to the local processes which it regulates, and internally specialized in that the central process is divisible into separate activities which can be performed in different places at different times". In this regard he follows Elman Service who focuses upon government, bureaucracy, and a hierarchy of offices; in sum, the focus is upon politics: "This political power organized the economy...." (Service 1974:xiii). While Adams (1981) attempts to document the processes involved in urban origins Wright eschews any concern for urbanism as it relates to his notions of state formation. Wright (1977:383) states forthrightly that "Indeed, the specialized production activities, in essence "urbanism" is merely (*sic*) an expected extension of the specialization of the strategy of central decision-making to local processes". Adams (1981:76) points out that it is not only the urban process that Wright deprecates but also class stratification, intensification of production, and militarism, as fundamental properties of the state as related to its emergence. Wright presents us with a rigidly unilinear scheme, in which "there is no reason why the period of state origin in any particular historical sequence cannot be specified" and differentiated from a chieftainship (Wright 1977:385).

The stress upon information processing and decision-making hierarchies, in short administrative bureaucracies, was the principle concern of Henry Wright and his student Gregory Johnson, in theorizing on the origins of the Mesopotamian state. In Mesopotamia the information processing metaphor, that is identifying specific artifacts believed to have an administrative function (seals, sealings, writing, standard units of measure, as indicated by specific ceramic types) within the context of a three or four tiered settlement hierarchy, became synonymous with identifying the presence of the state. Johnson's (1973:2) definition of the state did not differ from that of Wright. He defines the state as a "differentiated and internally specialized decision making organization which is structured in minimally three hierarchical levels." In this view the complexity of what we think of as "politics" becomes entirely subordinated to the routinization of administration, which together with settlement hierarchy define the state.

The theoretical notions on the origins of the state, as presented by Wright and Johnson, continue to have influence far beyond the borders of Mesopotamia. Almost 25 years have passed since they advanced their "model". Adams (1981:77) pointed out almost twenty years ago, but few were attentive, that Wright and Johnson's approach fails to comprehend the complexity of state origins in Mesopotamia:

> Nothing we know of the historic records of any society (wherever there are such records) however would allow even the full battery of administrative routines (assuming optimistically that they could ever be known archaeologically!) to stand as surrogate for its political system as a whole.
>
> The routines constitute not only a gross oversimplification of politics but also provide a misleading picture—one lacking in the pervasive but volatile and usually unexpressed elements of contingency, calculation, and coercion. Similarly missing from the analysis, in the face of overwhelming evidence not only of its importance as a historic force elsewhere but of incontrovertible archaeological evidence that it was the predominant preoccupation precisely in the Uruk period, is any concession of a special role for religion and religious institutions.

Adams concludes that Wright's definition of Uruk society as a state society [and its theoretical framework for state origins] "is theoretically too narrow to serve as a conceptual framework". Recent archaeological research has cast even a greater shadow upon the information-processing metaphor for state origins. The presence of seals and sealings, so integral to the presence of an administrative bureaucracy and the origin of the Mesopotamian state ca. 3500 B.C., have been recently recovered within individual household contexts from widely distinctive geographical and cultural regions as early as 6000 B.C. (Oates 1996; Lamberg-Karlovsky 1999).

None of the above approaches attract Eltsov's attention in examining the emergence of cultural complexity in the Harappan and Gangetic civilizations. Eltsov looks to both the material remains of the archaeological record and the ancient Sanskrit texts that discuss the evolution and nature of Gangetic society. The narrative content of the Sanskrit texts offer him the opportunity to relate them to the known archaeological record. His use of the direct historical approach (Lyman and O'Brien 2001) allows him to test this narrative against the archaeological record of the earlier Indus Civilization. It is to be noted that the Sanskrit texts differ from those recovered in Mesopotamia where there is little discussion as to the nature of the city and its social organization (but see Steinkeller 2006). Eltsov, on the other hand, is able, through a review of the rich Sanskrit literature, to inform the reader of the various attributes that defined the city and to reveal important elements of its social organization as revealed in the texts.

Piotr Eltsov began his study of Sanskrit in the Department of Oriental Studies at Leningrad University (present-day St. Petersburg University, St. Petersburg, Russia). His Sanskrit studies continued at the University of California, Berkeley, where he earned his M.A. His graduate studies were completed at Harvard University where Sanskrit studies were complimented by the study of archaeology in the Department of Anthropology. Over the course of his studies he participated in Pakistan in the excavations at Harappa, and at Panj Piye, Baluchistan, and undertook an archaeological survey in the region of Derai Ismail Khan. In India he made an extensive tour and study of the major sites and museums of the Gangetic Civilization. Eltsov's study, as presented in this volume, is a return to the grand tradition of historical narrative. His approach is in complete agreement with that of R. G. Collingwood (1946) who found that "history is different from what is ordinarily called science" and that "all history is the history of thought", thought being human agency and ideology (for the philosophy of R. G. Collingwood, see Mink 1969). While Eltsov does not abjure models, structures, or materialist causes he is explicit that "human agency is the driving force within history". His study of the Sanskrit texts informs him of what the authors of those texts considered important. This, in turn, leads him to the conclusion that ideology is of paramount significance in contouring what Robert Redfield (1977) called a "Great Tradition". To Eltsov "ideas and thoughts of historical agents" are of paramount importance and their signatures can be detected in the archaeological record. Thus, to Eltsov ancient texts become sources of ideas not merely of facts. This approach leads to some stunningly different and highly significant observations, ones that Eltsov is always cautious to indicate remain plausible hypotheses rather than concrete conclusions. Some of these include his belief, supported by the texts, that in South Asia city and village life remained undifferentiated. Thus, the Puranic model is utterly different from the western model in which cities and villages are hierarchically distinguished, and, as indicated above, implicated in State origins. In the Puranic model it is the village, not the city that offers the foundations of the social order. Urban life was rooted in the village wherein all forms of authority, ideology, and social life can be identified. Eltsov's conclusion, with reference to the Indus Civilization is both striking and provocative: "this civilization was unrelated to the emergence of cities, while cities, having emerged did not fundamentally alter the ethos of the civilization". Such a view offers a fundamental contrast to the Mesopotamian perspective in which the city is regarded as the dominant social institution within the "Heartland of Cities". In Mesopotamia the process of urban evolution remains the dominant concern resulting in the virtual absence of any archaeological excavation of Bronze Age villages. Interestingly enough, the primacy of the urban environment in Mesopotamia has been recently challenged by Piotr Steinkeller (2006). His study of the texts from Umma, a major city-state of southern Babylonia, suggests a dramatic difference in the archaeological settlement pattern than that recovered by Adams (1981). Steinkeller's study of the texts indicates the presence of a significant order of magnitude of villages around Umma that were not detected on archaeological survey. The conclusion seems unavoidable, and further supported by the study of the later Mari archives (Fleming 2004), the social landscape of Mesopotamia, if not dominated by cities, was certainly ameliorated by the presence of a very considerable number—perhaps even a majority—of villages and tribal entities. It is worth quoting Steinkeller's (2006) conclusions at some length for they dramatically alter our view of the Mesopotamian social landscape:

> It must be noted at this point that it is very difficult to pigeonhole Umma settlements into a few distinctive size and type categories. It is even harder to draw a sharp distinction between the "rural" and the "urban" features in their composition. Both the smaller and the larger ones show the same types of architectural structures and very similar elements of administrative and socio-economic organization.... In my reconstruction of Umma's physical landscape, there was no dichotomy, no fixed barrier between the town and the countryside, the two blend into each other. Urban space gradually and almost imperceptibly becomes countryside.... Indeed, it can be argued that it was precisely this exceedingly high level of urban-rural integration—the absence of sharp borders between the town and the countryside—that was largely responsible for the success of the southern Babylonian city-state as a political, social, and economic institution.... Thus, one encounters in villages characteristics that are usually associated with urban environments, such as the presence of temples and palaces. On the other hand, towns even the largest of them, display in their physical makeup and social organization features that must be analyzed as rural.

Thus, surprisingly, the settlement regime of the Indus Valley may mirror that of Mesopotamia where villages dominated the social landscape. A mirror image however is not a reality. The principle of equifinality reminds us that identical material expressions may exemplify very different cultural phenomenon. Nevertheless, Eltsov's textually derived emphasis upon the importance of the village and the absence of distinctions between cities and villages in South Asia is reminiscent of Steinkeller's Mesopotamian perspective. In this regard, one is reminded of Fairservis' (1976–1977) excavation of the village site of Allahdino. His excavation of this Harappan village, of less than two acres, recovered an identity of material culture, architectural complex, and village plan that mirrored, in all respects, that of the major city of Mohenjodaro.

It is perhaps not surprising that given the primacy of village life that Eltsov finds systems of authority allowed for a dominance of heterarchical principles, wherein power and authority was exercised by different social institutions. Again, such a view contrasts with the western view that hierarchical principles dominate. Eltsov offers convincing arguments that within the Indus Civilization many of the features regarded as "unique", i.e., the absence of temples and palaces, are the result of the heterarchical principles indicated in the Sanskrit texts. His emphasis upon the importance of orality sublimating the significance of writing, his arguments supporting the ideological rather than materialist roots of social organization, and his identification of such factors as animal sacrifice as implicated in the domestication of animals and agricultural practices, as well as his deliberations upon the significance of the varṇas and caste, are just a few of the original contributions emanating from his study.

Although it is never explicitly stated it is apparent that the author believes that archaeology is a branch of the historical sciences. It is not surprising that he follows in the great Russian tradition in which archaeology forms part of the historical discipline, itself richly informed in the differing genres of the philosophy of history. His passing references, from Vico to Toynbee, Marx and Bakhtin, place him squarely in that grand Russian tradition wherein history unfolds within an informed philosophical context of meaning, logic, and lesson (for a most recent exposition of this approach, in which historical knowledge reveals the past and informs the present, see Isaiah Berlin 2006).

When Eltsov writes of his concern for recognizing "the mind of the researcher and the mentality of historical agents" he grapples with the recognition that historians create the past by attempting to enter the minds of individual agents of the past. The imagined past of two ancient civilizations which he recreates in this book is filled with rich insights. They may not be fashionable to those that adhere to the "isms" of a particular social science agenda and there will be those that will categorically deny that the Gangetic world and Sanskrit texts have anything to do with the Harappan world. Denying a comparative approach and the merits of textual evidence to inform the archaeological record (and the reverse) results in being stuck in the vacuous arguments as to whether the Indus Civilization is a State or Chiefdom.

One final comment. All historical perspectives have modern permutations. Eltsov would seem to favor a linear continuity that weds a pre-Harappan village world to the Gangetic kingdom—a millennia long river of historical continuity. His argument has much conviction. Today in India such a view will be favored by many who embrace the notion of a primordial Aryan identity; a notion created, at least in part, by western Orientalists. In India, as in much of the rest of the world, the interpreted past is revived, manipulated and constructed in order to validate religious belief, ethnicity, racial and common grievances. A relevant question for our day is to what extent do historians self-censure their interpretation or perspective, or fabricate a more acceptable one, in order to either avoid, or allow, for its manipulation for political purposes? It is a sad reality of modernism that one sees a rapid rise in the industry of re-writing history to serve a present agenda.

This book offers both a new approach toward an understanding of two ancient South Asian civilizations as well as new insights into the applicability of a comparative approach. Eltsov's alien social landscape enriches the theory behind reconstructing ancient civilizations while providing the empirical evidence for a textually and archaeologically informed community.

—C. C. Lamberg-Karlovsky

Note

1. It might be pointed out that an extensive early settlement pattern study, predating Gordon Willey's Viru Valley project by over a decade, was undertaken by S. P. Tolstov in the 1920s and 1930s. Tolstov's settlement surveys in Khoresmia, between the Syr Darya and Amu Darya Rivers, to the east of the Aral Sea, were published in the 1930s and 1940s in numerous volumes. S. P. Tolstov was awarded the Stalin Prize (awarded for the best science book within a given year) for his publication of his Khoresmian settlement surveys (Tolstov 1939, 1948). Affiliated with Tolstov's Khorezmskaya Akheologo-Étnografichskaya Ékspeditsiya was B. V. Andrianov who undertook archaeological and topographic investigations in the Tash-kirman oasis in the mid 1950s. This remarkable study was perhaps the earliest field study to explicitly investigate the relationship between settlement patterns, irrigation technology, and socio-political formations (the results of his field seasons are summarized in Andrianov's 1969 book). The general absence of awareness of this work in the western literature has more to do with political and linguistic barriers than with its splendid intellectual contribution. An English edition of B. V. Andrianov's book, resulting from the successful collaboration of Maurizio Tosi (University of Bologna) and myself, has been completed and will soon be published by the Peabody Museum, Harvard University.

References

Adams, R. McC

1966 *The Evolution of Urban Society. Early Mesopotamia and Prehispanic Mexico*. Aldine, Chicago.

1981 *Heartland of Cities*. University of Chicago Press, Chicago.

Andrianov, B. V.

1969 *Drevnie Orositelnye Sistemy Priaralya*. Akademia Nauk, Moscow.

Berlin, I.

2006 *Political Ideas in the Romantic Age. Their Rise and Influence in Modern Thought*, edited by Henry Hardy. Princeton University Press, Princeton.

Chang, K. C.

1986 *The Archaeology of Ancient China*, Fourth Edition. Yale University Press, New Haven, CT.

2000 Ancient China and its anthropological significance. In *The Breakout: The Origins of Civilization*. Peabody Museum Monographs 9. Peabody Museum, Cambridge, MA.

Childe, V. G.

1936 *Man Makes Himself*. Watts & Co., London.

Church, R. L., and T. L. Bell
1988 An analysis of ancient Egyptian settlement patterns using location allocation covering models. *Annals of the Association of American Geographer* 78(4):701–714.

Collingwood, R. G.
1946 *The Idea of History*. Clarendon Press, Oxford.

Culbert, T. P., and P. S. Rice
1990 *Precolumbian Population History in the Maya Lowlands*. University of New Mexico Press, Albuquerque.

Earle, T. (ed.)
1991 *Chiefdoms: Power, Economy and Ideology. School of American Research Book*. Cambridge University Press, Cambridge.

Fairservis, W. A.
1976–1977 *Excavations at the Harappan Site of Allahdino*, Vols. 1–3. Papers of the Allahdino Expedition. American Museum of Natural History, New York, NY.

1989 An epigenetic view of the Harappan civilization. In *Archaeological Thought in America*, edited by C. C. Lamberg-Karlovsky. Cambridge University Press, Cambridge.

Flannery, K.
1999 Process and ageing in early state formation *Cambridge Archaeological Journal* 9:3–21.

Fleming. D. E.
2004 *Democracy's Ancient Ancestors*. Cambridge University Press, Cambridge.

Fried, M.
1967 *The Evolution of Political Society: An Essay in Political Anthropology*. Random House, New York, NY.

Johnson, G. A.
1973 *Local Exchange and Early State Development in Southwestern Iran*. University of Michigan Museum of Anthropology Papers 51, Ann Arbor, MI.

Kemp, B.
1989 *Ancient Egypt. Anatomy of a Civilization.* Routledge, London.

Kenoyer, M.
1998 *Ancient Cities of the Indus Valley Civilization*. Oxford University Press, Karachi.

Lamberg-Karlovsky, C. C.
1999 Households, land tenure and communication systems in the 6th–4th millennium greater Mesopotamia. In *Urbanization and Land Ownership in the Ancient Near East*, edited by Michael Hudson and Baruch Levine, pp. 167–202. Peabody Museum Bulletin 9, Peabody Museum, Cambridge, MA.

Liu L., and X. Chen
2003 *State Formation in Early China*. Duckworth, London.

Lyman, R. L., and M. J. O'Brien
2001 The direct historical approach, analogical reasoning, and theory in American archaeology. *Americanist Archaeology, Journal of Archaeological Method and Theory* 8(4):303–342.

Mink, L. O.
1969 *Mind, History and Dialectic. The Philosophy of R. G. Collingwood*. Wesleyan University Press, Middleton, CT.

Mughal, R.
1997 *Ancient Cholistan*. Ferozsons, Rawalpindi.

Oates, J.
1996 A prehistoric communications revolution, *Cambridge Archaeological Journal* 6:165–173.

Redfield, R.
1977 *The Primitive World and Its Transformations.* Cornell University Press, Ithaca, NY.

Renfrew, C.
1973 *Before Civilization.* Jonathan Cape, London.

Sahlins, M., and E. Service (eds.)
1960 *Evolution and Culture.* University of Michigan Press, Ann Arbor, MI.

Service, E.
1974 *Origin of the State and Civilizations.* Norton, New York, NY.

Steinkeller, P.
2006 City and countryside in third millennium Babylonia. In *Settlement in Society. Essays Dedicated to Roberts McCormick Adams.* Cotsen Institute, UCLA, Los Angeles, CA.

Tolstov, S. P.
1939 Drevnekhorezmiiskie pamyatniki Karakalpakii. *Vestnik Drevnei Istorii*, Vol. 3. Moscow.

1948 *Drevnii Khorezm.* Izdanie MGU, Moscow.

Trigger, B.
2003 *Understanding Early Civilizations.* Cambridge University Press, Cambridge.

Tyler, E. B.
1881 *Anthropology: An Introduction to the Study of Man and Civilization.* Macmillan, London.

Wengrow, D.
2006 *The Archaeology of Early Egypt.* Cambridge University Press, Cambridge.

Wright, H.
1977 Recent research on the origin of the state. *Annual Reviews in Anthropology* 6:379–397.

1984 Prestate political formations. In *On the Evolution of Complex Societies: Essays in Honor of Harry Hoijer*, edited by T. Earle, pp. 41–77. Undena Publications, Malibu.

Wright, H., and G. Johnson
1974 Population, exchange and early state formation in southwestern Iran. *American Anthropologist* 77:267–289.

Yoffee, N.
2005 *Myths of the Archaic State.* Cambridge University Press, Cambridge.

Preface

I became interested in ancient South Asia as an undergraduate in history while living in Saint Petersburg, Russia (at that time Leningrad, USSR). Soon I was greatly disappointed by the lack of communication between the scholars of philological and social orientations. Philologists scrutinized Sanskrit words and verses, while historians reconstructed the past in accordance with their dogmatic schemes. Understandably, the Soviet version of Marxist historiography prevented them from innovative and creative ways of thinking.

When after the collapse of the Soviet Union I moved to the United States, I thought that the interaction between philologists and social scientists of ancient South Asia would be more productive. I quickly found out that I was wrong. Although social scientists had immensely more freedom in expressing their ideas and creating new theoretical approaches, the interaction between specialists in texts and specialists in material culture was barely existent. Philologists still scrutinized words and verses, while anthropologists analyzed the past often without any knowledge of oral and literary traditions. Greatly dissatisfied with this situation, I began to look for a synthetic, conjunctive, and interdisciplinary method for the study of ancient South Asia; a method that would combine the efforts of historians, anthropologists, and philologists and would enable me to create a holistic and cross-disciplinary interpretation of the past.

Meanwhile, completing my doctorate in anthropological archaeology at Harvard University, I came to the conclusion that the epistemology of scientistic archaeologists in the west was not that much different from the epistemology of Soviet Marxism. Not unlike Marxists, scientistic archaeologists believed in the objectivity of the past and the intelligibility of human actions. As one well-known pandit of a "purely scientific approach" suggested, the craft of archaeology was similar to that of a car mechanic:

> ...one needs to know how the engine operates, in order to identify its relevant components—the carburetor, battery, cylinder, and so on—and to put them together correctly. In the same manner, archaeologists must identify each type of behavior that took place at each site they find and then begin to fit the pieces into place to make up a prehistoric system of land use (Binford 1983:132).

On the contrary, I was becoming more and more fascinated with the ideas of humanistically oriented thinkers, such as Benedetto Croce, R. G. Collingwood, Isaiah Berlin, Mikhail Bakhtin, and Hayden White. I gradually began to believe that the free will, or as anthropologists would put it "independent decision-making", rather than any other factor was the main driving force of history and that the sociopolitical consciousness of the historical agents was an innate component of the phenomena and structures of the past. This is how I arrived at the idea of subjective humanism formulated in the first chapter of this book and at the method of using the ancient Indian texts as sources of ideas rather than facts.

Thus, the present book is designed to pursue both theoretical and empirical goals. From a theoretical point of view, it is aimed at combining the efforts of philology, history, and archaeology and at finding a new way to study the nature and genesis of the earliest South Asian civilization through the analysis of archaeological and textual data. From an empirical point of view, the aim of this book is a new model of the ancient Indian city and civilization. For the convenience of the reader, I provide here a brief summary of my argument.

The first chapter is theoretical. Its argument is based on a simple, yet pivotal assumption that history is not just about writing chronicles or tracing *l'histoire événementielle*, for which ancient Indian literature has clearly very little to offer, but rather about grasping the illusory *longue durée*, discerning structures, and writing analytical narratives, for which ancient Indian literature has much more to offer. Consequently, instead of treating ancient Sanskrit and Pāli texts as sources of tedious factual information, I suggest that we treat them as sources of complex sociocultural ideas, which can be tested and conceptualized in the context of archaeological data. Epistemologically, I present this method as part of my broader research philosophy, aimed at combining the efforts of anthropology, archaeology, history, and philology, and contingent on four rules of thumb: first, that human agency is the main driving force in history; second, that the creation of structures and models is essential for the conceptualization of the human past; third, that there can be no purely objective interpretation of the past; and fourth, that the ideas and thoughts of the historical agents present an inseparable part of the events, phenomena, processes, structures, and models of the past. In summary, I argue that the ancient Indian texts are valuable primarily as sources of ideas rather than facts and propose to investigate the idea of the city based on three sets of data: a sample of Sanskrit and Pāli texts which can potentially shed light on how the city was envisioned in ancient India, a sample of archaeological sites of the Ganges civilization, and a sample of archaeological sites of the Harappan civilization.

The second chapter deals with the idea of the city in theory and in ancient Indian literature. First, after reviewing several theories of the city, I conclude that as an idea, the city has been innately dual. At some point, this duality was conceptualized in theological terms as a metaphorical opposition between the City of God and the Earthen City. Today, we see it as an opposition between the city as a product of poetic imagination and the city as an intelligible and objective whole. Consequently, I argue that neither as an idea nor as an historical phenomenon, the city can have a single and universally comprehensive definition. Instead, it can be investigated and conceptualized in a multitude of ways from the point of view of several academic disciplines. Moreover, as a phenomenon the city is inseparable from the idea of the city in the minds of the historical agents, and therefore, to understand the city properly one needs to find out how the historical agents themselves envisaged the phenomenon of the city.

Following these presumptions, I select excerpts from seven Sanskrit and Pāli texts, namely *Aṅguttara-Nikāya*, *Kauṭilīya Arthaśāstra*, *Vālmīki Rāmāyaṇa*, *Mahābhārata*, *Milindapañha*, *VāyuPurāṇa*, and *Lalitāmāhātmya of the BrahmāṇḍaPurāṇa*. Since these texts stand for more than a millennium of Sanskrit and Pāli literature and represent several very different literary genres and ideological traditions, I assume that their analysis is likely to produce inclusive, diverse, and socially representative results. After reviewing the relevant excerpts—abstract definitions of the city, conventional manuals of the layout of cities, and the panegyrics on divine, mythical and historical cities—I arrive at the conclusion that wittingly or unwittingly yet deeply in their minds, people responsible for the composition of these texts shared the similar view of the city. According to this view, the city was distinguished by two traits: fortifications and various forms of authority. Following my previous argument that, as a complex sociopolitical and cultural phenomenon, the city cannot have a single and universally comprehensive definition, I accept this view as a working hypothesis to be tested against the archaeological data of the Ganges and Harappan civilizations.

The third chapter presents the analysis of data on fortifications and authority from thirteen archaeological sites of the Ganges civilizations, namely, Ahicchatra, Atranjikhera, Bhita, Hastinapura, Kausambi, Mathura, Pataliputra, Rajghat, Rajgir, Sonpur, Sonkh, Sravasti, and Vaisali. As a result of this analysis, I conclude that the massive fortifications that surrounded many of these sites carried symbolic rather than utilitarian functions. Moreover, they served as the main material symbols of authority; no palaces, temples, rich burials, and objects of luxury were necessary for the expression, solidification, and glorification of power. Following this, I argue that the construction of fortifications in the Ganges civilization symbolized three codependent processes: the formation of territorially bound identities, the shaping of authority, and the emergence of cities. This in turn shows that the view of the city by the historical agents presents a plausible model for the conceptualization of the processes that took place in the Gangetic Doab in the mid-first millennium BC. Indeed, the first cities of the Ganges civilization were epitomized by the concurrent processes of the construction of fortifications and the formation of authoritative structures.

In the fourth chapter, I move back in time and take on testing the same model against the archaeological record of the Harappan civilization. I analyze data on fortifications and authority from Allahdino, Banawali, Chanhu-Daro, Dholavira, Harappa, Kalibangan, Kot-Diji, Lothal, Mohenjo-Daro, Nausharo, Surkotada, and Sutkagen-Dor. In several cases, I make significant revisions in the interpretation of existing cultural sequences and archaeological data. The conclusions that I arrive at are largely similar to the conclusions of the previous chapter. The systems of fortifications (platforms, gates, and freestanding walls) in the Harappan civilization carried symbolic functions and epitomized authority in the most explicit and opulent manner. Specifically, I suggest that through the elevation of certain areas, the control of access, the implementation of segregation, and the accentuation of important spaces, the Harappan fortification systems created three-dimensional and segregated mesocosms, characterized by restricted access and hidden monumentality. These mesocosms, i.e., the miniature replicas of the universe, were the products of a unique and complex worldview, possibly focused on the structure of the world. Thus, the construction of symbolic fortifications in the Harappan civilization, in the ways similar to those of the Ganges civilization, stood for the emergence of territorially bound identities and, along with the concurrent process of the formation of authoritative structures, epitomized the emergence of the first cities.

In the fifth chapter, I turn from the idea of the city to the idea of civilization. Since these two concepts have played a pivotal role in the study of ancient civilizations, I suggest that it is worthwhile to investigate their relationship in the context of ancient South Asia. I begin this investigation by reviewing several theories of civilization, and assert that identifying a civilization is like catching a glimpse of a murky, illusory, and to a large degree imaginary structure. Civilization, in my definition, is a transcendental, semi-objective, and reflective category; a deep structure of the most complex and inclusive sociocultural entity within vaguely outlined geographical boundaries. Epistemologically, the idea of civilization is in permanent transition, swinging between the data, the mind of the researcher, and the mentality of the historical agents. Importantly, what the historical agents thought of civilization or, in other words, how they categorized historical processes and culture change is not just an alternative view, but rather a constituent element of the idea of a given civilization. Following these presumptions, I propose to investigate the ideas of the historical agents, i.e., to determine whether ancient Indian literary traditions contain a concept or a set of concepts, that would be similar to or reminiscent of the idea of civilization. Such concepts, I argue, are found in the Yuga Story of the *VayuPurāṇa* and *BrahmāṇḍaPurāṇa*, the two Sanskrit texts dated roughly to the middle of the first millennium AD.

The first model is expressed in the concept of the Tretā Yuga, the second cosmic age in the ancient Indian story of cyclical time. This model is meant to mark a drastic cultural shift from the egalitarianism and hunting gathering to the sociocultural complexity and food-producing economy and is defined by the 11 following traits: 1) formation of a diversified economy divided into three main branches: agriculture, pastoralism and craft-production;

2) solidification of a sedentary lifestyle; 3) emergence of an orally transmitted behavioral code; 4) formation of a unique sociocultural system based on a mix of hierarchical and heterarchical relations; 5) emergence and institutionalization of sacrifices and rituals; 6) standardization of the means for achieving the ultimate liberation; 7) establishment of the unequivocal authority and unity of orally transmitted sacred scriptures; 8) institutionalization of kingship; 9) institutionalization of the means of coercion aimed at the maintenance of social order; 10) beginning of colonial expansion; and 11) increase in women's fertility. The second model is expressed in the five traits that emerge during the Tretā Yuga and maintain importance until the end of the cycle. These traits include: the vārttā, vedas, dharma, varṇāśrama, and yajña, or, in the language of contemporary social science, the agricultural economy, an orally transmitted code of conduct, an orally transmitted sacred knowledge, an idiosyncratic sociocultural system, and a set of ritual and sacrificial practices. Remarkably, in the context of these two models, the ethos of the ancient Indian civilization is temporally and causally linked to the agricultural revolution and is contingent on transformations in ethical, ritual, social, and economic spheres, yet is largely irrelevant to the emergence of cities, writing, and monumental architecture, the three traits that are often seen as the definitive markers of civilization.

In the sixth chapter, I place these theoretical models in the context of archaeological data and suggest that while the idea of the ancient South Asian city can be defined through the concurrent and codependent processes of the construction of symbolic fortifications and the formation of authoritative structures, the idea of the ancient South Asian civilization should be conceptualized with the help of four broadly defined traits: 1) agricultural economy and predominantly rural life style; 2) orality comparable in significance to literacy and maintained by highly sophisticated mnemonic devices used for the preservation of a large body of sacred and social information; 3) an idiosyncratic social system based on ideational differences, which are rooted in rural settings and structured predominantly along the heterarchical rather than hierarchical relations; and 4) a set of ritual and sacrificial practices materialized in water devices, hearths, ornaments, jewelry, figurines, iconographic motifs, burials, and the absence of monumental temples and lavish religious paraphernalia. Meanwhile the emergence of cities, writing, and monumental architecture are epiphenomenal to the idea of the ancient Indian civilization.

Finally in the postscript, I return to the three most controversial issues of this book, namely, the historicity of ancient Indian literature, the idea of the ancient South Asian city, and the idea of the ancient Indian civilization. Placing each of these issues in the context of broader theoretical and political debates, I conclude by asserting that the idea of the ancient Indian civilization proposed in this book is not meant to endorse any direct religious or ethnolinguistic continuities between pre-Harappan, Harappan, and Early Historic South Asia. Inclusive, reflective, and transcendental, this model can accommodate a multitude of discontinuities, and, most importantly, shows how one can speak of the "Great South Asian Tradition"—cum—the "Ancient Indian Civilization" and use ancient Indian literature in the analysis of archaeological data without falling into the ideology of "one people, one nation, one culture" and without having the Harappans speak Sanskrit and worship Shiva.

Note

Regarding the use of diacritical signs, I must note that since this book is written for a broad audience of readers interested in the archaeology of complex societies, ancient history, and the rise of civilization in the South Asian Subcontinent, the use of diacritical signs for the transliteration of Sanskrit words is selective. In the chapters and sections that deal predominantly with archaeological data, the use of diacritics is minimal. In the chapters and sections that analyze ancient texts, the diacritics are used more frequently.

Acknowledgments

This book is a result of my long-term search for a new humanistic and interdisciplinary approach to the study of ancient South Asia. All the ideas proposed in it are my sole responsibility. Yet the emergence of ideas is impossible without intellectual environment, the creation of which reflects the efforts of a group of individuals. Therefore I owe a great debt of gratitude to many dedicated scholars—teachers, friends, and peers in the United States, Russia, Italy, Germany, England, Pakistan, and India—who in one way or another influenced my ideas, directed my research interests, and simply helped me to become who I am. First and foremost, I must pay tribute to my late parents: my father, a long-term professor of organic chemistry at Saint Petersburg (Leningrad) Technological Institute, Andrey Vassilievich Eltsov, and my mother, a landscape architect and interior designer, Irina Nestorovna Surina. Without their unconditional support, love, and intellectual guidance, I would have developed neither a passionate interest in the study of ancient societies nor a strong humanistic bias in my perception of the past. As both of my parents left me unexpectedly and tragically while I was working on this book, to their memory I feel obliged to devote this modest effort. Equally, I owe an enormous debt to my Harvard mentor, professor of archaeology, Karl Lamberg-Karlovsky. Karl's charisma and intellectual power always served as a great inspiration for his peers and students. I was not the exception. Our conversations with Karl—either in his house in Massachusetts or in the villages of Baluchistan—inspired me to search for alternative ways of thinking about the roots of civilization and the nature of ancient societies. In 1997, Karl became interested in my ideas, and in 2001, after the unfortunate termination of the Harvard Archaeological Project in Baluchistan, supported and directed a major shift in my research. Without this support, it would have been difficult, if not impossible, to complete this project. Another person at Harvard to whom I am particularly indebted is a professor of Sanskrit and Indian Studies, Michael Witzel. Michael, unlike many South Asian philologists, sees things from a very broad humanistic perspective and always encourages his peers and students to look for culturally and socially significant information in the ancient Indian texts. To a large degree, it was because of Michael that I decided to continue my interests in ancient South Asia after coming to the United States. Richard H. Meadow is a Harvard archaeologist and the director of the Harappa Archaeological Project, to whom I also owe a great debt of gratitude. Aside from giving me a superb introduction to the archaeology of the Harappan civilization—both at Harvard and in the field in Harappa, Pakistan—Richard contributed greatly to my writing style, structure of argument, and knowledge of literature. In Cambridge and Boston, MA, I also would like to express my genuine thanks to Ofer Bar-Yosef, a Harvard professor of Stone Age archaeology, whose work ethic and dedication to the world of science are a remarkable example to all of his peers and students; to Rafique M. Mughal, currently a professor of archaeology at Boston University and previously the Director General of the Department of Museums and Antiquities of the Government of Pakistan, for his insights in the Harappan archaeology; to Joshua Wright for his very helpful comments on my writing; to Mariner Padwa for the unforgettable discussions that we had on many important issues of the Eurasian Bronze Age; to Vladimir Kozhemiakov for his genuine help at a very critical moment in the summer and fall of 1997; to John and Madeleine Carneys for their invaluable support in winter of 1995; and to Steven and Bobby Sands for their highly appreciated assistance at an early stage of this project. In Berkeley, CA, I would like to thank George L. Hart, Robert P. Goldman, Sally Sutherland, Aditya Behl, Usha Jain, and Kausalya Hart for coping with my efforts to master Sanskrit, Hindi, and Tamil. In Madison, WI, I would like to express my thankfulness to Jonathan Mark Kenoyer for training me in the field archaeology of the Harappan civilization and for sharing his passionate affection towards the cultures of ancient and modern South Asia. In Philadelphia, PA, I would like to thank Gregory L. Possehl for his genuine interest in my work, for many valuable insights and criticisms, and for inviting me to present ideas expressed in this book at the South Asian lecture series at the University of Pennsylvania. In New York, NY, I must thank Scott R. Evans for sharing with me my intellectual concerns and discussing many of my ideas.

In Saint Petersburg, Russia, I must, first of all, thank Svetlana Leonidovna Neveleva of the Russian Academy of Sciences Institute of Oriental Studies for her exemplary dedication to the ancient Indian philology and a genuinely enthusiastic desire to share her experience and knowledge with her peers and students. If it had not been for Svetlana Leonidovna who in 1992 encouraged me to continue my research, I would have most likely not pursued my academic interests in the study of ancient South Asia. In Saint Petersburg, I also would like to thank Mikhail I. Shevshuk, Vitaliy I. Startsev, Oleg B. Ostrovsky, Oleg Yu. Plenkov, and Abram D. Stoliar for their insights into ancient, medieval, and modern historiography; Nikita V. Gurov, Vladimir G. Erman, Tatiana I. Oranskaia, Iaroslav V. Vasilkov, and Ivan M. Steblin-Kamensky for their visions of the Indo-Iranian philology and South Asian studies, and Boris I. Marshak, Valentin G. Shkoda, and Mark G. Kramarovsky for my first training in field-archaeology. In Peshawar, Pakistan, I would like to thank F. A. Durani, Ihsan Ali, and Faruq Swati for their hospitality and willingness to cooperate. In Delhi, India, I would like to thank B. B. Lal, who kindly found time to explain to me his vision of Indian protohistory and who will hopefully forgive me my occasional criticisms of his work on the ensuing pages, S. P. Gupta for sharing with me his ideas in a very passionate and enthusiastic way, and R. S. Bisht for his invaluable help in organizing my visits to the sites of the Ganges Civilization in winter of 2002–2003. In Ravenna, Italy, I would like to express my gratitude to Maurizio Tosi for his sincere interest in my work and for inviting me to present the initial results of this study at an informal seminar on the Indus civilization held in Ravenna and Bologna in April of 2003. This seminar undoubtedly helped me shape and develop my (at that time) immature ideas. In Paris, France, I would like to thank Jean-Francois Jarrige, Catherine Jarrige, and Gonzaque Quivron for sharing with me their most recent interpretations of the data from Nausharo, a site that played an important role in the construction of my argument.

Importantly, I must thank the staff of three libraries: Tozzer Library of the Peabody Museum, Widener Library of Harvard University and the US Library of Congress. My research would have been impossible without full access to the resources of these three remarkable research centers. Special thanks among the staff of Tozzer Library must go to Emily Moss whose cataloguing project, in which I participated, taught me some invaluable skills for my own work with literature.

For the generous financial support, I must thank the Department of Anthropology at Harvard University, the American School of Prehistoric Research, the Cora Du Bois Charitable Fund, the Department of South and South East Asian Studies at the University of California at Berkeley, the International House at the University of California at Berkeley, Alexander von Humboldt Foundation, and Mr. Vladimir Anokhin for their generous financial support. Special thanks are due to Samuel and Christie Rileys of Cambridge, MA for their generous and greatly needed donation at the final and critical stage of completing this project.

For the illustrations, I am thankful to the American Institute of Indian Studies; American Oriental Society; Archaeological Research Faculty of the University of California, Berkeley; Archaeological Survey of India; Asia Publishing House; Cambridge University Press; Dietrich Reimer Verlag; Department of Ancient Indian History, Culture, and Archaeology of the Benares Hindu University; Directorate General of Archaeology and Museums, Government of Pakistan; Directorate of Archaeology, Bihar; Indian Archaeological Society; French Archaeological Mission in Pakistan; Harappa Archaeological Research Project; Kashi Prasad Jayaswal Research Institute in Patna; Motilal Banarsidas; and South Asia Program at Cornell University. Personally, for the assistance with getting permits for the illustrations, I would like to thank Arundhati Banerji, D. K. Chakrabarti, Harry Falk, S. P. Gupta, Lin Hart, Catherine Jarrige, Jean-Francois Jarrige, J. M. Kenoyer, B. R. Mani, R. H. Meadow, Purnima Mehta, U. S. Moorti, Mohana L. S. Ochani, G. L. Possehl, Gonzaque Quivron, Jonathan Rodgers, Jim Shaffer, and A. M. Stengle.

For the intellectually stimulating reviews of this book, I thank Dilip K. Chakrabarti, Professor of South Asian Archaeology at Cambridge University, UK, and Romila Thapar, Emeritus Professor of Ancient Indian History at the Jawaharlal Nehru University, India. Although not many of the requests of these two outstanding scholars were met (their views represent very different perceptions of ancient South Asia), some of the concerns raised in these reviews are addressed in the postscript. For additional reading of this book, I also would like to thank Ute Franke-Vogt of the German Institute of Archaeology and Harry Falk, director of the Institute of Indian Philology and Art History at the Free University in Berlin, Germany. For the final editing and formatting of the manuscript, I am greatly thankful to Wren Fournier, publications coordinator for the American School of Prehistoric Research at the Peabody Museum of Harvard University. And last but not least, I must thank my wife Vitessa and my daughter Tanaquil for their unconditional support and for courageously coping with my long absences and endless research.

1 From Historical Agents to Structure: A New Method for the Study of Ancient South Asia

Enfranchising itself from servitude to extramundane caprice and to blind natural necessity, freeing itself from transcendency and from false immanence (which is in its turn transcendency), thought conceives history as the work of man, as the product of human will and intellect, and in this manner enters that form of history which we shall call humanistic.

—Benedetto Croce (1921:94)

South Asia witnessed at least two urban revolutions. The first took place in the middle of the third millennium BC and brought into existence the Harappan civilization. The second occurred almost 2,000 years later and culminated in the emergence of the Ganges civilization. Being the earliest urban cultures of the South Asian Subcontinent that display sociocultural similarities and are comparable in the degrees of their sociopolitical complexity, these two ancient civilizations left behind invaluable material for the investigation of the ethos and genesis of protohistoric and Early Historic South Asia. During the last several decades, there has been much new research dealing with the various aspects of these two civilizations. Archaeologists, historians, philologists, and linguists have brought into play significant amounts of new data. Yet it would not be an exaggeration to say that after more than 200 years of research and despite all the new archaeological discoveries, there remains a striking lack of thorough studies that analyze both the Harappan and Ganges civilizations from a broad cross-disciplinary perspective and that are ultimately aimed at the creation of holistic and conceptual models of the nature and genesis of the ancient Indian civilization.[1]

In my view, there are several reasons for this situation. First, disciplines dealing with ancient South Asia—archaeology, history, philology, and linguistics—are still largely alienated from one another. Archaeology itself is split between several distinct theoretical approaches, i.e., anthropological archaeology, historical archaeology, art–historical archaeology, and the like. As a result, archaeologists, historians, philologists, and linguists who study ancient South Asia are neither sufficiently aware of each other's work, nor have much professional interaction.[2] Second, the Harappan and Ganges civilizations are separated from one another both geographically and chronologically; the Ganges civilization emerged over 1,000 years after the demise of the Harappan civilization, and with its emergence the center of political gravity in northern South Asia shifted hundreds of kilometers to the east. Third, the issues of ethnic, cultural, sociopolitical and linguistic continuity between the Harappan and Ganges civilizations have become exceedingly political; recently, several leading Indian scholars have fully revised the traditional models of South Asian protohistory (S. P. Gupta 1996; Lal 1998b, 2002c; Simha 1987, 1995). Fourth, the number of primary and secondary sources accumulated over 200 years of scholarly interest in ancient South Asia has grown to immense proportions. With dozens of archaeological reports and hundreds of ancient texts, it has become a challenge to master the data and to formulate a synthetic yet manageable research project.

Aimed to address at least some of these issues, this book will explore the ideas of the ancient city and civilization—the two key concepts in the archaeology of complex societies and ancient history—through the analysis of three sets of data: Sanskrit and Pāli literature, the archaeology of the Ganges civilization, and the archaeology of the Harappan civilization. By initiating this unusual project, I have sought to meet three main objectives: 1) to redirect attention from positivist and economically deterministic models of the study of ancient civilizations to humanistic, text-oriented, and reflective approaches; 2) to propose a novel method for the joint use of ancient texts and material culture in the context of ancient South Asia; and by doing so, to lay the foundation for a new interdisciplinary direction for the investigation of the nature and genesis of the earliest South Asian civilization; and 3) to address the issue of cultural continuities between proto-historic and Early Historic South Asia and to elaborate a viable analytical model for the study of the earliest South Asian city and civilization.

Intellectually, these objectives stem from the writings of a mixed group of historians, philosophers, philologists, anthropologists, and specialists in ancient South Asia. As far as the generic social thinkers are concerned, my ways of thinking have been affected by the ideas of Benedetto Croce, R. G. Collingwood, Isaiah Berlin, Hayden White, Mikhail Bakhtin, and Fernand Braudel. As far as the specialists in ancient South Asia are concerned, in one way or another, I have been under the influence of the writings by S. C. Malik, Romila Thapar, and D. K. Chakrabarti. More specifically, the ideas that affected me the most are: the equation of history with art by Benedetto Croce (1919), the concept of the text by Mikhail Bakhtin (1979), a model of the ancient Indian civilization by S. C. Malik (1968), the use of texts in the study of ancient India by Romila Thapar (1978, 2000a), the subjectivist and reflective philosophy of history of R. G. Collingwood (1946), the metahistorical theory of Hayden White (1973), a holistic approach to the study of the ancient Indian civilization by D. K. Chakrabarti (1972–73, 1995, 1999), the notion of historical time by Fernand Braudel (1949, 1969, 1987), and the emic-etic debate between Kenneth Pike (1954) and Marvin Harris (1979).

Between Archaeology, Anthropology, and History

The relationship between archaeology, anthropology, and history has been the point of controversy. Let me clarify a few points in this regard. Archaeology is like a prodigal son. Depending on the education, country of origin and academic traditions of its practitioners, it is seen as anthropology, history, art history, classics, area studies, or as an independent discipline. Protohistoric and Early Historic South Asia is a good example of how different perceptions of archaeology can be. Anthropological archaeologists working in South Asia deal mostly with the prehistoric or protohistoric cultures and, until recently, have displayed little interest in historical periods. Their methods, ideas, and jargon are heavily anthropological and have little to do with historical or literary thought. On the other hand, historical archaeologists focus predominantly on the periods beginning with the middle of the first millennium BC and rarely touch upon the cultures of the Bronze Age. Their primary interests lie in the reconstruction of culture histories and they employ historical methods of analysis.

As far as the definition of archaeology is concerned, I favor an old yet momentous distinction between "archaeology *per se*" and "archaeology as interpretation" proposed by Walter W. Taylor. "Archaeology *per se*", as Taylor (1948:44) defined it, is "nothing but an excavation technique," "no more than a method... for the gathering of cultural information". "The archaeologist, as archaeologist," in Taylor's view, is "a technician". Archaeology as interpretation or, as one could put it, archaeology as text is a much broader discipline, which is, in my view, coterminous with Mikhail Bakhtin's concept of the text as the essence of any scientific or intellectual activity. The text, as Bakhtin (1986:113–114) defined it, is "...the primary given reality and the point for departure for any discipline in the human sciences, ...the aggregate of various kinds of knowledge and methods called philology, linguistics, literary scholarship, scientific scholarship, and so forth...".

Given this, debating on whether archaeology is history, anthropology, or an independent discipline is pointless. All three disciplines are closely related, and their relationship is contingent upon research issues. If the research is undertaken by an archaeologist whose data comes primarily from excavations, history and anthropology can be seen as methods of interpretation. On the contrary, if a historian needs archaeological data for his interpretations, he or she is right in looking at archaeology as an auxiliary historical discipline. The relation of archaeology to history, anthropology or, for that matter, to any other academic discipline thus is an issue of constantly changing methods of data analysis and interpretation. While some archaeologists look for the truth in the ancient texts and philosophical treatises, others take recourse to zoology, botany, or stable isotope analysis. It is the new research topics and methodologies rather than strictly defined disciplinary boundaries that define the nature of our enquiries. Depending on the goals of research and the self-identification of the researcher, the relationship between archaeology, history, and anthropology thus is individual in every specific case. As far my own method is concerned, history and anthropology are kin disciplines and their kinship is obvious from a large number of similarities. Some of these similarities are outlined below.

History and anthropology have arisen from the same historico-philosophical roots. Voltaire, Vico, Compte, Condorcet, Kant, Herder, Hegel, Marx, and Durkheim laid the foundation of anthropology as well the foundation of history. For a long time, an impetus for the development of both disciplines was the search for the laws or structures that underlie human society. The main difference was that most historians looked for the rules and regularities in a diachronic perspective and most anthropologists in a synchronic. It is ironic that Evans-Pritchard (1962:122) spoke distastefully of Vico, Hegel, Marx, and Toynbee. Epistemologically, his own work was not that much different from Toynbee's. Both believed in the intelligibility of society and discerned regularities. Whether those regularities were synchronic or diachronic did not make their final interpretations fundamentally different.

Similar to anthropologists, many historians abandoned the idea of scientism and objected to the intelligibility of human society. To a person familiar with the philosophy of history, postmodern relativism and the neglect of scientific objectivism in anthropology do not offer anything fundamentally new. Postmodernists revitalized the debates, which, for a long time, had been held among the philosophers of history. Yet in the end of the nineteenth century, Benedetto Croce (1919) opposed the positivism of some of his famous contemporaries by comparing history with art. Soon after, Oswald Spengler (1918) published *Der Untergang des Abendlandes*, the treatise which, to many, would become the Bible of antipositivism in social sciences. Moreover, historians have continuously raised the questions of subjectivity, relativity, and reflexivity. Collingwood (1946:302–315), for example, wrote of reflexivity at the time when not many anthropologists expressed doubts in the objectivity of their knowledge. "Historical thinking", as Collingwood (1946:307) maintained in one of his famous works, was "always reflection: for reflection" and "thinking about the acts of thinking".

One of the biggest misconceptions about history is that it studies the past through the interpretation of written documents. As one distinguished American anthropologist puts it, "the "out there" for the historian is not in the heads of the natives in the field, but in what purposely or accidentally the natives have put down on paper" (Cohn 1980:208). In my view, this view of history is profoundly erroneous, if not derogatory. First, historians continuously take recourse to the study of sources other than written texts, e.g., numismatics, material culture, paleography, oral traditions, etc. Second, the vision of history as the study of written texts inevitably leads to the distinction between historical and a-historical societies (Gellner 1971), and consequently is not just wrong but also evolutionary, ethnocentric, and racist. Unsurprisingly, according to this point of view, most of America, Africa, and significant parts of Asia become "historical" only after contact with literate cultures. This means that people who created Chaco, Machu Pichu, Great Zimbabwe, and Jenne-Jenno had no history. In my view, this premise is absurd. Humans had history from the inception of their becoming human, i.e., from the Upper Paleolithic Revolution or, depending on one's definition of human culture, even earlier.

The juxtaposition of the self and the other is a driving force of research both in history and anthropology. The final product of both history and anthropology is the text, which, as Mikhail Bakhtin (1975) has vividly shown, does not exist without dialogue. Dialogue, on the other hand, is made possible through the dialectical juxtaposition of the self and the other; without this juxtaposition neither dialogue nor text exists. In other words, if there were no self, there would be no text; if there were no other, there would be no object of study, unless the self becomes the object. Diminishing the role of the self or the role of the other inevitably paralyzes the discipline, or, paraphrasing Bakhtin, makes dialogue impossible. Today, the imposing of self in the style of Malinowski or Radcliffe-Brown is not in fashion. Instead, anthropologists prefer to give more voice to the other. Doing so in history and archaeology is more difficult, yet not impossible. Ancient Romans or Egyptians can speak for themselves in the same way as the !Kung bushmen.

Synchronic and diachronic aspects of human societies interplay in history and anthropology. Neither human groups nor individuals can be properly studied from a timeless status quo perspective. It is a delusion to think that ethnography, ethnology, and anthropology can alienate temporal factors by studying local groups from a timeless perspective. By the same token, history cannot be limited to a temporal study of change within human society. To the historian, synchronic aspects are as important as diachronic. Temporal and spatial, synchronic and diachronic, structural and specific, self and other are the Hegelian opposites that characterize any meaningful enquiry into the human past.

In summary, anthropology and history have multiple, fluid, and coterminous identities. Consider the following. Bernard Lewis is a historian. His theoretical stance is anthropological. "Remembered, recovered, and invented history" is an anthropological construct suggested by a historian. The writings of Lewis (1975) are a good example of how anthropology and history can work together.

Subjective Humanism

Subjective humanism is a method that I initially designed for this study. I envision it however broader, as a theoretical basis for the conjunctive analyses of ancient texts and material cultures. Aimed at the creation of holistic interpretations and analytical models, this method is in essence a humanistic, reflective, and structural approach to the study of the remote human past. Its underlying philosophy can be summarized in four points.

The study of the past—whether anthropological or historical—is innately humanistic. In philosophical terms, this means that free will dominates necessity and that necessity plays minor or no role in an historical process. In this, I, to a large degree, follow the ideas of Benedetto Croce (1917, 1954) and Isaiah Berlin (1953, 1954), and strongly disagree with any kind of environmental, economical or biological determinism. The objects of historical and anthropological study—the events, phenomena and processes of the past—are, first and foremost, the products of human will, intellect and action, rather than of the environment, the forces of production, or any other non-human factor. Human agency—whether individual or in groups—is the main driving force within history. This premise I believe applies to the entirety of historical process. Biologically, the humans responsible for the transition from the Middle to the Upper Paleolithic are not any different from the humans responsible for the invention of writing in the Near East or the humans responsible for the Industrial Revolution in Europe. Having different technologies, ideologies and social institutions, they all acted consciously and were led by their intellect and will.

Regularities, patterns and structures as well as analytical models are the essential products of the study of the remote past, particularly if this past is known from fragmentary material remains. That the human agency is responsible for the course of history does not mean that we should divert our attention from the *longue durée* back to *l'histoire événementielle*. Being both the reflection of the past and the product of our thoughts, structures and models are bridges between the subject and the object, the past and the present, the self and the other, and the emic and the etic. Importantly, this transitional aspect of their existence neither prevents them from creating compelling pictures of the past, nor excludes the importance of human agency. If reflective of the thinking of the historical agents, structures and models can, in fact, reinforce the dominant role of the agency in a historical process.

There can be no purely scientific and objective interpretation of the past, for any anthropological or historical narrative that purports to represent the past has a poetic component in it and is subject to the same structural, stylistic, and linguistic analysis as any other narrative prose discourse. On this, I fully agree with Hayden White (1973:IX) and particularly favor his model of "the deep structure of the historical imagination". Although this model is designed primarily for the western historiography, its implications are, in my view, far-reaching, and can be applied to a wide range of texts that portray the past. For example, the levels of conceptualization distinguished by White (1973:2)—chronicle, story, mode of emplotment, mode of argument, and mode of ideological implication—are equally typical of many anthropological and historical narratives. The modes of argument—the Formism, Organicism, Mechanism, and Contextualism[3]—characterize even a wider range of analytical prose and, as I will show in the fifth chapter, can be applied to the analysis of ancient historical models. Importantly however, none of these fully discredits the positivistic component of the study of the past. Regardless of whether the truth exists and whether it is comprehensible, the desire to acquire it is what matters.

The sociopolitical mentality of historical agents is an intrinsic part of the events, phenomena, processes, structures and models of the past. By including the ideas and thoughts of the historical agents in anthropological and historical interpretations, we make the study of the past more thorough, intimate, and insightful. Thorough theoretical justifications for this premise can be found in the writings of several social thinkers, and in particular, in the works of R. G. Collingwood and Mikhail Bakhtin. To Collingwood (1946:214), the object of historical study was not "the mere event, but the thought expressed in it". Historical events, in his view, were meaningless without the ideas expressed in them. A good example of this point was the murder of Caesar, which, according to Collingwood, was to be understood through the thoughts of Brutus at the moment of stabbing. Following this, I would argue that not only the events, but also the phenomena, processes, structures, and models of the past become more meaningful when conceptualized with the help of the thoughts of the historical agents. The past as such does not exist without the ideas of those who lived through it or thought about it. Meanwhile, to Bakhtin (1975, 1979), one of the defining features of the novelistic discourse was multivocality, i.e., the simultaneous speech of several distinct characters. This multivocality, in my view, should be typical of not only the novelistic discourse but of any text aimed at a humanistic study of either the present or the past. The emic perspective of the historical agents is as important as the etic perspective of the researcher.

Applied to the study of ancient civilizations, these assumptions lead to a new method of using ancient texts in the interpretation of material cultures. The aim of this method is to discern structures and regularities from the phenomena and processes of the past. The objects of scrutiny, however, are humans, whose agency is conceptualized through the analysis of their sociopolitical views. Unlike some social scientists would like us to believe[4], such aims and objects are perfectly compatible; focusing on the human agency does not necessarily exclude structuralism, essentialism, or any other systemic methodology. Extracted from ancient texts and applied to the study of the *longue durée*, the ideas of the historical agents can, in fact, connect structure and agency in a holistic and humanistic picture of the past, one that will encompass both the emic and etic perspectives. In other words, regardless of whether history shapes ideas or ideas shape history; literature, mythology, and oral traditions absorb ideas of a sociopolitical nature. In one way or another, these ideas reflect the realities of time and are innately incorporated in a historical process. Their use in the creation of archaeological interpretations is a good alternative to epiphenomenal models of western scientific origin.

This method is nevertheless fundamentally different from the idea that the proper way to understand India is by using indigenous categories (Marriott 1990; Marriott and Inden 1977). By proposing to consider the ideas of the historical agents, I do not intend to diminish the importance of our own perspective. The mentality of the other cannot substitute the thinking of the self, and if there is such a thing as the true explanation, it is hidden deeply in between the data, the ideas of the historical agents, and the mind of the researcher. Projected on the study of ancient South Asia, these suggestions open multiple and unexplored directions for research. One of the directions that will be pursued in this book has to do with the idea of the most ancient city, a topic which has played a key role in shaping our knowledge about the genesis of ancient civilizations, yet in the context of ancient South Asia remains poorly explored. As F. R. Allchin (1989:15) has once noted, "the emergence of cities and states is a neglected subject, both for archaeologists and historians of South Asia, deserving far more attention than it has so far received." This book will address this neglected subject on five analytical levels.

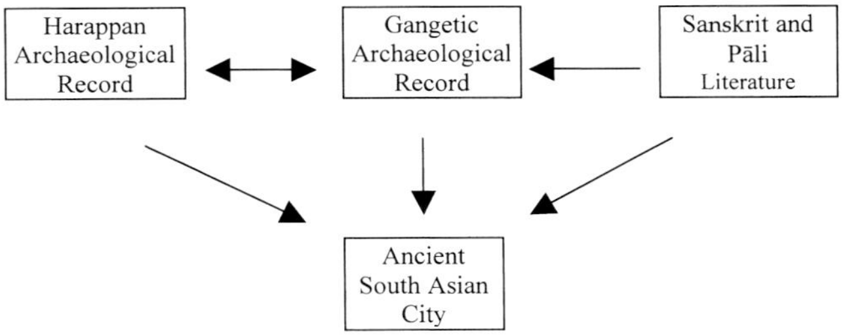

Figure 1.1 Archaeology and texts in ancient South Asia: Directionality of a conjunctive analysis.

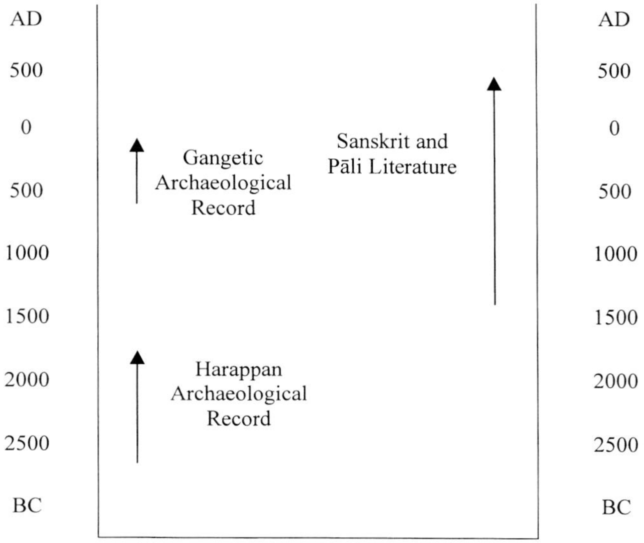

Figure 1.2 Archaeology and texts in ancient South Asia: Chronological correlations.

On the first level, I will bring together a representative sample of the Sanskrit and Pāli texts of the late first millennium BC and the early first millennium AD with the goal of extracting the definitions of the city and determining whether these definitions share an ideological nucleus, i.e., a quintessential concept of the city by the historical agents. On the second level, I will use this ideological nucleus as a model for the analysis of the archaeology of the Ganges civilization. The goal of this analysis will be to determine whether this model can enhance our understanding of the city in the Ganges civilization. On the third level, I will use the same ideological nucleus as a model for the analysis of the archaeology of the Harappan civilization. In a similar way, the goal of this analysis will be to determine whether the model extracted from the texts can enhance our understanding of the Harappan city. On the fourth level, I will introduce two ancient Indian theoretical models reminiscent of the contemporary ideas of civilization and complex society. Finally, on the fifth level, I will propose a hypothetical model of the ethos and genesis of the ancient Indian civilization. The investigation of the idea of the city in this book thus will involve the analysis of three main sets of data: the Pāli and Sanskrit literature, the archaeology of the Ganges civilization, and the archaeology of the Harappan civilization (see Figures 1.1–1.2). Clarifications need to be made on how these qualitatively different and chronologically unrelated data can work together.

As far as the relationship between ancient Indian literature and the archaeology of the Ganges civilization is concerned, it can be safely acknowledged that many well-known Sanskrit and Pāli texts were compiled and recorded at the time when the cities of Ahicchatra, Bhita, Kausambi, Mathura, Sravasti, and Vaisali were flourishing. Therefore, it is not unreasonable to assume that the descriptions of historical and mythical cities found in these texts were at least partly inspired by actual historical experience. The relationship between ancient Indian literature and the archaeology of the Harappan civilization is a much more contentious issue. The compilers of the Tipiṭaka, Epics, Sūtras, Śāstras, and Purāṇas were clearly not the historical agents of the Harappan cities.[5] In fact, their analytical perspectives may have been as distant from the realities of the third millennium BC as our analytical perspectives from the birth of Christianity or the fall of the Roman Empire. In both anthropological archaeology and history, comparing distinct cultural entities is nevertheless a widely practiced method. Scholars have compared state formation in Mesoamerica with state formation in Mesopotamia, early urbanization in China with early urbanization in West Africa, the American Revolution with the French Revolution, the industrialization in Europe with the industrialization in Asia, and so forth. In a similar way, if we leave aside the notorious correlations between the Harappan culture and Vedic literature, we can investigate the two earliest South Asian civilizations from a comparative perspective. Given the scale of their sociopolitical complexity and the amount of cultural similarities, the Harappan and Ganges civilizations are, in fact, the ideal candidates for a comparative study. Meanwhile, ancient concepts present an appealing alternative to the epiphenomenal models of western scientific origin. It is unfortunate that while many of these concepts are arguably as complex and profound as some contemporary social theories, we continue employing theoretical constructs that have very little to do with the culture-historical environment from which our data originate.[6] For example, the terms "Feudalism" and "Medieval" are European in origin, yet are still used in South Asian historiography.[7] Ancient Indian literature, in the meantime, provides great potential for the search of plausible analytical models. It is unfortunate that the historicity of this literature is still seen by some as dubious. Let me now turn to this important and contentious issue.

The Historicity of Ancient Indian Literature

Most genres of Sanskrit and Pāli literature—the Vedic canon, Tipiṭaka, Epics, Sūtras, Śāstras and Purāṇas—have been scrutinized from a variety of theoretical perspectives. The issue of their historicity is not the exception. The amount of scholarly literature dealing with whole genres or the separate texts from an historical angle is quite significant. Nonetheless, the value of Sanskrit and Pāli literature for historical and anthropological interpretation of South Asia's past remains highly controversial. Some scholars believe that any use of this literature in historical reconstructions is meaningless. The archaeologist D. K. Chakrabarti (1997:162), for example, asserts that "from the point of view of history-writing" the use of ancient Indian literature is "puerile, creating nothing more profound than a kind of Orientalist mist, beginning and ending in itself".[8] Other scholars believe that the ancient Indian texts not only have historical value but also can be seen as historical chronicles.[9] For example, the Sanskrit Purāṇas are still used for direct historical reconstruction and the precise date and the location of the Mahābhārata battle are being proposed (Singh 1994).

There is no need to get into a detailed analysis of literature dealing with the historical value of Sanskrit and Pāli texts; there are several good reviews putting this literature in a chronological and thematic perspective (Bongard-Levin 2000, 2001; Bongard-Levin and Iliin 1985, 2001). Suffice it to say that aside from the extreme opinions cited above, there have been some important contributions. The works of Wilhelm Rau (1956, 1971, 1972, 1974, 1976, 1983), Elena Elizarenkova (1999), Romila Thapar (1976, 1978, 1984, 2000a, 2003), George Erdosy (1988, 1989, 1994, 1995b, 1995c), and Michael Witzel (1987, 1989, 1991, 1995a, 1995b, 1997a, 1997b, 2001) deserve, in my opinion, particular attention; for each of these authors has found his or her own way to treat the ancient Indian texts as historical sources. Rau, Elizarenkova, and Witzel have looked at the Vedic Canon as the source of historical data. Erdosy has related the development of the earliest branches of Sanskrit and Pāli texts to state formation in Northern India. Romila Thapar, being the most prolific in her ability to see history beyond texts, has touched upon a large variety of sociopolitical issues of early North Indian history. Overall however, one must conclude that aside from the pioneering work on the identification of Early Historic sites by Alexander Cunningham (1871) and his followers, the study of the most ancient Indian literature has brought no great revelations for the analysis of archaeological data. A good example of how a recent attempt to relate the results of archaeological excavations to Sanskrit texts has ended unsuccessfully is the project "The Archaeology of the Rāmāyaṇa Sites". In 1975–1986, a distinguished Indian archaeologist B. B. Lal took on the project aimed at verifying the historicity of the great Sanskrit epics, the *Mahābhārata* and *Rāmāyaṇa*. Under this project, Lal excavated at Ayodhyā, Sringaverapura, Bharadvaja Asrama and Nandigrama, the sites featuring prominently in the *Rāmāyaṇa* and associated with the important events in the life of Rāma. Judging from the published results of this project, Lal (1981, 2002a) provided only minimal evidence in support of the existence of a historical core beyond the epics. Neither did he manage to relate archaeological and textual data directly and convincingly.

The question then arises whether we should follow the advice of skeptics and give up the attempts to relate the ancient Indian texts to history and archaeology or should continue looking into the alternative ways of using the texts in the interpretation of archaeological record. The answer to this question depends, in my view, not only on our readings of the texts but also on the definition of history as a scholarly discipline and on the

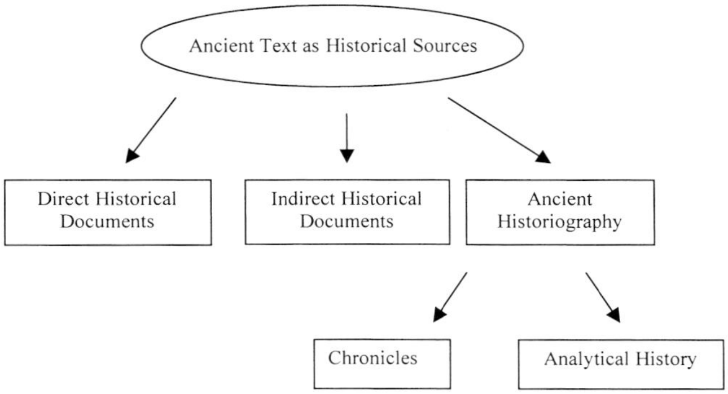

Figure 1.3 Ancient texts as historical sources.

ways in which the historicity of texts is evaluated; for it is my profound conviction that the reason why some scholars vehemently deny the historicity of Indian literary tradition while other scholars continuously misuse it in dubious historical reconstructions lies in the erroneous understandings of history rather than in the allegedly a-historical nature of ancient Indian literature.

There are many ways in which archaeologists as historians, archaeologists as anthropologists, and historians can classify ancient texts as historical sources. One can distinguish at least three types of such texts: direct historical documents, indirect historical documents, and the works of history *per se* or historiography (see Figure 1.3).

Direct historical documents are the records of economic, political, social or cultural life of the studied societies. These can be edicts, commercial transactions, laws, political treatises, and the like. The Narmer Palette, the Laws of Hammurabbi, and the hieroglyphic inscription on the staircase at Copan are the examples of this type of texts. In South Asia, aside from the undeciphered Harappan texts, the earliest well-dated historical documents are the Aśokan inscriptions. Arguably, parts of the Sūtras, Śāstras, and Purāṇas that deal with architecture, science, ritual and various aspects of daily life can be also seen as direct historical documents.

Indirect historical documents are any texts that accidentally absorb bits and pieces of historical information. The *Ṛgveda* is the earliest known indirect historical document in South Asia. Although it was not aimed at recording historical information directly, it contains data on material culture, sociopolitical organization, and even economic issues.

Historiography as the intentional writing of history is characteristic of many ancient societies. Classical Greece, Imperial Rome, Han China, and the Medieval Near East had highly sophisticated traditions of history-writing. Whether the earliest South Asian civilization had developed historiographic traditions is a debatable issue. On one hand, as a chronicle no text of Sanskrit or Pāli literature can stand a comparison with *The Record of the Historian* by Sima Qian or *The History of Peloponnesian War* by Thucydides. On the other hand, very few ancient civilizations can boast of having such an elaborate sociopolitical theory as the one of the *Kauṭilīya Arthaśāstra*. One must not forget that historiography is a very multifarious activity and it is profoundly erroneous to limit its scope to the arrangement of facts into chronologically structured narratives. In fact, the overwhelming majority of historical works are deeply interpretative; instead of presenting *l'histoire événementielle*, they expound on structures, concepts, functions, meanings, regularities, causes, and contexts.

Hayden White (1973:2), the historian whose ideas have largely inspired me for the search of alternative ways of using ancient Indian texts in archaeological and historical studies, defines historical work as "a verbal structure in the form of a narrative prose discourse that purports to be a model, or icon of past structures". White's definition is so broad that it can accommodate not only all the texts written by professional historians but also many myths, religious treatises, recorded oral traditions, and even historical novels. For example, the Greek myth of five ages as narrated by Hesiod, the *City of God* by Saint Augustine, the Biblical *Genesis*, *The Epic of Sundiata*, and the novel *The Three Kingdoms* by Luo Guanzhong, according to White's definition, must all be seen as historical works. In the context of Sanskrit and Pāli literature, this means that significant portions of the Purāṇa-Itihasa tradition, of the Buddhist canon, and of the Jaina literature are historical. For example, the story of the four Yugas, creation myths, the genealogical sections of the Purāṇas, and the early Pāli chronicles certainly qualify to be called the works of history. That many of Sanskrit and Pāli texts are recorded in verse is not, in my view, an obstacle. First, there are versions of creation myths, the Yuga Story, and the Purāṇic genealogical lists that are recorded in prose. Second,

I disagree with Hayden White that a historical work must be necessarily written in prose. Homer's *Odyssey* and *Iliad*, *The Song of Roland*, *The Elder Edda*, *The Tale of Igor*, and the Purāṇa-Itihasa tradition—either fully or in parts—can and, in my view, should be seen as the works of history. That significant portions of these texts are mythological does not mean that they are entirely a-historical. Modern social thought is rooted in mythology as well; in spite of all their scientism and claim of objectivity, many of the contemporary ideas and theories have predecessors both in the Greco-Roman mythology and in Judeo-Christian theology. Moreover, many social concepts are in essence myths. Ernst Cassirer has brilliantly demonstrated this on the example of the idea of the state. "If we try to resolve our contemporary political myths into their elements"—Cassirer (1946:277) wrote at the height of World War II— "we find that they contain no entirely new feature. All the elements were already well known. Carlyle's theory of hero worship and Gobineau's thesis of the fundamental moral and intellectual diversity of races had been discussed over and over again". If Cassirer was right, mythology can be separated neither from politics nor from historical thinking. As Levi-Strauss (1974:255) once wisely remarked, "it suffices... for history to move away from us in time or for us to move away from it in thought, for it to cease to be internalizable and to lose its intelligibility". When history loses its intelligibility, mythology comes to aid. Fortunately or unfortunately, this is simply unavoidable.

From this point of view, ancient Indian literature contains a wealth of historical information. That this information is useless for the reconstruction of *l'histoire événementielle* does not mean that it is equally useless for creating analytical models, discerning structures, and conceptualizing the *longue durée*. Let us consider one example. Sanskrit literature is known for its elaborate theories of the state. These theories are found in the *Kauṭilīya Arthaśāstra*, *Yājñavalkyasmṛti*, *Manusmṛti*, *Mahābhārata*, *Vālmīki Rāmāyaṇa*, as well as in several other texts. Scholars have studied the genesis, structure and textual development of these theories in great detail (Ghoshal 1959; Kane 1941–1953; Scharfe 1989, 1993; Spellman 1964). The least that these studies show is that many of these theories attained very high theoretical level and in terms of their analytical complexity, abstraction, and even historical practicality are not any worse than some contemporary and recent theories of the state. The Maṇḍala Theory found in the *Arthaśāstra* is particularly noteworthy; for it portrays the state both iconographically and conceptually. Iconographically, the state in the *Arthaśāstra* is defined as the saptanga, a maṇḍala (circle) that consists of seven constituent elements—the ruler, the minister, the ally, the country, the city, the treasury, and the coercive power—and is incorporated into two other maṇḍalas: aṣṭadaśakamaṇḍala (the circle of the eighteen) and caturmaṇḍala (the circle of the four). Conceptually, the state, according to the Maṇḍala Theory, is contingent on its constituent elements, political interactionism, and territorial expansionism. In spite of this theoretical sophistication, very few archaeologists and historians have looked upon the Maṇḍala Theory or, for that matter, at any other theory of the state found in Sanskrit literature as a potential source for the interpretation of archaeological data.[10] This is particularly unfortunate for the issues of the state in proto-historic and Early Historic South Asia—its existence, nature, and the time of emergence—are still highly controversial.

The same applies to other concepts widely used in anthropological and historical interpretations. The local versions of the ideas of social complexity, civilization, the city, evolutionary progression, culture, cyclicality, knowledge, and identity can be possibly found in ancient Indian literary traditions. The search, extraction, and analysis of these ideas can help us better understand the phenomena and events of the South Asia's past through the study of its material remains. Moreover, if we use texts as the sources for ideas rather than facts, meticulous text-historical methods will no longer matter. On this, I agree with Giorgio Bonazzoli (1979, 1980, 1981, 1982, 1983a, 1983b, 1985) who has argued that orality, ritualism, and the rules of recitation of the ancient Indian texts question the usefulness of many text-historical methods. The primary focus of Bonazolli's analysis was the Sanskrit Purāṇas, yet his observations, in my view, are applicable to some other genres of Sanskrit literature as well. The Purāṇas, according to Bonazolli (1983a:256), have a "multi-authenticity, each text of each age being authoritative for that particular period", and "the latest, and probably the final stage of the Purāṇas... is what should be taken as the starting text for any critical edition or any research". What this means is that the sociopolitical concepts found in Sanskrit and Pāli literature can be used regardless of their precise date and textual history. As works of history, such concepts deserve no less attention than, for example, the theory of sociopolitical formations by Karl Marx or the idea of civilization by V. Gordon Childe (neither of these concepts, by the way, are devoid of mythology in Cassirer's definition of myth).

That being said, I hope that this book will set the grounds for a new direction in the study of ancient South Asia. As an alternative to the epiphenomenal theories of the contemporary academe, the models from Sanskrit and Pāli literature may fill in a conceptual vacuum that is felt in the study of the earliest periods of South Asian history.

The Ideas of the City and Civilization in the Study of Ancient South Asia

The last 50 years have seen major advances in the archaeology of the Harappan and Ganges civilizations. Many new sites have been surveyed and excavated. Almost every single theory has been challenged and reconsidered. Nonetheless, if one carefully evaluates what has been written on the ideas of the city and civilization—arguably, the two of the most important concepts in the study of early complex societies—he or she will quickly discover that in spite of the enormous amount of new case-studies there have been not that many thorough conceptual and synthetic interpretations.

The Harappan/Indus Civilization

Theories about the nature of the Harappan civilization have been summarized in detail elsewhere (Kenoyer 1998; Maisels 1999; Possehl 1999, 2002c). The two most controversial issues seem to be its sociopolitical organization and ethnocultural identity. Marshall (1931), Mackay (1935, 1948), Piggot (1950) and Wheeler (1947, 1962) were the first to seriously discuss these issues. Marshall (1931) envisioned the Harappans as peaceful and trade-oriented burghers who created a monotonous and boring material culture. Wheeler (1947, 1962) and Piggott (1950) pictured the Harappan civilization as a socially hierarchical and elite-controlled polity. Both models relied on the analogies derived from European and Near Eastern archaeology. As Piggott (1950:133) admitted, "to a British archaeologist the inevitable parallel" was "the Roman Empire supervening upon prehistoric Iron Age barbarian settlements of his own country". The theory promulgated by Piggott and Wheeler emphasized social disparity, the despotism of priest-kings, and the supremacy of the Sumerian civilization. In his frequently quoted book *Prehistoric India to 1000 BC*, Piggott (1950:153) portrayed the Harappan civilization as "a state ruled over by priest-kings, wielding autocratic and absolute power from two main seats of government, and with the main artery of communication between the capital cities provided by a great navigable river". Comparative, holistic, and definitive, this view epitomized and concluded the first stage in the conceptualization of the Harappan sociopolitical system.

The next important contribution to the understanding of the Harappan sociopolitical organization was made by Walter Fairservis (1961, 1967, 1975, 1984a, 1984b, 1992), who envisaged the Harappan polity in rigid terms of cultural evolutionism. Based on his own "decipherment" of the script and the interpretation of archaeological record, Fairservis (1992:133) defined the Harappan sociopolitical system as "a hegemony of chiefdoms with paramount chiefs in each and a system of subsidiary chiefs responsible to the former". It is not known to me whether Fairservis arrived at this conclusion on his own or was inspired by the writings of the Indian historian S. C. Malik (1968:103–104), who, being under the influence of Elman Service, had proposed earlier that the Harappans lived in a chiefdom. One thing however is clear; the ideas of Malik and Fairservis inspired others to reconsider their understandings of the Harappan sociopolitical system. Shaffer (1982:45, 49), for example, concluded that the Harappan culture was unique, and its alleged homogeneity, being largely exaggerated, was a result of "an internal artifact distribution system" rather than of the control of the central government. Miller (1985:58) depicted the Harappan society as normative and "antagonistic to anything, which threatened it". The Harappans, according to Miller (1985:63–64), had no institutions of great power and wealth. They did not develop distinctive social and religious hierarchies. Their sociopolitical structure was monastic and possibly egalitarian in ideology. Possehl (1998) developed this line of argument suggesting that the Harappans lacked central government, territorial sovereignty, bureaucracy, and the monopoly of force. The Harappan sociopolitical system was unique and not to be understood with the help of a simplistic evolutionary progression of band-tribe-chiefdom-state. The Harappan society was localized and united by national ideology, which, according to Possehl (1998:289–290), was in "a constant battle against fissiparous forces: on one side, ideology, trade, ecological integration, and marriage; on the other, lineage, brotherhood, territory, history, one's occupational locus, and pride in one's social group and the memory of ancestors who helped to make it great". Recently, Possehl (2002c:55–57) has added to this model the notions of nihilism, heterarchy, and multi-leveled councils. Nihilism, according to Possehl, was an ideology that characterized the Harappan society after the alleged transition from the Early to Mature Harappan; heterarchy rather than hierarchy defined most of the relations between social groups; and a series of civic and regional councils performed the duties of the government.

The views of the Harappan civilization as a state-level society are found in the writings of Jacobson (1986) and Kenoyer (1989b, 1991a, 1992, 1994b, 1997). Jacobson argued that the Harappan sociopolitical structure was characterized not only by urbanization, writing, population size, geographic range, trade, colonialism, and religion, but also by social stratification, full-time centralized government, police power, communication, taxes, sovereignty and militarism. Kenoyer (1991a:369) developed this view by suggesting that the Harappan culture was a state "composed of several competing classes of elites who maintained different levels of control over the vast regions of the Indus and Ghaggar-Hakra Valley". In one of his more recent publications, Kenoyer (1997) drew parallels between the political structures of the Harappan and Ganges civilizations, and suggested that the Harappan political organization had the form of competing city-states.

Other noteworthy issues of the Harappan sociopolitical system that have been discussed in literature are the existence of caste and the meaning of urban segregation. On the issues of caste, Malik (1968:106–107) initially proposed that both the caste and the perpetuation of the caste by birth were present in the Harappan society. This view was contested by S. P. Gupta (1974:58), who, at that time, argued that "the material culture of the Harappans would not have died out without leaving any legacy of urbanization since the technical know-how of things would have been smoothly passing through the ages". Having changed, since then, his views on this and other issues, S. P. Gupta (1996, 1999) now advocates the full identity of the Harappan and Vedic cultures. Lamberg-Karlovsky (1999) entered the debate by assembling several archaeological traits as evidence for caste in the Harappan civilization. On the issues of urban segregation, Kenoyer (1989b, 1992) suggested that craft specialization might have been at least partially responsible for urban segregation; onerous occupations and ceramic production, according to Kenoyer, were localized and possibly segregated.

The issue of ethnocultural identity of the Harappan civilization is even more controversial.[11] Today, many Indian scholars identify the Harappan civilization with the Vedic literature and culture (Bisht 1999; S. P. Gupta 1996, 1999; Lal 1998b, 2002b, 2002c; Simha 1987, 1995). They argue that the *Ṛgveda* presents an authentic and legitimate source for the historical reconstructions of the religion, culture and sociopolitical organization of the Harappans. Evidence in support of this view is based on the conjunctive interpretation of the *Ṛgvedic* hymns and the Harappan archaeological record. S. P. Gupta (1996) and Simha (1987, 1995), for example, argue that the Harappans were responsible for the composition of the *Ṛgveda*, since the Harappan civilization was the only urban entity of ancient South Asia that fit the descriptions of the allegedly urban culture of the *Ṛgvedic* hymns. The proponents of this theory quote enthusiastically from the *Ṛgveda* yet rarely comment on the semantics of specific words, cultural contexts, and the mythopoetic nature of the Vedic literature. Evidence centers on numerous words for houses, architecture, pottery, and other attributes of material culture (S. P. Gupta 1996:146; Simha 1995:189–319). Sentences like "a very large house with a thousand gates" (RV VII:88.5) are cited to show the urban nature of the society described in the *Ṛgveda*.[12] Simha (1987, 1995) even claims that the *Ṛgveda* provides evidence for each of the ten characteristics of the early cities/civilizations as defined by Childe. In other words, monumental architecture, social stratification, and writing were all, from this point of view, characteristic of the Vedic society. It is both ironic and sad that in order to demonstrate the indigenousness and uniqueness of the Harappan and Vedic cultures, Simha needs Childe's ten points. Would it not make more sense to try to find analytical constructs in the rich legacy of ancient Indian texts, particularly when one is so keen to show the greatness of the Harappan civilization? Evolutionary and materialist, Childe's model is neither the only, nor, as I will be arguing later, the best way to think about ancient civilizations.

To conclude, both the sociopolitical system and ethnocultural identity of the Harappan civilization remain highly contentious. It is still debated whether the Harappan civilization was an early state, chiefdom, or an unique sociopolitical structure; whether caste, hierarchical ranking, or heterarchical relations characterized its social system; and whether it is appropriate to allude to the Vedic literature as a source for the reconstruction of the Harappan identity. The ethos of the Harappan civilization thus in many respects remains obscure. The phenomenon of the Harappan city, which is one of the most explicit achievements of this civilization, has not been properly analyzed either. In spite of myriads of case-studies summarizing data from separate sites, there is an apparent lack of conceptual syntheses that would focus on the idea of the Harappan city.[13]

The Ganges Civilization

The term "Ganges civilization" is not as common as the term "Harappan/Indus civilization". T. N. Roy seems to have been responsible for the first proper definition of this term in his book *The Ganges Civilization: A critical archaeological study of the PGW and NPBW periods of the Ganga Plains of India*. As Roy (1983:IX) asserted, his initial intention was "to re-examine the whole mass of material from the vaguely termed 'PGW and NBP periods of culture' in relation to the preceding black-and-red and black slipped wares and the succeeding Saka-Kushana culture". As a result of this study, Roy proposed that the composite culture, which evolved from the mingling of the PGW and the NBPW around 700 BC, could be seen as the first phase of the Ganges civilization. The next phase—the Mature Ganges—began around 400–300 BC and lasted until the beginning of the Saka-Kushana period. Both phases were defined by Roy through a set of distinctive cultural traits in a geographically distinct area.

Wittingly or unwittingly, Roy touched upon a very important issue—the meaning and usefulness of the terms used in the archaeology of Iron Age northern South Asia. Since the publication of the report on the excavations at Hastinapura, the Iron Age archaeology of northern India has been conceptualized with the help of a few types of pottery that served both as chronological and cultural markers. As it turns out however, these types of pottery—the OCP, PGW and NBPW[14]—are not only unable to represent complex cultural changes that took place in Northern India during the second and first millennia BC, but are also dubious in terms of their significance at the site of Hastinapura itself (Lal 1954–1955).[15] Other terms, such as Early Historical or Pre-Mauryan, are not much more helpful either. Vague and generic, they have been used in very different chronological, cultural and geographical contexts. For the lack of better terminology, the term "Gangetic or Ganges civilization" fits best the purpose of our enquiry; it is geographically focused and culturally inclusive. I will therefore use this term to designate a number of cultural and sociopolitical entities, which were located in the Gangetic Doab and were responsible for the second urbanization in the South Asian Subcontinent in the middle of the first millennium BC.

To my knowledge, there is no comprehensive up-to-date summary of the theories about the nature of the Ganges civilization. A very significant portion of the scholarly literature dealing with this civilization is descriptive rather than conceptual. Yet, in contrast to the studies of the city in the Harappan civilization, there has been a good deal of research dealing with the Early Historic cities from a holistic and comparative perspective.[16] Since much of this research is repetitive or conceptually lacking, it will suffice to mention just a few most significant publications. B. B. Dutt (1925) was one of the first to discuss the nature of the ancient Indian city from a holistic perspective. Based on the analysis of the *Vastuvidyā* and *Śilpa Śāstras* (the Sanskrit architectural treatises), Dutt (1925:299–320) defined the city "as the expression of civic life" and argued that the architecture and layout of Indian cities reflected the origins of communalism, patriarchism, and caste. Hindu religion and spiritualism, according to Dutt (1925:310–315), were also vividly expressed in the architectural layouts of towns and villages. Dutt (1925:320) concluded that ancient Indian cities were "great schools of nationalism in its most liberal and comprehensive sense." Dieter Schlingloff (1969) made an important contribution to the study of the city in the Ganges Civilization by bringing together, for the first time, both textual and archaeological sources in a comparative manner. Schlingloff (1969:45–46) discussed in detail various forms of fortifications and concluded that in scale the ramparts of Early Historic cities had parallels neither in the East nor in the Greco-Roman world; they could be compared only with protohistoric and Early Historic earthen works of the Nordic region. The defining markers of Indian cities, in contrast to their Greek counterparts, were massive fortification systems. Internal city planning and the residence of the king also played an important role in defining images of these cities. Schlingloff interpreted this layout in terms of rigid social distinctions between the king and the people. Some of Schlingloff's observations are quite remarkable and I will return to them in the second chapter. A. K. Ramanujan (1970), in a brief conference paper dealing with city images in Sanskrit and Tamil literature, also made a number of very revealing conclusions, some of which could be particularly interesting from a methodological perspective. Discussing the value of literature as a source of information for social scientists, Ramunajan (1970:224) for example suggested that the special contribution of literature was "its vision, its intuitive grasp of structure, its perspective; not the facts themselves so viewed by the facts as seen by the imaginative accuracy of a mind that is not merely factual". Literature, according to Ramunajan (1970:224), could provide a whole "repertoire of perceptions otherwise not available" to social scientists. It is the image of the city, not facts for which literature is important. From the point of view of my own argument which was partly exposed above and to which I will return shortly, these statements are very enlightening. The ideas, not the facts, matter when one evaluates the historical value of ancient texts. Aside from the theoretical assumptions, Ramanujan also made some stimulating general observations about the images of cities both in Sanskrit and Tamil literature. For classical Sanskrit, he suggested, the city was "civilization as it was to the Romans". "A contrast between the city and country or forest" was "realization of a more pervasive thematic contrast which might be described as the nature/culture opposition" (Ramanujan 1970:240). In Tamil poetry, however, the city was "not opposed to country or forest" (Ramanujan 1970:241). "The continuity of city and country, nature and culture" was, as Ramanujan (1970:242) believed, typical of Tamil esthetics. Amalananda Ghosh (1973) conceptualized the emergence of ancient Indian cities through the interpretation of archaeological data and a limited number of literary sources. The process of urbanization, in Ghosh's view, was autochthonous and spurred by the introduction of iron implements that allowed production of surplus. This surplus, through authority and trade, was diverted to support the non-food producing population. "No survival nor revival of the long dead Harappan urban tradition was necessary", and "any motivating foreign influence could be easily ruled out" (Ghosh 1973:89). Vijay K. Thakur (1981) attempted to create possibly the most comprehensive and theoretical picture of the ancient Indian city. He approached the city as a whole, consisting of economy, society, culture, and administration. As the point of departure, Thakur referred to the classical definition of the early cities by V. Gordon Childe, yet adjusted Childe's ten criteria to the Indian context. As Thakur (1981:19) concluded, ancient Indian cities were distinguished by thirteen criteria: dense population, non-food-producing classes, reliance on a variety of food resources, strong agricultural hinterland, the presence of ruling class, fortifications, monumental architecture, writing, craft and trade guilds, monetary exchange system, concentration of surplus and foreign trade, new artistic expressions, and urban consciousness. The causes that led to the second urbanization were fundamentally different from those of the first urbanization. Harappan cities, Thakur (1981:84) maintained, were ruled by theocratic priest-kings, while Gangetic cities were governed by the dharma. Chakrabarti (1970, 1972–73, 1974, 1985a, 1985b, 1988b, 1995, 2000) addressed the issue of Early Historic urban growth from an ideational perspective. Having done much research on the invention and spread of iron, Chakrabarti (1972–73, 1974, 1985a) concluded that political power rather than economy or the invention of iron had played the dominant role in the emergence of Gangetic cities. Erdosy (1985, 1987, 1988, 1995a) arrived at a somewhat similar conclusion through the conjunctive analysis of archaeology and ancient Indian texts. The Indian city, according to Erdosy (1987:17), was a center and agent of political power, "a predator on the countryside without the innovativeness exhibited by predators in some other cultural regions, such as Europe". F. R. Allchin made a noticeable contribution to the study of Early Historic urbanization by providing the main up-to-date synthesis (1995a) of archaeological data and by proposing several original interpretations (1989; 1990). Marked by the construction of massive ramparts and fortifications, the Early Historic urbanization, according to Allchin (1989:14), took off in two regions: the North West Frontier Province and the Ganga-Yamuna Doab. Last not the least, Brajadulal Chattopadhyaya attempted a brief yet comprehensive interpretation of the ancient Indian city from the point of view of Sanskrit and Tamil literature. According to Chattopadhyaya (2003:123, 128), "there could be as many views of the city as there were viewers", and "a city is what its inhabitants make of it", not the physical components. The city thus is primarily an idea, not a static empirical entity; the point which is quite novel when compared to the previous studies and which, to a large degree, is similar to my own view of the city, to which I will turn in the next chapter. Based on a comparative analysis of the texts, Chattopadhyaya distinguished normative and secular view of the city. In a normative view, the city was "a special place, to be separated from other spaces and protected, a place... accommodating workers, artisans, merchants, farmers and others, but only as ancillaries to the king and his rāṣṭra, because the city belongs to them" (Chattopadhyaya 2003:128). In a secular view, the city was "a beehive of secular activity, of movement..., and of convergence" (Chattopadhyaya 2003:128).

The study of the city in Early Historic India thus has been significantly more successful than the study of the city in the Harappan civilization. Without a detailed critique of the mentioned theories—my own views will be laid out in the ensuing chapters—it can be nonetheless safely concluded that much remains to be done in investigating the idea of the Gangetic city from the point of view of archaeology and ancient Indian literature. The historical agents are still mute. Their thoughts and ideas have not been properly utilized in the analysis of archaeological data.

Comparative and Holistic Interpretations

Aside from currently fashionable correlations of the Harappan archaeology with the Vedic literature (I purposely avoid here a detailed review of these theories as it has been done elsewhere (see, for example, Witzel 2001; or Bryant and Patton 2005), there has been a clear lack of conceptual studies of the Harappan and Ganges civilizations from a holistic and comparative perspective. Malik (1968, 1975, 1979) seems to have made the most innovative contribution to this topic. The concept of the Indian Style, presented in his brief monograph *Indian Civilization: A Formative Period,* is a good example of a holistic anthropological model. As Malik (1968:106–108) defines it, the Indian Style has three constituent elements: 1) "the unique institution of caste"; 2) "the genealogical means of the perpetuation of caste status by birth"; and 3) "the importance which is given to the memorization process, especially in descent reckoning, ritual prayers, etc., which are all learnt by oral repetition (substitution of writing)". The Indian Style is formed during the Mature Harappan period and maintains its significance throughout the second and first millennia BC, thus directly connecting the Harappan, Post-Harappan, and Early Historic eras. Aside from Malik, one must mention the works by D. K. Chakrabarti (1972–73, 1974, 1995), J. M. Kenoyer (1995, 1997), Jim Shaffer (1992, 1993), and most recently Monica L. Smith (2003, 2003, 2006). Chakrabarti has given the first thorough archaeological overview of ancient South Asian cities, which remains one of the most authoritative and interesting sources on this subject. The author's skeptical attitude to the ancient Indian literature is understandable as he approaches the texts from a positivist stance as a source of facts rather than ideas. His holistic view of the ancient Indian civilization is however quite evident. Judging from a few interpretative remarks in his recent overview of South Asian archaeology, Chakrabarti (see, for example, 1999:82) finds elements of the Great Tradition as early as in the Neolithic or even Upper Paleolithic periods. Shaffer (1992) must be credited with defining a comprehensive periodization of South Asian protohistory and with drawing convincing parallels between the first and second urbanization. Despite significant differences in sociopolitical organization, the archaeological record of the Harappan and Ganges civilizations display, in Shaffer view, a number of striking similarities, indicative of "a unique cultural tradition traceable for millennia" (Shaffer 1993:54). In a similar way, Kenoyer (1995) has advocated the notion of the Indo-Gangetic tradition, emphasizing the long-term cultural similarities between the Harappan, Post-Harappan, and the Gangetic cultural phenomena. Kenoyer's article, "Early City-States in South Asia: Comparing the Harappan phase and the Early Historic Period" deserves particular attention (Kenoyer 1997), for aside from its highly controversial argument regarding the Harappan state and city-states, it offers a novel methodological perspective, which, to a large degree, is similar to the method proposed above. Specifically, the author's reference to the Maṇḍala Theory in the context of archaeological data is not so different from my own suggestion of treating ancient texts as sources of ideas rather than facts. The author's explicit positivist and scientistic stance however prevents him from utilizing the ideas of the historical agents to their full potential. Relying primarily on archaeological data and feeling obliged to allude to the scientific models, such as the Central Place Theory, Kenoyer, in my view, undermines his otherwise very inspiring efforts to conceptualize archaeological data with the help of ancient sociopolitical ideas. Last but not least, M. L. Smith (2006) has recently attempted a comparative anthropological study of urban growth in the South Asian Subcontinent during the Indus, Early Historic, and Medieval Periods. Having analyzed an impressive amount of archaeological data, M. L. Smith (2006:130–132) arrives at a number of stimulating yet highly debatable conclusions. First, M. L. Smith defines three levels of distinctions: 1) "political involvement in urban activities"; 2) "the extent to which warfare and conflict are evident in the record of urban development"; and 3) "evidence for cultural discontinuities". On the level of political involvement, M. L. Smith argues that "each succeeding era of urban development shows an increasing visibility of elites and social hierarchy". On the level of warfare and conflict, she suggests that the purpose of fortification systems changes "from a principal emphasis on flood control and economic control in the Harappan period to a principal emphasis on warfare and defense in the Medieval period". On the level of cultural discontinuities, M. L. Smith maintains that the unity of the material culture during the Harappan and Early Historic period shifts to cultural discontinuities during the Medieval period. Second, M. L. Smith delineates the relations between shared motifs and urban development. In the Harappan period, she argues, shared motifs precede urban developments; in the Early Historic period, shared motifs emerge simultaneously with urbanism; and in the Medieval period, political factors begin to play a more important role than cultural. Third, as an overall conclusion, Smith suggests that the Harappan cities were "the economic nexus of trade routes"; the Early Historic cities were more distinctly juxtaposed to countryside; and the Medieval cities were an important element of state management. Although M. L. Smith's model of the South Asian city is elaborate and well-argumented, her entire research philosophy is the direct opposite of the one proposed in this study. Adhering to the ideas of positivist and scientistic archaeology, M. L. Smith (2006:101–102) believes that Childe's list of ten characteristics provides a useful tool for distinguishing between urban and non-urban settlements, and that the increase of research projects since Childe's time has "not resulted in any better criteria for defining ancient cities on the basis of materials found within them". The city, in M. L. Smith's view, thus is a concrete, empirical, and intelligible entity, which can be known and understood through the analysis of material culture. There is no reason, at this point, to critique M. L. Smith's model, as the present book, in its every empirical and epistemological aspect, offers a very different approach to the study of the past, the meaning of archaeological data, and the ideas of the ancient South Asian city and civilization. The ensuing chapters will address many of the issues raised in the writings of the aforementioned scholars both from the empirical and theoretical points of view.

Conclusion: Three Groups of Data

A new holisitic and conceptual analysis of the earliest forms of complex sociocultural organization in northern South Asia is what this book is designed to accomplish, and the ideas of the city and civilization, being the two key analytical units in the study of early complex societies, are the starting point. Our discussions will focus on three groups of data: a selection of excerpts from Sanskrit and Pāli texts, a sample of archaeological sites of the Ganges civilization, and a sample of archaeological sites of the Harappan civilization. Excerpts from Sanskrit and Pāli texts will shed light on how the ideas of the city and civilization were envisioned in ancient India, while the archaeology of the Harappan and Ganges civilizations will show whether these ideas have any merit and can be utilized in our own interpretations of the earliest tracks of South Asian history.

For the texts, I have chosen a sample of excerpts from eight different sources: *Aṅguttara-Nikāyā*, *Kauṭilīya Arthaśāstra*, *Vālmīki Rāmāyaṇa*, *Mahābhārata*, *Milindapañha*, *VāyuPurāṇa*, *BrahmāṇḍaPurāṇa*, and *Lalitāmāhātmya of the BrahmāṇḍaPurāṇa*. These texts cover more of than a millennium of ancient Indian history and stand for a wide range of ideological, literary, and sociopolitical traditions. I will discuss the reasons for the choice of these texts prior to their analysis in the second and fifth chapters. For archaeological data, I have selected excavation reports from thirteen sites of the Ganges civilization and twelve sites of the Harappan civilization. The sites of the Ganges civilization are: Ahicchatra, Atranjikhera, Bhita, Hastinapura, Kausambi, Mathura, Pataliputra, Rajghat, Rajgir, Sonkh, Sonpur, Vaisali, and Sravasti. The sites of the Harappan civilization are: Allahdino, Banawali, Chanhu-Daro, Dholavira, Harappa, Kalibangan, Kot-Diji, Lothal, Mohenjo-Daro, Nausharo, Surkotada, and Sutkagen-Dor.[17] I will explain why these particular sites were chosen in the beginning of the third and fourth chapters. Without further ado, let me now proceed with my next subject, the idea of the city in theory and in ancient Indian literature.

2 The Chimera of the City: From Saint Augustine to Doxiades and to Ancient Indian Literature

Ancient and modern cities share only traits of so general a character that they are virtually useless for classificatory or analytical purposes.

—Paul Wheatley (1972:601)

The idea of the city has produced an immense amount of literature in several fields of knowledge. Architects, geographers, sociologists, economists, historians, archaeologists, ethnographers, philosophers, and theologians have tackled the idea of the city for many centuries. On one hand, thinkers like Spengler, Weber, Mumford, and Doxiades have brought about generic definitions highlighting morphological or functional traits that are allegedly shared by all cities. On the other hand, anthropologists, historians and ethnographers have produced a myriad of case studies pointing to the uniqueness of each individual case. To reconcile generic definitions with case studies is difficult and unnecessary. The city both as an idea and an historical phenomenon is so multifarious that it can accommodate almost any approach, whether it is the Central Place Theory, Ekistics or a murky historical poeticism in the style of Oswald Spengler.

In this chapter, I will revisit some of the grand theories of the city, the ones that, in my view, made the most significant impact on the perceptions of this phenomenon in western Europe and North America. By tracing the differences between these concepts, I will present my own thoughts with regard to the intelligibility and phenomenology of the city. I then will turn to the perceptions of the city in Sanskrit and Pāli texts and will determine whether these perceptions share a quintessential ideological nucleus. I will conclude by discussing whether this nucleus has merit for the analysis of archaeological record.

Torn Between the Two Cities

The intellectual legacy beyond the idea of the city is so immense that it would be unrealistic and unnecessary to attempt a comprehensive review.[1] It is sufficient to refer to several key thinkers whose ideas represent different disciplines and mark major developments in the western understanding of the city. Let Saint Augustine speak for theologians, Oswald Spengler for philosophers, Max Weber for sociologists, Lewis Mumford for historians, Walter Christaller for geographers, and Konstantinos Doxiades for economists. In conclusion, I will juxtapose the views of these generic thinkers with one recent case-study, an ethnography of the Newar city of Bhaktapur by the anthropologist Robert Levy. This will consequently allow me to present my own understanding of how we should investigate the idea of the city.

De Civitate Dei by Saint Augustine is a theological treatise having to do with a holistic picture of the world and the church, written from a perspective of an early Christian mystic.[2] Aside from theology and mysticism, *De Civitate Dei* presents a multiplicity of ideas on history, philosophy, and politics. It would not be an exaggeration to say that many of these ideas laid the foundation for western historical and sociopolitical thought for many centuries ahead. The ideas of linearity, inevitability, rationality, statehood, civility, and even the prototype of the idea of progress can be found in *De Civitate Dei*.[3] One of the main themes of *De Civitate Dei* is the dualism of two cities: the *Civitas Terrena* (*The Earthly City*) and the *Civitas Dei* (*The City of God*). This theme was not new at the time of Saint Augustine. In the Old and New Testaments, there were many references to the duality of the city. Moreover, the theme of the city featured prominently in the Latin literature of the fourth century AD, e.g., the writings of Cicero, Marcus Aurelius, and Seneca. Nonetheless, Saint Augustine's approach was truly novel. He narrated world history in the form of two intermingled processes: the history of the Earthen City and the history of the City of God. The idea of the city, although not explicitly defined, played an important role in his narrative.

The use of the word *civitas* (city) by Augustine is allegorical and figurative. There is a debate among scholars on what exactly Augustine meant by using this term—the state, the two communities of men, or some kind of a sociopolitical system (see Donnelly 1995b:203). In spite of what the answer is, it is clear that Augustine used this term consciously and by using it implied a high degree of historical realism. Manifestations of this realism are found throughout the treatise and can be exemplified in the three following observations. First, the notions of the two cities are inspired by real historical examples. Aside from mysticism and scholastic speculations, Augustine describes in detail Rome, Jerusalem, Athens, and Babylon. The history of Rome plays a particularly important role in his narrative. Second, the City of God and the Earthly City are intermingled in history. Depending on the context, Jerusalem becomes either the City of God or the Earthly City. For example, in the same sentence of book XVII, Jerusalem is described as the Earthly City "which is in bondage with her children" and "the true city of God... eternal in the heavens, whose children are all those that live according to God in the earth" (Augustine 1993:570). Third, the description of the Earthly City displays elements of positivist historical analysis (see Book XV.4). The Earthly City is torn by wars, conflicts and disasters. "...it desires earthly peace for the sake of enjoying earthly goods,...it makes war in order to attain to this peace" (Augustine 1993:481).

From the point of view of the conceptual development of the idea of the city, it does not, in fact, make much difference whether the city, in Augustine's view, was the state, a community of men, or something else. That the idea of the city was grounded in the historical examples of Rome, Babylon, Jerusalem, and Athens, that the history of the earthen city displayed historical realism and, most importantly, that the city was seen as a key analytical concept were great achievements in and unto themselves. By envisioning the entire world history through the idea of the city, Saint Augustine envisioned the city as an analytical whole of unprecedented significance and elevated it to the highest theoretical levels. In my view, this was one of his greatest and long-lived theoretical achievements, which in many respects laid the foundations for the further development of the idea of the city. Following Augustine, many thinkers have referred to the idea of the city as a key element of the historical process. Yet, it was not until the beginning of the twentieth century that the view of the city as the quintessence of human history reached its apogee in the writings of the German philosopher, Oswald Spengler.

Der Untergang des Abendlandes (Spengler 1918) was a popular read in Europe at the beginning of the twentieth century. Published at the end of World War I it met the aspirations of its time and audience very well. As a new philosophy of history, it aimed at discerning the ethos of history, civilization, and culture. The theme of the city appears in the second volume, in the chapter titled "The soul of the city". Extremely expressive and in parts poetic, this chapter is a powerful panegyric, in which the city is presented as the greatest achievement of civilization, history, and culture. In making his point, Spengler (1926:II.90–91) is categorical: "All great Cultures... are town-cultures... Higher man... is a town-tied animal. ...World history is the history of civic man". The ethos of the city, in Spengler's view, lies in its soul. The birth of this soul is a miracle. This soul is a totality and organism, which "lives, breathes, grows and acquires a face and an inner form and history." The presence of this soul, not the size, is what distinguishes the city from the village. The city, is "a place from which countryside is... regarded, felt and experienced". The city is "a unit objectively expressing the form-language and style-history that accompanies the Culture throughout its life course". Spengler (1926:II.97–98) classifies cities in three categories: the town, the city, and the world-city. The distinction is the matter of spirit, not the number of inhabitants. The world-city is the ultimate goal. It arises as "the monstrous symbol and vessel of the completely emancipated intellect". It is "the center in which the course of a world-history ends by winding itself up". The fate of the city is doomed; it self-destructs. As Spengler (1926:II.107) puts it: "...growing from primitive barter-center to Culture-city and at last to world-city", the city "sacrifices first the blood and soul of its creators to the needs of its majestic evolution, and then the last flower of that growth to the spirit of Civilization—and so, doomed, moves on to final self destruction". The vision of the city by Spengler, I believe, dwells on the ideas of Saint Augustine. Both in *De Civitate Dei* and in *Der Untergang des Abendlandes*, the city is portrayed as the key element of history. As Spengler (1926:II.95) concludes:

> ...we cannot comprehend political and economic history at all unless we realize that the city, with its gradual detachment from and final bankrupting of the country, is the determinative form to which the course and sense of higher history generally confirms.

Aside from Spengler, no work on ancient or modern urbanism is written without a reference to Max Weber. *Wirtschaft und Gesellschaft* by Weber (1922) is the classic of urban sociology and of western-oriented approaches to urban studies. In contrast to Spengler's poetic and anti-structural approach, Weber created a very prosaic concept of the city. Urban communities, according to Weber (1958:80) "appear... only in the Occident". In other words, China, southeast Asia, India, Mesoamerica and many other parts of the world did not know urbanism whatsoever! There are a few exceptions in the Near East, e.g., Syria, Phoenicia and Mesopotamia. Nevertheless, even in these regions, the emergence of urban communities is occasional and rudimentary. This startling conclusion stems from Weber's formalist sociological method of defining an urban community. The true urban community, according to Weber (1958:81), must display "a predominance of trade-commercial relations" and be characterized by five traits: "a fortification, a market, a court of its own and at least partially autonomous law, a related form of association, and at least partial autonomy and autocephaly, thus also an administration by authorities in the election of whom the burghers participated". Strictly following this definition, even many cities of Europe would not classify as urban communities. Neither could most contemporary urban conglomerates be called cities. Aimed at rigid scientific analysis, Weber's theory is impeccably formalist yet barely applicable to actual case-studies.

Another frequently quoted example of a western-oriented approach to the study of the city is *The City in History* by Lewis Mumford (1961). The definition of the city suggested by Mumford in this lengthy treatise is systemic, structural, cosmic, symbolic and closely associated with the idea of civilization. The city is defined by Mumford (1961:30) as:

> a structure specially equipped to store and transmit the goods of civilization, sufficiently condensed to afford the maximum amount of facilities in a minimum space, but also capable of structural enlargement to enable it to find a place for the changing needs and the more complex forms of a growing society and its cumulative social heritage.

So far as the cosmic role of the city is concerned, Mumford (1961:31) envisions it as "the means of bringing heaven down the earth" and as "a symbol of the possible". Adhering to the ideas of Mircea Eliade, he believes that the symbolic purpose antedates any other functions of the city. The western centrism of Mumford is striking. Teotihuacan, Monte Alban and Anyang are not even mentioned, and it is asserted that urbanism diffused from the Old World to the New World. Some archetypal ideas, according to Mumford, must have been borne by traders, explorers or religious missionaries. A possibility of independent invention is totally excluded because of the alleged parallelism in urban forms (Mumford 1961:91).

Understandably, the writings of Weber and Mumford are not very popular among specialists in the early complex societies. Today, archaeologists seem to prefer theories from geography and economy. Central Place Theory has played a particularly prominent role in the recent archaeological literature. In 1933, the German scholar Walter Christaller (1933) published a book on settlement geography (*Siedlungsgeographie*). Christaller's task was to establish patterns of settling a large area, i.e., the laws determining number, distribution and sizes of settlements. Christaller (1966:201) characterized the nature of his research as either national economics or economic geography, and emphasized that the questions and problems he dealt with were purely geographical. Following the ideas by his predecessor Robert Gradmann (1913), Christaller (1966:16) tentatively defined the town as a "center of its rural surroundings and mediator of local commerce with the outside world". Given this, it is important to realize that Christaller purposely avoided using the terms "town" or "city". The idea of centrality, in Christaller's view, applied not only to towns but also to market shops and other places. Meanwhile, there were towns, which did not, or only in a very small measure, showed centrality. Christaller unambiguously stated that he dealt neither with settlement or economic units, nor with political communities. The unit of his study was the central place, not the town or for that matter any other settlement(!). Christaller (1966:16–17) distinguished four types of central places: central places of higher order, central places of a lower order, central places of the lowest order, and auxiliary central places. The dispersed places were the opposite of the central places. Christaller distinguished three types of dispersed places: "the areally-bound ones—those settlements the inhabitants of which live on their agricultural activities, which are conditioned by the land area surrounding them," "the point-based ones—those settlements the inhabitants of which make their living from resources found at specific locations", and "those which are not bound to a central point, and area, or an absolute point". Again, it is important to realize that dispersed places were not necessarily equal to rural settlements or villages. Like the central place, the dispersed place was a term in itself with its own independent meaning. The network of central and dispersed places constituted settlement systems, which were the object of Christaller's investigation. Christaller (1966:164–166) convincingly managed to show that from the point of view of market economy, these systems revealed regular patterns of size, distribution and numbers of settlements.

Another attempt at a systematic analysis of human settlements was undertaken by the Greek scholar, Konstantinos Doxiades, whose intention was to create a new discipline that would deal exclusively with human settlements. Doxiades named this discipline Ekistics. Ekistics, according to Doxiades, had both practical and theoretical implications. On one hand, it was expected to solve the crisis in human settlements. On the other hand, it was driven by the desire to bring together "the facts, concepts and ideas related to human settlements" and "to readjust the disciplines and professions connected with the settlements" (Doxiades 1968:15). Ekistics was meant to have a truly holistic nature and to systematize human settlements in their totality. Based on size and function, Doxiades defined eight types of settlements: isolated settlements, nomadic settlements, agricultural settlements, urban-agricultural settlements, towns and cities (one category), metropolis, dynametropolis, and dynamegalopolis. Each of these eight categories was carefully defined, described and subdivided. For example, the category of towns and cities was characterized by Doxiades (1968:91) as follows:

> Their main characteristic is that they are static. This, in the past, was expressed by the fact that they were usually surrounded by walls, and even when they were not, they remained compact since no urban dweller could live out in the open countryside… they contain two to twenty thousand people and sometimes even up to fifty and a hundred thousand; but they seldom go beyond this. Only very few cities of the past are known to have had a population in the hundreds of thousands and these were the administrative capitals of empires….

In addition, each of the eight categories was subdivided into types. For example, towns and cities were classified into 11 types in accordance with their anatomy, structure and dynamics (Doxiades 1968:156–157). In a sense, Doxiades created an evolutionary progression. Settlements developed like organisms from the earliest prehistoric forms that would eventually merge into the single city of the future, the Ecumenopolis.

Such is a brief summary of the six grand theories that aim at the generic definition of the city. What unites these concepts is that they assume the existence of one true definition. Despite all the differences between their teachings, Saint Augustine, Spengler, Weber, Mumford, and Doxiades believed that the city was an organic and intelligible whole. Not denying the value of this premise for broad cross-cultural and philosophical studies, I nonetheless believe it has very little use for the study of specific historical cases. To demonstrate this, let us consider one example: a recent ethnography of the Newar city of Bhaktapur by the anthropologist Robert Levy (1984).

Theoretically, Levy follows the long-forgotten yet in my view still interesting ideas of the nineteenth century French historian Fustel de Coulanges (1864) who saw the city in a very particularistic way, as a self-sufficient and idiosyncratic entity consisting of autonomous units. The main theme of Levy's study is the poetic imagination of Bhaktapur. Levy spends a good deal of time describing and analyzing symbolic forms, spheres, structures and opposites which make, in his view, Bhaktapur's system meaningful. Among other traits, Levy looks at the pantheon, religion, purity and power. Levy (1984:601–615) distinguishes what he terms "resources for intelligibility", which include hierarchical levels of phenomena and ideas, discrete categories, membership in assigned domains, amorphous boundaries between the spheres, and the systematic ordering of Bhaktapur's mesocosm. The conclusions that Levy arrives at stand in striking contrast to generic urban theories. "In both fact and ideology," Bhaktapur is depicted by Levy (1984:68) as self-sufficient and "turned in on itself". Very little of its world is part of larger economic or political networks. Both economy and politics are of local nature and significance. Levy concludes with a myriad of statements, all in one way or another reiterating the holistic, self-sufficient, idiosyncratic and symbolic nature of Bhaktapur's world. On one occasion, Levy (1984:615) maintains that "bits and pieces" of Bhaktapur's mesocosm construct "an aesthetic and philosophical unity" like a "Wagnerian multidimensional artwork". On another occasion, Levy (1984:616) characterizes Bhaktapur's mesocosm as "a powerful device for turning accident and history into structure, for trying to escape the contingencies and consequences of history, for trying to capture change, to make change seem illusory within an enduring order".

In the context of grand and generic theories, Levy's ethnography is enlightening; it shows that despite all the developments in positivist scholarship, *the city remains an object of humanistic studies. Moreover, its humanistic side cannot be adequately conceptualized by means of scientific methods*. If juxtaposed to the positivistic and systemic concepts, studies like the one by Levy highlight the uniqueness of individual cases and raise a number of eternal questions about what the city is, as a phenomenon, as an idea, and as an object of scholarly enquiry (see Table 2.1). Is the city an objective historical phenomenon or an idea in the minds of the historical agents? Is it a sociopolitical and cultural whole or a myriad of sporadic elements? Is it an object of scientific enquiry or a product of poetic imagination? Is it a part of complex systems or a thing in itself? Is it a static entity or a live organism?

It is my profound conviction that these questions do not have unambiguous answers. For as an idea and a historical phenomenon, the city is innately dual. In the fifth century AD, Saint Augustine conceptualized this duality in theological terms, as an opposition between the City of God and the Earthen City. Today we see it as an opposition between the city as a product of poetic imagination and the city as an intelligible and objective whole. Figuratively speaking, we are still torn between the two cities. Our scholarly ways of thinking have not moved us far from the theology of the medieval mystic.

Table 2.1
What is the City?

	OR	
An objective historical phenomenon?		An idea in the minds of historical agents?
A sociopolitical and cultural whole?		A myriad of sporadic elements?
An object of scientific enquiry?		An object of poetic imagination?
A part of complex systems?		A thing in itself?
A static entity?		A live organism?

Against this theoretical background, what I would like to propose follows my discussion in the previous chapter and can be summarized in three brief points:

1) *There cannot be a single and universally comprehensive definition of the city.* For generic concepts of the city, whether scientific or humanistic, are not able to reflect the city in its totality. Being valuable for broad cross-cultural studies, these concepts have little use for the anthropology and history of spatially and temporally restricted cases. Moreover, many generic urban theories are Eurocentric and, by definition, fail to explain the specificity of cases outside of the western world.[4] Choosing to use these theories in the study of ancient civilizations, anthropologists end up concluding that these civilizations had no cities.[5] To give credit to generic theoreticians, at least some of them were well aware of the limitations of their theories.[6]

2) *The city as a complex sociopolitical and cultural phenomenon can be studied and conceptualized in a multitude of ways from the viewpoint of several academic disciplines*. One can investigate and classify cities based on size, layout, economy, political structure, social organization, artistic life, and so on. One can look at cities from a morphological, structural or functional angle. One can approach the city internally as a system consisting of numerous elements or one can approach the city externally as part of a large network of settlements. Importantly, most of these approaches are complementary to each other, not mutually exclusive. For example, showing that Central Place Theory works in the context of a given ancient culture does not mean that other approaches cannot be used in the context of the same culture.

3) *The city as an historical phenomenon is inseparable from the idea of the city in the minds of the historical agents.* In other words, how the people themselves define the city is crucial for our own understanding of the phenomenon of the city. In this, I again follow the subjectivist and reflective ideas of R. G. Collingwood (1946:214), to whom the object of an historical study was "not the mere event, but the thought expressed in it". I would add that this applies not only to historical events, i.e., the actions by the historical agents, but also to historical phenomena, i.e., the products of the actions by the historical agents. The city is exactly this kind of phenomenon and is consequently incomprehensible without the thought expressed in it. The thought expressed in the phenomenon of the city is, in my view, the perception of the city by the historical agents. Keeping all these in mind, let us turn to the Sanskrit and Pāli literature.

The Idea of the City in Ancient Indian Literature

In Sanskrit and Pāli texts, there are many terms that designate units of settlements. The most frequent ones are kuṭi, gāma, nigama, durga, pura, pattana, puṭabhedana, and nagara. Nagara can be also subdivided into nagaraka, mahānagaraka, rājadhānīya nagara, mula nagara, sakha nagara, kuḍḍa nagaraka, ujjangala nagaraka, paccantima nagara, and so forth. The *Kauṭilīya Arthaśāstra* has its own settlement terminology differentiating between droṇamukha, sthānīya, karvatika, and sangrahana. Scholars have tried to define and classify these terms. Yet, variations in their meanings remain obscure. In my opinion, it is erroneous to assume that each of these terms must have an inflexible and static meaning that correlates with the size and function of a specific settlement. Some of the terms may be synonymous; other might have been ambiguous from the time of their emergence. For example, it is still debated whether the word nigama designates an urban or rural settlement. Given that the object of our enquiry is the idea of the city in its broad conceptual meaning, it is important to focus on the texts and passages that utilize the least ambiguous terms. The terms durga, pura and nagara seem to fit this purpose the best.

Cities are described in many Sanskrit and Pāli texts of the late first millennium BC and early first millennium AD. The Buddhist Canon, Śāstras, Sūtras, Epics, Purāṇas as well as other genres of Sanskrit and Pāli literature contain descriptions of historical, divine and ideal cities. For the analysis in this chapter, I have chosen a sample of excerpts from the seven texts: *Aṅguttara-Nikāya*, *Kauṭilīya Arthaśāstra*, *Vālmīki Rāmāyaṇa*, *Mahābhārata*, *Milindapañha*, *VāyuPurāṇa*, and *Lalitāmāhātmya of the BrahmāṇḍaPurāṇa*. A few brief remarks need to be made with regard to the nature and date of these texts.

The *Aṅguttara-Nikāya* or as it is sometimes called *Ekuttara* is the fourth book of the *Sutta-Piṭaka* which is the second part (basket) of the Buddhist canon of Tipiṭaka (three baskets). The precise date of the compilation of the *Aṅguttara-Nikāya* is unclear yet most researchers agree that the core of the *Sutta-Piṭaka* had been formed by the Mauryan period (third to second century BC; Geiger 1916; Hinuber 1996; Law 1933; Somapala 1994).[7] In content, the *Aṅguttara-Nikāya* is a religious treatise; it expounds on the foundations of the Buddhist teaching, the dhamma. The *Aṅguttara* consists of 11 sections each arranged according to the ascending sets of numbers. For example, the first section deals with the sets of one, the second section with the sets of two, and so on until the section of the 11s.

The *Kauṭilīya Arthaśāstra* is a treatise on warfare, politics, and statehood, composed allegedly by one of the ministers of Chandragupta Maurya, either Kauṭilīya or Chanakya. The actual authorship and date of this treatise are debated (Hillebrandt 1923; Kalianov 1959; Kangle 1960, 1963, 1965; Rangarajan 1992; Scharfe 1993; Trautman 1971). Trautman (1971) argued that some of its chapters had been composed earlier than the other. In fact, if Trautman is right, the extant *Arthaśāstra* presents a compilation of several treatises composed roughly between the third century BC and the fourth century AD. The section of the *Arthaśāstra* that will be analyzed in this chapter is dated by Trautman (1971) to the second century AD.

The *Vālmīki Rāmāyaṇa* and the *Mahābhārata* comprise their own genre of Sanskrit literature, the Epics. Orally transmitted and recited for hundreds of years, they had not been recorded in a written form until the middle of the first millennium AD. There is an immense amount of philological literature dealing with the chronology and textual history of these two texts.[8] Given the tremendous length, orality and lengthy composition time of the *Mahābhārata*, I believe it is impossible to reconstruct the precise history of its compilation, yet it is likely that its earliest oral components date to the middle of the first millennium BC.

The *Milindapañha* (*The Dialogues of Milinda*) is a non-canonical Buddhist text composed in the form of dialogues between the Indo-Greek ruler Milinda (Menander) and the Buddhist monk Nāgasena. In it, Nāgasena asks questions about the various aspects of the Buddhist teaching. The answers given by Milinda reflect the Theravāda view of Buddhism and are not any different from the teachings of the canonical texts. Most scholars date the *Milindapañha* to the second century AD and believe that its original version was composed in the northwestern India. It is also believed that the extant *Milindapañha* presents a collection of the earlier texts (Basu 1978; Demieville 1924; Fussman 1993; Hinuber 1996; Paribok 1989).

The Purāṇas form a separate genre of Sanskrit literature, comprising 18 major texts, the Māhapurāṇas, and 18 minor texts, the UpaPurāṇas. As in the case with the epics, the study of the Purāṇas has produced an immense amount of scholarly literature.[9] The dating of the Purāṇas is very difficult, for like the epics they were transmitted orally and absorbed concepts and narratives of different time and origin. The *VāyuPurāṇa* is usually seen as one of the earliest and most authoritative texts of the Purāṇic corpus. Most researchers date its compilation to the fourth or fifth centuries AD (Hazra 1940; Kirfel 1927; Rocher 1986:243–249).

Finally, the *Lalitāmāhātmya* (*The Glorifications of Lalitā*) or as it is also called the *Lalitopākhyāna* (*The Tale of Lalitā*) belongs to the genre of devotional texts attached to the Purāṇic corpus. Although technically the *Lalitāmāhātmya* is part of the *BrahmāṇḍaPurāṇa*—one of the eighteen canonical Māhaurāṇas, which in date and content is similar to the *VāyuPurāṇa*—most scholars believe that it is a later independent treatise compiled and added to the *BrahmāṇḍaPurāṇa* by the devotees of Śakti (Rocher 1986:156–160).

The chosen texts thus span over a millennium-long history of Sanskrit and Pāli literature and represent several literary genres and ideological traditions. There are two main reasons why I believe these texts can be analyzed conjointly. First, the texts speak for a diverse and comprehensive spectrum of ideological and literary traditions. Since the goal of my inquiry is not to reconstruct the textual history of the idea of the city, but to determine whether there was a conceptual nucleus that united the definitions of cities found in different Sanskrit and Pāli texts, any ideological, chronological, or literary diversity makes it more likely that at the end we will arrive at representative and inclusive conclusions. Second, the descriptions of cities found in these texts represent each of the three main types of city descriptions found in Sanskrit and Pāli literature. I believe these types include: 1) definitions of the city as an abstract sociopolitical concept; 2) conventional manuals on the layout of cities; and 3) panegyrics on divine, mythical, and historical cities. As far as the specific breakout of the selected texts, excerpts, and types of descriptions is concerned, the description of the Frontier City from the *Aṅguttara-Nikāya* and the description of the City of Virtuousness from the *Milindapañha* represent the abstract definitions; the description of fortified settlements from the *Kauṭilīya Arthaśāstra* represent the conventional manuals; and the descriptions of Ayodhyā from the *Vālmīki Rāmāyaṇa*, of Hastināpura from the *Mahābhārata*, Sāgala from the *Milindapañha*, and the divine abode of the goddess Lalita from the *Lalitāmāhātmya* represent panegyrics.

Aside from these two reasons, one must remember that in social science it is not uncommon to lump together ideas, facts, and phenomena of very different nature. For example, when investigating the idea of the city in the western intellectual tradition, most researchers will find it justified to bring together the theories of Oswald Spengler and Walter Christaller, even though the difference between the milieus of these two scholars is no less significant than the difference between the milieus of the compilers of the *Aṅguttara-Nikāya* and the *Arthaśāstra*. Meanwhile, in archaeology it is common to make general and far-reaching conclusions through the excavation of very small areas. The trajectories of state formation, nature of urbanism, social organization, and many other grand theoretical issues are frequently reconstructed based just on a few excavated squares and soundings. Keeping all these in mind, let us now turn to the selected texts.

Several scholars who previously looked into the descriptions of cities found in these texts held the opinion that since by style and context all of these descriptions

Table 2.2

Definition of the city in the *Anguttara-Nikaya* VII.63

City Characteristics	Auspicious Qualities
Pillar	Faith
Moat	Conscientiousness
Encircling road	Fear of blame
Armory	Learning
Troops	Heroism
Gate-keeper	Concentration
Rampart	Wisdom

Stores	Meditations
Grass, wood and water	First meditation
Rice and corn	Second meditation
Sesame, beans, vetches, etc.	Third meditation
Ghee, butter, oil, honey, etc.	Fourth meditation

are repetitive, standardized, and hyperbolic, they have no use for historical studies (Erdosy 1988:11; Ghosh 1973:49–50). Obviously, I disagree with this interpretation. Since the object of our enquiry is the idea of the city, not the description of real historical places, I believe it is quite reasonable to assume that beyond the unreal and repetitive details, these descriptions contain abstract visions of the city as a sociopolitical phenomenon.[10] These visions are expressed in the attributes and features of the ideal cities; and the hyperbole and repetition are the best proof of this. In other words, if every single panegyric or conventional manual depicts the city as having attributes "x", "y" and "z", this may indicate that in the view of these texts, the city was defined by having attributes "x", "y" and "z".

One of the earliest manifestations of the idea of the city in Sanskrit and Pāli literature is found in the *Book of the Sevens* (*Sattaka Nipāta*) of the *Aṅguttara-Nikāya*. This book is called the *Book of the Sevens* because each of its suttas expounds on various sets of seven; e.g., seven auspicious qualities (AN VII.6), seven obsessions VII.12), seven suns (VII.62), and so forth. Sutta 63 of the *Book of the Sevens* presents a definition of the king's frontier city, raňño paccantima nagara (AN VII.63.1) (see Table 2.2). In the beginning of this sutta, Buddha tells the monks that in order to be properly protected, the frontier city must have seven characteristics[11] and four types of storage.[12] The seven characteristics are further defined as: the deep-seated, well dug in, immovable and unshakable pillar;[13] the deep and wide moat;[14] the wide encircling road;[15] the great armory of spear and sword;[16] the large quantity of troops;[17] a clever, intelligent and wise gate keeper;[18] and the high, wide and plastered rampart.[19] The four types of storage include: the great stores of grass, wood and water;[20] the great stores of rice and corn;[21] the great stores of sesame, beans, vetches and cereal;[22] and the great stores of medicines, such as ghee, fresh butter, oil, honey, sugar, and salt.[23] In the concluding segment of the sutta, the seven characteristics are matched with the seven auspicious qualities of the Aryan disciple, while the four types of storage are matched with the four meditations. Specifically, it is said that just like the city has a pillar, the Aryan disciple has faith;[24] just like the city has a moat, the Aryan disciple has consciousness;[25] just like the city has an encircling road, the Aryan disciple has fear of blame;[26] just like the city has a great armory, the Aryan disciple has learning;[27] just like the city has troops, the Aryan disciple has great energy;[28] just like the city has a gate-keeper, the Aryan disciple has concentration;[29] just like the city has a rampart, the Aryan disciple has wisdom.[30] The four meditations equated with the four types of storage are the first meditation, the second meditation, the third meditation and the fourth meditation (AN VII:63.20–23).

The frontier city thus is conceptualized with the help of a rigid numerical formula typical of the *Aṅguttara-Nikāya* (see Table 2.2). Although this makes the concept of the city somewhat dogmatic, I believe it is unlikely that the traits of the city were chosen randomly and thoughtlessly just to match the formula. As the contents of other suttas indicate, there is a large degree of mundane practicality in the analogies provided by the Buddha. Used as succinct illustrations for the norms of the Buddhist teaching, these analogies are usually rational, logical, and quite realistic.[31] The sutta discussed here is not the exception and the definition of the frontier city represents this kind of analogy. In other words, the traits selected for the Sutta VII.63 must have been seen by the Theravadins as characteristic of the ideal frontier city. *From a morphological perspective, these traits represent five constituent elements: a pillar, fortifications, an encircling road, troops, and storehouses.* Spoken by the Buddha and correlated with the qualities of a virtuous devotee, these traits, in my view, are indicative of the conceptualization of the idea of the city in the early Buddhist literature.

A later version of this definition is found in one of the chapters of the *Milindapañha*.[32] When the king Milinda enquires of the monk Nagasena whether Nagasena himself or any of his teachers have ever seen the Buddha, Nagasena answers negatively. Milinda then concludes that the Buddha did not exist. In response, Nagasena provides a scrupulous explanation for the existence of the Buddha. The essence of this explanation is in the juxtaposition of the two cities: the nagara, the ordinary city built by an architect, and the dhammanagara, the City of Righteousness built by the Buddha. As the City of Righteousness is the work of the Buddha, Nagasena concludes that the Buddha did once exist. Prior to arriving at this conclusion, Nagasena describes the Ordinary City and the City of Righteousness in great detail.

The Ordinary City is said to be regularly planned; with moats and ramparts all around; with strong gateways, watchtowers and battlements; with wide squares, open places and junctions; with king's highways; with lines of shops; with parks, gardens, lakes, lotus ponds, and wells; with storehouses of food; with the four varṇas; with troops and barracks; with numerous craftsmen and street performers; with actors and prostitutes; and with foreigners from different countries. The City of Righteousness is described somewhat similarly, yet with a stronger emphasis on its abundant bazaars and diverse inhabitants. The main difference between the two cities is that the City of Righteousness is given a rigid definition, whereas the Ordinary City is described in plain narrative prose. The City of Righteousness has 11 traits: a rampart, moat, upper battlement, watchtower, pillar, gatekeeper, upper terrace, market place, cross-ways, and a judgment hall. Just as in the *Aṅguttara-Nikāya*, each of these traits is paired with an auspicious quality, e.g., righteousness, fear of sin, knowledge, energy, faith, concentration, wisdom, suttantas, abhidhamma, vinaya, and constant self-possession (see Table 2.3). Unlike the traits of the frontier city however, the traits of the City of Righteousness are directly equated rather than compared with auspicious qualities; the rampart in the City of Righteousness is righteousness, the moat is the fear of sin, the upper battlement is knowledge, and so forth.[33]

Thus, by the time of the composition of the *Milindapañha*, the concept of the city had become more abstract and acquired two new morphological traits:

Table 2.3

The City of Righteousness in the *Milindapañha*

Structural Element	Auspicious Quality
Rampart	Righteousness
Moat	Fear of sin
Upper battlement	Knowledge
Watchtower	Energy
Pillar	Faith
Gatekeeper	Concentration
Upper terrace	Wisdom
Market place	Suttantas
Cross-ways	Abhidhamma
Judgment hall	Vinaya
Main street	Self-possession

a market place and a judgment hall. The main emphasis in the definition had nevertheless remained similar to that of the *Aṅguttara-Nikāya*; fortifications—a rampart, moat, watchtower and a gatekeeper—continued to play a paramount role in the definition of the city.

In contrast to abstract definitions, the conventional manuals dealing with the construction and layout of cities are found in a larger variety of texts. The *Kauṭilīya Arthaśāstra* devotes two full chapters to this issue by describing the ideal fortified settlement, the durga (KA 4.3–4). In the first chapter, we are introduced to the basic principles of construction. We are told that the durgas must be built in the four corners on the borderlands of the janapada, the country. The sthānīyas, or the centers for tax-collection, must be built in the center of the country. Three moats must be dug around the durga. An earthen rampart must be build next to the moat. On the rampart, a brick pavement must be erected for the movement of chariots. Towers, covered roads with hidden traps, gateways and stores for weapons must be built in various parts of the fortified settlement (KA 4.3.1–35). In the second chapter, we are given details on the internal layout of the durga (KA 2.4.1–31). Given the significance of this chapter, it is worthwhile to quote it at length:

> The layout of the site is as follows: three eastern royal roads and three northern royal roads, 12 gates with proper water drains and secret paths. General roads are four daṇḍas in width. The royal roads, the roads of regional centers, droṇamukha, the roads of regional centers, sthānīyas, country

roads, the roads passing through the pastures, military roads, the roads leading to the places of cremation and the village roads are eight daṇḍas in width. Roads passing through irrigation works and forests are four daṇḍas in width. Roads for elephants and roads passing through the fields are two daṇḍas in width. Chariot roads are five aratnis in width, cattle roads are four aratnis, and roads for small animals and men are two aratnis. The residence of the king must be in the best place of the site that is of access to the four varṇas. In the ninth part of the area to the north from the heart of the construction site, the king must have the palace built in accordance with the prescribed regulations, facing east or north. In the northeastern quarter, there must be places for priests, teachers, sacrifices and ablutions. Ministers should reside there too. In the southeastern quarter, there must be a kitchen, elephant stables and storage. Beyond them, in the eastern quarter, the traders in perfumes, flower garlands, and juices, as well as artists of ornament and kṣatriyas. In the southeastern quarter, there must be storage, depository of legal records, and workmen's shops. In the southwestern quarter, there must be storage for metals and armory. Beyond them, traders in city grain, supervisors of production, military commanders, sellers of cooked food, drinks and meat, prostitutes, actors and vaiśyas must reside in the southern quarter. In the southwestern quarter, there must be stables for donkeys and camels and a workshop. In the northwestern quarter, houses for carriages and chariots. Beyond them, craftsmen working on wool, carpets, bamboo, leather, coats of mail, arms, and shields as well as śūdras, must reside in the western part. In the northwestern quarter, there must be shops with commodities and medications. In the northeastern part, treasury, cows, and horses. Beyond them, the deities of the city and the king, blacksmiths, jewelers and Brāhmaṇs must live in the northern quarter. In free spaces on the construction site, guilds of craftsmen and foreign traders must reside. In the middle of the city, he (the king) must build walled-in little shrines for Aparājita, Aparatihata, Jayanta, Vaijayanta, and temples for Śiva, Vaiśravaṇa, Aśvins, Śrī, and Madirā. He must set up household deities in accordance with the appropriate regions.[34] (He must also erect) the gates devoted to Brāhma, Indra, Yāma, and Senāpati. Outside, one hundred dhanuses away from the moat, there must be religious monuments, holy places, groves, irrigation works, and the deities of the cardinal points in accordance with the cardinal points. The northern or the eastern areas of the cremation ground are for the higher varṇas, southern areas of the cremation ground are for the lower varṇas. For the violation of this, one must pay the lowest fine. The residence of heretics and caṇḍālas must be at the end of the cremation ground. He should draw boundaries for householders in accordance with their cultivated fields.[35] In these fields, by permission they (householders) should set up gardens with fruits and flowers as well as stores of grain and goods. Each enclosure of ten families must have a well. He must prepare, for several years of use, stocks of all kinds of fats, grain, sugar, salt, perfumes, medications, dried fruit, fodder, dried meat, hay, wood, metal, leather, coal, tendons, poison, horns, bamboo, bark, strong timber, weapons, shields, and stones. He must be replacing the old (stuff) with new. He must set up (an army of) elephants, horses, chariots, and infantry under the command of several leaders. Since the leaders would fear each other, the army would not commit treason. The building of frontier cities has thus been explained (KA 2.4.1.31).[36]

Scholars have previously discussed and analyzed information provided in this excerpt (Kalianov 1959; Kangle 1965; Rangarajan 1992). Yet no one has approached it as a peculiar definition of the city. If treated this way, the durga can be defined by the presence of fifteen attributes: namely, royal residence; construction plan; the alignment of streets and houses according to the cardinal directions; a network of roads; an elaborate defense system; segregation of residential areas in accordance with occupation, origin and the varṇāśrama affiliation of residents; ritual places; storehouses; stables for animals; temples; cremation grounds; an army; boundaries between households; and agricultural fields.[37] Various versions of this definition are found in many Sanskrit Purāṇas. In the *VāyuPurāṇa*, for example, the layout of durgas is discussed in the context of the innovations of the Tretā Yuga, the third stage in the sequence of cosmic ages. The *VāyuPurāṇa* describes durgas very briefly. One feels that the Paurāṇikas who compiled the Vāyu had a reference text in mind. Possibly, this text was the *Arthaśāstra*. In the view of the *VāyuPurāṇa*, fortified cities ought to have huge mansions, ramparts, gates and a moat (*VP* 1.8.103–105). The difference between the city and the village is purely a matter of scale. We are told that a hamlet must be two times smaller in diameter than a city, whereas a village is bigger than a hamlet (*VP* 1.8.111.2). Similar descriptions are found in other Māhapurāṇas.

Like the conventional manuals, panegyrics are numerous and can be found in a large variety of Sanskrit and Pāli texts. The description of Hastināpura of the *Mahābhārata*, Ayodhyā of the *Vālmīki Rāmāyaṇa*, Sāgala of the *Milindapañha*, and the divine abode of Lalitā provide good examples of this type of city descriptions.

The description of Hastināpura in the *Mahābhārata* is extremely conventional. In one of the episodes of the Sabhāparva, the second book of the *Mahābhārata*, we are told that Hastināpura was adorned with ponds and trees and its buildings were like the Kailāsa peaks all beautiful, attractive and perfectly furnished. It had gold lattices, the floors were laid with jewels, the stairs rose smoothly and so on.

> ...towered like Kailāsa peaks, attractive and well-furnished, on all sides surrounded with high stuccoed walls... The lattices were made of gold, the floors were paved with precious stones; the stairs rose gently, and the seats and appointments were large. The residences were decked with wreaths and garlands and redolent with superb aloes, white like goose feathers, quite visible from as far as a league, never too crowded, with doors equally wide, and adorned with a variety of features. Their elements were made of many metals, and thus they appeared like the Himalayan summits (*MBH* II.31.20–25; Buitenen 1973:II.90).

In the *Vālmīki Rāmāyaṇa*, the description of Ayodhyā is not much more informative, though more reminiscent of the one in the *Arthaśāstra*. In the second book of the *Rāmāyaṇa*, the *Bālakaṇḍa*, Ayodhyā is portrayed as:

> ...a great and majestic city, twelve leagues long and three wide, with well-ordered avenues... adorned with a great and well-ordered royal highway, always strewn with loose blossoms and constantly sprinkled with water... provided with doors and gates... It was a fortress with deep moat impossible to cross, was unassailable by its enemies, and was filled with horses, elephants, cows, camels, and donkeys... it was filled with every kind of jewel and adorned with palatial buildings... its houses were built in close proximity to one another... it had plentiful store of Śāli rice... king Daśaratha had populated the entire city with thousands of great chariot warriors...the king also peopled the city with great Brahmans who tended the sacred fires and had mastered the Vedas with their six adjunct sciences... (*RM* II.5; Goldman and Sutherland 1985:134–135).

Compared to Hastināpura and Ayodhyā, the description of Sāgala from the *Milindapañha* is a bit more informative. The city of Sāgala, according to the *Milindapañha*, has many attributes that can be assembled in seven groups. Group 1 includes parks, gardens, groves, lakes, and tanks. Group 2 is comprised of rivers, mountains, and woods. Group 3 is represented by various types of fortifications: towers, ramparts, gates, entrance archways, and moats. Group 4 is commercial: it consists of shops, merchandise and money. Group 5 includes architectural features, such as residential houses and the royal palace. Group 6 has different types of storage, that is a variety of warehouses full of goods and food. Group 7 includes a large variety of animals (MiP I.2).

Finally, the description of the divine city found in the *Lalitāmāhātmya*, a devotional attachment to the *BrahmāṇḍaPurāṇa*, follows a similar pattern. In the *Lalitāmāhātmya*, we are told that the city of the goddess Lalitā has towers, city walls, and gates, as well as numerous stables for elephants, horses and chariots.

> It looks magnificent due to its royal roads and has beautiful houses for sāmantas, ministers, soldiers, the twice-born, vetālas, and the female and male śūdras. In its center stands a divine royal residence decorated with doors and gates. This residence has numerous halls... There is a luminous and beautiful throne hall, decorated with nine precious

Table 2.4

Traits of the city from the selected Sanskrit and Pāli texts

Traits	Pn	Dn	Vn	Dg	Hs	Ay	Sg	Vp	Lm
Agricultural fields	–	–	–	+	–	–	–	–	–
Animals	–	–	–	+	–	+	+	–	+
Army	+	+	+	+	–	+	–	–	–
Authority	+	+	+	+	+	+	+	–	+
Cardinal directions	–	–	–	+	–	–	–	+	–
Construction plan	–	+	+	+	–	+	+	+	–
Cremation grounds	–	–	–	+	–	–	–	–	–
Fortifications	+	+	+	+	+	+	+	+	+
Household boundaries	–	–	–	+	–	–	–	–	–
Judgment hall	–	+	–	–	–	–	–	–	–
Parks, gardens, etc.	–	+	+	–	–	–	+	–	–
Pillar	+	+	–	–	–	–	–	–	–
Roads	+	+	+	+	–	+	–	+	+
Storehouses	+	+	+	+	+	+	+	–	–
Temples	–	–	+	+	–	–	–	–	–
Trade and money	–	+	+	–	–	+	+	–	–
Social diversity	–	+	+	+	–	+	+	–	–

Key

Pn	The King's Frontier City, pacantima nagara, the *Aṅguttara* N VII.63
Dn	The City of Virtuousness, dhammanagara, the *Milindapañha*
Vn	An Ordinary City, nagara, the *Milindapañha*
Dg	The Fortified Settlement, Durga, the *Kauṭilīya Arthaśāstra* 2.3–4
Hs	Hastinápura, the *Mahābhārata* II.31.20–25
Ay	Ayodhyā from the *Vālmīki Rāmāyaṇa* II.5
Sg	Sāgala from the *Milindapañha*
Vp	An ideal city from the *VāyuPurāṇa* 1.6.103–105
Lm	The abode of Lalitā, the *Lalitāmāhātmya*

stones. A divine throne, made of Cintāmani, stands in the center of it: self-shining, matchless, reminiscent of the rising sun... (*LM* 14.9–13).

Such is a brief summary of the selected excerpts. Taken together, they reveal an interesting pattern. In all of the quoted texts the city is conceptualized through various morphological traits (see Table 2.4). Yet most of these traits are not uniquely urban.[38] Roads, construction in accordance with cardinal directions, stores, animals, temples, cremation grounds, boundaries between households, trade, and the system of varṇas and aśramas are characteristic of both rural and urban settlements. The only two traits that are unmistakably urban and feature prominently in most of the quoted excerpts are fortifications and authority. Consider the following.

Fortifications play an important role in every single description of the city discussed above. In the *Aṅguttara-Nikāya*, of the seven traits that define the frontier city, two—a rampart and a moat—are parts of fortifications and the remaining five are directly related to fortifications. Of the 11 traits, that define the City of Righteousness in the *Milindapañha*, four—a rampart, a moat, an upper battlement, and a watchtower—are parts of fortifications; several other directly relate to fortifications. In the *Arthaśāstra*, of the two chapters that describe the fortified settlements (durgas), the first chapter deals solely with an elaborate system of fortifications: three moats, an earthen rampart, a brick pavement on top of the rampart, towers, hidden traps, gateways, and so forth. The panegyrics on the legendary cities—Hastinápura, Ayodhyā, Sāgala, and the abode of the goddess Lalitā—always speak of deep moats, high walls, massive ramparts, towers, bastions and gates. Even in a very brief description of the durgas in the *VāyuPurāṇa*, the Paurāṇikas refer to fortifications rather than any other trait of the durgas.

Similar to fortifications, authority is present in most of the discussed descriptions and definitions of the city. The *Arthaśāstra* unambiguously states that the place for the king's residence needs to be properly selected and planned. The *Mahābhārata* describes Hastināpura as the capital of the Kauravas. The *Vālmīki Rāmāyaṇa* depicts Ayodhyā as the capital of Kośala and the place of residence of king Daśaratha. Sāgala of the *Milindapañha* and the abode of Lalitā are portrayed as the seats of great power. Even the definitions of the Frontier City in the *Aṅguttara-Nikāya* and of the City of Virtuousness in the *Milindapañha* indicate the importance of authority. Although authority—whether divine or secular—is not mentioned in the list of traits, its presence is unambiguously clear: for the City of Virtuousness is built by the Buddha and the full name for the Frontier City is the King's Frontier City. The only example when authority is not mentioned is the description of the durga in the *VāyuPurāṇa*. As I have noted above however, the Paurāṇikas who compiled the *VāyuPurāṇa* must have had a text of reference in mind and more importantly the reference to durgas in the *VāyuPurāṇa* is too fragmentary to be taken seriously.

In summary, fortifications and authority are the two traits that unite the definitions of the city discussed in this chapter. The work of Schlingloff mentioned above, seems to support, at least indirectly, this conclusion as well. Although Schlingloff did not discern a specific definition of the city, he observed at some point that the system of fortifications, the planning of the city, and the residence of the kings are particularly important in the description of the city found in the *Arthaśāstra*. "Sehr zutreffend behandelt das Staatslehrbuch zuerst die Anlage der Befestigung, dann erst die Plannung des Stadtkerns und—als dessen wichtigstes Bauwerk—der Residenz des Königs" (Schlingloff 1969:46). The planning of the city does not seem to me to be of such a great importance, particularly when compared with the descriptions of cities found in other texts. The notion of authority—whatever form it takes—is nevertheless very important. Whether fortifications and authority present an ideological nucleus within the aforementioned definitions or, in other words, stand for a quintessential concept of the city by historical agents is a question that needs to be addressed with the help of archaeological data. At this point, I will treat these two traits as a hypothetical theoretical model. The further analysis of archaeological data will show whether this model is helpful for the conceptualization of the Gangetic and Harappan city and whether it can be seen as the Collingwoodean thought expressed in the phenomena of the past.

Conclusion: From Texts to Material Culture

It has not been my intention to add another redundant definition of the city. Focusing on only two traits—fortifications and authority—the model defined above is not meant to portray the city in its complexity. The value of this model is in its potential application. If used in the study of material culture, it may draw a link between agency and structure and reveal the previously unknown aspects of the ancient Indian city; particularly so, since the archaeological data of the Harappan and Ganges civilizations provide great potential for investigating the processes of the construction of fortifications and the formation of authoritative structures.

Fortifications[39] are an innate feature of the archaeological landscape both in the Ganges and Harappan civilizations. Where the Ganges civilization is concerned, it is not an exaggeration to say that, when compared to the data on settlement patterns, domestic architecture, and other aspects of material culture, the remains of fortifications form the most extensive body of the currently available archaeological data on this civilization. One could even argue that our current knowledge about the archaeology of the Ganges civilization is, to a large degree, defined by its grander fortifications, i.e., ramparts, moats, walls, gates, and bastions. Although scholars have previously analyzed some of these structures, their interpretations did not go beyond description and typology (Erdosy 1987; Mate 1969–1970; T. N. Roy 1986; U. N. Roy 1954). In the Harappan civilization, fortifications present yet another very distinctive structural feature. Consisting of walls, gates, and platforms, they not only define the layout of sites as sociopolitical and economic entities, but also implement the norm of urban segregation, i.e., create distinct sectors and quarters. Although many of these fortifications have been extensively excavated, not much research has been undertaken with the purpose of determining their meaning and role in the process of the Harappan urbanization.

In contrast to fortifications, authority is difficult to trace in archaeological record. While fortifications are, in the overwhelming majority of cases, an objective structural feature, authority is a concept that needs to be shown theoretically through a combination of archaeological traits. Since the texts reviewed in this chapter are the products of several distinct ideologies, their views on authority vary. *What unites these views is that authority—whether an individual ruler, a deity, or a group of secular governing officials—is seen as a distinct institution of power. This institution of power, i.e., a group of full-time specialists whose sole business is to govern, is what can be shown archaeologically*. Authority nonetheless takes different forms in different cultures. In some cultures, it is expressed in architecture and settlement layout. In other cultures, its presence is evident from burials or the objects of ritual paraphernalia. There are cultures, in which authority is barely distinguishable through material record. Overall, one must admit that there is no universal archaeological signature of authority and whether architecture, settlement pattern, burials or some other traits of material culture can be used as evidence of authority must be decided on a site-by-site and culture-by-culture basis.

Most archaeologists who worked in South Asia at the turn of the twentieth century brought with them preconceived notions of authority from West Asian and European archaeology. Eager to find palaces, rich burials, and assembly halls, they were ready to impose their interpretations on the newly discovered data. For example, Bloch (1904:94) and Spooner (1914:99) saw the discovery of a palace as one of the main goals of their mission in Vaisali. Not surprisingly, the "pillared hall" excavated around the same time by Spooner (1913) in Kumrahar, Pataliputra, was quickly labeled a Mauryan assembly hall.[40] In a similar way, despite of the lack of palatial structures and grandiose temples in the archaeological record of the Harappan civilization, the first explorers were eager to see the Harappans oppressed by the ruling elites and heavily influenced by the Sumerian civilization (Piggott 1950; Wheeler 1962). In more recent literature, the forms and mechanisms of the formation of authority in the Harappan and Ganges civilizations remain equally questionable. Obviously, in order to create a new and credible interpretation, we need to abandon any preconceived notions and to approach the existing data in its totality. *The emergence of authority then can be established by tracing drastic and simultaneous changes in the settlement size, layout and at least several aspects of material culture*, such as architecture, sphragistics, numismatics (in the case of the Ganges civilization), figurines, pottery, weapons, agricultural tools, and the like. Archaeological records of both the Ganges and Harappan civilizations offer a broad range of traits to be tested for such changes. Of course, the number and nature of these traits will vary depending on the quality, quantity, availability, and credibility of archaeological data on each specific site.

The two following chapters will focus on the analysis of data from the twenty-five sites; thirteen sites of the Ganges civilization and twelve sites of the Harappan civilization. This analysis will be carried out on three interrelated levels: fortifications, authority, and the idea of the city. On the first level, I will focus on the date of construction, structural history, and, when possible, function of fortifications. On the second level, I will discern the traits of material culture indicative of the formation of authority, and will try to place these traits in a chronological frame. On the third level, I will investigate the relations between the processes of the formation of authority and the construction of fortifications. This in turn will allow me to theorize on whether the construction of fortifications and the emergence of authority symbolized, in any manner, the first cities of the Ganges and Harappan civilizations.

3 The Idea of the City in the Ganges Civilization

... the surviving ramparts represent the size of the cities from the time of their first construction, however much their superstructures may have been renewed in later times. It is our view that this major operation was, as far as any one thing can be, the hallmark of the emergence of a city, or city state.

—F. R. Allchin (1989:14)

D. K. Chakrabarti (1988a, 2003) well-described the history of exploration of the Ganges civilization. During the 1860–1870s, Alexander Cunningham (1871) discovered, explored, and excavated a number of large urban sites, which, in his view, could be identified with places known from Sanskrit and Pāli literature.[1] At the turn of the twentieth century, Hoey, Vogel, Spooner, Marshall, Bloch, and several other individuals continued Cunningham's undertakings and initiated new excavations.[2] As a result, Bhita, Mathura, Pataliputra, Rajgir, Sravasti, Vaisali, and several other sites of the Greater Gangetic Doab were explored, mapped, and excavated. A new dimension to the archaeology of the Gangetic Doab was given in the 1950s, when B. B. Lal (1954–1955) excavated the site of Hastinapura and defined the sequence of the Ochre-Colored Pottery (OCP), the Painted Gray Ware (PGW) and the Northern Black Polished Ware (NBPW). Since the 1950s, many more Early Historic sites of the Gangetic Doab have been excavated and published.

In 1983, based on the similarities in material culture between these sites, T. N. Roy defined the concept of the Ganges civilization.[3] According to Roy (1983:256), more than 400 sites were known at the time as belonging to the mature phase of this civilization (ca. 400–100 BC). At least several dozen of these sites had been excavated. Today, the number of surveyed and recorded sites of the Ganges civilization must be much higher than 400. On the survey of Kanpur district conducted in 1977–1979, M. Lal (1984) recorded 150 sites dating from the middle of the second millennium BC to the beginning of the Mauryan Period. Erdosy's survey (1988) recorded 72 sites in the Allahabad District. Chakrabarti (2001) has recently published a gazetteer of several hundred Early Historic sites for the Lower and Middle Ganges River. Overall, the Gangetic Doab contains many hundreds of archaeological sites dating to the first millennia BC, and around 100 of these sites have been partially excavated.

Given such a massive amount of data, it was not an easy task to choose a proper sample of sites for the analysis in this chapter. While reviewing the existing data, I considered the following factors.

Quality and Availability of Archaeological Data. This was by far the most important factor. Sringaverapura, for example, is a very interesting and potentially important site. It features prominently in the *Vālmīki Rāmāyaṇa*, and reveals a continuous sequence of cultures from the OCW to the British Period. B. B. Lal excavated at Sringaverapura for almost 10 years; yet, save for a volume on water tanks (Lal 1993) and one article briefly describing the cultural sequence (Lal and Dikshit 1978–1979), Lal did not publish a comprehensive report. Kampilya is another interesting site that features prominently in the *Mahābhārata*. A team of Italian archaeologists and Indologists surveyed and mapped Kampilya, yet did not conduct any excavations (Filippi and Marcolongo 1999). Some sites were excavated on a very small scale. For example, Ghosh's 1951 excavation of Rajgir was basically a scraping of a section at the foot of one of the surrounding hills. At the same time, the sites of Atranjikhera, Rajghat, Vaisali and Sravasti were excavated and published relatively well.

Geographic Diversity. I tried to include sites representing several distinct regions of the Ganges civilization. However, the quality and availability of archaeological data prevented me from representing all distinct areas equally. For example, the Lower Gangetic Doab is still

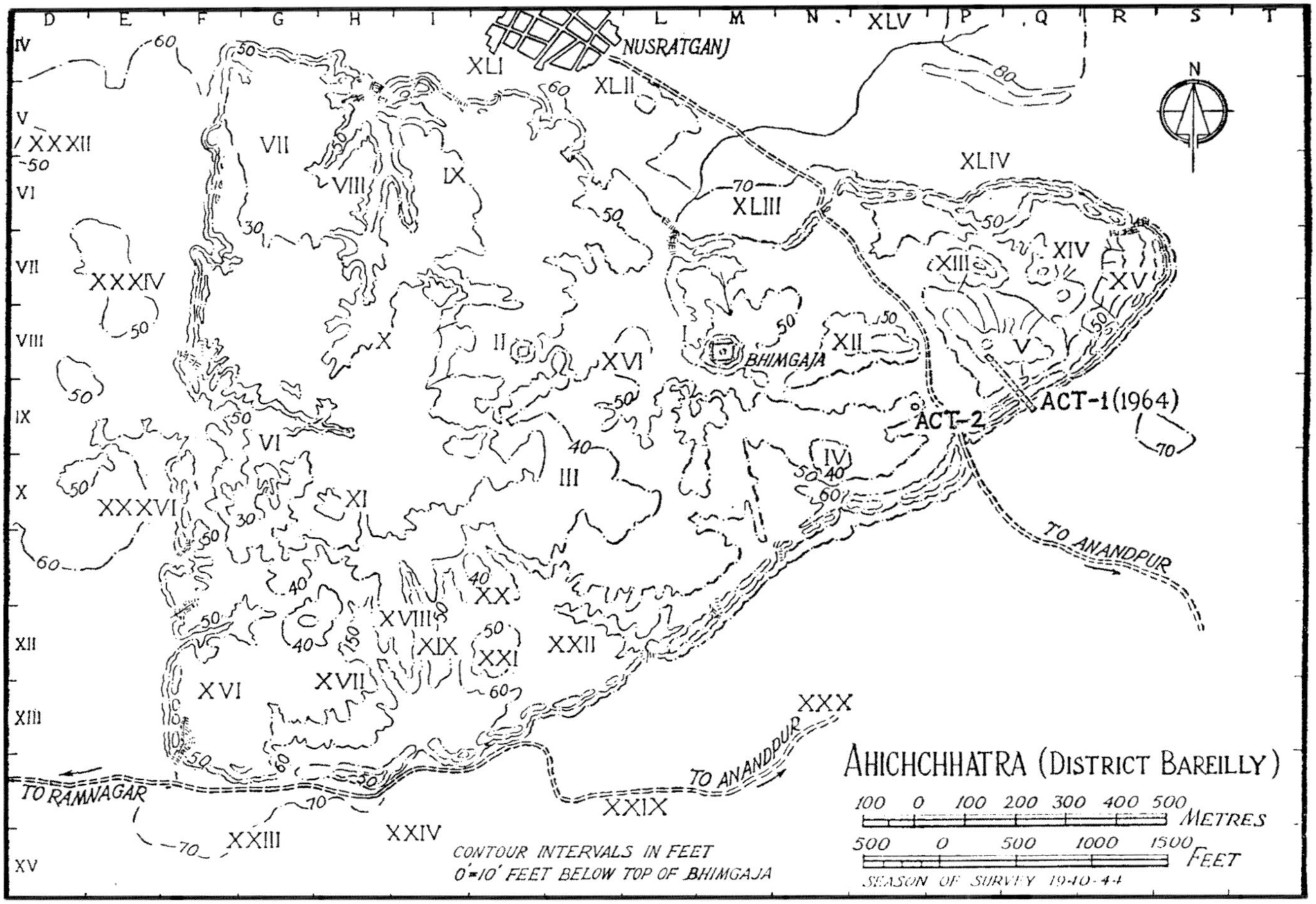

Figure 3.1 Contour plan of Ahicchatra. Illustration used with the courtesy and permission of the ASI, *Indian Archaeology: A Review* 1964–1965.

poorly known.[4] Consequently, I was unable to analyze any sites from that region.

Diversity in Scale. Archaeologists have used the size of settlements to distinguish between cities and villages. For example, the emergence of multiple tiers in settlement patterns, i.e., settlement hierarchy, has been seen by some as direct evidence for urbanization and state formation.[5] Ethnographic and historic examples however show that scale alone can be a very misleading factor for distinguishing a city from a village. During both antiquity and more recent periods, there were cities which were smaller than villages. The Ganges civilization as it is known from its archaeological record had several enormously large sites. Kausambi, for example, occupied an area of almost 8 km^2. Ahicchatra was spread over 180 ha. The size of Pataliputra during the Mauryan period must have been close to the size of modern Patna. Investigating the phenomenon of the city in the Ganges civilization based exclusively on the data from these sites would be disorienting. For example, the sites of Prahladpur, Sonpur, Sonkh, and Hastinapura each occupied only several hectares (ha). As attention was mostly paid to large sites, I selected several sites of a smaller scale to be analyzed along with the large and well-known settlements.

Historical Role. Many sites of the Ganges civilization feature prominently in Sanskrit and Pāli texts. For example, Rajgir was allegedly the first capital of Magadha. Sravasti was the capital of Kośala. Vaisali was the capital of the republic of Licchavis. Some places played an important role in the life of Buddha, Mahavira and other

Figure 3.2 Rampart of Ahicchatra (photo by the author).

important characters of the early Indian history. As in the case with the excavation of Hastinapura, archaeology, however, often failed to confirm the glory assigned to these sites by the literary tradition.

Limitations of the Present Research. The comparative and cross-disciplinary nature of this book makes it difficult and unnecessary to utilize all of the existing data. Inevitably, the final list of sites reflects my personal preferences and familiarity with archaeological data, formed as a result of a brief survey that I conducted in the Ganges Valley in January of 2002.

Ahicchatra

Located near the town of Aonla in the Bareilly district of Uttar Pradesh, Ahicchatra covers an area of ca. 180 ha (see Figures 3.1–3.2). As the capital of the north Panchalas, Ahicchatra played an important role in the political history of northern India. Yet the archaeology of this site is poorly known.[6] After sporadic excavations by Cunningham and Fuhrer, K. N. Dikshit conducted the first extensive excavation at Ahicchatra in 1940–1944. Nine strata were identified as a result of this project (Ghosh and Panigrahi 1946; see Table 3.1). From 1963 to 1965, N. R. Banerjee, under the auspices of the ASI, conducted further excavations in Ahicchatra. The sequence defined as the result of this excavation was significantly different from that of Dikshit and Gonda. Its final revised version included four periods (IAR 64–65:39–42; see Table 3.2).

Fortifications

Ahicchatra has an impressive well-preserved defense system. A high rampart, almost 6 km in circuit, revetted on the interior wall, encircles Ahicchatra from all sides. A long partition wall running north–south divides the site into eastern and western sectors. The western sector is smaller and appears to have been occupied significantly earlier. Except for a few brief reports that appeared in *Ancient India* and the IAR, the results of the excavations conducted at this site by the ASI have never been published.

Table 3.1

Ahicchatra: Periodization by Dikshit (after Ghosh and Panigrahi 1946)

Stratum	Approx. Dates	Defining Characteristics
IX	before 300 BC	two pits cut into the natural soil
VIII–VII	300–100 BC	remains of mud-brick houses
VI–V	100 BC–AD 100	first brick-built structures
IV	AD 100–350	described as "the most prosperous period of building activity in the city"
III	AD 350–750	intensive structural activities
II	AD 750–850	two small houses and a number of pits filled with ashes and potsherds
I	AD 850–1110	blocks of houses separated from eachother by streets and lanes

Table 3.2

Ahicchatra: Periodization by Banerjee (IAR 64–65:39–42)

Period	Defining Characteristics
I	Ochre Colored Ware
II	Painted Gray Ware
III	Northern Black Polished Ware
IV	Kushana and Gupta periods

Dikshit and Banerjee both investigated defenses. Under Dikshit's project, defenses were excavated in two places. Two successive earthen ramparts were established below the brick wall. Based on pottery found within the core of the rampart and in the soil below it, Ghosh and Panigrahi (1946:38) dated the construction of initial rampart to ca. 100 BC, i.e., to the advent of the Panchala rulers. On behalf of the ASI, Banerjee laid out a trench (ACT 1) across the defenses in the western sector. Based on the excavation of this trench, Banerjee defined five phases in the construction of defenses all dated to period IV, combining both the Kushana and Gupta periods. During the first phase, the rampart was built of mud. During the second phase, the rampart was first damaged and then buttressed at its top by a brick wall, 4.98 m in width and 2.59 m in height. The wall ran through the entire length of the rampart. Interestingly, rectangular gaps, 2.13 x 1.32 m, were left in the wall at regular intervals; the openings were filled with rubble and clay. The excavators explained this by the desire to economize bricks(?). During the third phase, the brick wall was covered with mud. During the fourth phase, the wall was strengthened at intervals by packing. During the fifth phase, fragmentary walls of brick and brickbats were built inside the gaps in the outer wall (IAR 63–64:44).

The construction of fortifications at Ahicchatra thus underwent several developmental stages. During the first stage, due to its vulnerability, the rampart was unlikely to carry a defensive function; or at least, defense was not its primary concern. The function of the partition wall was also quite ambiguous. Since the western sector was smaller and contained evidence for earlier occupations, it would be tempting to hypothesize that the partition wall marked the perimeter of the earlier site. However, this wall was built over architecture of the Gupta period and consequently must have been built during the late Gupta or even post-Gupta time. The excavators proposed that the construction of the partition wall might have been due to "the excessive vulnerability" of the northeastern part of the fortified area where the habitation was concentrated during later periods (IAR 53–64:44). Given the presence of a massive fortification system around the whole city, this argument, in my opinion, is dubious. It is more likely that after the western sector had been abandoned, the new wall marked the new city boundaries. In sum, whatever the true function of the partition wall was, military concerns were unlikely to play a significant role in it.

Authority

Dikshit and Ghosh correlated the construction of fortifications in Ahicchatra with the advent of the Panchala rulers around the first century BC. Stratigraphically, this corresponded to Strata VI, which was characterized by the first brick-built structures and Pancala coins (Ghosh and Panigrahi 1946:39). Prior to Strata VI, little structural activity had been recorded. Banerjee's chronology assigned the construction of fortifications to period IV (originally, period III), which stood for the rule of the Kushanas and the Guptas. In association with this period, Banerjee recorded typical Kushana ware and copper coins of the Kushanas, Panchalas and Achyus. Prior to period IV, the recorded structural activity was limited to postholes, mud-floors, ovens, and burnt brick fragments. Period IV had numerous walls of burnt bricks and brickbats. Houses were allegedly aligned according to the cardinal directions. Period IV also provided a large variety of artifacts, including coins, iron objects, figurines, beads, and so forth (IAR 1963–1964:44). Overall, Strata VI–V of Dikshit's chronology and period IV of Banerjee's chronology appear to mark a time of change in the sociopolitical life of Ahicchatra. Allegedly, this was the period when Ahicchatra became an important political center.

Atranjikhera

Atranjikhera is a large site (ca. 1,200 m x 400 m) located in the district Etah in Uttar Pradesh (see Figures 3.3–3.4). A series of mounds lies on the western bank of the Kali Nadi, a tributary of the Ganges River, 10 km from Mirahchi, a small town on the Etah-Kasganj road. R. C. Gaur excavated this site in 1962–1968.[7] His excavations revealed continuous occupation from the beginning of the second millennium BC to AD 1650. Gaur (1983) distinguished seven periods (see Table 3.3).

Fortifications

On the surface, the defenses of Atranjikhera are less noticeable than some defenses of other Gangetic sites. Yet, as established by Gaur, like many other Gangetic sites Atranjikhera had a rampart with a parapet wall on top of it. Gaur (1983:6–10) defined four structural sub-phases for the rampart. All of these sub-phases belong to period IV which in turn is divided into four phases (see Table 3.4). The construction of the first rampart belongs to period IVB dated to ca. 500–350 BC. Gaur (1983:254) calls this rampart a "mud-bund" and describes it as a "massive clay deposit laid in slope after the great flood". The width of this rampart at its base is estimated to be approximately 30 m. During sub-phase 2, the existing "bund is extended to surround the whole town as a rampart" (Gaur 1983:255). Sub-phase 3 is a period of several structural changes. The rampart is strengthened and raised. A tower-like circular structure with a diameter of 4.5 m is built at the top of the rampart in the southwest corner of C1 trench. Two successive mud-brick walls are attached to this structure. During sub-phase 4, the tower is renovated and its height is raised. A flank-wall on the northern side of the tower is built, and the height of the rampart is raised. Finally, parapet walls with gaps at regular intervals are built on the top of the rampart. The maximum height of the parapet wall is traced up to 13 courses of bricks which measure at 3.7 m. The maximum height of the rampart is 3.05 m.

With regard to the function of the rampart, Gaur emphasizes the role of floods. Phases IVA and IVB allegedly end in floods and destruction. Consequently, Gaur explains that the construction of both the mud-bund and the encircling rampart as a protective measure against floods. I believe this explanation is a bit simplistic. If the sole reason for the construction of the rampart had been the protection against floods, there would have been no need to build towers and a parapet wall on top of the rampart. Military defense does not seem to explain the functionality of the rampart either. On one hand, period IV provides some evidence for warfare; most of the arrowheads, spearheads, and spear shafts come from the deposits of period III and IV (see Table 3.5). On the other hand, the rampart, being low and gradually sloping, was unlikely to provide sufficient protection from a military attack at least until the parapet wall was built. The function of the rampart at Atranjikhera thus remains an open question. What one can say at this point is that non-utilitarian and symbolic explanations seem to be more in line with the data than military defense or protection from floods.

Authority

Transition from period III (PGW) to period IV (NBPW) marks several drastic changes in the life of Atranjikhera.

Settlement Expands in Size. During period III, Atranjikhera was small. Gaur excavated several exploratory trenches with the sole purpose of determining the size of the settlement during period III. He discovered that until the end of period III, the settlement had been confined to the eastern part of the mound. Occupation in the rest of the mound began during the first phase of period IV (IAR 1967–68:45–46; 1968–1969:37–38).

Architecture Becomes More Complex. Wattle-and-daub structures give way to structures made of mud and burnt brick. Although Gaur did not expose any large horizontal areas—his focus was predominantly on defining a cultural sequence by excavating deep soundings—he nonetheless collected enough data to give a sense of changes. Period III lacked evidence of significant structural activities and it was unlikely that this was the result of a limited scale of excavations. The size of trenches laid out at Atranjikhera was big enough to detect structural activities if there were any. Period IV, on the contrary, witnessed a significant intensification of structural activities. In this respect, phase C, which immediately followed the construction of the earliest

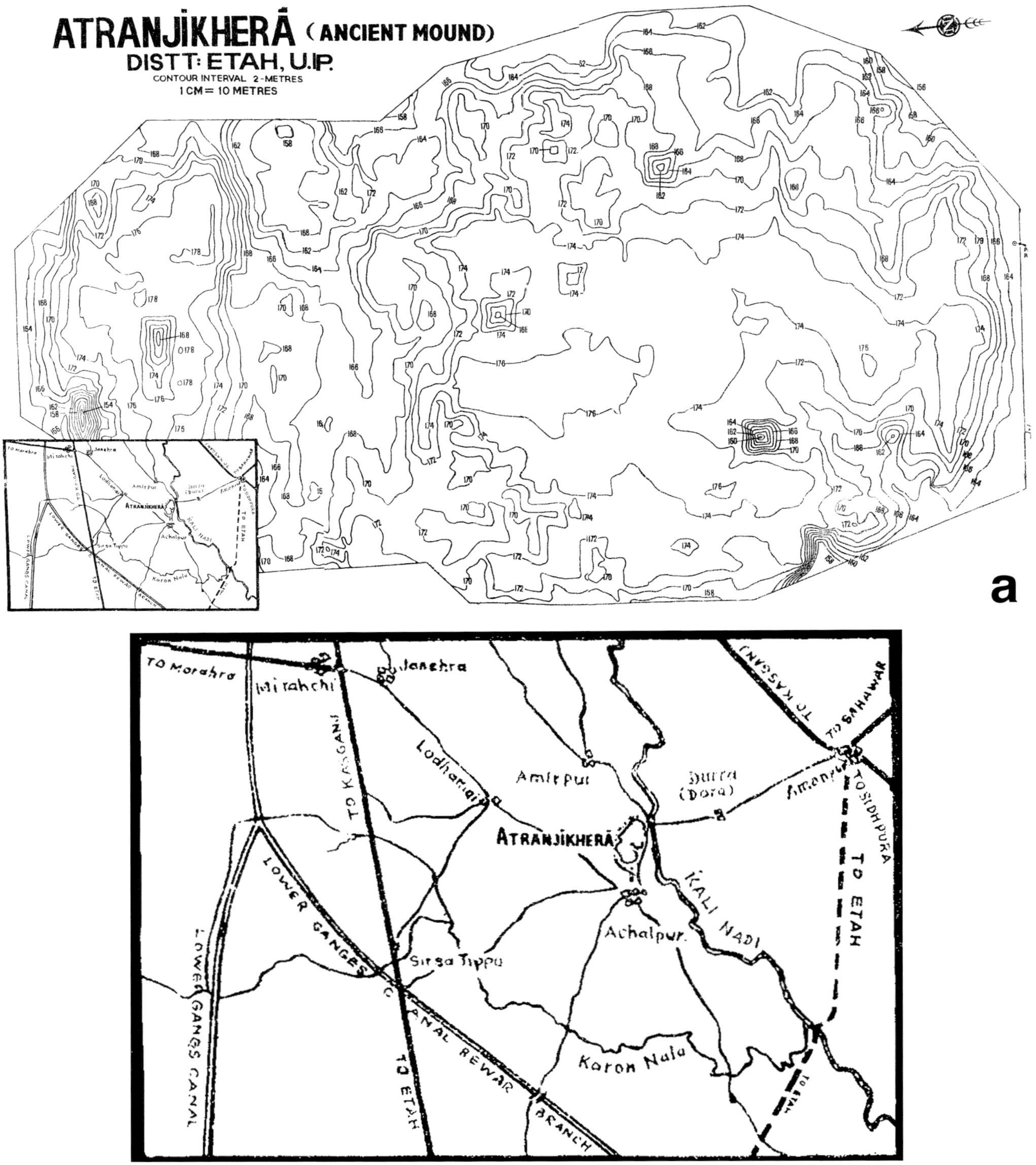

Figure 3.3 a) Contour plan of Atranjikhera. Illustration used with the courtesy and permission of Motilal Banarsidas, *The Excavations at Atranjikhera: Early Civilization of the Upper Ganga Basin* (Gaur 1983); b) magnification of inset.

Figure 3.4 Atranjikhera: The main mound (photo by the author).

Table 3.3

Atranjikhera: Periodization (Gaur 1983)

Period	Approx. Dates	Defining Pottery Types
I	before 1450 BC	Ochre Colored Pottery
II	1450–1200 BC	Black and Red Ware
III	1200–600 BC	Painted Gray Ware
IV	600–50 BC	Northern Black Polished Ware
V	50 BC–AD 350	
VI	50–1100 AD	
VII	1100–1650 AD	

Table 3.5

Atranjikhera: Weapons (Gaur 1983)

Weapon Type	Period III All Phases	Period IV Phase A	Phase B	Phase C	Phase D
Bone arrowheads	53	68	40	9	15
Iron arrowheads	21	10	9	8	3
Iron spearheads	8	16	6	8	3
Iron shafts	5	3	1	1	0

Table 3.4

Atranjikhera: Phases of period IV and sub-phases of the rampart (Gaur 1983)

Period / Phases	Rampart Sub-Phases	Approx. Dates
Phase A		600–500 BC
Phase B	Sub-Phase 1	500–350 BC
Phase C	Sub-Phase 2	350–200 BC
Phase D	Sub-Phase 3	
	Sub-Phase 4	200–50 BC

mud-bund, was particularly important. In the context of this phase, Gaur (1983:249) identified numerous mud-brick walls, ring-wells, barns, granary, kitchens, and rooms. Regardless of whether Gaur's identifications of structures were accurate, one thing was clear: the first evidence for active structural activity came from period IVC, dated to ca. 350–300 BC.

System of Coinage Emerges. Twenty-three coins were attributed to period IV. Thirteen coins were discovered in a well-stratified context. Gaur (1983:447–452) classified the coins into three groups: punch-marked, uninscribed, and inscribed.

Sealings Appear. The total of three sealings were discovered in the deposits of period IV: two in terracotta and one in bone (1983:452).

Agricultural Tools Made of Iron Appear. In the deposits of period IV, Gaur (1983:427–431) identified five types of agricultural tools made of iron: sickles, spuds, ploughshares, hoes, and diggers.

Human Terracotta Figurines Appear. The total of 21 human (1983:362–363) and 37 animal figurines (Gaur 1983:366–372) were discovered in the deposits of period IV.

Weapons Increase in Number (see Table 3.5). Interestingly enough, the largest number of arrowheads comes from period IVA and period IVB, the time immediately preceding the construction of the first rampart.

As evidence for the emergence of authority, these changes are of different value. Since period IV lasted for almost 600 years, one would need to know in which phases the changes took place. Unfortunately, as many finds and features were poorly stratified, some changes were ascribed to periods and not to specific phases. Nonetheless, based on the traits that were dated more credibly—settlement size, architecture, pottery, seals, and coins—one can conclude that phases IVB and IVC witnessed a number of important qualitative changes, e.g., the site significantly expanded in size, architectural practices became much more complex, coins and sealings emerged, and pottery became more standardized and mass-produced. It is difficult to imagine that the implementation of these changes would have been possible without social stratification and the emergence of authority.

Bhita

Bhita is located near Allahabad, downstream from Kausambi.[8] John Marshall (1915a) excavated at this site in 1909–1912 (see Figures 3.5, 3.7). During this excavation, Marshall exposed a large area in the southeastern part of the city, which provided evidence for occupation from the Mauryan to Gupta periods. Following the methods employed by many British archaeologists at that time, Marshall did not define a consistent chronology for Bhita. Nonetheless, judging from his report, he excavated stratigraphically and on several occasions defined sequences of strata. For example, based on the excavation of the house and shop of Nagadeva (Buildings 12–13) located among the group of structures near the gate in the southeastern part of Bhita (see Table 3.6, Figure 3.6), Marshall (1915a:33–35) defined five consecutive strata.

Later, Marshall reconfirmed this sequence in the excavations of another structure, the adjacent house of Jayavasudha. As far as the earliest occupation was concerned, Marshall believed that the site had been settled well prior to the Mauryan period; the lowest floor reached in the trench dug under High Street between the buildings 12 and 22 was dated by him to ca. 800 BC, and, on one occasion, he even mentioned the discovery of Neolithic artifacts. Later investigations reconfirmed and developed many points of Marshall's chronology. First, when the concept of the NBPW was defined it became clear that Bhita had a significant presence of this type of pottery (Ghosh and Panigrahi 1946). Second, in the early 1990s, the Lucknow circle of the ASI under the directorship of G. T. Shendey conducted a small-scale excavation on the Garh, a fortified mound at Bhita (IAR 1995–1996:74–75). It was established that the earliest occupation had "a thin deposit (20 cm) of black-slipped ware" dated roughly to the eighth to seventh centuries BC (IAR 1995–1996:74). The next deposit was represented by the NBPW and the excavators dated it to the seventh–second centuries BC. The uppermost deposit, according to the excavators, belonged to the Sunga period. The deposits of the Kushana period were discovered on the Garh mound.

Fortifications

Marshall spotted the remains of fortifications in the southeastern section of Bhita and traced them for a length of 40 ft at the southeast end of Bastion Street. The discovered remains consisted of an earthen rampart, an 11 ft thick wall on top of the rampart, and a quadrangular bastion projecting 15 ft from the outer side of the wall. Marshall (1915a:40) suggested that the wall

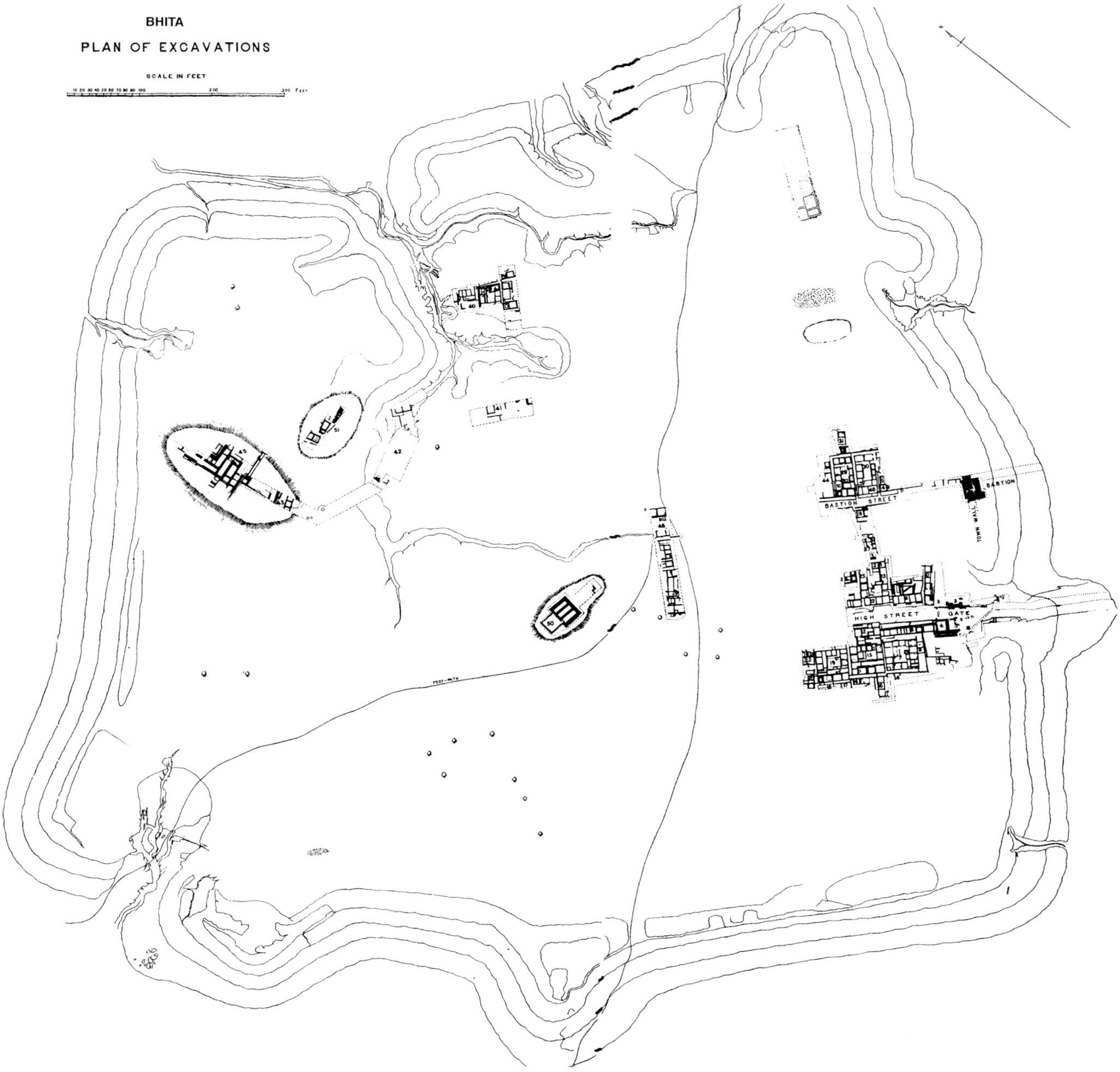

Figure 3.5 Bhita. Illustration used with the courtesy and permission of the ASI, *Excavations at Bhita, Annual Report of the Archaeological Survey of India 1911–1912* (Marshall 1915).

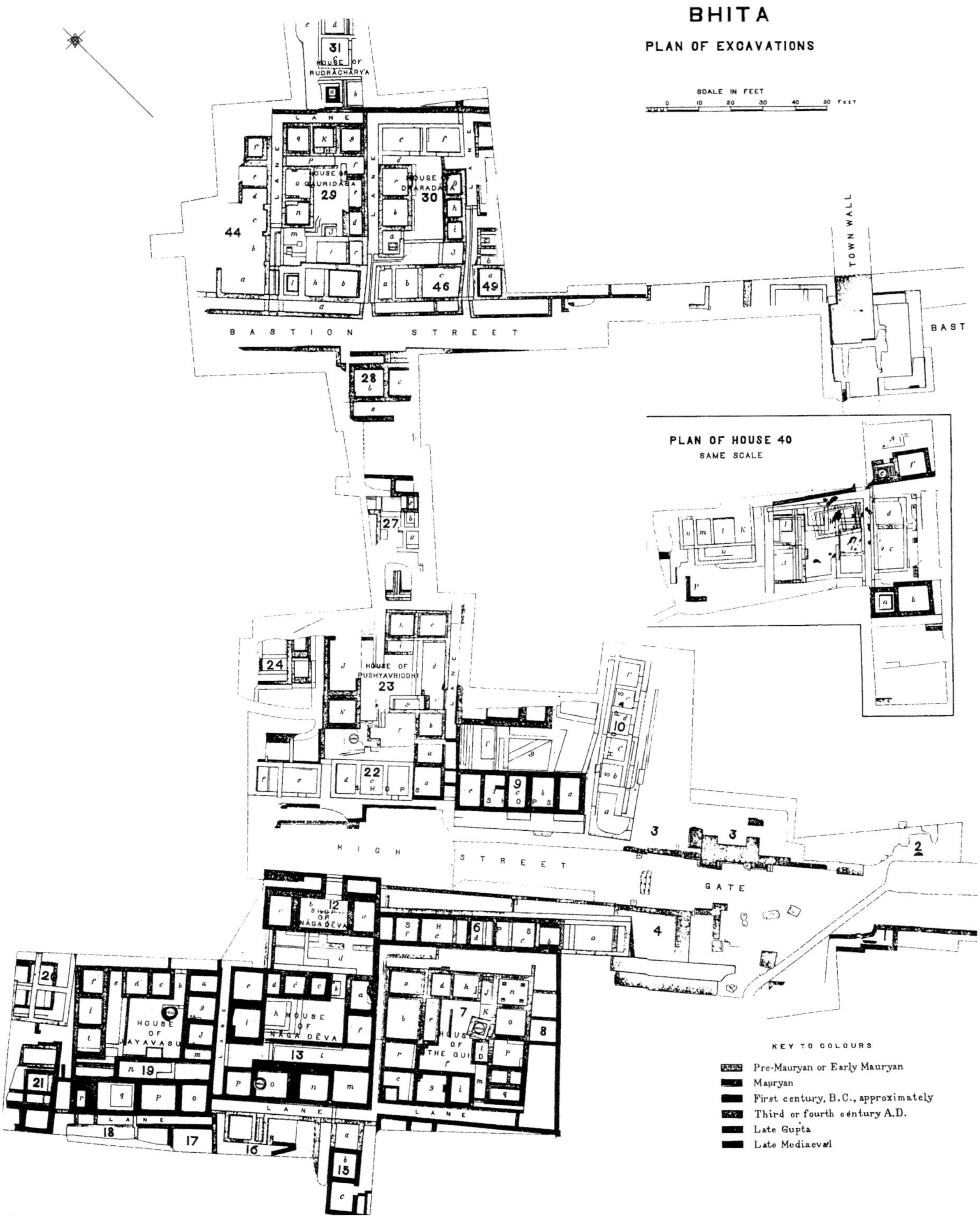

Figure 3.6 Bhita: Plan of main excavations. Illustration with the courtesy and permission of the ASI, *Excavations at Bhita, Annual Report of the Archaeological Survey of India 1911–1912* (Marshall 1915).

Figure 3.7 Bhita today: Remains of John Marshall's trench (photo by the author).

was built during the early Mauryan or pre-Mauryan periods and was pierced originally by a gateway. The bastion, according to Marshall, was built during the Mauryan period in order to strengthen the wall. The wall in turn was strengthened by a casing, 4 ft in thickness.

As I noted above, the team of the Lucknow circle of the ASI under the directorship of G. T. Shendey established that the occupation in Bhita started with the Black-Slipped Ware and continued through the NBPW to the Sunga and Kushana periods (IAR 1995–1996:74–75). Structural activities and the expansion of the settlement seem to have begun with the NBPW period, since no structures were discovered in association with deposits of the Black-Slipped Ware period. Considering this information as well as Marshall's description of fortifications, it is tempting to suggest that the initial rampart was built in Bhita at the beginning of the NBPW periods. Later, during the Mauryan period, it was reinforced by parapet walls and bastions. Such structural history would follow a pattern observed on several other sites of the Ganges civilization. In addition, fortifications divide Bhita into two parts: Garha, the fortified mound, and Garhi, the lower mound outside the fortified area *(*IAR 95–96:74). It is not clear whether this layout was confirmed by excavations or was assumed based on a surface survey and general observations. If Bhita indeed consisted of the fortified and non-fortified parts of town, this would be an interesting and rare pattern of planning for an Early Historic site in the Gangetic Doab.

Table 3.6

Bhita: Cultural sequence of buildings 12–13 (Marshall 1915)

Strata	Approx. Date	Defining Characteristics
I	pre-Mauryan	No structural activities
II	Mauryan	First architectural features
II	1st century BC	Foundation of the house; terracotta figurines; pottery
IV	Kushana period	Defined by the floor of the house
V	3rd century AD	Defined by a floor in the house

Marshall does not provide any explanations of the function of the fortifications. Given the lack of credible chronology and structural history, it is difficult to assess his data. What one can say at this point is that by the Mauryan period the size and complexity of fortifications at Bhita exceeded the needs (if any) to protect the site from floods. Moreover, if the division of Bhita into the fortified mound and the lower mound is correct, then the fortifications at Bhita must have performed a segregational function. It is also interesting that in shape and design fortifications at Bhita are similar to those of Ahicchatra, Atranjikhera, Sravasti, and some other Gangetic sites. Therefore it is not unreasonable to assume that the function was also somewhat similar.

Authority

Bhita is one of a few sites of the Ganges civilization excavated on a very large horizontal scale. Near the city-gate in the southeastern part of Bhita, Marshall unearthed the whole district with the remains of several streets and houses (see Figure 3.6). Judging from structural features and artifacts uncovered in this district, Bhita had become an important local center the latest by the Mauryan period. Authority must have emerged at the site around the same time, for the settlement layout, architecture, seal/sealings, terracotta objects, and coins provide ample evidence for the existence of a complex sociopolitical system.

That the site was big is clear from the Mauryan deposits discovered by Marshall in several remote trenches, such as trench 40 on the northeastern side of town and several trenches near the southeastern gate. Most structures assigned by Marshall to the Mauryan period were imposing, architecturally sophisticated, and possibly indicative of social differentiation. Building 7, or as Marshall (1915a:30–31) called it "The House of the Guild", was one of the largest and most interesting structures on the site. It consisted of a rectangular courtyard surrounded by twelve rooms on four sides. A row of rectangular rooms in front of it, "the shops" according to Marshall's interpretation, faced "High Street" that ran from the southeastern gate inside the city. Buildings 3–4, which faced each other on the opposite sides of the southeastern end of "High Street", were also quite interesting. Marshall (1915a:30) suggested that these two buildings were either guardhouses or were somehow functionally connected with the defenses. Indeed they were located right next to the southeastern gate and were very different from other houses on High Street. Some Mauryan structures must have been rebuilt during later periods. For example, the "House of Pushyavriddhi", building 23, located on "High Street" across from the "House of the Guild" had Mauryan portions. The house of Nagadeva, building 13, located next to the "House of the Guild" also on "High Street", had Mauryan remains underneath its foundation (Marshall 1915a:35–36). Near the northeastern side of town, a thick layer of Mauryan occupation was detected in Trench 40. Architectural remains of this layer were standing to a height of 8 ft 8 in. including house foundations, walls of baked brick and floors laid with brick, earth, and concrete (Marshall 1915a:40–41). Finally, the Mauryan debris composed of burnt bricks and brickbats were unearthed in a pit dug underneath High Street between the shops of Nagadeva (Building 12) and the shops of Pushyavriddhi (Building 22).

Seals and sealings constitute an important portion of finds recorded by Marshall (1915a:44–61) at Bhita. A total of 210 seals and sealings comprising 120 varieties and 67 duplicates were found. Although most of the discovered seals and sealings date to the Kushana or Gupta periods, there are also seals of the earlier periods. Some of these seals are quite interesting. For example, seal 1 found underneath the walls of the House of the Guild, judging from both language and stratigraphy, dates to around the third century BC. The seal is inscribed with the words sahijitiye nigamasa. The meaning of the word nigama is debatable. It has been translated as "a city", "a village" or even "a corporation, guild". The discovery of this seal led Marshall (1915a:47) to call Building 7 "the House of the Guild", since he assumed that the seal might have marked the "site of the office of a nigama or corporation". Regardless of whether Marshall's interpretation was correct, the use of the term nigama on a seal that dates around third century BC is quite interesting. Whether it designates a type of settlement or a governing body, it points to the presence of authority on the site.

Nonetheless, the most interesting period for tracing the emergence of authority must be the one that immediately preceded the Mauryas. Unfortunately, because of the lack of dating techniques at the time of excavation and the emphasis that the excavator seemed to have placed on the Mauryan and post-Mauryan periods, many finds and architectural features of the earlier periods were poorly stratified and not given sufficient attention. On one occasion, Marshall (1915a:41) mentions architectural remains of the pre-Mauryan period in Trench 40. Allegedly, they consisted of "two walls of pakka brick" and "the foundations of the chamber".

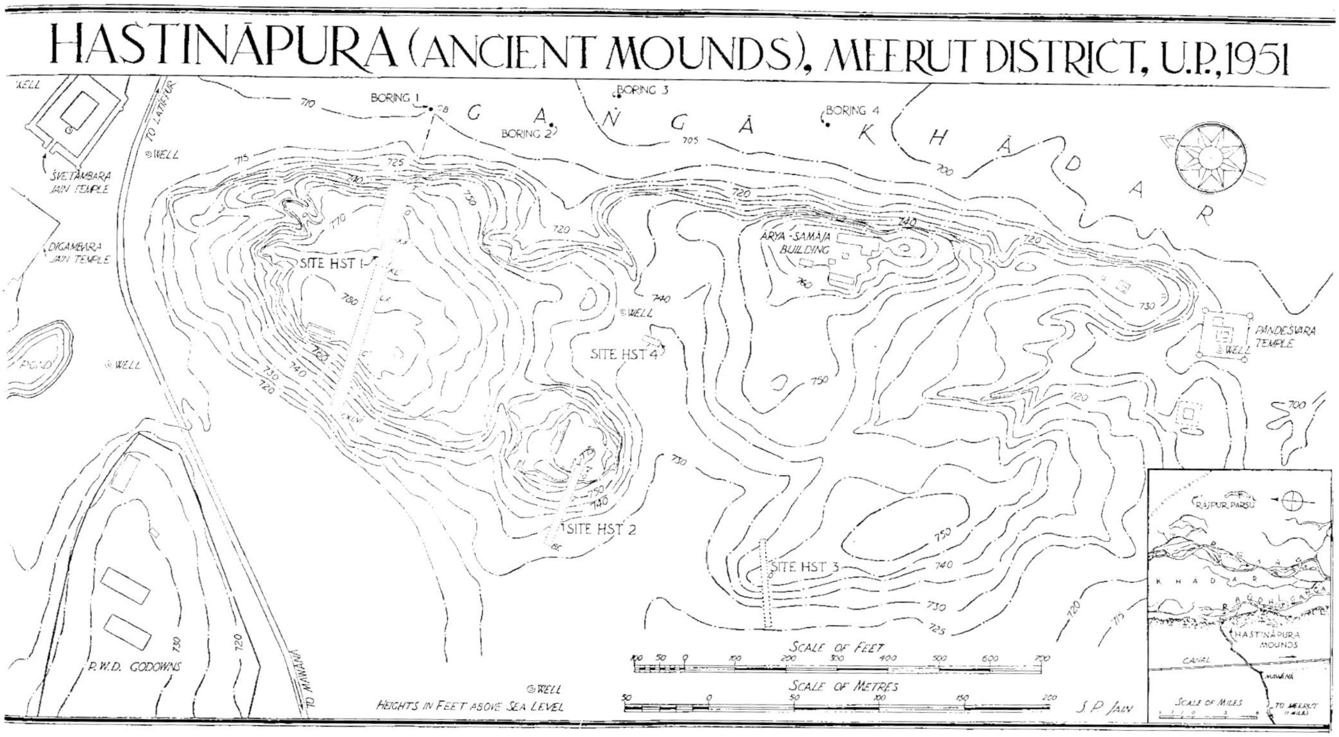

Figure 3.8 Contour plan of Hastinapura. Illustration used with the courtesy and permission of the ASI, *Excavation at Hastinapura and other explorations in the Upper Ganga and Sutlej Basins 1950–1952, Ancient India 10–11* (Lal 1954–1955).

The earliest baked bricks were found in the pit dug underneath High Street. Marshall dated them to the fourth to fifth centuries BC. Also, the later excavations established that the NBPW, not defined as an important pottery type at the time of Marshall, was present in Bhita in large amounts. In size, the pre-Mauryan settlement was quite large; both Marshall and Shende found pre-Mauryan deposits in the remote parts of the site.

Considering all of this information, it seems reasonable to suggest that Bhita had become an important settlement prior to the Mauryan period. In a similar way, the process of the emergence of authority must have taken several hundred years prior to the third century BC. One hopes that further excavations will clarify this.

Hastinapura

Hastinapura is a type-site of the Ganges civilization (see Figure 3.8). It is located in the District Meerut near the town of Mawana, on the right bank of an old bed of the Ganges River. As the capital of the Kurus, Hastinapura plays a very prominent role in the *Mahābhārata*, and is frequently mentioned in the various texts of the Jaina and Purāṇic literature. B. B. Lal (1954–1955) excavated at Hastinapura in 1950–1952 and three years later published a report in *Ancient India*. The cultural sequence of Hastinapura consists of five periods covering almost 3,000 years, from the late second millennium BC to the middle of the second millennium AD.[9] Each of these periods ends in the abandonment of the site, and is defined by a distinctive pottery type: Ochre Colored Ware (OCW), Painted Gray Ware (PGW), Northern Black Polished Ware (NBPW), Red Ware (RW), and pre-Mughal Glazed Ware (PMGW; see Figure 3.9, Table 3.7).

Hastinapura was an important project that revitalized interest in the archaeology of the Ganges civilization; however, as I noted above, the cultural aspect of the chronology defined by Lal is highly questionable. Needless to say, the alleged links between the distribution of the PGW and the migration routes of the "Aryan-speaking people" are also outdated (Lal 1954–1955:147).

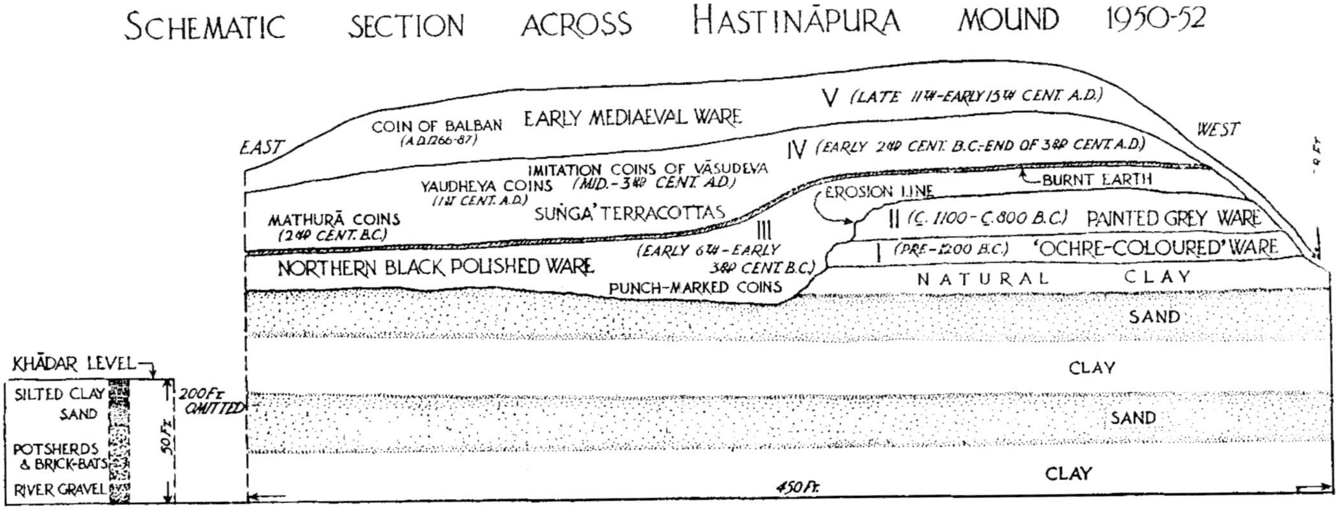

Figure 3.9 Cultural sequence of Hastinapura. Illustration with the courtesy and permission of the ASI, *Excavation at Hastinapura and other explorations in the Upper Ganga and Sutlej Basins 1950–1952, Ancient India 10–11* (Lal 1954-1955).

Table 3.7

Hastinapura: Periodization (Lal 1954–1955)

Period	Approximate Dates	Defining Pottery Type
I	before 1200	Ochre Colored Ware
II	1100– 800 BC	Painted Gray Ware
III	600–300 BC	Northern Black Polished Ware
IV	200 BC–AD 300	Red Ware of the Sunga Kushana period
V	AD 1100–1500	Pre-Mughal Glazed Ware

Fortifications

Lal did not report any fortifications at Hastinapura. Of the four trenches that he excavated, HST 1 was the largest and most informative. Its total length was 590 ft and its width varied from 44 to 21 ft. The trench cut all the way from east to west across the main mound (see Figures 3.10–3.11). Given this, one would expect that if a wall or a rampart had surrounded the mound, the excavator would have certainly hit it. Three scenarios are possible here. Firstly, it is possible that parts of fortifications were eroded or destroyed due to floods, conflagrations or other calamities. Indeed, every period defined by Lal ended with the abandonment of the site. The PGW ended with the heavy flood that washed away a considerable portion of the settlement. The NBPW ended in a large-scale conflagration and a 100-year-long break in occupation. After the Sunga-Kushana period, the site was deserted for almost 800 years. In addition, Lal reported that on the eastern, widest end of HST 1, there was a very deep and wide rain gully. This might have significantly confused the uncovering of the remains of fortifications. Also, the width of HST 1 might have been insufficient for finding fortifications. Secondly, it is possible that the excavators missed fortifications. The analysis of some architectural features by Lal is not always clear. The function of the wall 86 located in the western end of the HST 1 (see Figure 3.10) and assigned by Lal (1954–1955:27) to the period V could have been misunderstood. Lastly, it is possible that Hastinapura was never fortified. In my view, this last scenario is the most likely one. The ensuing analysis of archaeological data on authority seems to support it quite convincingly.

Authority

Given the role assigned to Hastinapura in the *Mahābhārata*, one would expect the archaeological evidence for authority to have appeared in Hastinapura by period III, the NBPW. The archaeological record nevertheless reveals the opposite.

Settlement Size. The size of Hastinapura is an interesting issue. The deposits of the OCP, PGW, NBPW, and the Sunga-Kushana periods were traced only in Trenches 1

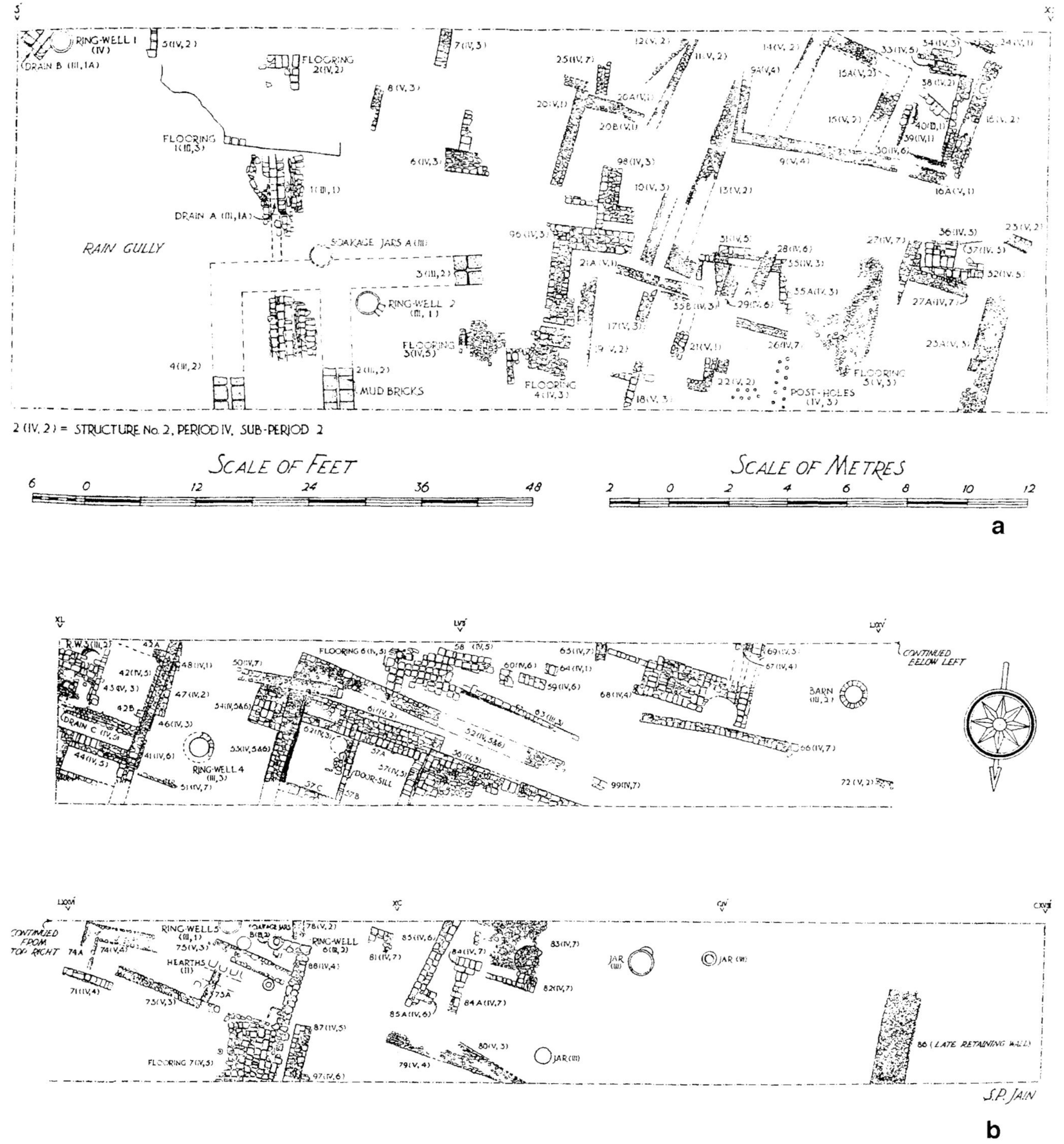

Figure 3.10a–b Hastinapura: Trench HST 1. Illustration used with the courtesy and permission of the ASI, *Excavation at Hastinapura and other explorations in the Upper Ganga and Sutlej Basins 1950–1952, Ancient India 10–11* (Lal 1954–1955).

Figure 3.11 Hastinapura today: Remains of the main trench (photo by the author).

and 2, both located on the main mound. Judging from Lal's map, the size of this mound is about 2 ha (see Figure 3.8). Trenches 3 and 4 excavated on the adjacent mounds revealed the remains of period V which starts, according to Lal, around AD 1100! If the results of Lal's excavations are taken as indicative of the dynamics of settlement expansion, Hastinapura must have been quite a small settlement until the twelfth century AD.

Architecture. Period II deposits revealed no house plans. Fragmentary remains of mud-brick walls were encountered. Lal suggested that the presence of mud-plaster with reed impressions indicated that some houses might have had reed walling. The use of baked bricks during this period is dubious since only a fragment of a baked brick was reported from one of the pits (Lal 1954–1955:13). The deposits of period III did not reveal house plans either. A number of mud, mud-brick, and burnt-brick walls were encountered. Two burnt-brick drains and several terracotta ring-wells were found as well. In trench 1, three structural sub-periods were defined (Lal 1954–1955:15–16). Period IV marked a significant proliferation in structural activities. Walls and floors were made of burnt bricks. A section of a 16-ft wide street with houses on either side was detected. Although no complete house plans were obtained, rooms, walls, floors, doorways, and platforms give a good sense of structural activity during this period. Seven structural sub-periods were defined. Based on the orientation of some walls, Lal argued that houses were constructed in accordance with cardinal directions.

Pottery. As noted above, each of the five cultural periods at Hastinapura is defined by one distinctive pottery type. Other pottery types are either given little attention or completely disregarded. For example, no ratio between the PGW and other wares is provided in the context of period II. Only 101(!) NBPW sherds are reported from the deposits of period III. Most of these sherds come from the lower levels and only 10 sherds(!) are indicative of shapes (Lal 1954–1955:52). Briefly mentioning other wares of period III, Lal does not specify their types and amounts. Instead, he treats the NBPW as a chronological and cultural marker of the period that lasted for over 400 years. Given this, it is basically impossible to determine changes in pottery production that took place between periods II and III. The pottery of period IV seems to be characterized by a higher degree of standardization and mass production. All pottery of this period is wheel-made, mostly unpainted and is entirely of Red Ware.

Figurines. Of the 39 recorded human figurines, only four were discovered in the deposits of period III. Most of the human figurines were attributed to period IV. Out of 105 recorded animal figurines, most came from period V. Only three figurines were attributed to period II. It is not clear what the exact ratio between the figurines of periods III and IV was. Yet according to the illustrated examples, as compared to the preceding periods, period IV provided the largest and most diversified collection of animal figurines (Lal 1954–1955:85–87).

Coins. Of the 85 coins found, most were discovered in the deposits of period IV. The deposits of period III revealed a number of punch-marked and uninscribed coins (Lal 1954–1955:101–105).

Other traits potentially important for tracing authority would be seals, weaponry, and inscribed objects. None of these however were unearthed in Hastinapura. Lal seemed to believe that this was due to the excavation methods which were traditionally focused on vertical soundings and lacked horizontal exposures; he did not seem to consider the possibility of Hastinapura simply not having these types of artifacts. In my view, given the size and location of trenches HST 1 and HST 2 (see Figures 3.8, 3.10), there was no reason to treat the results of Hastinapura excavations as deficient. That the seals and inscribed objects were lacking in the deposits of all the periods while structural activities had been minimal until period IV must have reflected the sociopolitical organization of Hastinapura rather than Lal's excavation methods.

To conclude, the existing archaeological data does not support the presence of strong authority in Hastinapura at least until period IV. Settlement size, the nature of architecture, coins as well as the lack of seals, weaponry and inscribed objects indicate quite a modest nature of settlement. This of course does not exclude a religious or ritual significance, which is difficult to trace archaeologically.

Kausambi

Kausambi is one of the largest Early Historic sites in northern South Asia. Located near Allahabad, on the left bank of the Yamuna River, it is spread over eight square miles and is enclosed by a chain of well-preserved massive ramparts (see Figures 3.12–3.13). According to literary sources, Kausambi was the capital of the janapada of the Vatsas and played an important role in the early history of northern South Asia. Cunningham was the first to recognize the importance of Kausambi in the second half of the nineteenth century. Majumdar conducted a small-scale excavation in Kausambi near the Asokan pillar in 1937–1938. Unfortunately, the results of this excavation were not published. G. R. Sharma undertook a major archaeological project in Kausambi from 1949 to 1967. Having excavated in four areas—near the Asokan pillar in 1949–1950, in the Ghoshitarama Monastery in 1950–1956, in the area of defenses in 1957–1959, and in the area of the so-called palace in 1960–1967—Sharma unearthed massive amounts of archaeological data and defined several cultural sequences.[10] One must say a few words about these sequences, since the periodization of Kausambi has been a controversial issue.

Based mostly on the stratigraphy of defenses, Sharma (1960) distinguished four cultural periods, covering a span of time from 1165 BC to AD 580 (see Figures 3.14–3.15, Table 3.8). In addition to these periods, Sharma defined a number of structural sub-periods, each characterized by a set of construction activities and renovations in the defense complex. Dates for periods III and IV were based on coins, seals, terracotta figurines, and arrowheads. The earlier periods were dated by conjecture.

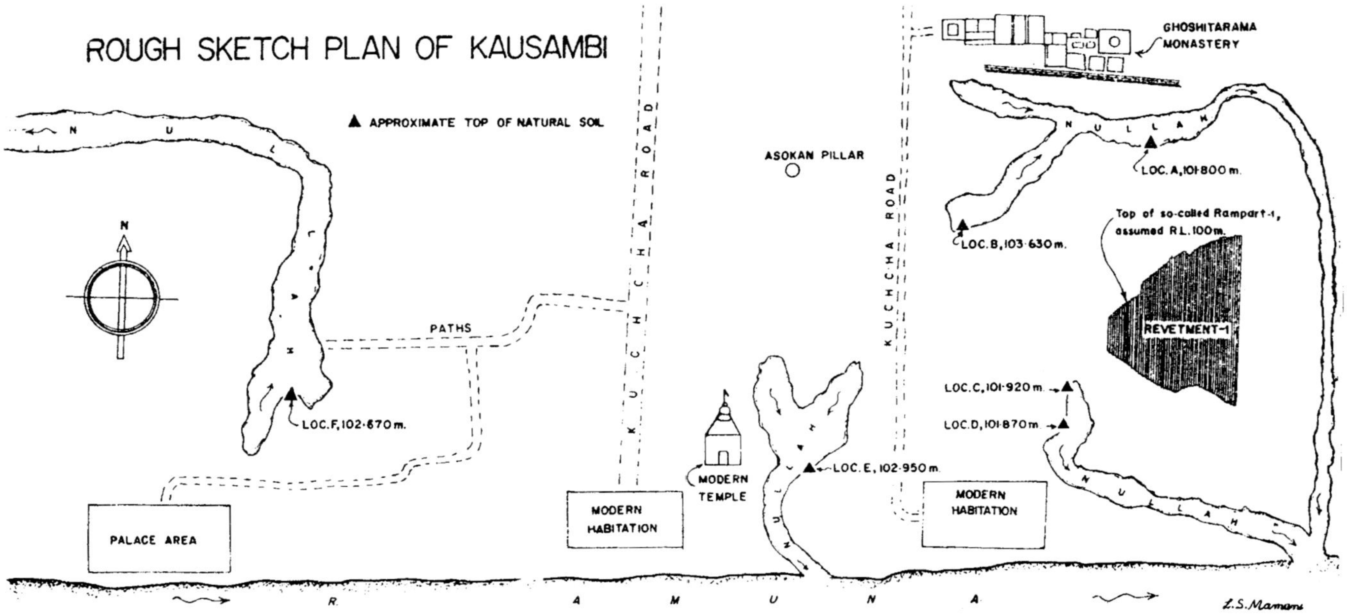

Figure 3.12 Sketch plan of Kausambi. Illustration used with the courtesy and permission of The Indian Archaeological Society, *Are the defences of Kausambi really as old as 1025 BC, Puratattva 1979–1980* (Lal 1979–1980).

Figure 3.13 Kausambi today: Rampart and bastion (photo by the author).

Sharma simply assumed that structural periods associated with ramparts 2 and 1 had the same average span of life—seventy-five years—as the structural periods associated with ramparts 3, 4, and 5. Consequently, he proposed the exact dates for each structural period. For example, period SP I.3 defined by the construction of the first rampart and the plastered revetment was dated precisely to 1025 BC–955 BC (Sharma 1960:22)!

Understandably, scholars have criticized Sharma's dating and identification of architectural features (Erdosy 1987:3–6; 1988:51–55, 59–61; Ghosh 1973; Lal 1979–1980; Sinha 1973). Lal (1979–1980:90), for example, argued that rampart 1 was "natural soil" and that revetment 1 was built to "protect the edge from further erosion". In Lal's view, the first rampart was what Sharma called rampart 2 and it was constructed no earlier than the sixth century BC. Erdosy (1987:3–6) developed Lal's argument by showing the absurdity of some of Sharma's early dates. The most obvious contradiction was the presence of coins in early levels. According to Sharma's own report (1960:80), uninscribed square coins were found throughout structural periods II.5–III.[10] If Sharma's dates were correct, this would mean that coins had been used in northern India by the ninth century BC! Not seeing anything wrong with this, Sharma (1960:81) concluded that "the beginning of coinage" could be "placed... in the early centuries of the first millennium BC".

Another obvious contradiction is the incongruity of chronologies defined by Sharma for different excavated areas. Aside from the main chronology based on the stratigraphy of defenses, Sharma formulated three other chronologies: one for the area of the Asokan pillar, one for the Ghoshitarama Monastery, and one for the palace. Had all these chronologies been correct, the first rampart would have been built in 1025 BC; structural activities in the area of the Asokan Pillar would have intensified in the fourth century BC; the palace would have been erected in the eight century BC; and the area of the Ghoshitarama Monastery would have been settled around the sixth or fifth century BC. One wonders, under this scenario, whether Sharma ever asked himself what the relationship between the four excavated areas was and whether these areas had always been parts of the same site.

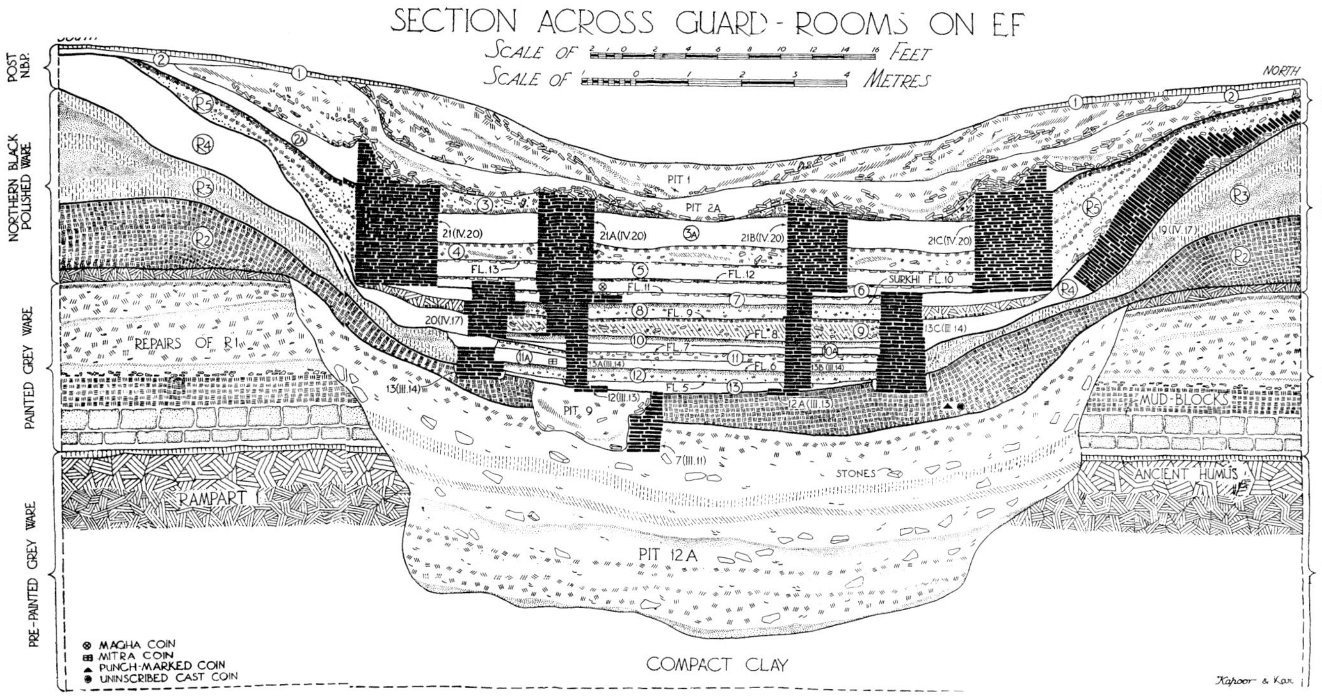

Figure 3.14 Kausambi: Section across the guardrooms of EF. Illustration used with the courtesy and permission of the ASI, *The Excavations at Kausambi (1957–1959): The Defences and the Syenaciti of the Purusamedha* (G. R. Sharma 1960).

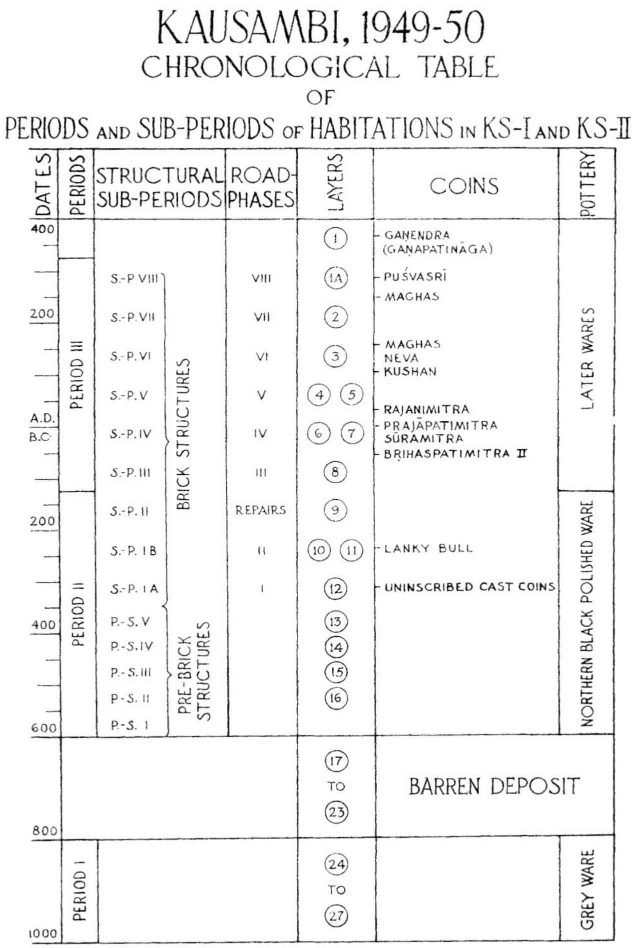

Figure 3.15 Cultural sequence of Kausambi. Illustration used with the courtesy and permission of the ASI, *The Excavations at Kausambi (1957–1959): The Defences and the Syenaciti of the Purusamedha* (G. R. Sharma 1960).

Table 3.8

Kausambi: Periodization (Sharma 1960)

Period	Structural Period	Dates	Defining Characteristics
I	1–4	1165–885 BC	Ochre Colored Ware, Rampart
II	5–8	885–605 BC	Painted Gray Ware, Black and Red Ware
III	9–16	605–45 BC	Painted Gray Ware, Northern Black Polished Ware, and Black and Red Ware
IV	17–25	55 BC–AD 580	Palace Complex

Fortifications

Kausambi has by far the most impressive defense system among the sites of the Ganges civilization (see Figures 3.13–3.18). Considering the scale of its ramparts, walls, moats, and towers, it is not surprising that Sharma saw the investigation of defenses to be one of the prime goals of his project and worked out an elaborate structural history. Not all of the 25 structural periods that Sharma defined were however meaningful. As noted above, Sharma's structural history was dubious and many periods that he defined must have erroneously marked contemporaneous structural activities. One must not however discard the entirety of his sequence. At least some of the structural periods (SP) reflect major modifications in the defense system and it is certainly worthwhile to revisit them. In my opinion, nine of the 25 structural periods indicate important qualitative changes that may have actually taken place in different periods of time (see Figure 3.15). These nine structural periods are: 1) SP I.3, ca. eleventh to tenth centuries BC: The first clay rampart and the first burnt brick revetment are constructed. The revetment is 9 ft thick at the base, available to a height of 40 ft, and is covered by a 2–3 in. layer of thick plaster made of mud and lime (Sharma 1960:27–28); 2) SP II.5, ca. ninth century BC: The first moat is dug (Sharma 1960:29); 3) SP III.10, ca. sixth to fifth centuries BC: Rampart 2 and Revetment 2 are built. The moat was re-excavated and road 3 is laid out (Sharma 1960:31–32); 4) SP III.13, ca. fourth to third centuries BC: The system of guardrooms, towers and flank walls is established. This constitutes the new system of defense, which fully replaces the old system by the SP III.15, ca. second century BC. SP III.13 (Sharma 1960:33–34); 5) SP III.14, ca. third to second centuries BC: The first evidence for a calamity comes from this period. Sharma (1960:34) believes that massive deposits of ash as well as the destruction of Revetment 2 "offer unmistakable evidence of invasion". As additional evidence, he notes that many double-tanged arrowheads were discovered in ash deposits and in the destruction debris of the Revetment 2; 6) SP III.15, ca. second century BC: A highly debatable identification of the fallen debris with the Syenaciti of the Purusamedha,—a type of human sacrifice known from the Vedic literature—belongs to this period (Sharma 1960:34–35); 7) SP III.16, ca. first century BC: Second

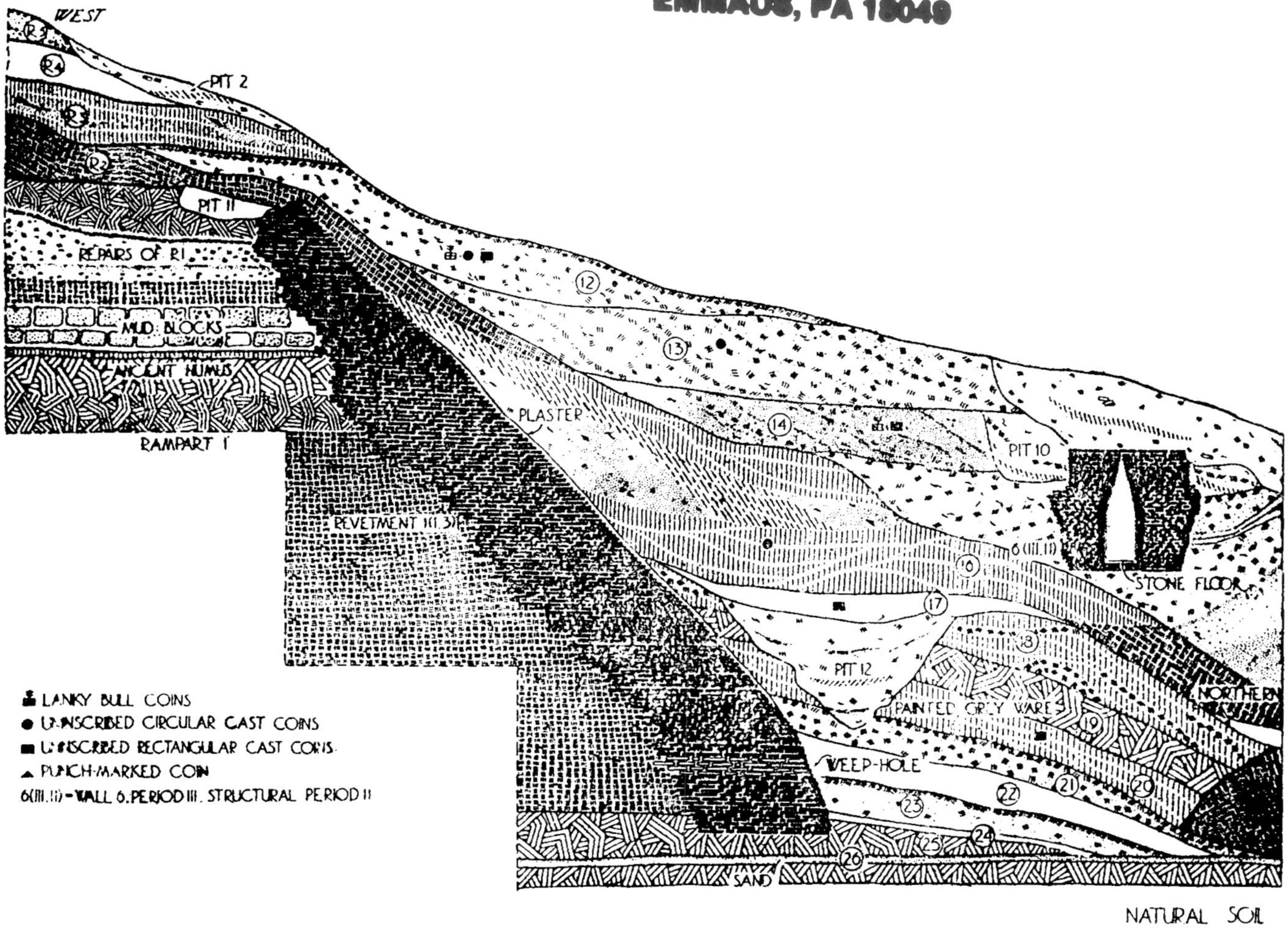

Figure 3.16 Kausambi: Section across defenses. Illustration used with the courtesy and permission of the ASI, *The Excavations at Kausambi (1957–1959): The Defences and the Syenaciti of the Purusamedha* (G. R. Sharma 1960).

major destruction on the site occurs. Sharma (1960:35) points to "extensive burning of the site, forming an accumulation of an ash layer in which are buried fragments of bones and a few pieces of skull". This is also the final period of the NBPW; 8) SP IV.19, ca. second century AD: Another destruction takes place. Sharma (1960:36) argues for "the extensive conflagration and destruction indicating an invasion during which all the buildings were razed to the ground"; 9) SP IV.24, ca. fifth to sixth centuries AD: The greatest destruction takes place. Everything is burnt down. Sharma (1960:37) hypothesizes that "it was the result of a violent assault that shook the city to its very foundations. The defenses... were finally abandoned and henceforth throughout its remaining life, the town was defenseless. The barbed arrow-heads Type (K), which make their appearance for the first time in large numbers, were obviously the instruments of massacre, pillage and unprecedented devastations".

A careful reassessment of data recorded in association with these nine periods allows us to make two hypothetical conclusions. First, the rampart appears to have been built not earlier than the sixth century BC. Second, neither military threat nor protection from floods appears to have played a significant role in the construction of the defense system. The first conclusion is based on the fact that the earliest structural levels contain coins characteristic of the mid first millennium BC

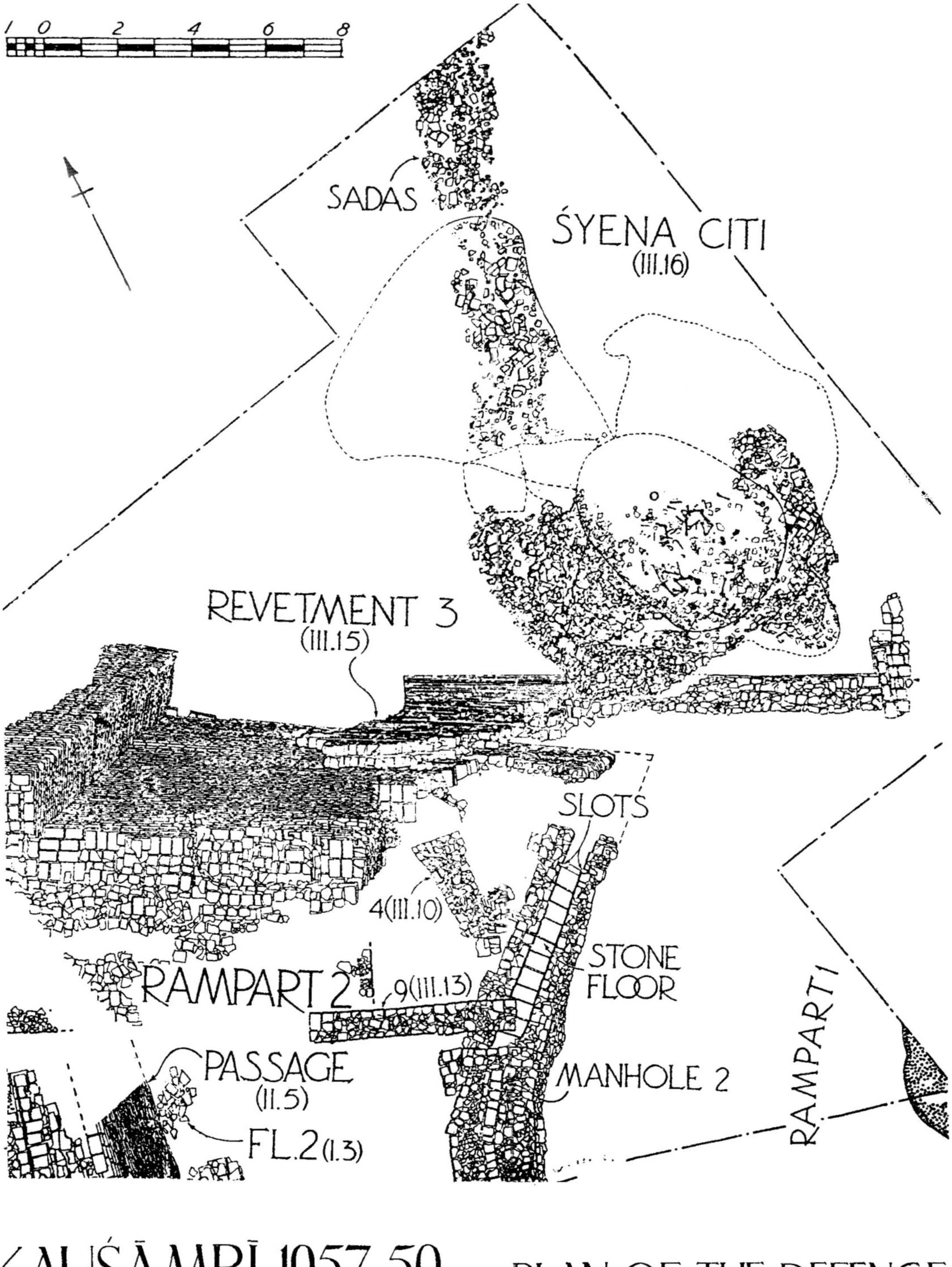

Figure 3.17 Kausambi: Plan of defenses. Illustration used with the courtesy and permission of the ASI, *The Excavations at Kausambi (1957–1959): The Defences and the Syenaciti of the Purusamedha* (G. R. Sharma 1960).

Figure 3.18 One of the minor ramparts of Kausambi today (photo by the author).

(see Figures 3.15). The argument for the second conclusion can be summarized as follows.

On one hand, given the grandiose scale of fortifications warfare would be the easiest explanation. This is particularly so, because structural periods III.14, III.16, IV.19 and IV.24 allegedly indicate destruction and contain a significant amount of weapons, 370 arrowheads and 58 fragments of spears for periods III and IV (Sharma 1960:45–48). On the other hand, the layout of fortifications has several very puzzling features. First, fortifications are truly massive in only two areas: around the so-called palace in the southwestern corner of the site (see Figure 3.13), and on the eastern side of the site south of the Ghoshitarama Monastery. In other areas, ramparts are much less imposing (see Figure 3.18). Second, there are many wide openings between the ramparts and some parts of the site are unprotected. For example, the rampart along the Yamuna River has long gaps, which make protection from floods impossible. Third, the chronology of the ramparts has never been properly determined. Yet differences in size, structural history, and most importantly in the time of initial occupation of the adjacent areas indicate that different ramparts may have been built in different periods of time. If this was the case, Kausambi was fortified not as a one-time event but during a long period of time. Finally, judging from Sharma's structural history, fortifications at Kausambi underwent two main stages of development:

the first one centered on ramparts, revetments, and the moat; the second one centered on guardrooms, towers, and flank walls. The transition from the first to the second stage marked a significant technological shift, which was likely to be caused by a shift in the function of fortifications as well.

In summary, to explain the construction of the fortification system at Kausambi exclusively as a response to warfare and floods appears to be erroneous. Explanations emphasizing non-utilitarian or symbolic factors seem to be more appropriate and I will return to this issue in the concluding part of this chapter.

Authority

The main evidence for authority at Kausambi is the defense complex itself. Obviously, massive ramparts, bastions, and revetments could not have been built without organization of labor and strong authoritative control. The three other excavated areas of Kausambi provide solid evidence for authority as well. The traits particularly indicative of the emergence of authority in these areas are architecture, weapons, figurines, coins, and seals.

Architecture. Along with the area of defenses, all other excavated areas revealed significant architectural remains. In the area of the Asokan pillar, a whole district with roads, alleys, and houses was exposed. In the Ghoshitarama Monastery, a stupa and monastic establishments were excavated. In the area of the palace, a complex of large stone structures was detected.

For the area of the Asokan Pillar, Sharma defined a sequence of three periods. The deposits of period 1 revealed no traces of structural activities except for a few circular pits measuring ca. 6 in. in diameter at the top (Sharma 1969:16). The pottery chosen to represent this period was the PGW, even though very few PGW sherds were discovered. The period was dated vaguely to the first quarter of the first millennium BC. Period II was associated with the NBPW and dated to ca. sixth to second centuries BC. The structural history of this period consisted of pre-structural phases and structural sub-periods (Sharma 1969:23). The main difference between the phases and sub-periods was the use of burnt brick. Dated to ca. sixth to fourth centuries BC, prestructural phases were defined by pits, postholes, mud-brick walls, ring-wells, and concrete pavements. Transition to structural sub-periods marked drastic qualitative changes. In sub-period 1A, the main road was built, a street made of powdered brickbats was laid out, and burnt bricks began to be used in the construction of houses (Sharma 1969:24–25). As Sharma (1969:37) justly asserted, "this sub-period marked a new epoch in the history of habitation in this area". Based on coins and stratigraphy, Sharma convincingly dated this sub-period to the mid-fourth century BC.

For the area of the Ghoshitarama Monastery (see Figure 3.19), Sharma defined a sequence of sixteen structural phases covering a period of 1,000 years from the sixth century BC to the sixth century AD (IAR 55–56:20). Phase I, dated to the sixth century BC, marked the earliest occupation at the site and was characterized by pits/postholes and the NBPW (IAR 55–56:20). During phase II, dated to ca. fifth century BC, the main stupa was built. During phase III, dated to ca. fourth to third centuries BC, the stupa was renovated. Prior to phase VI, no clear evidence of other architectural activities was established.

For the area of the palace, Sharma defined a sequence of three structural phases. During phase I, the walls were reportedly built of "random rubble" with "huge undressed stones being set in lime mortar." In phase II, the core of the walls remained of rubble, while the facings were made of dressed stones of relatively regular size. Towards the end of this phase, the palace was destroyed. In phase III, the core of the walls was made of bricks, the facings were covered with dressed stones, and the dressed stones were coated with lime plaster (IAR 60–61:34). The dating of these three phases was very controversial. Stratigraphically, Sharma related the initial construction of the palace to the pre-NBPW deposits and consequently dated phase I to ca. 600 BC (IAR 60–61:34). Later, he pushed this date even earlier, to ca. 800 BC (IAR 1961–1962:51). The last phase was dated to the first to second centuries AD (IAR 61–62:52). Thus, the palace, in Sharma's view, functioned for almost 1,000 years, from the beginning of the first millennium BC to the beginning of the first millennium AD. It is not surprising that these dates raised severe criticism of other scholars. Lal (1985c), for example, responded by proposing that the palace was built not earlier than the sixteenth century AD!

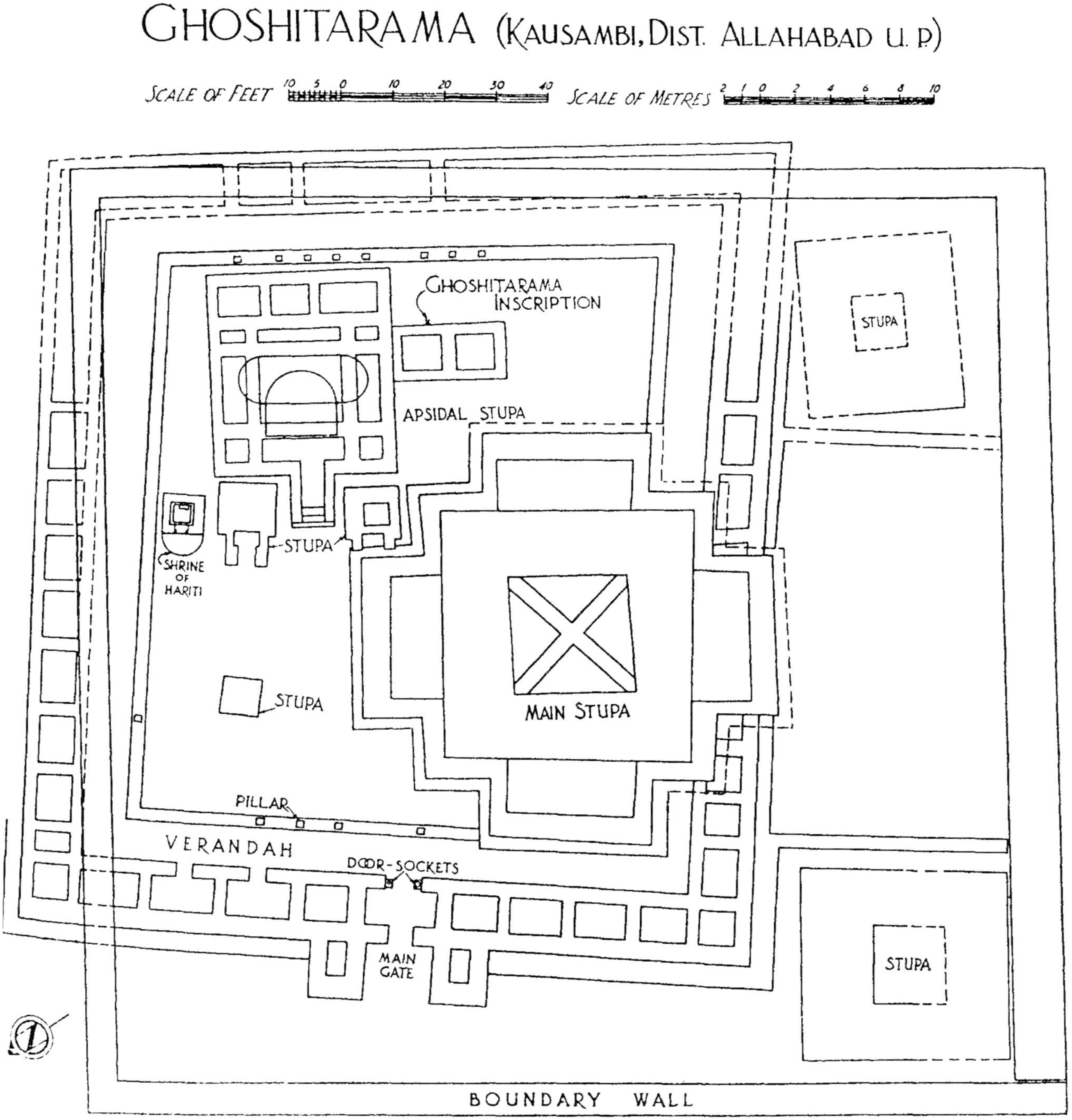

Figure 3.19 Kausambi: Ghoshitarama Monastery. Illustration used with the courtesy and permission of the ASI, *The Excavations at Kausambi (1957–1959): The Defences and the Syenaciti of the Purusamedha* (G. R. Sharma 1960).

Thus, architectural remains in these three areas provide ample evidence for authority, yet the chronology is very problematical. The most obvious incongruence is an early date for the construction of the palace. It is highly unlikely that the palace was built at the time when in other parts of Kausambi there were wattle-and-daub huts or even no occupation at all. Unfortunately, the data published in the IAR are not sufficient for evaluating Sharma's argument. That Sharma connects phases in the construction of the palace with sub-periods in the structural history of fortifications is convincing and reasonable (IAR 1961–1962:50–51). The palace is located in the southwestern corner of fortifications, right next to the rampart and an imposing tower topped by a bastion. If the construction of fortifications is placed in the middle of the first millennium BC, the construction of the palace must be dated soon after. The dates and structural histories of other architectural remains are more reasonable. They show that by the fifth to fourth centuries BC, structural activities indicative of social changes and the presence of authority were underway in the areas of the Asokan Pillar and the Ghoshitarama Monastery.

Settlement Size. Since the excavations were conducted in four different areas and some of these areas were quite far away from the others, one would expect that comparing the dynamics of habitation and structural activities in these areas would provide some hints for the creation of a larger picture in regards to the expansion of the site. Unfortunately, all the early dates provided by Sharma are dubious. As discussed above, the method of assigning equal periods of time to each structural modification is simply meaningless. Sharma's later dates are more reasonable, yet they do not allow tracing the expansion of the settlement. At this point, what one can say is that even if the four excavated areas had been occupied by the sixth or fifth century BC as parts of one settlement, this alone would have put Kausambi in an exceptional position as an incredibly large site.

Coins. In the area of the Asokan pillar, the earliest uninscribed coins are dated to the third century BC. The earliest inscribed coins belong to Brihaspatimitra, the ruler who lived around the second century BC (Sharma 1969:82–83). In the area of the defenses, the earliest uninscribed coins are associated with structural period II.5; the first punch-marked coins are associated with the deposits of structural period III (Sharma 1960:80–83). The chronological implications of these stratigraphic associations have been discussed above. If one does not follow Sharma's lower chronology and dates the first rampart to the sixth or fifth century BC, the first uninscribed coins appear right after, i.e., during the fifth or fourth century BC. Considering the emergence of coins on other Gangetic sites, this scenario is most likely.

Terracotta Figurines. In the area of the defenses, 323 complete terracotta figurines were discovered. The earliest hand-made figurines are associated with sub-period III.10, the NBPW, dated by Sharma (1960:74) to ca. sixth to fifth centuries BC. Unfortunately, Sharma does not provide any further information on intensification, standardization, or any other changes in the production of figurines. For the area near the Asokan Pillar, Sharma provides more information. The earliest figurines come from the deposits of pre-structural phase IV, dated to the fifth century BC (Sharma 1969:47). With the transition from pre-structural phases to structural sub-periods, figurines become more standardized and mass-produced. As Sharma (1969:47) notes "figurines from earlier levels, viz., pre-structural IV to sub-period IB, were of better quality, while those of the later sub-periods were cruder in appearance and were seemingly prepared out of coarse and gritty paste". This transition chronologically coincides with the proliferation of architectural activities and a general growth of complexity on the site.

Weapons. A large number of arrowheads, spears, and javelins were discovered in the area of defenses. Iron and bone arrowheads appear in SP II.5, the period of the initial construction of a moat. The largest number of weapons is associated with the deposits of period III, the NBPW.

To conclude, Kausambi contains ample evidence for authority. The latest by the fourth century BC, drastic sociopolitical changes were underway in the areas of defenses, the Asokan pillar, the Ghoshitarama Monastery, and possibly the palace. If the dating had been more accurate, the palace would have been the most unambiguous proof of authority. Judging from literary sources, it may have been the residence of King Udayana, a legendary ruler of Kausambi. According to Sharma's estimations, the palace occupied an area of 315 by 150 m (IAR 60–61:33). It stood on a 2.5-meter high platform of mud and mud-brick. At the junction of its walls, there were circular towers varying from 4.5 to 8 m in diameter. Inside, the palace consisted of a hall, flanked by rooms with lime flooring. All walls were reportedly covered with lime plaster of uniform thickness. There was a flight of steps leading to the tower from the central hall (IAR 60–61:34). Given the lack of palatial structures in the Ganges Civilization, the re-excavation and dating of the remains of this structure could greatly contribute to the understanding of the early history of Kausambi. So far, fortifications and architecture remain the most unambiguous proof of authority, and it is still unclear whether the excavated areas were all parts of the same site or represented separate and independent localities.

Mathura

Mathura is a city of great history, art, and literary tradition. It is located on the Yamuna River in the district that carries the same name (Figure 3.20). Owing to its beautiful sculptures and antiquities, as well as to the leading political role that it played during the time of the Kushanas, Mathura has always attracted the attention of archaeologists. Cunningham, Burgess, Fuhrer, Vogel, and others undertook occasional excavations in Mathura in the end of the nineteenth century. These excavations focused mostly on unearthing sculpture and other objects of art. In 1954–1955, M. Venkataramayya and B. Saran of the ASI excavated the Katra mound and defined the first consecutive sequence of cultures for Mathura. In 1973–1977, the ASI under the directorship of B. K. Thapar and M. C. Joshi carried out another project in Mathura. By the end of the project, they had excavated 14 sites and defined a sequence of the five periods (IAR 1975–1976:53–55; M. C. Joshi 1989:167; Table 3.9). Besides this chronology, the ASI project conducted by Thapar and M. C. Joshi brought many important results. Unfortunately, aside from four brief publications in the IAR and a few occasional articles, no comprehensive report on this excavation has been published.[11]

Fortifications

A massive crescent-shaped mud wall, called Dhulkot, surrounded ancient Mathura from the west, north, and south. The Yamuna River protected the fourth, eastern side of the settlement (see Figure 3.20). One of the tasks of the project headed by B. K. Thapar and M.C. Joshi in the 1970s was to examine the character of Dhulkot. In the season of 1973–1974, two trenches (MTR-1, MTR-3) were laid across the Dhulkot. It was established that the original fortification was built of mud on "the uneven natural soil resulting from successive floods". In other words, the excavators argued that natural mounds were utilized in the construction of defenses. Gaps between the mounds were filled with layers of compact clay (IAR 1973–1974:31–32).

During the 1974–1975 season, another trench (MTR-4) was dug across the Dhulkot. Based on the data from this trench, the excavators distinguished two constructional phases (IAR 1974–1975:48–50). The first phase was characterized by a rampart made of compact earth mixed with kankar with a maximum height of 6.45 m. The outer face of this rampart was strengthened with oblique packings. At the end of this phase, around the first century BC, the excavators argued, the mud fortification lost its utility (IAR 1974–1975:49). During the second phase, at the time of the Sakas and Kushanas, fortifications were revived and renovated. The wall was enlarged and its eroded portions were repaired (IAR 1974–1975:49).

In the 1975–1977 seasons, the study of the defense system at Mathura continued. First, it was established that period IV witnessed the construction of an inner mud-fortification. A trench (MTR-9) cut through this fortification showed that the inner fortification was built of wet mud and clay on top of architecture of the previous period. On the outer edge, the inner fortification was strengthened by "a retaining wall of discarded bricks, brick-bats, tiles, and burnt lumps of mud" (IAR 1975–1976:55). The width of the retaining wall varied from 22 to 40 cm. Its height varied from 80 cm to 1 m. The basal width of the inner fortification reached in some places 17 m (IAR 1975–1976:55). Second, the remains of a semi-circular bastion (trench MTR-14) were discovered at the northwestern turn of the inner fortification (IAR 1976–1977:55). Third, a moat was built on the Katra mound, on the northwestern side of fortifications (M. C. Joshi 1989:169).

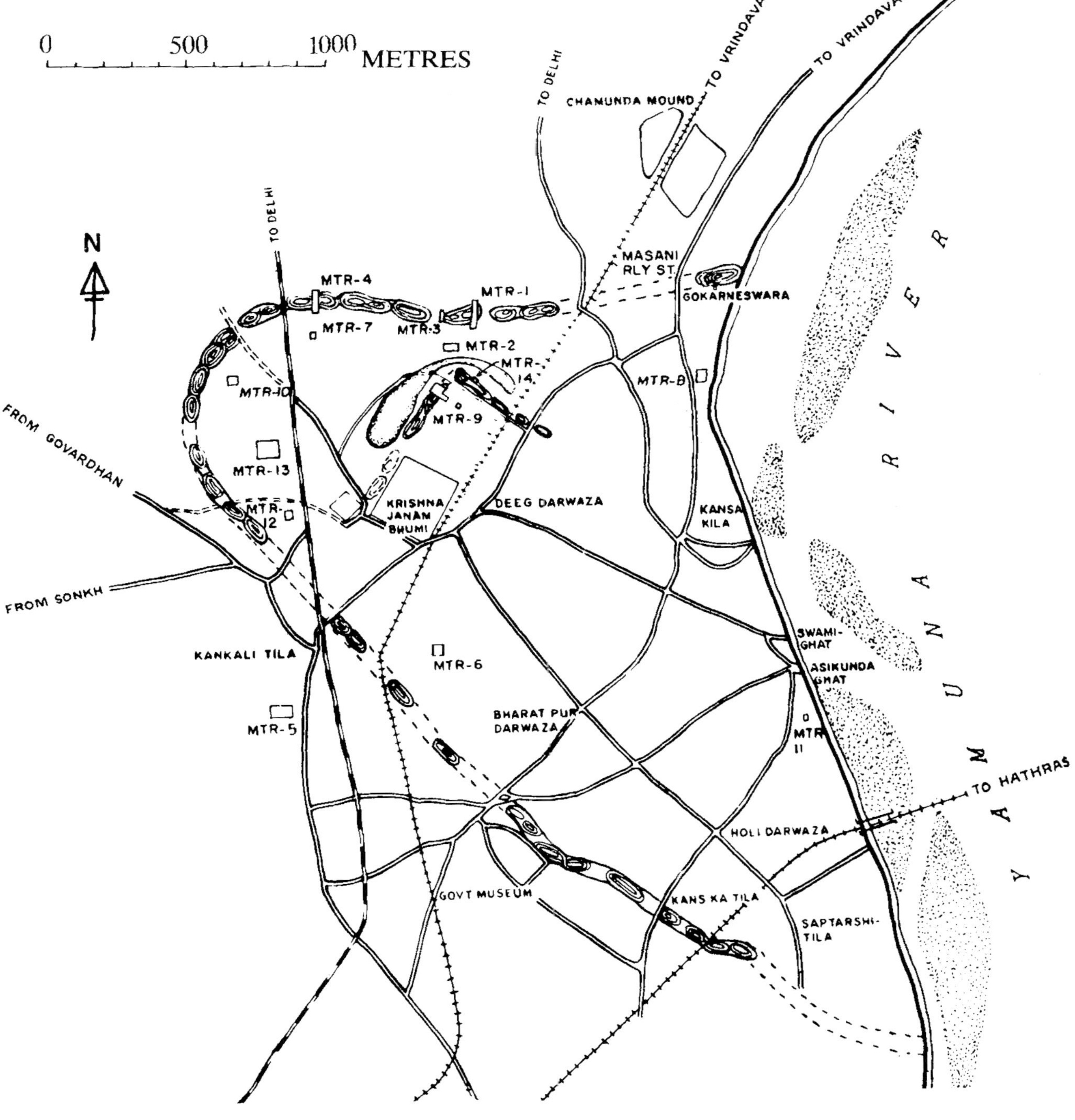

Mathura: Ancient fortifications.

Figure 3.20 Mathura. Illustration used with the courtesy and permission of the American Institute of Indian Studies, New Delhi, India. "Mathura, as an ancient settlement", in *Mathura: The Cultural Legacy* (M. C. Joshi 1989).

As far as the absolute chronology is concerned, phases in the construction of defenses can be easily correlated with the revised cultural sequence by Thapar and M. C. Joshi (IAR 1975–1976:53–55). The construction of the first mud rampart belongs to the early part of period II, the NBPW, dated to the fourth to early third centuries BC. The decay of the rampart falls into period III, the late NBPW, dated to the second to first centuries BC. The renovation of the rampart and the construction of the inner fortification system belong to period IV, culturally associated with the Sakas-Kushanas, and dated to the first century BC to third century AD.

As far as the function is concerned, the evidence is ambiguous. On one hand, it is not unreasonable to suggest that military function played an important role; the dimensions of the walls and bastions are massive, the line of fortifications is solid, and in addition to the main fortification system there is a massive internal fort. On the other hand, some traits of the structural history and layout of the outer rampart challenge both military and ecological explanations. First, the rampart does not protect the site fully. Encircling the site from the west, north and south, it leaves the bank of the Yamuna River completely unprotected. The ecological function, under this scenario, can be completely excluded: even if the site had some protection from floods, the rampart clearly played no role in it. The military function is not certain either; the length of the Yamuna embankment in Mathura was over 3 km and it is difficult to imagine how without additional protection the river could properly defend the site. If there had been a necessity to defend the site from military threat by building a high and massive rampart, the bank of the Yamuna River would not have been left unprotected. Second, M. C. Joshi (1989:168) notes that in period III the defense wall lost its original function "as a defensive or protective enclosure for the occupants". M. C. Joshi explains this by the presence of occupational deposits over portions of the wall. Yet during period IV, M. C. Joshi (1989:169) notes, the function of the wall was rejuvenated. From the point of view of military conflict in northern India, this structural history makes no sense. If the wall had indeed protected the site from the military threat during period II, it would not have lost its function during period III; for it is widely known that the second and first centuries BC, to which period III belongs, was a time of significant military conflict. Moreover, Mathura was directly involved in this conflict; during the reign of Pushyamitra Shunga the city was allegedly lost to the Greeks.

Table 3.9

Mathura: Periodization (IAR 1975-1976; M. C. Joshi 1989)

Period	Approx. Date	Defining Characteristics
I	6th–4th centuries BC	Painted Gray Ware, Black Slipped Ware
II	4th–2nd centuries BC	Northern Black Polished Ware, fortifications
III	2nd–1st centuries BC	Northern Black Polished Ware
IV	1st century BC–3rd century AD	Major structural activities: water tank, inner fortifications
V	4th–6th centuries AD	Mud platforms

In summary, it appears that the fortification system at Mathura had a non-utilitarian function. At some point, the excavators hinted at a possibility of a ritual use; as they found the remains of animal bones and ash in a pit at the base of the inner fortification wall (IAR 1975–1976:55). Also, from the time of its initial construction the rampart was smoothly incorporated in the natural landscape (IAR 1973–1974:31–32). The use of landscape by itself of course does not exclude the military or ecological function, yet if combined with the aforementioned traits it provides a sense of the symbolic rather than utilitarian use of the fortification system.

Authority

Archaeological evidence for authority in Mathura seems to appear in period II. The traits indicative of authority are scarce and difficult to verify since the excavators have not published the final report. Nonetheless, judging from brief reports in the IAR and a summary of the excavation by M. C. Joshi (1989), the transition from period I to period II marks important and drastic changes in material culture, settlement size, and settlement pattern.

Settlement Size. The settlement significantly expands in size. During period I, the settlement is limited to the area around Ambarish Tila (MTR-8). In period II it covers the entirety of the fortified area.

Architecture. The only remaining traces of structural activity from period I are mud-floors and postholes. During period II, mud-floors and postholes are also present, yet structural activity intensifies. Houses are built on mud platforms and are often associated with ring wells. Other features include U-shaped ovens, drains, and the occasional use of baked brick (IAR 1975–1976:55; M. C. Joshi 1989).

Coins. Coins have been an important source for the reconstruction of Mathura's dynastic history as well as for the study of its separation from Magadha. The first square punch-marked coins appear in Mathura during period II. P. L. Gupta (1968) believes that the minting of an independent coin series started in Mathura as early as in the third century BC.

Terracotta Figurines. Human figurines appear for the first time during period II. "Mother-goddesses" and elephant-riders are the most common types. M. C. Joshi (1989:168) argues that during period II, figurines were manufactured in large numbers and on a commercial scale.

Weapons. Arrowheads and spearheads noticeably appear in period I and period II. Unfortunately, M. C. Joshi does not provide exact amounts, ratios or typologies.

Pottery. In pottery production, Plain Gray and Red Wares dominate during the both periods. On a noticeable scale, the NBPW is introduced in period II, although the first occasional sherds appear in period I.

Settlement Pattern. M. C. Joshi (1989:167–168) makes an important observation with regard to the settlement pattern of the Mathura area. Many sites of the Mathura region were not under occupation during Mathura's period I, yet they were occupied during period II.

If these observations are correct, authoritative structures were present in Mathura by the fourth century BC. Meanwhile, in period I Mathura must have been a small helmet-type settlement, not the capital of the Surasena janapada, as the texts make us believe.

Pataliputra

Pataliputra lies on the right bank of the Ganges River underneath the modern city of Patna (see Figure 3.21). It is one of the largest Early Historic sites in South Asia. According to literary sources, Pataliputra was the second capital of Magadha and the capital of the Mauryan Empire; it maintained political and cultural importance from the fifth century BC until the sixth century AD. Archaeologically, Pataliputra is known by the names of its districts: Kumrahar, Bulandibagh, Panc Pahari, Mahabirgarh, Sadargaly, and Lohanipur. Over the years, excavations at these districts revealed numerous artifacts, structural features, and two occupational sequences. L. A. Waddell carried out the first systematic excavation at Pataliputra in 1892–1899. D. B. Spooner excavated at Pataliputra in 1912–1916. J. A. Page and M. Ghosh conducted further excavations in 1926–1927. Altekar and Mishra of the Jayaswal Research Institute undertook excavations in 1951–1955.[12] The latter project was the first to result in a cultural sequence for Pataliputra. This sequence was based on nine cuttings in the area of Kumrahar and included six periods (Altekar and Mishra 1959:14–21; IAR 1953–1954:9–10; see Table 3.10). Judging from pottery, coins, terracotta figurines, seals, and inscribed sherds, this sequence is quite accurate. One must however keep in mind that the sole basis for the formulation of this sequence was Kumrahar, an area in the eastern part of Pataliputra where Spooner discovered the "pillared hall". In 1955–1956, B. P. Sinha and L. A. Narrain of the Directorate of Archaeology and Museums at Patna continued excavations at Pataliputra. Six trenches were laid out in the four separate parts of town: Mahabirghat, Shah-Kamal Road, Begum-Ki-Haveli, and Government Press Play Ground. Trenches varied from 8 ft to 15 ft in width and from 18 ft to 51 ft in length. As a result of this project, a sequence of three long periods was defined (IAR 1955–1965:22–23; Sinha and Narain 1970:10–14; see Table 3.11). In many respects, this sequence reconfirmed the sequence of Altekar and Mishra. Most importantly, the two sequences showed that the settlement had been under continuous occupation roughly for a millennium, from the sixth century BC to the sixth century AD.

Fortifications

According to Megasthenes, Pataliputra was "of the shape of a parallelogram," and was "girded with a wooden wall, pierced with loopholes for discharge of arrows". The wall had "a ditch in front for defense and for receiving the sewage of the city" (McCrindle 1877:66). Today,

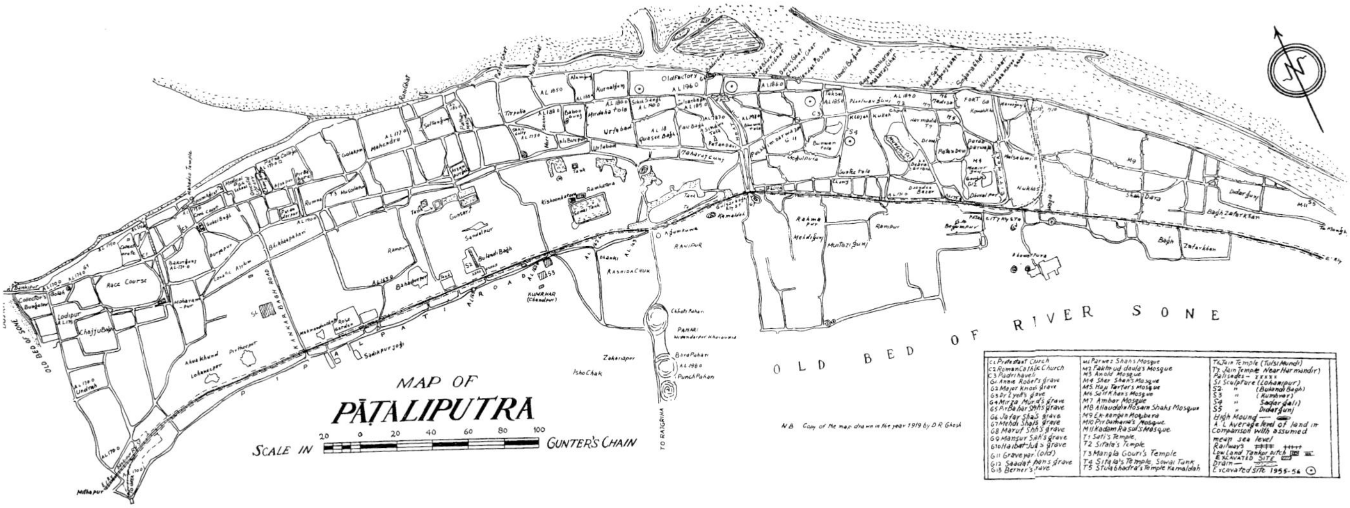

Figure 3.21 Pataliputra. Illustration used with the courtesy and permission of the Jayaswal Research Institute, Patna, Bihar, *Report on Kumrahar excavations, 1951-1955* (Altekar and Mishra 1959).

Pataliputra lies underneath the modern city of Patna, making further excavations almost impossible. Yet some archaeological data were made available to verify the words of Megasthenes. The main evidence for the wooden fortification wall comes from Bulandibagh, an area in the western part of Patna.

In 1915–1917, Spooner excavated at Bulandibagh on behalf of the ASI. During this excavation, he unearthed a structure consisting of two parallel walls made of wooden poles. Underneath this structure, he found a "floor composed of long squared timbers, with their ends fitted into sockets into the uprights of the walls" (Patil 1963:394). The wooden walls were 24 ft long. The floor extended for at least 350 ft. Due to the trimmed ends of the floor timbers, it was concluded that the wall originally extended to the same distance as the floor. The height of the wooden walls was estimated to rise at least 9 ft above the floor level. Based on the depth of the deposit and on stratigraphic association, the entire structure was dated roughly to the Mauryan period (Patil 1963:394). Spooner's discovery was not the exception. In 1926–1927, J. A. Page and M. Ghosh resumed excavations at Bulandibagh and exposed a timber floor and wooden poles over a length of 137 m. In 1935, a very similar wooden structure was discovered at Gosain Khanda, an area to the east of Bulandibagh. The uncovered wall fragment at Gosain Khanda was 100 ft long, about 7 ft high, and 5 ft 6 in thick. It was argued that the wall

Table 3.10

Kumrahar, Pataliputra: Periodization (Altekar and Mishra 1959; IAR 1953-1954)

Period	Approx. Date	Defining Characteristics
I	?–150 BC	Gray Ware, a few sherds of Northern Black Polished Ware, coins
II	150 BC–100	Northern Black Polished Ware, Red Ware, Gray Ware, Sunga terracottas, coins, stone pillars, a sherd inscribed in Brahmi
II	AD 100–300	Northern Black Polished Ware, Gray Ware, Kushana coins and terracottas
IV	AD 300–450	Coins of Chandragupta I, seals in Gupta script, Gupta terracottas
V	AD 450–600	Red Ware, Brick structures
	— No signs of occupation —	
VI	AD 1700–?	Muslim Glazed Pottery, Mughal coins

Table 3.11

Pataliputra: Periodization (Sinha and Narain 1970; IAR 1955–1965)

Period	Approx. Date	Defining Characteristics
I	600 BC–150 BC	Northern Black Polished Ware, Black and Red Ware, Gray Ware
II	150 BC–AD 500	Sunga-Kushana terraccotta, brick architecture
	— No signs of occupation —	
III	1700 AD	Muslim Glazed Ware, figurines, coins

continued further north and south (Patil 1963:396). Another group of wooden structures was reported by Waddel and then by Mukherji from Rampur, an area west of Bulandibagh. Lohanipur, an area rich in antiquities, located a mile west of Bulandibagh, also produced evidence of a wooden palisade (Patil 1963:398–400).

Thus, Megasthenes appears to have been accurate in mentioning wooden walls around Pataliputra. Although most of the cited data are poorly published or lost, the overall number of references to wooden walls is too large to be discarded as erroneous. The chronology and structural history of these walls are unclear, yet a few words can be said about their function. Megasthenes recorded mostly military attributes: "loopholes for the discharge of arrows", "570 towers", "four-and-sixty gates", and the encircling ditch (McCrindle 1877:66, 68). I would not however take the words of Megasthenes as solid evidence of military function. Walls made of wood are a poor way to protect a large city from a military attack and they are ineffective in protecting a city from floods.

Authority

According to the Jaina and Purāṇic literature, the ruler of Magadha Ajatshatru founded Pataliputra as a fort in the fifth century BC. Ajatshatru's successor, Udayi, moved the capital of Magadha from Rajgir to Pataliputra. Thus, in the view of literary sources, Pataliputra was a seat of authority from the fifth century BC. Archaeologically it is difficult to reconfirm this claim, as the results of previous excavations are not sufficient enough for tracing specific changes that might have characterized the genesis of Pataliputra's material culture in the sixth to fourth centuries BC. According to the chronology by Sinha and Narain, period I begins around the sixth century BC and lasts until the middle of the second century BC. The early phases of this period are not well defined. The data on architecture, figurines, coins, and weapons are too vague to make even hypothetical conclusions. For example, no significant structural remains are associated with period I: ring wells, postholes, and a brick floor were recorded on the site of Mahabhirgat; a wall was traced on the site of Government Press Play Ground; two walls, a brick floor, and several ring wells were unearthed on the site of Begum Ki Haveli (Sinha and Narain 1970:15–19). Figurines are not very informative either. Human figurines are found throughout the period. The figurines found in the earlier levels are all hand-made and abstract. The human figurines from the middle and upper levels are more realistic and the plaques are produced from moulds (Sinha and Narain 1970:41). As far as coins are concerned, the first uninscribed cast coins and the first punch-marked coins appear in the middle levels of period I (Sinha and Narain 1970:48). Finally there is a good number of bone arrowheads associated with period I, but none of them are chronologically and spatially differentiated (Sinha and Narain 1970:55).

A potentially better archaeological proof of authority is the "Pillared Hall" discovered by Spooner at the area of Kumrahar (see Figures 3.22–3.23). The remains of this hall consisted of the foundations, sites, and fragments of 80–84 monolithic stone pillars. The hall was constructed during the Mauryan period and destroyed soon after the Guptas (Spooner 1913:77–78) or in the second century BC (Altekar and Mishra 1959:23). Judging from the structures built on top of the hall, the latter view is more likely. The function of the hall is very obscure. No walls, floors, railing or any other structural elements were found inside the hall. Neither were found any significant Mauryan structures in the immediate vicinity of the hall. Most of the structures excavated at Kumrahar belonged to the later periods.[13]

Thus paradoxically and in contrast to the literary tradition, the archaeology of Pataliputra has provided the least amount of credible data to reconfirm its status as a great center of power and the capital of the first South Asian empire.

Rajghat

Rajghat is located on the outskirts of Varanasi (see Figure 3.24). According to the literary sources, it was the capital of the janapada of Kasi and played an important role in the early history of northern India. K. Deva conducted a brief season of excavations in Rajghat in 1940. A. K. Narain undertook several seasons of excavations at Rajghat during 1960–1967 (Narain and Roy 1976:21–35). As the result of the latter project, a continuous sequence of six periods was defined (see Table 3.12, Figure 3.26). Compared to other Gangetic sites, Rajghat was excavated on a large horizontal scale.[14]

Fortifications

The defenses at Rajghat are well documented and the

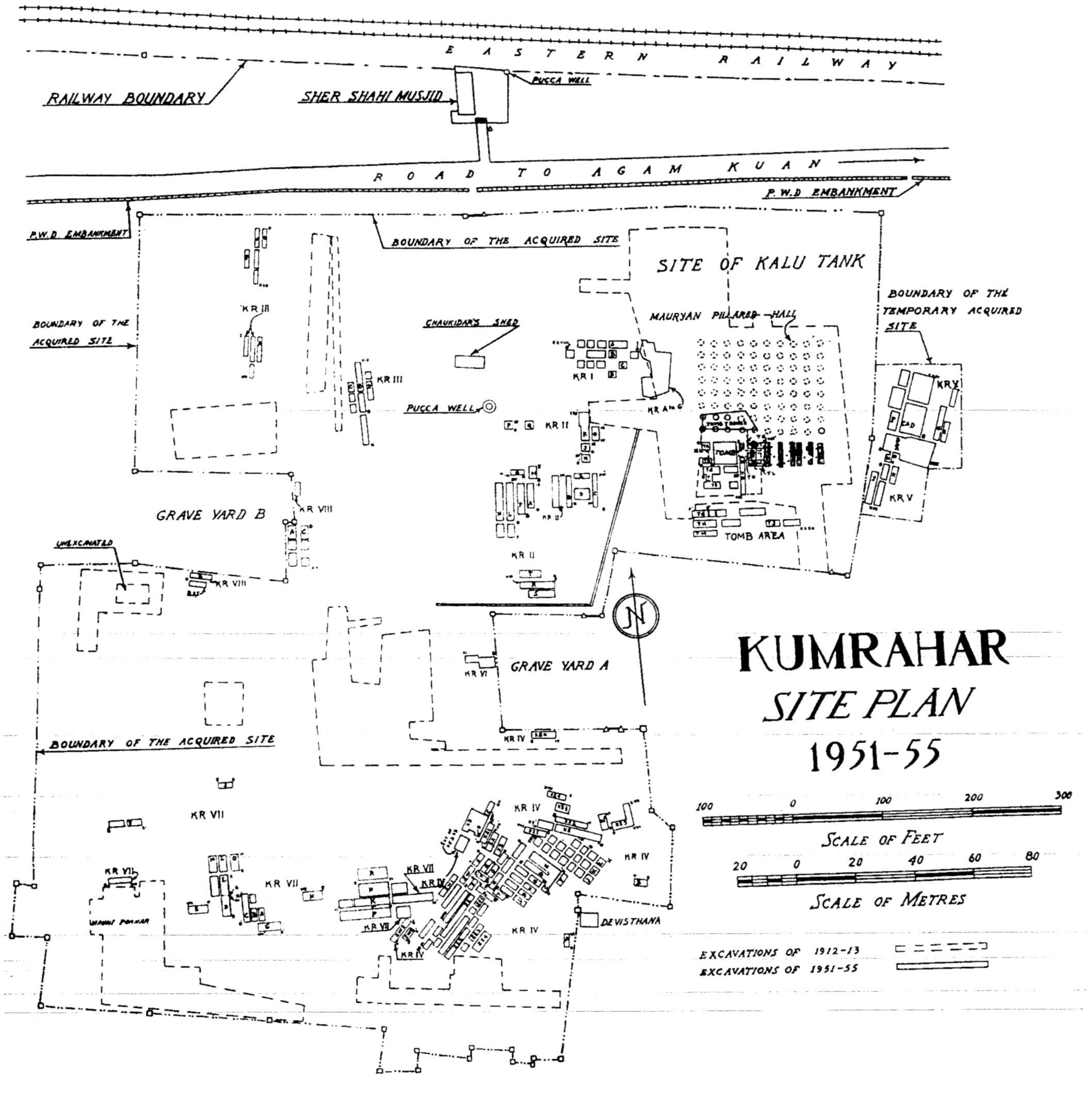

Figure 3.22 Pataliputra: Kumrahar. Illustration used with the courtesy and permission of the Jayaswal Research Institute, Patna, Bihar, *Report on Kumrahar excavations, 1951–1955* (Altekar and Mishra 1959).

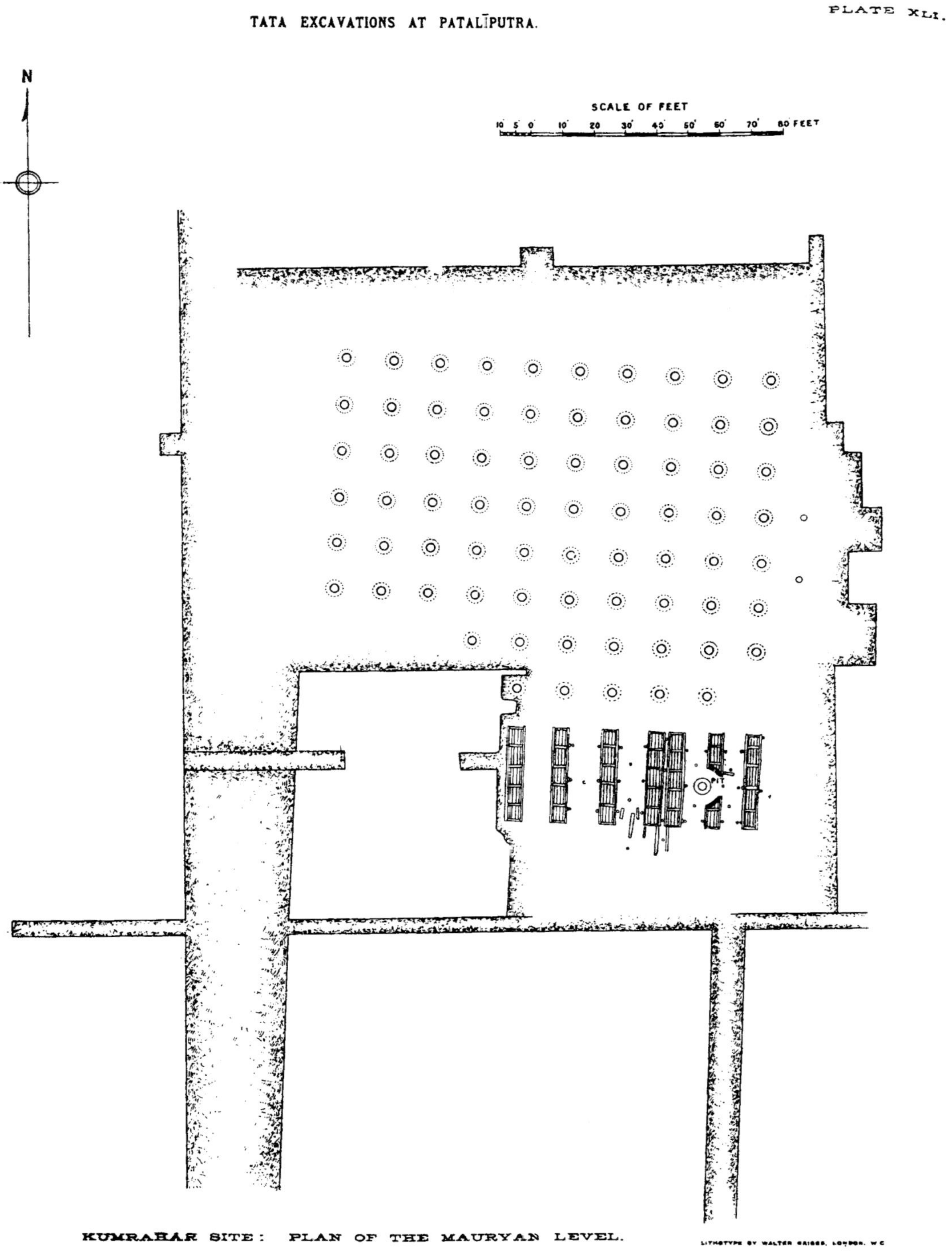

Figure 3.23 Pillared hall at Kumrahar, Pataliputra. Illustration used with the courtesy and permission of the ASI, *Mr. Ratan Tata's excavations at Pataliputra, Annual Report of the Archaeological Survey of India 1912–1913* (Spooner 1913).

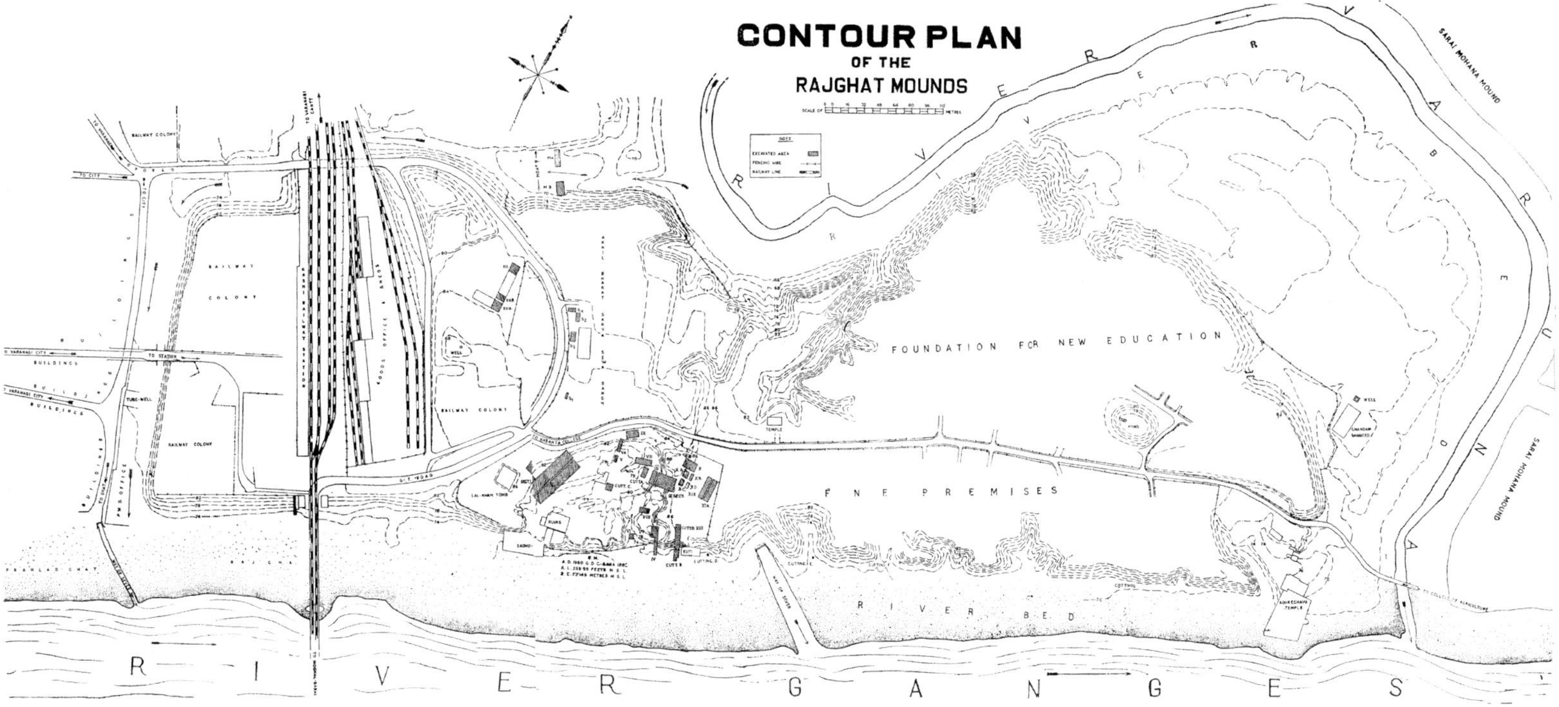

Figure 3.24 Contour plan of Rajghat. Illustration used with the courtesy and permission of the Department of Ancient Indian History, Culture, and Archaeology, Benares Hindu University, *Excavations at Rajghat, 1957/58–1960/1965*, Part I (Narain and Roy 1976).

Table 3.12

Rajghat: Periodization (Narain and Roy 1976)

Period	Approx. Dates	Defining Characteristics
I	800–300/200 BC	
Sub-Period IA		Black and Red Ware, Black Slipped Ware, Slipped and Unslipped Red Ware; numerous terracotta objects: discs, wheels, balls, etc.; no structures
Sub-Period I B		Northern Black Polished Ware, wooden platform (first structural phase), massive clay embankment channel; terracotta figurines
Sub-Period IC		Coarse Gray Ware, deterioration of the Northern Black Polished Ware
II	300/200 BC–0	Red Ware, general decline of the ceramic industry; first burnt-brick structures
III	0–AD 300	Red Ware, burnt-brick structures, seals, coinage, figurines
IV	AD 300–700	Red Polished Ware, sealings, beads, terracotta objects
V	AD 700–1200	Red Ware, Grayish-Black Ware, architectural fragments, sculptures, terracotta objects, beads
VI	AD 1200–1700	Coarse Red Ware, various glazed wares, terracotta, figurines, beads, bangles, coins

studies are quite interesting. Since the view of the excavators on the date, nature, and function of these defenses has significantly changed over time, it is worthwhile to review the main stages of research.

For a long time, it was thought that Rajghat had a massive rampart. During the first season of excavations conducted on behalf of the Banaras Hindu University, the excavators noticed "the remains of a rampart with gates" (IAR 1957–58:50). As a goal of the next season, it was decided "to ascertain the nature of defenses" (IAR 1960–61:35). A long trench measuring 16.48 m in length and 3.05 m in width (RGT-4) was dug in the southeast corner of the main mound. Later it was extended for another 12 m north into the town. The excavators reported (IAR 1960–1961:37).

> The most noteworthy discovery of the season was that of an enormous clay rampart dating back to the earliest occupations of the site. Built directly over the natural soil and available to a height of about 10 metres, the rampart has a pronounced slope towards the river.

The rampart was dated to sub-period IA, ca. 800–600 BC (IAR 1960–1961:37), and two structural phases were distinguished (IAR 1961–1962:58; Narain and Roy 1976:49): 1) phase 1 was represented by a structure made of "well rammed, compact, brownish clay." The vertical extant of this structure was 5.10 m; its basal width was 19.8 m; 2) during phase 2, the structure was raised by 1.10-m thick mud filling and its inner side was patched by a similar filling towards the beginning of its slope.

It took another important discovery for the excavators to realize that they were dealing with the embankment against floods, not the rampart. In the season of 1964–1965, a wooden platform was uncovered on the bank of the Ganga River. The excavators reported (IAR 1964–65:45):

> In the last year's cutting, the outer slope of the massive clay structure was further traced up to a height of 4.24 m from its base, exposing wood-remains all over the trench. It was noticed that a 25 m thick layer of ash, charcoal and potsherds intervened between the defences and the wood remains. A cross-section of the wood remains in one of the corners revealed that, despite heavy decomposition, its thickness varied from 3 to 5 cm. The smooth laying of the wooden planks in the nature of a platform and their possible stretch to a length of 34 m, from the present cutting along the bank of the Ganga, leads on to infer that the structure served as an ancient wooden platform. As a result of rise in the level of the Ganga and consequently deeper penetration of the floodwater, this wooden platform fell in disuse and floods became a source of constant danger to the city. It was at this stage that a massive clay embankment was built as a defensive measure against floods; it was not planned to be a regular fortification, a fact which is corroborated by three more cuttings laid in the same alignment.

It took another couple of years for the excavators to come to the conclusion that Rajghat might not have had a rampart at all, for the trial trenches dug in various locations around the site revealed no traces of fortifications whatsoever. The revised picture thus was quite different. Sub-period I had three structural phases. In phase 1, a wooden platform was constructed along the bank of the Ganga. In phase 2, around 500 BC a massive

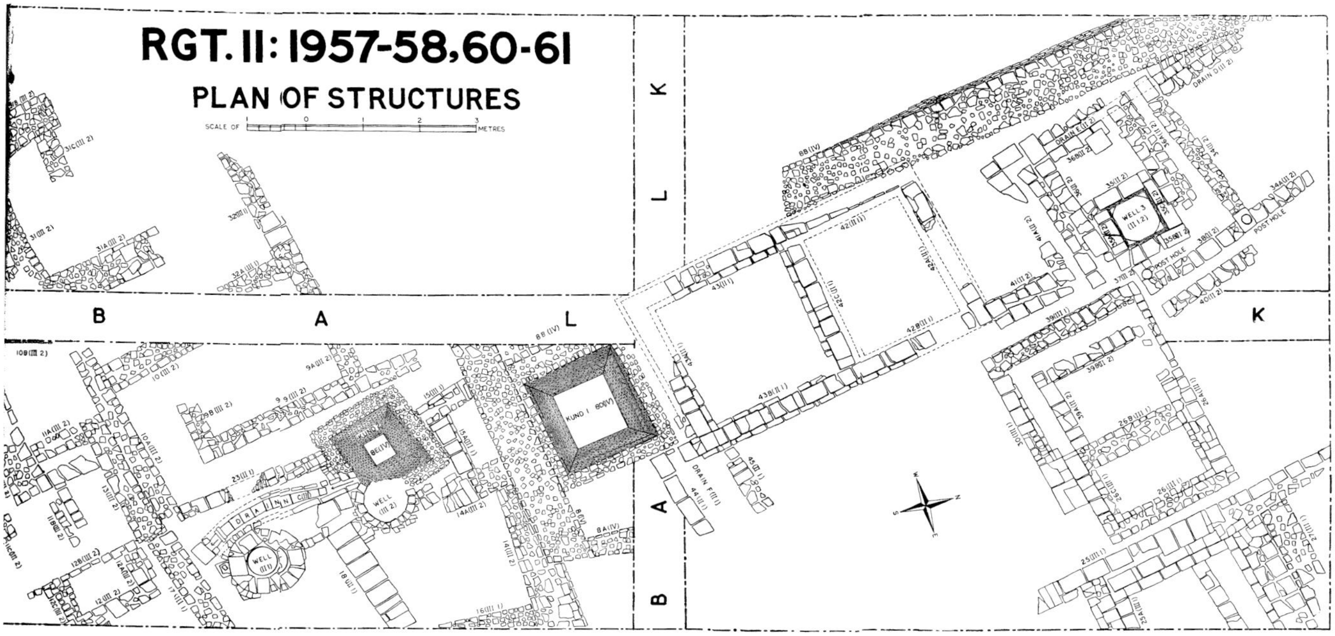

Figure 3.25 Rajghat: Trench RGT II. Illustration with the courtesy and permission of the Department of Ancient Indian History, Culture, and Archaeology, Benares Hindu University, *Excavations at Rajghat, 1957/58–1960/1965*, Part I (Narain and Roy 1976).

embankment was built between the river and the settlement in order to protect the settlement against floods. In phase 3, the embankment was enlarged and renovated (Narain and Roy 1976:22–24). Besides the embankment, the only other structure that could have possibly carried a defensive function was a channel on the northern side of the settlement. In the first phase of its construction, it was almost 8 m wide at the top and about 2.4 m deep. Later, the channel was widened to about 37 m (IAR 1961–1962:58) at the top. Narain and Roy (1976:58) nevertheless argued that it was a channel, "not a full-fledged moat".

Thus, the construction of massive structures at Rajghat—the wooden platform and the embankment—was roughly contemporaneous with the advent of the NBPW. As far as the nature and function of these structures are concerned, the situation remains unclear. Narain and Roy never established the actual size of the settlement. It is not however impossible that the site was bigger than the excavated areas and the remains of the rampart on the eastern and western sides are still to be found. Also, the shift in interpretation makes one wonder whether the revised explanation is credible. If the massive structure between the site and the river was indeed the embankment, what was the function of a channel on the northern side of the site? Judging from its extraordinary width (37 m), it must have been either a moat or a water reservoir.

In sum, in spite of many seasons of excavations at Rajghat much remains to be done. I strongly believe that circumvallation is to be found. The Ganges is a powerful river and a short embankment would not have sufficiently protected the site from floods, particularly when the site is located in the immediate proximity to the water.

Authority

The beginning of period II around third or second centuries BC marked several significant changes in the cultural history of Rajghat (see Figure 3.25). During period I, structural activities were minimal. Besides the wooden platform and the embankment, excavators spotted a number of pits, post-holes, terracotta ring-wells, mud-floorings, and occasional mud-walls. No complete rooms or house plans were detected. The use of mud plaster and the discovery of reed impressions led Narain and Roy (1976:23) to propose that houses may have

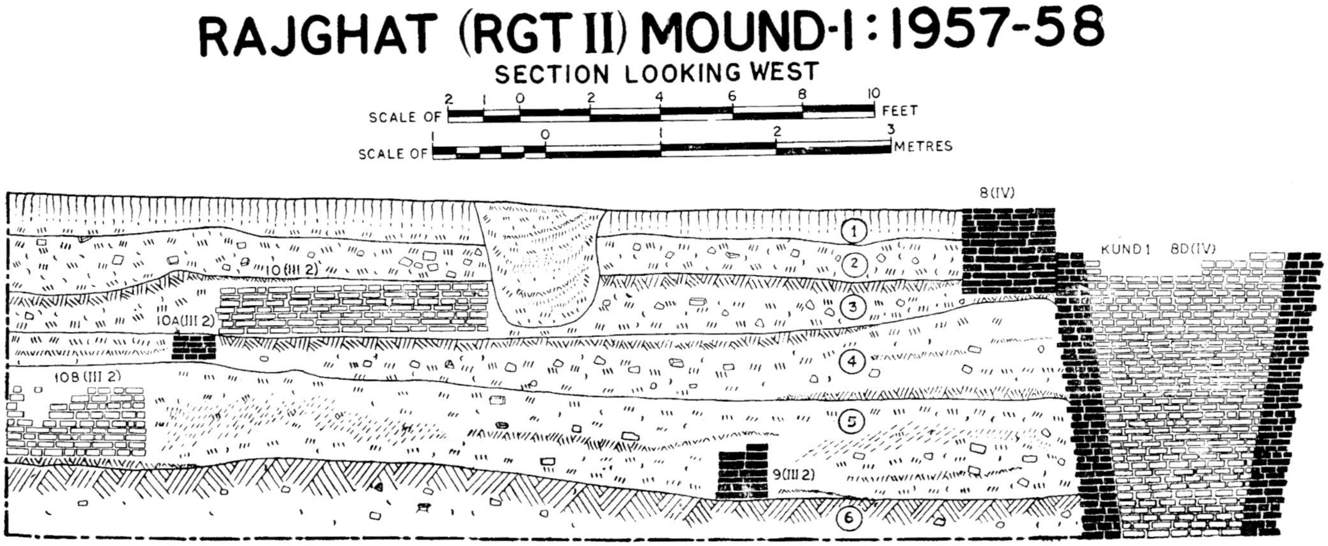

Figure 3.26 Rajghat: Section of trench RGT II. Illustration with the courtesy and permission of the Department of Ancient Indian History, Culture, and Archaeology, Benares Hindu University, *Excavations at Rajghat, 1957/58–1960/1965*, Part I (Narain and Roy 1976).

been made of reed and plastered with mud. Toward the end of period I, the first copper-cast coins appeared and moulds began to be used for the production of figurines. During period II, burnt brick replaced mud and mud-brick in construction. Structural remains of this period were characterized by high standing burnt-brick walls, complete rooms and houses, foundations made of brick-bats and mud, sanitary soakage jars with perforated bottoms, drains and bathing platforms. Houses were arguably built according to cardinal directions. In one of the trenches, a whole domestic unit was excavated. It consisted of two rooms with a doorway, a vestibule, an internal well, a bathing platform, and an attached drain. Among other innovations, period II saw the introduction of seals and sealings. A large variety of terracotta figurines, coins, arrowheads, points, beads and other artifacts also characterized this period.

Unfortunately, many of these finding were recorded in a way that does not allow placing the relevant cultural changes in a temporal perspective. For example, on several occasions, the excavators mentioned the presence of bone arrowheads and points. Yet they did not specify their exact numbers and stratigraphic context. Figurines were analyzed from a typological and artistic perspective but changes that must have taken place from period to period were not clearly specified. With regard to pottery, the excavators emphasized the spread of large size vessels of more utilitarian shapes in period II as compared to period I. With regard to demography and the patterns of settlement expansion, Narain and Roy (1976:26) argued that period II was characterized both by a significant increase in population and the expansion of settlement. It is not exactly clear on what data this assumption was based since the deposits of both period I and period II were detected in almost all of the trenches. Overall however, traits of period II seem to provide some evidence for the formation of authoritative structures in Rajghat. This means that before the third or even second century BC, Rajghat was a relatively insignificant rural settlement.

Rajgir

Rajgir, or Rajagriha, is located in Bihar in the district Nalanda, southwest of Biharsharif (see Figure 3.27). Judging from the literary sources, it had been the capital of Magadha until the fifth century BC when the capital was moved north to Pataliputra. The remains of ancient Rajgir are thought to consist of two parts: Old Rajgir and New Rajagriha. Both parts have been sporadically explored and excavated since the middle of the nineteenth century. A. Cunningham, J. Marshall, V. H. Jackson, T. Bloch and D. R. Sahni excavated and surveyed at Rajgir at the turn of the twentieth century. As a result of these explorations, detailed maps of the site and fortifications were compiled. A number of structures of the Mauryan, Kushana, and Gupta periods were identified and excavated. Yet no systematic culture history was generated. In 1950, A. Ghosh carried out a small-scale excavation by the inner defenses of Old Rajgir. Based on this excavation, Ghosh (1951:70–72) defined a sequence of four cultural periods (Table 3.13). Referring to this sequence, one must keep in mind that it was defined with the help of section cut by a stream at the foot of one of the hills at Rajgir. No excavation was undertaken to reconfirm this sequence in other parts of the site. When in the early 1960s, R. Singh launched a new project at Rajgir, a sequence of three cultural periods was defined (Table 3.14). Although the main criterion for Singh in defining cultural periods was the structural modification of defenses, this section was reconfirmed in several separate locations, including the habitation areas (IAR 1962–1963:5–6).

On the whole, the archaeological remains of Rajgir remain poorly investigated.[15] First, it is still unclear whether a distinction between Old and New Rajgir suggested by A. Cunningham is appropriate. There does not seem to be any mentioning of two Rajgirs in the literary sources. Neither is there a solid proof of Old Ragir being actually settled earlier than New Rajgir. Second, if Rajgir was indeed the first capital of Magadha, one would expect it to have left significant structural remains datable to the sixth century BC. No such remains have been so far detected.

Fortifications

Looking at the maps of Rajgir and surrounding areas, one can see a truly grandiose network of inner and outer fortifications (see Figures 3.27–3.29). The outer walls run for about forty km over the surrounding hills. They are made of massive stones that are carefully adjusted and bonded together. The maximum height of these walls is about 12 ft. On the average however, they reach 7–8 ft. The thickness of the walls is about 15 ft. There are several rectangular bastions. The chronology of these walls is controversial, yet most scholars place their initial construction before or during the Mauryan period. The structural history of these walls is not very well known either.

The structural history of the internal fortifications is better known. In 1961–1962, R. Singh of the ASI laid out a 66 m x 5 m cutting across the southern defenses at New Rajgir. The excavation was carried to a depth of 18 m below the extant top of the defenses and, as I mentioned above, a sequence of three structural periods was defined (IAR 1961–62:6–8). The main finds of period I included the NBPW, Red Ware of medium-to-fine fabric, terracotta figurines, copper objects, and punch-marked coins. The final layers of this period reportedly contained evidence of conflagration. Period II saw the construction of a mud-rampart, a brick parapet wall, and a moat. Singh distinguished two structural sub-periods within this period. In sub-period A, the rampart and moat were built. The main extant part of the rampart was 7.3 m high. The southern side of the rampart was retained by a brick wall. On the top, the rampart was covered with mud and brickbats. Sub-period B saw the construction of a brick parapet wall on top of the rampart (IAR 1961–62:7). Period III had two sub-periods and was defined by several consecutive renovations and enlargements. The chronology of this fortification complex is confusing. Based on pottery and other finds, the excavator placed period II in the sixth and fifth centuries BC (IAR 1961–62:8). A radiocarbon sample from the pre-defense period I(!) however gave the date of 245+105 BC (IAR 1962–1963:5).

The function of fortifications at Rajgir is not as clear as it may first seem to be. There are three sets of fortifications: the outer fortification, the inner Old Rajgir fortification, and the New Rajgir fortification. The scale of the outer fortifications is truly unique.

Table 3.13

Rajgir: Periodization (Ghosh 1951)

Period	Approx. Date	Defining Pottery Types
I	before 5th century BC	Crude and Coarse Red Ware;
II	5th–2nd centuries BC	Northern Black Polished Ware
III	1st century BC	Red Ware
IV	AD 4th century	Thick jars and bowls and bright terracotta color

Table 3.14

Rajgir: Periodization (Singh in IAR 1962–1963)

Period	Defining Characteristics
I	Pre-defense occupation, Northern Black Polished Ware
II	Mud-rampart with a brick wall on top of it
III	Renovation of the defense system

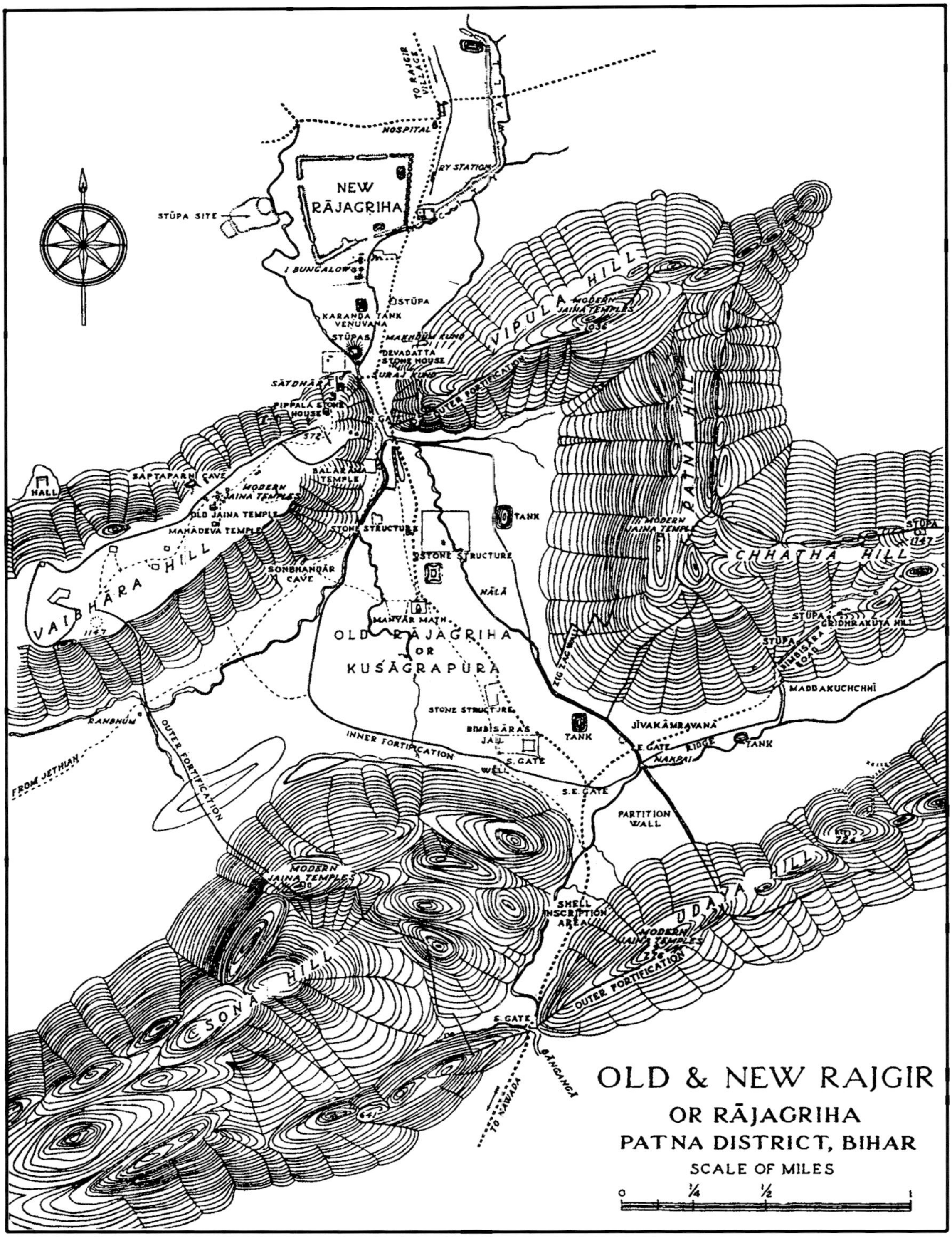

Figure 3.27 Rajgir/Rajagriha. Illustration used with the courtesy and permission of the ASI, *Rajgir* (Ghosh 1958).

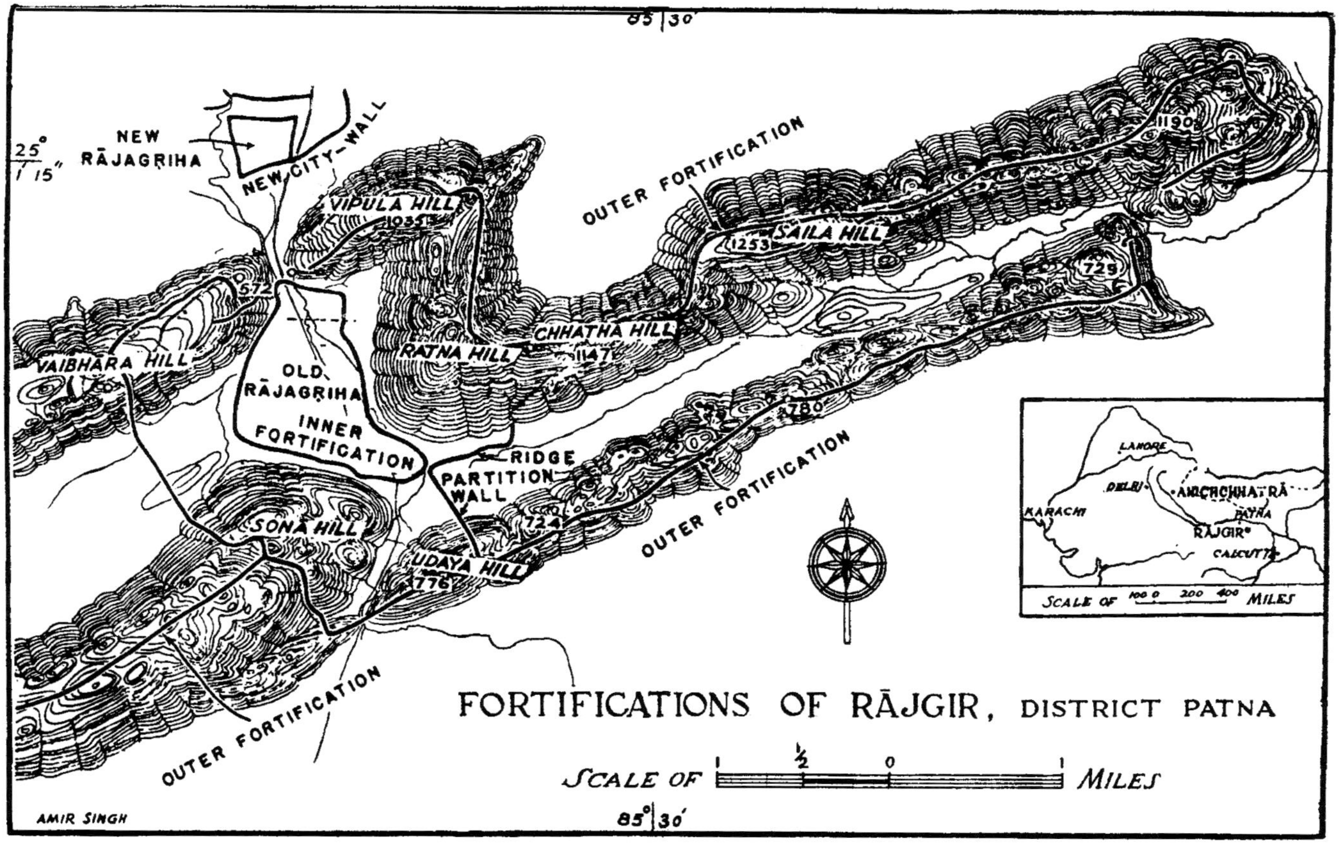

Figure 3.28 Fortifications of Rajgir. Illustration used with the courtesy and permission of the ASI, *Rajgir* (Ghosh 1958).

No other Early Historic site in northern India has such a long system of walls. Built of massive and carefully trimmed stones on top of high hills, these walls must have required a very significant consumption of time and labor. Given the role that Rajgir played in the political history of northern India according to the texts, it is reasonable to assume that the sole reason for the construction of such an elaborate network of fortifications was military conflict. Indeed, as the first capital of Magadha, Rajgir was involved in several military conflicts during the sixth and fifth centuries BC. Under Bimbisara and his son Ajatashatru, Magadha waged at least three important wars: with the kingdom of Anga, with the kingdom of Kośala, and with the confederacy of Vrijji. Nevertheless, the complexity of the three-leveled fortification system of Rajgir seems to exceed its military needs. The internal ramparts and parapet walls surrounded by high hills with narrow passes must have provided sufficient defense without long and massive outer fortifications. In fact, Rajgir was the only Early Historic site in northern India that had such an advantageous location from the viewpoint of defense. Furthermore, if the outer fortification wall had been built prior to the transfer of the capital from Rajgir to Pataliputra, one would expect for the fortification system of Pataliputra to have been at least as powerful as the fortification system at Rajgir; for in the fifth century, military conflicts between the janapadas intensified yet the location chosen for Pataliputra was more vulnerable than the location of Rajgir. If the outer wall had been built after the transfer of the capital from Rajgir to Pataliputra, one would still expect for the fortification system of Pataliputra to have been more powerful; for after the transfer of the capital the center of power, trade, and military defense would have certainly gravitated towards the capital. Texts and archaeology nevertheless show the

Figure 3.29 Rajgir: The remains of outer fortifications today (photo by the author).

opposite. Wooden palisades that surrounded Pataliputra (see above) clearly did not match the strength and elaboration of the fortification system of Rajgir.

The magnitude of the defense system of Rajgir thus appears to have been militarily unjustified. In my opinion, it seems likely that the construction of the outer fortifications was motivated by a combination of military and symbolic concerns. Considering that Rajgir gave birth to a consecutive chain of dynasties, one of which eventually united northern South Asia under the imperial rule, it is not unreasonable to suggest that its fortifications played a certain role in the glorification and solidification of power. Moreover, fortifications are, at present, the only archaeological proof for the institution of authority in Rajgir, both during the pre-Mauryan and Mauryan periods.

Authority

From the literary sources, we know of Rajgir as an important political, cultural and religious center. As early as in the sixth and fifth centuries BC, Rajgir was famous for its religious and philosophical schools. As well, it was intimately connected with the activities of Buddha and Mahavira. Even if a small percentage of what the texts tell us is true, Rajgir must have been a flourishing and bustling settlement by at the latest the sixth century BC. Unfortunately, besides the remains of fortifications, the archaeology of Rajgir is currently unable to provide any data to prove this assumption. The cultural sequence of Rajgir formulated by Ghosh is useless for tracing the emergence of authority. The results of the excavation conducted by the ASI under the directorship of Singh are slightly more informative, yet still not sufficient for tracing the emergence of authoritative structures. In Rajgir, there are many architectural remains having to do with authority, yet all of them date to the later periods. In fact, most Buddhist monuments, the remains of which can be currently seen in Rajgir, belong to the period between sixth and eleventh centuries AD.

The case of Rajgir thus is quite intriguing. The site of great history, it has so far provided nothing to reconfirm its fame except for a massive and elaborate fortification system. This fortification system epitomizes authority and complexity of Rajgir prior to the Mauryan and during the Mauryan periods.

Sonkh

Sonkh is located in the Mathura district, about 30 km southwest of Mathura (see Figure 3.30). The extant mound occupies an area of approximately 320–280 m. The original settlement may have been larger, up to 200,000 m^2. H. Härtel of the Berlin Museum of Indian Art carried out eight seasons of excavations at Sonkh during 1966 to 1974.[16] Based on the results of these excavations, a continuous sequence of seven periods from the PGW of ca. eighth century BC to the Jats of the seventeenth century AD was defined (see Table 3.15).

Fortifications

In association with period I, Härtel (1993:25) reports the remains of a ditch system and possibly a rampart, which may have been "part of an enclosure... anticipating the elements of later defensive works", yet are currently insufficient for assuming the existence of "a fortification like that of the Early Historic time with its parapets and ditches of bigger extent". Interestingly enough, none of the later periods until the very last one reveals any traces of fortifications. Apparently, Sonkh had no defense system until the advent of the Mughals and Sher Shah.

Authority

The cultural history of Sonkh as defined by Härtel (1993:17) provides good potential for investigating the formation of authoritative structures. Revisiting this sequence from the point of view of construction materials used in different periods, one can distinguish four structural phases: 1) the phase of Wattle-and-Daub Structures, characteristic of period I, the PGW, ca. 800–400 BC; 2) the phase of Mud-Wall Structures, characteristic of all but one level of period II, the NBPW, ca. 400–200 BC; 3) the phase of Mud-Brick Structures, characteristic of the last level of period II and levels 29, 28, dated to the end of the Sunga period and the beginning of the period of the Local States; 4) the phase of Baked Brick Structures, characteristic of period III, which starts around the second century BC.

As far as evidence for authority is concerned, the fourth phase is the most interesting. Aside from the use of baked brick, it marks a number of significant changes in settlement layout, architecture, and material culture. In architecture, the regular planning of houses is introduced; a standard house now has an inner courtyard, terracotta ring-wells, and gable roofs made with tile and pinnacles. Other changes include inscribed copper coins, seals, new weapons, iron tools, terracotta human plaques, and terracotta votive tanks. Evidently, all of these changes are related to the political situation in neighboring Mathura, for layer 27 (ca. second century BC), in which the changes initially take place, is contemporaneous with the reign of Suryamitra, a famous ruler from the dynasty of the Mitras of Mathura.[17] Härtel characterizes this layer as a period of major transformations (see Figure 3.31). "The solidity and comfort of structures as well as the abundance of finds", according to Härtel (1993:85), "create an impression of a great prosperity". As far as the type of settlement is concerned, Härtel (1993:33) asserts that the use of mud-brick marks the formative phase of the early urbanism, yet does not clarify whether the use of baked brick indicates the

Table 3.15

Sonkh: Periodization (Härtel 1993)

Period	Approx. Dates	Defining Characteristics
I	800–400 BC	Painted Gray Ware, Black and Red Ware, post-holes, no walls
II	400–200 BC	Northern Black Polished Ware, mud and mud-brick structures
III	200–100 BC	Mithras, Red Ware, baked brick structures, planning
IV	100 BC–AD 100	Ksatrapa and Ramdata, Red Ware, baked brick
V	AD 100–300	Kushanas, Red ware, much architecture, temples
VI		Gupta to Early Medieval
VII		Medieval
VIII		Mughals to Jats

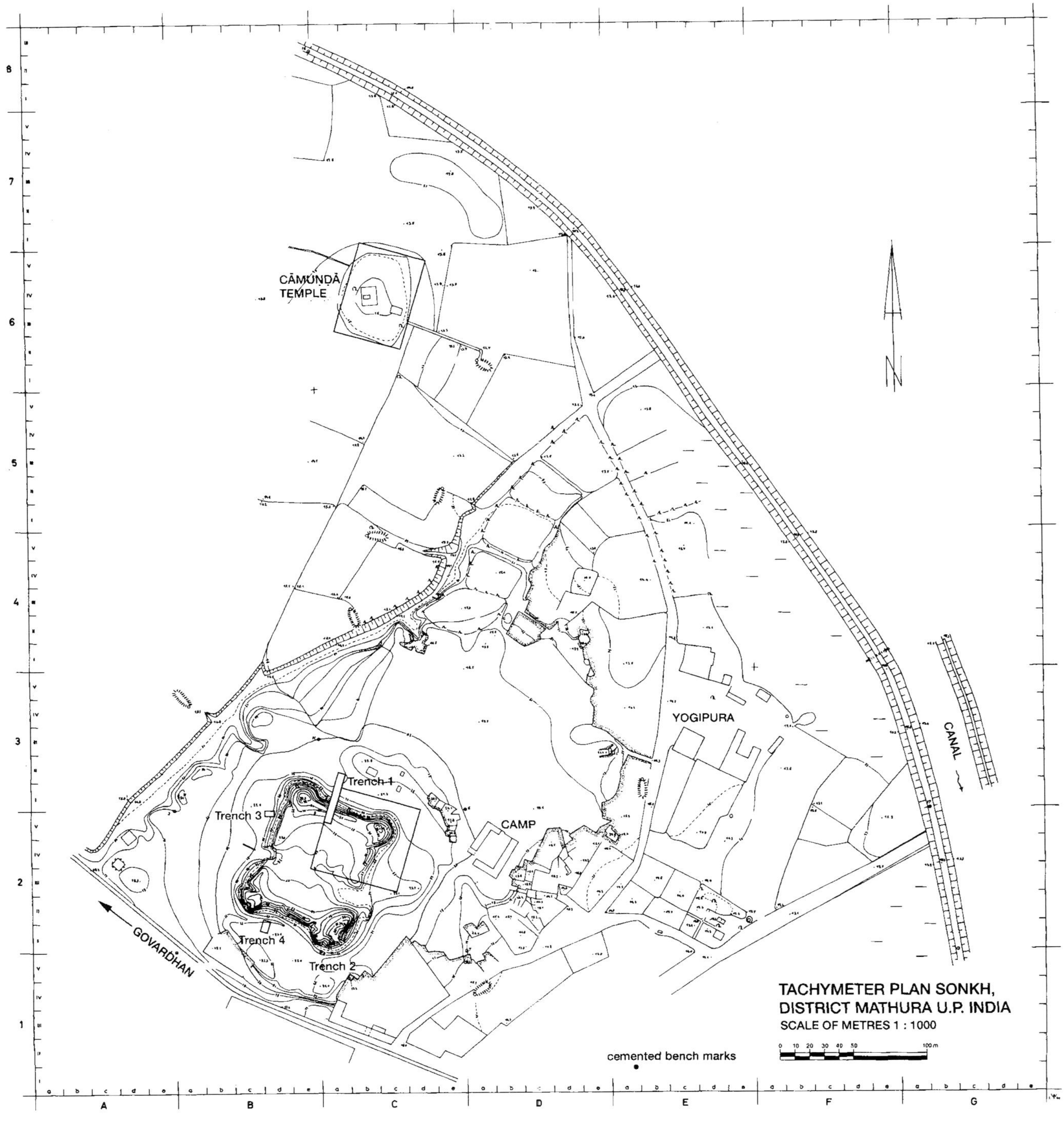

Figure 3.30 Sonkh. Illustration used with the courtesy and permission of D. Reimer Verlag, Berlin, *Excavations at Sonkh: 2500 Years of a Town in Mathura District* (Härtel 1989).

beginning of urbanism. Leaving aside this issue—I will return to it in the end of this chapter—what one can conclude at this point is that the transition to layer 27 of period III provides the first solid and convincing evidence for the presence of authority at Sonkh (see Figure 3.31).

Sonpur

Sonpur (sometimes Sonepur or Sonitpur) is a small site, located south of Patna in the district Gaya, Bihar. Some researchers identify it with the capital of Bana, Sonitapura, mentioned in the Epic and Purāṇic literature. No convincing evidence however has been provided to substantiate this claim. In 1956, the Jayaswal Research Institute of Patna together with the Directorate of Archaeology and Museums, Bihar, began the excavation at Sonpur. During the next several seasons, they exposed large areas of the site and defined a cultural sequence of three consecutive periods (Table 3.16).[18] The absolute dates of this sequence are very speculative. For example, period I is dated on pure conjecture. Dates for period II are borrowed from the report on the excavation at Hastinapura by B. B. Lal. Dates for period III are approximated from coins (Sinha and Verma 1977:12).

Table 3.16

Sonpur: Periodization (Sinha and Verma 1977)

Period	Approx. Date	Defining Pottery Types
IA	1100–1000 BC	Black and Red Ware
IB	1000–650 BC	Fine Black and Red Ware
II	650–200 BC	Northern Black Polished Ware
III	200 BC–AD 200	Post Northern Black Polished Ware

Fortifications and Authority

No fortifications were found in Sonpur during the excavation by the Jayaswal Research Institute. With regard to authority, the results of Sonpur excavation are also negative. Structural activities are minimal until period III (ca. 200 BC–200 AD). Period IA reveals no structural activities whatsoever and the excavators assume that the houses must have been made of perishable materials such as reed and leaves. Period IB has circular lime floors and circular pits. Based on their shape and quantity, the excavators hypothesize that circular huts were built during this period.

Likewise, several post-cremation pit burials from this period have a circular shape. Period II has traces of a mud wall, a platform and several terracotta ring-wells. In period III, burnt brick is introduced and several structures made of burnt brick are found in the upper levels of this period (see Figure 3.32). Yet no complete room or a house has been excavated (Sinha and Verma 1977:10–11). The first coins appear during period II. Of 108 discovered coins, 48 are from stratified context. Of these 48, 16 belong to the deposits of period II and 32 to the deposits of period III (Sinha and Verma 1977:89). There are three types of coins: punch-marked coins, die-struck copper coins, and uninscribed cast copper coins. Importantly, there are no inscribed coins. There are quite a few terracotta sealings, yet there are absolutely no seals. Of the total of 41 sealings, 39 come from stratified layers. Inscribed sealings indicate the names of individuals, divinities or places. Most of these seals belong to period III (Sinha and Verma 1977:99–100). Most terracotta figurines come from period III (Sinha and Verma 1977:115). Most beads are associated with periods II and III (Sinha and Verma 1977:101). There are quite a few arrowheads, styli, and pins. Interestingly enough, the majority of them come from period I (Sinha and Verma 1977:130). As far as the size of the settlement is concerned, the plan of the mound is not provided. The exact size, save for an approximate height, is not reported either. Nonetheless, based on the information about the cuttings, some conclusions can be made with regard to the expansion of the site. It appears that during period IA, the site was very small. Of the thirty excavated trenches, only three (SPR VII, VIII and IX) revealed the deposits of period IA. Moreover, these three trenches were located right next to each other in the center of the northern mound (Sinha and Verma 1977:15–16) and occupied an area of 106 m^2. By period IB, the settlement significantly expanded and, judging from the excavated trenches, stayed as such until the end of occupation. The deposits of periods IB and II were detected in all 30 trenches. The deposits of period III were detected in 29 trenches.

In summary, the cultural history of Sonpur does not provide sufficient evidence for the presence of authority at least until period III or even during the entire occupational sequence: structural activities are minimal throughout all the periods; in size, the settlement stays unchanged in periods II and III; seals and inscribed coins, often seen

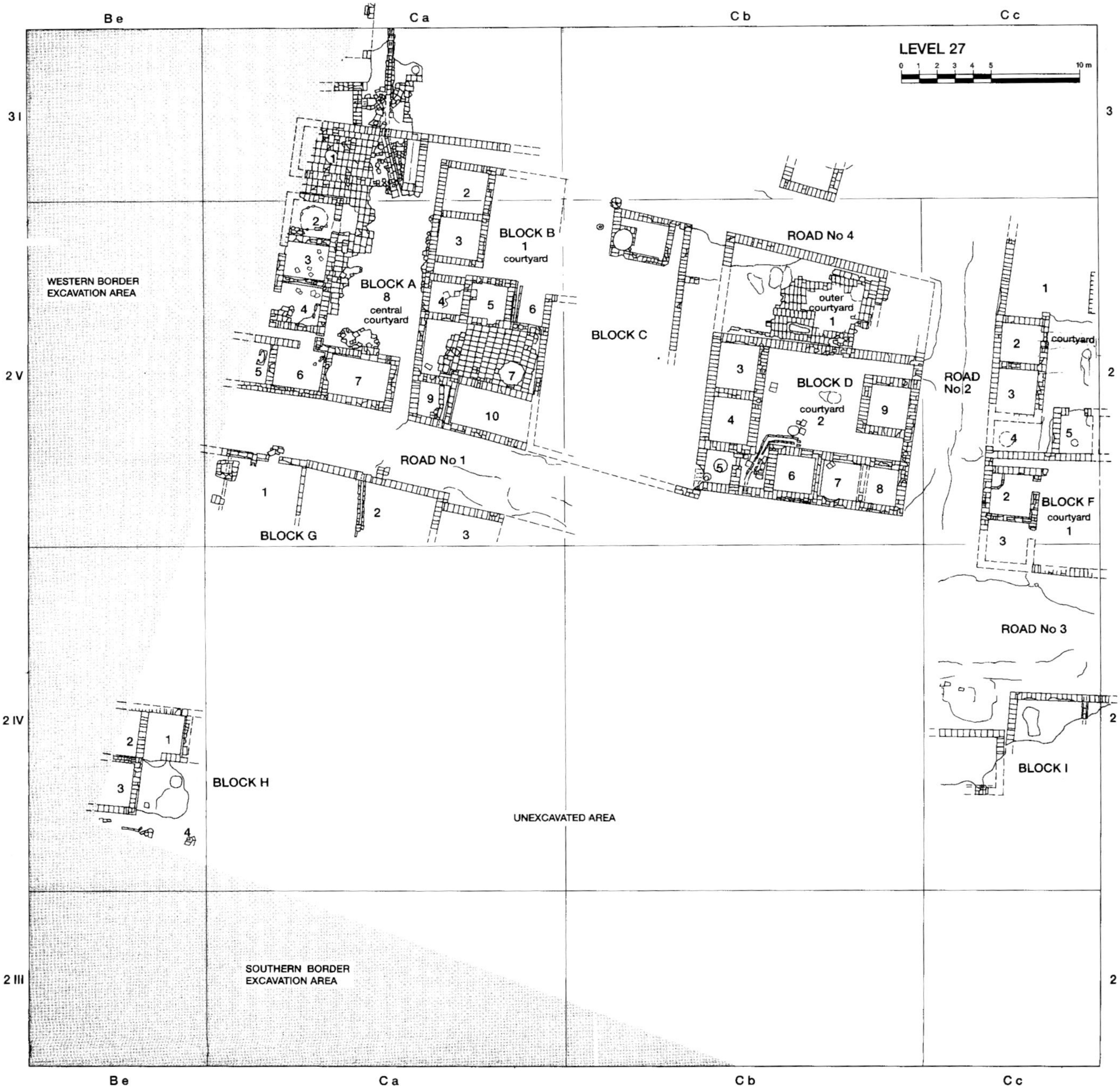

Figure 3.31 Sonkh: Level 27. Illustration used with the courtesy and permission of D. Reimer Verlag, Berlin, *Excavations at Sonkh: 2,500 Years of a Town in Mathura District* (Härtel 1989).

as an important indicator of authority, are completely absent; and there is a clear dearth of signs of drastic changes in sociopolitical complexity. Sinha and Verma (1977:11) claim that the scale of excavation was responsible for at least some of these shortcomings. For a small site however, thirty trenches covering an area of 905 m^2 are not a small-scale horizontal exposure! In my view, the results of the excavation at Sonpur by the Jayaswal Institute must be seen as quite representative.

Sravasti / Saheth-Maheth

Sravasti is a very large site, located in the districts of Gonda and Bahraich, not far from the border between India and Nepal (see Figure 3.33). According to literary tradition, it was one of the two capitals of Kośala, a janapada that played a very important role in early Indian history. The archaeological remains of Sravasti are scattered on two sites, Saheth and Maheth that are separated from each other by a small strip of land. Saheth is a Buddhist establishment; Maheth is a large fortified city. The history of explorations at Saheth and Maheth goes back to the middle of the nineteenth century. In 1863, A. Cunningham briefly explored these two sites and identified them with the city of Sravasti, known from Sanskrit and Pāli literature. W. Hoey followed Cunningham by exploring the site first in the mid-1870s and then in the mid-1880s. In 1908, J. P. Vogel began the first systematic archaeological excavation at Saheth and Maheth. He reconfirmed Cunningham's identification with Sravasti and compiled the first comprehensive map of the site. In 1910–1911, J. Marshall and D. R. Sahni conducted excavations at Saheth. In 1959, Sinha of the ASI excavated at Maheth. Finally, Kansai University in collaboration with the ASI has carried out excavations at both Saheth and Maheth since 1986.[19]

Based on the most recent excavations, the cultural sequence of Saheth begins with the Sunga period around the first century BC, and the cultural sequence of Maheth with the Black and Red Ware phase (BRW) in the beginning of the first millennium BC. There are two cultural sequences of Maheth that are worth mentioning: the first one formulated by Sinha based on his excavation in 1959; the second one formulated by the Kansai University–ASI team based on their most recent excavation. The first sequence consists of three periods (Sinha 1967:7–16; see Table 3.17) The second sequence consists of five periods (Aboshi et al. 1999:135; see Table 3.18).

Fortifications

Maheth is surrounded by a massive rampart with a brick wall on top of it. The length of the rampart is about 5.2 km (see Figure 3.33). The area enclosed by the rampart is almost 160 ha. According to recent excavations, the maximum width of the rampart reaches 36 m and the maximum height reaches 7 m. Cunningham, Hoey and Vogel explored the fragments of the rampart, yet it was K. K. Sinha who in 1959 carried out the first recorded and stratigraphic excavation of it. Sinha laid a trench (SRV I) measuring 120 ft x 12 ft across the northern side of the rampart. Based on this trench he defined a sequence of five structural phases, all of which belonged to period II.

In phase I, the basal width of the rampart was 90 ft and the maximum height was 7 ft.[20] Phase II, did not witness any significant renovations. Yet based on the presence of "a heterogeneous deposit consisting of pottery dump," Sinha (1967:18) suggested that during this phase the area of defenses was used as a "temporary dumping ground". During phase III, a wide brick wall was built on top of the rampart. During phase IV, the height of the mud-rampart was raised further up. Phase V saw the construction of a brick wall right over the rampart filling of phase IV. According to Sinha (1967:19), there was no time gap between phases IV and V.

Table 3.17

Sravasti: Periodization (Sinha 1967)

Period	Approximate Dates	Defining Characteristics
I	< 275 BC	Pre-defense
II	275–50 BC	Northern Black Polished Ware; Painted Gray Ware; defenses
III	50 BC	Site largely deserted

Table 3.18

Sravasti: Periodization (Aboshi et al. 1999)

Period	Approximate Dates	Defining Characteristics
I	< 6th century BC	Black and Red Ware
II	6th–4th century BC	Early Northern Black Polished Ware
III	3rd–1st century BC	Late Northern Black Polished Ware
IV	1st–3rd century AD	The Kushanas
V	7th–8th century AD	Post-Gupta

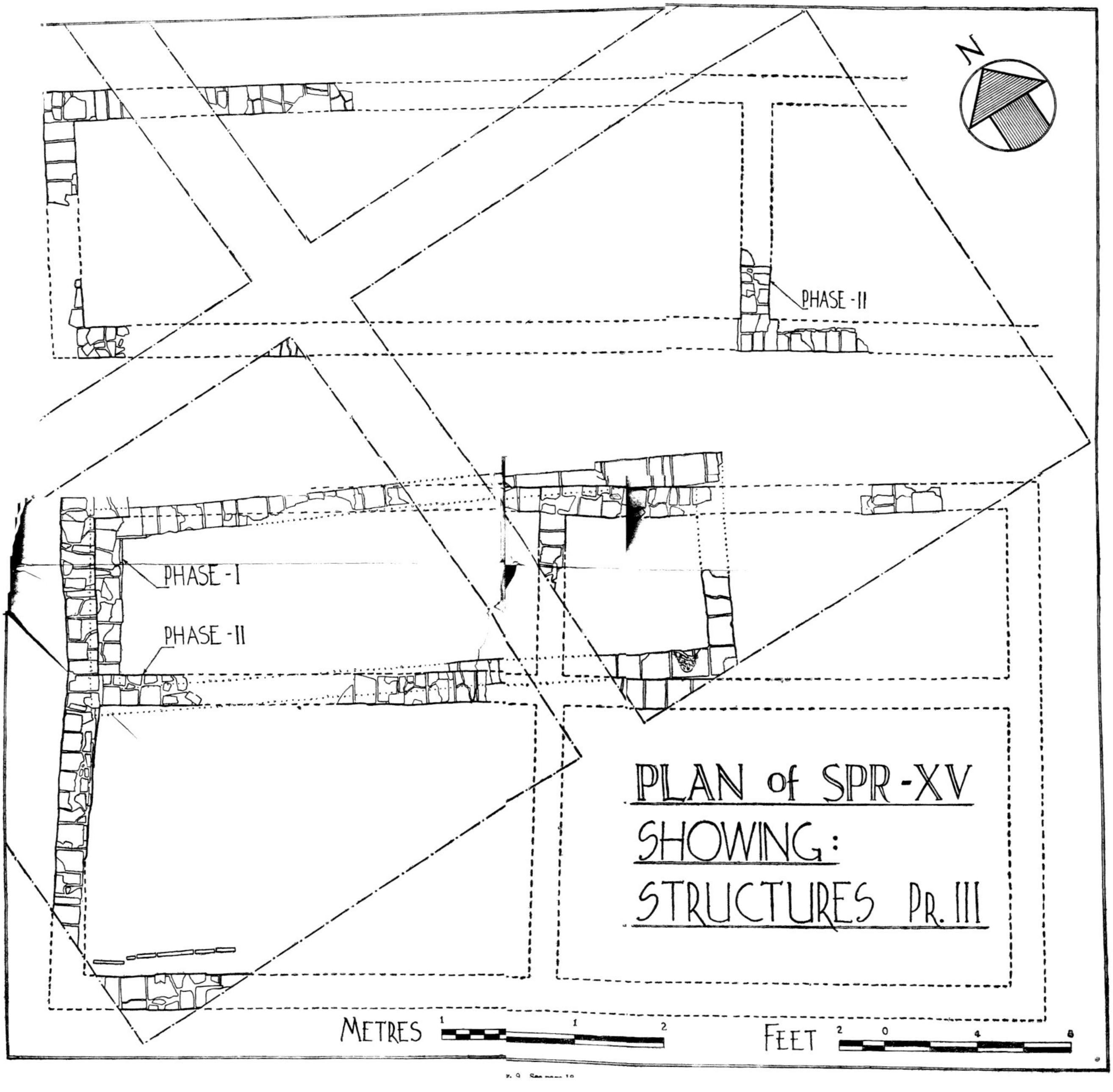

Figure 3.32 Sonpur: Period III. Illustration used with the courtesy and permission of the Directorate of Archaeology, Patna, Bihar, *Sonpur Excavations, 1956 and 1959–1962* (Sinha and Verma 1977).

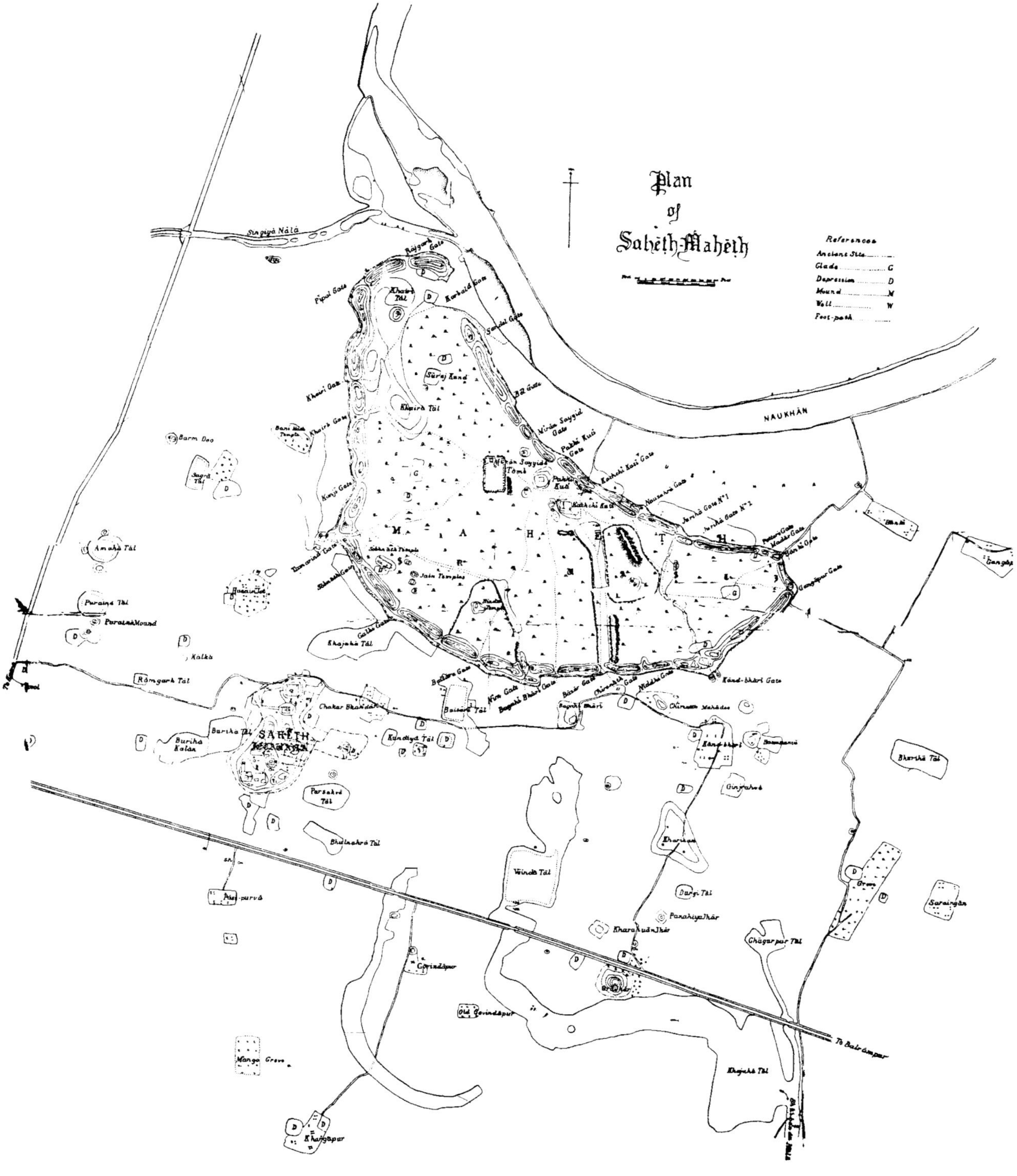

Figure 3.33 Sravasti. Illustration used with the courtesy and permission of the ASI, *Excavations at Saheth-Maheth, Annual Report of the Archaeological Survey of India 1907-1908* (Vogel 1908).

Figure 3.34 Sravasti today: Rampart with a gap (photo by the author).

To verify Sinha's sequence, Kansai University in collaboration with the ASI has recently re-excavated the rampart. The new sequence is generally in agreement with that of Sinha's. Most importantly, Sinha and Aboshi seem to agree on the date of the initial construction of the rampart; period II of Sinha's chronology and period III of Aboshi's chronology are placed roughly in the third and second centuries BC. The difference between the two sequences is that Aboshi dates the construction of the brick wall on top of the rampart by the second half of his period IV (ca. third century AD), while Sinha dates the same wall by his period II.B (ca. second century BC).

As far as the function of fortifications is concerned, neither Sinha nor Aboshi have proposed any explanations. The existing data are nonetheless sufficient for a preliminary hypothesis. Six following traits are particularly revealing: 1) the rampart had many wide openings located at similar intervals from each other. None of these openings revealed the remains of "gates" (see Figure 3.34); 2) in phase I, the rampart was low and had a very gradual slope; 3) in phase II, the rampart was arguably used as a "dumping area"; 4) there are signs of occupation beyond the rampart; 5) the rampart was built during the Mauryan period, after the struggle for power between the janapadas was over; 6) the parapet wall was built either during the late Mauryan period or in the third century AD.

What unites all these traits is that, according to them, neither military defense nor protection from floods can sufficiently explain the function of the rampart. Wide openings and the gradual slope makes the rampart vulnerable. The use of the rampart as a dumping area makes no sense from a military perspective. The fact that the rampart was built well into the Mauryan period is odd given the history of the military conflict in northern India. Finally, if Aboshi is right in dating the wall on top of the rampart by the third century AD, this means that the major strengthening of the fortification system was carried out past many important military conflicts.

Given all these, it is reasonable to suggest that the rampart at Maheth performed a symbolic rather than practical function. The division and circumvallation of space based on ideological principles would perfectly explain the wide openings at regular intervals as well as other military impracticalities during the first two structural phases. The presence of the walled monastery and other occupational deposits in the proximity to the rampart would also make perfect sense if the function of the rampart were to symbolically divide the space rather than to protect the site from floods or military attacks.

Authority

Although Sinha's project was quite modest in scale—he excavated only one trench, 15 x 36 ft, in the habitation area—it produced sufficient results for tracing main qualitative changes in the cultural history of Sravasti. These changes took place between periods I and II of Sinha's chronology. Period I had no structural remains, no coins, no inscribed seals. Its material culture was defined on pottery, beads, terracotta figurines, terracotta discs, and glass bangles. The transition to period II brought several important innovations. Burnt brick architecture laid in mud-mortar was introduced (Sinha 1967:19–20). Red Ware became mass produced, simple, and utilitarian (Sinha 1967:41–46). Human figurines appeared for the first time and became one of the defining characteristics of this period (Sinha 1967:52–57). Most arrowheads came from the deposits of period II (Sinha 1967:69–71). Finally and most importantly, inscribed seals (Sinha 1967:71) and coins (Sinha 1967:73–77) appeared for the first time. Based on all these data, Sinha (1967:9) suggested that the changes that had taken place by period II "might have been brought about by a central authority". One must agree with Sinha; for even given the small scale of excavations, burnt-brick structures, inscribed seals, coins, and mass-produced pottery were undoubtedly indicative of major sociopolitical changes.

The excavation by the joint ASI-Japanese team reconfirmed Sinha's conclusions. Of the three excavated trenches, the one at Suraj Kund (area A) revealed the entire cultural sequence from period I to period V. Periods I and II, which were contemporaneous with Sinha's period I, revealed minimal structural activities such as pits of various sizes and hearths (Aboshi et al. 1999:138). The transition from period II to period III, being almost exactly contemporaneous with the transition from period I to period II in Sinha's chronology, brought important changes. The deposits of period III revealed workshops of an iron maker, glassmaker and stone bead maker (Aboshi et al. 1999:138). Period IV, also contemporaneous with Sinha's period II, disclosed the first burnt brick structures, domestic complexes with internal courtyards including a storeroom of roof tiles (Aboshi et al. 1999:138–140; IAR 1995–1996:76–82). As far as other objects of material culture are concerned, Aboshi et al. (1999:165) recognize that period III marked several radical changes in the life of the site. Both excavation projects thus unambiguously show that archaeological evidence for authority in Sravasti emerges by the third century BC.

Vaisali

Vaisali or Basarh is located about 22 mi north of Patna, Bihar. According to literary tradition, it was the capital of the republic of Licchavis and was founded by King Visala of the Iksvaku lineage. Vaisali comprises several localities (see Figure 3.35), the most known of which is Raja-Visala-ka-Garh, a rectangular fortified mound measuring ca. 500 m x 240 m (see Figures 3.36–3.38). Other important localities are Kharauna tank, Buddhist stupa, Bhimsen-ka-Palla, Chakramdas, Baniya, Lalpura and Virpur. Vaisali has a long history of excavations. Most of these excavations have been well published. In 1903–1904, T. Bloch took on the first substantial excavation project at Vaisali. Spooner continued his work in 1913–1914. In 1950, K. Deva and V. Mishra carried out a season of excavations on the site of Raja-Visala-ka-Garh. The most extensive archaeological exploration of

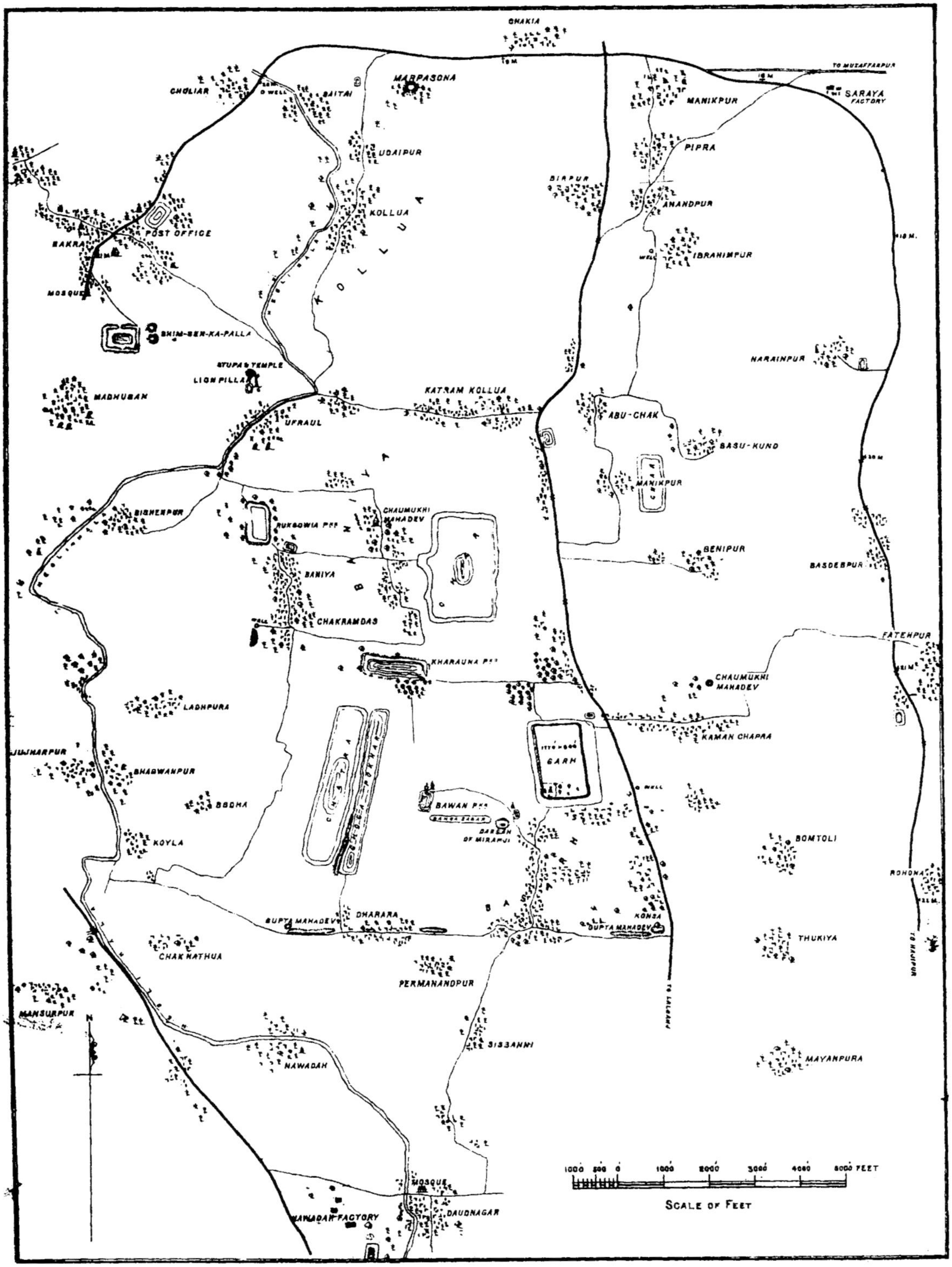

Figure 3.35 Sketch plan of Vaisali. Illustration used with the courtesy and permission of the Directorate of Archaeology, Patna, Bihar, *Vaisali Excavations, 1958–1962* (Sinha and Roy 1969).

Vaisali was carried out on behalf of the Jayaswal Research Institute in 1958–1962. Finally in 1988–1989, B. K. Sharan conducted a small-scale project on Raja-Visala-ka-Garh.[21]

As far as chronology of Vaisali is concerned, there are two main sequences: one defined by Deva and Mishra, and another one by the Jayaswal Research Institute. Deva and Mishra (1961:5–7) distinguish four periods (see Table 3.19). The main deficiency of this sequence is that it is based exclusively on the data from Raja-Visala-Ka-Garh; other localities were left unexcavated. The sequence defined by the Jayaswal Research Institute is more inclusive; for it is based on the data from several localities and comprises five periods (Sinha and Roy 1969:7–8 (see Table 3.20). I will be referring to these two sequences interchangeably.

Table 3.19

Vaisali: Periodization (Deva and Mishra 1961)

Period	Approx. Dates	Defining Characteristics
IA	500–300 BC	Northern Black Polished Ware, Black and Red Ware, Red Ware; structures of mud and bamboo; traced only on the site of Chak Ramdas
IB	300–150 BC	Northern Black Polished Ware; structures of square brick; the earliest occupation on the Garh area and the latest at Chak Ramdas; simple structures of square brick
II	150 BC–AD 100	Time of efflorescence, artistic activity, well-planned single course structures
III	AD 100–300	Red Ware, carnelian beads, brick structures on top of the brick concrete
IV	AD 300–600	Red Ware, brickbats, Gupta terracottas and sealings in Brahmi script

Table 3.20

Vaisali: Periodization (Sinha and Roy 1969)

Period	Approx. Dates	Defining Characteristics
I	< 600 BC	Coarse Black and Red Ware, Pale-Red Wares
II	600–200 BC	Northern Black Polished Ware
III	200 BC–AD 200	Red Ware, Gray Ware; Sunga seals/ings, coins, figurines
IV	AD 200–600	Gupta terracotta seals/ings and figurines
V	> AD 600	Pre-Mughal Glazed Ware

Fortifications

The mound of Raja-Visala-ka-Garh is rectangular in shape and measures roughly 500 x 240 m (see Figures 3.36–3.38). Its height varies from 2 to 3 m and its slopes reveal a regular sharp pattern. Even to an unaccustomed visitor, Garh gives the impression of being fortified. The first excavators of Garh, A. Cunningham and T. Bloch sensed this, yet failed to show the existence of defenses archaeologically. Following their steps, T. B. Spooner (1914:103) noticed "an earthen embankment" at the edge of the mound, yet, having evaluated it, concluded that this was "all the circumvallation that the site possessed" and no "ancient masonry ramparts" ever existed in Vaisali. It took another several decades until Deva and Mishra (1961:13–14) unearthed a complex defense system on the mound of Raja-Visala-ka-Garh in 1950. In a trench laid across the western edge of the mound (VS III), Deva and Mishra uncovered a mud-rampart of more than 65 ft in width and over 9 ft in extant height. On top of the rampart, there was a mud-brick structure. Deva and Mishra placed the construction of the rampart in period IB, ca. 300–150 BC. A mud-brick wall, according to their chronology, was constructed later to "prevent erosion of the hump of the rampart".

The Jayaswal Research Institute continued the study of defenses at Vaisali in 1958–1962. Several trenches were laid in the southeastern corner of Raja-Visala-ka-Garh with the sole purpose of investigating the defenses. Based on the excavation of trench VSG II, three structural phases were defined (IAR 1958–1959:12; Sinha and Roy 1969:25–26). The first phase saw the construction of a baked brick wall and was dated to the beginning of period III of the revised chronology, ca. second century BC. The wall reportedly measured 20 ft in thickness. The second phase witnessed the digging of a moat and the erection of a rampart. The rampart was 68 ft in width at the base, 21 ft in width at the extant top, and 13 ft in extant height. At some point before the third phase, the rampart was destroyed. Based on a sealing discovered in a post-rampart layer, the construction of the rampart was dated to the first century BC. During the third phase, a brick-defense wall, about 9 ft thick, was built on top of the rampart. In association with this phase, a group of similar structures was uncovered. Judging from a large number of weapons found in these structures and from the proximity of defenses, Sinha and Roy (1969:27–28) called these structures "military barracks". The construction of the wall and the barracks were dated roughly to the time of the late Kushanas or the early Guptas. These

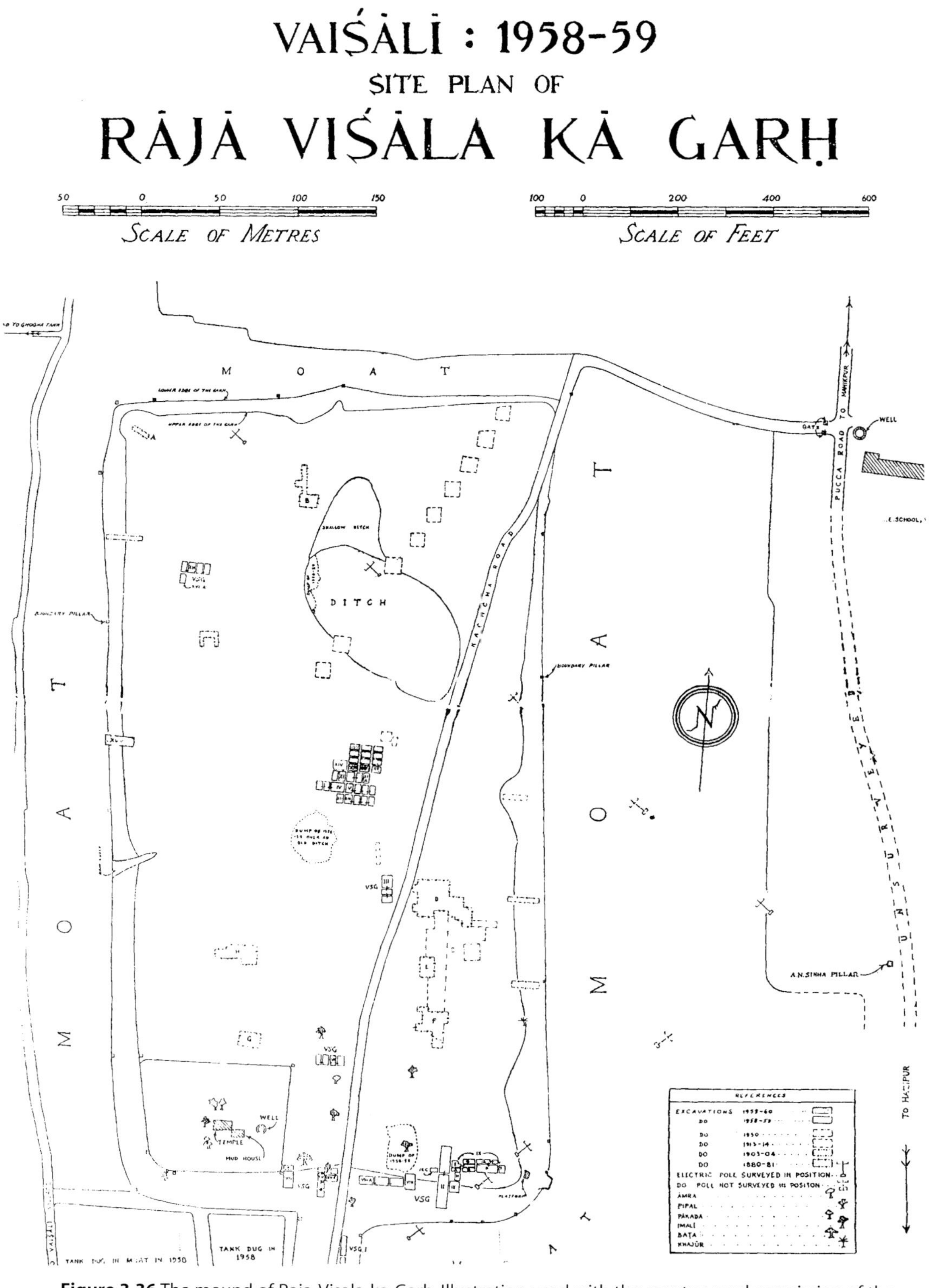

Figure 3.36 The mound of Raja-Visala-ka-Garh. Illustration used with the courtesy and permission of the Directorate of Archaeology, Patna, Bihar, *Vaisali Excavations, 1958-62* (Sinha and Roy 1969).

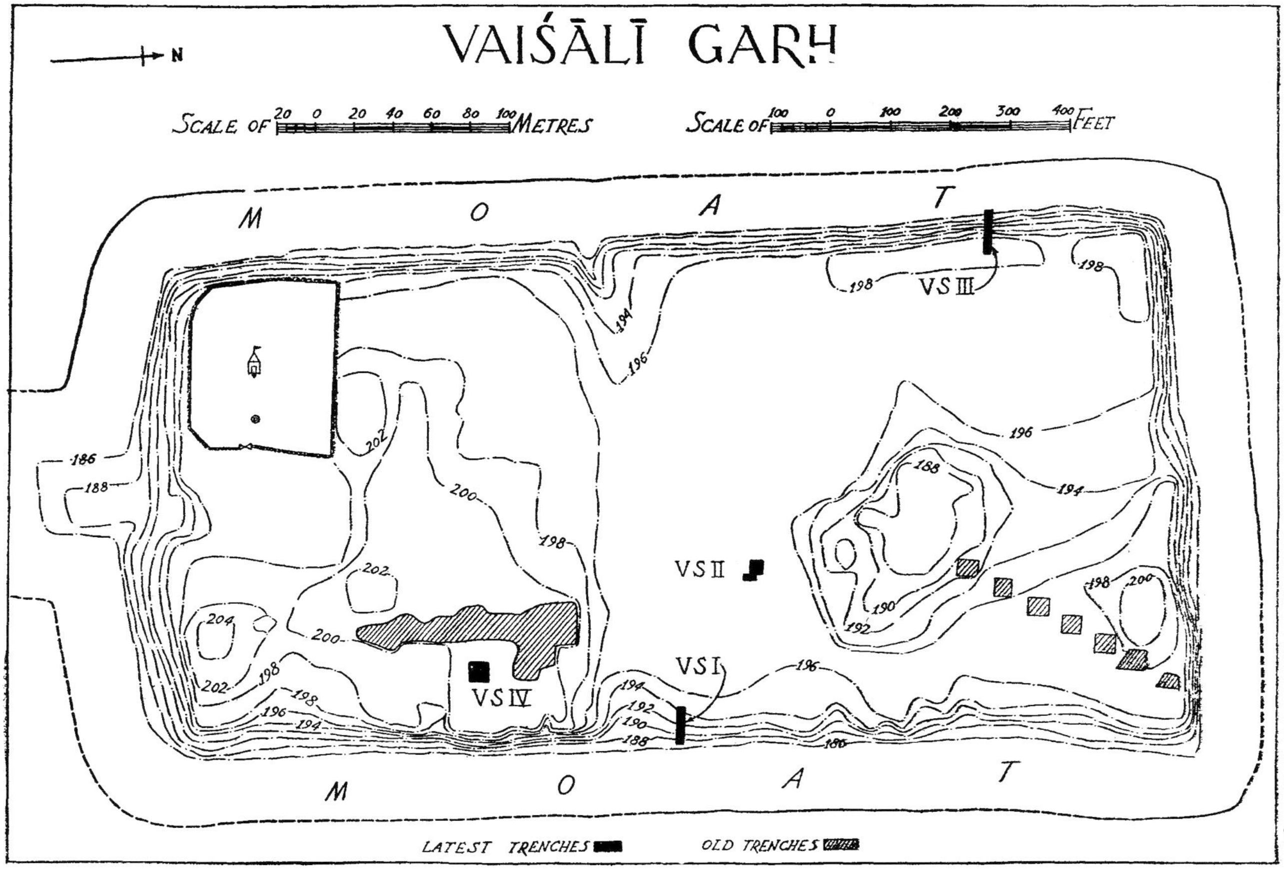

Figure 3.37 The mound of Raja-Visala-ka-Garh. Illustration used with the courtesy and permission of the Directorate of Archaeology, Patna, Bihar, *Vaisali Excavations 1950* (Deva and Mishra 1961).

results were verified on other locations, including trench VSG XVIII on the western side of Raja-Visala-ka-Garh (IAR 1959–1960:14–15). All the trenches revealed similar structural sequences.

Fortifications at Vaisali thus present an intriguing case. Three points are particularly important. First, fortifications at Vaisali appear to have been built relatively late, in the beginning of the Sunga period around the second century BC. Second, the structural history of fortification at Vaisali is quite unusual; the construction of a brick wall precedes the construction of a rampart and moat and not the vice versa. Third, the relations and the degree of integration between separate localities of Vaisali—Raja-Visala-ka-Garh, Kharauna tank, Buddhist Stupa, Bhimsen-ka-Palla, Chakramdas, Baniya, Lalpura and Virpur—are very unclear. Are these localities parts of a single entity or separate sites? No one, to my knowledge has properly addressed this question yet everyone treats these sites as innate parts of Vaisali. In my view, the nature of the relationship between these localities is directly related to the function/s of fortifications on Raja-Visala-ka-Garh. If the mound of Raja-Visala-ka-Garh represented only one district of Vaisali, the rampart must have carried a segregative or symbolic function. If the localities in fact were isolated from each other, the rampart may have carried a defensive function.

In this respect, it is worth mentioning that based on the reading of several seals, Sinha and Roy proposed that Raja-Visala-ka-Garh was a market place. "It was wise", Sinha and Roy (1969:118) maintained, "to make a market place on a comparatively higher ground that the surrounding ground level, so that the place might not

Figure 3.38 The mound of Raja-Visala-ka-Garh at Vaisali today (photo by the author).

become damp and spoil the articles stored therein". Consequently, "the ramparts in different periods were nothing but strong revetments of this artificial elevated ground". If Sinha's and Roy's suggestion is correct, the function of fortifications on Raja-Visala-ka-Garh was very unusual. Taking into consideration the proximity of localities to each other, as well as the small size of Raja-Visala-ka-Garh, I tend to believe that the localities of Vaisali were parts of one entity. Under this scenario, its fortifications did not carry a military or ecological function, but rather symbolically marked the border of an important locality. Whether this locality was a market, an administrative center, a palatial complex, or something else remains an open question.

Authority

Two cultural sequences defined for Vaisali reveal similar patterns of the emergence of authority. According to the sequence by Deva and Mishra, period I A (ca. 500–300) has no structural activities and is encountered only on the site of Chak Ramdas. Period IB (ca. 300–150 BC) evinces the earliest occupational phase on the site of Raja-Visala-ka-Garh, yet structural remains and other artifacts that could mark the formation of complex social organization and the emergence of authority are still lacking. Period II (150 BC–100 AD) is the first to show significant changes in several aspects of material culture. In architecture, this period is characterized by burnt-brick houses with the use of the English bond technique in foundations (Deva and Mishra 1961:11–13). In pottery, the NBPW gradually disappears giving place to red and buff wares. Mass production, simplicity, and standardization become the main characteristics of ceramic production during this period (Deva and Mishra 1961:18). Among other noticeable innovations, the emergence of human figurines and coins must be mentioned.

In the cultural sequence defined by Sinha and Roy, changes become evident by period III (ca. 200 BC–AD 200), or more precisely in the beginning of Sunga period. Settled around the third century BC (Sinha and Roy 1969:118), Raja-Visala-ka-Garh has hardly any structure associated with period I and II (Sinha and Roy 1969:29). The first significant structures, such as the complex of "military barracks" are built around the second and first centuries BC (Sinha and Roy 1969:26–28). Judging from coins and terracotta figurines, the intensification of structural activities on two other important localities of Vaisali, Kharauna tank and Bhimsen-ka-Pala, takes place also in period III (Sinha and Roy 1969:9–16, 33–35). The excavated deposits of Chak Ramdas, Baniya, Lal Pura, and Virpur reveal no archaeological traits that could help in reconstructing the formation of authoritative structures (Sinha and Roy 1969:35–39).

As far as small artifacts are concerned, seals and sealings from Raja-Visala-ka-Garh are the most abundant and conspicuous signs of authority in Vaisali. Seals and sealings discovered during the early excavations by Bloch and Spooner are out of context and stratigraphy. Seals and sealings found during the excavation by the Jayaswal Research Institute are much better recorded (Sinha and Roy 1969:110–131). Of the 98 seals, sealing, and tokens, 86 come from Raja-Visala-ka-Garh. The nine earliest seals, sealings, and tokens date to the end of the Mauryan period. Sixteen seals, sealings, and tokens belong to the Sunga period. Most of the remaining seals, sealings, and tokens belong to the Kushana period (Sinha and Roy 1969:114). Many seals and sealings directly point to the presence of authority. Sealing #10, for example, is the main cause of the aforementioned hypothesis of Raja-Visala-ka-Garh being a fortified market place (1969:116–119). Sealing #7 can be interpreted as belonging to a government functionary at Vaisali during the time of the Mauryas (Sinha and Roy 1969:115). A fragment of the sealing #11 carries the name of king Agnimitra, the son and heir of Pursyamitra Sunga. As Sinha and Roy (1969:119) propose, this seal constitutes evidence of the Sunga's sway over Vaisali. A number of seals, sealings. and tokens belong to random individuals, merchants, and officials. For example, the legend of token #19 is translated as "of the chief counselor" (Sinha and Roy 1969:120).

In sum, archaeological evidence for the formation of authority in Vaisali is associated mostly with the beginning of the Sunga period. This was the time when the site expanded, Kharauna tank was built, seals were actively circulated, and the vigourous construction activity began on the mound of Raja-Visala-ka-Garh.

Conclusion: The Idea of the Gangetic City

Of the 13 reviewed Gangetic sites, most are fortified and contain evidence for authority. The patterns of the formation of authority and the structural history of fortifications on these sites reveal some interesting regularities. I will discuss these regularities under two broad themes: the function of fortifications and the nature of authority. These two themes in turn will lead to the main question: whether the model that I have extracted from Sanskrit and Pāli texts in the second chapter can enhance our understanding of the idea of the city in the Ganges civilization.

Function of Fortifications

In his report on the excavation at Sravasti, K. K. Sinha (1967:11) asserted that the defenses in north India were "constructed as a measure against the threat of Indo-Greek invasion". Sinha's view is representative of a significant amount of scholarly literature. Military conflict and floods are still seen by many as the key factors in the construction of defenses on the sites of the Ganges civilization. I believe this view is misleading. The archaeological data reviewed above have demonstrated that warfare and protection from floods were by far not the main factors that motivated the construction of fortifications on the Gangetic sites and that the meaning and functionality of these fortifications were much more complex. At least nine of the 13 reviewed sites are fortified. Hastinapura, Sonkh and Sonpur have no fortifications. The case of Rajghat is questionable. As I have stated above I believe it has a circumvallation, yet at this point we do not have a solid proof of it. Out of the nine fortified sites, five, in my view, provide substantial evidence in support of a symbolic function of their fortification systems. These sites are Kausambi, Mathura, Rajgir, Sravasti, and Vaisali. Let me reiterate the main points of my argument that have led me to this important conclusion.

The scale of fortifications in Kausambi is striking. Particularly massive are the walls, revetments and bastions in the southwestern corner and on the eastern side of the site. Yet from the viewpoint of military defense, both the layout and size of the Kausambi fortification system raise serious doubts. On one hand, the size of some ramparts and bastions clearly exceeds military demands of its time. On the other hand, some traits of layout and structural history are inefficient from the military point of view. For example, there are many long gaps in the ramparts; the ramparts significantly vary in size; and most importantly, the initial rampart did not encircle the whole site. Fortifications at Mathura are massive and surround the site from the west, north and south. From the literary sources, we know that Mathura was directly involved in military conflict. Nonetheless, neither military nor ecological considerations sufficiently explain the construction of fortifications at Mathura. First, the bank of the Yamuna River was left unprotected. Second, during the period of political unrest portions of the wall were covered with occupational deposits. Third, from the time of its initial construction the rampart was smoothly incorporated into the natural landscape. Rajgir has the longest and one of the most elaborate fortification systems of all the reviewed sites. Besides the two massive internal forts, it is encircled by a stone wall that runs for about 40 km over the adjacent hills. The construction of this massive fortification system must have required a very significant expenditure of labor, time, and authoritative control. Its complexity however seems to exceed the military needs of Rajgir. As we know from the literary sources, in the fifth century BC the capital of Magadha was moved from Rajgir to Pataliputra. This happened as military conflict intensified. Hence, if the outer wall were built prior to the transfer of the capital from Rajgir to Pataliputra, one would expect the system of defense in Pataliputra to be stronger or at least comparable in strength with the system of defense at Rajgir. If the outer wall were built after the transfer of the capital, one would still expect the system of defense in Pataliputra to be stronger; for with the transfer of the capital, the center of political and military gravity would have certainly moved to Pataliputra. Texts and archaeology nevertheless show the opposite. The system of defense in Rajgir is clearly more elaborate and labor consuming than the wooden palisades of Pataliputra. Sravasti consists of two parts: the Buddhist establishment of Saheth and the city of Maheth. Maheth is surrounded by a rampart with a brick wall on top of it. Despite of the massive size and technological sophistication of this rampart, there are many indicators of its symbolic use. First, the rampart had too many wide openings to make the defense of the site effective. Second, during the first two structural phases (ca. third to second centuries BC), the rampart was low, its slope was gradual and at some point it might have been used as a "dumping ground". Third, the site of Saheth is not well protected and there are numerous signs of occupation beyond the rampart of Maheth. Finally and most importantly, the current dating of the rampart places its initial construction in the third century BC, i.e., after the struggle for power between the janapadas was over and a significant portion of northern South Asia was united under the rule of the Mauryas. Vaisali comprises a number of localities scattered around a large area. No trace of a fortification system that would enclose all of these localities has been discovered. The only locality that has a circumvallation is Raja-Visala-ka-Garh, a rectangular mound measuring approximately 500 m x 240 m. This circumvallation was built around the second century BC and consisted of a rampart, a moat, and a brick wall. The construction of a brick wall however preceded the construction of a rampart and a moat. Since Raja-Visala-ka-Garh is only part of Vaisali, the function of its circumvallation must be approached in terms of the relationship between Raja-Visala-ka-Garh and other localities.

Such is a brief summary of my argument in support of the symbolic function of fortifications on the five aforementioned sites. In short, this argument can be presented in a list of six distinctive traits: 1) excessive monumentality of ramparts, bastions and revetments; 2) militarily impractical layout of ramparts expressed in wide openings and large unprotected areas; 3) inefficient military characteristics of ramparts such as low height and gradual slopes; 4) alleged disuse of ramparts in certain periods expressed in the creation of dumping areas and the construction of buildings on top of ramparts; 5) chronological incongruity between the construction of fortifications and the history of military conflict in northern India, i.e., the construction of fortifications in the periods of a relative political stability and the absence or disuse of fortifications in the periods of active military conflict; 6) presence of habitational areas beyond the fortifications. Each of the five aforementioned sites reveals at least several of these traits; two sites—Mathura and Sravasti—reveal all of them. Moreover, fortification systems of these five sites are characterized by structural similarities. Massive ramparts, parapet walls with gaps and wide openings are characteristic of most of these sites. This in my view makes a strong case for a certain pattern in the functionality of the Gangetic fortifications.

By using the term "symbolic" with regards to these fortification systems I mean that their overall significance was non-utilitarian and ideational, rather than military, ecological, and overall practical. Now I believe we can go a step further by suggesting that the symbolism of fortifications on these five sites was similar. Similarities in design, use, structural history and other traits seem to support this argument. Moreover, the four other fortified sites—Ahicchatra, Atranjikhera, Bhita, and Pataliputra—are likely to follow a similar pattern; for in spite of the lack of data, there are indications that their fortification systems are distinguished by similar traits. For example, the rampart at Ahicchatra is excessively monumental, displays military inefficiencies during its early structural phases, and is possibly characterized by chronological incongruities with the history of military conflicts in northern India. The rampart at Atranjikhera is too small during the first two structural phases and the parapet wall is not built until the end of the Mauryan or even Sunga periods. Bhita is divided into two parts so its rampart must have carried a segregative function. The wooden palisades of Pataliputra are too week to provide an effective military defense of the site which was the capital of the first great South Asian empire and one of the biggest cities of the ancient world.

What kind of symbolism these fortifications conveyed, of course, is a more difficult question. Fortifications remain the main symbols of conspicuous consumption and control of labor in Early Historic India; the archaeology of the Ganges civilization does not provide much evidence for the existence of many other forms of monumental architecture. Thus, by delineating space in such a monumental manner, the walls, ramparts, and bastions of the Ganges civilization must have epitomized some important sociopolitical changes and processes. Figuratively speaking, fortifications created the inner worlds or the mesocosms of the first urban centers. This is not to say that the military or ecological concerns played no role whatsoever; in one way or another, warfare and floods may have contributed to the construction of fortification. Yet the main cause and meaning of these massive dividing structures was ideological not utilitarian. What kind of ideas they conveyed of course is a much more difficult question. Archaeological evidence for authority comes handy as an aid for answering this question.

Nature of Authority

To show the emergence of authority on each of the 13 chosen Gangetic sites, I have traced significant and concurrent changes in various aspects of their material culture. The analyses of data from Ahicchatra, Atranjikhera, Kausambi, Mathura, Rajghat, Sravasti, Sonkh and Vaisali have revealed substantial evidence for authority. Importantly, the emergence of authority on these sites could be placed in a chronological context. The analyses of data from Bhita, Pataliputra, and Rajgir have provided enough evidence for showing the presence of authority, yet not for establishing the chronologies of its genesis. The available data from Hastinapura and Sonpur have not revealed evidence for authority whatsoever. From site to site, my argument can be summarized as follows.

Archaeological data from Ahicchatra is very scarce, yet there are changes indicative of authority. These changes include the construction of fortifications, the emergence of brick structures, site expansion, the introduction of coinage, and planning in accordance with cardinal directions. All these changes are attributed to a relatively short period of time and appear in Strata 6 (first century BC) of the periodization by Dikshit and Ghosh and in period IV (Kushana period) in the periodization by Banerjee. In Atranjikhera, evidence for authority is more substantial. It includes the construction of fortifications, the expansion of settlement, intensification of structural activities, the emergence of brick architecture, the introduction of coinage, increase in weaponry, the appearance of human terracotta figurines, and the manufacture of agricultural tools made of iron. All these changes occur during phases B and C of period IV (500–200 BC). Bhita provides ample evidence for the presence of authority. Fortifications, architecture, regular planning, seals, and coins point to the presence of authority roughly by the Mauryan period. It is however impossible at this point to reconstruct the precise chronological context for the emergence of authority at Bhita because the chronology and periodization of this site are basically nonexistent. The archaeology of Hastinapura does not provide sufficient evidence for authority. The size of the site does not increase until period V (AD 1100–1500). Structural activities are minimal until period IV (200 BC–AD 300). In addition, the deposits of all the structural periods display a striking lack of seals, weaponry and inscribed objects.

In Kausambi, the main criteria for tracing authority are fortifications, architecture, and coins. Since the chronologies of the fortifications and the palace are poorly defined, archaeological evidence for the formation of authority is best traced in the areas of the Asokan pillar and the Ghoshitarama Monastery. Each area has its own periodization. In the area of the Asokan pillar, major qualitative changes can be attributed to Sub-period IA (mid-fourth century BC). In the area of the Ghoshitarama Monastery, changes indicative of authority are associated with the construction of the stupa and can be attributed to phase II (fifth century BC). In Mathura, evidence for authority includes the construction of fortifications, the expansion of the settlement, the emergence of brick architecture, the introduction of coins, the manufacture of human figurines, simplification and mass production of standardized pottery, and hierarchy in the settlement patterns of the adjacent region. All these changes are associated with the transition from period I to period II of M. C. Joshi's periodization (fourth century BC). Pataliputra provides no evidence for authority during the pre-Mauryan period. In the Mauryan period, the only possible indication of authority is the famous Pillared Hall of Kumrahar. The function, archaeological context and structural history of this hall however remain enigmatic. In Rajghat, the changes that are indicative of authority include the emergence of complex burnt brick architecture, seals, sealings, and coins. The changes become evident in the beginning of period II (third to second centuries BC). In Rajgir, the main evidence for a complex sociopolitical organization and authority in the pre-Mauryan and Mauryan periods is the system of fortifications. In Sonkh, the formation of authority is associated with the emergence of baked brick architecture, regular planning of houses and residential units, inscribed coins, new weapons and iron tools. All these innovations are attributed to layer 27 (second century BC) according to the periodization by Härtel. Sonpur provides no sound evidence for authority during its entire cultural history. In Sravasti, evidence for authority includes fortifications, burnt-brick architecture, planning of houses and residential units, mass-produced, simple and utilitarian red ware, human figurines, inscribed seals, and several workshops. All these innovations are the result of the transition from period I to period II in Sinha's periodization and from period II to period III in the periodization by Aboshi. In both periodizations, this transition takes place around the third century BC. Lastly, in Vaisali the emergence of authority is associated with the construction of fortifications and burnt brick house complexes on Raja-Visala-ka-Garh, with the expansion of the site and the establishment of new neighborhoods, with the production of simplified and standardized Red and Buff Wares, which gradually replace the NBPW, with the emergence of human figurines, and with the introduction of coinage, seals, and sealings. In Deva and Mishra's periodization, all these changes occur in period II (150–100 BC). In the periodization defined by Sinha and Roy, these changes are attributed to the first part of period III (second to first century BC).

Thus, tracing the emergence of authority from site to site, I have pinpointed changes such as settlement expansion, intensification and sophistication of structural activities, the introduction of burnt-brick architecture, the beginning of regular planning, the minting of coins, the emergence of seals and sealings, the manufacture of human figurines, the transition to mass produced and simplified pottery, the increase in the amount of weaponry, and the emergence of hierarchies in settlement patterns. In its own unique way, each of these changes is indicative of social transformations. Settlement expansion usually points to the increase in population density. Population density in turn implies a higher social complexity, and, potentially, the shaping of authority. The drastic sophistication and differentiation of architecture often indicates changes in kinship and sociopolitical organization that result in the emergence of elites and forming of authoritative structures. Coins and seals are indicative of authority as their production, use, and circulation require the existence of complex trade mechanisms, ownership rights, control of minting, high-level political decision-making, the existence of steady sociopolitical or religious groups, and generally a high degree of economic complexity. One by one, these traits are not necessarily indicative of authority. Conjointly, they constitute a much more substantial proof of social transformations and the emergence of authoritative structures. In some cases, I have traced concurrent changes in all of these traits. In other cases, I have used changes in architecture, settlement size, and seals to argue for social transformations.

Nevertheless, when placed in the context of cross-cultural and comparative studies, most of these traits leave a sense of deficiency. For example, changes in architecture—being important in the local context—are modest if compared to the changes that took place at the initial stages of urbanization in Mesopotamia, Egypt, or Mesoamerica. There are no pyramids, monumental palaces, and spacious assembly halls at the sites of the Ganges civilization; the pillared hall at Pataliputra and the alleged palace at Kausambi are neither properly identified, nor credibly dated. As far as the ritual or authoritative paraphernalia, monumental art, and inscribed seals are concerned, none of these traits are present on the sites of the Ganges civilization at least until the Mauryan period. The only archaeological feature which is unmistakably indicative of major social transformations and the emergence of strong authoritative institutions is an elaborate system of fortifications. In a sense, fortifications have become the epitome and symbol of complexity, social disparity, and power in the Ganges civilization. In Rajgir, the stone wall, which runs for more than 40 km over several ranges of hills, is currently the only archaeological proof of a sociopolitical complexity prior to the Gupta period. In Kausambi, colossal bastions, ramparts and revetments surpass in magnitude all other structural remains and constitute the main evidence for authority and control of labor. In a similar way, ramparts, bastions, parapet walls, and revetments are the most unambiguous evidence for the existence of authority in Ahicchatra, Atranjikhera, Bhita, Mathura, Sravasti, Vaisali, and possibly Rajghat.

The archaeological signature of authority in the Ganges civilization thus is quite unique. In a number of ancient civilizations, authority is symbolized by lavish material expressions, monumental architecture, elite burials, luxurious objects of art, writing, seals, and the like. In the Ganges civilization, evidence for authority comes mostly from fortifications and, to a lesser degree, from the dynamics of settlement expansion, the sophistication of architecture, the introduction of regular planning, and the emergence of inscribed seals. For some reason, authorities of the Gangetic sites did not need palaces, temples, rich burials, and objects of luxury; their ethos was expressed in ramparts, walls, bastions, and revetments.

This unusual expression of power evokes a number of possible scenarios for the genesis of sociopolitical complexity. In one way or another, each of these scenarios points to the same sociocultural process that is the formation of territorially bound identities. In other words, the crystallization of authority in the Ganges civilization went hand in hand with the formation of new local identities, while the delineation of space by massive ramparts, walls, and bastions was the material expression of the division between ours and theirs, internal and external, domestic and alien. This shaping of identity, i.e., the emergence of a sense of belonging to a certain place, group, sociocultural entity, or any other imagined world, was an impetus and an essential part of the processes of the formation of authority. The emergence of authority and the formation of territorially bound identities thus were the two facets of the same process, which was materialized in the encircling of important sites by massive fortifications. In this respect, it is worth noting that many of the Gangetic fortifications had their own original shapes; the top plans of the fortifications at Bhita, Mathura, Sravasti, Vaisali, as well as at several other Gangetic sites presented unique and individual patterns. It is not impossible that these patterns were also part of the symbolic expression of local identity.

All of the reviewed sites that have provided evidence for authority match this model. Even Sonkh, which has no fortifications, falls in the same pattern. Located only 30 km away from Mathura, Sonkh was in the shade of Mathura's political power. Before the rise of Mathura there was an attempt to build a circumvallation at Sonkh. At that time, Sonkh was equal to Mathura and its population must have experienced similar processes of the formation of identity and authority. The further rise of Mathura to political power overrode these processes. Sonkh did not develop the form of authority that would need to define its identity by constructing massive fortifications. It is no coincidence that qualitative changes that characterize level 27 in the cultural sequence of Sonkh were chronologically contemporaneous with the reign of Suryamitra in Mathura.

This model also agrees with the information provided by literary sources. The rise of the janapadas could not be complete without the formation of janapada identities. Given that most of the reviewed sites were the

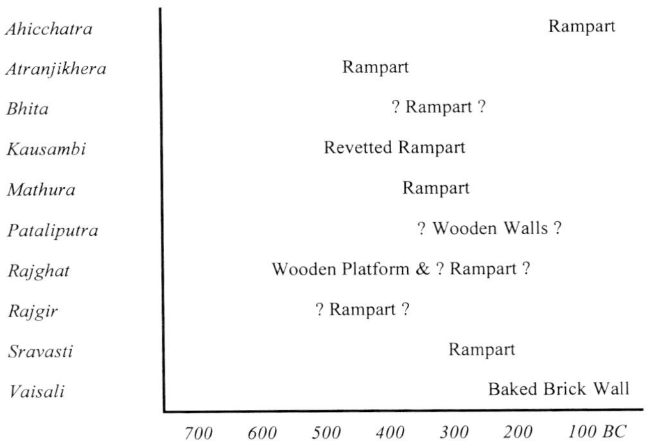

Figure 3.39 Fortifications of the Ganges civilization: Approximate dates of construction (dates are indicated by the first letter in the name of a type of fortification).

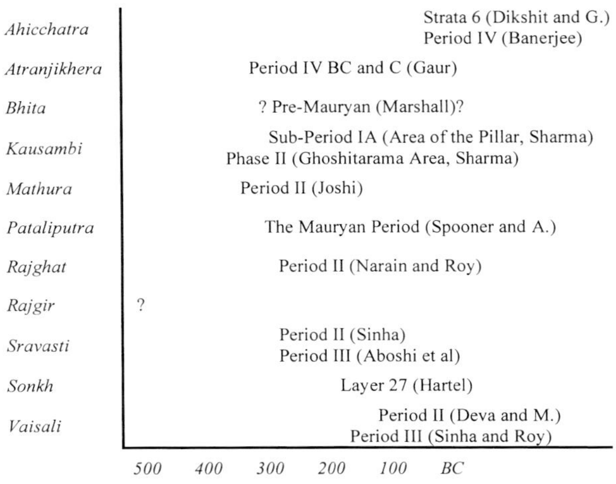

Figure 3.40 Authorities in the Ganges civilization: Approximate time of emergence (dates are indicated by the first letter in the name of a period, phase, stage or layer).

capitals of janapadas, the notions of space, territory, and of one's own local world must have played a key role in this process.

To conclude, it is difficult to reconstruct the precise form of authoritative structures of the Gangetic sites from the existing archaeological record. What the current state of data allows us to do instead is to understand some processes involved in the genesis of these structures. One of such processes was the formation of local identities expressed in the symbolic delineation of space by means of the construction of massive fortification systems.

The Idea of the Gangetic City

In the second chapter, I proposed that as an object of anthropological and historical studies, the phenomenon of the city is meaningless and incomprehensible without the ideas of historical agents about the city. Paraphrasing Collingwood (1946:214), the city does not exist without "the thought expressed in it". In the same chapter, based on the analysis of several Sanskrit and Pāli texts I provided a definition that could potentially serve as "the thought expressed in" the phenomenon of the Gangetic city. The analysis of archaeological data undertaken in this chapter shows that the definition of the city extracted from Sanskrit and Pāli texts indeed can be a helpful and meaningful tool for conceptualizing the phenomenon of the Gangetic city; for its basic premise of defining the city as a combination of fortifications and authority adequately reflects the archaeology of Gangetic sites.

On most of the reviewed sites, the emergence of authority went hand in hand with the construction of fortifications (see Figures 3.39–3.40). Ahicchatra, Atranjikhera, Kausambi, Mathura, Vaisali and Sravasti provide enough data for correlating the construction of fortifications with changes in material culture. The analysis of these data has shown that, on all of these sites, the construction of fortifications was roughly contemporaneous with all the other changes indicative of authority. Moreover, the archaeology of Kausambi has provided potential for correlating the structural history of fortifications directly with the structural history of the buildings that may have been used by authorities; the phases of the southwestern rampart and bastion can be correlated with the phases of the so-called palace, while the phases of the Ghoshitarama Monastery can be correlated with the phases of the northeastern rampart. The other fortified sites, in my view, are likely to follow the same pattern. In Bhita, evidence for fortifications and authority is present by the Mauryan period. Pataliputra provides very little archaeological data, yet from the literary sources we know that as the new capital of Magadha it was founded and fortified roughly around the same time in the fifth century BC. Rajgir also provides little archaeological data, yet the texts ascribe the construction of fortifications and the formation of authority (it was the first capital of Magadha) on this site to the sixth century BC. Finally, Rajghat is a confusing case, yet the cause for this confusion is the lack of data and poor interpretations rather than the innate uniqueness of its archaeology.

Fortifications and authority thus define the city in the texts for good reasons: being contemporaneous and codependent, the construction of fortifications and the emergence of authority can be seen as an epitome of urban growth in the Ganges Civilization. Ahicchatra, Atranjikhera, Bhita, Kausambi, Mathura, Pataliputra, Rajgir, Vaisali, Sravasti and possibly Rajghat were ancient cities. Hastinapura, Sonkh and Sonpur were mid-size villages. The contemporaries, i.e., the compilers of the cited Sanskrit and Pāli texts, conceptualized the urban nature of these sites in simple terms—through their grandiose fortifications and the explicit expressions of authority. I do not see the reason why we should not follow the same pattern in our own interpretations.

4 The Idea of the City in the Harappan/Indus Civilization

We must turn more firmly to the Harappan civilization to view the origins of at least some major traits of Indian civilization. Probably the great gap between this ancient civilization and medieval India that we are prone to emphasize does not exist. If we direct our attention to these possibilities, we may be able to define far more of India's beginnings that has hitherto been possible.

—Walter Fairservis (1967:44)

Possehl (1999, 2002b, 2002c) well-described the history of exploration of the Harappan civilization. From its initial discovery in the beginning of the twentieth century and the first excavations at Harappa and Mohenjo-Daro in the 1920s and 1930s, tremendous progress has been achieved in the accumulation of data and the exposition of this civilization. As of 2001, Possehl records 1,052 sites as belonging to the Mature Harappan period (ca. 2600/2500–1900 BC). Ninety-seven of these sites are claimed to have been excavated (Possehl 2002a; 2002b:65). The number of surveys conducted in different areas of the Harappan civilization is also quite impressive (for a comprehensive list, see Possehl 2002a). Although the precise numbers are contentious—the definition and use of the term Mature Harappan as well as the notion of being excavated are debatable—they show that we are dealing with a very significant amount of archaeological data. While investigating these data and selecting sites for a detailed analysis, I considered factors similar to those that I had taken into account when analyzing the archaeology of the Ganges civilization. The factors that most influenced my choice can be summarized as follows.

Quality and Availability of Archaeological Data. As is the case with the Ganges civilization, the quality and availability of archaeological data was an important factor. For example, the results of the excavations of Kalibangan, Banawali, and Dholavira are neither well published, nor easily available. The sites of Rakhigarhi and Ganweriwala have not even been properly excavated. Meanwhile, the sites of Harappa, Nausharo, Lothal, and Surkotada are known much better. Although I made an effort to review as many sites as possible, the lack of data prevented me from including at least several potentially important sites.

Geographic Diversity. As far as the geographical diversity was concerned, it was easier to find quality data from the geographically remote sites of the Harappan civilization than from the geographically remote sites of the Ganges civilization. This can be explained by the fact that more sites of the Harappan civilization are properly excavated and published. As a result, the sites that I have chosen for analysis represent the remote areas of Gujarat, Rajasthan, Haryana, Punjab, Sindh, Baluchistan, and the Dasht Valley of the Makran Desert.

Diversity in Scale. As in the previous chapter, diversity in scale has played a significant role in determining which sites should be included in the final review. It seemed to me equally important to include the small sites such as Allahdino or Sutkagen Dor along with the grandiose sites such as Harappa and Mohenjo-Daro. In fact, as the excavations at Allahdino and Sutkagen Dor show, small sites can be very important for understanding the Harappan urban phenomenon. Allahdino is only about 100 m in diameter, yet reveals "the presence of almost every major artifact category of the Mature Harappan culture" (Shaffer 1982:45). Sutkagen Dor and Shortugai, located in the remote and alien territories, signify the nature and directionality of the Harappan expansion.

Chronological Diversity. As several sites of the early Harappan period were fortified and likely reached a high degree of sociopolitical complexity well prior to the transition to the Mature Harappan, it seemed to me necessary to consider them along with the Mature Harappan settlements; particularly so since the cultural meaning of the distinction between the Early and Mature Harappan is a highly debatable issue.

Limitation of the Present Research. Like the choice of data for the previous chapter, I found it impossible and unnecessary to utilize more than a certain amount of data from the Harappan civilization. Inevitably, the final selection of sites also reflects my personal biases and familiarity with archaeological data.

Allahdino

Allahdino (Nel Bazaar) is a very small site—around 100 m in diameter (Hoffman and Shaffer 1975:95) or approximately 40,000 m^2 (Hoffman 1974b:1)—located on the outskirts of modern Karachi (see Figure 4.1). Discovered by Majumdar in 1934, it was excavated under the directorship of Walter Fairservis for two seasons in 1973–1974.[1] The total excavated area at Allahdino measured about 2,800 m^2. Based on the 4.5 m deep sondage, excavated during the first season, Shaffer (1974:141–147) defined a sequence of six consecutive levels. During the second season, this sequence was modified into a cultural periodization consisting of three phases. Phase 3, the earliest, had no structures and was defined based on lithics and pottery. Phase 2 was characterized by structures made of mud-brick, pise, and wood. Phase 1, particularly its earlier levels, presented the main occupational period defined by mud-brick and stone architecture (Hoffman and Shaffer 1975:96–99). No absolute dates were determined. Yet judging from pottery and other objects of material culture, all occupational levels of the Allahdino sequence were assigned to the Mature Harappan period. Moreover, Hoffman and Shaffer (1975:96) argued that the occupation throughout all cultural phases lasted between 100 to 300 years. Fairservis (1982:111) believed that Allahdino was occupied for no longer than 100 years.

Fortifications and Authority

No perimeter walls, retaining walls or any other forms of fortifications were found at Allahdino (Fairservis 1982:110; Hoffman 1974b). As far as authority is concerned, the archaeological record of Allahdino is more informative. On one hand, the cultural history of Allahdino displays a remarkable continuity. All stratigraphic units are characterized by Mature Harappan traits and are consequently classified as belonging to the Mature Harappan culture (Shaffer 1974:149). On the other hand, at least two important transitions characterize the cultural sequence of Allahdino.

Transition from phase 3 (level V) to phase 2 (level IV) witnesses the abrupt introduction of structures made of mud-brick, pise, and wood (Shaffer 1974:19–27, 143–144). The earlier levels (VI–V), although defined as Mature Harappan, have neither structures nor features. Phase 2 (level IV), on the other hand, is characterized by the fully developed mud-brick architecture, which, according to Shaffer (1974:150), demonstrates "a rather sophisticated knowledge of construction techniques." Based on parallel changes in lithics, architecture, and ceramics, Shaffer (1974:153) argues that this transition reflects a shift from pastoral nomadism represented by levels VI–V to sedentary agriculturalism represented by levels IV–I. The second transition takes place between phase 2 (level III) and phase 1 (level II). That Shaffer (1974) in his original report on cultural stratigraphy of Allahdino does not view this transition as an important cultural change seems to me erroneous. Phase 1 (level II) marks a significant intensification of structural activities. In fact, the overwhelming majority of architectural remains unearthed in Allahdino are stratigraphically associated with level II. The most important structures of this level include a household water system, a small-scale irrigation network, and several public structures of enigmatic function. The houses according to Hoffman (1974b:26) were laid out according to the northwest–southeast axis. In addition, public structures were grouped in one part of the site (see Figure 4.1). In summary, if Shaffer's hypothesis is right, the first transition led to the establishment of an agricultural hamlet, consisting just of three or four mud-brick houses. The second transition led to the formation of a fully developed agricultural village with an irrigation channel, a household water system and some public buildings (Hoffman 1974b).

The role of authority, if any, in the first transition must have been minimal. A shift from pastoral nomadism to agricultural sedentism does not require rigid social differentiation and authoritative decisions. The second transition however indicates a more complex picture. Phase 1 (level 2) reveals a whole set of artifacts and architectural features that are typically characteristic of a large-scale Harappan settlement. Judging from the

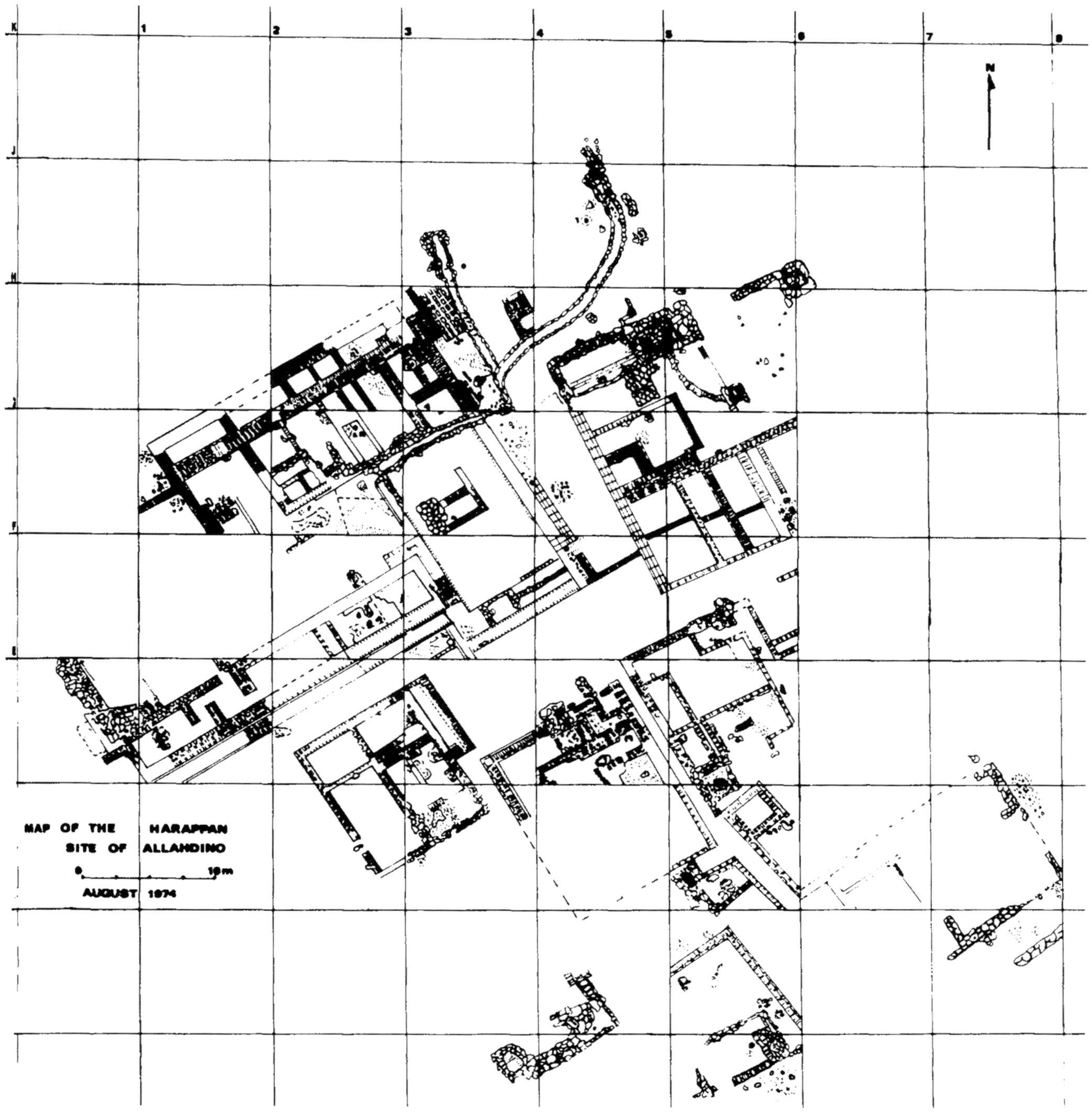

Figure 4.1 Allahdino. Illustration used with the courtesy and permission of Jim Shaffer and the South Asia Program, Cornell University; "The Harappan settlement at Allahdino: Analyzing the sociology of an archaeological site", in *Ecological Backgrounds of South Asia Prehistory* (Hoffman and Shaffer 1975).

Table 4.1

Banawali: Periodization (after IAR 1987–1988)

Period / Phase	Name of Period / Phase
Period I	Pre-Harappan (Kalibangan) culture
Phase IA	Pre-Defense phase
Phase IB	Defense phase
Phase IC	Transitional (Proto-Harappan) phase
Period II	Mature Harappan phase
Period III	Post Harappan phase

results of the excavation, however, none of the artifacts were locally produced. As Shaffer (1982:45) justly noted, this implies the existence of a very developed internal trade and distribution network. In my view, it also has implications for the understanding of the role and origins of authority on the site. Interestingly enough, among other artifacts, phase 1 (level 2) reveals several seals, sealings, and inscribed objects. According to Fairservis (1982:111), this indicates that Allahdino was characterized by a social system and mechanisms of leadership familiar on a larger scale at other Harappan sites. Fairservis' argument is well taken, for the least that Harappan seals and sealings must indicate is the existence of a social system, of which the Indus script was representative, as well as the presence of individuals who were familiar with this script. In other words, artifacts and features associated with the deposits of phase 1 (level 2) indicate that by the beginning of this phase Allahdino had been fully acculturated in the world of the Harappan civilization. If authority played any role in this acculturation, it must have been introduced to Allahdino from outside, from already existing Mature Harappan settlements; for as a sedentary community Allahdino emerged long after the formations of the Mature Harappan culture.

To conclude, it is likely that Allahdino was a small center of local administration that was fully incorporated within the larger network of the Harappan sociopolitical order and like most artifacts and features discovered in Allahdino had external origins.

Banawali

Banawali is located on the bank of the lost Hakra River in the district Hissar in Haryana (see Figure 4.2). It occupies a relatively small mound measuring ca. 400 x 400 m. In 1974–1977, R. S. Bisht conducted the first three seasons of excavations at Banawali on behalf of the Department of Archaeology and Museums of Haryana. In 1983, Bisht resumed the work at Banawali, this time on behalf of the Archaeological Survey of India. Between 1983 and 1988, he conducted three more excavation seasons at this site.[2] The cultural sequence as defined by Bisht for Banawali begins with the pre-Harappan local phase, similar to that of Sothi or Kalibangan I and subdivided into three cultural subphases, then transforms into the Urban Harappan phase, and ends with the post-Harappan cultural entity (see Table 4.1), reminiscent of that of the Bara Culture (Y. D. Sharma 1973). As far as the dates are concerned, there are at least two publications offering precise chronological brackets for each of the three periods (Bisht 1976; Ghosh 1989:II.45–46). It is not clear on what kind of argument these publications are based since the existing ^{14}C dates are scarce and contradictory. Period I for example does not have any absolute dates. Based on pottery, Bisht (1987:145) equates it with Siswal B and Mitathal I, as well as draws broader parallels with the pre-Harappan levels at Kot-Diji and Amri. Period II has a few radiocarbon dates, yet some of these dates are clearly erroneous. Based on the dates that are more reasonable, this period should be placed approximately between 2500 BC and 1800/1750 BC (Bisht 1997:257). Period III has no radiocarbon dates, yet based on similarities in pottery. Bisht (1997:260) equates it with Sanghol IB, Mitathal IIB, Bhagwanpura IA, and Dadheri IA. In sum, the periodization and absolute chronology of Banawali remain tentative.

Fortifications

Banawali, although being a relatively small site, has an elaborate and impressive system of fortifications (see Figure 4.2). Besides being surrounded and divided by mud-brick walls, it has a moat and a channel on the eastern side, several bastions and gates, a ring road running on the outer side of the perimeter wall, an internal system of roads related to fortifications and gates, and at least one platform. According to the data gathered by Bisht, the construction of fortifications began during period IB and continued throughout period IC and period II when the settlement entered the Mature Harappan phase.

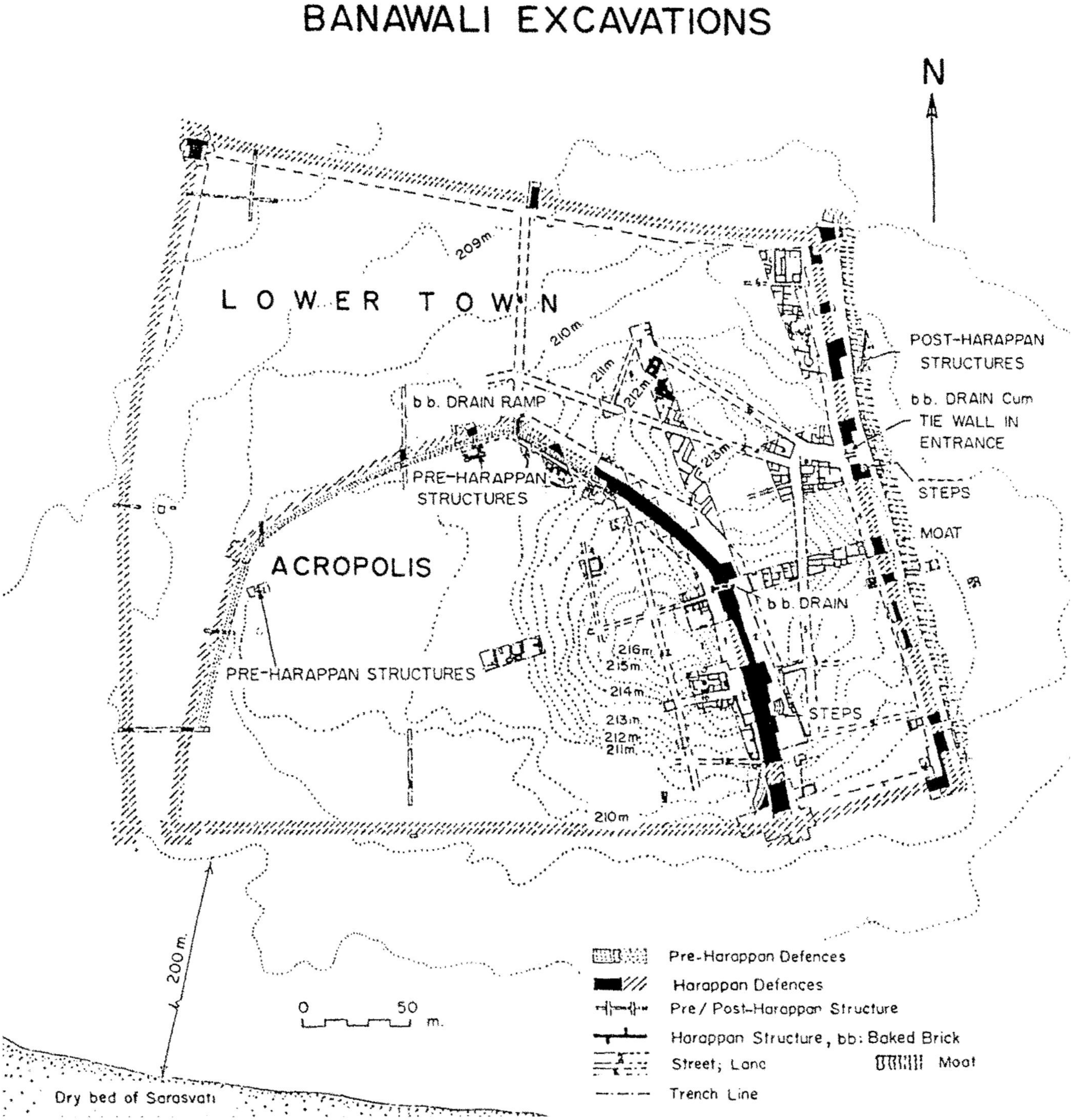

Figure 4.2 Banawali. Illustration used with the courtesy and permission of the ASI, *Indian Archaeology: A Review 1987–1988.*

Table 4.2

Chanhu-Daro: Periodizations (after Mackay 1943; Piggot 1943; and Possehl 2002c)

Scholar	Periodization
Mackay	Harappan period
	Harappa III
	Harappa II
	Harappa I
	Jhukar period
	Jhangar period
	Trihni period
	Islamic period
Piggot	Chanhu Daro I period
	Chanhu-Daro IA
	Chanhu-Daro IB
	Chanhu-Daro IC
	Chanhu-Daro II period
	Chanhu-Daro III period
Possehl	Mature Harappan period
	Mature Harappan A
	Mature Harappan B
	Mature Harappan C
	Mature Harappan D
	Jhukar period, Post-Urban
	Harappan period
	Trihni period
	Jhangar period

Built and modified gradually during several hundred years, the fortifications underwent many structural modifications. The initial perimeter wall was only 1.4 m wide. Toward the end of period IB, however, this wall was strengthened and widened to ca, 2.5–3.2 m (Bisht 1998–1999:18; IAR 1987–1988:23). In period IC, the wall was further widened, the whole fortification system was noticeably renovated, and the division into the two distinct sectors was established (Bisht 1998–1999:15–16). In period II, a gate complex, a V-shaped moat, a berm, and a channel parallel to the moat were constructed on the eastern side of the settlement (Bisht 1998–1999:18). Around the same time, a platform was built under the Acropolis (IAR 1987–1988:25). Interpreting these data, one must remember that the size of the moat, the berm, and the perimeter wall has been conjectured rather than precisely determined. For example, the moat was traced only for 75 m along the eastern side (IAR 1983–1984:27) and was not traced at all on any other side of the settlement. Also, since there are no precise dates for period I, it is unclear what the actual chronological gaps were between the initial construction of the perimeter wall, the division of the settlement into two distinct sectors, and the rebuilding of fortifications. This being said, the existing data nevertheless provide sufficient grounds for theorizing on both the structural history and function of the fortification system at Banawali.

The structural history was gradual. When during period IC almost the entire settlement was erased and built *de novo*, many elements of the previous structure and design were incorporated in the construction of new fortifications (Bisht 1998–1999:16). Some structural modifications however were significant enough to be caused by changes in sociopolitical organization at the site. One such modification was the construction of a fortified settlement with two distinct sectors divided by a mud-brick wall. Another one was the construction of a moat, berm, and gate complex on the eastern side of the settlement. As far as the function is concerned, it seems that at least until the Mature Harappan period, fortifications at Banawali had played mostly a symbolic role. The following observations support this hypothesis: 1) the main wall was too insignificant to perform a military function; 2) the construction of a fortified settlement with two distinct sectors implied the segregation of space, which may in turn be indicative of sociopolitical or religious changes; 3) although Banawali was excavated on a large horizontal scale, the excavators detected only one platform, which given its location and size, was very unlikely to serve as protection from floods, and more likely elevated an important structure for political or religious purposes (IAR 1987–88:25); 4) from the earliest stages of occupation, the wall did not mark the actual boundary of the settlement; for as the excavators report, structures were detected on the outer side of the fortifications wall (Bisht 1998–1999:15–16), and the earliest wall was built right on top of the structures constructed during period IA (Bisht 1987:142); 5) the shape and direction of the pre-Harappan wall were smoothly incorporated in the natural landscape. The wall was "designed like a large oval following the existing natural elevation" (IAR 1987–1988:23). Taken together, these traits can, in my view, be seen as indicative of a non-utilitarian function. At least until the construction of the gate and moat on the eastern side of the settlement, the walls at Banawali could not protect the site from floods or military threat. Instead, they must have marked the boundary of some symbolic significance.

Authority

The first drastic transition that is indicative of the emergence of authority in the cultural history of Banawali takes place during phase IC. Bisht (1998–1999:16) equates this phase with Siswal B and Mitathal I as well as with the pre-Harappan levels at Kot-Diji and Amri. Given the nature of changes that take place during this phase, it would make more sense to distinguish it as a separate cultural period. In fact, Bisht (1987:145) recognizes this at some point, but nonetheless continues to classify it as part of the pre-Harappan cultural complex. The innovations of this phase are quite drastic (Bisht 1998–1999:16–17). The material culture is characterized by bricks of the ratio 4:2:1, triangular terracotta cakes, 8-shaped terracotta nodules, chert blades, and a substantial increase in beads and bangles. The pottery is represented by a mix of local and the new Harappan shapes and designs. Most importantly, however, the whole settlement is rebuilt anew and the division into the lower and upper sectors is established. Architecture becomes more sophisticated and significantly differentiated in size and quality (Bisht 1984). A new street system is laid out and the houses are oriented according to the cardinal directions.

Interestingly, in his earlier publications, Bisht (1976, 1977, 1978, 1982) did not pay much attention to the cultural transformation associated with phase IC. The main shift in sociopolitical complexity, according to him, took place in period II. Since more recently however, Bisht (1987:143–145; 1998–1999:16–17) began to emphasize the significance of phase IC as a transitional "Proto-Harappan" period. In my view, this is a much more appropriate approach; for judging even from the scarce data that are currently available in print, it is quite clear that the innovations of phase IC could not have occurred without the presence of authoritative structures on the site. The rebuilding of the settlement, the reinforcement of fortifications, and the creation of two distinct sectors alone seem to constitute solid evidence for the emergence of authority. Hopefully, the publication of the previously excavated data as well as further research will add more information about the nature of technological innovations and cultural changes that took place during phase IC.

Chanhu-Daro

Chanhu-Daro is located next to the village of Jamal Kirio in the Nawabshah District of Sind, Pakistan, about 12 mi from the left bank of the Indus River which once flew next to the site (see Figure 4.3). Chanhu-Daro was discovered and briefly explored in 1931 by Majumdar.
In 1935–1936, it was excavated by Mackay under the auspices of the American School of Indic and Iranian Studies and the Boston Museum of Fine Arts. The history and significance of this well-acclaimed project was described in detail by Possehl (1999:95–101). Although Chanhu-Daro is an extensively excavated site, its cultural history, settlement layout, and the dynamics of expansion remain poorly known.[3] This is due, at least in part, to the fact that the excavation methods employed by Mackay were quite rudimentary. At the time of the excavations, the site consisted of three mounds. However, both Majumdar and Mackay (1943:59) thought that the site occupied only one mound and was later divided into three parts by floods and erosion, for numerous traces of occupation were detected between the mounds. Considering the size of gaps between the mounds as well as the size of mounds themselves, the site must have occupied at least 5 ha (see Figure 4.3). To date, there are three versions of the cultural sequence of Chanhu-Daro: the original one defined by Mackay, the one revised by Piggott, and the one revised by Possehl (see Table 4.2). Mackay (1943) distinguished five occupational periods: Harappan, Jhukar, Jhangar, Trihni, and Islamic. Piggott (1943:179) generally followed this sequence, yet renamed the periods. Possehl (2002c:74), in one of his recent summaries of the Harappan archaeology, proposed yet another sequence; the Harappan period, in Possehl's view, should be divided into four rather than three sub-periods and the Trihni Ware period should precede rather than follow Jhangar. Since it is unclear on which grounds the latter periodization is based, in my own analysis, I will be referring to the terminology defined originally by Mackay. Also, it is important to note that all of the major occupational periods including the Harappan sub-periods are structurally unrelated to one another. Mackay (1943:34, 37) saw this discontinuity as a result of population movements.

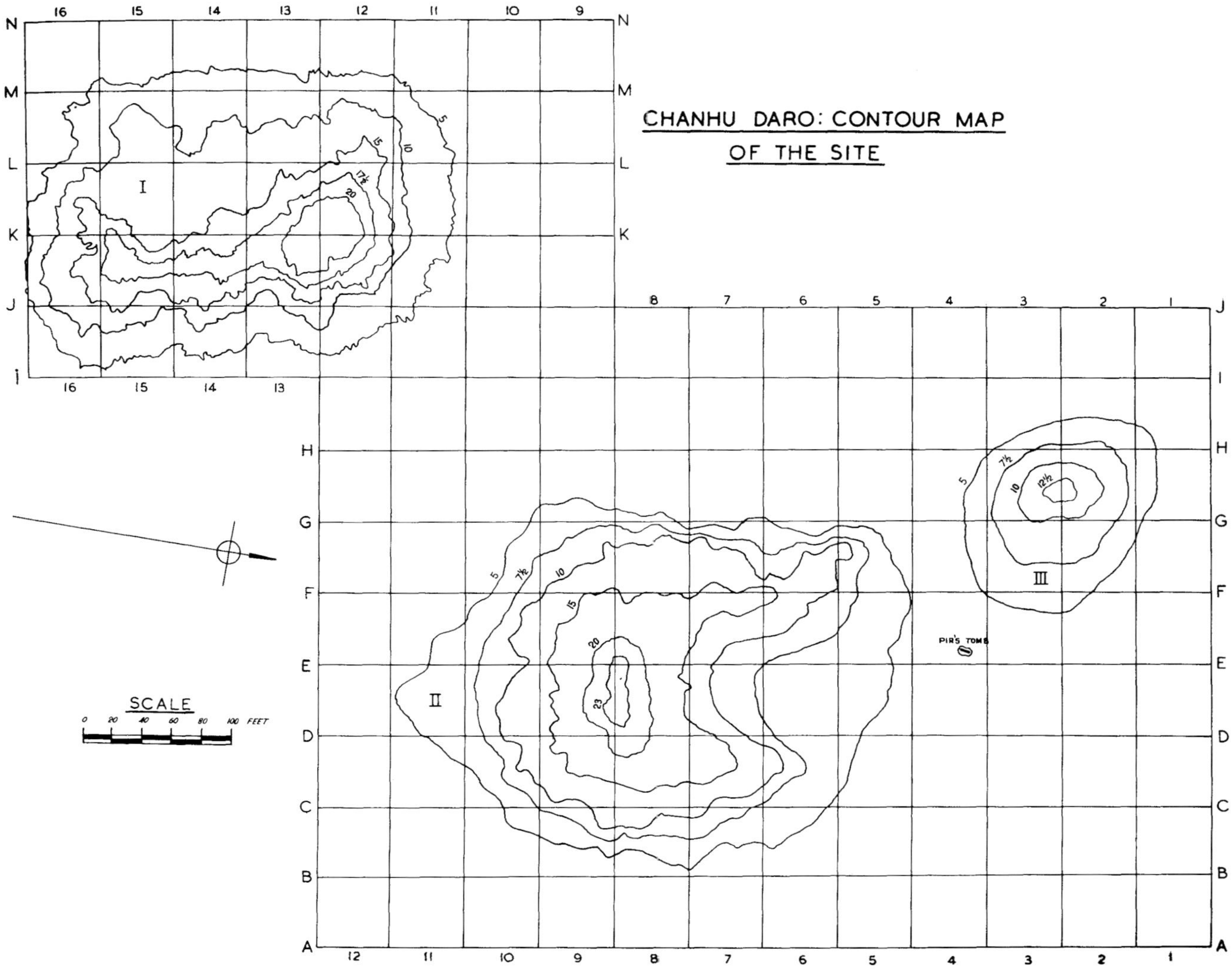

Figure 4.3 Chanhu-Daro: Contour plan. Illustration used with the courtesy and permission of the American Oriental Society and American Oriental Series, *Chanhu-Daro Excavations 1935–1936* (Mackay 1943).

Fortifications

There is still no consensus on whether Chanhu-Daro or any of its sectors were fortified. I believe that the currently available data provide convincing evidence for the existence of a fortification system that consisted of at least one perimeter wall and several mud-brick platforms (see Figure 4.4). Consider the following. The first trench excavated by Mackay (1943:1–2) in Chanhu-Daro revealed the remains of a massive wall, which was characterized by the following features: 1) the wall was significantly bigger than any other wall unearthed in Chanhu-Daro (80 ft long, from 4.9 to 5.4 ft wide); 2) the ends of the wall were not reached (the excavation was stopped due to the presence of crops on one end and the tomb of a local saint on the other end); 3) standing at the foot of mound 2 and at a distance from other mounds, the wall was positioned on the edge of the settlement; 4) on its eastern side, the wall had a revetment, which varied from 6 to 3 inches in width and was traced for 22 ft in length; 5) structural remains discovered in the direct association with the wall were sporadic and fragmentary, no rooms were detected. Taking these traits into account, one

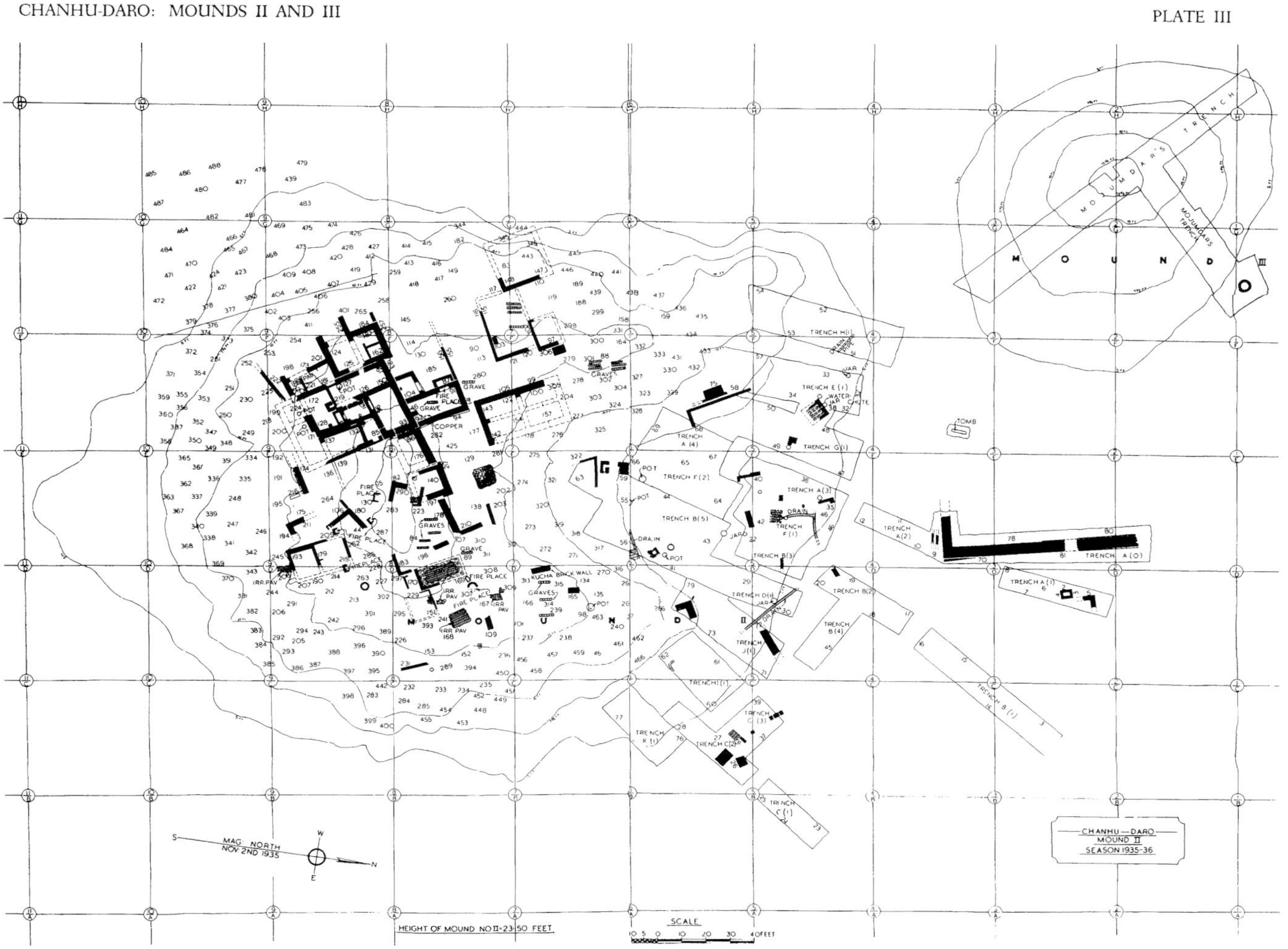

Figure 4.4 Chanhu-Daro: Mounds II and III. Illustration used with the courtesy and permission of the American Oriental Society and American Oriental Series, *Chanhu-Daro Excavations 1935–1936* (Mackay 1943).

may suggest, with a high degree of certainty, that this structure was not part of any building, but a freestanding wall that encircled either the entire site or a significant section of the site. Moreover, judging from the alignment of this structure and stratigraphic notes taken by Mackay, it was built in the "Harappa II" period, the time of cultural efflorescence and active structural activity on the site. In association with this period, Mackay also reported the construction of massive mud-brick platforms. In particular, he noted that in several trenches on mound 2 he had reached "the upper portions of solid platforms of unburnt brick", and, in the deep trench, the base level of one of these platforms (Mackay 1943:37). Mackay seemed to believe that these platforms were initially underneath the entire site. Later some of them were eroded due to frequent floods. Given the current state of the data, it is difficult to verify these conclusions. What is clear is that by the second Harappan sub-period, a significant part of mound 2 had rested on several massive mud-brick platforms. Interestingly, the structures that stood on top of these platforms were very modest (Mackay 1943:40).

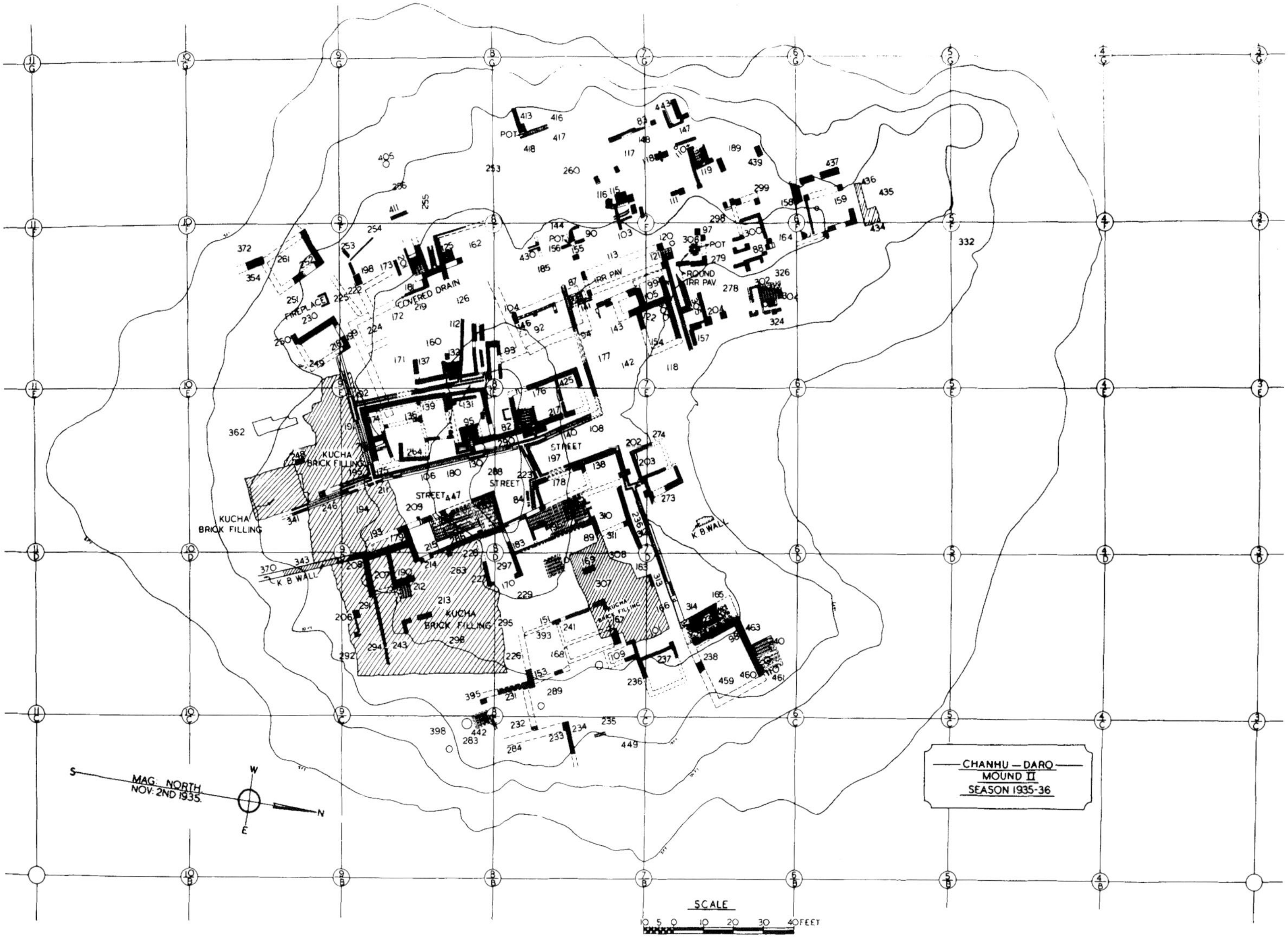

Figure 4.5 Chanhu-Daro: Mound II, Harappa II level. Illustration used with the courtesy and permission of the American Oriental Society and *American Oriental Series, Chanhu-Daro Excavations 1935-1936* (Mackay 1943).

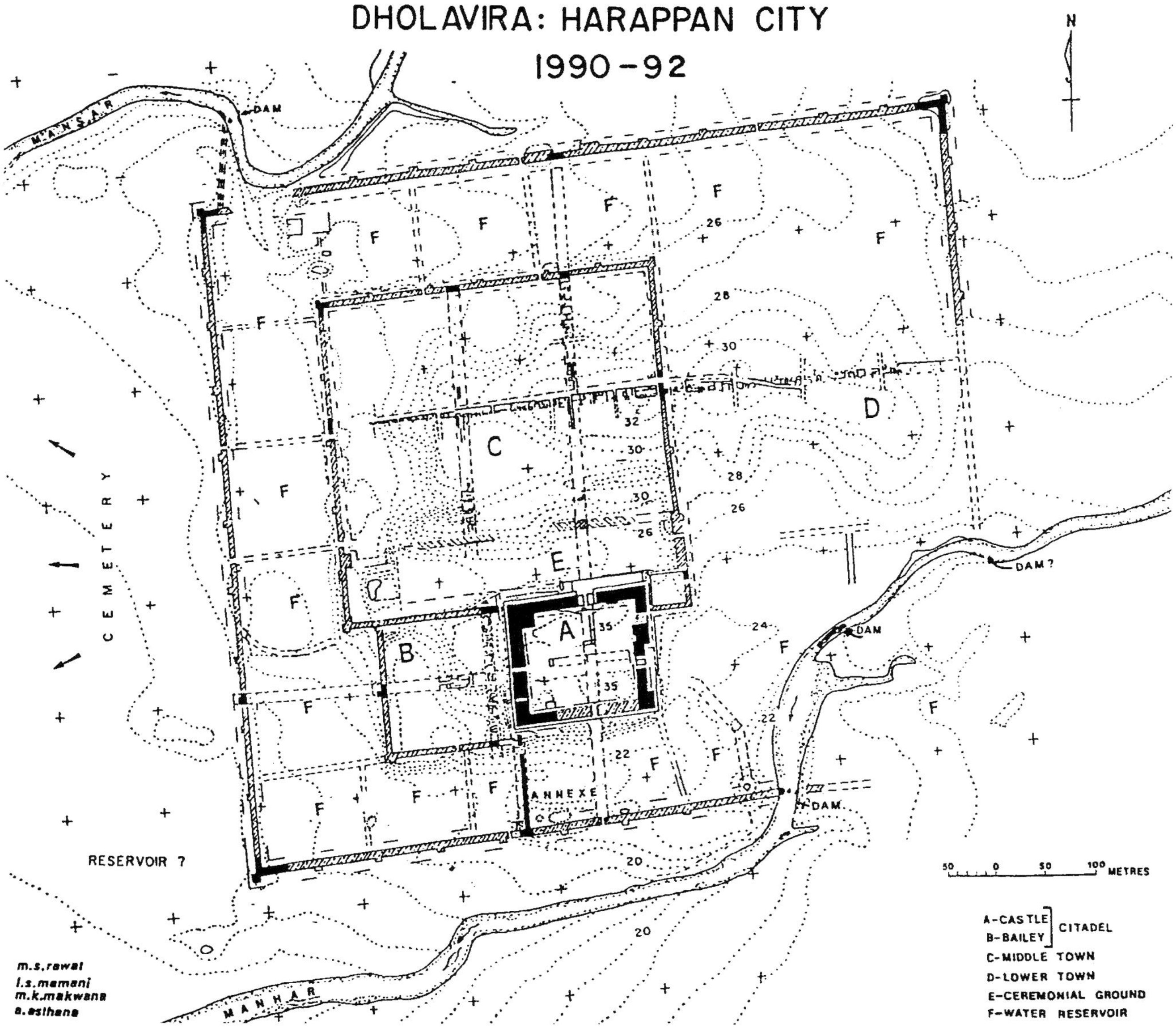

Figure 4.6 Dholavira. Illustration used with the courtesy and permission of the ASI, *Indian Archaeology: A Review 1991–1992.*

To conclude, both the wall and mud-brick platforms appear to have been built at Chanhu-Daro during the second Harappan sub-period. Due to the paucity of data, their function remains enigmatic.

Authority

Since the culture history of Chanhu-Daro is poorly defined, it is difficult to place the emergence of authority on this site in a chronological context. It is clear that authority was present at Chanhu-Daro by the second Harappan sub-period. Judging from the architecture, seals, the discovery of a bead factory, and several other traits of material culture, Harappa II was the period of active structural activities and overall cultural efflorescence (see Figure 4.5). The dimensions of the platforms associated with this period are indicative of massive consumption of

Table 4.3

Dholavira: Periodization (after Bisht 1999; IAR 1991–1992; Possehl 2002c)

Stage	Name of Stage	Approximate Dates
I	Early-Mature Harappan Transition A	2650–2500 BC
II	Early-Mature Harappan Transition B	2550–2500 BC
III	Mature Harappan A	2500–2200 BC
IV	Mature Harappan B	2200–2000 BC
V	Mature Harappan C	2000–1900 BC
VI	Post-Urban A	1850–1750 BC
VII	Post-Urban B	1650–1450 BC

labor, growing social complexity, and the possible presence of authoritative structures. It is also clear that the formative period, if any, was short; for so far no Early Harappan occupations have been detected.[4] Given this, it is likely that Chanhu-Daro presents an example of Harappan expansionism, when social complexity and authority were exported from outside and planted on virgin soil. Of course, further excavations and the discovery of earlier occupational levels could alter this picture.

Dholavira

Dholavira is located on Kadir Island off the Great Rann of Kutch in the district Kutch of Gujarat, India (see Figure 4.6). Discovered in 1967, it has been continuously excavated since 1989, under the directorship of R. S. Bisht and on behalf of the ASI.[5] The exact size of the site is still unclear. Bisht (1998–1999:21) believes that in its heyday, the site covered over 100 ha; for the fortified area alone measures at 800 by 650 m, or 52 ha. The cultural sequence of Dholavira, as defined by Bisht, begins ca. 2650 BC (Bisht 1999:403; IAR 1991–1992: 26–31). Combined with the periodization and dates proposed by Possehl (2002c:67), it can be summarized in seven stages (see Table 4.3).

Fortifications

An elaborate and grandiose system of fortifications is one of the defining and most fascinating features of urban layout at Dholavira (see Figures 4.6–4.9). Judging from the currently available data, it had evolved gradually from the local pre-Harappan traditions (see Figure 4.8). Three pre-defense layers (10–7) were detected during the excavations. None of these layers had Harappan material. Layers associated with the earliest perimeter wall (6–5) were non-Harappan as well. Bisht (1991:76) nevertheless combined pre-defense and defense layers in the same cultural period. The first perimeter wall, according to Bisht, was built during Stage I, soon after the founding of the site. During the next two stages, the fortifications underwent drastic modifications and by stage III, i.e., the beginning of the Mature Harappan period, transformed into a complex network of walls, gates, passages, bastions, and encircling roads.

The immensity and complexity of the fortification system at Dholavira have no parallels on other excavated Harappan sites. Bisht has put together several informative descriptions of the structural history and the layout of this fortification system. Based on these data, one can highlight four traits, which, in my view are the most characteristic of this unique architectural complex. Firstly, from the time of its initial construction during Stage I, fortifications at Dholavira were truly grandiose. For example, the earliest perimeter wall reached 11.1 m in width and 4 m in height (IAR 1991–1992:26). The so-called castle, built by stage IIIA, was surrounded by double ramparts with stone walls and stood to a height of 16 m (IAR 1984–1985:14)! Some of the 14 city gates—particularly those surrounding the castle—were immensely high and wide, yet had narrow passages (Bisht 1998–1999:30). Secondly, many architectural elements incorporated within the fortification system at Dholavira had conspicuous non-utilitarian or non-military significance. The following two examples illustrate this point: a) of the two stadia detected between the citadel and the middle town, the smaller one was surrounded by massive walls on three sides, while the larger one did not have any circumvallation (Bisht 1999:404); b) the east gate of the castle had symmetrically arranged, neatly cut and highly polished limestone blocks and pillar bases incorporated in the design of its internal elevated chamber. Bisht (1998–1999:79) proposed that the arrangement of blocks and pillar bases was based on esthetic principles. Other gates of the castle display similar structural elements. Thirdly, during its heyday Dholavira was a highly segregated place. The three main sectors were the citadel, the middle town, and the lower town. The citadel in turn was divided in two sectors termed by Bisht "the castle" and "the bailey". North of the citadel, there was a walled passage. South of the citadel, there was

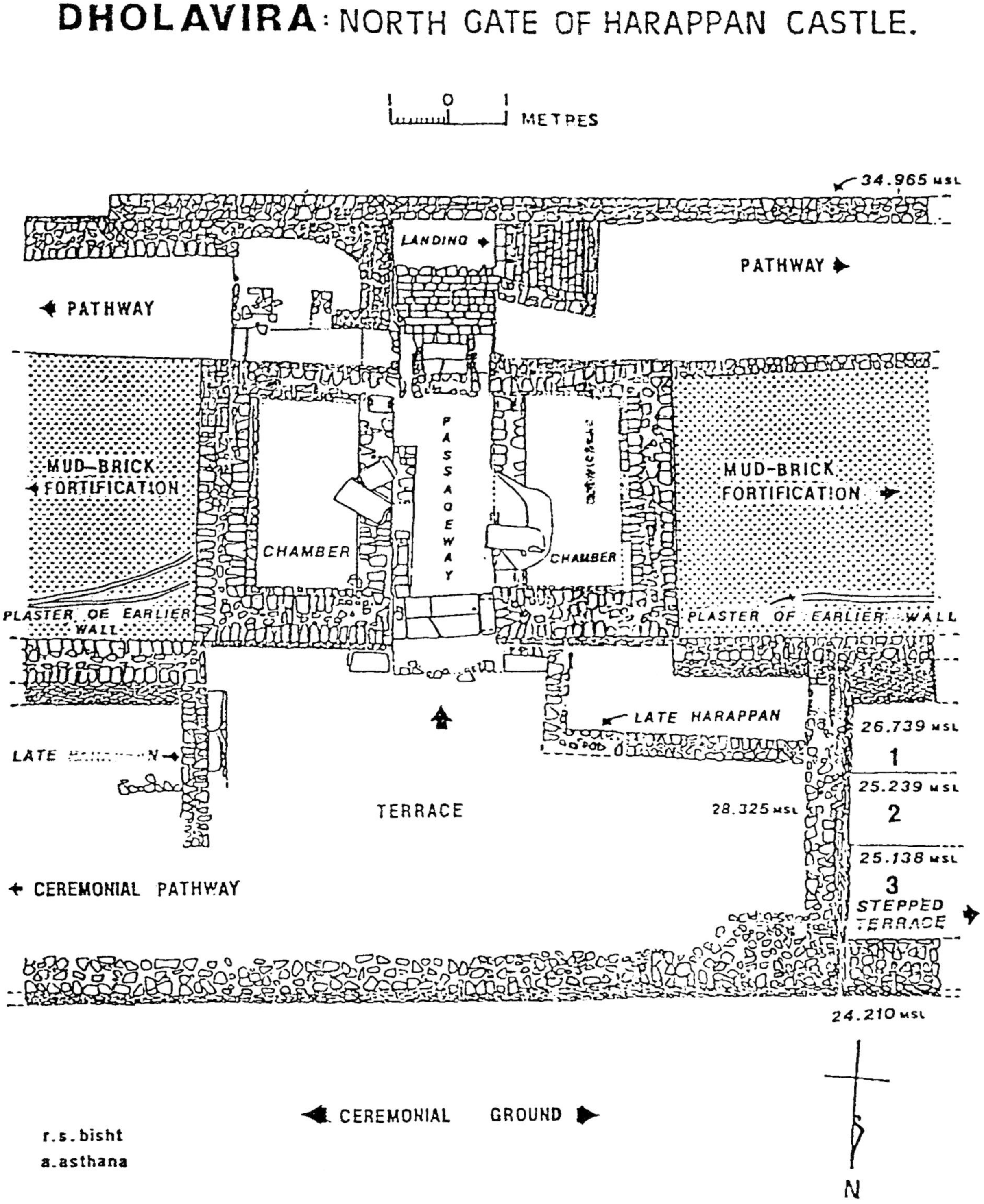

Figure 4.7 Dholavira: North gate of the castle. Illustration used with the courtesy and permission of the ASI, *Indian Archaeology: A Review 1991–1992*.

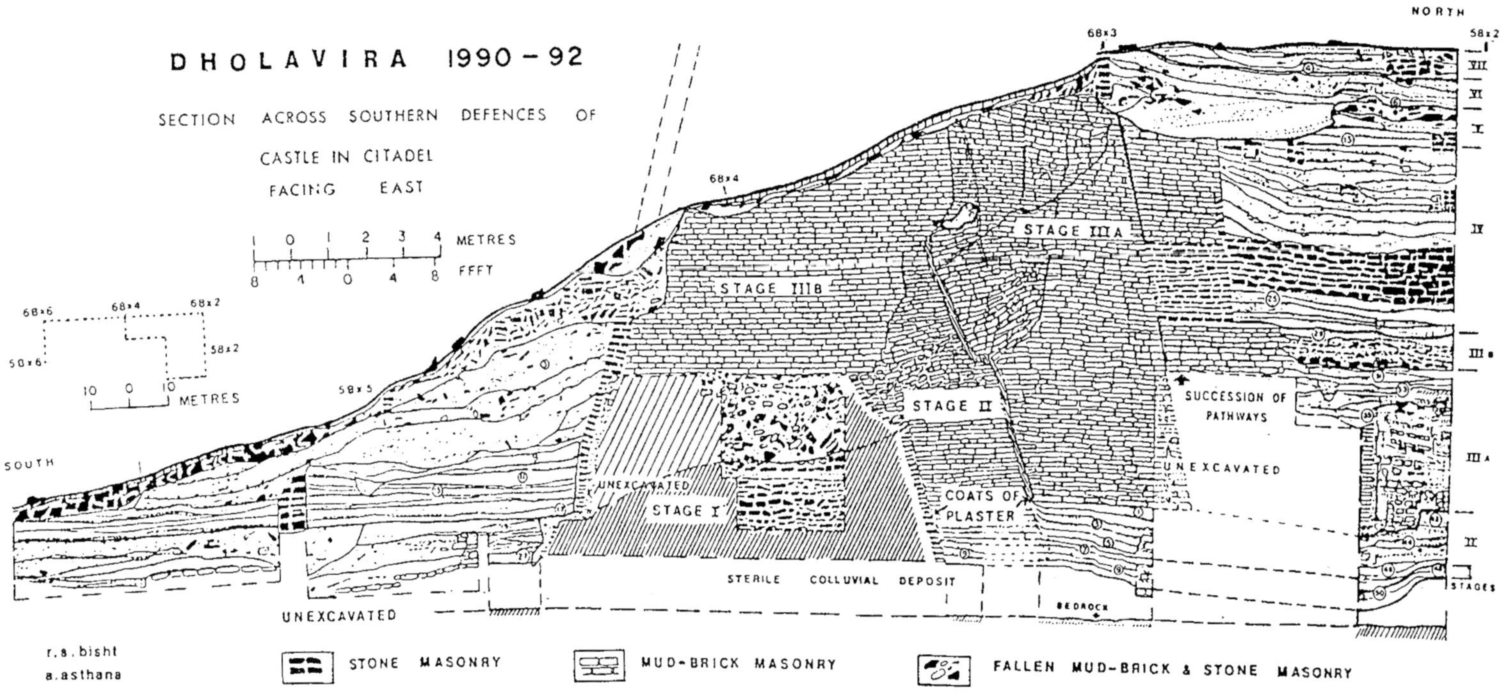

Figure 4.8 Dholavira: Section across southern defenses of the castle. Illustration used with the courtesy and permission of the ASI, *Indian Archaeology: A Review 1991–1992*.

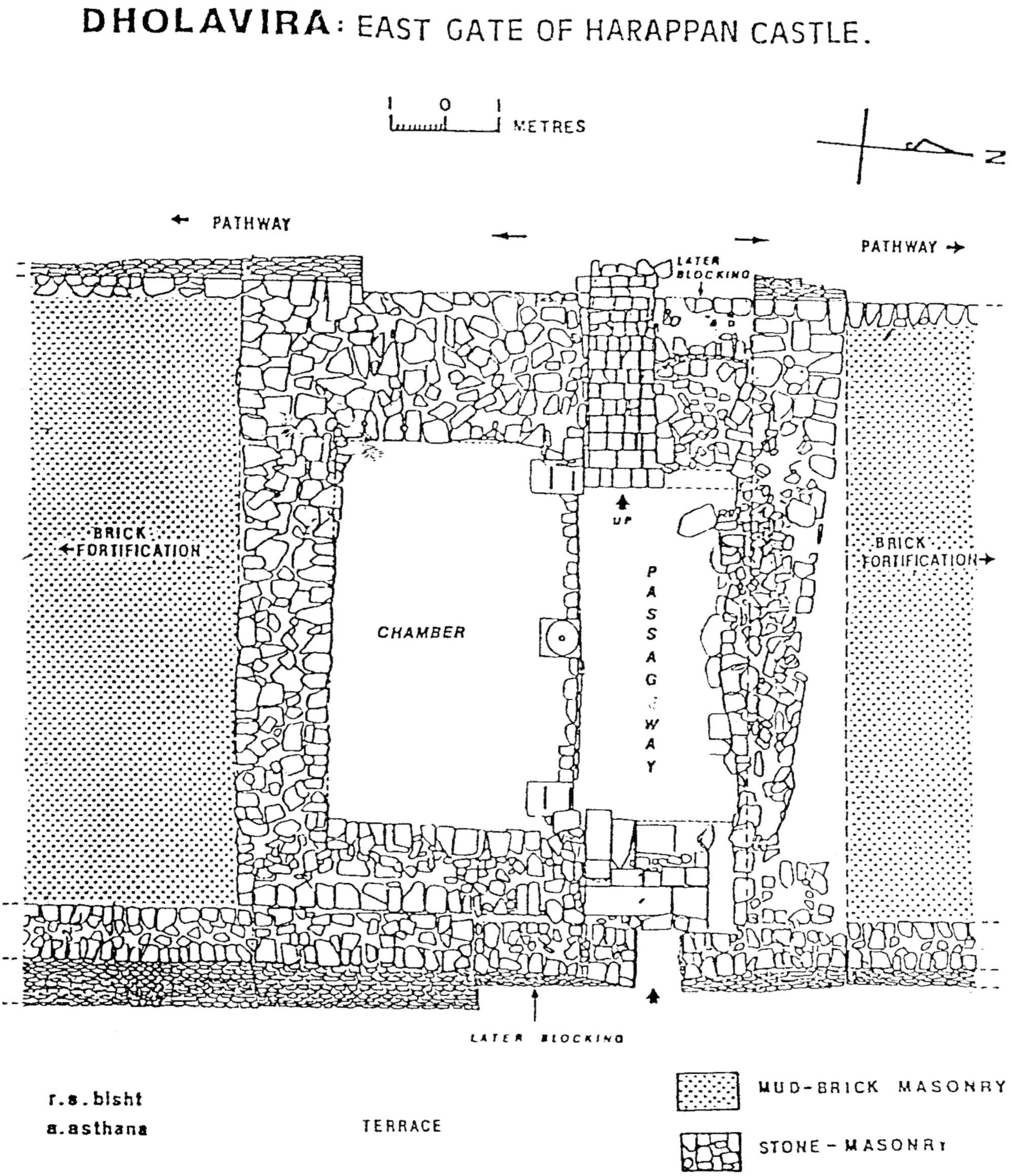

Figure 4.9 Dholavira: East gate of the castle. Illustration used with the courtesy and permission of the ASI, *Indian Archaeology: A Review 1991–1992.*

Table 4.4

Dholavira: Fortification system—distinctive traits and possible interpretations

Traits	Interpretative Options
Grandiose scale	Military defense
	Expression of power and authority
Non-utilitarian elements	Ritual or symbolic functionality
	Expression of esthetic values
Urban segregation	Maintenance of social hierarchy
	Maintenance of social heterarchy
	Maintenance of ritual purity
Empty spaces and open areas	Ritual and religious ceremonialism
	Performance of sociopolitical functions
Free-standing internal walls	Social segregation
	Defense
	Symbolism of space and border

a partly walled sector. On the eastern side of the lower town, there were several water reservoirs, all protected by massive walls with bastions and towers. Lastly, one of the most intriguing features of the layout of Dholavira was the existence of the so-called empty spaces and open areas encircled and accentuated by free-standing walls (see Figures 4.6–4.7, 4.9). Some of these spaces and areas reached 140 m in width (Bisht 1998–1999:72). The most interesting empty space was located between the northern side of the citadel and the southern side of the middle town (IAR 1991–1992:31). Connecting the grandiose north gate of the castle with the main stadium of the middle town, it likely had a strategic position (see Figure 4.7). Bisht proposed that it performed a ceremonial function and served as the main entrance to the castle. As far as the free-standing walls are concerned, they not only divided the city into sectors, but also surrounded—partially or fully—one of the stadia, the southern annex of the castle, water reservoirs, empty spaces, and several residential units.

In terms of functionality, each of these traits is indicative of sociopolitical structures and deeper meanings (see Table 4.4). The grandiose scale of architectural elements is too overwhelming to be explained by military demands. The conspicuous consumption of labor necessary for the construction of massive ramparts, walls, gates, and bastions may be indicative of the desire to express power and authority by means of architecture. The presence of non-military and non-utilitarian elements shows that ritual, symbolic and esthetic considerations were an integral part of the fortifications' function. The intricate urban segregation augmented by empty spaces and open areas points to the great role that social considerations played in the construction of Dholavira fortification system. Lastly, the large number of free-standing walls makes one wonder whether some kind of symbolism of space and border played a role in the creation of Dholavira's urban landscape. Like the Wasserluxus was a key element in the ideology of Mohenjo-Daro (see Jansen 1993a), the division of space must have played an important role in the worldview of Dholavirites. In summary, by the Mature Harappan period, ideological factors overpowered any other concerns that may have led to the construction of fortifications at Dholavira. The segregation, accentuation, and symbolization of space began to play a crucial role in conveying the meaning of these fortifications to the people who lived in this remarkable city.

Authority

There is no need to argue that Dholavira was an important seat of authority during the Mature Harappan period. The size, layout, architecture, writing, and material culture unequivocally show that this site was a center of power. The chronological frame for the emergence of authoritative structures however could be the point of debate. On one hand, it is obvious that stage IIIA, the beginning of the Mature Harappan period, marked the most drastic transition in the history of Dholavira. On the other hand, stages I and II foreordained the efflorescence of stage III, and although the data on these early stages are currently scarce, one can cite at least three lines of evidence in support of the growth of authoritative structures during these stages (IAR 1991–1992:26–28). First, the structural history of fortifications shows that monumentality had been attained long before stage III; the earliest wall was 11 m in width and 4 m in extant height! In a similar way, demand for the strengthening of the wall had emerged long before stage III; the wall was widened for 2.8 m in the beginning of stage II. Thus both the initial construction and the further structural modification of the perimeter wall required a high expenditure of labor and implied, in my view, the existence of a strong authority. Second, several "definitive principles of planning and architecture" evolve prior to stage III (IAR 1991–1992:28). For example, bricks of the typical Indus proportion 4:2:1 were used both in fortifications and domestic structures as early as in stage I. During stage II, white and pink plasters were applied to fortifications and domestic architecture all over the site. The latter phenomenon was quite remarkable, for the application of plasters was truly extensive—13 coats on the inner side of the defensive wall and numerous coats on the floor and wall of various structures (Bisht 1999:403). Taking into consideration the frequency, standardization, and esthetic nature of these colorful plasters, it is not unreasonable to assume that authoritative decisions were responsible for both their use in stage II and the abrupt disappearance in stage IV. Third, the first noticeable expansion of the site took place in the beginning of stage II. Yet the expansion itself was not as significant as the resultant spatial segregation indicative of the ongoing social stratification and the shaping of authoritative structures. In sum, authoritative structures appear to have evolved in Dholavira gradually and locally during the first two cultural periods. The genesis of these structures went hand in hand with the construction of fortifications.

Harappa

Harappa, located in the district Sahiwal in Punjab, Pakistan, is one of the most extensively investigated archaeological sites in South Asia.[6] From its discovery in the nineteenth century, it was excavated by D. R. Sahni, M. S. Vats, R. E. M. Wheeler, M. R. Mughal, and from 1986 by the American-Pakistani Archaeological Research Project (HARP) first under the directorship of G. Dales, and more recently under the directorship of R. H. Meadow, J. M. Kenoyer, and R. P. Wright.[7] The first relative chronology of Harappa was defined by Vats. Following Marshall's chronology of Mohenjo-Daro, Vats (1940:I.8–9) distinguished three periods: the early, the intermediate, and the late, and traced each of these periods in five areas of the site. The currently accepted sequence was initially defined by G. Dales and later modified by Kenoyer and Meadow (2000). The most recent version of this sequence consists of five periods (see Table 4.5).[8] Besides serving as chronological markers, each of these periods is characterized by a large number of cultural and technological traits.

Table 4.5

Harappa: Periodization (after Kenoyer and Meadow 2000)

Period	Period Name	Approximate Dates
1	Ravi (Aspect of the Hakra) phase	3300–2800 BC
2	Kot Diji (Early Harappa) phase	2800–2600 BC
3A	Harappa phase A	2600–2450 BC
3B	Harappa phase B	2450–2200 BC
3C	Harappa phase C	2200–1900 BC
4	Harappa / Late Harappa Transitional	1900–1800 BC
5	Late Harappa phase	1800–1300 BC

Fortifications

The site of Harappa consists of the four main mounds: mound AB, mound E, mound ET, and mound F (see Figure 4.10). Each of these mounds is fortified. When in 1946 Wheeler explored Harappa, he assumed that mound AB, the highest of the four mounds, was a citadel. Consequently, one of the main purposes of the excavation that he undertook was to determine whether mound AB was fortified and, in the case if fortifications were found, to determine their character and structural history. The results of Wheeler's excavations were positive (see Figures 4.11–4.12). In most of his trenches, Wheeler traced the remains of massive mud and mud-brick structures. Having connected these remains on the map, Wheeler (1947:64) claimed that the plan of the defenses on mound AB fell "roughly within the limits of a parallelogram, 400 yards by 200 yards". As far as the structural history was concerned, Wheeler (1947:64–67) distinguished five main structural elements: mud-brick rampart, mud-brick wall, revetment, platform, and rectangular towers. All of these elements, according to Wheeler, dated to the Mature Harappan period. Moreover, based on the alleged differences in pottery, Wheeler (1947:93) assumed that mound AB was fortified by an alien group of people. In 1970, Mughal questioned the credibility of Wheeler's argument with regard to the date of the initial fortification on mound AB. Mughal reasonably suggested that level 26A defined by Wheeler (Trench HP XXX) as containing Early Harappan Pottery was associated with the fortifications. Consequently, the construction of the initial fortification, Mughal (1970:127–131) argued, took place during the Early Harappan period.

In 1997, Kenoyer reopened Wheeler's trench HP XXX. When originally excavated, this trench measuring 111 x 12/18 ft was cut across the western side of the

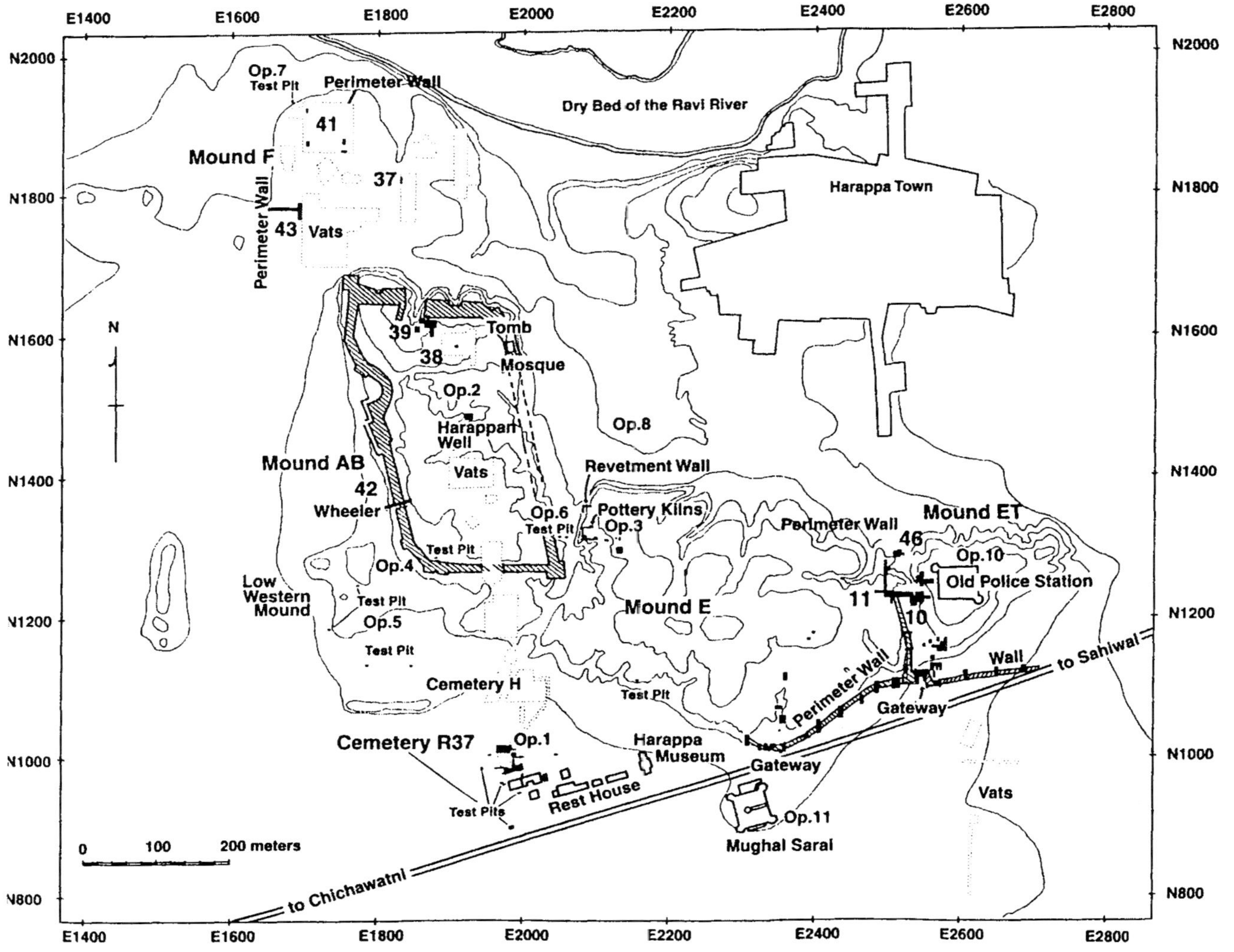

Figure 4.10 Harappa: Plan. Illustration used with the courtesy and permission of Richard H. Meadow, HARP Director, Harappa Excavations 1999. *Report submitted to the Director General, The Department of Archaeology and Museums, Government of Pakistan* (Meadow et al. 1999).

mound AB and reached natural soil. The reopened trench was renamed as HARP 42. The cleaning and redrawing of the sections revealed that a complete Early Harappan (Kot-Diji phase) period perimeter wall had underlain the Harappa phase fortifications (Meadow et al. 1997:14–15). Besides the walls, massive mud-brick platforms were detected on different sides of mound AB. At least some of these platforms were constructed during the Kot-Diji phase (Meadow et al. 1999:3).

Mound F lies to the north of mound AB and like mound AB it drew much attention of the early explorers and excavators. Sahni, Vats, and Wheeler excavated on mound F extensively and disclosed a large number of structures the most known among which were "workman quarters", "granary", and circular platforms. No city walls however were found. In 1997, Kenoyer opened four trenches on mound F. One of these trenches (41 NE) revealed two mud-brick perimeter walls: the first one built on natural sediment, and the second one built on top of the first one. Meadow and Kenoyer (2000:13) suggested that these walls were constructed as a bund to protect the area of the "granary" from flooding. The investigation of the city wall on mound F continued during the season of 1998 and 1999. It was established that the

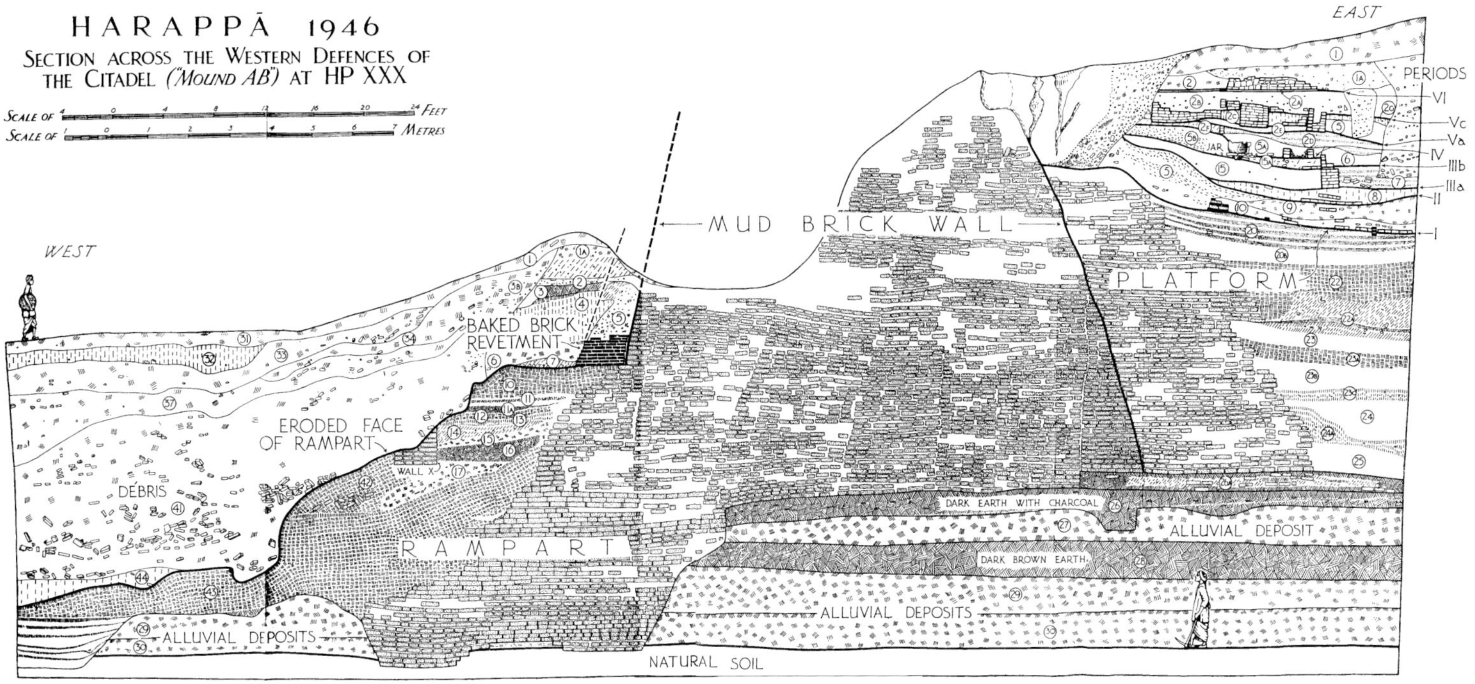

Figure 4.11 Harappa: Mound AB, section across the defenses. Illustration used with the courtesy and permission of Cambridge University Press, *The Indus Civilization, The Cambridge History of India, supplementary volume* (Wheeler 1962).

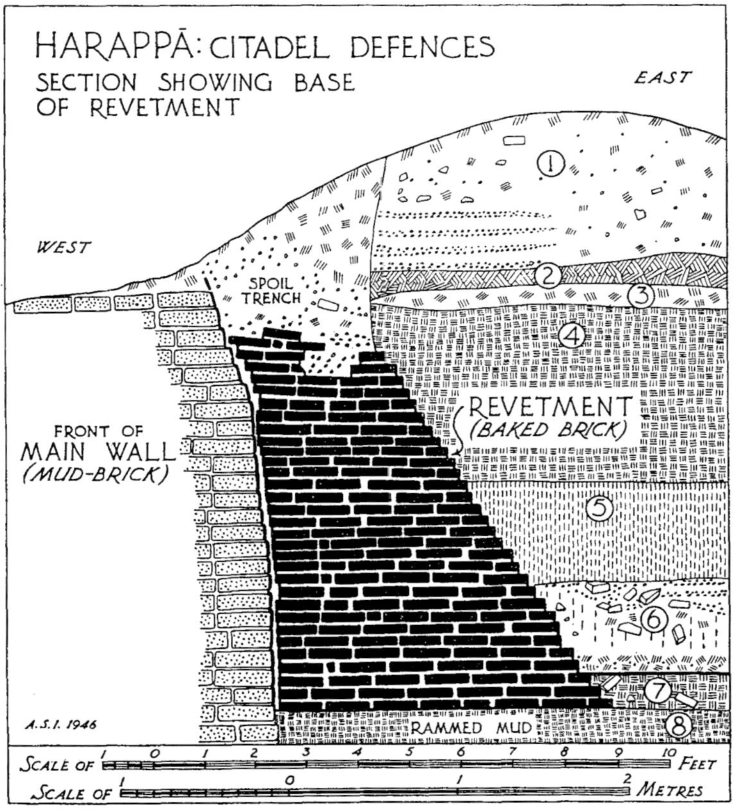

a

Section of revetment of baked bricks in cutting HP XLV

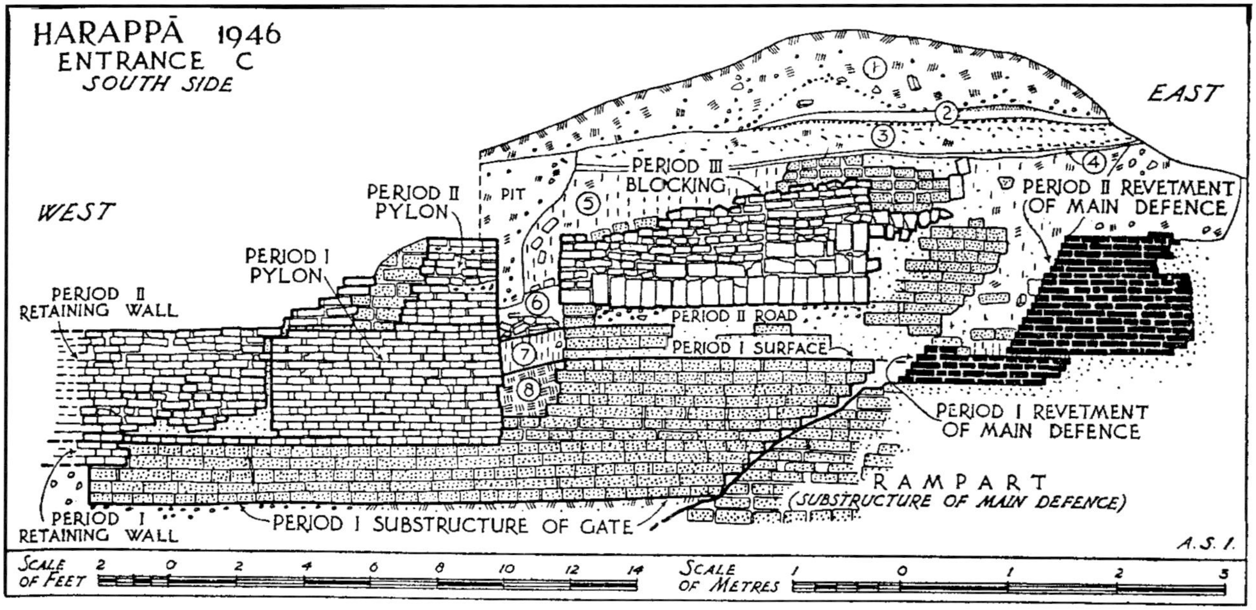

b

Figure 4.12 a–b) Harappa: Sections of defenses. Illustration used with the courtesy and permission of the ASI, *Harappa 1946: The Defenses and Cemetery R-37, Ancient India 3* (Wheeler 1947).

perimeter wall was at some point 14 m wide and included several phases of construction. No precise date of the initial construction was established, yet the pottery associated with the houses constructed against the interior face of the later wall [74–203] was assigned to period 3C. Also, more evidence was collected in support of the interpretation of the function of the wall as a bund against flooding (Meadow et al. 1999:13–14).

Mound E lies to the southeast of mound AB. Noticed and trenched in a limited fashion by Cunningham, this mound nonetheless remained unexcavated until 1987, when the HARP began active explorations on the mounds that were not given sufficient attention by the previous excavators. During the 1988 and 1989 seasons, perimeter walls made of large mud-bricks were unearthed in the northwestern corner of mound E. Some of these walls were associated with Early Harappan (Kot Dijian) ceramics. Dales and Kenoyer (1991:230) suggested that since the exterior face of these walls was eroded (and the interior face was not), the walls may have served as "retaining or revetment walls". The earliest mud-brick platforms of mound E were likely to be constructed during the Kot Diji phase as well. The remains of these platforms were detected on the western side of mound E. Further excavations revealed walls on southern, eastern and western sides of mound E. It was determined that the wall on the southern and southeastern sides was freestanding and reached a height of at least 2 m. The wall on the east side was possibly retaining. These walls were initially constructed during period 3A, rebuilt during period 3B and repaired during period 3C (Meadow and Kenoyer 1993:9, 36). The remains of a robbed baked brick wall were traced on the western side of mound E. The earliest phases of this wall were dated to Kot Diji phase. In addition, a thin curtain wall paralleling the perimeter wall was discovered on the east side of the mound E. The area between the curtain wall and the perimeter was filled with rubble (Meadow et al. 1997:4–6). Besides the walls, excavations on mound E revealed a city gate and a corner bastion, both located on the southern side of the mound (Meadow and Kenoyer 1993:9, 36).

To the east of mound E lies mound ET, the smallest of the four main mounds of Harappa. Excavations on this mound by the HARP revealed perimeter walls on the southern and western sides. The initial construction of the wall on the southwestern side was dated to ca. 2470 BC, period 3A of the HARP sequence. Excavations showed that in the Harappan period, this wall was likely to surround the entirety of mound ET (Meadow et al. 1995:7). Another important feature of fortifications excavated on mound ET is the Gateway Complex located in the southwestern corner, next to the southeastern corner of mound E. As excavated by the HARP, the complex consisted of a gateway, side rooms, a sewage drain, and a corbelled drain built in the middle of the gateway during its last structural phase (see Figure 4.13). Interestingly enough, the entrance street was quite narrow, measuring ca. 2.6 m in width. The gate underwent at least three stages of construction: the initial construction in period 3A, renovations in period 3C, and the blocking of the entrance in the last phase of the gate's use (Meadow et al. 1995:4–5).

Thus, recent excavations by the HARP have significantly altered our knowledge of the fortification system at Harappa. During the Kot-Diji phase, the site had already been divided into two distinct areas—mound AB and mound E. Whether these mounds were surrounded by walls completely and as a one-time event remain open questions. What is clear is that the earliest Kot Dijian fortifications were massive enough to require a significant consumption of labor and the existence of authoritative structures. By period III, Harappa had at least four fortified areas: mound AB, mound E, mound ET, and mound F. It is difficult to imagine that the construction and maintenance of this elaborate system of walls, platforms, and gates were motivated by practical reasons. Military defense, protection from floods, or even the necessity of having retaining structures would not have led to the creation of an internal segregarion; one must keep in mind that access to certain areas and communication between the areas (as in the case of the gate passage that was 2.6 m wide at the time of construction and was blocked during a later period) were restricted and controlled. Neither can one explain the three-dimensional layout of Harappa, reinforced by platforms of different heights, exclusively by erosions, a complicated structural history, or the necessity of protecting the site from floods. Explanations need to be sought in the sphere of ideology, social structure, and symbolism of space.

Figure 4.13 Artist's reconstruction of the southern gateway at Harappa, mound ET. Drawing by Chris Sloan, courtesy of J. M. Kenoyer, HARP.

Three-dimensional accentuation, internal demarcation, restriction of access, and the lack of communication are too impractical to be caused by utilitarian considerations. There may have been changes in the meaning and function of fortifications through time; the blocking of gates, disuse of the perimeter wall, and other structural modifications are indicative of such changes. The overall role that the walls, gates, and platforms played in the life of Harappa must have nonetheless been ideological.[9]

Authority

Archaeological evidence for authority appears at Harappa during period 2 (Kot Diji phase). Besides the construction of fortifications on mound E and mound AB, which in itself implies the existence of highly sophisticated authoritative structures, this period marks a number of important changes in settlement size, settlement layout, as well as several aspects of material culture. The main changes that are indicative of authority can be summarized as follows.

Settlement Size. The transition from period 1B to period 2 at Harappa marks a significant increase in size of the settlement. Although the deposits of period 1 were detected both on mound E and mound AB, there is no evidence that these deposits represented the same settlement. On the other hand, the size of the Kot Dijian settlement at Harappa, according to the estimates by HARP, was about 20 ha. and covered both mound AB and mound E.

Settlement Layout. A very important innovation of the Kot Dijian period at Harappa is the segregation of residential areas expressed in the emergence of distinct fortified sectors on mound AB and mound E. Whether this was a result of social stratification, of the idea of ritual purity, or of a combination of the two is an open question (Kenoyer 1989a). It is however clear that some unique social system based on a mix of heterarchical and hierarchical relations was responsible for such a layout. Another innovation of the Kot Diji phase at Harappa is the alignment of streets and houses in accordance with cardinal directions; walls and streets in several trenches on mound AB and mound E were oriented north–south and east–west. Moreover in the northwest corner of mound E, the layout of walls during the Harappan period was found to be similar to the one of the Kot Diji phase (Dales and Kenoyer 1992a:6; Meadow et al. 1999:60–66).

Architecture. Besides the construction of fortifications, the architectural innovations of the Kot Diji phase at Harappa include brick standardization and a general increase in structural activities. Mud-bricks with the measurements ratio of 1:2:4 have been found in the Kot-Dijian deposits on the northern side of mound AB (Meadow et al. 1999:6) as well as in the northwestern corner of mound E (Dales and Kenoyer 1991:240). Also, it has been suggested that clay used for the bricks in the northwestern corner of mound E was brought from different sources within the mound of Harappa (Dales and Kenoyer 1991:230, 235).

Seals and Writing. There is no evidence of a fully developed writing system during the Kot-Diji phase. There are nonetheless many inscribed sherds. For example, a step trench on the northern side of mound AB has produced several interesting sherds and seals that are inscribed with the early Indus script (Meadow et al. 1999:6).

Standardized Weights and Measures. At least one weight has been found in the stratigraphically sealed Kot Dijian context on mound AB (Meadow et al. 1999:3). Otherwise, evidence for the existence of standardized weights and measurements during the Kot Dijian phase at Harappa is still scarce.

Crafts. Craft technology and its implications for sociopolitical organization at Harappa has been the focus of much research by the HARP. It is clear that many important technologies that characterize craft and jewelry production at Harappa were developed long before the transition from the Kot Diji to the Harappa phase. For example, the beads of the Kot Diji phase at Harappa were made of blue glazed faience, steatite, pecked/drilled carnelian, banded agate, lapis lazuli, serpentine, and amazonite. Some of these materials constitute direct evidence for long-distance trade and exchange networks with areas as remote as Afghanistan and Gujarat (Meadow et al. 1999:7).

Kalibangan

Kalibangan is located in the District Hanumangarh, Northern Rajasthan, on the southern bank of the Ghaggar River (see Figure 4.14). It was excavated for nine seasons in 1961–1969 by the ASI under the directorship of B. B. Lal, B. K. Thapar, and J. P. Joshi.[10] The site rests on three mounds (KLB 1, KLB 2, and KLB 3) and has a perimeter of ca. 2 km. The sequence defined by Lal (2003b) consists of two periods separated by a break in occupation of approximately 100 years. Period I is Pre-Harappan and is characterized by a fortified settlement and an adjacent agricultural field, both located on mound KLB 1, which occupies an area of ca. 4.5 ha. (see Figure 4.15). Lal dates this period to ca. 3000–2700 BC. Period II is Mature Harappan and is characterized by two fortified sectors and an unfortified area, all lying on mounds KLB 1 and 2. Taken together, the fortified sectors occupy an area of ca. 11.5 ha. "With a margin of about fifty years on the earlier side and of about hundred years on the later," Lal (1997:245–246) dates this period to 2550 BC–2000 BC.

Fortifications

Kalibangan was surrounded by walls both in period I and period II. The structural history of these walls can be subdivided into three main phases: the initial construction in period I; the widening of the perimeter wall in period I; and the construction of a new system of walls, bastions, gates, and platforms in period II. The earliest wall built at the beginning of the Pre-Harappan period was made of mud-brick and was covered with plaster on both the external and internal side. The basal

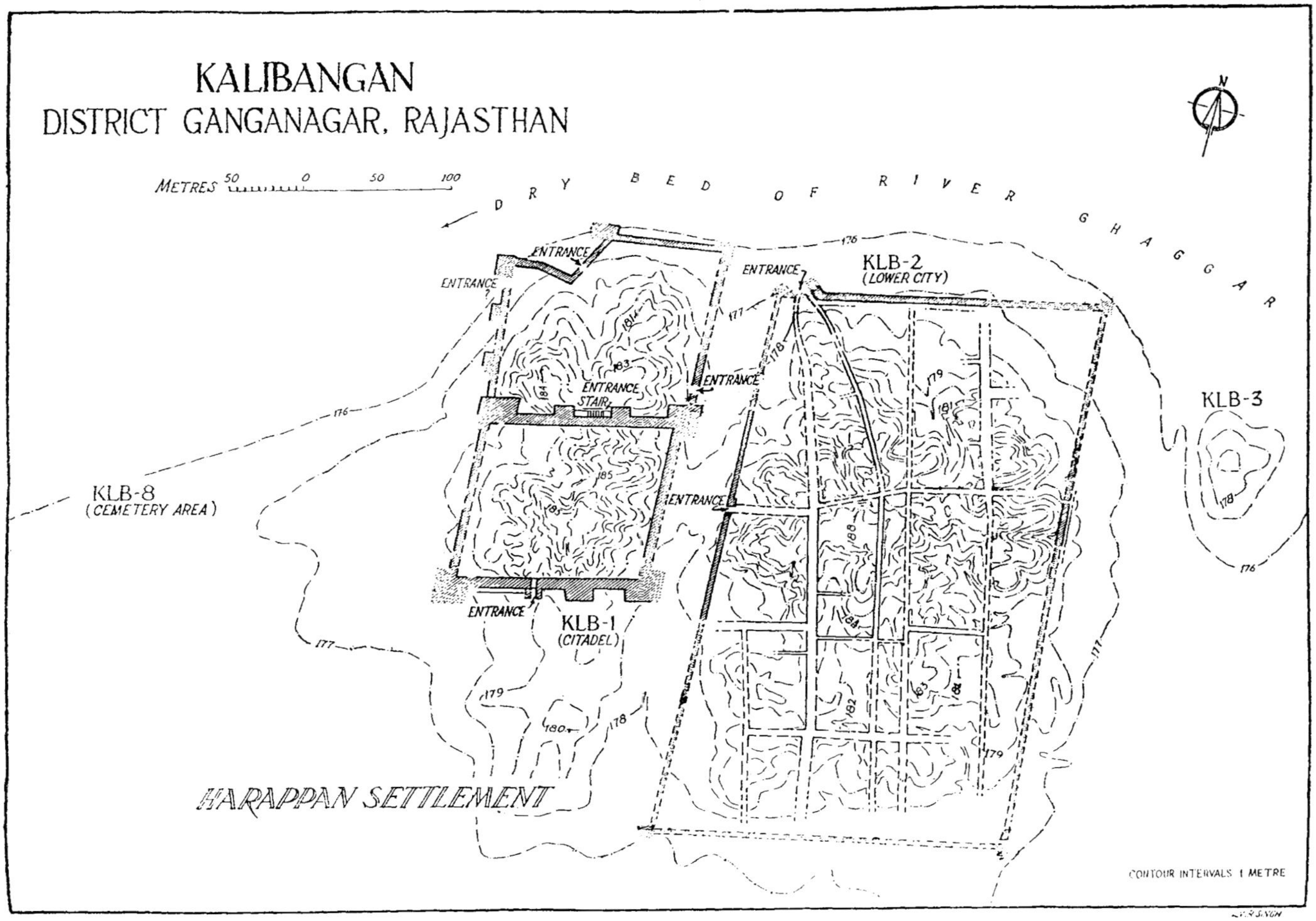

Figure 4.14 Kalibangan: Period II. Illustration used with the courtesy and permission of the ASI, *Indian Archaeology: A Review 1968–1969.*

width of this wall varied from 1.90 to 2.20 m. In the second phase, the perimeter wall was widened and attained the width of 3.60–4.20 m.[11] In the northwestern corner of the settlement there was an entrance (Joshi 2003b:52–53). In period II, fortifications were drastically modified. First, in response to the new layout, perimeter walls were built to encircle two distinct sectors: the western sector, built on top of the previously existing Early Harappan settlement; and the eastern sector, founded on the adjacent mound.[12] Second, the western sector was divided into southern and northern parts. The southern part was fortified heavier than the northern; it had thicker walls (up to 11 m), corner towers, salients, and several mud-brick platforms. Unlike Harappa and Mohenjo-Daro, the platforms were separated from the walls and had no traces of structures on top of them (Lal 1979:76–77). Thus, the beginning of the Harappan period was marked by the creation of a fundamentally new fortification system, which was likely to be the result of a new sociopolitical order. By dividing the space of Kalibangan into four distinct areas—the southern part of the western sector, the northern part of the western sector, the eastern sector, and the unfortified area south of the western sector—this fortification system performed a segregative function (see Figure 4.14) and reinforced the differences between areas of the site. The southern part of the western sector, for example, had mud-brick platforms and was heavily fortified. The eastern sector, being the largest, was regularly planned and had much domestic architecture. There are many possible ways of interpreting these differences. One thing however is clear. To protect the site from floods or military attack, there was no need to divide it in sectors. Consider the following. During the initial phase, the walls were too thin to protect the settlement from any significant threat. No evidence for flooding was established in association with stratigraphic levels. Despite the drastic nature of innovations that took place in the beginning of period II, there was a significant degree of continuity between the fortifications of Pre-Harappan and Harappan periods. For example, the walls built on the western mound during the Pre-Harappan period were fully incorporated into the fortification system of the Harappan period (IAR 1965–1966:51; Joshi 2003a:41; Lal 1979:76). Last but not least, south of the fortified area the excavators discovered the remains of an agricultural field (Lal 2003a). If the identification and dating of this field is correct, it is not unreasonable to suggest that one of the functions of perimeter walls in period I was to separate spaces between agricultural and domestic worlds. In sum, each of these traits points to ideological rather than utilitarian meanings of the fortification system at Kalibangan. Moreover, some elements of these meanings must have been shaped already during the Pre-Harappan period.

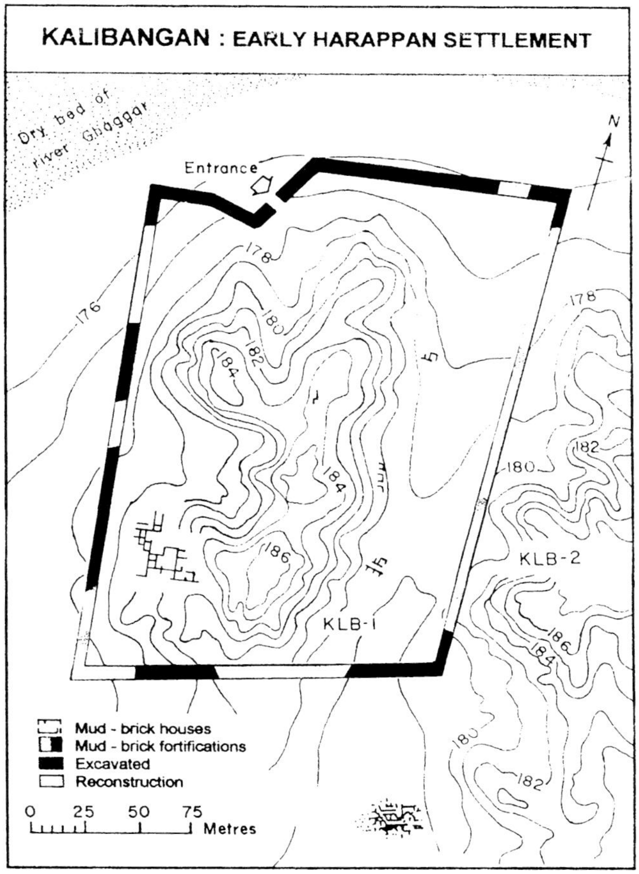

Figure 4.15 Kalibangan: Period I. Illustration used with the courtesy and permission of the ASI, *Memoirs of the Archaeological Survey of India 98, Excavations at Kalibangan: The Early Harappans, 1960–1969* (Lal et al. 2003).

Authority

Even a brief comparison of the main traits of period I with the main traits of period II shows that archaeological evidence for the emergence of authoritative structures in Kalibangan must be associated with the beginning of period II. The traits that are most indicative of social transformations in this period are the size of the settlement, layout, and architecture.

Settlement Expansion. In period I, settlement did not exceed 4.5 ha. including the fields. The area encircled by a mud-brick wall was roughly ca. 3 ha. By period II, the site significantly expanded and covered at least 13 ha. Whether the site grew in size during period I is unclear. As mentioned above, the excavators believe that the site was surrounded by a mud-brick wall from the very beginning of period I. Judging from currently available data, the most significant and abrupt expansion took place in the beginning of the second period.

Segregation and Planning. The excavators give contradictory information about the orientation of streets and houses of Pre-Harappan Kalibangan. Lal (2003c:27) maintains that they were "oriented roughly along the cardinal direction". J. P. Joshi (2003b:51) states that they "do not follow strict cardinal direction and run slightly oblique". Judging from the top plans provided in the recently published report (Lal et al. 2003:Figures 11–17), Joshi's comment seems to be more in line with actual evidence. The orientation of streets and walls of the Pre-Harappan period provides no evidence of regular planning. The layout of period II, on the other hand, is characterized by two important innovations, e.g., the division of the site in four distinct sectors and a grid-like layout introduced both in the western and eastern sectors.

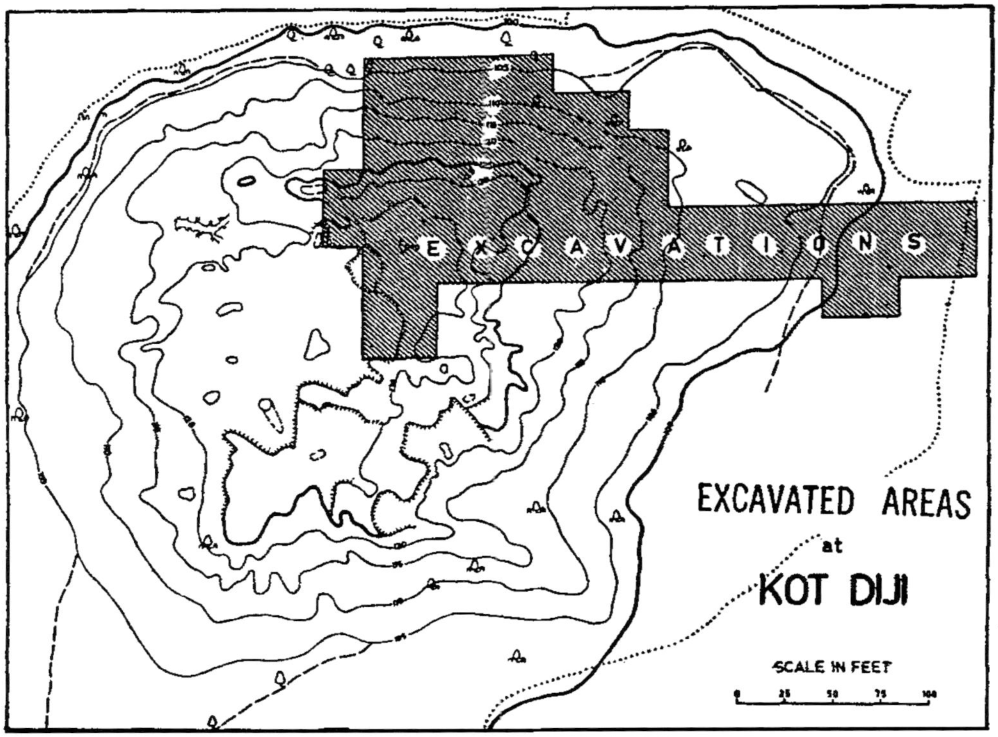

Figure 4.16 Kot Diji: Contour plan. Illustration used with the courtesy and permission of the Directorate General of Archaeology and Museums, Government of Pakistan, *Excavations at Kot Diji, Pakistan Archaeology 2* (Khan 1965).

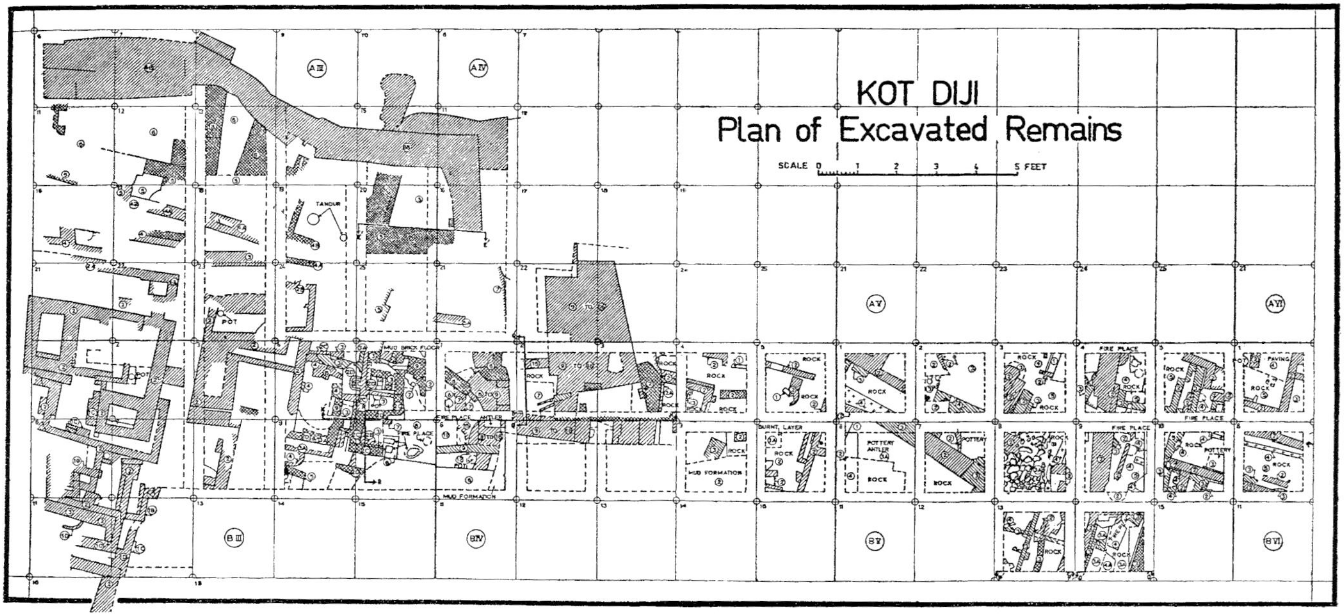

Figure 4.17 Kot Diji: Excavated areas. Illustration used with the courtesy and permission of the Directorate General of Archaeology and Museums, Government of Pakistan, *Excavations at Kot Diji, Pakistan Archaeology 2* (Khan 1965).

Architecture. The pre-Harappan architecture of Kalibangan is quite homogenous and modest. J. P. Joshi (2003b:51) justly characterizes it as oblique and lacking structural maturity. In period II, most traits of domestic architecture remain the same. Houses consisting of several rooms around the courtyard, the means of sanitation and the lack of noticeable differentiation in wealth are characteristic of both period I and period II (J. P. Joshi 2003b:53; Lal 1979:83–84). Nonetheless, two important innovations take place in the beginning of period II. First, the new system of fortifications is constructed. Second, four large mud-brick platforms are built in the southern part of the western sector.

That at least some of these transformations indicated changes in ideology and social structure was discussed by Lal. The division of the settlement into fortified sectors, according to Lal (1984:61), showed the emergence of a three-tier social hierarchy. Lal suggested that the northern part of the western sector was populated by religious leaders who conducted ritual ceremonies in the southern part of the western sector. The eastern sector was populated by "agriculturalist-cum-traders". The area south of the western sector was populated by "the working class which, although not living below the poverty-line, was certainly under-privileged for it was the only section of the society which was left "unfortified". To me, this interpretation appears both simplistic and inaccurate, for aside from the division into fortified sectors, which is clearly not sufficient for postulating the existence of a rigid social hierarchy, the homogeneity and relative modesty of architecture, artifacts, and burials point to the heterarchical rather than hierarchical structure of social organization. In one respect however, Lal is right. Regardless of a precise form of social organization at Kalibangan, it is clear that the changes that took place in the beginning of period II are indicative of major social transformations and, possibly, of the emergence of authoritative structures. Whether these structures were religious, political, or a combination of the two is an open question. Judging from the lack of evidence for conspicuous consumption by the elites, it is likely that these structures were part of a social system based predominantly on heterarchical rather than hierarchical relations.

Kot Diji

The site of Kot Diji is located next to the Pakistan national highway 15 mi south of Khairpur (see Figures 4.16–4.17). The mound on which the site lies occupies ca. 2.2 ha and measures ca. 600 x 400 ft (Khan 1965:13–14). Kot Diji was excavated by F. A. Khan on behalf of the Department of Archaeology, Government of Pakistan, in 1955–1957.[13] During two seasons of fieldwork, Khan excavated two large trenches: 160 x 40 ft and 160 x 140 ft. As the result of this project, Khan divided the site in two parts: the citadel or area A and the outer city or area B;[14] and defined two occupational periods: Kot-Dijian (Pre-Harappan) and Mature Harappan. There are only four radiocarbon dates for Kot Diji, which roughly place the Kot-Dijian levels in the middle and before the middle of the third millennium BC (Khan 1965:85). The stratigraphy of Kot Diji is complicated. Khan (1965:31–35) defined two separate sequences: one for area A and another one for area B. The sequence of area A consisted of 16 layers while the sequence of area B of only five. The correlation between these two sequences in Khan's original report was very confusing. In 1970, M. R. Mughal (1970:52) revised Khan's chronology and until today Mughal's correlation of the two sequences remains the main source on the periodization of Kot Diji.

Fortifications

The earliest fortification wall at Kot Diji was detected in a small sounding in area A in association with layer 15, the second layer (from the bottom) of the area A sequence. The remains of this wall were made of stone (Khan 1965:28). The later wall (see Figure 4.17)—not clear of which Kot Dijian layer—varied from 12 to 14 ft in height (Khan 1965:29). Its core was made of mud-brick yet the lower part was built with undressed limestone blocks set with mud mortar. In addition, it had some stone revetments and was strengthened with bastions. The bastion excavated in the northeastern corner measured 31.5 x 20 ft. Interestingly, this wall ceased to be used during the later phases of Kot Dijian period. Khan (1965:26) notes that the thick debris was formed on top of the wall in layer 8. Moreover, "a wide drain... lined with small stone blocks" going right over the fortifications wall was uncovered in layer 7. No perimeter walls were detected by Khan (1965:17–21) in the Harappan layers.

Fortifications at Kot Diji thus present a very interesting and obscure case. The case is interesting because fortifications were built very early, were used throughout the most of Kot Dijian period, and fell in disuse during the Harappan period. The case is obscure because the structural history of the perimeter wall, revetments, and bastions was poorly investigated. The excavator did not correlate structural modifications with the stratigraphic layers. Moreover, the wall was traced only in a limited area, and no entrance or gate was detected. As a result, the current data on fortifications at Kot Diji raise more questions than provide answers. The most intriguing among these questions is the function of the wall in light of its disuse in the final stages of Kot Dijian period. Khan's report and Mughal's revision of Khan's periodization provide a few helpful hints for addressing this question. First, both Khan's stratigraphy and Mughal's revised chronology show that the wall falls into disuse before area B is settled. The first structural activities above the wall are associated with layers 8 and 7 (Khan 1965:26), and the earliest layer of the area B correlates with the layer 7 of area A (Mughal 1970:52). In other words, the expansion of the settlement starts with structural activities above the walls (layer 8) and leads to the establishment of the new residential area beyond the walls (layer 7). For the understanding of the function, this means that the wall never divided area A and area B; by the time area B was established the wall was no longer in use. Second, judging from the expansion of the site, new patterns in architecture, and new traits of material culture, the most efflorescent period at Kot Diji begins with layer 7 (Khan 1965:25–26). This means that the wall was functional during the formative portion of the Kot Dijian period and dysfunctional during its cultural peak. Third, the disuse of the wall has no clear parallels in material culture. If the wall had played an important role in the sociopolitical life of the community, one would expect that its degeneration would have been accompanied by similar changes in material culture, settlement layout, or architectural pattern. The archaeological record, however, displays the opposite; the layers that follow the degeneration of the wall show the gradual sophistication of sociopolitical complexity.

The least that these three observations show is that the sociopolitical or religious segregation that characterized fortifications of other Harappan settlements was not important at Kot Diji. Paradoxically, the sophistication of the sociopolitical organization made it possible for the fortification system to degenerate. This could be possible under many scenarios. The fortification system at Kot Diji could be built as a symbolic demarcation of the site's border, as a support for the houses located on the interior of the wall, or as a protection from military attacks.

Authority

Khan viewed social organization of Kot Diji as a direct reflection of its bipartite layout and discontinuous cultural history. With regard to the layout, Khan (1965:15) noted:

> The Kot Diji site consists of two parts: one comprising the citadel area where lived the ruling classes; and the other, the outer part of the city, which must have been inhabited by the artisan classes.

With regard to the break in cultural sequence, Khan (1965:22) offered another straightforward explanation:

> This prominent and clearly marked burnt layer strongly suggests that the last occupation level of the early settlers (that is, the Kot Dijians) was violently disturbed, and probably totally burnt and destroyed. The sudden disaster was indeed connected with the movement of newcomers into this part of the country.

Evidently, these comments are based on the erroneous understanding of the site's layout and cultural history, both of which need to be reconsidered prior to any discussions on social organization and authority. As I noted above, the wall was not functional at the time when "the outer city" was established. Moreover, located on the same mound, the areas A (the citadel) and B (the lower city) were neither separated from one another nor displayed any significant differences. Distinguishing the two distinct sectors such as "the citadel" and "the outer city" was therefore groundless. Needless to explain, the use of the layout as evidence for social division, under this scenario, was also erroneous.

As far as the periodization is concerned, the division into two periods—Kot Dijian and Harappan—is too simple to reflect even those few cultural changes that were recorded during the excavation (Khan 1965:31–35; see Table 4.6). According to the existing periodization, conflagration marks the end of period I, while period II begins with the reoccupation of the site and the spread of the Mature Harappan pottery. Khan thus sees only one turning point in the cultural history of Kot Diji; that is a break in occupation stratigraphically associated with layers 4 and 3A. In my view, at least two more turning points can be distinguished. The first additional turning point is stratigraphically associated with layer 7 and is defined by several transformations; i.e., the site grows in size, fortifications are no longer in use, the new architectural patterns emerge, and a number of typically Harappan artifacts appear. The second additional turning point is stratigraphically associated with layer 2 and is marked by the abandonment of area B. Both turning points are significant enough to divide the sequence into more periods. The sequence thus should consist of the four periods, each defined by a distinctive set of traits and tied to the concrete stratigraphic layers of area A (see Table 4.7).

Now turning to authority, one faces an interesting situation. Archaeologically, Pre-Harappan periods seem to provide more evidence for social complexity and authority than Harappan periods. In period I, evidence for authority is provided by the structural history of fortifications. Even though specific phases of this history are very poorly known, it is clear that the construction of massive walls, bastions, and revetments must have required a significant organization of labor. In period II, the formation of authoritative structures can be envisioned as part of the general growth of social complexity. I believe, this period presents the cultural apogee of ancient Kot Diji—the settlement expands in size, architecture becomes more durable and socially differentiated, and the new cultural elements emerge. Undoubtedly, these changes were accompanied by the sophistication of social organization and possibly the emergence of new social order. The new social order in its turn made it possible to no longer maintain massive fortifications. Somewhere in this picture there must be a place for authority, the scale and nature of which remain an open question. The next two periods nevertheless display little evidence for the growth of social complexity. The site gradually decreases in size, architectural remains are minimal, and despite the emergence of the Indus script there is very little evidence for its use at the site. To conclude, Kot Diji appears to have been an important site during the Pre-Harappan periods and the

Table 4.6

Major cultural transformations at Kot-Diji (after Khan 1965)

Major Cultural and Structural Changes	Layers
Beginning of occupation in area A	16
Construction of the first fortification wall	15
Construction of revetments and bastions	?
Emergence of an architectural pattern characterized by stone foundations and mud-brick superstructures	7
Degeneration of fortifications	8–7
Expansion of the settlement	7
Emergence of the typically Harappan objects	7
Conflagration and the abandonment of the site	4–3A
Reoccupation of the site	3A
Spread of Mature Harappan pottery	3A
Abandonment of area B	2
End of occupation	1

Table 4.7

Alternative Periodization of Kot-Diji

Period	Stratigraphic Layers	Defining Characteristics
I	16–8	Mud-brick and occasional stone architecture; construction, renovation and degeneration of the fortification system; Kot Dijian pottery; and Kot Dijian assemblage of artifacts
II	7–4	Expansion of the settlement; complete degeneration of fortifications; emergence of the new architectural; pattern; stone foundations with mudbrick superstructures; coexistence of the Harappan and Kot Dijian elements in pottery and other traits of material culture
III	3A–2	Mature Harappan material culture; no fortifications; minimal architectural remains
IV	2–1	Abandonment of the area B; Mature Harappan material culture; minimal architectural remains

site of little significance at the time of the efflorescence of the Indus civilization. If authority was indeed present at any time at Kot Diji, it must have been present during period II of my periodization, or the later part of period I according to Khan's periodization.

Lothal

Lothal is located between the Bhogawo and Sabarmati Rivers, 80 km southwest of Ahmadabad, Gujarat. It was discovered in 1954 by S. R. Rao during his exploration of the Sabarmati River. From 1955 to 1962, Rao conducted systematic excavations at Lothal[15] and defined a sequence of two periods, both of which were of the Mature Harappan cultural affiliation (Rao 1979b:24–36). These two periods in turn consisted of five structural phases, each subdivided into two or three sub-phases (see Table 4.8). Based on comparative stratigraphy and a small number of radiocarbon samples, the dates of the phases (Rao 1979b:37–46) are tentative and should be used with caution. Consider the following. None of the dates of the second series confirms the dates of the first series (Rao 1979b:39), while the dates for phases IV and V vary from place to place in the same report (Rao 1979b:37–46). Also, it is not unlikely that Lothal was occupied long before 2450 BC; the first signs of human occupation were associated with a local Chalcolithic culture, which both preceded and overlapped with the Mature Harappan cultural phenomenon in Gujarat (Rao 1979b:53–70).

Fortifications

A system of fortifications at Lothal consists of a mud-bund, a mud-brick perimeter wall (Rao calls it "peripheral wall") and several platforms built of mud and mud-brick (see Figures 4.18–4.19). The initial mud-bund, 52 ft wide at the base and 42 ft at the extant top, was reportedly built in phase 1, at the time when Lothal was a small pre-Harappan settlement (Rao 1979b:85). In phase 2, the mud-bund was reinforced by a mud-brick wall. The height of this wall varied from 6 to 8 ft and the width varied from 42 to 72 ft. The northern and western sides of the wall were reportedly revetted from outside. Judging from Rao's excavations, there were no gates or bastions. Most platforms were built during phase IIA, allegedly as a response to the massive flood that destroyed much of the previously existing settlement around 2350 BC. Since the site was excavated on a large horizontal scale, Rao (1979b:115) was able to investigate

Table 4.8

Periodization of Lothal (after Rao 1979b)

Period	Phase	Approximate Dates
A	I	2450–2350 BC
	II	2350–2200 BC
	III	2200–2000 BC
	IV	2000–1900 BC
B	V	1900–1600 BC

the technology and structural history of these platforms. The first layer was typically made of rammed kankar, clay, or earth. The top layer was laid with several courses of mud-bricks. Most platforms underwent several stages of reconstruction. In sum, by period IIA the entirety of the excavated settlement stood on terraced platforms and was surrounded by a mud-bund with a mud-brick wall on top. The total enclosed area measured ca. 550 m x 365 m (Rao 1979b:85).

As far as the function of this fortification system is concerned, Rao (1979b:87) asserts that both the system of platforms and the wall were built to protect the site from floods, rather than from military attacks. I believe Rao is right in saying that the element of defense was either minimal or did not play any role at all. Indeed, the shape and height of the wall, as well as the lack of bastions and gates convincingly demonstrate that military defense was not the primary concern for the people who had these fortifications built during phase IIA. Yet I also believe it is too simplistic to explain the construction of fortifications at Lothal exclusively as a necessity to protect the site from floods. In this respect, I would suggest taking into consideration the following traits. Firstly, there is only one entrance to the space enclosed by the fortifications at least until phase III. This entrance is located in the south of the site behind the so-called Acropolis. Rao (1973:66) describes the Acropolis as "a formidable fortress, in the shadow of which stood the Lower Town providing shelter to the ordinary citizens". If Rao were right and the ruler or a group of rulers indeed lived on the Acropolis, the commoners, who according to Rao lived in the Lower Town, would have to bypass the residence of the ruler and the warehouse every single time they needed to enter or exit the city. Obviously, such a scenario is unlikely. Secondly, the entrance has no traces of a gate. Instead, it presents a plain opening in the mud-brick wall. Either as protection from floods or as military defense, such an opening would have been very ineffective. Thirdly, all buildings in the fortified area stand on platforms of different height. For example, the Acropolis stands on platforms rising ca. 12 ft above the ground level (Rao 1979b:86). The adjacent block A, or as Rao (1979b:88) called it "the bazaar part of the Lower Town" stands on platforms that on average are only 2 ft to 4 ft in height.

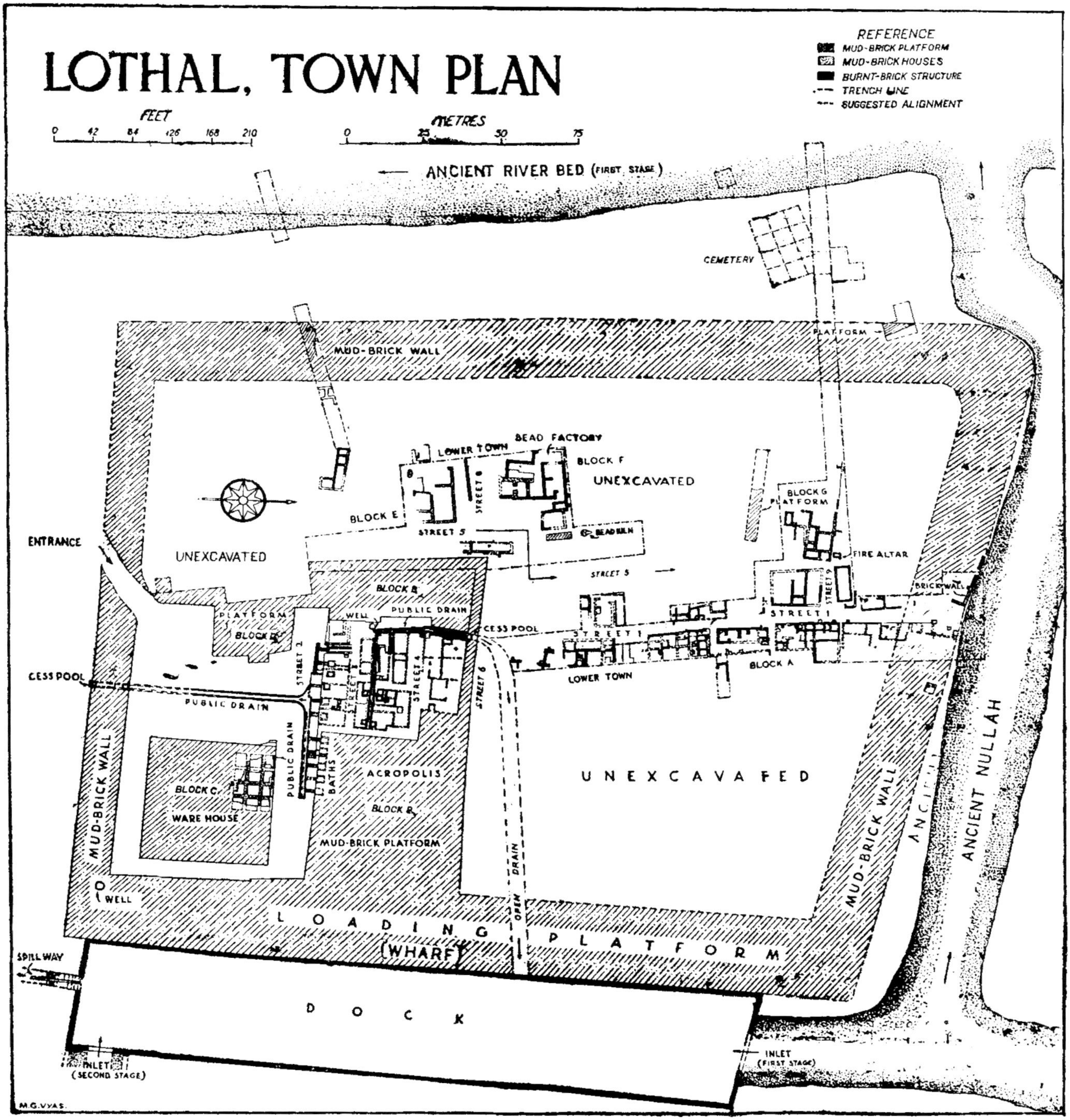

Figure 4.18 Lothal. Illustration used with the courtesy and permission of the Asia Publishing House, *Lothal and the Indus Civilization* (Rao 1973).

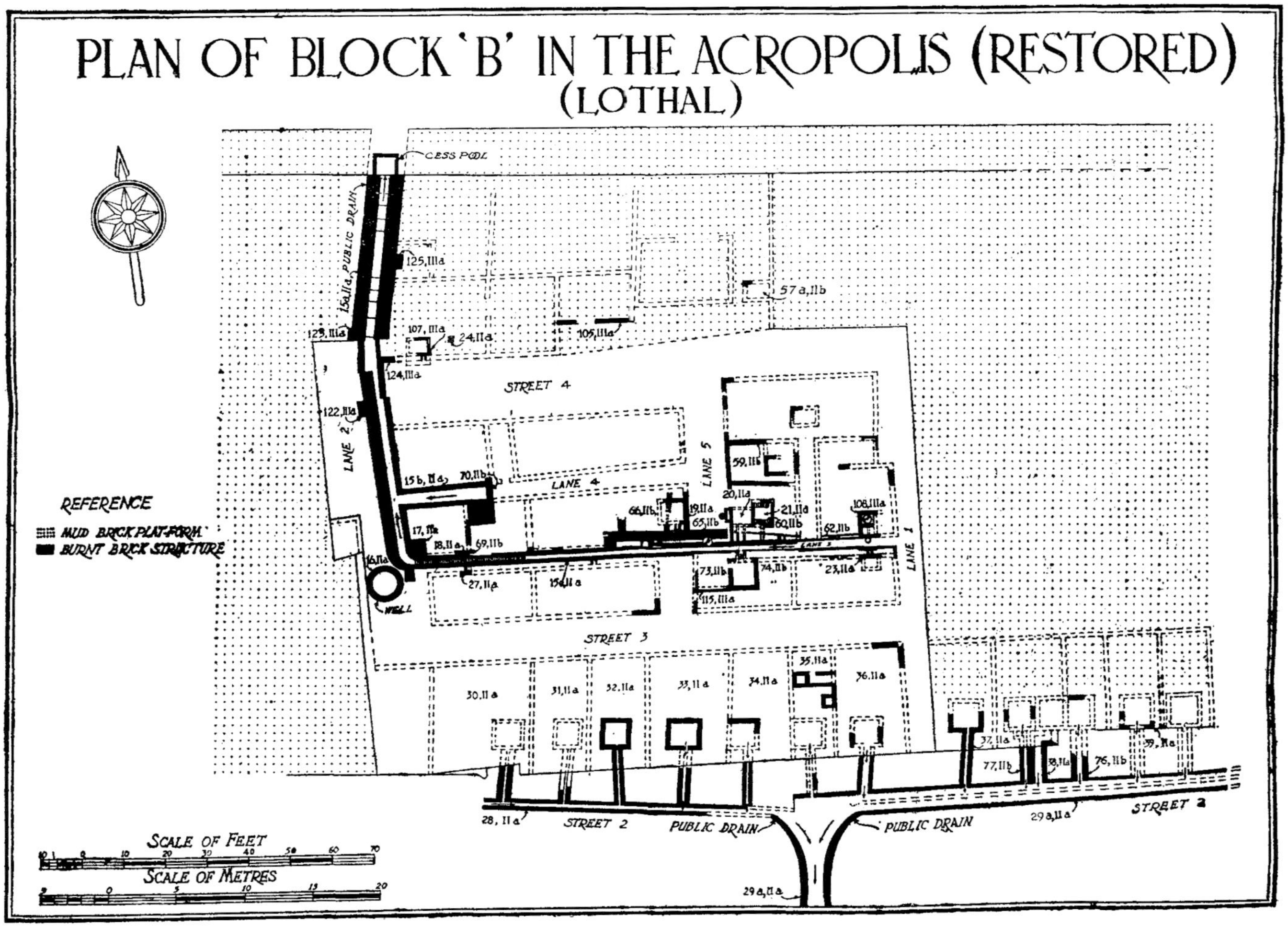

Figure 4.19 Lothal Acropolis. Illustration used with the courtesy and permission of the Asia Publishing House, *Lothal and the Indus Civilization* (Rao 1973).

The desire to protect the city from floods is an understandable cause for the construction of platforms, yet it is clearly insufficient for explaining why the height of platforms was different in different parts of town. Lastly, some platforms did not have structures on top of them. Rao (1979b:111, 113, 115) calls such platforms "peripheral" and seems to believe that originally they had superstructures, yet in the course of time these superstructures were completely eroded. For example, block D is represented by a platform measuring 96 x 80 ft in size and 9 ft in height (Rao 1979b:115). This platform is located across from the warehouse, next to the ruler's residence. It was initially built in phase IIA and underwent several stages of reconstruction. Based on its massive size and strategic position, Rao (1973:66) suggests that this platform supported a "public building no less important than the warehouse". In a similar way, a significant part of the platform that underlies the alleged warehouse itself (block C) is empty. Rao (1979b:111–113) seems to believe that originally the entirety of this platform was covered by a superstructure that later eroded. Obviously, Rao's interpretations are hypothetical and no archaeological evidence has been so far obtained to verify them. The fact remains that some of the platforms on the Acropolis are either completely or partially empty and have no remains of structures on top. A similar situation was observed during the excavation of Kalibangan, and Lal interpreted this as a sign of ritual activities (B. B. Lal 1984).

Taken together these traits lead to an interesting observation. Aside from serving as protection from floods, the fortification system at Lothal must have had a non-utilitarian function. The lack of entrances may indicate the intentional restriction of access due to the existence of social segregation. Great variability in the height of platforms points to the symbolism of three-dimensional space and the use of elevations for ideational purposes. Last not the least, the circumference of the settlement by a mud-brick wall may reflect the desire to demarcate the ideologically significant space of the inner city and to separate it from the adjacent areas.

Authority

The excavator of Lothal, S. R. Rao, had a rather clear vision of the sociopolitical situation in Lothal. According to Rao (1973:62), Lothal was governed by the ruler who lived on the Acropolis in block B. Explaining the choice of location for the ruler's mansion, Rao (1973:56) noted:

> ...an impressive structure had to be erected for accommodating the ruler in such a vantage position that he could supervise the transactions of the warehouse on the one hand and the movement of ships in the dockyard on the other.

The ruler, according to Rao, was responsible for the important architectural modifications and the daily functioning of the community. As Rao (1979b:227) asserted, "the ruler derived his authority not from any religious sanctions but from the willing co-operation of the common people... He provided civic amenities in the Acropolis as well as the Lower Town and enforced regulations strictly...". During phase IV, Rao believed, the authority of the ruler—at this point, Rao (1979b:228) called him a merchant-prince—waned following a general decline of Lothal. The Acropolis at this time, according to Rao, was occupied by artisans and craftsmen (Rao 1979b:228). As far as the location of the ruler's residence is concerned, Rao apparently relied on the fact that block B stood on the highest platform and the rooms unearthed on it were significantly bigger than the rooms of the lower town. As far as the ruler's functions and various mechanisms of power are concerned, Rao's statements and assumptions are purely speculative and there is no way to test them against the existing archaeological record. Also, it is unclear how Rao arrived at the conclusion that the structural remains of block B represented one large mansion instead of several separate houses.

Leaving aside Rao's speculations, one must admit that the archaeological record of Lothal is currently mute with regard to the form and mechanisms of authority. What it provides enough data for is the emergence of authority *per se*, and the correlation of its emergence with the relative chronology of Lothal. Phase I of the Lothal's cultural sequence is very poorly known. To a large degree, it may be due to the fact that the remains of phase I are hidden under the mud-brick platforms and architecture of phase II. On several occasions Rao (1979b:88, 100, 111) manages to trace the remains of mud-brick walls and even possibly of a mud-brick platform in the context of phase I. Otherwise, the remains of phase I are too fragmentary to display the level of complexity indicative of a strong authority. The clear evidence for authority emerges in Lothal with the transition to phase II A. Besides the construction of a fortification system discussed above, this phase is characterized by a number of drastic changes in settlement size, settlement layout, and the various aspects of material culture.

Settlement Size. On one hand, it seems reasonable to assume that during phase I the settlement was smaller than the fortified settlement of phase II; Rao (1979b:85, 88, 100, 111) reports that the deposits of phase I were detected only in parts of blocks A, B and C, located mostly on the southern side of the fortified settlement underneath the Acropolis and the Warehouse. On the other hand, one must remember that the fortified settlement was quite small. As mentioned above, the total area enclosed by peripheral walls occupied an area of ca. 20 ha. Importantly, the circumference of the initial mud-bund was identical with the circumference of the later peripheral wall. In fact, Rao believes that the wall was built on top of the mud-bund. If Rao's structural analysis is correct, and the mud-bund was initially built during phase I and then strengthened by a mud-brick wall during phase IIA, the enclosed settlement of phase I must have been identical in size to the enclosed settlements of all the later phases. This of course does not mean that Lothal maintained the same size in all the periods. Evidence for the settlement expansion must be sought in the areas lying on the outer sides of the peripheral walls. Although no thorough survey of these areas has so far been conducted, Rao (1979b:85) reports two signs of occupation; the remnants of a brick structure at a distance of 1,000 ft south of the southern peripheral wall, and the scatter of pottery and bricks at a distance of 1,500 ft southeast of the tank. If any further research takes place in Lothal, it would be very important to determine the actual size of Lothal during phase IIA. At this point, I hypothetically suggest that during phase I, Lothal was the size of the fortified area. By the beginning of phase IIA, it expanded beyond the previous circumference, and consequently a mud-brick wall was built on top of the mud-bund.

Settlement Layout. The transition to phase IIA significantly altered the layout of Lothal. First, through the construction of terraced platforms, three-dimensionality was introduced into the landscape of the fortified settlement. Second, a grid-like layout of streets and houses was established. Third, the fortified area was subdivided in sectors.

Architecture. All main public structures of Lothal were built in phase IIA. These included the so-called "dock", "warehouse", and the buildings of Block B on the Acropolis. Also, many new architectural elements were introduced; different types of baths and drains, corbelled roofs, headers and stretchers, buttresses, cesspools, and the like.

Other changes and innovations include the introduction of new industries, the establishment of a cemetery on the outer side of the perimeter wall and the appearance of exported materials that indicate the development of long-distance trade. In sum, the greatest advantage of Lothal's cultural sequence is that all these changes can be placed in a relatively short period of time; for regardless of whether the absolute chronology of Lothal is accurate, phase IIA took no longer than 50 years. The emergence of all the aforementioned traits within such a short period of time unequivocally implies the presence and proper functioning of the sophisticated mechanisms of authority. Whether this authority was of local origin or the result of the expansion of Harappan culture from the west cannot be definitely answered at this point. It is my impression however that the emergence and genesis of the Harappan authority at Lothal by phase IIA was a result of both local and foreign developments; for both Harappan and local cultural traits characterized archaeological record of phase IIA.

Mohenjo-Daro

Mohenjo-Daro is located in the Larkana District, Sind, Pakistan (see Figure 4.20). The history of archaeological research—at this ultimately the most famous site of Bronze Age South Asia—has been discussed in detail elsewhere (Jansen 1991, 1993a; Possehl 1999:70–83). In short, there were four main archaeological projects at this site. From 1922 to 1932, Banerjee, Marshall, and Mackay carried out the first and most extensive excavations. From 1934 to 1936, Moneer undertook a smaller excavation on the mound, later called after his name. In 1950, Wheeler took on the excavation on the Stupa mound. In 1964–1965, Dales excavated on HR mound. Finally, in the 1970s and 1980s, a joint German-Italian team carried out a systematic survey and recording project at Mohenjo-Daro without actual excavations.[16] Despite all this research, the stratigraphy and cultural history of Mohenjo-Daro are poorly known. Marshall and Mackay who exposed almost everything of what we see today on the surface at Mohenjo-Daro did not pay much attention to the internal relative chronology. Marshall was, however, the first to define a consecutive stratigraphic sequence. Based on the three 40 ft deep trenches dug in the Stupa courtyard, he defined seven strata and three periods: the late (strata 1–3); the intermediate (strata 4–6); and the early (stratum 7). It was clarified that this sequence was based exclusively on the stratification of structural remains, not on the antiquities found in association with these remains (Marshall 1931:10). Mackay (1938:XIV–XVI) generally followed this sequence, yet slightly modified the correlation of strata and periods. One must remember that both sequences were based on the preconceived ideas and was not meant to reflect major cultural or sociopolitical changes. Ironically, Vats (1940) who served as a supervisor at Mohenjo-Daro defined a very similar sequence for Harappa. Wheeler was very critical of Marshall's approach to chronology, and his own excavations on the Stupa mound resulted in the formulation of several sequences. The first sequence was originally published by Wheeler (1962:44) and consisted of five phases. The second sequence was recorded by Alcock (1986:499) and

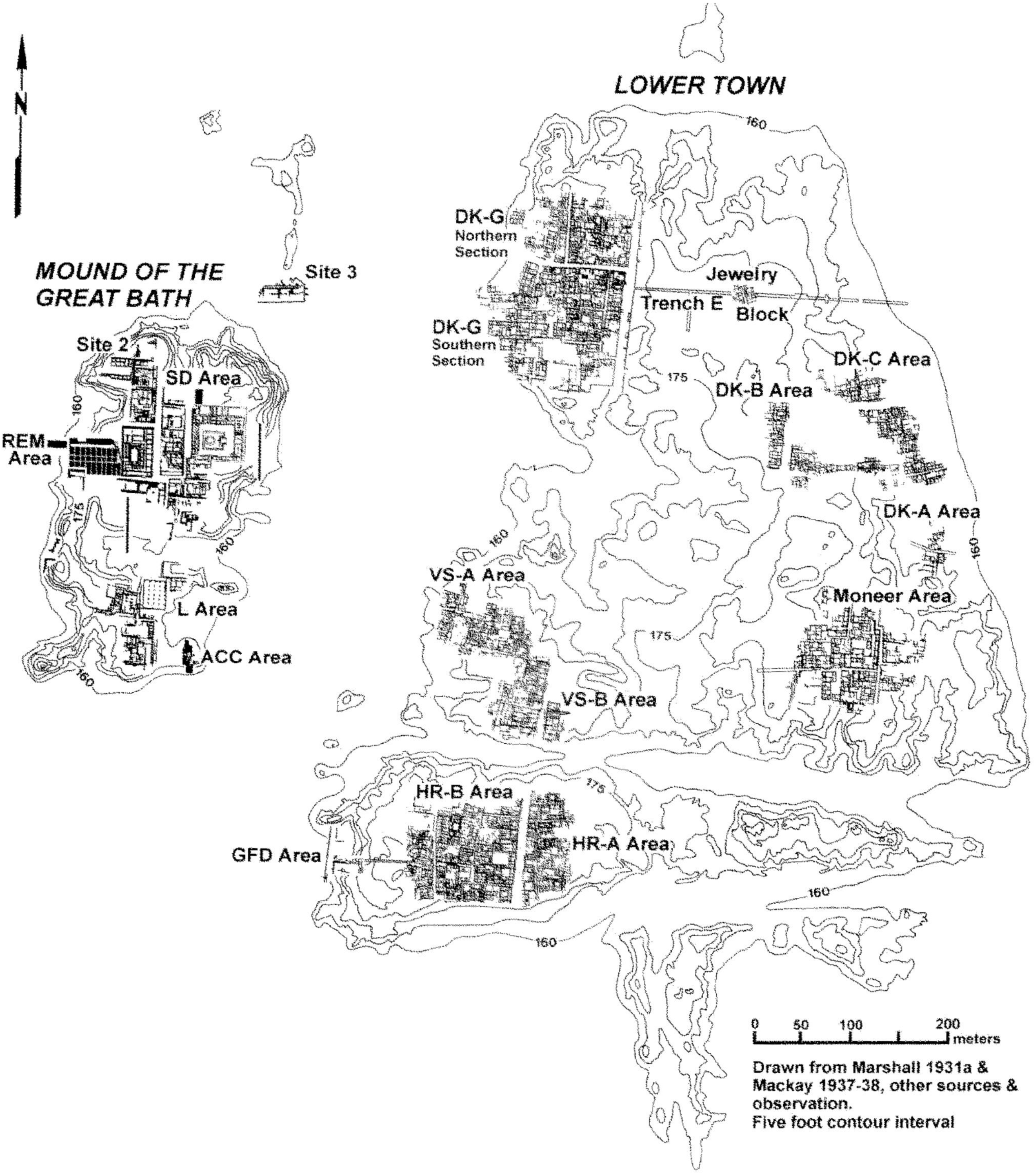

Figure 4.20 Mohenjo-Daro. Illustration used with the courtesy and permission of Gregory L. Possehl, *Indus Civilization: A Contemporary Perspective* (Possehl 2002c).

had 11 phases. The third sequence was formulated on the basis of the Trench ACC (supervised by A. H. Dani) and comprised seven periods (see Alcock 1986:501). Based exclusively on the pottery, Alcock (1986) formulated yet another, the fourth, sequence which consisted of four stages. The stratigraphy of Dales' excavation was never fully published, yet the analyzed pottery was placed in a temporal frame, and grouped into three phases: phase A, phase B and late phase B (Dales and Kenoyer 1986a:466–486). The defining characteristics of each of these phases had cultural implications and were possibly connected with the changes in structural activities. Finally, the German-Italian project added yet another perspective to the internal chronology of Mohenjo-Daro. Based on the reconsideration of all the previous chronologies, Franke-Vogt (1993:95) distinguished two phases: the earlier and the later; while Jansen (1991:163–165) defined five periods: Pre-platform period, Platform period, Urban period (subdivided into two phases: Mature Urban and Later Urban), Post-Urban period, and Kushana Urban period. As the main focus of the German-Italian project was the recording of the existing data rather than new excavations, no absolute chronology was defined. Instead, each of the periods was characterized by a large number of structural activities and technical innovations. Moreover, period 0 (Pre-Platform) was defined exclusively on the analogies with the Early Harappan occupations at other sites; Mohenjo-Daro so far did not produce any evidence for human occupations before the Mature Harappan period (Franke-Vogt 1994). Being most recent and based on a thorough review of the large amount of data, Jansen's periodization seems to be the most accurate. My further analysis will rely mostly on this periodization.

Fortifications

Mackay (1931:282) excavated at Mohenjo-Daro for many years and did not find any fortifications, yet he still believed that the burnt-brick perimeter walls existed at some point and were later demolished by brick-robbers. The desire to find fortifications must have been among the main reasons that brought Wheeler to Mohenjo-Daro as well. Having spotted the massive walls on mound AB at Harappa, Wheeler possibly wanted to repeat his success on the "citadel" of Mohenjo-Daro. It is therefore not surprising that after excavating for only one season, Wheeler claimed to have discovered the remains of fortifications in the southeastern corner of the Stupa mound (Alcock 1986). Later research at Mohenjo-Daro showed that Wheeler's conclusions were premature. No walls, bastions, or any other traditional forms of defenses were detected at Mohenjo-Daro. Instead, Mohenjo-Daro was found to stand on grandiose earthen platforms encircled by retaining walls and possibly a moat (see Figure 4.21). Taken together, these structures formed a unique fortification system that encompassed the entirety of the Stupa mound and the excavated areas of the Lower City.

Banerji, Marshall and Mackay were the first to spot platforms and retaining walls under the Stupa mound. In the final excavation report, Marshall (1931:I.125) recorded that the space between the sixth and the seventh strata which, according to his own periodization, marked the transition from the early to the intermediate periods, was "occupied... by crude brick or alluvial mud heaped up artificially so as to form an immense platform over the whole of this stupa area, as well as over a big expanse of ground to the north of it...". On the eastern and western side of the Stupa mound, Banerjee and Marshall unearthed portions of a retaining wall (Marshall (1931:I.125). The illustrations and plates included in Marshall's final report fully support this information (Plates XVIII, XXI). Wheeler's deep trench on the western side of the Stupa mound reconfirmed the conclusions of Banerjee, Marshall, and Mackay. Different versions of Wheeler's section were published and discussed by Wheeler (1962:44), Alcock (1986:499), and Jansen (1987:12). Having compared these sections, Jansen suggested distinguishing at least three stages of the mud-brick bund construction: the lowest part at 45 m a.m.s.l. or lower; the upper inner extension above 45 m a.m.s.l.; and the upper outer extension. Owing to Jansen's research, it is clear that the structures of the Stupa mound rest on a gigantic platform filled with alluvial sediments and encircled by a retaining wall. Jansen (1987:13) estimates that the amount of clay and sediments required for the construction of this platform was ca. 400,000 m^3.

The lower city also stands on a platform. Mackay was the first to trace this platform in several locations under the DK area. For example, on one occasion Mackay (1938:I.42–43) noted the presence of a "very thick mud-brick platform", which did not have any objects in it and was constructed in several phases. Mackay however admitted that it was very difficult to distinguish any precise structural phases in the construction of this platform and that the densely built architecture of later periods would not allow the exposure of this platform for further investigations (Mackay 1938:I.42–43). A new light on the structural history and functions of platforms and revetments in the Lower City was shed by remote sensing, surface stripping, and core drilling conducted in the HR east area by the German-Italian project (see Leonardi 1988). It was established that the entirety of the HR east area stood on a massive mud-brick platform encircled by a revetment wall. The platform was initially built in the beginning of the urban phase and underwent several reconstructions. Following Leonardi's presentation of data, one can distinguish at least five anthropic phases in the structural history of the platform complex: 1) the initial construction of the platform; 2) the construction of a mud-brick wall on the edges of the platform; 3) the filling of the gaps between the wall and the mud-brick platform; 4) the construction of a mud-brick structure next to the mud-brick wall; and 5) the construction of the baked-brick revetment (Leonardi 1988:56). Given the extent of the platform, it is not unreasonable to suggest that similar patterns of structural development characterized other parts of the lower city.

In summary, it appears that all the excavated areas of Mohenjo-Daro stood on artificial platforms surrounded by retaining walls and revetments. Moreover, as Jansen (1987:13) proposed, the city could have been surrounded by a ditch, resulting from the digging required for the construction of the platforms. Altogether, these structures formed a complex fortification system that may have carried at least three functions: 1) it protected the city from floods; 2) it divided the city into distinct urban sectors; and 3) it symbolically elevated the Stupa mound. Judging from recent investigations by the German-Italian project, protection from floods must have been a key concern at the initial stages of the construction of the platforms. Yet as Jansen himself points out, it would be too simplistic to view this unique fortification system exclusively as a response to the environment. The internal layout of mounds and the structural history of the investigated platforms show that symbolic and segregative considerations played at least an equally important role

Figure 4.21 Mohenjo-Daro: Remains of the eastern retaining wall of the Stupa mound (photo by the author).

in the construction of platforms, retaining walls, and revetments. In order to protect the city from floods, there was no need either to raise the Stupa mound above other areas of Mohenjo-Daro, or to demarcate residential areas by retaining walls and revetments (see, for example, Figure 4.21). Neither was there a practical need to renovate the retaining wall on mound HR east at the time of urban and technological decay (Leonardi 1988:64). The elevation of the Stupa mound thus must have been caused by symbolic or religious reasons, i.e., the desire to emphasize the ritual, political, or social significance of this place. The construction of retaining walls, on the other hand, could be the result of urban segregation based on the professional or social affiliation of its residents. Taken as a whole, the system of platforms, retaining walls, and revetments was the means of demarcations between the inner and outer local worlds of Mohenjo-Daro; by acting as such, it served as one of the definitive characteristics of the urban nature of this city.

Authority

There are at least two possible scenarios for the early history of Mohenjo-Daro. According to the first scenario, Mohenjo-Daro was a founder's city. This means that it was built in a short period of time—as Jansen (1987:15) believes in no longer than eighty years—by specialists who were well familiar with the environment and had prior technical experience. The key elements of architectural layout and building technology, according to this scenario, were planned well in advance and the city was basically built on an empty or abandoned spot (Jansen 1994:271–272). This scenario assumes the arrival of population and specialists from some other place. According to the second scenario, Mohenjo-Daro had an Early Harappan settlement. Around 2600–2500 BC, this settlement expanded and underwent radical changes in its layout, architecture, and ideology. This scenario implies that it was the local population of Mohenjo-Daro that was primarily responsible for the changes and that most technological and ideological prerequisites for the emergence of Mohenjo-Daro had been acquired prior to the alleged transition from the Early to the Mature Harappan period. Based on the analogy with other Harappan sites (particularly Harappa), I believe, the second scenario is more likely. The fact that an Early Harappan settlement has not been found at Mohenjo-Daro is not surprising.[17] The remains of such a settlement must be well hidden under the platforms and thick layers of alluvium.

With regard to authority however, both scenarios reveal very similar patterns. The construction of platforms and the initial structural activity on top of these platforms required the presence of a strong authority regardless of whether there was or was not an Early Harappan settlement in Mohenjo-Daro. The construction of the platforms involved the removal of clay and sediments in the amount of 4,000,000 m^3 (Jansen 1987:13). This by itself would have required an immense consumption of labor and the permanent presence of authority on the site during the entire time of construction. In this sense, the construction of these platforms is not fundamentally different from the examples of conspicuous consumption in other ancient civilizations. The time immediately following the construction of the platforms (period IIA according to Jansen and intermediate period III and II according to Marshall-Mackay) witnessed more structural activities. Both the chronology of Marshall (1931:10)—Mackay (1938:XIV–XVI) and the periodization by Jansen (1991:161–165) indicate that most buildings of the Stupa mound, cylindrical fired-brick wells, main streets of the Lower City, and densely built residential houses were laid out right after the construction of the platforms. Taking into consideration time constraints, scale of construction, and sophistication of technology, none of this could have taken place without the existence of powerful authoritative structures.

Nausharo

Nausharo is located on the Kachi Plain at the foot of the Bolan Pass, about 6 km south of Mehrgarh (see figures 4.22–4.23). Archaeological remains occupy two mounds that rise 6 m to 9 m above the surrounding fields and measure ca. 6 ha in area (C. Jarrige 2000). The excavation at Nausharo began in 1985 as part of the long-term project conducted by the French Archaeological Mission in Pakistan under the directorship of Jean-François Jarrige.[18] Several seasons of excavations resulted in the opening of large horizontal areas and the definition of a long occupational sequence. The most recent version of the sequence consists of six periods (see Table 4.9).[19]

Fortifications

The discovery of fortifications at Nausharo has a long history. In the 1988–1989 season, a fragment of a massive structure consisting of a drain, a wall, and a mass of mud-brick was discovered on the south side of the northern mound (see Figure 4.23). One of the discovered structures was a water reservoir dated to period II and possibly similar to the one excavated at Lothal (J.-F. Jarrige 1989:48). The discoveries of the following seasons reconfirmed this interpretation (Quivron, personal communication). In the proximity from the reservoir, the excavation also revealed a network of perpendicular walls and a large circular structure. The circular structure was dated to period II and was found to measure 11.5 m in diameter. The perpendicular walls, dated to Period ID, were excavated along the length of 10 m and were found to measure over 5 m in width. J.-F. Jarrige suggested that that these walls be viewed as a "compartmented platform" that both in length and width extended beneath the northern mound (J.-F. Jarrige 1990:230–231). The main wall connected to the network of compartmented walls was found to be built in period ID and consequently renovated in periods II and III (J.-F. Jarrige 1990:222, 227–228). The earliest part of this wall was reportedly 8.5 m wide at its highest point; it was later widened to 11 m (C. Jarrige 2000:241). In the same season, the remains of a massive mud-brick wall ("surrounding wall") were discovered under the cultivated fields on the southern side of the southern mound. This wall reached 3.8 m in extant height and 3–6 m in basal width and must have surrounded the site from all the sides. Based on ceramics, it was dated to period II. During the later seasons it was established that this wall had also a large gateway leading to the main thoroughfare of the southern mound (Quivron 2000:148). Walls were also detected on the southern and eastern side of the "acropolis", a massive complex of structures elevated high above the other sectors of the site and located on the northern mound. The massive L-shaped wall spotted in the middle of the northern mound must have marked the remains of a monumental structure built during period II.

Taken together these data allow us to make some preliminary generalizations. As far as the structural history is concerned, Nausharo was initially fortified in period ID and fortified most extensively in period II. The first walls, compartmented platforms, and some structures of the architectural complex located between the southern and northern sectors were built in period ID. Period II, associated with the beginning of the Mature Indus phase ("The First Indus" in the current periodization), was marked by the construction of new fortifications, the circular platform, the first reservoir, and a number of structures on the acropolis. As far as the meaning of the system of walls and platforms is concerned, it is clear that at least some of these structures were built to "counterbalance the slopes created by the ruined structures of the preceding periods, to counter the action of erosion, and to consolidate the structures which adjoined them" (Quivron, personal communication). Complicated stratigraphy, site formation processes, and the fact that many of the walls were free standing only on one side can be cited in support of this explanation. The currently available data nonetheless provides us with sufficient evidence for looking into the explanations emphasizing the ideational meaning of this fortification system. First, the structure dividing the northern and southern sectors of the settlement is strikingly monumental. Consisting of a massive platform and a mud-brick wall, it must have been more powerful and visually imposing than the outer fortifications of the site. Second, the site of Nausharo was divided in at least two distinct sectors: the "acropolis" and the southern town. It is not impossible that further excavations would reveal other sectors as well. Third, the acropolis with the monumental structure marked by the L-shaped wall was elevated high above the other sectors of the site and was delineated by walls on at least the eastern and southern sides. Separately and together, these traits indicate that aside from any retaining function, this system must have had an ideational purpose—an explanation also advocated by the excavators (Quivron, personal communication). Most likely, this purpose was a three-dimensional segregation based on political, social, or religious differences. The amount and layout of mud-brick walls seem to support this thesis as well. The fact of the matter is that aside from being surrounded and divided by free-standing walls Nausharo was laid out on a rigid rectangular grid, oriented in accordance with the cardinal points. Several blocks of the southern sector have been fully exposed and one can see that the mud-brick wall was a crucial element in conveying rectangular

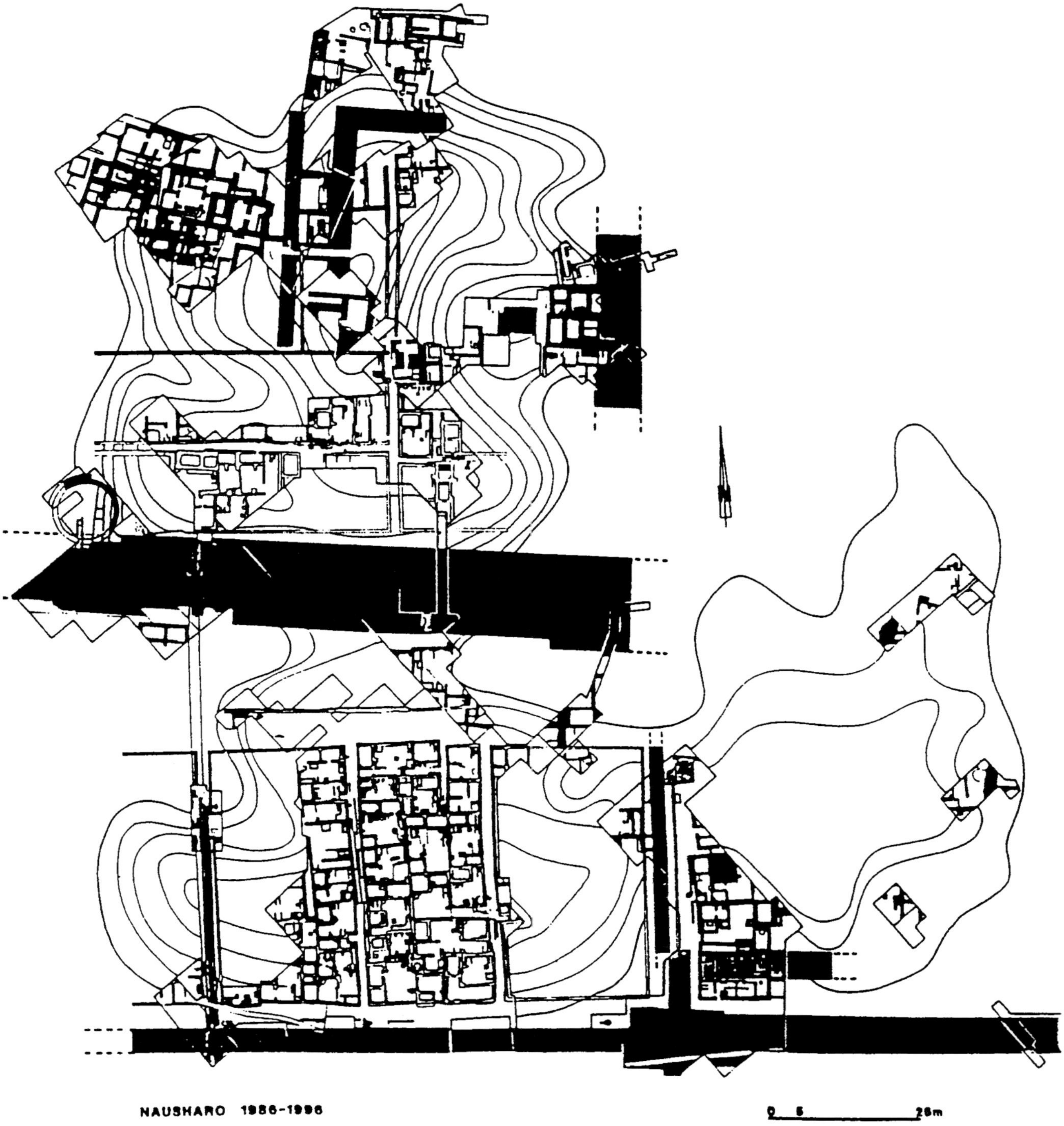

Figure 4.22 Nausharo. Drawing by Gonzaque Quivron. Illustration used with the courtesy and permission of the artist, the French Archaeological Mission in Pakistan, *Excavations at Mehrgarh-Nausharo* (J.-F. Jarrige 1995–1996).

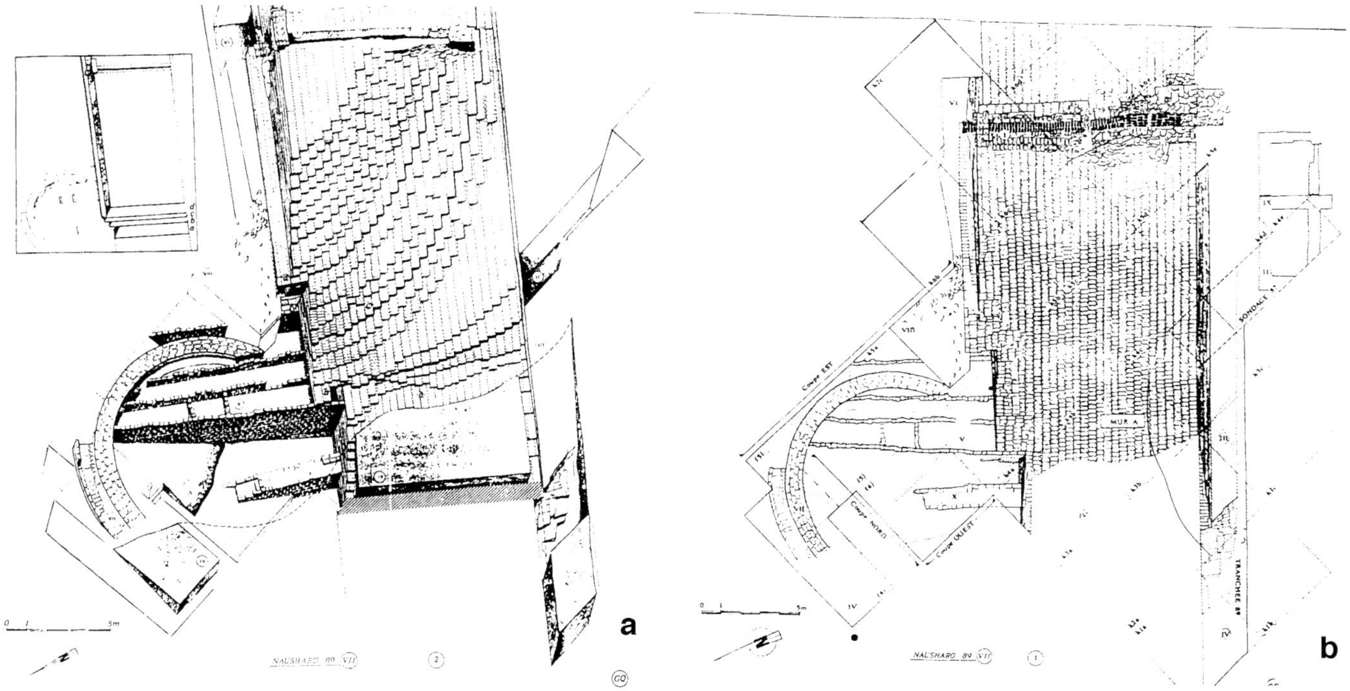

Figure 4.23 Nausharo: Dividing wall and the circular structure. Drawings by Gonzaque Quivron. Used with the courtesy and permission of the artist, the French Archaeological Mission in Pakistan, Excavations at Nausharo1988–1989, *Pakistan Archaeology* (J.-F. Jarrige 1990).

linearity as the main principal of settlement layout; long solid walls that surrounded each block served both as the backside for the houses and as the marker of access and border for their respective sectors. Judging from the number of entrances to each block, access was restricted. It is difficult to imagine that such a layout was created exclusively in response to practical needs. Esthetic and symbolic considerations must have played an important role as well. The symbolism of the wall as the divider of space and the conveyor of ideologically significant information must have been a key principle in the construction of internal fortifications and the block walls of Nausharo.

Authority

When the French Archaeological Mission started the excavation of Nausharo, it was thought that this was a large Indus village; in one of his first reports, J.-F. Jarrige (1974–1986:119) characterized Nausharo as "a sizable rural center" that had neither large scale craft activities nor a complex sanitary system. After several seasons of excavations, this view drastically changed; in one of the more recent reports, Nausharo of Periods II and III is described as "a true city with a large surrounding wall and an important drain network in fired bricks" (J.-F. Jarrige 1995–1996:4). Judging from the currently available data, the latter point of view seems to be more in line with the archaeological data. Clearly, by period II Nausharo had become an important regional center distinguished by a very complex social organization and powerful institutes of authority. Consider the following. All the major structural innovations of Period II (fortifications, platforms, the water reservoir, and the monumental structure of the acropolis), as well as the

Table 4.9

Nausharo: Periodization (Quivron, personal communication)

Period / Phase	Name of Period / Phase	Approximate Dates
Period 0	similar to Mehrgarh VI	3100–2900 BC
Period I (A, B, C)	Pre-Indus	2900–2600 BC
Phase ID	Proto-Indus	2600–2500 BC
Period II	First Indus	2500–2300 BC
Period III (A, B, C)	Second Indus	2300–2100 BC
Period IV	Third Indus	2100–1900 BC
Period V	similar to Late Pirak	800–500 BC

implementation of grid planning, the maintenance of urban segregation, and the renovation of public buildings were labor-intensive and required control, which in turn would certainly indicate the existence of strong authoritative structures. Therefore, the point of controversy must be not the existence of authority *per se*, but the temporal frame of its emergence. Did it appear in the beginning of period II or during the later phases of period I? Did it gradually emerge from the local socio-political traditions or was it the result of external influence? To answer these questions, one must reassess the archaeological record of period ID, the one that immediately precedes period II.

As J.-F. Jarrige (1993:162) justly argued, period ID signified a major transitional stage between "the late Quetta/Sadaat III, Mehrgarh VIIC tradition and the Harappan civilization in its early stage", and marked a brief yet drastic transition from the Pre-Mature Harappan to Mature Harappan phase at Nausharo (termed "Proto-Indus" in the most recent periodization; see Figure 4.9). From the point of view of the formation of authoritative structures, this short intermediate period was also very important. For the first time in the cultural history of Nausharo, it displayed the signs of conspicuous consumption, control of labor, and possibly social differentiation. It must be kept in mind that aside from the construction of the walls, this period was marked by the erection of the first massive complex of structures on the Northern Mound. Terraces, platforms, regularly planned houses, basic elements of sanitation, the foundation of the acropolis and, consequently, the first principles of urban segregation were also introduced during this period. Moreover, Nausharo during period ID, II, and III may have occupied a much larger area than it was thought before. Judging from the discovery of a perimeter wall—with structural remains on both of its sides—deep under the alluvium of agricultural fields, the actual size of the site in period II may have reached more than 6 ha (C. Jarrige 2000). The size of the site during period ID may have also been quite significant.[20] In sum, period ID witnessed major social transformations, which among others included the formation of authoritative structures. Whether these transformations were rooted in local traditions or brought from outside remains a point of controversy. J.-F. Jarrige seems to believe that the Harappan cultural elements of Nausharo evolved from the local pre-Harappan traditions. Period ID however ends in massive burning and all the period II structures of the northern sector are built anew. It thus is not impossible that external impulses played a role. One thing however is certain. By period ID Nausharo was fully ready for drastic sociopolitical transformations.

Surkotada

Surkotada is located in the District Kutch of Gujarat, possibly on the bank of a lost river. J. P. Joshi (1990:14–15) discovered it in 1964 on a survey of northern Kutch, and excavated it in 1970–1972 on behalf of the ASI.[21] Surkotada is quite small. The mound on which it lies occupies an area of 2 ha (see Figure 4.24). The size of the fortified site is even smaller, measuring 120 x 55 m or 0.66 ha (J. P. Joshi 1990:49, 56). Considering that only two excavation seasons were conducted, the scale of horizontal exposure is quite impressive. The main trench laid on the southern side of the mound measured 140 x 45 m, an area roughly equal to the entire fortified site. Several additional trenches were dug on the northern side of the mound as well in the cemetery lying to the northwest of the fortified area (J. P. Joshi 1990:15). Based on these excavations, three cultural periods were defined: period IA (ca. 2300–19070/40 BC), period IB (ca. 1940–1790 BC), and period IC (ca. 1790–1660 BC; see Figure 4.25). Criteria for the definition of these periods are not very clear. Transitions between the periods are smooth and not well defined. This possibly explains why Joshi named the periods IA, IB, and IC instead of I, II, and III; he wanted to emphasize the cultural continuity between the stages of this sequence.

Fortifications

Owing to extensive horizontal excavations, the plan and structural history of fortifications at Surkotada are well-known (see Figure 4.26). From the beginning of occupation, Surkotada was encircled by a massive rampart, which also divided the site into two parts: the eastern and western.[22] The inner core of the rampart was made of mud-bricks and mud lumps. On the outer and inner sides, the rampart had a veneer of dressed stones. The layout of the rampart did not seem to change over time; however, it underwent several renovations, was numerously revetted on both sides, and was rebuilt

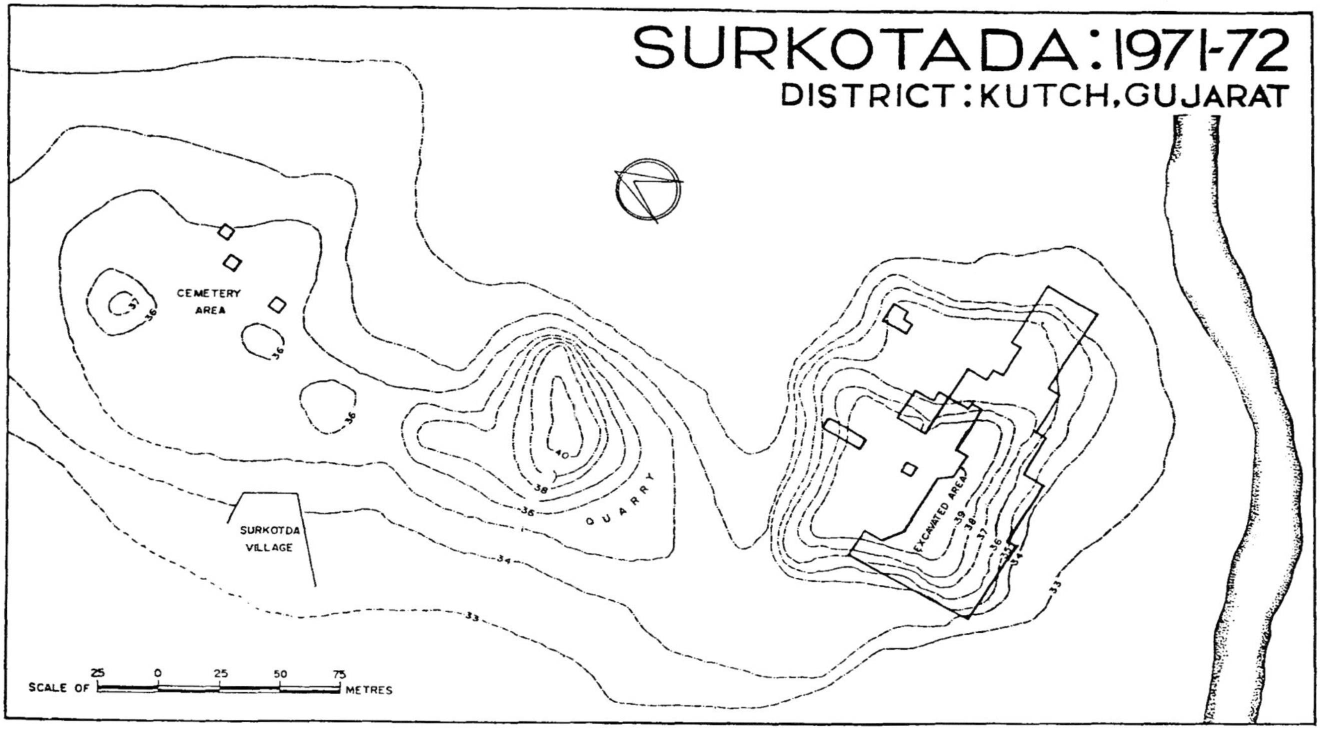

Figure 4.24 Surkotada: Contour plan. Illustration used with the courtesy and permission of the ASI, *Memoirs of the Archaeological Survey of India 87, Excavation at Surkotada 1971–1972 and Exploration in Kutch* (J. P. Joshi 1990).

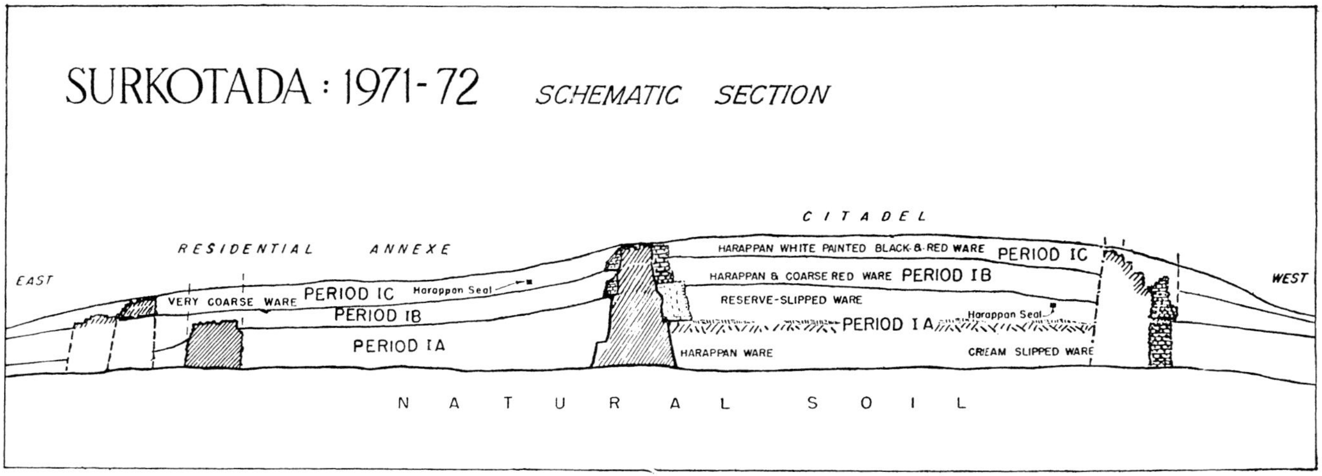

Figure 4.25 Surkotada: Cultural sequence. Illustration used with the courtesy and permission of the ASI, *Memoirs of the Archaeological Survey of India 87, Excavation at Surkotada 1971–1972 and Exploration in Kutch* (J. P. Joshi 1990).

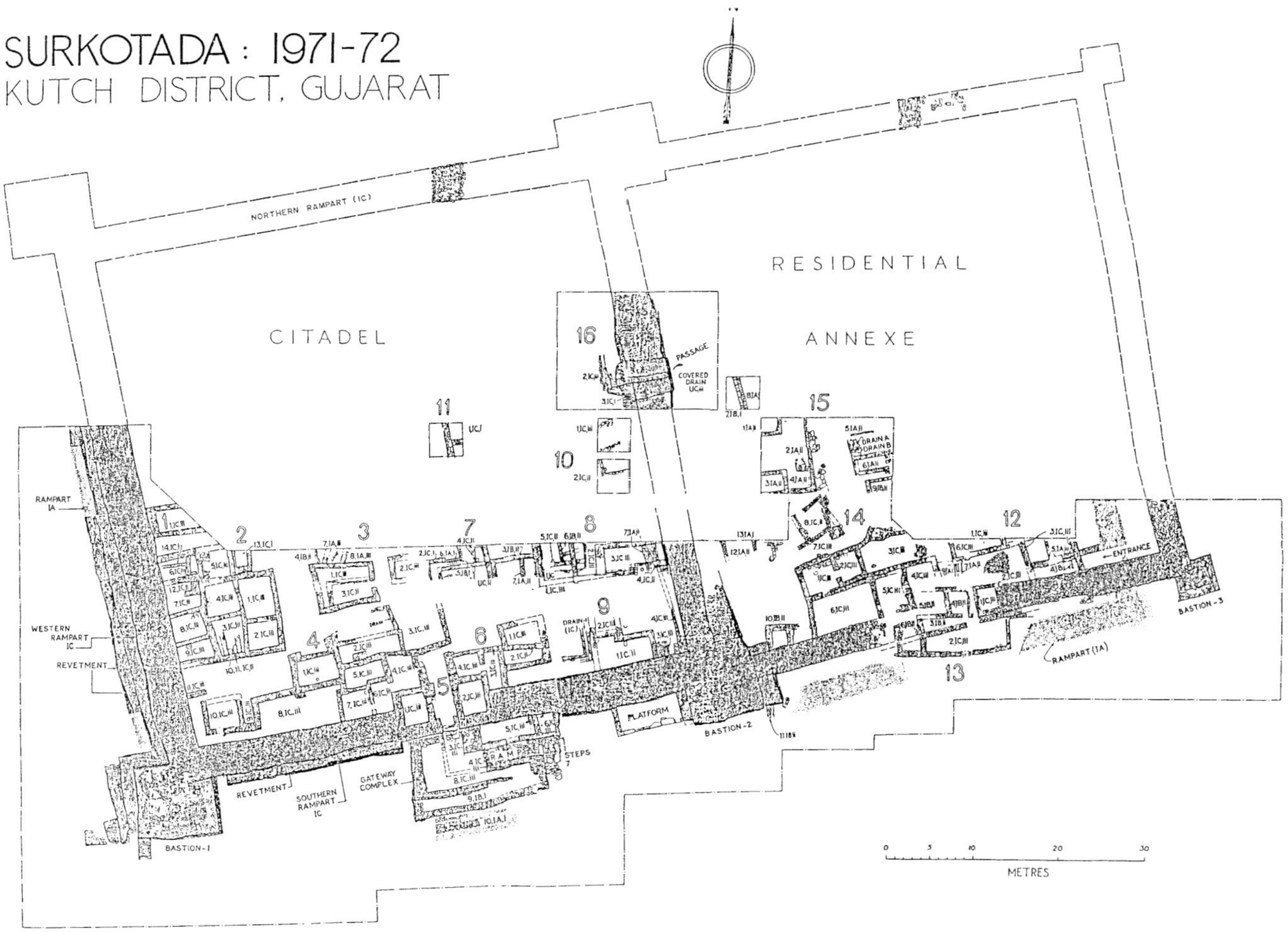

Figure 4.26 Fort of Surkotada. Illustration used with the courtesy and permission of the ASI, *Memoirs of the Archaeological Survey of India 87, Excavation at Surkotada 1971–1972* and *Exploration in Kutch* (J. P. Joshi 1990).

de novo in the beginning of period IC. As far as the dimensions of the rampart are concerned, the western sector was fortified slightly heavier during periods IA and IB. The basal width of the rampart in the western sector during these periods was on average 6–7 m, whereas the width of the rampart in the eastern sector was 3.5 to 5 m. Nonetheless, by period IC, which the excavator seems to view as the efflorescence of the Harappan culture at Surkotada, the basal width of the rampart decreased to an average of 4 m. The height of the rampart is much more difficult to determine. J. P. Joshi (1990:33) maintains that initially the rampart was only 1 m high and was raised during the later innovations. It is not clear however how J. P. Joshi arrives at this conclusion.

In several places, the rampart was pierced by gates and entrances. The most imposing gate was detected in the middle of the southern rampart. It occupied an area of 190 m^2 and had ramps, parapet walls, and stairs. The structural history of this gate however is not very clear. J. P. Joshi (1990:43, 47, 51–52, 57) believes that in period IA it was a simple open entrance, 1.8 m wide. Hence, the first gate complex was constructed either in period IB or in period IC. In addition to this gate complex, there were several simple entrances located both in western and eastern sector of the site. None of these entrances revealed any traces of gates or additional structures throughout all the three cultural periods. Bastions detected at the corners of the rampart were built in period IC. Dressed stones and burnt bricks were used in this construction. The bastions underwent several phases of renovations all within period IC. Given the size of the site, the two excavated bastions of the western sector were quite big; at the final phase, the first one occupied an area of 110.25 m^2 and the second one occupied an area of 109.8 m^2. Thus, pierced by gates and topped by bastions, the rampart must have made Surkotada look like an imposing fort. That such a small settlement was so heavily fortified and divided into two sectors raises a number of intriguing questions with regard to the function of this fortification system. J. P. Joshi (1990:49) believes that at least during period IC Surkotada was fortified for the purpose of military defense. In my view, this explanation is too simplistic. First, if in period IA, the rampart was only 1 m high, it could not properly perform a military function. One can easily jump or even step over such a rampart. Second, if the rampart carried a purely defensive function, one would expect it to increase rather than decrease in width. Nonetheless, the width of the rampart in the western sector (the alleged "citadel") significantly decreased from period IA to period IC. Third, neither from a military nor from an ecological perspective was there a need to divide the settlement into two equal parts and build a massive wall in the middle. The division into sectors must have had a sociopolitical or religious subtext. Fourth, since the fortified area covered only a third of the mound, the actual size of the settlement may have significantly exceeded the size of the fortified area. With the cemetery on the north and the fortified area in the south, it is, in fact, very likely that the central part of the mound was also populated. Save for making a few generic observations, J. P. Joshi never properly addressed this issue.[23] Lastly, one must keep in mind that during all the three periods of the occupational sequence, the walls of both sectors had openings, which revealed no traces of gates, ramps, stairs, or any other protections. Similarly in later periods, there was an open passage connecting eastern and western sectors.

Directly or indirectly, each of these traits seems to indicate that there was much more to the meaning of the fortification system at Surkotada than a military defense and protection from floods. Although it is possible that military concerns played a role during period IC (when the rampart was strengthened by bastions and the new gate complex was built), the necessity to segregate the site due to sociopolitical or religious differences seems to have been more important both at the time of the initial construction and during the further maintenance of the fortification system.

Authority

Evidence for authority is present at Surkotada throughout all three cultural periods. In other words, Surkotada is a founder's settlement, established by the Harappans on virgin soil in the second half of the second millennium BC. The three following lines of argument show how the settlement layout, architecture, and material culture indicate the presence of authoritative structures in Surkotada.

Layout. Surkotada was divided in two or possibly three distinct sectors. The only noticeable difference between the two sectors however is the strength and magnitude of fortifications. For example, the bastions of the western sector were significantly larger than the bastions of the eastern sector; ca. 110 m^2 versus ca. 10–11 m^2. And the gate complex in the south of the western sector was much more imposing than the entrances in the eastern sector. What is more important however is that these differences characterized mainly the final occupational period IC. In the two earlier periods, fortifications, layout, architecture, and material culture of the two sectors were very similar. Moreover, even in period IC, domestic architecture, internal layout and material culture of the two sectors were also similar.

Massive Architectural Projects. There is evidence for three massive construction projects that took place at Surkotada and would have clearly required a significant expenditure of labor: 1) The construction of a mud platform underneath the entirety of the fortified site in period IA; 2) The construction of the rampart and the dividing wall in period IA; and 3) The construction of a new rampart, massive bastions and a gate complex in the beginning of period IC.

Material Culture. As in many other Harappan sites, all periods at Surkotada had large numbers of Mature Harappan artifacts. Among those that may be indicative of authority are seals, inscribed objects, and weights (J. P. Joshi 1990:337, 359). Except for the pottery however, temporal variations in the material culture of Surkotada have not been properly investigated. J. P. Joshi (1990:18) argues that in period IA the percentage of "Harappan" pottery was significantly higher than in periods IB and IC.

Taken together, these traits lead to contradicting observations. On one hand, settlement layout and construction projects provide ample evidence for the existence of authority; neither division in sectors nor the construction of bastions and gates would have been possible without control and leadership. On the other hand, material culture, domestic architecture, and burials display a high degree of homogeneity, and provide no clear evidence for the presence of a ruler or a ruling group. Given this, it seems reasonable to suggest that during period IA and possibly during period IB the sociopolitical system of Surkotada was operated through heterarchical rather than hierarchical mechanisms. In these two periods, even the communication between the two sectors was easy; it was carried out with the help of a wide passage that was laid over the dividing wall. By the beginning of period IC, however, the heterarchical system must have attained hierarchical features. Archaeologically, this became expressed in the strengthening of the western sector, the construction of the gate-complex, and the replacement of the interconnecting ramp. Importantly, heterarchical relations do not exclude the existence of authoritative structures. In the case of Surkotada, massive structural projects are the best evidence for this.

Sutkagen-Dor

Sutkagen-Dor is located in the Dasht Valley of Makran, Pakistan, 35 km east of the present Iranian border. It was discovered and briefly explored by Major E. Mockler in 1875. Stein visited and excavated at Sutkagen-Dor in 1928. G. Dales conducted a small-scale excavation at this site while surveying the Makran Coast in 1960.[24] Dales' project lasted for only two weeks and, as Dales and Lipo (1992:58) asserted, given the size of the site, this project was "ridiculously small". Nonetheless, it provided some important information and raised a number of interesting questions. Although Dales' (1992a:135) main interest at that time was to investigate coastal contacts between the Indus civilization and the Near East, the results of Dales' excavation at Sutkagen-Dor were far-reaching; this project raised a number of important questions about Harappan expansionism and the nature of urbanism in the Harappan civilization in general.

The site of Sutkagen-Dor occupies an area of at least 4.5 ha (Possehl 2002c:80). One must note that the actual size of the site has never been established and it is possible that the citadel measuring 117 m x 103.3 m, ca. 1.2 ha, constituted only a small portion of the site (see Figure 4.27). Since the excavations were very brief, the cultural sequence could not be properly defined (see Figure 4.28). Nonetheless, the L-shaped trench A-A1 excavated under the supervision of M. R. Mughal next to the interior face of the western citadel wall revealed a stratigraphic sequence that allowed Dales to define what he called a sequence of human events, which included seven phases. Phase 1 marked the arrival of the Harappans. Phase 2 was defined by the construction of the citadel. Phases 3 to 6 were characterized by a number of various structural modifications. Phase 7 signified the post-Harappan occupation. It is in the context of this sequence that we can discuss the construction of fortifications and the formation of authoritative structures.

Fortifications

The system of fortifications is the most distinctive feature of the archaeological remains of Sutkagen-Dor. Many of its elements are still well preserved and greet the visitor with their grandeur. Mockler (1877) and Stein (1931:36–60) recorded the measurements and made the first maps of the massive wall surrounding the citadel area. It was not until Dales and his team spent two weeks at the site however that the first elements of structural history and stratigraphy were established. For the understanding of structural history and relative chronology, Dales and his team made two important discoveries. First, they found out that the citadel wall stood on natural soil; the supervisor of Trench A reached the bottom of the inner face of the western citadel wall and discovered that there was no occupational deposits underneath the wall (Dales and Lipo 1992:58). Second, they determined that all the structural phases in the construction of the wall were stratigraphically associated with Mature Harappan deposits. What this meant for the broader understanding of the history of Sutkagen-Dor was that the citadel was constructed by the Harappan newcomers immediately after their

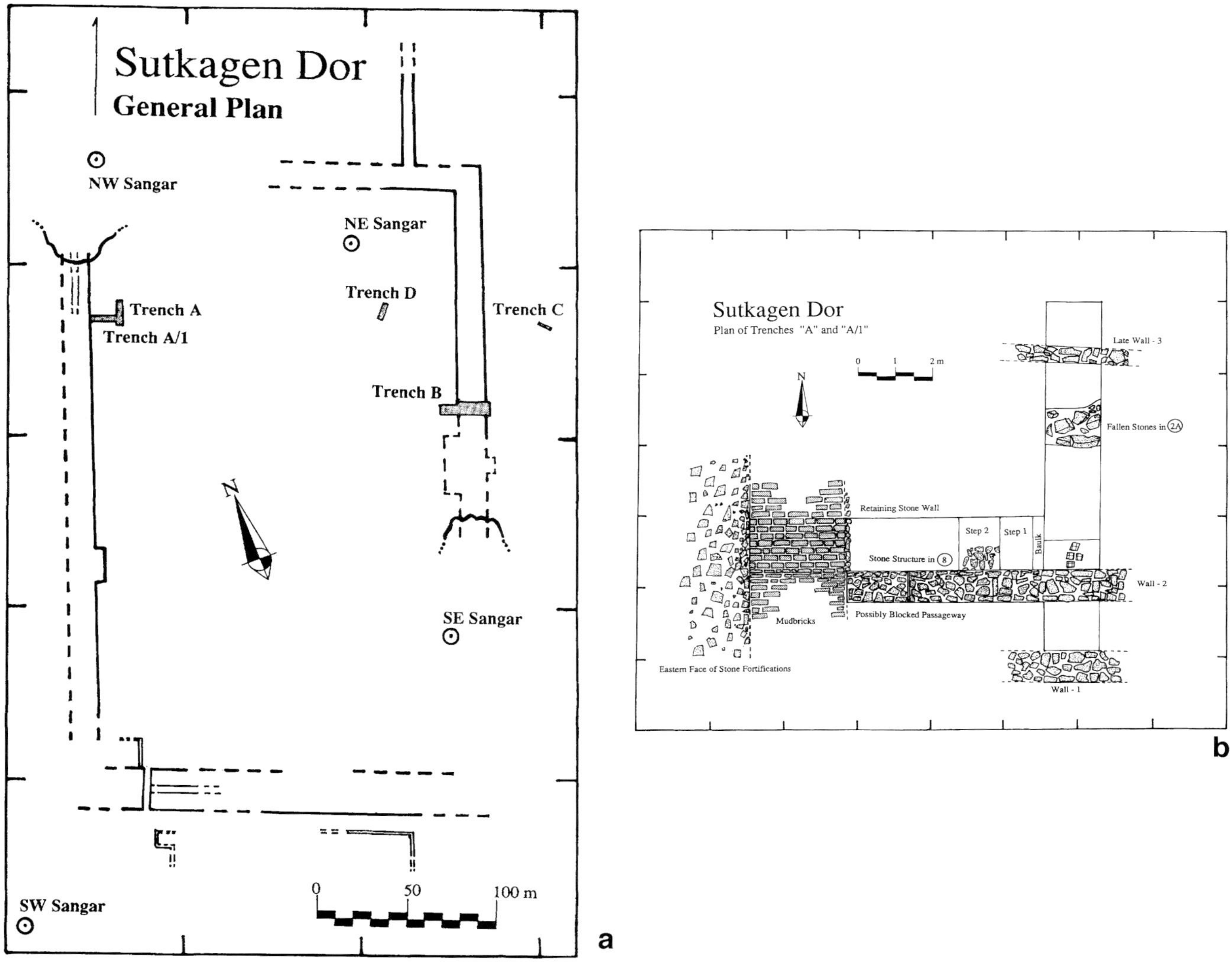

Figure 4.27a–b Sutkagen-Dor: Plans of excavations. Illustration with the courtesy and permission of *Explorations on the Makran Coast, Pakistan: A Search for Paradise, Contributions of the Archaeological Research Faculty, University of California, 50* (Dales and Lipo 1992).

arrival, and that these newcomers had a clear plan in mind prior to settling on the new territory. In this context, the function of the fortification system at Sutkagen-Dor was most likely focused on military defense. Moreover, other available evidence speaks in favor of military function as well. First, the dimensions and strength of the citadel wall were truly immense. Made of roughly shaped stones, the citadel wall at Sutkagen-Dor was different from the typical mud-brick walls surrounding other Harappan settlements. The basal width of the eastern wall was estimated at ca. 7.5 m. The extant height of the western wall was 3.3 m (Dales 1992a:147). Moreover, the wall was strengthened by towers and had a massive narrow gate in the southwestern corner. Second, some mud-bricks structures being incorporated in the fortification complex likely performed a military function. Trench A1, for example, revealed a long mud-brick platform built on a stone foundation against the inner face of the western citadel wall. This platform was 2.3 m wide x 3.35 m high. Dales (1992a:137, 147) justly suggested that these were the best dimensions to allow guards to walk unnoticed behind the western wall. Finally, the segregative function typical of fortification systems on many other Harappan sites does not seem to have played an important role in

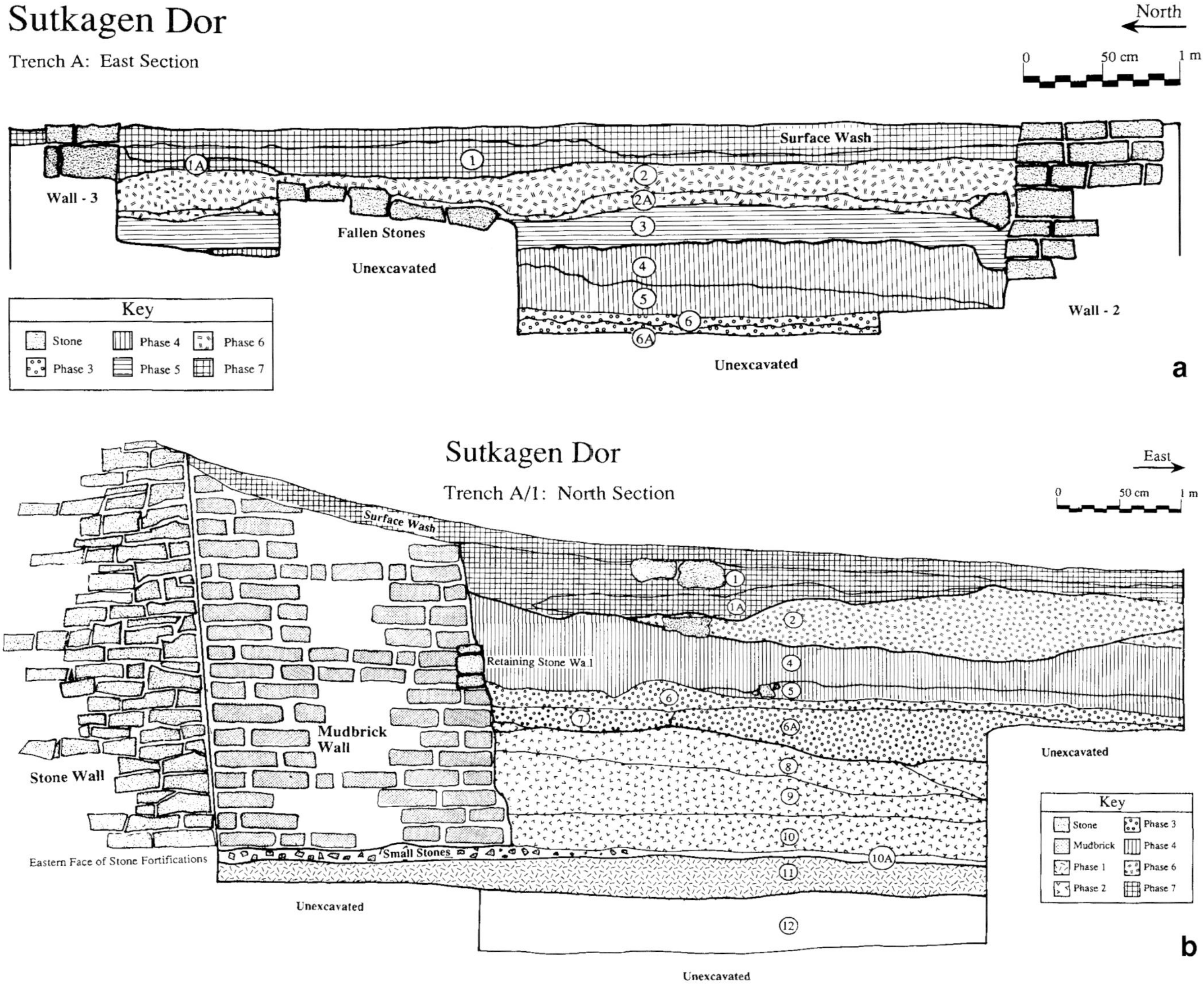

Figure 4.28 a–b) Sutkagen-Dor: Sections. Illustration used with the courtesy and permission of *Explorations on the Makran Coast, Pakistan: A Search for Paradise, Contributions of the Archaeological Research Faculty, University of California, 50* (Dales and Lipo 1992).

the construction of this citadel; unlike some other Harappan settlements, Sutkagen-Dor was not divided into distinct sectors and its fortification system was too imposing to perform a sociopolitical function.

Authority

An intriguing feature of the material culture at Sutkagen-Dor is the lack of certain classes of artifacts typically found on Mature Harappan sites. Among others these artifacts include seals, figurines, beads, and faience objects. Interestingly, a similar situation is observed at Sotka-Koh, another Harappan site in the Makran. Dales (1992a:156) does not provide an explanation for this intriguing phenomenon except for noting that this "may reflect the difference in activities and function between these coastal sites and those more closely associated with central Indus Valley sites". Considering recent studies on the relationship between crafts and sociopolitical structure in the Harappan civilization, I believe this puzzling phenomenon is reflective of a unique sociopolitical

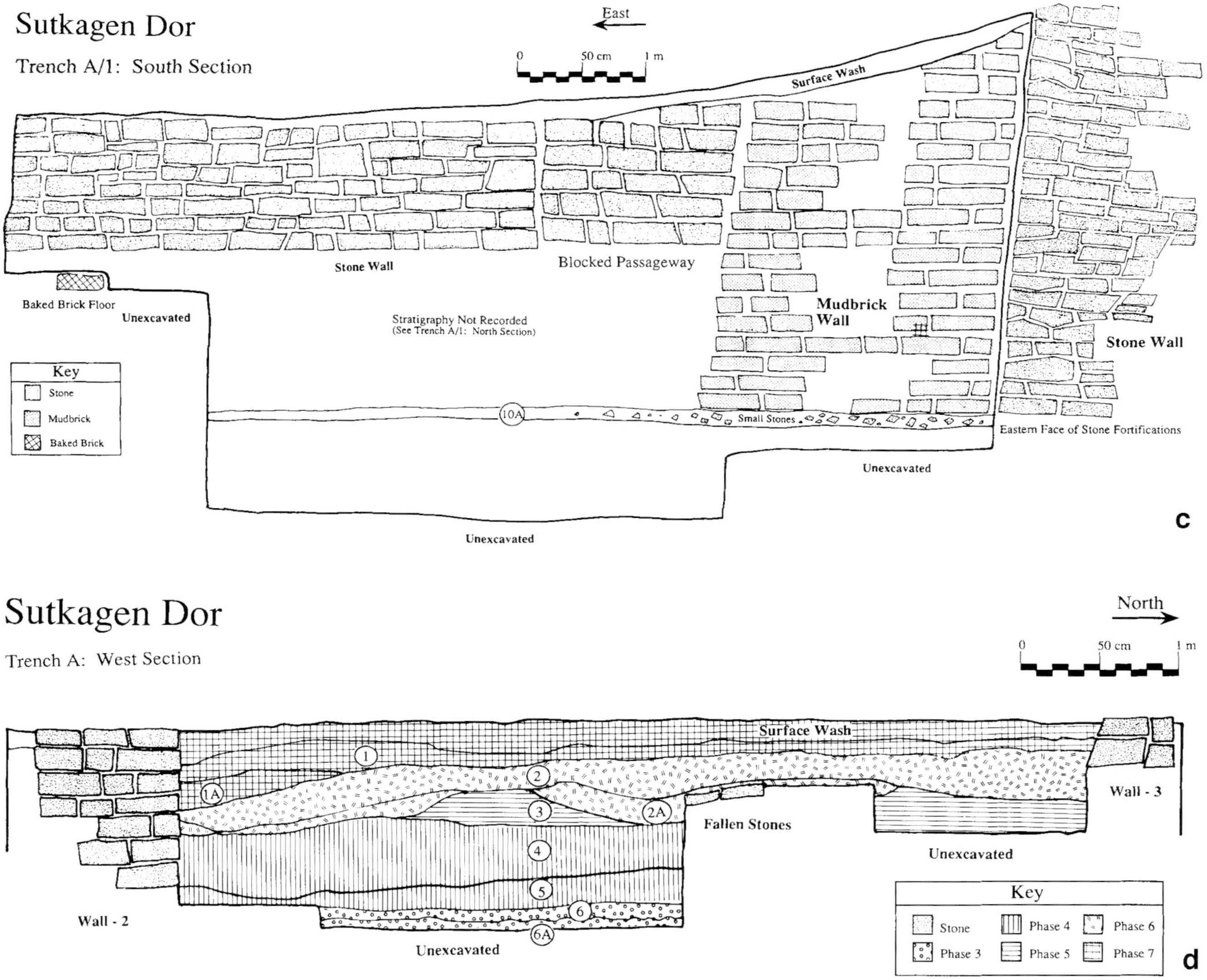

Figure 4.28 c–d) Sutkagen-Dor: Sections. Illustration used with the courtesy and permission of *Explorations on the Makran Coast, Pakistan: A Search for Paradise, Contributions of the Archaeological Research Faculty, University of California, 50* (Dales and Lipo 1992).

organization at Sutkagen-Dor. Craft specialization and sociopolitical organization do not have universal and simplistic equations. The equifinality of material culture often makes the reconstruction of sociopolitical structures almost impossible. In the context of the Harappan civilization, the complexity of the interrelationship between crafts and social structures has been justly advocated by several scholars. Nonetheless, as Kenoyer and a few others have shown, there are ways to use technology, crafts, and even specific artifacts in the analysis of social, economic, and political structures. Bhan et al. (1994:145–147), for example, have discussed in detail the significance of major Harappan crafts with an emphasis on specific artifacts, e.g., lithics, semi-precious stones, steatite, faience, shell, terracotta, and so forth. For example, bead ornaments, in their view, were "a critical feature of all Harappan settlements"; steatite was "more than just a versatile raw material and undoubtedly had significant socio-ritual implications"; and shell working was the industry that provided the best evidence for urban segregation. Furthermore, based on spatial distribution of artifacts, craft standardization, access to resources, and other criteria, Kenoyer (1989b:189) has argued that the social organization of Harappan cities displays "some form of socioeconomic ranking". To Kenoyer, in other words, the patterns of craft production and distribution are indicative of the patterns of sociopolitical organization. Now, if one generally agrees with the proponents of studying social organization through craft and technology, one must also agree that the artifacts listed by Dales as missing, in one way or another, are all indicative of sociopolitical structures and mechanisms. Seals for example are reflective of social structures in at least four ways: 1) through the acquisition of resources required for their production; 2) through the technology of their production; 3) through the texts inscribed in the Indus script; and 4) through the iconography of inscribed images. In spite of all the diversity of possible interpretations, to which each of these four paths may lead, one thing is nevertheless clear; the presence of seals in the archaeological record is indicative of complex sociocultural structures. Bead ornaments, in a similar way, being the result of sophisticated technology and "a critical feature of all Harappan settlements" are indicative of esthetic, social, technological, and possibly ethnic distinctions. Terracotta figurines requiring local raw material and simple technologies (Bhan et al. 1994:143; Kenoyer 1989b, 1992) are likely to be indicative of local sociocultural and religious norms. Finally, faience objects can be seen as an indicator of complex socioeconomic mechanisms. Now turning the argument upside down, we must ask whether the lack of these artifacts and technologies may indicate the absence of sociopolitical structures and mechanisms, for which they stand. I believe that in the case of Sutkagen-Dor we can disregard the frequent equifinality of material culture and answer this question positively. The reason for this lies in the diversity of archaeological evidence that makes Sutkagen-Dor look different from other Harappan sites. The location, layout, fortifications, and cultural history of Sutkagen-Dor display many unique features. Founded far from the core area of Harappan culture, Sutkagen-Dor was likely located in a culturally alien environment. The layout of Sutkagen-Dor, consisting of a citadel and the outer town, does not show a rigid division into sectors like some other Harappan sites. Massive stonewalls strengthened by towers and connected with mud-brick platforms form a formidable system of military defense.

This being said, I believe, it is not unreasonable to propose the following explanation. Sutkagen-Dor was founded by a group of Harappan colonists. The sociocultural order of their community was relatively homogeneous; for it neither required rigid residential sectioning nor produced the usual products of the Harappan social order, such as writing, seals, and bead ornaments. The members of this community were united and led by a clear goal; resources, political control, exploration of new territories, etc.... They had a clear plan in mind before the construction of the citadel. Despite their social homogeneity however, they had enough power and authority to organize and supervise labor for the construction of a massive citadel. To maintain the citadel and its defense, they must have had among them a group of at least part-time military specialists. Thus, as far as the existence of authoritative structures is concerned, one can safely conclude that some form of authority had been present on the site prior to the construction of the citadel. Moreover, one may suggest that during the initial stages of occupation this authority was responsible for at least three tasks: 1) they constructed and maintained the citadel; 2) they provided military defense; and 3) they performed the task/s that led the colonists to this remote area. To test this hypothesis, one would certainly need to conduct further excavations both inside and outside the citadel. What would further develop the proposed theory is the discovery of culturally diverse material remains outside the citadel.

Conclusion: The Idea of the Harappan City

The reassessment of the data on fortifications and authority from twelve Harappan sites has brought interesting results. Most of these sites are fortified and provide ample evidence for authority. As in the case with the Ganges civilization, the patterns of the emergence of authority and the construction of fortifications reveal a number of intriguing regularities. As in the concluding part of the previous chapter, I first will summarize these regularities under two themes: the function of fortifications and the nature of authority; and, then, will turn to the main issue, the idea of the city in the Harappan civilization.

Function of Fortifications

Utilitarian considerations played at least some role in the construction of the Harappan fortifications. For example, military defense was a prime factor in the construction of the perimeter wall at Sutkagen-Dor. The fort at Sutkagen-Dor was built immediately after the arrival of the Harappans. Compared to the area it occupied, the dimensions of its walls were immense. Moreover, several structural elements were directly indicative of the fort's military function. Besides Sutkagen-Dor, military considerations may have played a role in the construction of fortifications at Dholavira and Banawali; the fortification systems of these two sites were effective from the military point of view. On the rest of the reviewed sites, fortifications were less likely to perform any military function; most of the reviewed fortification systems were inefficient from the military point of view, and evidence for warfare was very scarce. Ecological factors may have played a role in the construction of fortifications on the sites built in the immediate proximity to the water. Indeed, many Harappan sites are located next to the rivers: Banawali and Kalibangan on the Ghaggar-Hakra, Chanhu-Daro and Mohenjo-Daro on the Indus, Harappa on the Ravi, Lothal between the Bhogawo and Sabarmati, and Surkotada on a nameless river. On some of these sites perimeter walls reveal patterns of erosion caused by water. On the whole however, ecological factors seem to have played a secondary role. Retaining function seems to be of importance on several sites and particularly at Harappa. The excavations by the HARP has shown that not every wall was free standing and at least some of the walls were built for the purposes of maintaining, protecting, and stabilizing the new layers of construction. Nonetheless, as in the case with the fortifications systems of the Ganges civilization, most of the reviewed Harappan sites provide substantial evidence for the ideational meaning of their fortification systems. Data from Banawali, Dholavira, Kalibangan, Harappa, Lothal, Mohenjo-Daro, Nausharo, and Surkotada are particularly revealing.

At Banawali, the first fortification wall is vulnerable to military attacks, the moat is built only on one side of the site, the site is divided into two fortified sectors, there are very few platforms, occupational deposits are likely to extend outside the city walls, and the perimeter walls are smoothly incorporated in the natural landscape. At Dholavira, fortifications of the castle are strikingly more monumental than the outer walls, the site is divided into four fortified sectors, the design of the walls and gates incorporates non-utilitarian and esthetic elements, and the layout of free standing walls creates several empty spaces and open areas. At Harappa, fortifications divide the site into four sectors, access to certain parts of the site is restricted, and the communication between some parts of the site is complicated. At Kalibangan, the earliest fortification wall is vulnerable, the site is divided into three sectors, fortifications significantly vary in scale, and some platforms have no structures on top of them. In Lothal, access to the site is restricted, the site is divided into two fortified sectors, many buildings stand on platforms of different heights, and several platforms have no structures on top of them. In Mohenjo-Daro, platforms and elevations are used for ideological purposes, and the site is divided into distinct and possibly fortified sectors. In Nausharo, the site is divided into two fortified sectors, the wall dividing the northern and southern sectors is significantly bigger than the outer walls, and the southern sector is divided into distinct rectangular blocks. In Surkotada, the first rampart is vulnerable, its width decreases rather than increases in time, there are several openings in the walls, the fortifications of the western sector are significantly more monumental than fortification of the eastern sector, and the site is divided into two fortified sectors. Taken together, these traits reveal recurring patterns that can be grouped and discussed under five themes: elevation, scale, access, segregation, and accentuation of space.

Elevation. The landscapes of the Harappan sites are uneven. The elevation of certain sectors and structures by means of mud and mud-brick platforms is a key element of planning. In this chapter, I have treated platforms as part of fortification complexes, for the platforms are often directly connected to perimeter walls. In terms of their function, platforms seem to be part of fortification complexes as well; for there are at least three indications of their ideational use. First, platforms can be of different heights within the same site or even within the same area of the site (Mohenjo-Daro, Lothal, Nausharo). Second, there are platforms that have no structures on top (Kalibangan, Lothal). Third, platforms do not necessarily cover the whole sites or even the whole areas of the site. Banawali has a few occasional platforms, while in Kalibangan platforms cover only the southern part of the western sector.

Scale. Fortifications of many Harappan sites are monumental and their construction is labor consuming. Monumentality however characterizes mainly platforms (Mohenjo-Daro, Harappa, Lothal, Kalibangan) and internal fortifications (the castle of Dholavira, the dividing wall at Nausharo, the southern part of the western sector at Kalibangan). Most external fortifications (the outer walls) are not monumental.

Access. There are numerous indications that the construction or non-construction of gates on Harappan sites has ideational causes. The southwest gate on mound ET at Harappa is blocked at some point. Some sites have very few entrances (Lothal), whereas other sites have several wide openings (Surkotada). Some gates are monumental (northern Gate at Dholavira), while other gates are very simple and barely protected. Several gates have very narrow passages (Dholavira, Harappa).

Segregation. One of the most obvious features of the Harappan fortification systems is segregation. Most of the reviewed fortified sites are divided into two or more sectors encircled by walls. Banawali has two fortified sectors. Dholavira has four fortified sectors. Harappa has four fortified sectors. Kalibangan has three fortified sectors. Lothal has two fortified sectors. Mohenjo-Daro is a controversial case, yet the recent research by the Italian team shows that some or possibly all of the mounds and areas of Mohenjo-Daro have perimeter walls. Nausharo has two fortified sectors. Surkotada has two fortified sectors. In addition, most of these sites reveal occupational deposits beyond the city walls; in other words, besides fortified sectors, they have sectors not protected by the walls yet symbolically separated from the rest of the site.

Accentuation of Space. In addition to segregating sites into large distinct sectors, freestanding walls divide and accentuate important places. On some sites, they create empty spaces, long passages, and open areas, some of which may have had ritual or political significance (Dholavira). On other sites, they divide fortified areas into relatively small and distinct sectors (Kalibangan, Surkotada). On many sites, walls delineate block borders and residential complexes (Nausharo).

Traits grouped under each of these five themes point to ideational meanings. Platforms accentuate the significance of certain buildings and areas by using elevations as means of ideological significance. Monumentality, being a feature of platforms and internal fortifications, conveys a message from one group to another, often within the area of the same site. Gates restrict access to the sites, making the passage of people and vehicles restricted and controlled. Free-standing walls that divide the sites into distinct sectors maintain the existing sociopolitical order. The creation of small sectors, passages and empty spaces reflects ritual or political ceremonialism; no military, ecological or any other practical reason would justify splitting the western sector at Kalibangan or the creation of a long passage in front of the north gate at Dholavira. Finally, differences in the date of construction and the magnitude of some fortification systems—Harappa was surrounded by perimeter walls long before Nausharo, or Dholavira had more elaborate fortifications than Banawali and Lothal—point to the internal (sociopolitical or ritual) rather than external (military) functions. Figuratively speaking, fortifications of Banawali, Dholavira, Harappa, Kalibangan, Lothal, Mohenjo-Daro, Nausharo, and Surkotada created three-dimensional and segregated worlds characterized by restricted access and hidden monumentality. The ethos of these worlds was ideological rather than utilitarian. They conveyed ideas rather than protected the enclosed areas from floods or foes. To theorize on what kind of ideas these could be, we need to turn to the data on authority.

Nature of Authority

To trace the emergence of authority in each of the 12 Harappan sites, I have followed the same method as in the previous chapter, i.e., have traced concurrent and drastic changes in the material culture of each of these sites (see Figure 4.30).

In Allahdino, evidence for authority is associated with the transition from phase 2 to phase 1. The innovations of phase 1 include structures of possible public function, a household water system, a small-scale irrigation network, and the grouping of public structures in one part of the site. In phase I, although remaining a small village, Allahdino becomes fully acculturated in the world of the Harappan civilization. Given the rapidity of cultural changes (the entire sequence of Allahdino lasts no longer than 150 years), authority plays a role in this acculturation. Yet like most artifacts in Allahdino are from outside, authority is exported from a larger center of power. In Banawali, authority becomes evident during phase IC, which marks a transition from the pre-Harappan to Mature Harappan layers and is dated roughly to the middle of the third millennium BC. During this phase, the whole settlement is rebuilt anew, the fortification system is renovated, the division into two fortified sectors is established, architecture becomes more sophisticated, and the new street system oriented in accordance with cardinal directions is laid out. In Chanhu-Daro, authority is present by the second Harappan period. The periodization and chronology of this site are however so poorly defined, that it is currently impossible to trace the emergence of authority with better precision. In Dholavira, authority emerges either during stage IIIA or during stage II. Based on three lines of evidence—monumentality, site expansion, and the principles of planning and architecture—I have argued that stage II foreordains the efflorescence of stage III. Harappa provides clear evidence for authority by period II (Kot Diji phase) which starts around 2800 BC. The innovations of this period that are directly indicative of authority include: the construction of fortifications and the emergence of distinct fortified sectors, the expansion of the site, the intensification of structural activities, brick standardization, the emergence of seals and possibly standardized weights and measures, and the sophistication of craft technology and development of long-distance trade. In Kalibangan evidence for authority appears in the beginning of period II around 2600/2500 BC. The innovations indicative of authority include settlement expansion, the renovation of fortifications, the division into three fortified areas, orientation along the cardinal directions, and the construction of platforms in the southern part of the western sector. In Kot Diji, evidence for authority (if any) is associated with period II (layers 7–4) of my periodization, and the later part of period I (Kot Dijian) of Khan's periodization. This period witnesses the expansion of the settlement, complete degeneration of fortifications and the emergence of new architectural patterns. Interestingly, evidence for authority becomes less evident during periods III and IV of my periodization or period II (Harappan) of Khan's periodization. In Lothal, archaeological evidence for authority is associated with the transition from phase I to phase IIA. This transition witnesses settlement expansion, the construction of platforms, the renovation of fortifications, the division of the site into distinct fortified sectors, the construction of the "dock" and the "warehouse", a general intensification of structural activities, and the establishment of street layout in accordance with cardinal directions. Importantly, all these changes can be placed in a relatively short period of time; phase IIA arguably lasts for less than 100 years. Mohenjo-Daro provides the strongest case for authority of all the reviewed sites. The Stupa mound alone is as an epitome of authority in the Harappan civilization. Platforms, public architecture, planning and most other characteristic features of Mohenjo-Daro would not have been possible without the existence of a very complex social system (whether hierarchical or heterarchical) and powerful authoritative structures. The emergence of authority on this site is nonetheless obscure. Evidence for authority is found throughout all the cultural periods and nothing is known about the pre-Harappan levels. In Nausharo, the emergence of authority can be ascribed either to period II dated to 2500–2300 BC or to period ID dated to 2600–2500 BC. Period II is defined by fortifications, platforms, monumental architecture, grid planning in accordance with cardinal directions and the division in sectors. Period ID sees the construction of the first fortifications, the beginning of the division into fortified sectors and the building of a massive architectural complex on the northern mound. Following Jarrige, I have argued that the traits of period ID are sufficient to indicate the emergence of authority. Surkotada is a founder's settlement. Evidence for authority on this site is found throughout all three periods and includes massive architectural projects, the division into two fortified sectors, and a large number of characteristically Harappan artifacts. Based on the structural history of fortifications and the site layout, I have suggested that during period IA and IB Surkotada was characterized by a heterarchical sociopolitical system.

In period IC the heterarchical system must have attained hierarchical features—strengthening of the western sector, the construction of a gate-complex, and the replacement of an interconnecting ramp with a passage support this interpretation. Sutkagen-Dor is another founder's settlement, possibly surrounded by culturally alien populations. Like in Surkotada, evidence for authority is present in the deposits of all periods and includes massive architectural projects. Interestingly enough, the site lacks the division into fortified sectors and some typically Harappan artifacts, such as writing, seals, and bead ornaments. I have explained this as a result of relative social homogeneity of those who resided at the site, and have proposed that Sutkagen-Dor was founded by a group of Harappan colonists united by a clear goal; such as resources, political control, or the exploration of new territories.

Thus, in reassessing data from site to site, I have come across a large number of archaeological traits, which in one way or another can be used as indicators of major social transformation and the formation of authoritative structures. The significance of these traits as evidence for authority can be discussed under four general topics: size, layout, architecture, and material culture.

Size. A drastic and fast site expansion almost universally implies increase in social complexity and possibly the emergence of ruling groups. Unfortunately, many Harappan sites lack quality data to trace the dynamics of site expansion. Of the 12 sites discussed in this chapter, only Dholavira, Harappa, Kalibangan, Kot Diji, and Nausharo provide some data for establishing the time frame and scale of expansions. Sutkagen-Dor and Surkotada seem to have been founded from scratch on a new territory. Allahdino is a small agricultural village, which did not undergo any major increase in size. Other sites either lack data on the pre-Harappan occupations, or the existing data are not sufficient for establishing the size of early settlements.

Layout. An idiosyncratic layout is one of the most evident manifestations of the Harappan urban phenomenon. Advance planning, the grouping of public structures, and the division into distinct fortified sectors are usually quoted as typical of Harappan sites. Each in its own way, these traits imply authoritative decisions. Not all of them however are equally present on Harappan sites. The most unique and widely spread feature is the division in sectors, or putting it in more interpretative terms, urban segregation.

Structural Activity. Many Harappan sites conceal the remains of massive architectural projects; such as mud and mud-brick platforms, perimeter walls and public buildings. Massive architectural projects in turn are among the best indicators of social transformations, such as the emergence of authority, for they require the organization of labor, advance planning, acquisition of resources, and most importantly a good reason for construction. All of these preconditions are impossible without a high degree of social differentiation—either hierarchical or heterarchical—and authoritative decision-making. Of the reviewed twelve sites, all but Allahdino reveal traces of massive architectural projects.

Material culture. There are several types of Harappan artifacts, potentially indicative of authority. These include inscribed seals, inscribed objects, standardized weights, bricks of the standard ratio, precious jewelry, and the objects of long distance trade. The use of these artifacts as direct evidence for authority can be however very misleading. For example, the reassessment of data from Kot-Diji and Allahdino shows that the presence of writing does not necessarily imply the presence of authority. On the other hand, the cases of Dholavira and Harappa during the Pre-Harappan period or Sutkagen-Dor during the Mature Harappan period show that the lack of writing does not necessarily imply the lack of a strong authority. The matter of the fact is that on many sites authority emerges prior to or after the appearance of the aforementioned artifacts.

Thus, archaeological evidence for authority in the Harappan civilization rests on four sets of data: size, layout, structural activity, and material culture. Importantly, since the dynamics of site expansion are in most cases obscure and the traits of material culture by themselves can be misleading, layout and structural activity become the two key material expressions of authority on most of the reviewed sites. More specifically, this means that in Banawali, Dholavira, Harappa, Kalibangan, Lothal,

Mohenjo-Daro, Nausharo, and Surkotada, evidence for the major social transformations, such as social differentiation, conspicuous consumption of labor, and the emergence of authoritative structures comes primarily from the idiosyncratic layout (the division in sectors) and massive architectural projects (platforms, walls, gates, moats and public buildings). Besides a few public buildings however, these traits are all facets of fortification systems, whose quintessential meaning, as I have argued above, is the creation of three-dimensional and segregated worlds with restricted access and hidden monumentality. The material expression of authority thus can be described in the same terms as the meaning of fortifications. Indeed, aside from several public buildings—"granaries", the great bath, etc.—authority on these eight sites expressed itself most conspicuously in the implementation of massive public works and the segregation of space. Neither public works nor the segregation of space however had a clear utilitarian cause. As I have argued above, the construction of platforms and walls had in most cases an ideational rather than utilitarian significance. Thus, as in the Ganges civilization, the ethos of authorities in the Harappan civilization was materialized predominantly through the construction of fortifications. The authoritative structures of the Harappan sites did not need palaces, rich burials, and lavish objects of art. Instead, they built various kinds of walls, gates, passages, dividing structures, and massive mud-brick platforms. Encircling and dividing space, they must have solidified their identities and local worlds the way similar to those of the Ganges civilization. In other words, the processes of sociocultural differentiation and the formation of territorially bound identities must have played an important role as an impetus for these activities. Yet in the contrast to the Ganges civilization, these identities were more confined. For judging from the division of sites into sectors with restricted access, a sense of belonging to a certain religious, professional, or any other sociocultural group must have been more restricted in terms of territorial boundaries and access to some areas. Furthermore, in the contrast to the Ganges civilization, the local worlds created by the Harappan fortifications were segregated and three-dimensional. What this means is an intriguing question. Platforms, walls, and urban segregation present a unique and enigmatic pattern of authority in an ancient civilization. In my view, the very existence of this pattern on a number of important sites in a given civilization implies that the rulers or ruling groups of these sites shared many common traits in ideology, function, and the mechanisms of power. It is certainly very difficult to reconstruct the precise nature of these traits. Given the lack of variables and the frequent equifinality of archaeological explanations, there can be at least several competing theories. The one that I would like to propose makes an emphasis on the holistic and idiosyncratic worldview.

I believe, authorities at Banawali, Dholavira, Harappa, Kalibangan, Lothal, Mohenjo-Daro, Nausharo, and Surkotada brought into play a unique and complex worldview. This worldview was focused on the structure of the universe and possibly foreordained the later cross-cultural concepts of terrestrial axis and the world tree (Eliade 1949). Archaeologically it became expressed in a three-dimensional and segregated layout of the sites and the restricted access to certain areas. Three-dimensionality of the Stupa mound at Mohenjo-Daro, empty spaces at Dholavira, the massive dividing wall at Nausharo as well as other traits that embody the world as a multi-tiered, compartmented, yet single whole are the products of this view. Without a credible decipherment of the Harappan script or new readings of the Harappan iconography, it is difficult to say anything more concrete, yet one cross-cultural analogy comes to mind. Despite drastic cultural, linguistic and sociopolitical differences, the early Mesoamerican city-states and culture-areas shared a cosmovision, i.e., a set of beliefs, ideas and rituals that made it possible to view them as a cultural whole (Carrasco 1990). I believe the ideology that accompanied the formation of authority on the Harappan sites should be approached in a similar way.

The function of the Harappan authorities was affected by their views. The initiation of massive structural projects, such as platforms, gates and dividing walls was driven by the desire to implement this ideology in practice, to mingle the view of the world with the daily life of metropolitan sites, and ultimately to create mesocosms, or the miniature replicas of the universe. This model I believe is applicable to the major Harappan sites, the key centers of power and ideological control. Clearly, there are exceptions. Intermediate centers, small rural settlements, colonial outposts, and the sites not fully belonging to the Harappan ideological realm do not have to follow the same pattern. Of the twelve sites discussed in this chapter, four belong to the latter type of sites. The location and material culture of each of these four sites provide explanations why they do not reveal the pattern of the metropolitan ideological centers. Allahdino is a small rural settlement. Although fully incorporated in the Harappan trade networks and, as I have suggested above, affected by authoritative decisions from outside, Allahdino is insignificant as a political or ideological center. Chanhu-Daro is an important intermediate center, significant economically, yet not ideologically. Kot Diji is an interesting case, for it seems to have been an important flourishing center in the early part of the third millennium yet a place of minor significance in the second half of the third millennium, which marked the time of the efflorescence of the Harappan civilization. Sutkagen-Dor is a colonial outpost. As I have argued above, it must have been founded by a small and socially homogenous group of Harappan colonists united and led by an exploratory goal. A strong authority must have been present at Sutkagen-Dor, yet its nature and function are fundamentally different from those of the major sites.

The Idea of the Harappan City

In the end of the third chapter, I arrived at the conclusion that the model of the city extracted from the Sanskrit and Pāli texts in the second chapter adequately reflects the archaeology of the Ganges civilization and enhances our understanding of the phenomenon of the Gangetic city. The analysis of archaeological data, conducted in this chapter, provided yet another example of how this model can work in the context of South Asian archaeology. A model of the city defined through the concurrent processes of the construction of fortifications and the formation of authority appears to be helpful not only in the context of the Ganges civilization, a culture which was roughly contemporaneous with the genesis of this view, but is also applicable to the archaeology of the Harappan civilization, a culture whose emergence had preceded this view by at least 2,000 years. The relationship between the construction of fortifications and the emergence of authority on the Harappan sites is not as straightforward as on the Gangetic sites (see Figures 4.29–4.30). Of the 12 sites reviewed in this chapter, 11 reveal sound evidence for authority and at least nine are fortified. One can distinguish three types of sites based on the temporal relationship between the construction of fortifications and the emergence of authority.

On the sites of the first type, the earliest perimeter walls precede the emergence of authority. This type includes Banawali, Kalibangan, and Lothal. In Banawali, the first perimeter wall is built in period IB dated roughly before 2600 BC. The scale of the wall and the traits of material culture attributed to this period do not indicate the presence of authority. The following period IC however provides unambiguous evidence for authority as well as sees the construction of the new system of fortifications that divide the site in sectors. In Kalibangan the first perimeter wall is built in the beginning of period I soon after 3000 BC. This period in my view does not provide enough evidence for authority, which emerges after a significant break in occupation in the beginning of period II around 2600–2500 BC. In Lothal initial fortifications are built during the Pre-Harappan phase 1. Clear evidence for authority as well as more substantial fortifications and platforms are associated with the Harappan phase 2. On the sites of the second type, the construction of fortification is roughly contemporaneous with the genesis of authority. This type includes Dholavira, Harappa and Nausharo. In Dholavira, the earliest perimeter wall is constructed during Stage I dated by Bisht to ca. 2650–2550 BC. Evidence for authority begins to emerge during periods I and II (2650–2500 BC). In Harappa both authority and segregated fortifications are present at the site the latest by the Kot Diji phase (2800 BC). In Nausharo, authority and fortifications appear during period ID around 2600–2500 BC. The third type is represented by the so-called founder's settlements. The two sites that certainly belong to this type are Sutkagen-Dor and Surkotada. Both of these sites seem to have been planned and founded on virgin soil by newly arriving groups. Whether Mohenjo-Daro and Chanhu-Daro belong to the same type of settlements is a controversial issue. Currently, neither of these two sites provides clear evidence for the pre-Harappan occupations.

Thus, in some cases the construction of perimeter walls precedes the emergence of authority.[25] In other cases, the emergence of authority is contemporaneous with the construction of fortifications. Under both scenarios however, authority and fortifications can be viewed as an epitome of the city; for it is their mutual presence that marks the time of most drastic qualitative changes. What this means is

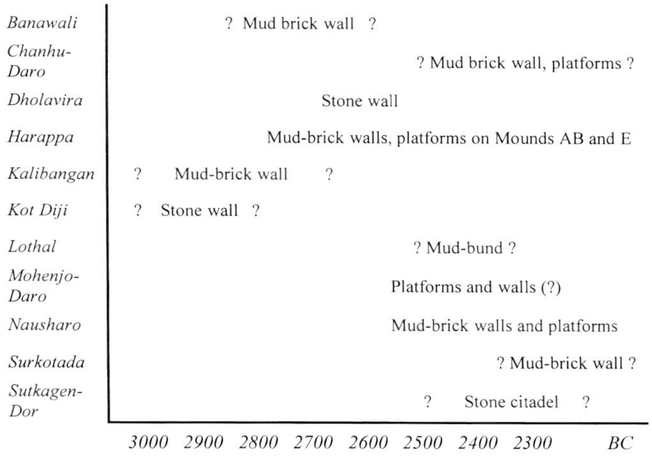

Figure 4.29 Fortifications of the Harappan civilization: Approximate dates of construction (dates are indicated by the first letter in the name of a type of fortification).

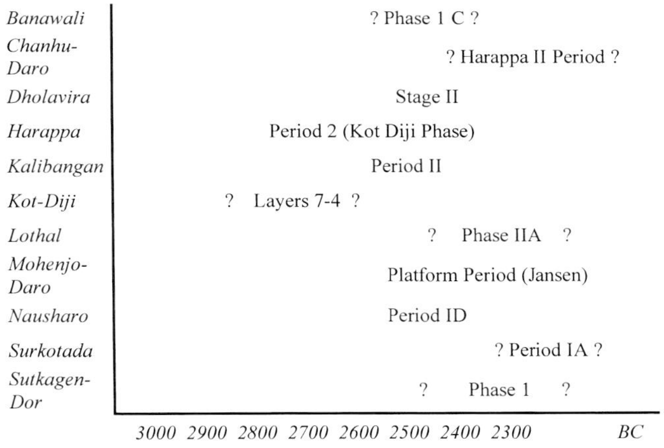

Figure 4.30 Authorities in the Harappan civilization: Approximate time of emergence (dates are indicated by the first letter in the name of a period, phase, stage or layer).

that from the viewpoint of the model formulated in the second chapter, Banawali, Dholavira, Harappa, Kalibangan, Lothal, Mohenjo-Daro, Nausharo, Sutkagen-Dor, and Surkotada are cities. Allahdino is a rural settlement existing in the shadow of larger centers of power and interaction. Chanhu-Daro and Kot Diji are middle size settlements, which from the view of this model do not qualify to be called cities. Returning to Collingwood and ancient Indian literature, one may conclude that the definition of the city from the point of view of the historical agents makes perfect sense in the context of the Harappan archaeology.

5 The Idea of Civilization: From Voltaire to Braudel and to the Sanskrit Puranas

> *Civilizations, like sand dunes, are firmly anchored to the hidden contours of the earth; grains of sand may come and go, blown into drifts or carried far away by the wind, but the dunes, the unmoving sum of innumerable movements, remain standing.*
>
> —Fernand Braudel (1972–1973:II.757)

In anthropological and historical theory, the concept of the city has for many years been closely associated with the concept of civilization. In the archaeology of early complex societies, the city is still seen as the hallmark of civilization and the emergence of cities is often argued to mark the emergence of civilization. This premise stems from the writings of several social thinkers and in particular from the definition of the Urban Revolution proposed by V. Gordon Childe. The relationship between the phenomena of the city and civilization is nevertheless much more complex. As Paul Wheatley (1971:386) has justly noted:

> The etymological link between the words "city" and "civilization" is wholly inadequate as a guarantee of their synonymity, and the attempt to combine them in a conjoint definition only engenders unnecessary difficulties. This, of course, is not to deny the very real broad correspondence that commonsense establishes between urban life on the one hand and civilization in any of its multitudinous manifestations on the other, but this is not ground for an *a priori* assumption that cities and civilization developed contemporaneously.

Since the Enlightenment, the idea of civilization has been a key analytical tool for the generations of social thinkers. It has produced an immense amount of literature with a multitude of mutually exclusive interpretations. One thing is nevertheless certain. Regardless of how the city and civilization are defined, the concept of civilization is much broader than the concept of the city. In this chapter, I turn to the idea of civilization, for in my view it logically continues my investigation of the idea of the city. Following the theory laid out in the first chapter, I will present several analytical options. First, I will revisit some of the old meanings of the term "civilization". Second, I will present my own thoughts on this issue. Third, I will turn to the Sanskrit and Pāli literature in order to find out whether the people of ancient India, i.e., our historical agents, had any concepts, similar to the concept of civilization, and in which particular ways these concepts were different from the contemporary definitions of civilization. In conclusion, I will discuss whether the ideas of the historical agents can be useful for creating our own models of the ancient South Asian civilization through the analysis of archaeological data.

The Idea of Civilization in Theory

As an idea, civilization went through a number of drastic conceptual transformations.[1] Formulated by the thinkers of the French Enlightenment as an antonym to barbarism, the term "civilization" had for a long time carried ethnocentric and moral connotations. As Braudel (1980:180) vividly put it, "the substantive civilization had to be... invented, and made up", it was "enlightenment", which could "hardly be imagined without a well-bread, well-mannered, and "polite" society to sustain it". By the middle of the nineteenth century, the purely idealistic notion of civilization in the singular had nonetheless been replaced by the notion of civilization in the plural. As the disciplines of history, ethnology, anthropology, archaeology, and sociology branched and developed during the nineteenth and twentieth centuries, the idea of civilization obtained numerous and often very different meanings. By the middle of the twentieth century, civilization became an extremely multifaceted and interdisciplinary concept. As "one of those words which show a new vision of the world" (Benveniste 1971:289), civilization was conceptualized in a multitude of meanings, at least some of which by that time had very little to do with the meanings originally implied by Francois Guizot (1828, 1829–1832), Victor de Riqueti (1756) and Voltaire (1756, 1769).[2] To give an example of how diverse the perceptions of civilization had become, one could refer to the meanings of culture, a term that is closely related to the idea of civilization. Over 50 years ago, two prominent American anthropologists—Alfred Kroeber and Clyde Kluckhohn (1952)—collected 161 definitions of culture. Without a doubt, had one decided to collect all the definitions of civilization, he or she would have come up with a comparable number. In fact, it would not be an exaggeration to say that in the nineteenth and twentieth centuries almost every social scholar whose intention it was to create a holistic model of world history had to deal with the idea of civilization.[3] To get a sense of how it was done, let us revisit the ideas of four very influential social thinkers.

In the classic work by Engels (1884) *Urspung der Familier, des Privateigentums und des Staats*, civilization is "a stage of development in society". Human progress—from primitive society to communism—would have been impossible without attaining this stage. Civilization thus is defined in socioeconomic terms, by the division of labor, the exchange between individuals... and the commodity production which combine them both. In civilization, these three innovations are argued to have come to their full growth and have revolutionized the whole of previous society. In archaeological terms, this means that all the attributes of early complex societies pinpointed by archaeologists—writing, monumental architecture, state-level sociopolitical organization, or urbanism—are not the essence of civilization but mere reflections and consequences of drastic changes that took place in the economic infrastructure. Although obsolete in the view of many contemporary social thinkers, this kind of economic determinism is alive in some quarters. Viewing the means of production as a driving force of social evolution has by no means lost its significance. To give an example, a prominent Russian assyriologist and ancient historian, Igor Diakonoff (1994), in his recent conceptual synthesis of world history, has attempted to present similar ideas on a new empirical level. Although Diakonoff avoids the direct use of the term "civilization", the spirit of this term is hidden within his linear eight-stage-model which is designed to explain the course of human history. The third phase in this model is called "The Early Antiquity" and its association with the Childean notion of civilization is quite apparent.

In contrast to the linear, mechanistic, and positivistic view of civilization by Engels, civilization of Oswald Spengler is idealistic, poetic, and decadent. To solve "the problem of civilization" is one of the main tasks of Spengler's famous treatise *Der Untergang des Abendlandes*. Civilization, in this treatise, is "the organicalogical sequel, fulfillment and finale of a culture". Every Culture has its own Civilization", and "the Civilization is the inevitable destiny of the Culture" (Spengler 1926:I.31). Civilizations in the plural are:

> the most external and artificial states of which as species of developed humanity is capable. They are a conclusion, the thing-become succeeding the thing-becoming, death following life, rigidity following expansion, intellectual age and the stone built, petrifying world-city following mother-earth and the spiritual childhood of Doric and Gothic. They are an end, irrevocable, yet by inward necessity reached again and again (Spengler 1926:I.31).

Regardless of the contemporary value of Spengler's ideas, his theory highlights two very important traits that until today are closely associated with the idea of civilization. These two traits are urbanism and culture. As I pointed out in the second chapter, the city, according to Spengler, was the decadent culmination of culture. Since civilization is the culmination of culture as well, it is unattainable without cities. At some point, Spengler unequivocally states that the city and money are the two most obvious and degenerate expressions of civilization.

The two great twentieth century historians to whom the idea of civilization has been particularly dear are Arnold Toynbee and Fernand Braudel. According to Toynbee (1934–1961:XII.273), it is important to distinguish between the idea of civilization and the idea of civilizations.[4] Civilization in the singular is a process that is still going on. In concrete historical terms, it is "an attempt to attain the kind of culture that had been attained by citizens of a Graeco-Roman (... Hellenic) city-state", and is consequently synonymous with the process of Hellenization that took place in the Near East after the third century BC. In broader philosophical, or as

Toynbee (1934–1961:XII.279) puts it, in "spiritual" terms, civilization is "an endeavor to create a state of society in which the whole of mankind will be able to live together in harmony, as members of a single all inclusive family". Civilizations in the plural mean to Toynbee (1934–1961:XII.282, 284) "particular historical exemplifications of the abstract idea" of civilization in the singular. Defined objectively, they are "one species of the genus "culture", and "the common ground between the respective individual fields of action of a number of different people".

The concept of civilization advocated by Braudel is more prosaic. Not particularly interested in defining civilization as a spiritual and idealistic phenomenon, Braudel (1980:208–209) instead focuses on civilizations in the plural. Given his passion for structural analysis, the study of a civilization, in Braudel's view, is the building of models. Civilizations are just another form of the *longue durée*, which can be investigated in a multitude of ways. On one occasion, Braudel (1980:202–203) defines a civilization as contingent upon three sets of criteria: cultural areas with frontiers, intercultural borrowings, and the refusals of intercultural borrowings.[5] On another occasion, Braudel (1993:9–22) offers a more functional definition, according to which a civilization combines a multitude of traits grouped under four topics: the geographical area, society, economy, and the way of thought. At last, Braudel (1993:35) portrays a civilization in purely ideational terms. It is:

> neither a given economy nor a given society, but something which can persist through a series of economies or societies, barely susceptible to gradual change. A civilization can be approached, therefore, only in the long term, taking hold of a constantly unwinding thread—something that a group of people have conserved and passed on as their most precious heritage from generation to generation, throughout and despite the storms and tumults of history.

This definition, in my view, is quite remarkable. Wittingly or unwittingly, Braudel admits that civilization has become one of those grand generic concepts which everyone uses and everyone knows yet no one can properly define. The idea of civilization thus has outgrown its intellectual roots. To Guizot, de Riqueti, and Voltaire, it had a clear cultural, evolutionary, and ethical meaning. Today, civilization is much more than a term; it is a powerful conceptual framework used in different social sciences and humanities. In the second chapter, when discussing the intelligibility of the idea of the city, I presumed that the city as a complex sociopolitical and cultural phenomenon can be studied and conceptualized in a multitude of ways from the point of view of several academic disciplines. Without a doubt, the same can be said about the idea of civilization. Like cities, civilizations can be investigated and classified based on the infinite variety of criteria. Political structure, social organization, religion, and economy are only a few among these criteria. What is more, civilization is a broader and more inclusive concept than that of the city. In fact, it is the most comprehensive analytical unit for the conceptualization of society and culture.

Like many other anthropological and historical concepts originating within western thought, civilization has carried ethnocentric, moral and even racist meanings. Yet, the negative legacy of this term must not overshadow its great analytical achievements. As the prominent linguist Emile Benviniste (1971:289) once noted, "the whole history of modern thought and the principal intellectual achievements in the western world are connected with the creation and handling of a few dozen essential words which are all the common possession of the western European languages". Civilization is certainly one of these words. Since its introduction into the vocabulary of modern European languages in the middle of the eighteenth century, this word has obtained a multitude of meanings many of which have little to do with its original ethnocentric roots. For example, there is a great difference between "civilization" of Lewis Morgan (1877) and "a civilization" of Fernand Braudel (1993:35); the former implies the notions of savagery and cultural superiority, while the latter is focused on something essential yet illusory, which lies at the foundation of society and culture and "can persist... barely susceptible to gradual change". Should the civilization of Lewis Morgan be discarded, the civilization of Fernand Braudel remains a powerful analytical tool. That fire causes death and destruction does not exclude the fact that fire is the source of life. If one believes in the validity of all-inclusive structural analyses of large geographical, cultural, and temporal entities, one must not see anything wrong with the idea of civilization.

Several scholars who have analyzed the history and semantics of the term "civilization" have emphasized the importance of distinguishing between civilization in the singular and civilizations in the plural. Civilization in the singular is a generic category, which in my view has little interest to the specialist in a specific cultural locus. As Braudel (1993:36) has justly noted, if we wish to understand what civilization is, we must study real instances, rather than any theory of civilizations; and generic definitions—whether archaeological or historical—are not going to provide much help. Whether as Toynbee's (1934–1961:XII.279) idealistic "endeavor to create a state of society in which the whole of mankind will be able to live together in harmony" or as Childe's (1950) materialistic 10 traits of an ancient urban center, civilization in the singular is too generic to reflect the specificities of concrete historical cases. On the contrary, perceived as spines of society and culture, as the largest imaginable cultural entities, as the Braudelian sand dunes, whose "unmoving sum of innumerable movements remain standing" (Braudel 1972–1973:II.757) for hundreds and thousands of years, civilizations in the plural present a viable analytical device for a holistic and all-inclusive study of the past.

Having said this, I tentatively accept the core assumption of the Braudelian view. To me, *a civilization is a deep structure of the most complex and inclusive sociocultural entity within vaguely defined geographical boundaries*. Synchronically, to define a civilization is to discern and describe this deep structure, or a component of this structure that remains unchanged for a significant period of time. Diachronically, to define a civilization is to establish the time of the emergence and the time of the disintegration of this structure. The epistemology of this definition directly relates to the theory that I have laid out in the first chapter. Specifically, I have suggested that there can be no purely objective interpretation of the past; and that the sociopolitical mentality of the historical agents is an intrinsic part of the events, phenomena, processes, structures, and models of the past. As far as objectivity is concerned, a civilization, in my view, is neither thing in itself nor an object subject to a purely objective study. Civilization is a transcendental and semi-objective category,[6] an idea with the help of which one conceptualizes massive amounts of cultural data. Defining a civilization then is like catching a glimpse of a murky, illusory, and to a large degree imaginary structure. As for the ideas and thoughts of the historical agents, they clearly constitute an innate part of any given civilization.[7] Epistemologically, the idea of civilization is in permanent transition, swinging between the data, the mind of the researcher, and the mentality of the historical agents. In previous interpretations, the emphasis has been placed on two of these three factors: the data and the mind of the researcher; not much attention has been given to the ideas of the ancient people, i.e., the historical agents. To make the study of civilizations meaningful, one must nevertheless consider these ideas carefully and thoughtfully. What the Romans, Chinese, or Greeks thought of history and of themselves and how they perceived progress, culture, and civilization is not just an alternative view; it is a constituent element of the Roman, Chinese, and Greek civilizations.

Thus, for the proper investigation of a given ancient or modern civilization, it is important to consider the sociopolitical ideas of the historical agents. In the context of ancient South Asia, this means that we need to find a concept or a set of concepts, which would be similar to or reminiscent of the idea of civilization. I believe such a concept exists in the ancient Indian literature; it is hidden within the Yuga Story in the rendition of the *VāyuPurāṇa* and *BrahmāṇḍaPurāṇa*.

World History in the Yuga Story

The earliest elaborate concept of time, history and cultural change in the ancient Indian literature is found in the Story of the Yugas, the four cosmic ages that follow one another in the course of universal time. Although absent in the Vedas, this story is present in several main genres of Sanskrit literature—the Śāstras, the Epics, and the Purāṇas.

Despite significant differences between its versions, the Yuga Story has a common core. According to this core, time is divided into the Kalpas, Manvantaras, Mahāyugas, and Yugas. One Kalpa, also called "The Day of Brahmā", consists of 1,000 Mahāyugas or 14 Manvantaras. One Mahāyuga also called Caturyuga (the fourfold Yuga) consists of the four Yugas, which are named Kṛta, Tretā, Dvāpara and Kali, each to identify the upside of a die cast in the game of dice. The four

Yugas are characterized as historical ages similar to those found in the Greek mythology. Kṛta is the Golden Age, in which the dharma (virtue) is fully present, sickness does not exist, and rivers flow with wine. Tretā is the Silver Age, in which sacrifices come to be practiced, the Veda appears and the dharma deteriorates. Dvāpara is the Copper Age, in which the Vedas multiply, sacrifices and austerities increase in number, and lawlessness becomes common. The Kali Yuga is the Iron Age, in which lawlessness prevails, the dharma is not respected, mlecchas (barbarians) rule, and the degeneration of the world is observed.

Scholars have analyzed the Yuga Story many times and have proposed a large variety of interpretations.[8] Most of these interpretations focus on textual history, cross-cultural parallels, and the place of the Yuga Story in Indian mythology. Having undergone a long genesis, the Yuga Story nonetheless contains many analytical layers. One of the most neglected and poorly investigated among these layers is historical. Aside from mythology, didactics, and the notion of deteriorating dharma, the Yuga Story has incorporated a sophisticated model of world history. The most detailed account of this model is found in the *VāyuPurāṇa* and *BrahmāṇḍaPurāṇa*, the two closely related Sanskrit texts that date roughly to the mid first millennium AD (Rocher 1986:156–160, 243–249).

The nucleus of the Yuga Story in the *VāyuPurāṇa* and the *BrahmāṇḍaPurāṇa* is standard. The historical process is divided into eight periods: the four Yugas (cosmic ages)—Kṛta, Tretā, Dvāpara, and Kali—and the four Sandhyās (transitional periods)—the Kṛta Sandhyā, the Tretā Sandhyā, the Dvāpara Sandhyā and the Kali Sandhyā—each placed between the respective Yugas. As in the other versions of the Yuga Story, the cycle of the Yugas is depicted as a progression from the Golden to the Iron Age and defined by the gradual corruption of the dharma (virtuousness). Aside from the standard characteristics however, the Yugas and Sandhyās of the *VāyuPurāṇa* and the *BrahmāṇḍaPurāṇa* include a number of unusual traits of purely historical nature. It is worthwhile to review these traits in a word-by-word translation.[9]

During the first Kṛta Yuga, god creates people who are described as "mobile gatherers" (VP 1.8.21), and who:

> ...took refuge by the rivers, waterfalls, seas and mountains (VP 1.8.46)... These people ate food produced from the juice of the earth. Having acquired mental perfection, they moved wherever they wished (VP 1.8.47)... They took refuge by the mountains and oceans having neither houses nor shelters (VP 1.8.52)...

There is neither dharma (virtuousness) nor a-dharma (non-virtuousness) in the first Kṛta Yuga. People are socially undifferentiated. No system of varṇas and āśramas exists.

> In the beginning of the Kalpa, during the Kṛta Yuga there was neither dharma nor adharma. In the Kṛta Yuga (people) were born with their own and different duties and rights (VP 1.8.49)... In the Kṛta Yuga, the doing of good or evil did not take place. There was no system of varṇas and āśramas. Neither was there mixture of castes through unlawful intermarriage... there were no low class and high class people (VP 1.8.60–61).

During the Kṛta Sandhyā, the period of junction between the Kṛta and Tretā Yugas, two important changes occur—climatic deterioration and the transition to a sedentary lifestyle:

> When little time remained, because of the nature of the transitional period, extremes (of climate) began to take place. (People) were severely troubled by cold winds and burning sunshine. Tormented by these extremes they made shelters. Fighting with the extremes of climate they found recourse in houses. Before, they wandered wherever they wanted without having a base in houses. Now, depending on circumstances and their desire, they lived in houses, in deserts, in deep ravines, on the mountains and by the rivers... (VP 1.8.91–94).

The innovations of the Kṛta Sandhyā are developed in the Tretā Yuga. First, sacrifice is institutionalized:

> yajña (sacrifice) was established by the gods, namely by Yāmas, Śuklas, and Japas with all their requisites (VP 1.57.61)... Then, Indra, the consumer of the world, together with all the gods established yajña and all its requisites. When the aśvamedha (horse-sacrifice) was established, the Great Sages assembled and performed sacrifices with animals. After having heard about it, everyone assembled there (VP 1.57.91–92).

Secondly, agriculture is introduced. There are several stories found throughout the Purāṇas that expound on the transition to agriculture during the Tretā Yuga. According to one of them:

> ... success befell them... As they wished, agriculture, the accomplishment of artha (welfare), became another means of their subsistence. Rainwaters, which poured downwards, became known as 'rivers'. Streams flowing in the ditches became known as 'streams'. Thus, in the second creation by rain, the rivers appeared. The little water that was left afterwards on the surface of the earth was mixed with dirt and became plants. Plants then produced flowers, roots and fruits. Fourteen types of not sown and non-cultivated trees and bushes that grew in the villages and forests gave birth to seasonal fruits and flowers. Such was the emergence of agricultural plants during the Tretā Yuga. Since then, in the Tretā Yuga people subsisted on these plants (VP 1.8.124–134; 1.2.7.124–130).

In another version of this story, the god Brahmā is held responsible for initiating agriculture:

> Then seeing the success of his actions, the self-existent lord Brahmā instituted agriculture for the sustenance of (people). Since that time plants were cultivated (VP 1.8.153).

In both versions, the introduction of agriculture is related to the emergence of the varṇāśrama system, dharma, daṇḍa (coercive power), pastoralism, craft production, and the study of the Vedas. The establishment of the varṇas—the first institutionalized system of social disparity in ancient South Asia—is presented as having particularly strong ties to the emergence of agriculture:

> When agriculture became fully perfected by (people), the Self-Existent (Brahmā) established rules in due order one by one. The ones who had power and means established themselves as Kṣatriya for the protection of their deeds.... The ones who spoke "The truth is Brahmā" and narrated the story of the past were Brahmāṇs. The others who were weak were prescribed the duties of Vaiśyas... They were called Vaiśyas because they sustained their living by cultivation. Those who moaned, relented, and were engaged in serving others, those who were powerless and had little potency; he (Brahmā) called them Śūdras. When the system of the four varṇas was established everywhere, the lord Brahmā assigned specific karmas (duties) and dharmas (virtues). Yet again, out of ignorance people violated their dharmas. They did not live according to the dharmas of their respective varṇas and confronted each other. After having observed this in reality, the lord Brahmā assigned force, daṇḍa (coercive power, punishment) and war as the means of livelihood for the Kṣatriyas. To the Brahmāṇs the lord assigned these three duties: sacrifice, study of the Vedas, and the receiving (of gifts). He gave cattle breeding, trade and agriculture to the Vaiśyas, and devised crafts as the means of sustenance for the Śūdras. There are also duties common for the Brahmāṇs, Kṣatriyas, and Vaiśyas. These are sacrifice, study of the Vedas, and the giving of gifts (VP 1.8.153–164)... When the varṇas were set up, he established āśramas (VP 1.8.168)...

Among important innovations of the Tretā Yuga, mention must be made of the Śrauta ritual:

> In the beginning of the Tretā Yuga, Manu and the seven Sages spoke. The seven Sages spoke of the orally transmitted Śrauta dharmas, such as Agnihotra, the taking of a wife and the like; all prescribed by Brahmā in accordance with the Ṛgveda, Yajurveda, and Sāmaveda, ... (BaP 1.2.29.43–45).

Also, the Tretā Yuga witnesses the conceptualization of three means for achieving mokṣa (the final liberation): kāma (love), artha (wealth), and dharma (virtuousness):

> Artha, dharma, kāma, glory and victory are acquired by the kings one by one without any hostility (BaP 1.2.29.81).

In the sphere of sacred scriptures, the Tretā Yuga is characterized by the undivided four-partite (lit. four-footed) Veda and the compilation of the Mantras and Brahmāṇas.

> In the beginning of Tretā, being the outcome of dharma, the Veda Samhita was an entity... (VP 1.57.47)... One four-partite Veda was known at the time of Tretā (VP 1.57.83)... The mantras and Brahmāṇas were compiled by the Sages (VP 1.57.60).

In the political sphere, the Tretā Yuga witnesses the emergence of kingship and daṇḍa (coercive power, punishment):

> Thenceforth arose the kings carrying the staff of daṇḍa. The rulers came to be called Rājas since they conciliated the people (VP 1.57.58).

An important institution of Cakravartins (the rulers, lit. the turners of the wheel) also emerges during the Tretā Yuga:

> The future, past and present Cakravartins are born during the Tretā Yuga (BaP 1.2.29.79).

Colonization of the earth takes place during the Tretā: Manu Svāyambhuva had ten grandsons who were similar to him. This whole earth with its seven dvīpas (continents) was settled by them during the first Tretā Yuga of the Svāyambhuva Manvantara (VP 1.33.4–5).

Finally, women's fertility is discussed in the context of the Tretā Yuga:

> Today women's menstruation continues until the end of their life. At that time that did not happen because of the nature of the (Tretā) Yuga. The menstruation of those women took place month by month. Sexual intercourse took place in accordance with menstruation (BaP 1.2.7.78–79).

The transitional period of the Tretā Sandhyā is not distinguished by any major transformations, save for generic statements about the deterioration of the dharma. The Dvāpara Yuga is the next to witness significant changes. Numerous vices overpower people during this age. "Greed, unhappiness, trade, war, indecisiveness in the issues of truth, breakdown of the varṇāśrama system, uncertainty of duties, restraint of sacrificial plants and animals, drunkenness, deceit, impatience, and violence" commonly characterize the people and manners that prevail during the Dvāpara Yuga (VP 1.58.3–4). Also, during the Dvāpara, difference of opinion starts among men; sacred scriptures split and multiply; philosophical schools and new branches of knowledge emerge; the twice-born begin to disregard the system of varṇāśrama; droughts, deaths and epidemics take place… The following excerpt from the *VāyuPurāṇa* gives a succinct theological explanation to the perturbations that take place during the Dvāpara Yuga:

> Owing to the incompetence with regards to the causes and the uncertainty of the cause, there arises a confusion of opinions that results in the split of knowledge. A multitude of texts are created by individuals of different beliefs. The single Veda is made four-fold during the Tretā… The Vedas are further divided by the sons of the Sages who, confused by different opinions, misinterpret sounds and syllables and compose Mantras and Brahmāṇas. Because of the minor and occasional (textual) modifications, the Samhitas of Ṛg, Yajur and Sāma are collated by the Sages who are proficient in the sacred knowledge of Śruti and hold different opinions. The teachings of Brahmāṇas, Kalpasūtras and Mantras are compiled by the teachers, while other texts are opposed. During the Dvāpara, the twice-born live in a confused system of varṇas. Before, there was one Yajurveda. Now there are two. The entirety of Śāstras is perverted by generally confusing commentaries. Much confusion is brought by discussions on the Yajurveda. In a similar way, because of the unending uncertainties during the Dvāpara much confusion is made by the people of different views with regards to the Ṛg, Atharva and Sāma Vedas… Calamities, such as droughts, deaths, diseases, and uprisings, take place in the Dvāpara. Verbal and mental actions bring despair. Despair results in discussions on the liberation from suffering. These discussions lead to asceticism; asceticism leads to the realization of suffering, the realization of suffering leads to the birth of knowledge during the Dvāpara. The Śāstras of the Dvāpara confront the Śāstras honored earlier during the Svāyambhuva Manvantara. There are uncertainties in the Āyurveda (medicine), Jyotiṣa (astrology) and Vedāṇga (auxiliary Vedic sciences). Also there are uncertainties in the Arthaśāstra (political science) and Hetuśāstra (science of logic). The distinctions between Smṛti (the sacred knowledge) and the Śāstras (sciences) are established here and there (VP 1.58.9–24).

In addition to all these perturbations, the Śruti and Smṛti are divided during this Yuga (BaP 1.2.7.31.6) and the significant deterioration of the dharma takes place. The worst degeneration of the dharma however takes place in the two final periods of the cycle, during the Dvāpara Sandhyā and the Kali Yuga. Descriptions of the Kali Yuga are found in most Purāṇas, the *Mahābhārata*, and several other texts of Sanskrit literature. According to these descriptions, in the Kali Yuga the world is shaken by a multitude of social, religious, and political perturbations. The deterioration of the dharma, fatal diseases, fear of hunger, danger of drought, loss of the authority of scriptures, neglect of the Vedas, cessation of sacrifices, the advent of rulers from the Śūdras, Yavanas (Greeks), and Mlecchas (foreigners, barbarians), propaganda of heretic ideas, slaughter of children in the womb, mixture of castes,... these and other troubles lead to the end of the world and, ultimately, following the cycle, bring the return of the Golden Age of Kṛta. A vivid version of this story is told by the Sage Mārkaṇḍeya in his conversations with the Paṇḍavas in the Forest Book of the *Mahābhārata*. This story is well-known and has previously attracted the attention of scholars (Fleet 1911; Gable 1920; Pargiter 1913; Varma 1978–79). At the end of the Kali Yuga, during the transitional period of Kali Sandhyā, Kalki Viṣṇuyaśas, the tenth incarnation of the god Viṣṇu, comes to kill the Mlecchas and heretics and to turn the cycle back to the Golden Age of Kṛta (VP 2.36.105–125; MBH 3.188.85–93, 189; as well as in many other Purāṇas). Thus ends the Story of the Yugas in the *Mahābhārata* and the Purāṇas.

As I noted above, there is a significant amount of philological literature dealing with the origin and textual history of this story. For example, it has been argued that the historical component is a relatively late incursion (ca. fourth to fifth century AD) and was not part of the earlier versions of the Yuga Story. At this point however, I am purposely avoiding the text-historical aspects of the *VāyuPurāṇa* and *BrahmāṇḍaPurāṇa* (these two texts are, in many respects, identical, and possibly originated from the earlier text). As I argued in the first chapter, if we use texts as the sources for ideas rather than facts, meticulous text-historical methods do no longer matter. In other words, whether the historical component of the Yuga Story emerged during the Mauryan, Kushana, or Gupta periods is not going to change its value as a reflection of the ideas by the historical agents. In a similar way, when we refer to contemporary sociopolitical theories, we rarely recall when their authors lived and what sociopolitical milieu was like at the time they wrote. Eventually, it would be helpful to know whose views this narrative represented and from which sociopolitical milieu it originated. I will return to this issue in the postscript, yet at this point will limit my task to determining whether as a work of history, this narrative can be of help for our own interpretations.

The Yuga Story and the Idea of Civilization

The first striking feature of the historical narrative of the Yuga Story is that it contains an elaborate model of cultural change. According to this model, the genesis of human society is cyclical, hierarchical, and unilinear. It consists of six distinct stages (see Table 5.1): 1) Kṛta Yuga: egalitarian society of mobile gatherers from the creation of humans until the transition to sedentary life style; 2) Kṛta Sandhyā: transition to sedentary life style caused by climatic deterioration; 3) Tretā Yuga: a highly complex society characterized by a long list of social, economic and ideological traits; 4) Dvāpara Yuga: a partial crisis and the decadence of dharma, when society still functions but evinces traits of decay and degeneration; 5) Kali Yuga: a catastrophic collapse, disintegration of sociopolitical system, de-urbanization and ideological breakdown; 6) Kali Sandhyā: the total collapse of all societal and religious institutions eventually transforming into the new Kṛta Yuga.

Without a doubt, this model is both a work of history and a historical framework. Its mode of argument is organicist (see my reference to Hayden White in the first chapter). Its method of envisioning world history is structural and synthetic. Its generalizations aim at abstraction and discerning patterns and regularities. No individuals are of significance. Brahmā, the Seven Sages, and Kalki are the personifications of inevitable destiny rather than meaningful historical agents. What matters are the laws and regularities manifested in the cycle of the Yugas, Manvantaras and Kalpas, not the peculiarities of historical process. It is the inevitability of fate or in the vivid words of the Paurāṇikas "the power of the essence of the future", which makes the Age of Kṛta return after the perturbations of the Age of Kali (VP 1.58.102).

Most importantly, this model displays an advanced level of social thinking grounded in empirical knowledge. Consider the story of transition to agriculture. Both in the *VāyuPurāṇa* and *BrahmāṇḍaPurāṇa*, climatic deterioration is seen as the prime cause of sedentary life and the domestication of plants. The understanding of the relationship between sedentism and agriculture is also quite realistic. Sedentism precedes agriculture and is classified in a

Table 5.1

Sociocultural traits of the Yugas and transitional periods

Yugas	Main Traits
Kṛta Yuga	Creation of people
	Mobile gatherers
	No dharma, no varṇāśrama system
Kṛta Sandhyā	Climatic deterioration
	Sedentary life style
Tretā Yuga	Agriculture, cattle-breeding, crafts
	Life in helmets, villages, and cities
	Rule of the dharma
	Proper functioning of the varṇāśrama system
	Institutionalization of the yajña (sacrifices) and the Śrauta Ritual yet the placement of a taboo on the killing of animals
	Kāma, artha and dharma as means for achieving mokṣa
	Authority and unity of sacred scriptures: the single four-fold Veda and some Brahmāṇas
	Reign of kings: The Cakravartins and the Rājas
	Kings carrying the staff of daṇḍa (coercive power, army)
	Colonization of the earth
	Women's fertility
Tretā Sandhyā	No specific traits, except for the deterioration of the dharma
Dvāpara Yuga	Deterioration of the dharma
	Formation of the Vedic cannon, i.e., classification and division of the Vedas by the Vedavyāsas and the compilation of the Samhitās
	Confusion of the Vedas by people of different views
	Emergence of a large variety of texts commenting on the Vedas
	Division of the Yajurveda into Śuklas and Kriṣṇa recensions
	Formations of schools of thought and sciences, emergence of Śāstras
	People begin to disregard the varṇāśrama system
	Draughts, premature deaths, and epidemics
Dvāpara Sandhyā	No specific traits, except for the deterioration of the dharma
Kali Yuga	Deterioration of the dharma
	Fatal diseases, hunger, droughts
	Loss of the authority of scriptures
	Neglect of the Vedas
	Cessation of sacrifices
	Advent of rulers from the śūdras, yavanas (Greeks), and mlecchas (foreigners)
	Warfare
	Women outnumber men
	Mixture of the varṇāśrama system
	Propaganda of heretic ideas
	Slaughter of children in the womb
Kali Sandhyā	Dharma completely destroyed
	Very few people left on the earth after droughts and slaughter
	Complete collapse of the varṇāśrama system
	Twice born flee to the forests
	Kalki, an incarnation of Viṣṇu, comes to kill the mlecchas and infidels

separate sub-phase, namely the Kṛta Sandhyā. The consequences of the introduction of agriculture are very similar to those advocated by contemporary anthropologists. Sacrifices, violence, social differentiation, the formation of an elaborate ideology, diversification of kingship, development of religion, and even women's fertility, in one way or another, are mentioned in the *VāyuPurāṇa* and *BrahmāṇḍaPurāṇa*. The concepts of the Dvāpara and Kali present yet another example of highly developed social thinking. In them, the Paurāṇikas conceptualize the sociopolitical crises that result in the collapse of complex societies. Most premises of these crises—the intensification of religious debates, warfare, corruption of the varṇāśrama system, propaganda of heretic ideas, slaughter of children in the womb, the advent of foreign rulers, and the like—are all based on the observation and rethinking of real historical events that took place in the second half of the first millennium BC. Moreover, there are indications that the historical concepts of the Yuga Story may have had practical and theoretical implications already at the time of its formation and codification.

The Aśokan inscriptions, for example, mention the term kapa/kalpa, which is frequently associated with the word "Yuga". The Girnar version of the Rock Edict 4 uses the term savata-kapa/samvarta-kalpam when speaking of the promotion of the right dharma by the sons, grandsons, and grand-grandsons of Aśoka. The Kalsi version of the Rock Edict 5 uses the term ava kapam/ yavat kalpam. Savata kappa/samvarta kalpa literary means "the era of destruction", and ava kapam/yavat kalpam means "throughout the era" (Hultzsch 1925). In spite of the existence of the different interpretations of these terms (Barua and Chaudhuri 1990:77; Nikam and McKeon 1958:31; Sen 1956:74–75), it is quite likely that the term kapa/kalpam refers to the idea of cyclical time, and if so it is quite remarkable that it marks actual time periods in historical documents of the Mauryan Period. Another, more direct indication of the use of the Yuga terminology is found in the *Kauṭilīya Arthaśāstra*, which unequivocally includes the term "Yuga" in the list of measures to be learned by the supervisors of measurements (KA 2.20.28–29).

Yet, the most remarkable use of the Yuga terminology is found in the sections of the Purāṇas that describe the continents and people of the earth.[10] The full sequence of the Yugas is not ascribed in these sections to every single continent. The ages of the Kṛta, Tretā, Dvāpara and Kali are known primarily in the Bhāratavarṣa, which is a traditional name for India (VP 1.57.22; 1.24.1). In other mythical continents and subcontinents, the full sequence is often unknown. The continent of Puṣkara, for example, is characterized as being at the stage of the Kṛta (VP 1.49.115–117). The continents of Plakṣa and Śāka are described as being permanently in the time of the Tretā (MP 122.40; VP 1.49). In some continents, no Yugas are known at all (VP 1.33.49). In other words, some regions of the world never leave the stage of the Kṛta, some remain at the stage of the Tretā, some go through the full cycle of the four Yugas and some never enter the evolutionary cycle at all. Thus, the Paurāṇikas use the historical model of the Yuga Story as a conceptual device to differentiate the stages of cultural evolution, and, similar to the thinkers of the Enlightenment, distinguish between the "civilized" and "uncivilized'. The Bhāratavarṣa, or India, is "civilized" as it has gone through the full cycle of the Yugas, and by the time of the composition of the Epics and Purāṇas has entered the final period of the Kali.

Thus we have approached the main issue of our enquiry, the concept of civilization. Although it has not been my intention to find a direct equivalent to this concept—the historical constructs of the Yuga Story are clearly self-sustaining[11]—one cannot help noticing that some of the ideas that the Yuga Story conveys are reminiscent of the concepts of civilization as used in ancient history and archaeology. The analysis of these ideas, in my view, can significantly deepen our own understanding of the ancient South Asian civilization.

The highest level of sociocultural complexity in the sequence of the Yugas is attained with the transition from the Kṛta to the Tretā Yuga. Following the transitional period of the Kṛta Sandhyā, the Tretā Yuga witnesses the largest number of drastic cultural innovations, which can be summarized in eleven traits: 1) agriculture, cattle-breeding, crafts; 2) life in hamlets, villages and cities; 3) rule of dharma; 4) proper functioning of the varṇāśrama system; 5) practice of the yajña and the Śrauta ritual, with a taboo on the killing of animals; 6) kāma, dharma and artha, as the means for achieving mokṣa (final liberation); 7) authority and unity of sacred scriptures: the single four-fold Veda and the principle Brāhmaṇas; 8) reign of kings:

the Cakravartins and the Rājas; 9) kings carrying the staff of daṇḍa (coercive power, army); 10) colonization of the earth; 11) changes in women's menstrual cycles.

Moving a step forward from the succinct wording of the Purāṇas, one can render each of these innovations into the language of contemporary social science. The traits of the Tretā Yuga then become noticeably more theoretical and can be presented as follows: 1) formation of the diversified and specialized economy divided into three main branches: agriculture, pastoralism and craft-production; 2) solidification of a sedentary lifestyle by creation of permanent villages and the emergence of cities; 3) emergence of an orally transmitted behavioral code, dealing with a large variety of legal, social and ethical issues (dharma); 4) formation of the unique sociocultural system based on a mix of hierarchical and heterarchical relations (the system of the four varṇas and four āśramas); 5) emergence and institutionalization of sacrifices and rituals, yet the placing of a taboo on the killing of animals; 6) standardization of the means for achieving the ultimate liberation (implies the existence of religious system/s aimed at liberation); 7) establishing of the unequivocal authority and unity of the orally transmitted sacred scriptures, the Vedas; 8) institutionalization of kingship; 9) institutionalization of the means of coercion for the maintaining of social order (daṇḍa): army, supervisors and institutionalized punishment (the state?); 10) beginning of colonial expansion; 11) increase in women's fertility.

Without question, either of these two lists represents very a sophisticated concept. Like the idea of civilization in archaeology, the Tretā Yuga marks a drastic qualitative shift to the most complex period in human history. The Paurāṇikas seem to be purposely emphasizing the magnitude of this shift: no other Yuga or Sandhyā is defined by such a diverse and long list of changes. The traits that define these changes are of two types: generic and idiosyncratic. The sedentary lifestyle in villages and cities, the institution of kingship, the means of coercion (the state), colonialism, the increase in women's fertility, and agricultural economy are the generic traits; not uniquely South Asian, they could equally characterize many other parts of the ancient world. The dharma, varṇāśrama, yajña, Śrauta, and all the other remaining traits are idiosyncratic; one does not find them in Greece or Mesopotamia. Yet taken together, all of these traits are closely interrelated. Sacrifices, agriculture, the system of varṇas and āśramas, dharma, kingship, daṇḍa, etc., are conceptualized interdependently; their emergence is interrelated and is contingent on one another.[12] The societal organization of the Tretā Yuga thus is perceived as an organic whole, as an entity consisting of codependent elements.

Remarkably, five of these elements, namely the vārttā, dharma, veda, varṇāśrama, and yajña continue to play the key role in the descriptions of the subsequent periods; a complex sociopolitical organization does not perish at the end of the Tretā Yuga, and the state of affairs during the Dvāpara and Kali Yugas is defined by the degree of degeneration of the dharma, veda, varṇāśrama, and yajña. Thus, if there is a deep structure beyond the definitions of the Yugas and Sandhyās that stand for the most complex periods of the cycle, this structure rests on five pillars: 1) agricultural economy (vārttā): 2) an orally maintained and transmitted code of legal, ethical and social conduct (dharma); 3) an orally maintained and transmitted sacred knowledge (the Vedas); 4) an idiosyncratic semi-hierarchical and semi-heterarchical sociocultural system (varṇāśrama); and 5) a set of ritual and sacrificial practices (yajña).

Who of the modern social thinkers would have come up with a better structural definition of the ancient Indian civilization? Are not these five traits reminiscent of the deep structures of the Braudelian *longue durée*? The historical narrative of the Yuga Story thus contains two models reminiscent of the idea of civilization (see Table 5.2). The first one, diachronic, is expressed in the concept of the Tretā Yuga and is meant to designate a drastic cultural shift from the egalitarianism and hunting-gathering to the sociocultural complexity and food-producing economy. The second one, synchronic, is expressed in the five aforementioned traits that emerge during the Tretā Yuga and maintain importance until the end of the cycle; it stands for the quintessential sociocultural core or the deep structure that maintains importance from the Tretā to Kali Yuga. Importantly, both of these models are the products of Brahmanic ideology, and unlike the definition of the city extracted from the ideologically diverse texts in the second chapter, omit the views of other contemporary social and religious groups.

The question then arises whether being so ideologically biased these models have any value for the analysis of archaeological data. In my view, the answer to this

Table 5.2

Two models of complex society based on the Yuga story

Model 1—Defined diachronically from the point of view of the transition to the TretāYuga

1. Formation of diversified and specialized economy with the foundation in agriculture, cattle-breeding, and crafts
2. Solidification of sedentary lifestyle in rural and urban centers
3. Emergence of rigid legal and ethical code of dharma
4. Formation of the idiosyncratic sociocultural system of varṇas and āśramas based on a mix of hierarchical and heterarchical relations
5. Institutionalization of the sacrifices (yajña) and the Śrauta Ritual the imposition of a taboo on the killing of animals
6. Formulation of the kāma, artha and dharma as the main three means for achieving mokṣa (ultimate liberation)
7. Establishing of the authority and unity of the sacred scriptures, such as the single four-fold Veda and the main Brāhmaṇas
8. Institutionalization of kingship through the rule of Cakravartins and Rajas
9. Maintaining of social order by means of the institution of coercive power (the daṇḍa)
10. Beginning of territorial expansionism
11. Changes in women's productive behavior

Model 2—Defined synchronically as a deep structure of the Tretā, Dvāpara and Kali Yugas

1. Agricultural economy (vārttā)
2. An orally maintained and transmitted code of legal, ethical and social conduct (dharma)
3. An orally maintained and transmitted sacred knowledge (the Vedas)
4. An idiosyncratic sociocultural system (varṇāśrama)
5. A set of ritual and sacrificial practices (yajña)

question lies in the choice of a proper theoretical angle. On some levels, the Paurāṇikas adhere to rigid religious and ideological dogmas; for example, they ascribe unreasonably early relative dates to the typically Brahmanic traits such as the vedas, varṇāśrama, and Śrauta ritual. On other levels, they rely on sophisticated empirical knowledge and critical thought; the story of the transition to agriculture and the concept of sociopolitical crisis are both empirically grounded and theoretically sophisticated. The two theoretical models presented above thus exist on several levels. While, on the surface some of their traits reflect the dogmas of faith, in subtext they display the patterns of highly sophisticated critical thinking. As an analogy to this kind of historical analysis, one can refer to the works of the Soviet Marxists. Paying the tribute to the required dogmas—the class struggle, forces of production, etc.—the Marxist historians often managed to convey original and even anti-Marxist ideas. The Paurāṇikas responsible for the compilation of the *VāyuPurāṇa* and *BrahmāṇḍaPurāṇa* must have been in a somewhat similar situation. Using the required terminology and framework—the veda, yajña, Śrauta, etc.—they encoded their critical thoughts and empirical knowledge in subtext. Whether they did it wittingly or unwittingly is a question for a separate study. What matters is that their theoretical models contain a great mix of ideas, many of which may have merit in the context of the contemporary studies of ancient South Asia.

Conclusion: From the Paurāṇikas to V. Gordon Childe

In archaeology, the most influential and frequently quoted definition of civilization is the one proposed by V. Gordon Childe. Yet it is often forgotten that the goal of the article, in which this definition was originally formulated, was not to define civilization but to define the city. As Childe (1950:3) asserted in the beginning of this article, he intended "to present the city... prehistorically as the resultant and symbol of a 'revolution'...". The reason why the contemporaries and successors of Childe turned his argument into the definition of civilization owed to the fact that Childe faithfully adhered to the evolutionary paradigms of Lewis Morgan and the Marxists, and in particular to the ideas of savagery, barbarism, and civilization. The ten famous traits[13] defined by Childe (1950:17) "to distinguish... the earliest cities" consequently became associated with the concept of civilization.

In archaeological theory, many changes have taken place since the time of Childe and his contemporaries. Today, instead of civilization, many Anglo-American archaeologists prefer the term "complex society". In my view, this terminological shift is futile. First, as I tried to show above, the term civilization remains a powerful analytical tool which despite its past meanings can be used in the study of both the ancient and the modern world. Second, caused mainly by the desire to avoid derogatory and racist language of the past, the terminology shift *per se* does not change the essence of the Childean ideas, which still lie in the foundation of protohistoric archaeology. For example, the concept of the two revolutions—agricultural and urban, with the latter marking the threshold of civilization—remains the dominant theoretical framework for the explanation of cultural change in protohistory. The field of South Asian archaeology is not the exception. In the view of most Indian, Pakistani, and Western scholars, the first civilization of the South Asian subcontinent is the Harappan civilization. Consequently, the emergence of the ancient Indian civilization as such is associated with the formation of the Harappan phenomenon, either in its early or mature forms.

Evidently, the Purāṇic models discussed above present a significantly different picture. The first model contains a highly sophisticated theory of transition to agriculture yet has no concept of urbanism. In fact, the emergence of cities is not even distinguished in a separate stage or a phase. Briefly mentioned among other innovations of the Tretā Yuga, cities play a relatively insignificant role. The three Yugas that mark various stages in the development of a complex society are the Tretā, Dvāpara, and Kali. The Tretā begins with the transition to agriculture, the Dvāpara marks a partial systemic crisis, and the Kali is the collapse of a complex society. The history of civilization thus is conceptualized in three phases: the emergence-efflorescence, the decadence, and the collapse. Cities play no important role in either of these phases. Neither their emergence nor disintegration is presented as a major event comparable in significance to the transition to sedentism, the introduction of agriculture, the formation of the varṇāśrama system, or the deterioration of the dharma. Conceptually, this means that unlike many contemporary archaeologists who, treading in Childe's footsteps, distinguish between the agricultural and urban revolutions, the Paurāṇikas envisioned the transition to agriculture and the emergence of cities under the single analytical unit, the concept of the Tretā Yuga; for some reason, the emergence of cities was not as significant to them as the transition to agriculture.

In continuation of this, the second Purāṇic model presents the ethos of the ancient Indian civilization as contingent on transformations in ethical, religious, ritual, social, and agricultural spheres. Meanwhile, cities, writing, and monumental architecture—the traits that for a long time have been seen as the definitive markers of civilization—are epiphenomenal to the ethos of ancient India. Both temporally and causally the formation of the ancient Indian civilization is linked, in the second model, to the transition to agriculture.[14] Taken together and projected on South Asian archaeology, these two models present an interesting and unusual story of the rise of civilization in ancient South Asia. According to this story, the genesis of the ancient South Asian civilization begins during the Neolithic Period and its ethos—the deep structure that maintained its significance over a long period of time—is defined through five traits; namely, agricultural economy, an orally transmitted code of conduct, an orally transmitted sacred knowledge, an idiosyncratic sociocultural system, and a set of ritual and sacrificial practices. Although different from most mainstream interpretations, this story, in my view, is not anathema to the contemporary archaeology. Yet this is a question for the next and concluding chapter.

6 The Idea of the Ancient Indian Civilization: A Framework of Enquiry

...there is something about India which not only anthropologists are able to characterize as a "unique configuration" but ... is also evident to the non-academic "lay". We must thus say that there is a specific quality of an "Indianness" of its civilization as opposed to Chinese or the European ones, etc.

—S. C. Malik (1968:58).

I began this study by proposing a theory aimed at a humanistic and structural investigation of the past. Given that this theory has been of utmost importance in directing my analysis of texts and material cultures and that this concluding chapter will follow it in every respect, let me reiterate its main assumptions. According to the first assumption, human agency is the key driving force within history. Consequently, the objects of anthropology and history are the products of human will, intellect, and action. According to the second assumption, the creation of structures and models is essential for the conceptualization of human past, particularly if this past is known from fragmentary material remains. According to the third assumption, there can be no purely scientific and objective interpretation of the past; regardless of whether the correct interpretations exist, the desire to acquire them is what really matters. According to the fourth assumption, the ideas and thoughts of the historical agents present an intrinsic part of the events, phenomena, processes, structures, and models of the past. By incorporating these ideas and thoughts in our interpretations we make the study of the past more intimate and insightful.

The first three of these assumptions are not new. I have formulated them under the influence of the ideas of several well-known thinkers who advocated humanistic and literary methods in the study of the past. The fourth assumption, I believe, is rather new, for by proposing to treat the ancient texts as sources of ideas rather than facts, I have brought into play the sociopolitical thinking of the historical agents, i.e., a medium which is not commonly used by archaeologists in the analyses of material cultures, particularly so in the context of ancient South Asia. It is this assumption that paved a path for my study of the ancient Indian city, and ultimately allowed me to formulate a tentative definition of the ancient Indian civilization.

Aside from the vārttā (agriculture), the traits that are included in this definition—dharma, veda, varṇāśrama, and yajña—are quite specific. Needless to say, it would be absurd to take them literally and to attempt to trace their origins in the archaeological cultures of Neolithic, Chalcolithic, and Bronze Age South Asia. As in the case with the idea of the city, it is not the content of the ideas of the historical agents that matters; it is the theoretical framework within this content that may have merit from the point of view of archaeology. As I suggested above, these five traits can be rendered in the language of contemporary social science as agricultural economy, an orally transmitted code of conduct, an orally transmitted sacred knowledge, an idiosyncratic sociocultural system, and a set of ritual and sacrificial practices. To determine whether these traits form a plausible model for the conceptualization of South Asian protohistory and the idea of the ancient Indian civilization, we need to place them in the context of archaeological data, e.g., chronology, culture history, and the specific aspects of material culture. Evidently, it would be very difficult to find archaeological evidence for "an orally transmitted sacred knowledge", "an idiosyncratic social system", and "a set of ritual and sacrificial practices"; yet one can amass circumstantial data and determine whether in the context of these data, these traits reflect the processes and structures that may have actually characterized South Asian past. For one thing is clear; taken together, these five traits can be maintained for thousands of years in different linguistic, religious, ethnic, and political contexts, and their material expressions can be hidden within a large variety of archaeological cultures. Let me discuss these traits under four general topics: agricultural economy and rural life style, orality and mnemonic devices, social organization, and religious practices.

Agricultural Economy and Rural Lifestyle

In the Purāṇic historical model analyzed in the previous chapter, the notions of rural life style and agriculture play a prominent role. According to this model, the first hamlets and villages appear during the transitional period of the Kṛta Sandhyā, while the invention of agriculture takes place in the stage immediately following it, i.e., in the Tretā Yuga. Marking the threshold of civilization and causing a chain of drastic innovations, agriculture, henceforth, maintains importance as one of the definitive characteristics of the remaining Yugas until the collapse of complex society during the transitional stage of the Kali Sandhyā. The transition to sedentism thus sets the scene for the transition to agriculture, while the transition to agriculture sets the scene for the emergence of civilization in ways very similar to those proposed in contemporary archaeology. Given this, one could, not unreasonably, draw comparisons between the Kṛta Sandhyā and the South Asian Epipaleolithic or Mesolithic, and between the initial stages of the Tretā Yuga and the South Asian Neolithic. The difference between the Purāṇic and modern periodizations, then is conceptual and has to do with the idea of the city. In the Purāṇic model, the city and the village are not clearly differentiated. Neither is there any equivalent to the concept of the urban revolution. In our ways of thinking, the city and the village constitute a dichotomy or even a dialectical opposition, and the concept of the urban revolution both temporally and causally is separated from the concept of the agricultural revolution. Conceptually, in my view, the Purāṇic model reflects the genesis of the ancient Indian civilization more accurately and the currently available archaeological data support this point.

To begin with, the story of the transition to food-production and village life in South Asia is complicated and multilineal. There are several distinct areas where Neolithic cultures have been detected and investigated, yet the origins, regional classification, absolute chronologies, and periodizations of these cultures are still debated.[1] Some scholars tend to view domestication in South Asia as an autochthonous process, which took place independently, without any external impulses (Chakrabarti 1997:240–241, 1999:205–209, 326–329; Misra 1999). Others point to the diffusion from the west (in the case of the northwestern Neolithic zone) and from the east (in the case of the northern and eastern Neolithic zones) (Agrawal and Kharakwal 2002:157–224; Possehl 1999). The internal dynamics of the spread of Neolithic cultures are also debated, for as the story stands now, there is a significant chronological gap between the domestication of plants and animals in the northwestern region and the remaining parts of the South Asian Subcontinent. In Baluchistan, the earliest Neolithic communities are dated roughly to the seventh and sixth millennia BC, while in northern, eastern and southern India, full-fledged agriculture does not appear until the third millennium BC. Consequently, the nature and degree of interaction between the Harappan and non-Harappan South Asia remains one of the most interesting and poorly understood issues in South Asian protohistory.

Nonetheless, what matters the most is that whether in the areas of the later distribution of the Harappan civilization or in the areas not directly related to the Harappan cultural phenomenon, rural lifestyles and agricultural economy established during the Neolithic and Chalcolithic periods set the grounds for the genesis of the ancient Indian civilization. In other words, it is the villages not the cities that were responsible for shaping the ethos of this civilization. The analysis and interpretations proposed in the previous chapters with regard to the most ancient South Asian city seem to support this assumption.

Our historical agents, the people of different social and religious backgrounds who lived in northern South Asia roughly between the mid-first millennium BC and the mid-first millennium AD, conceptualized the phenomenon of the city in many different ways. These ways, however, shared something in common. Wittingly or unwittingly, they emphasized the importance of two traits: fortifications and authority. My consequent analysis of archaeological data has shown that this view had merit. Indeed, the construction of fortifications and the formation of authoritative structures were the two coterminous and concurrent processes that epitomized the emergence of the first cities both in the Harappan and Ganges civilizations. Surrounded by walls, ramparts, and moats, the first cities symbolized new territorially-bound identities, the formation of full-time authoritative institutions, the further social differentiation, and certainly a number of other innovations in sociopolitical and cultural spheres. Being qualitatively very similar to the villages, cities did not, however, alter the deeply agricultural and rural ethos of the ancient Indian civilization.

Walter Fairservis (1961:33) once noted that one of the most peculiar features of the Harappan culture was that it possessed civilization but its people dwelled largely in villages. Consequently, "to know more about the Harappan culture"—he continued—"we must know more about Indian village life". Fairservis was neither first nor the only one in making this important observation. Some scholars even questioned the usefulness of the term "urbanization" in the context of ancient South Asia. A. Ghosh (1972–1973:34), for example, in his comments on Chakrabarti's (1972–1973) article, *Concept of Urban Revolution and the Indian Context*, asserted that in "both the periods, the Indus and Early Historic, there was no large-scale drift to the city" and despite all the glamour of the sites such as Mohenjo-Daro, Harappa, Taxila and Kausambi, the fact remained that India "had all along been a rural country". In a similar way, Niharranjan Ray (1978:890) believed that the South Asian city was "always in tune and harmony with the countryside." On one occasion, Ray asserted that:

> since Indian civilization was essentially village-based, Indian cities were, relatively speaking, smaller and much less complex than those in West Asia, in Eastern Mediterranean countries and in Europe. Conversely, the Indian village was characteristically larger and more complex... The Indian village had a more elaborate division of labour and a much more complex social organization....

Leaving aside the claims that ancient India had no cities—I find such claims pointless if not derogatory, for the idea of the city is so multifarious and conditional that it can be defined and conceptualized in a multitude of ways—one must nevertheless admit that the ancient Indian city was always a logical and natural continuation of the ancient Indian village. The archaeology of both the Harappan and Ganges civilizations support this point.

The village of Allahdino was smaller than 1 ha, yet the artifacts and features that it disclosed were not much different from those of Kalibangan, Lothal, or any other important Harappan city. In fact, as Shaffer (1982:45) noted, Allahdino had almost every major artifact category of the Mature Harappan Culture, including quantities of metal objects and semi-precious stones. In a similar way, the Gangetic village of Sonkh was significantly smaller than the neighboring city of Mathura, yet its layout, architectural patterns, and material culture were very similar to those of major cities of the Ganges civilization.

As far as agriculture is concerned, it evidently played an important role in the life of both the city and the village. The excavation at Kalibangan, disclosed the remains of an agricultural field in the immediate proximity from the walls of an early Harappan settlement (Lal, et al. 2003:95–98). In Early Historic cities, agricultural fields were an innate part of the city life as well. As the Kauṭilīya Arthaśāstra prescribed the ways, in which the rulers drew boundaries between households, it mentioned agricultural fields located inside the fortified settlements (KA 2.4.24—see my discussion and translations in Chapter 2). Agriculture and rural life style thus were a thread that connected cities and villages rather than separated them. What divided them was the idea in the minds of the historical agents.

As I suggested earlier, fortifications in the Harappan and Ganges civilizations delineated inner and local worlds and possibly created the mesocosms that symbolized new identities. In the Harappan civilization, these mesocosms were expressed in a three-dimensional layout created by platforms and perimeter walls, by segregation implemented by dividing walls, by restricted access enforced by blocked and narrow gates, and by hidden monumentality conveyed through the massive consumption of human labor. In the Ganges civilization, these mesocosms were materialized in the excessive monumentality, military inefficiency, incongruity with the history of military conflicts, and the alleged periods of disuse of the fortification systems. Indeed, in the context of both the Harappan and Ganges civilizations, the term "fortification" misrepresented these architectural complexes, for they served primarily ideational functions, i.e., symbolized authority, marked the emergence of new territorially bound identities and local worlds, created mesocosms, and, ultimately, epitomized the first cities. In this sense, the most ancient Indian city was an idea and imagined world to no less a degree than it was a historical reality. As agriculture and rural life style continued to determine the ethos of both the Harappan and Ganges civilizations, the city was an ideational phenomenon symbolizing transformations in sociopolitical sphere.

Somewhat similar conclusions were made by D. K. Chakrabarti (1972–1973, 1974, 1995) and G. Erdosy (1987, 1988) with regards to the second urbanization. In one way or another, both authors emphasized the sociopolitical nature of transformations that led to the emergence of cities in the Greater Gangetic Doab. In my view, both in the Harappan and Ganges civilizations, the city was a by-product of ideational transformations, in particular, the formation of authoritative structures and the creation of new territorially bound identities. Despite all their inherent significance and innovations, cities were epiphenomenal to the ethos of the ancient Indian civilization. Their initial emergence in the middle of the third millennium BC, gradual disintegration in the first half of the second millennium BC, and the re-emergence in the mid-first millennium BC did not destroy the ethos of ancient India; for this ethos was deeply rooted in rural life style and agricultural economy.

Orality and Mnemonic Devices

Literally, the dharma and Veda imply very concrete information; the rules of social conduct and sacred hymns. On a more generic level, they indicate the formation of a large corpus of sacred knowledge and a code of sociocultural conduct, both of which are preserved by oral means. As many other traits of a complex sociopolitical system, the dharma and Veda emerge in the beginning of the Tretā Yuga and, henceforth, play a definitive role in the description of the remaining periods. The dharma gradually deteriorates until it is completely annihilated during the Kali Sandhyā. The Veda, which initially comes fourfold and undivided, undergoes a gradual corruption; it is divided and misread during the Dvāpara Yuga, neglected during the Kali Yuga, and is lost during the Kali Sandhyā.

Obviously, it would be absurd to take the words of the Paurāṇikas for granted and to assume that the dharma and Veda emerged with the introduction of agriculture. Taken in their direct meaning neither dharma nor Veda has use from the standpoint of protohistory. Taken generically, as orally transmitted sacred knowledge and orally transmitted norms of conduct, they may however have some merit for archaeology while retaining a uniquely South Asian character.

Orality *per se* is not exclusively a South Asian phenomenon. Merely every pre-literate and literate culture had oral traditions. Yet in the context of the Indian civilization—whether ancient or modern—orality has played a truly vital role. There is no need to reiterate the well known facts about the oral nature of composition and transmission of the Vedas, Śāstras, Epics, Purāṇas, as well as many other genres, corpuses, and separate texts of ancient Indian literature. Evidently, memorization, recitation, and oral transmission had, for a very long time, been the main means of preservation of an immense body of information in ancient India. Importantly, this body of information was not restricted to the issues of ritual and religion, but also served the needs of social, political, legal, poetic, and scientific spheres. The commonly quoted fact that the *Ṛgveda* was transmitted in its ancient form for hundreds of years by oral means should not be underestimated.[2] The oral composition, memorization, recitation and transmission of texts such as the *Ṛgveda* and *Mahbhrata*—whether with or without significant changes and modifications added during later periods—required the existence of very elaborate mnemonic techniques and a class of people able to teach them. The *Ṛgveda* and other texts of course were not the exceptions. As one author justly observed, mnemonics must have played an important role in merely every aspect of ancient Indian life.

> ...the mnemotechnics evolved for the preservation of the Rigveda in its authentic form were again put to use for the oral preservation of much of these auxiliary products of the textual tradition. But, more significantly, analogous mnemotechnics were evolved to support the development, teaching, and preservation of structurally complex performing art forms, vocal and instrumental music, dance, and so on. In other words, although the Indian tradition, in the large, was oral, it functioned within a highly literate framework. Despite undervaluing writing as a technology, articulations usually unavailable to oral societies were made accessible within the Indian tradition through a variety of intellectually sophisticated techniques (Narasimhan 1991:179).

The last part of this statement challenges many postulates of the so-called "literacy theory" which being initially elaborated in the writings of Eric Havelock (1963, 1976), Walter J. Ong (2002) Marshall McLuhan (1962) and

Jack Goody (1977, 1986, 1987, 2000) has played an important role in the studies of orality and literacy by western scholars during the second part of the twentieth century. As D. R. Olson (1991:251) succinctly summarized this theory, its central claim was "that writing had, historically, been responsible for the evolution of new forms of discourse... that reflected a new approach or understanding of language and a new, more subjective and reflective frame of mind". Literacy was seen as leading to "new forms of social organization, of states rather than tribes" and, in general, as a route to modernity, "exportable to developing countries that... aspired to this modernity". This theory has been severely criticized by a number of anthropologists, particularly so in recent years (see Street 1984:44–65). Interestingly, the case of ancient India has been repeatedly used in these debates, particularly by those who oppose the postulates of the "literacy theory".

The argument that once and again is brought up by a broad range of specialists in ancient Indian culture is that orality enabled by the highly sophisticated mnemonic devices was one of the pillars of the ancient South Asian civilization, a tool without which many of its cultural achievements would have never come into play. Moreover, the relationship between literacy and orality in South Asian context must not be seen in terms of a simplistic dichotomy, for the written texts in India were often more malleable than oral traditions, while oral traditions were more fixed than the written texts (see Fuller 1984; Oliver 1979; R. M. Smith 1966).[3]

It is beyond my purpose to get into the details of this debate. What is important from the archaeological standpoint is that, as an innate part of the identity of the ancient Indian civilization, orality and mnemonics were not, by any means, contingent on the emergence of cities and states. This, then, raises an intriguing question. Could a massive corpus of ideational information, prototypal of the Veda and dharma, and preserved by similar mnemonic techniques, have developed prior to the formation of the Harappan civilization? Evidently, this question alone could form the basis for another book and there is no way I can address it thoroughly in this chapter without a separate investigation of archaeological data from Neolithic and Chalcolithic South Asia. Nonetheless, judging from the currently available circumstantial evidence and following my preceding argument, I would like to propose the following hypothesis. A massive corpus of ideational information, most likely some kind of sacred knowledge and the norms of sociocultural conduct, enabled and reinforced by highly sophisticated mnemonic devices, was formed, developed, and began to be practiced in western South Asia in the areas of the first agricultural communities prior to the emergence of the Harappan civilization. Thereafter, it played a significant role in defining the identity of the Harappan civilization, the post-Harappan cultures of the Indo-Gangetic tradition, and of the Ganges civilization. Notably, it was the form not the content that kept the thread of tradition alive for several millennia in different social, ethnic, linguistic, and political environments. In other words, it was the highly sophisticated mnemonic technique rather than the Vedas or dharma that formed in the Pre-Harappan period. Remarkably, this technique was not limited to the realm of religion and ritual, and played an important role in social and political spheres. Despite how speculative this hypothesis may seem to be, it provides a good explanation for several puzzles of South Asian protohistory and can be tentatively supported by four lines of evidence.

Nature and Function of Writing and Literacy in the Harappan and Ganges Civilizations. Notwithstanding the numerous attempts at cracking the Indus script, the first known writing system of the South Asian subcontinent remains undeciphered. Moreover, it has not yet been unequivocally shown that the Indus script represents a fully-fledged writing system. Conveying relatively short messages and preserved mostly on square stamp seals, the function and nature of this script stands in striking contrast to other known writing systems of the ancient world. Judging from the available evidence, it appears that the role that this script played in the life of the Harappans was fundamentally different from those of the Egyptian, Mesopotamian, Chinese, and other ancient writing systems. The Early Historic writing was also quite unique. Appearing relatively late and serving limited functions of political nature, it played no crucial role in either sociopolitical, cultural, or economic life of the Ganges civilization. Meanwhile, we know from other sources that both formative and mature phases of the Ganges civilization witnessed the formation of a massive body of religious, philosophical, sociopolitical, literary, and early scientific information. Characteristically, this information was codified, canonized, and preserved by oral means.

This brings us back to the aforementioned anthropological debate on the idea of literacy and the relation between literacy and orality in the context of ancient South Asia. From the viewpoint of an archaeologist, what this debate highlights is that a very complex sociopolitical system of the Ganges civilization functioned without a significant use of writing, yet figuratively speaking was highly literate. As Narasimhan (1991:179), asserted "articulations usually unavailable to oral societies were made accessible within the Indian tradition through a variety of intellectually sophisticated techniques". To this, one must add that many of these articulations, particularly those that were regarded by the advocates of the "literacy theory" as sociopolitical changes allegedly caused by the invention of writing, were made fully available to the ancient Indian society by means of mnemonic techniques without the use of writing.[4]

The question then arises whether the Harappan society could have functioned in a similar way, with orality and mnemonic techniques playing a crucial role in the storage and transmission of important information. The nature of the Harappan script may hold an answer to this question. In fact, the use of the script may, in one way or another, be related to the development of orality. The brevity of inscriptions, a large number of signs, the association of inscriptions with iconographic scenes, and the unusual context of the discovery of seals can all be interpreted as circumstantial evidence of seals being at least in part the mnemonic devices. As Goody (1987:122) suggests "the development of certain important memorizing techniques for speech seems almost to require the prior reduction of language to a visual form, providing speech with a spatial dimension". Needless to say, at this point this is just a suggestion. If this suggestion turns out to be correct, it will not be unreasonable to suggest that the roots of this type of orality and mnemonic techniques must be sought in the pre-Harappan agricultural communities.

Lack of Monumental Material Expression of Religious and Social Practices. It has been frequently noted that the cities of the Harappan civilization oddly lack temples, lavish religious paraphernalia, and palaces. Neither do the first cities of the Ganges civilization reveal any of these archaeological traits; the first Buddhist stupas are built well after the emergence of the Ganges civilization and are located outside the city walls. In the case of the Ganges civilization, we nonetheless know that the people residing in its cities and villages had elaborate religious practices and followed intricate social laws. The preservation, transmissions and control of these practices and laws were implemented by oral means. The power of the spoken word thus performed a very important role. What in many other ancient cultures was conveyed with the help of architecture and material culture was communicated through speech and preserved by memory.

Moving 2,000 years back in time, one finds a similar situation. On one hand, religion and social hierarchy have no unequivocal material expression. On the other hand, the traits such as urban segregation, fortifications, massive platforms, occasional public buildings, and script, indicate that this society was socially very complex. As in the case with the Ganges civilization, the existence of orally transmitted sacred knowledge and orally transmitted norms of conduct would explain how it functioned. The power of the spoken word and mnemonic devices would have simply excluded the necessity to built palaces and temples.

Pace of Harappan Urbanization. One of the controversial issues in recent literature dealing with the emergence of the Harappan civilization has been the pace of its initial urbanization. On one hand, Possehl (1990, 1999, 2002c), Jansen (1994), and Shaffer and Liechtenstein (1989) have advocated a theory, according to which the transition to the Mature Harappan Phase was a sort of "rapid, paroxytic change" occupying only about one century. Possehl (1999:568) places this century between 2650 BC to 2550 BC, while Shaffer and Liechtenstein (1989) place it between 2600 BC and 2500 BC. On the other hand, Mughal (1970), Kenoyer (1991a), and S. P. Gupta (1996, 1999) believe that the process of urbanization was gradual rather than rapid, taking at least several hundred years.

From the point of view of my own argument, the outcome of this debate does not really matter, for even if "the gradual theory" reflects the overall picture of the earliest urbanization more appropriately, not all the cities had to follow the same pattern by evolving gradually over significant periods of time and, in contrast to the overall genesis of the Harappan civilization, could have been built as "founder's settlements". The most famous example of such a settlement is Mohenjo-Daro. Michael Jansen (1994:271), a scholar who spent many years investigating the architectural history of this remarkable city, stunningly concludes that in order for it to have been built, "any earlier settlement must have been abandoned and the design of the city must have been perfectly planned by master builders" who "had prior experience of the technology involved and have already developed the script". Given that there is no evidence of script prior to the construction of Mohenjo-Daro, this statement poses an intriguing puzzle. Could the technological, social, and ideological knowledge, necessary for the rapid construction of the city such as Mohenjo-Daro be elaborated, preserved, conveyed and implemented without a script? In my view, it certainly could, but only provided the existence of highly elaborate mnemonic devices. The emergence of the first Harappan cities, from this point of view, was an outburst of information accumulated and transmitted orally over a long period of time.

Social Organization

With regard to the social organization, the Purāṇic model is clear-cut. The varṇāśrama system, being a distinctive trait of the Tretā Yuga, emerges after the introduction of agriculture and remains a key criterion for describing the further stages of a complex sociocultural organization; viz. in the Tretā Yuga it is properly followed, in the Dvāpara Yuga it is partially disregarded, in the Kali Yuga it is confused, and in the Kali Sandhyā it is annihilated. As in the case with the dharma and Veda, it would be absurd to take this scheme literally. On a more generic level however, the idea of the varṇāśrama could stimulate some fruitful theorizing.

To begin with, the system of the varṇas and āśramas is usually closely associated with caste, a concept which, from the beginning of European interest in India, has been one of the most exploited topics in Indology and related academic disciplines. It would not be an exaggeration to say that the topic of caste alone is responsible for producing a large portion of scholarly literature that deals with ancient and modern South Asia, as well as for instigating many heated debates on the issues of sociocultural organization in different parts of the ancient and modern world. Given this, it is not surprising that there is no consensus on what caste means, in which contexts it should be used, and even on whether it is a meaningful concept at all. It is beyond my purpose to get into a thorough analysis of the concept of caste; without doubt this would require a separate study. For the sake of my own argument however, I cannot completely avoid discussing this issue, and therefore would like to make some clarifications.

Recent studies of caste represent, in my view, three main theoretical directions. The first direction, to a large degree, continues previously established Indological traditions and presents caste as a constitutive institution of the ancient and modern Indian civilization. A classic example of an authoritative study that represents this direction is the book *Homo Hierarchicus* by Louis Dumont (1966). Another more recent example is a study of the concept of varṇa by B. K. Smith (1994). It is precisely about this type of studies that the anthropologist Ronald Inden (1990:82) has made the following observation:

> ...virtually all of the hegemonic accounts of India, beginning with Mill and Hegel, have made caste into the central pillar of their constructs. Caste, they have held, is the type of society characteristic of India, the institution that distinguishes it from the other civilization of Asia as well as from the West.

The second direction can be seen as part of the ongoing anthropological critique aimed to disavow various colonialist, Orientalist, and Euro-centric analytical models and, as far as caste is concerned, to deconstruct the latter "as the central problematic of Indian society, and of hierarchy as its most compelling trope" (Appadurai 1984:745).[5] The most illustrative example of such a deconstruction is the book *Imagining India* by Ronald Inden. In this book, Inden (1990:82) contends that the importance of caste in ancient and medieval South Asia has been largely overstated and, based on his own research on the history of Bengal, argues that it was kingship or a polity rather than caste that formed the constitutive institutions of Indian civilization. Other examples that fall within this direction include a number of case-studies, specially aimed to renounce the authority of caste as the main analytical device for the conceptualization of Indian civilization and society (see Daniel 1984; Khare 1984).

The third direction is often overlooked by specialists in South Asia, as it is concerned with the holistic and cross-cultural uses of the term "caste" and involves the study of non-South Asian social systems. The history of this direction goes back to the term "casta" used in the sixteenth century by the Portuguese and Spanish to designate human clans and lineages of the newly discovered lands.[6] As these lands included both India and the New World, the term "casta" acquired a cross-cultural meaning.[7] Today this meaning is alive, and there is a significant body of scholarly literature dealing with caste both in cross-cultural and case-oriented contexts.[8]

Turning to South Asian archaeology, one discovers that the idea of caste has played a noticeable role in the analysis of protohistoric social structures. S. C. Malik (1968:106–107) suggested that both caste and the means of perpetuation of caste by birth were present already during the Harappan period. Although Malik neither properly defined caste nor provided sufficient archaeological evidence in support of its existence in the third millennium BC, his ideas were nonetheless innovative and stimulated discussion (Allchin 1971; Gupta 1974). One of the most respected Indian archaeologists, B. B. Lal (1997:229–233, 1998a:100–101, 2002b:120–132), in several of his recent publications, has gradually tilted towards the idea of caste as well. Having suggested that data from Kalibangan and other sites indicate a threefold social division—"a priestly class inhabiting the citadel, an agriculturist-cum-merchant class occupying the Lower Town; and a workers' class living outside the two fortified areas"—Lal (1997:230) made an explicit connection between the Harappan archaeological record and the system of varṇas.

> It would appear that the priestly elites of the Citadel may have been the forerunners of the Brāhmaṇas, the middle class agriculturists and merchants of the Lower Town, those of the later day Vaiśyas and the out-of-fortification dwellers of Kalibangan and the occupants of the Harappan barracks could, in the course of time, have led to the class which came to be known as the Śūdras (Lal 1997:232).

The proponents of the equation between the Harappan civilization and the Vedic culture understandably agree with Malik's and Lal's allusions (Bisht 1999; Simha 1987, 1995); for the varṇas mentioned, for the first time, in the Ṛgveda are traditionally seen as an early form of caste (Smith 1994). Another recent attempt to use the concept of caste in the analysis of Harappan archaeology has been undertaken by C. C. Lamberg-Karlovsky (1999) whose approach seems to fall between the first and the third of the three aforementioned methodological directions.[9] Among the archaeological traits that may indicate the presence of caste in the Harappan society, Lamberg-Karlovsky mentions a distinctive layout of residential units, an extraordinary degree of expansionism, the unprecedented geographic span, a striking level of attention given to the control of water, cultural uniformity in material inventory and settlement design, the absence of temples, and the lack of imported commodities. Finally, a noteworthy approach to the issue of the Harappan social organization is found in the writings of J. M. Kenoyer, whose stance may appear as somewhat contradictory. On the one hand, Kenoyer (1998:131) states:

> ...we have no indication that during the Harappan Phase, occupational specialists were organized into rigid social categories called jati or caste, a feature that became common only much later. The social hierarchy and stratification of different classes in the Indus cities may have been somewhat flexible, especially for individuals who wanted to change professions, exploit new resources or develop new technologies.

On the other hand, Kenoyer (1989b:189, 1992:42) proposes that a system of hereditary reciprocal exchange, such as jajmani, may have characterized the Harappan social organization. Apparently Kenoyer believes that the jajmani system does not have to be related to caste, a viewpoint which disagrees with many interpretations of jajmani.[10] Furthermore, some of the recent studies have questioned the meaningfulness of jajmani as such (Fuller 1989; Inden 1990:143–145).

Against such a diverse theoretical background, it is difficult to imagine that any consensus will ever be achieved with regards to either definition or applicability of the concept of caste. It appears that, as in the case with other grand anthropological and historical concepts, the idea of caste will always remain highly contentious. The least that we can do in this situation is to follow the advice of Julian Pitt-Rivers (1971:253), who believed:

> recognition that a word that in origin meant no more than offspring should have done so much heavy… duty in the cause of one ideology or another should surely incline the anthropologist to prudence in the choice of his analytical vocabulary….

For the purpose of my own argument, my prudence is to treat the idea of the varṇāśrama separately from the idea of caste and to determine whether aside from its rigid brahmanic content it reflects any sociocultural traits that may be of interest to the archaeologist.

In a recent study of the varṇa system, Brian K. Smith (1994:18) has proposed that the varṇas presented "a taxonomical system with universal scope, designed and deployed in order to classify the cosmos as a whole". This interpretation is not new, as in many respects it develops the argument of tripartition initially proposed by George Dumezil (1958) for the analysis of Indo-European mythology. Smith however elevates the epistemological power of the varṇa system to an unprecedented level. The varṇas, according to B. K. Smith (1994:19), presented a holistic, universal, categorical, multi-faceted, and generalized system of "enormous and wide-ranging epistemological capabilities". On the social level, Smith (1994:82) argued that the varṇas system must be seen as a "mutlifaceted and generalized classificatory scheme," which "had the first of foremost goal to rationalize and represent an ideal form of a hierarchical social structure by projecting that form into the domains of the supernatural, the metaphysical, the natural, and the canonical". Even if in presenting the varṇas in this manner the author largely overstated his case, it is not unreasonable, I believe, to accept the premise of the varṇas being a unique classificatory device and to treat them and the āśramas as the first attempts to subdivide society on the basis of sociocultural differences. Needless to say such attempts were undertaken in many other parts of the ancient world. The Romans, Greeks, Iranians, Northern Europeans, and other ancient ethnocultural groups did classify themselves and the others into various social, political, and cultural categories. The South Asian system, in its varṇāśrama version, is however quite distinctive. From the point of view of social relations, this distinctiveness can be summarized in the three following traits.

Varṇāśrama Implies both Heterarchical and Hierarchical Relations. It is primarily the occupational, ideological, or, in the case of the aśramas, age differences, rather than the idea of hierarchy, that delineate the relationship between, on the one hand, the brāhmaṇs (priests), kṣatriyas (warriors), vaiśyas (peasants), and śūdras (outcasts), and, on the other hand, the brahmacarya (the stage of being a student), gṛhasthya (the stage of being a householder), vānaprastha (the stage of being a hermit), and sanyāsa (the stage of a wandering beggar). The caste system, regardless of how it is defined, presents even a more complex net of heterarchical and hierarchical relations. Moreover, its heterarchical component is arguably much more complex that the hierarchical one. In other words, within the system of castes there are many more groups which display heterarchical relations than the groups which can be placed in a simple hierarchical scheme.

Varṇāśrama Reflects Mostly Ideational Rather than Economic Differences. Acquired by birth and expressed in different professions and dharmas, the statuses of the brāhmaṇs, kṣatriya, vaiśya, and śūdra are, in my view, the products of ideology rather than of the means of production, economic infrastructure, or any other materialistic factor. The statuses of the brahmacarin, gṛhasthya, vānaprastha, and sanyāsin, being determined by age, the successful completion of the previous stage, and the proper implementation of the dharma, are even more so unrelated to any economic, materialistic, or technological factors.

Formation of the Varṇāśrama is Rooted in Rural Settings, and is in no way Contingent on the Emergence of Cities and States. With regard to the varṇa system, this thesis is particularly characteristic of the thinking of our historical agents; for both the *VāyuPurāṇa* and *Brahmā ṇḍaPurāṇa* place the emergence of the varṇāśrama in the context of the Tretā Yuga and draw an implicit causal link between the introduction of agriculture and the subsequent division of society into the four varṇas. Evidently, this is quite an unusual development for ancient Indian thought, for other references to the varṇa system offer significantly different explanations.[11] What this development may indicate is that since its initial mentioning in the tenth maṇḍala of the *Ṛgveda*, the varṇa concept underwent modifications and, by the time of the composition of the early Purāṇas, had absorbed some elements of critical thinking about society, historical process, and the ancient past. Importantly, the idea of the city plays no significant role in this thinking as the formation of the varṇas, being linked to the introduction of agriculture, takes place in the rural setting. With regard to the four āśramas, the cities and states play no significant role either. By designating differences in age, virtuousness, and religious activities, the āśrama system is functional primarily in the rural setting.

Turning to archaeology, first of all, one must admit that it would be absurd to trace the varṇāśrama, in its primary brahmanical meaning, in the archaeological cultures of the Harappan and pre-Harappan South Asia. Clearly, I am not suggesting that the four varṇas and four āśramas could have emerged in the context of the Harappan or pre-Harappan cultures. As in the case with the dharma and the Veda, it is the form, not the content, that matters from the standpoint of protohistory. In other words, the Paurāṇicas' assumption that the varṇāśrama emerged in the beginning of the Tretā Yuga and then defined the subsequent complex Yugas must be treated not as an indication of the great antiquity and importance of the brahmanic classification, but as a general recognition of the long-term existence of a unique sociocultural system, which stood for ideational rather than economic differences, was dominated by heterarchical rather than hierarchical relations, and, being unrelated to the emergence of cities and states, was rooted in rural settings. Only when we look at the idea of the varṇāśrama this way, we then can turn to archaeology and ask ourselves whether the existence of a social system characterized by such traits could have linked some archaeological entities of the South Asian subcontinent from the time of the pre-Harappan agricultural communities to the formation of the Mauryan Empire. My preceding argument with regard to the idea of the city in the Harappan and Ganges civilizations has set the ground for looking into this question.

In the third and fourth chapters, I attempted to verify and trace the emergence of authoritative structures in the first cities of the Harappan and Ganges civilizations. To do so, I pinpointed parallel and drastic transformations in the material culture, settlement layout, and settlement size of the twenty-five archaeological sites. The analysis of these transformations led to the suggestion that in the Harappan and Ganges civilizations, the formation of authority was part of the process of urbanization and had analogous material expressions. In the Ganges civilization, evidence for authority and control of labor comes from the construction of fortifications, settlement expansion, sophistication of domestic architecture, introduction of regular planning, and emergence of inscribed seals. In the Harappan civilization, evidence for authority includes the construction of fortifications and platforms (I viewed the latter as part of fortification complexes), urban segregation, layout, and certain changes in material culture. Yet most vividly, I argued, both in the Harappan and Ganges civilizations, authority and conspicuous consumption of labor are evident from the construction of massive fortification complexes, which until today stand as the main markers of the earliest form of South Asian urbanism. Moreover, the term "fortification" is in essence a misnomer, for the structures of circumvallation, division, and segregation present on the sites of the Harappan and Ganges civilizations appear to have served mainly non-utilitarian purposes. I suggested that one of such purposes was to delineate space or, figuratively speaking, to create mesocosms that reflected the newly formed and territorially bound sociocultural identities.

Expressed spatially, these identities did not have opulent material expressions. Neither the Harappan nor Ganges civilizations provide evidence for the existence of palaces, temples, and lavish ritual paraphernalia. Yet, it is quite clear that the society of neither of these two civilizations was socially homogenous. In the case of the Harappan civilization, craft specialization, settlement hierarchies, writing, urban segregation, and long-distance trade unequivocally tell us that the sociocultural structure of this civilization was comprised of a significant number of groups, identities, and local worlds. In the case of the Ganges civilizations, we know from the texts that complex sociocultural systems existed in the area of distribution of this civilization well prior to its emergence. Thus, both the Harappan and Ganges civilizations were socially complex, yet the forms of their complexity did not leave any material signs, which were indicative of rigid hierarchies as found in other ancient civilizations.

This unusual expression of power, authority, and social organization can be explained in a number of ways. The three traits identified above in connection with the varṇāśrama system seem to provide a good point of departure for constructing such explanations. Let us briefly consider the potential applicability of these traits to the archaeology of the Harappan and Ganges civilizations.

Heterarchy versus Hierarchy. From the Sanskrit and Pāli texts, we know that aside from hierarchical relations expressed mostly in the institution of kingship, social structures of the Ganges civilization had much room for heterarchy. Contingent on territory, religion, dharma, occupation, age, and a myriad of other factors, the identities of Vedic, Buddhist, and Jaina society could be better envisioned as long and meandering branches of a low-standing tree rather than as a clear-cut linear hierarchy. The social relations of the Harappan society must have been somewhat similar. Delineated in space through segregation, restricted access, and possibly elevation, Harappan identities can also be better conceptualized with the help of heterarchical rather than hierarchical social models (see Ehrenreich et al. 1995). Although for the construction of massive fortifications and the maintenance of relevant ideologies, some ranking, institutions of power, and authoritative control had to be in place already in the early stages of urbanization, the overall picture of the social organization of the first Harappan and Gangetic cities was likely dominated by heterarchical principles.

Ideational Nature of Sociocultural Identities. There is a significant amount of literature on the growth of sociopolitical complexity in Early Historic India. Most of this literature points to the ideational rather than economic roots of social differentiation (see Chakrabarti 1972–1973, 1974, 1995; Erdosy 1987, 1988; R. Thapar 1984, 2003). My argument with regard to the authoritative institutions which were materialized most vividly in the construction of fortifications and had predominantly non-utilitarian use goes along with this type of interpretations. Ideology rather than the means of production appears to have been responsible for major sociopolitical transformations. Considering similarities in the processes that epitomized the emergence of the first cities, as well as the lack of lavish expressions of power in both civilizations, it seems quite reasonable to suggest that the criteria that determined social identities in the Harappan civilization were also ideational.

Rural Roots. If the conventional interpretation of the society responsible for the composition of Vedic literature as non-urban is accurate, many characteristic features of the ancient Indian sociocultural mosaic formed well prior to the emergence of the first cities and were perfectly functional in the rural context. What the emergence of cities introduced was a new set of territorially bound identities augmented by hierarchical elements, i.e., authoritative structures necessary for the creation of large fortified communities. In the case of the Ganges civilization, the texts tell us of chakravartins, the rulers whose emergence marks the formation of the institute of kingship. In the case of the Harappan civilization, we do not know the precise nature of authority yet judging from the similarities between the two processes of urbanization, it is reasonable to suggest that the social foundation of the Harappan society had, in a similar way, been formed prior to emergence of the first cities. The existence of such a foundation, distinguished by heterarchical relations and rooted in village life style, would explain the rapid emergence of massive fortified communities in some cases (Mohenjo-Daro) and the gradual transition from villages to cities in other cases (Harappa).

To conclude, I would like to emphasize that the above is just a hypothetical reconstruction of continuities that may have characterized the structures of Indo-Gangetic social systems for several thousand years. Despite all the dogmatism of their historical constructs, the Paurāṇikas may turn out to be quite right in assuming that some of the distinctive social traits began to form as early as during the periods following the introduction of agriculture and survived until the historical period.

Religious Practices

The concept of yajña (sacrifice) plays a prominent role in the religious practices of Early Historic India. It is, therefore, not surprising that the Paurāṇikas place its origins in the context of the Tretā Yuga. In fact, the yajña, according to the Purāṇic civilizational model, not only emerges at the very beginning of the Tretā Yuga, but arguably precedes the introduction of agriculture and even possibly surpasses it in significance. Likewise, in many recent studies of sacrifice—both philological and anthropological—the emergence of sacrificial practices is conceptualized in conjunction with the domestication of plants and animals. Jonathan Z. Smith (1987a:199), a historian of religions from Chicago University, calls sacrifice "a meditation on domestication" and asserts that "a theory of sacrifice must begin with the domesticated animal and with the sociocultural process of domestication itself". Some anthropologists have even suggested that domestication of animals in certain parts of the world could have been motivated by the desire to find victims for sacrificial ceremonies (Isaac 1962, 1963a, 1963b, 1970).[12]

In Sanskrit, the term yajña usually refers to a set of very specific sacrificial practices discussed in the later Vedic texts, the Brāhmaṇas and Śrautasūtras. There is a significant amount of literature dealing with these practices in detail and from different theoretical perspectives.[13] Furthermore, there is an immense amount of literature on sacrifice in other culture-historical settings, as well as in a cross-cultural context.[14] Some scholars today even question the meaning and usefulness of the term sacrifice as such. The classicist M. Detienne (1989:20), for example, claims that sacrifice is an outdated category, while J. Z. Smith (1987b:179) maintains that scholars imagine sacrifice and "then go out and find it". It is clearly beyond my current purpose to get into this serious and long-standing debate, for its proper handling would require a separate study. What is important to me in the context of our current discussion is that, if we leave aside the categorical and, in my view, unconstructive opinions that sacrifice is a useless category which does not reflect any phenomena and activities of the past, the assumption of the Purāṇic civilizational model that the origins of South Asian sacrificial practices go back to the agricultural revolution is not at all off the mark.

Most Vedicists seem to hold that the study of yajña is important not only for the understanding of Vedic Weltanschaung, but also for the understanding of later Indian religious and philosophical traditions. In spite of whether they are right or wrong, the concept of yajña is clearly very broad. In defining the Vedic worldview, it itself is a worldview, not just a set of religious practices. Having said this, I am by no means suggesting that we should look for agnihotra, aśvamedha, and their underlying ideology in the archaeology of the Vindhyan Neolithic, Harappan civilization, or Deccan Chalcolithic. As in the case with the Veda, dharma, and varṇāśrama, it is once again the form not the content that should matter to us from the standpoint of protohistory. Following the advice of Heestermann (1993:9):

> ...it seems wiser to speak... of a "family" of phenomena called "sacrifice", for it is still more than likely that we are dealing here with a ritual complex of great antiquity—whether we derive it from the experience of Paleolithic hunters or from the habits of Neolithic cattle keepers—and of a wide geographic distribution that shows its resilience in its capacity for developing and evolving variant forms as well as penetrating thought.

In other words, what I am suggesting is that, while we should clearly avoid projecting later historical beliefs and practices directly onto protohistorical contexts, we must not see anything fundamentally wrong in assuming that some formal, structural, and prototypal elements of these beliefs and practices began to emerge during the Neolithic, Chalcolithic, and Bronze Age periods. The archaeology of protohistoric South Asia provides much data for testing this assumption.

The sequence of Mehrgarh, being the best studied record of culture change from the Neolithic to Bronze Age in Western South Asia, contains numerous ornaments, jewelry, figurines, and burials, many of which convey symbolic and religious messages. Despite of many years of remarkable research by the French Archaeological Mission in Pakistan, the beliefs, worldview and religious practices of its people are still awaiting to be carefully investigated. The same could be said about the religious worlds of the Northern and South Indian Neolithic.

In the context of Chalcolithic Deccan, the situation is somewhat better. Based on the excavation of Inamgaon (Lukacs and Walimber 1986–1988) and Daimabad (Sali 1986), the two key sites of Chalcolithic Maharashtra, Dhavalikar (1970, 1978, 1982, 1987, 1988:55–70) has argued that there is evidence of beliefs and practices prototypal of those of later Hinduism, e.g., sati, the sacredness of bull, and the worship of deities reminiscent of Śiva, Śākambari, Pālghat, and even Ganeśa. Although many of these suggestions are likely to be the fruit of scholarly imagination, a significant portion of Dhavalikar's argument is compelling.[15]

As far as the Harappan civilization is concerned, scholars have argued for continuities between the Harappan and later historical religious beliefs and practices since the time of John Marshall (1931).[16] The evidence referred to in support of these arguments usually includes a standard set of archaeological traits and features; viz., wells and water devices, hearths, ornaments and jewelry, figurines, iconographic motifs, burials, and the alleged ritual objects. As evidence for religious practices, each of these traits has nonetheless different value. For example, the interpretation of wells and water devices found in excessive amounts in Mohenjo-Daro as signs of ritual purity and ablutions is very compelling, while the interpretation of hearths found in Kalibangan and Banawali as altars indicative of the worship of fire is more dubious. Iconographic motifs on seals, tablets, and pottery have been by far the most widely used medium for theorizing and have produced the largest number of the boldest speculations. To the aforementioned traits, one could add the three-dimensional layout of cities created by urban segregation, restrictions of access, and the elevation of certain areas by means of massive mud-brick platforms. As I suggested above, this three-dimensionality may have carried some symbolic and ritual meanings, particularly so in the case of the Stupa Mound at Mohenjo-Daro or the southern section of the western mound at Kalibangan. Also, although the absence of evidence does not constitute any solid evidence, one must mention the lack of monumental religious architecture and lavish religious paraphernalia;[17] combined with other lines of evidence, it emphasizes the uniqueness of Harappan religious practices. In any rate, based on the currently available evidence, scholars have brought up a large number of topics all, in one way or another, dealing with the issue of religious, sacrificial, and ritual continuity. These topics can be summarized as follows: 1) the worship of proto-Shiva and the beginnings of Shaivaism; 2) the dichotomy of the male god and the female goddess and the beginning of Shaktism; 3) the notion of ritual purity, the sanctity of water, and the performance of ritual ablutions; 4) the practice of Yoga; 5) the cult of mother goddesses; 6) the worship of fire; 7) the sacredness of certain animals, possibly of a cow, and the nagas (snakes); 8) the worship of human genitalia (linga and yoni); 9) the worship of trees, particularly of the pipal tree; 10) the performance of human and animal sacrifices; 11) the making of an intoxicating concoction and the burning of incense.

Evidently, each of these topics encompasses a large array of opinions and there is hardly any consensus on the specific interpretations of archaeological traits. Importantly however, the focal point of controversy is not whether the Harappan and later Indian religious practices share a number of common expressions—most scholars seem to agree that the existence of such expressions is archaeologically undisputable—but whether these common expressions, e.g., hearths, wells, iconographic motifs, etc.—imply the commonality of religious beliefs. In other words, it is not whether the Harappans worshipped fire is what matters, but whether the reasons why they worshipped it and the procedures that they followed while worshipping it were similar to those of the Vedic ritual of Agni. Answers to these questions depend not only on the evaluation of specific archaeological traits but rather on one's stance on the issue of equifinality of archaeological record, i.e., the situation when different cultural phenomena have identical material expressions. As a result, on one hand, there are interpretations, which by assuming continuities both in form and in content, draw a direct link between the Harappan and later Hindu religious practices.[18] On the other hand, there are interpretations, which, while alluding to continuities, exercise caution in making far-reaching conclusions.[19]

From the point of view of our argument, what is important is that the existence of common traits and features indicative of religious practices in the Harappan civilization and Early Historic India has become almost undisputable. The most conspicuous among these traits is the use of water in Mohenjo-Daro and Dholavira—the water splendor or "Wasserluxus" as Michael Jansen (1993a) termed this phenomenon—and certain iconographic motifs, indicative of the worship of nagas (snakes), trees, animals, and possibly the early elements of Shaktism and Yoga. It is nevertheless important to realize that the presence of the same objects of worship, iconographic motifs, and non-utilitarian artifacts in the archaeological record of two temporally distinct cultures does not necessarily mean that the people who created these cultures believed in the same gods, spoke the same language, or belonged to the same ethnic groups. On the contrary, as numerous ethnographic and historical examples show, the same structures, motifs, and objects can stand for very different religious and ideological values; the Aya Sofia of Istanbul is a symbol of both Christian and Moslem faith, the images of the Buddha at Gaya are worshiped by the Vaishanavites who believe that the Buddha was the ninth avatara of the God Vishnu, and water plays an important role in at least several Indian religions. What this means is that if the Harappans, the Vedic Aryans and succeeding ethnic or religious groups indeed shared certain ritual and sacrificial practices, the meaning and religious foundations of these practices could be very different.

At any rate, I believe it is very likely that the Harappans exercised some religious practices prototypal of those of Early Historic India. Judging from the absence of temples and lavish paraphernalia, these practices were performed predominantly in rural and domestic settings aided by an orally preserved body of sacred knowledge. Moreover, it is not at all unreasonable to suggest that many elements of these practices were rooted in the preceding periods. The birth of gods and religious practices in South Asia did not have to follow a unique pattern and, most probably, were coterminous with the origins of agriculture in the ways similar to those in the Middle East (Cauvin 1994). The yajña, under this scenario, can be seen as a convenient category for the conceptualization of the archaeological traits that point to continuities in religious beliefs and practices from the Neolithic Period to the Iron Age. Once again, both in terms of its historicity and conceptual depth, this category of the historical agents is not as off the mark as it may first seem to be.

Conclusion: The Ideas of Civilization and the City in Ancient South Asia

Thus, if civilization is defined as a deep structure, which maintains importance over a long period of time, the model discussed in this chapter appears to present a plausible option for a holistic study of the rise of civilization in South Asia (see Table 6.1). Illusory and to some degree imaginary, this model is meant to connect the historical reality, the mind of the researcher and the mentality of historical agents. As I suggested earlier, to define a civilization is to provide a glimpse of this structure from each of these three perspectives. My analysis of archaeological and textual data, one must hope, has set the grounds for doing so in the context of ancient South Asia.

The specifics of the proposed model are, to a large degree, hypothetical. Before being reasserted in a more affirmative manner, each of them needs to be thoroughly investigated in the context of specific protohistoric cultures, the archaeological entities of Neolithic, Chalcolithic, Bronze Age, and Iron Age South Asia. This is why I would prefer to call it, at this point, a framework of inquiry into the idea of the ancient South Asian civilization (see Table 6.1).

With regard to the idea of the city, this model enhances our preceding argument. In particular, it is incongruous that in the context of ancient South Asia most scholars equate the idea of civilization with the idea of the Urban Revolution. As the last two chapters suggest, the idea of the ancient South Asian civilization is much more inclusive than the idea of the ancient South Asian city. Rooted in the transformations that took place as early as in the Neolithic and Chalcolithic periods, this civilization was unrelated to the emergence of cities, while cities, having emerged, did not fundamentally alter the ethos of this civilization. Thus, in the context of ancient South Asia, it makes sense to distinguish between the emergence of civilization and the urban revolution, for these two important processes of cultural transformations were very different from one another both in time and in magnitude.

In other parts of the world, one must add, the earliest civilizations and cities have been conceptualized in ways that challenge the equation of the city and civilization and the materialistic models of complexity as well. In the case of ancient China, K. C. Chang (1983, 1989) advocated the idea that neither the genesis nor the nature of the earliest Chinese civilization followed the Childean models. Western hypotheses, according to Chang (1989:165), simply failed to explain the genesis of ancient China:

> To the social scientist seasoned in the theories of Marx, Engels, Weber, Childe, and other with regard to social evolution and the rise of urbanism and state society... the Chinese road to civilization appears to be an aberration....

Table 6.1

The ancient Indian city and civilization: A framework of enquiry

The Ancient Indian Civilization	The Ancient Indian City
Agricultural economy and rural lifestyle as the basis of rural and urban worlds.	Massive fortifications that served mostly ideational functions, e.g., delineated space, marked territorially-bound identities, epitomized authority, and possibly reated symbolically charged mesocosm.
Orality comparable in significance to literacy and maintained by highly sophisticated mnemonic devices used for the preservation of a large body of sacred and social information.	Full-time authorities whose identity was expressed mainly in the construction of fortification systems and whose relation to other social groups and identities was to a large degree heterarchical.
A social system based on ideational differences, rooted in rural settings, and structured predominantly along the heterarchical rather than hierarchical relations.	
A set of religious beliefs and practices expressed in similar archaeological traits, such numerous wells and water devices, hearths interpreted as fire altars, ornaments and jewelry, figurines, iconographic motifs, burials, and the absence of monumental temples and lavish religious paraphernalia.	

Instead, Chang believed that the road to civilization in China was gradual and displayed "continuity between man and animal, between earth and heaven, and between culture and nature". Moreover, political processes and complex rituals, not the innovations in the means of production and trade, were responsible for the growth of sociopolitical complexity that ultimately led to the emergence of civilization. Most importantly, the ethos of this civilization was seen by Chang (1989:161) as deeply ideational: it was created and existed "within a framework of cosmogonic holism". In a similar way, several recent case-studies of ancient Greece (see Osborne 1987; Polignac 1984; Rich and Wallace-Hadrill 1997) and Mesopotamia (see Steinkeller 2006) present the cities and civilization in terms that are very different from those of the traditional archaeological paradigms of civilization and urban revolution.

Coming back to the ancient South Asian civilization, one must add that one of the byproducts of this study is the re-evaluation of ancient Indian sociopolitical thought. The people responsible for the composition of the Epics, Sūtras, and Purāṇas were apparently well aware of the historical past, yet for some reasons did not record it in the form of chronicles or secular analytical history. The memory of the past and thinking about the past was absorbed in theoretical models hidden within their theology and myths. As the *VāyuPurāṇa* portrays the transition from civilization to sociopolitical collapse and back to civilization, the memory of the past is said to be preserved and maintained by a few survivors.

> Miserable and struck by droughts they abandoned agriculture. They left their countries (janapadas) and lived in the borderlands. They found shelter by the rivers, seas, wells and mountains. Very miserable, they subsisted on honey, meat, roots, and fruit. They wore garments of bark and tiger skin. They had neither wives nor sons. Having fallen off the system of varṇas and āśramas, they started a horrific mixture of castes. These people reached the abyss. There were very few of them remaining. They were old, ill, and hungry. From grief they turned to infidelity… Infidelity led to contemplation, contemplation to serenity. In the state of serenity they awoke. Having awaken they turned to dharma. When these survivors from the Kali obtained this knowledge, the Yuga changed after one day and night… When the Kṛta Yuga started again, the survivors of the Kali became the subjects of the Kṛta Yuga (VP1.58.96–101, 103).

It is tempting to hypothesize that this story stems from a real historical experience, for the genesis of civilization in South Asia seems to follow this pattern. It is not impossible that the memory of the Harappan civilization passed through generations to the residents of the Gangetic states and the Mauryan Empire. Yet this is a topic for another study.

Postscript: On Theory and Politics

More than a year after the initial version of this book was completed, and several months after it was extensively revised for publication, I decided to write this addition, a brief postscript that would clarify the most important of my ideas, address anticipated criticisms, and place the whole discussion in the context of current political debates. This decision came as a response to several reviews that the manuscript of this book had received, and as an outcome of my own realization that, without further clarifications, the methods and ideas put forward in this book could be misinterpreted and used for wicked, political purposes.

Throughout this book, I have touched upon the three grand questions of South Asian studies: the historicity of ancient Indian literature, the idea of the ancient Indian city, and the idea of the ancient Indian civilization. Aside from being broad, cross-disciplinary, and controversial, each of these questions is also extremely political. It would therefore be not only irresponsible but quite cowardly of me not to address at least some of the related theoretical and political controversies in the most forthright manner.

Historicity of Ancient Indian Literature. Despite many attempts at correlating archaeology and texts of ancient South Asia, almost every aspect of the historical and archaeological value of ancient Indian literature remains a point of great controversy. Scholars still debate chronology, authorship, nature of composition, mechanisms of transmission, and sociocultural milieu of most Sanskrit and Pāli texts. Moreover, these debates are becoming more and more politicized, with the chronologies of texts and the identities of material cultures being unapologetically used to promote current political and religious agendas.

By proposing to treat ancient Indian literary traditions as sources of ideas rather than facts, I intended to divert attention from these politically charged controversies to an aspect of the ancient Indian literature, which has received the least attention of archaeologists. By doing so, I did not intend to convey a message that the ongoing political debates were unimportant, or that other ideas and theories—whether modern or ancient—were inappropriate for the conceptualization of the ancient South Asian past. All that I intended to do was to show that aside from the fruitless attempts at finding archaeological proof of the events described in the Sanskrit Epics or Purāṇas or from the endless debates on the archaeological identity of the Indo-Aryans (for a recent summary of opinions on this controversial issue see Bryant and Patton 2005), one could look at the ancient Indian literature as a source of historical information from a meaningful and completely unexplored epistemological perspective. Specifically, I proposed that treating ancient Indian texts as sources of complex sociocultural ideas, such as the idea of the city, and the idea of civilization, could be currently more productive and interesting than the reconstruction of illusive *l'histoire événementielle*. If the goal of anthropology and ancient history were seen as the creation of models and structures rather than chronicles and chronologies, which, in fact, are interpretative as well, the ancient Indian literature could provide a wealth of invaluable historical information. This information, i.e., the ideas of the historical agents, could be the focus of archaeological and historical studies, and most importantly a tool for the analysis of archaeological data.

New for South Asian archaeology, this analytical perspective may open new trajectories for research.

Why not test the ancient ideas of the city, complex society, state, civilization, collapse, social structure, and the like against the archaeological record? As archaeologists, historians, and anthropologists, we utilize a tremendous number of theories, many of which are mutually exclusive and deeply epiphenomenal to the data. Yet we omit potentially the most rewarding analytical perspective, namely the ideas and thoughts of the historical agents. This is not to say that the proper way to understand the other is by utilizing the other's theoretical constructs. I would like to reiterate that there is a significant difference between my suggestions and the ideas of those victimized anthropologists who substitute their own perspective with the perspective of the other. To me, the ideas and thoughts of the historical agents are neither an additional thought-provoking perspective nor the exclusive path for the understanding of the other, but rather an inseparable component of the past, the study of which enriches rather than diminishes our own ways of thinking.

This preamble set the grounds for my selection of texts and should explain why I did not pay any attention to the questions of textual history, authorship, and audience. Let me clarify my take on these issues again. The excerpts that I selected for analysis in the second chapter cover more a millennium of Sanskrit and Pāli literature and stand for very different social, religious, and literary traditions. Although there are many more descriptions of cities found in Sanskrit and Pāli texts, the selected excerpts are quite representative. In other words, their authors and audiences are not limited to one social or religious group, but rather speak for a wide spectrum of society, and this is exactly what I intended to achieve at this stage of research. Ideally, one would want to discuss the ideology, religion, and politics of the authors and audiences of the analyzed texts as well. To do this thoroughly however, one would need to write a separate book on each of the analyzed texts; for the authors, transmitters, and audiences of the Buddhist canon, Epics, Purāṇas, Śāstras, and the later Buddhist texts such as the *Milindapañha* are not only multilayered, but also extremely illusive. Oral forms of composition and transmission made the history of these texts extremely complicated, and it is therefore not surprising that much of the philological scholarship during the last 200 years was preoccupied with the reconstruction of this history. More importantly however, the details of textual history are irrelevant to the goals and theoretical stance pursued in this study and, under no conditions would they alter the proposed model of the city. All that they could do is to enrich this model by detailed text-historical information. Also one must realize that in order to deduce a preliminary conceptual pattern of the city, neither is there a need to cite all the descriptions and panegyrics of cities, nor is it necessary to investigate the social and political backgrounds of their authors. In a similar way, if one wants to investigate the general trends of the perceptions of the city in Western intellectual traditions; neither must one review every single work on the city, nor should one immerse himself into the biographies of their authors. Overall, it was not my intention to trace the developments of the idea of the city in ancient Indian literature, but rather to formulate a model of the city by finding conceptual similarities between different descriptions, panegyrics, and manuals.

My choice of excerpts from the two Sanskrit Purāṇas follows a very different methodological and conceptual pattern. Unlike the descriptions of cities which stand for diverse ideologies, the Yuga Story in the rendition of the *VāyuPurāṇa* and *BrahmāṇḍaPurāṇa* is a product of one ideology and possibly of a single compiler. In fact, if Wilibald Kirfel (1927) was right in his critical assessment of the Purāṇic corpus, the Yuga Story of the *VāyuPurāṇa* and *BrahmāṇḍaPurāṇa* may be the work of one author! Thus, while making use of ideologically diverse texts for discerning the model of the city, I focused on a single and ideologically-biased text for formulating the idea of the ancient Indian civilization. There are three reasons for this inconsistency. First, the Yuga Story of the *VāyuPurāṇa* and *BrahmāṇḍaPurāṇa* is significantly more conceptual than the descriptions of cities discussed in the second chapter. Second, there are not that many historical narratives in ancient Indian literature that can stand a comparison to this story in their analytical complexity. Third, many elements of this story go beyond religious dogmatism and display the elements of rationalistic and empiricist knowledge. My goal in the fifth and sixth chapters was to expose these elements and to determine whether they could be used in the analysis of archaeological data and the reconstruction of the past.

In sum, I am aware that the ways in which I used ancient Indian texts to formulate my analytical models may raise many questions. What my efforts have hopefully achieved is to have shown that ancient Indian literature contains ideas that can be used to contextualize material culture and to enhance our understanding of the ancient South Asian civilization.

Idea of the Ancient South Asian City. A model of the ancient South Asian city that I proposed in this book is clear-cut. The concurrent processes of the construction of fortifications and the formation of authoritative structures mark the emergence of the first cities both in the Harappan and Ganges civilizations, and consequently epitomize the idea of the city in the minds of the historical agents for many centuries ahead. There are numerous urban theories that I avoided in my analysis. I did it deliberately and in accordance with my argument that the city cannot have a single and all-inclusive definition. Perceived either as a fruit of poetic imagination or as an intelligible whole, the idea of the city is doomed to have multiple interpretations. Moreover, as a phenomenon, the city is inseparable from the idea of the city in the minds of the historical agents. Given this, my model of the ancient South Asian city is not meant to portray either the Harappan or Gangetic cities in their entire complexity. By connecting agency and structure, it is meant to highlight just a few important aspects of the first and second urbanizations and to create a model of the ancient South Asian city as an idea and a historical phenomenon.

Evidently, this model may open itself to criticism, and its most vulnerable point is the notion of authority. While fortifications are an easily deductible archaeological feature, authority is a complex concept that needs to be shown theoretically. Moreover, there is a multitude of forms that authoritative structures may take in different sociocultural settings. The reason why I, while tracing the emergence of authority in the archaeological record of twenty-five sites, did not try to determine specific forms of authority lies within the nature of my model of the city and the quality of the analyzed archaeological data.

The primary goal of my enquiry was to determine whether the model of the city extracted from the texts is appropriate for the analysis of archaeological data. Compiled from ideologically different texts, in which authorities take very different forms, this model had simply no room for the forms of authority. In other words, the forms of authority mentioned in the discussed descriptions and definitions of cities were not as theoretical and abstract as the idea of the city, and since the goal of my enquiry with regards to the texts was to extract the ideas rather than facts, I felt it was more justified to utilize the ideas of the city and complex society rather than the factual information about authority. Moreover, the selected archaeological data was not really helpful for discerning the forms of authority from site to site. With only few sites horizontally exposed and much data remaining unavailable, it would have been quite difficult, if not impossible, to theorize on the precise forms of authority from site to site through the analysis of archaeological data.

This is not to say that South Asian archaeology and ancient Indian texts totally lack data for theorizing on the sociopolitical organization of the Harappan and Ganges civilizations. Following the theoretical premises formulated in the beginning of this book, one could certainly investigate whether the Harappan and Ganges civilizations shared similar forms of authority. As far as the texts are concerned, theories of the state found in the *Kauṭilīya Arthaśāstra* and several other Sanskrit texts provide solid foundation for launching such an investigation. The archaeological record of the Harappan and Ganges civilization is not lacking either. The very fact that authorities both in the Harappan and Ganges civilization expressed their ethos in similar material symbols—various forms of fortification and circumvallation—indicates that the forms of authorities in these two civilizations may have been similar as well.

In sum, the forms of authority and sociopolitical organizations in the Harappan and Ganges civilizations remain to be investigated. This book sets the grounds for such a project, and I anticipate undertaking it shortly.

Idea of the Ancient Indian/South Asian Civilization. The most audacious of my theoretical models concerns the idea of the ancient Indian civilization. Not only did I place the Harappan and Ganges cultures within the same sociocultural entity, but I also suggested that some elements of this entity may have been formed during the Neolithic Period. Moreover, I theorized that while being shaped for several millennia, the ethos of this entity was contingent on four traits, namely rural lifestyle, orality used for the preservation of sacred and social information, an idiosyncratic social system, and a set of ritual and sacrificial practices (see Table 6.1), yet was irrelevant to the three traits that are most frequently associated with the formation of the early complex societies, namely, cities, writing, and monumental architecture.

Anticipating all kinds of misinterpretations, I need to clarify, once again, the premises that lie in the foundation of this model. As far as the theory of civilization is concerned, I believe that aside from being transcendental, semi-objective, and reflective, the idea of civilization is very inclusive. Like Braudelian sand dunes, whose "grains of sand may come and go" but "the dunes... remain standing", civilizations can preserve their unique configurations by accommodating a multitude of ethnolinguistic and cultural discontinuities. South Asia is a good example of such a civilization. Whether in its most ancient or more recent manifestations, it has always been a multiethnic and multilinguistic entity, in the shaping of which an important role has been played by interaction, external influxes, and internal diversity. The uniqueness of this civilization has, to a large extent, been in the capacity to absorb, reshape, and melt down these influxes and diversities. For good reasons, Rabindranath Tagor called India "bharattirtha" and placed it in the center of the universe as a great melting pot of cultures, languages, and religions. In a similar way, the model of the ancient Indian civilization that I proposed in this book is broad enough to accommodate a large number of very different religious and ethnolinguistic traditions.

Thus, by taking recourse to the idea of the ancient Indian civilization, my intention was to show that one can define the Great South Asian Tradition without falling into the ideology of "one people, one nation, one culture" and without having the Harappans speak Sanskrit and worship Shiva. Not unlike in later historical South Asia, the Great Tradition of protohistoric South Asia could be maintained in multilingual, multiethnic, and religiously diverse settings. Throughout the formation of the Harappan civilization, the consequent disintegration of the Harappan civilization, the infiltration or, for that matter, the local genesis of the Indo-Aryan languages, and the formation of the Ganges civilization, this tradition could be preserved in the ways of life, forms of ritual, means of maintaining important information, and norms of social differentiation. Meanwhile, religion, culture, language, and ethnicity could be in the process of permanent transformation.

The fact that I formulated this model based on the re-reading of a dogmatic religious text compiled around the mid-first millennium AD is quite remarkable. The least that it shows is that the intellectual legacy of the ancient Indian literature contains much unexplored potential for the analysis of archaeological data and the rethinking of South Asian protohistory.

Endnotes

Chapter One

1 Being fully aware of the modern political implications of the term "Indian", I use it throughout this book interchangeably with the term "South Asian", and do not imply any long-term cultural continuities *a priori*.

2 Similar concerns have been expressed in a large number of publications. Most recently, Fuller and Boivin (2002:160) has reasserted that "a clear picture of the trajectory of cultural development" in South Asia "will only come about when the various isolated specialists on the Harappan Civilization, the Deccan Chalcolithic, the Southern Neolithic, the Historical period, the ancient texts and the Stone Age... are finally able to operate as a single community"

3 Formism is defined by White (1973:14) as dispersive, focused on the data rather than integrative schemes. Its goal is "the depiction of the variety, color, and vividness of the historical field". Organicist and Mechanistic modes are seen as aimed at abstraction. Individual entities become less important "than the classes of phenomena to which they can be shown to belong; ...these classes in turn are less important... than the laws their regularities are presumed to manifest" (White 1973:17). Both modes are integrative, structural and aim at discerning the laws of history. The difference is that Organicism is synthetic whereas Mechanism is reductive. Finally, the Contextualist mode is aimed at functions and hidden meanings, or implies that "what happened in the field can be accounted for the specification of the functional interrelationships existing among the agents and agencies occupying the field at a given time" (White 1973:18).

4 For example, Ronald Inden, a well-known historian of South Asia from the University of Chicago, has argued that essentialism, structuralism, and other similar methods are innately opposite to the study of agency. In his well-acclaimed book *Imagining India*, Inden (1990:263) writes, "Studies of India have employed the presuppositions and assumptions of empiricism and its supposed opposite, idealism, to constitute their object. Whichever of these positions they have favored, they can almost always be seen as trying to know and control a human world ordered in systems that consist of mutually exclusive of dichotomously defined but interdependent parts. Those parts and the systems to which they belong are all assumed to be reducible to essences, to stable, objective and determinate features of natures presumed to underlie the surface phenomena of observation. Such thinking runs counter to a social science that wishes to study people and institutions as agents because it consistently devalues the actions of transient, historical agents". Inden seems to ignore the fact that thoughts of the historical agents can also be structuralist and essentialist. These thoughts form a constituent part of the past and should not be ignored in our own interpretations.

5 I am aware that today some scholars believe that the Vedic culture was urban and created by the Harappans (S. P. Gupta 1996, 1999; Simha 1987, 1995). Although I am open to these interpretations, I personally adhere to a more traditional view, according to which the first hymns of the *Ṛgveda* were composed roughly in the middle and the second half of the second millennium BC and the *Ṛgveda* society was predominantly pastoralist. Nonetheless, I want to avoid this whole issue in this book, for one of my main purposes is to show that there are more productive ways of using ancient Indian literature in the analysis of archaeological data and the reconstruction of South Asia's past, and I will reiterate this point several times throughout the book and particularly in the postscript.

6 Historical Materialism, Evolutionism, Processualism, Postmodernism, and other theoretical settings are often deeply alien to the data that we are discussing.

7 The concept of feudalism in the Near Eastern and Asian context was refuted even by a Russian Assyriologist, Igor M. Diakonoff, who followed many evolutionary and materialistic paradigms until his last days. In one of his last publications, a conceptual treatise on world history, Diakonoff (1994:7–8) unambiguously stated that Feudalism is a socioeconomic system typical of Western Europe and completely alien to most of non-European political traditions.

8 See also a separate chapter on this issue in Chakrabarti's book *Theoretical Issues in Indian Archaeology* (1988c:35–49).

9 The latter view goes back to F. E. Pargiter (1910, 1912, 1913, 1914, 1922a) who having analyzed the Sanskrit Purāṇas came to the conclusion that in spite of their mythological narrative these texts had a historical nucleus; the Purāṇic lists of the lunar and solar dynasties according to Pargiter included the names of the actual North Indian rulers.

10 An article by J. M. Kenoyer (1997) on the Harappan and Gangetic city-states and a chapter by F. R. Allchin (1995d) on the Mauryan State in *The Archaeology of Early Historic South Asia* are exceptions. Both authors, however, seem to be reluctant to use the texts to their full potential. I discuss the significance of Kenoyer's article in the end of this chapter.

11 For example, see a debate between B. B. Lal (1998b) and M. Witzel (2001).

12 Interestingly, neither Gupta nor Singh properly investigate the meaning of the word "pur". This has however been an important question for reconstructing the lifeways of the Vedic people. Wilhelm Rau (1976) has written a whole book on this issue. A more recent interpretation has been proposed by Erdosy (1994). Rau believed that the word "pur" in the *Ṛgveda* meant a temporary fortified settlement consisting of earth mounds with palisades and gates. People would use them primarily for keeping cattle and occasionally would hide there themselves. Recent archaeological discoveries in Central Asia and Kazakhstan have good examples of such settlements. Some Russian archaeologists see parallels between the *Ṛgvedic* "pur", the "var" of Yima in the *Avesta* and the archaeological sites, such as Arkhaim and Sintashta (Kuzmina 1995). The proponents of the "Vedic Harappans" Theory believe that the word "pur" indicates actual cities.

13 Some of the publications by Michael Jansen (1979, 1984b, 1993a) could possibly qualify as conceptual works on the Harappan city, yet mostly they focus on the architectural aspects of Mohenjo-Daro.

14 For most recent syntheses on the PGW and NBPW, see T. N. Roy (1986) and Tripathi (1975).

15 The PGW, as Lal (1954–1955:32–33) proposed in his initial report, was the only homogenous and well-defined distinctive ceramic industry of the "Dark Age" that could be "used as a cultural label". Moreover, Lal (1954–1955:147) hypothesized that the distribution of the PGW may have reflected "the movement of Aryan-speaking people in western Asia and southern Europe". As far as the NBPW was concerned, Lal reported that this ware had "quite a wide distribution ranging from Nasik in the west to Bangarh in the east. Although confined principally to northern India, it penetrated as far south as Sisupalgarh in Orissa. The remarkable uniformity in technique and appearance of this ware throughout does suggest a common centre of origin. It is observed that at the sites located in the Ganga plain it is more abundant and, in fact, outnumbers the other local ware in the main strata of its occurrence. Some of the sites in this belt are, therefore, likely to give a clue to the place of manufacture of this typical pottery" (Lal 1954–1955:50–52). As it now turns out, both the PGW and NBPW were defined based on relatively small assemblages. Most importantly the relationship between PGW and NBPW to other pottery types present at Hastinapura is unclear.

16 For archaeological perspectives, see Allchin (1989, 1990, 1995b), Chakrabarti (1970, 1972–1973, 1974, 1985a, 1985b, 1995), Erdosy (1984, 1987), and Piggott (1945). For textual perspectives, see Dutt (1925), Puri (1966), Ramanujan (1970), Sarao (1990), and Chattopadhyaya (2003). For both texts and archaeology, see Schlingloff (1969), Erdosy (1988), and Ghosh (1973). Also, see J. P. Sharma (1968), R. S. Sharma (1959, 1968, 1974, 1975–1976), Y. D. Sharma (1964, 1973), and Thakur (1981).

17 The names of sites in the Harappan and Ganges civilizations are given without diacritical signs, because this way they are usually quoted in archaeological and historical literature. Most of the Sanskrit terms are given in their proper transliteration, as this is more typical of philological and text-historical research.

Chapter Two

1 An example of a recent holistic study of the city in history is the book *The City in Time and Space* (Southall 1998).
2 Saint Augustine wrote this treatise soon after Rome fell to the Goths in 410.
3 Not surprisingly, *The City of God* still attracts the attention of scholars from different academic disciplines. For recent interpretations, see Donnelly (1995a) or O'Daly (1999).
4 Theories by Mumford (1961:91) and Weber (1922) are the best examples of Eurocentrism.
5 For example, Egyptologist J. A. Wilson (1951:35) came to the conclusion that until the eighteenth dynasty, Egypt had no cities; all of its settlements, in his opinion, were agricultural villages. In a similar way, Michael Coe (1961), at some point of his career, argued that the Classical Maya had no cities.
6 Christaller (1933) was certainly well aware of the fact that his theory was not universal. Doxiades (1968) also seemed to realize that the Ekistics although designed as a universal and holistic theory was not able to explain the multifarious nature of the city in its entire complexity.
7 The first written compilation of the Buddhist canon was carried out in Sri Lanka in the first century BC. The language of compilation was Pāli.
8 For a recent substantial synthesis of the Sanskrit Epics, see J. L. Brockington (1998). For the most recent research, see separate chapters and bibliographies in Brockington and Schreiner (1999); Brockington (2002); and Koskikallio (2005). For a comprehensive bibliography, see Stietencron et al. (1992).
9 For the most recent research, see separate chapters and bibliographies in Brockington and Schreiner (1999); M. Brockington (2002); and Koskikallio (2005). For the best synthesis of the Purāṇic studies, see Rocher (1986). For a comprehensive bibliography, see Stietencron et al. (1992).
10 An anthropologist, Jan Vansina (1965:149), once made a very revealing observation about the historical value of panegyric poetry: "It is obligatory to use a large number of stereotype phrases in this category of poems, so the poems serve as a source of information about the social ideals prevalent at the time when they were composed". Vansina (1965:149–150) unfortunately stops short in stating that "any attempt to study the poem itself in order to learn something about the history of the institution to which the person whose praises are sung belonged comes up against the difficulty of deciding whether a statement is merely a stereotype phrase, or one which describes actual facts". Vansina's skepticism evidently stems from the conviction that history is about writing chronicles, rather than discerning structures and formulating analytical models. It is not surprising that in his elaborate classification of oral traditions, Vansina leaves the idea of history undefined, yet accepts that panegerics may reflect "social ideals prevalent at the time when they were composed". The social ideals, pinpointed by Vansina, indicate in my view the historical thinking of ancient people and are worth being conceptualized in the context of other historical and archaeological sources.
11 sattahi nagaraparikkhārehi (AN VII.63.1).
12 catunnañ ca āhārānaṃ(AN VI.63.1).
13 esikā... gambhīraranemā sunikhātā acalā asampavedhi (AN VII.63.2).
14 parikhā... gambhīrā ... vitthatā ca (AN VII.63.3).
15 anupariyāyapatho (AN VII.63.4).
16 bahuṃ āvudhaṃ sannicitaṃ (AN VII.63.5).
17 bahu balakāyo (AN VII.63.6).
18 dovāriko... paṇḍito vyatto medhāvī (AN VII.63.7).
19 pākāro... ucco c' eva vitthato ca vāsanalepanasampanno ca (AN VII.63.8).
20 bahuṃ tiṇakaṭṭhodakaṃ sannicitaṃ (AN VII.63.9).
21 bahuṃ sāliyavakaṃ sannicitaṃ (AN VII.63.10).
22 bahuṃ tilamuggamāsāparaṇṇaṃ sannicitaṃ (AN VII.63.11).
23 bahuṃ bhesajjaṃ sannicitaṃ hoti, seyyathīdaṃ sappi navanītaṃ telaṃ madhu phāṇitaṃ loṇaṃ (AN VII.63.12).
24 seyyathā... nagare esikā hoti..., evam eva... ariyasāvako saddho hoti (AN VII.63.13).
25 seyyathā... nagare parikhā hoti..., evam eva... ariyasāvako hirimā hoti (AN VII.63.14).
26 seyyathā... nagare anupariyāyapatho hoti..., evam eva... ariyasāvako saddho hoti (AN VII.63.15).
27 seyyathā... nagare bahuṃ āvudhaṃ sannicitaṃ hoti..., evam eva... ariyasāvako bahussuto hoti (AN VII.63.16).
28 seyyathā... nagare bahu balakāyo hoti..., evam eva... ariyasāvako āraddhaviriyo viharati (AN VII.63.17).
29 seyyathā... nagare dovāriko hoti..., evam eva... ariyasāvako satimā hoti (AN VII.63.18).
30 seyyathā... nagare pākāro hoti..., evam eva... ariyasāvako paññavā hoti (AN VII.63.19).
31 For example, on one occasion the Enlightened One refers to horse training (AN IV.111). On another occasion, he mentions the political role of Kośala AN X.29).
32 This section is called Anumānapañha, which can be translated as "The issues of inference".
33 Grammatically, this duality is expressed by means of Pāli compounds: sīlapākāra, hiriparikhā, añāṇadvārakoṭṭhaka, viriyaaṭṭālaka, saddhāesikā, satidovāriko, paññāpāsāda, suttantacaccara, abhidhammasinghāṭaka, vinayavinicchaya, satipaṭṭānavīthika (MiP:332).
34 This sentence allows different translations.
35 This sentence is ambiguous (see endnote 37, the same chapter).
36 Quoting from the *Mahābāhrata* and *Rāmāyaṇa*, I use translations by Buitenen and Goldman, for these translations are, in my view, very good. Otherwise, all translations of

Sanskrit and Pāli passages (including this one) are mine.

37 The last attribute—agricultural fields—is controversial and depends on the translation of the sentence karmā ntakṣetravaśena kuṭumbinām sīmānam sthāpayet (KA 2.4.24). I believe the sentence should be translated as follows: "[He the king] should draw boundaries for householders in accordance with their cultivated fields". Yet there are different interpretations (Kalianov 1959:61; Kangle 1963:81; Rangarajan 1963:81).

38 The distinction between the city and the village is murky in many ancient Indian texts. In the *Arthaśāstra*, for example, the titles of administrators, such as nāgarika, samāhartṛ, gopa and sthānika, are present both in urban and rural contexts (KA 2.35.1–2, 6; 2.36.1–4).

39 The term "fortification" carries a functional connotation. Unfortunately, the English language does not have a good neutral term that would designate various types of dividing and circumvallating structures. The term "circumvallation", in my view, is not a much better option, because it implies the surrounding of a settlement from all the sides. Yet, as we will see later, some of the walls and ramparts did not surround sites entirely. Therefore, I will continue using the term "fortifications" generically for various kinds of perimeter walls, bastions, ramparts, and platforms. No defensive or any other function is implied at this point.

40 In his report on the excavation at Kumrahar, Spooner (1913:80) drew a direct parallel between the Mauryan pillared structure and the Hall of a Hundred Columns in Persepolis. Spooner (1913:80) even asserted that the similarity between the two structures indicated "a greater debt of India's part to Persepolitan civilization". As far as the use of the Mauryan Hall is concerned, Spooner (1913:80) suggested that it "may have been the Hall of Conference of an exceptionally vast and important monastery…, a Hall of Audience, or even the Throne-room of the Mauryan palace". To give Spooner some credit, he (1913:80) added that "one can only guess at this stage of the excavation, and guesses are unprofitable".

Chapter 3

1 The reports on archaeological explorations by Alexander Cunningham appeared in a number of periodicals and were eventually summarized in Cunningham (1871), a volume which, in many respects, predetermined the development of the archaeology of the Ganges civilization.

2 W. Hoey (1892) explored the site of Maheth. J. P. Vogel (1905, 1908, 1909a, 1909b, 1909c, 1914, 1915, 1994) explored Kasia, Saheth-Maheth, and Mathura. B. D. Spooner (1913, 1914) conducted research at Pataliputra and Basarh. T. Bloch (1904, 1909) excavated at Lauria and Basarch. John Marshall (1905, 1909, 1913, 1914, 1915a, 1915b, 1916, 1925–1926, 1927, 1928, 1929, 1930, 1934), Marshall and Konow (1908, 1909), and Marshall and Vogel (1903) excavated the sites of Lauriya, Rajagriha, Taxila, Saheth-Maheth, Bhita, Sarnath and Charsadda.

3 The meaning of this term has been discussed in the first chapter.

4 Chakrabarti (2001) has recently published a gazetteer of archaeological sites of the Middle and Lower Gangetic Doab. Although this area is very rich in archaeology, very few sites have been properly excavated. Moreover, the data from the excavated sites are not easily available.

5 A classical example of the application of this method to the Near Eastern archaeology is the study of urbanization and state formation by Robert Adams (1966, 1972, 1981). In South Asia, this method was used by M. R. Mughal (1990a, 1990b) in his analysis of the Harappan archaeology .

6 The excavations of Ahicchatra are very poorly published. For brief reports, see IAR (1963–64:43–44, 1964–65:39–42), Agrawala (1947–1948), Dikshit (1952), and Ghosh and Panigrahi (1946). The summaries by Bajpai (1986), M. Lal (1986), Law (1942), and S. B. Singh (1979) can be also helpful. Today, Ahicchatra is covered by agricultural fields making further excavations problematical.

7 The excavations at Atranjikhera are well published. (For brief annual reports see IAR 1960–61:35, 1962–63:34–36, 1963–64:45–49, 1965–66:44–47, 1967–1968:45–46, 1968–69:37–38, 1979–1980:75–76). For a more substantial report, see Gaur (1983). Currently, Atranjikhera is not covered by agricultural fields and provides a great potential for future excavations.

8 Protected by the ASI, Bhita is still in a very good condition. Owing to of its size, location, and long occupational history, it remains a very important site of the Ganges civilization.

9 Soon after, Gordon (1957) wrote a critical review of Lal's excavations. Chronology was revised many years later by M. Lal (1986).

10 The results of the excavation near the Asokan pillar and at the defense complex are published in two separate volumes, in Sharma (1960) and Sharma (1969). For a preliminary report, also see Sharma (1958). The results of the excavation at the Ghoshitarama Monastery and in the area of the palace, as well more results of the excavations near the Asokan pillar and at the defense complex, can be found in brief reports of the IAR (1953–1954:9, 1954–1955:16, 18, 1955–1956:20–22, 1956–1957:28–29, 1957–1958:47–49, 1958–1959:46–47, 1959–1960:46, 1960–1961:33–35, 1961–1962:50–52, 1962–1963:32–33, 1963–1964:40, 1966–1967:38–39). For later critical reviews and interpretations, see also Erdosy (1984, 1988), B. B. Lal (1979–1980, 1985b, 1985c), Mate (1969–1970), and K. K. Sinha (1973). For coins, see Shastri (1979). For historical synthesis, see N. Ghosh (1935). For the literary

perspective, see Law (1939). Today, agricultural fields and villages cover a significant portion of Kausambi making a possibility of further excavations highly questionable.

11 For the reports of the early excavations, see Vogel (1909c, 1914, 1915). For brief reports of later excavations (no substantial reports of these projects have been published), see IAR (1954–1955:15–16, 1966–1967:41–43, 1968–1969:40, 1969–1970:42–43, 1970–71:39–40, 1971–1972:47–48, 1972–1973:33–35, 1973–1974:31–32, 1974–1975:48–50, 1975–1976:53–55, 1976–1977:54–56). Also see a volume edited by Srinivasan (1989), with summary of the 1973–77 excavations by M. C. Joshi (1989), the analysis of pottery by Härtel (1989), the interpretations of coins by P. L. Gupta (1989), Narrain (1989), and Ray (1989), a study of etched beads by Margabandhu (1989), the outlines of the early history by Chattopadhyaya (1989) and R. Thapar (1989), and a review of prehistoric material by Shaffer (1989).

12 For the reports and notes of explorations and excavations at Pataliputra, see Mukherji (1898), Waddell (1892, 1903), Spooner (1913), Page (1927), Altekar and Mishra (1959), and Sinha and Narain (1970). For brief reports by the ASI, see ARASI (1926–1927:135, 1935–1936:54) and IAR (1953–1954:9–10, 1954–1955:18–19, 1955–1956:22–23). Since many excavations are unpublished, see Patil (1963), whose summary is helpful as a secondary source. For a general overview of the archaeology of Pataliputra and Nalanda, see Kumar (1987). For the history of Patna/Pataliputra, see Devi et al. (1980) and Ahmad (1988). For the English translation of Megasthenes' notes about Pataliputra, see McCrindle (1877).

13 For interpretations of the pillared hall, see Spooner (1913), Altekar and Mishra (1959), S. P. Gupta (1980), and Allchin (1995c:237–238).

14 For brief reports of the excavation at Rajghat, see IAR (1957–1958:50–51, 1960–1961:35–39, 1961–1962:57–59, 1962–1963:41–42, 1963–1964:58–59, 1964–1965:44–45, 1965–1966:54–55, 1966–1967:44, 1968–1969:41). For more substantial reports, see Narain and Roy (1976, 1977), Narain and Singh (1977), and Narain and Agrawala (1978). Today, a significant part of Rajghat is either covered by the modern city of Varanasi or washed away by the Ganges River.

15 Many of the early excavations at Rajgir are unpublished. For the earliest published reports, see Marshall (1909), Jackson (1914), and Sen (1918). For the excavations of 1950, see Ghosh (1951). For brief reports of further excavations by the ASI, see IAR (1953–1954:9, 1954–1955:16–17, 1957–1958:11, 1958–1959:13, 1961–1962:6–8, 1962–1963:5–6, 1974–1975:10–11). For general overviews of the archaeology of Rajgir, see Ghosh (1958), Kuraishi (1956), and Narayan (1983). For the history of early excavations at Rajgir and a general overview of issues, see Patil (1963). A recent study of the archaeology of Rajgir by Robert Harding is not yet available to me. Today, Rajagriha is a bustling resort for Indian tourists, which apparently complicates further excavations.

16 For brief reports of the excavation at Sonkh, see IAR (1966–1967:41–43, 1968–1969:40, 1969–1970:42–43, 1970–71:39–40, 1971–1972:47–48, 1972–1973:33–35). For a more substantial report, see Härtel (1993). For a review of pottery, see Härtel (1989).

17 Many identifiable coins, found in good context in Layer 27, support this chronological correlation.

18 For brief reports on the excavation at Sonpur, see IAR (1956–1957:19–20, 1959–1960:14, 1960–1961:4–5, 1961–1962:4–5, 1970–1971:5–6). For a more substantial report, see Sinha and Verma (1977). For a review of issues, see Patil (1963).

19 For the earliest explorations and excavations at Sravasti, see Hoey (1892), Vogel (1908), and Marshall (1914). For the general overviews of the archaeology of Sravasti, see Venkataramayya (1981). For the excavations of the 1959, see Sinha (1967). For brief reports by the ASI, see IAR (1958–1959:47–50, 1986–1987:76, 1987–1988:106–108, 1988–1989:82–84, 1991–1992:102–104, 1992–1993:91–92, 1995–1996:76–82). For the ongoing excavations by the joint Indian-Japanese team, see Aboshi et al. (1999). For the review and analysis of relevant literary sources, see Law (1935).

20 One must note that a report published in IAR gives different dimensions. The basal width is 95 ft and maximum height is 12 ft (IAR 1958–1959:50).

21 For the main reports on the excavations at Vaisali, see Bloch (1904), Spooner (1914), Deva and Mishra (1961), and Sinha and Roy (1969). For brief reports by the ASI, see IAR (1957–1958:10–11, 1958–1959:12, 1959–1960:14–16, 1960–1961:6, 1961–1962:5–7, 1974–1975:11, 1988–1989:9). For an overview of issues, see Patil (1963). For a general introduction to the site and museum, see Mishra and Roy (1964).

Chapter 4

1 There are four published reports on the excavation of Allahdino: three by Fairservis (1973, 1976, 1977), and one by Hoffman and Cleland (1977). There are also three unpublished reports: two by Hoffman (1974a, 1974b) and one by Shaffer (1974). The unpublished reports are the courtesy of Richard H. Meadow. For brief summaries and interpretations of the archaeology of Allahdino, see Fairservis (1982) and Hoffman and Shaffer (1975).

2 Unfortunately, no comprehensive report on the excavation of Banawali has been published. For brief reports by the ASI,

see IAR (1983–1984:24–29, 1986–1987:32–34, 1987–1988:21–27). For summaries and interpretations, see Bisht (1976, 1977, 1978, 1982, 1984, 1987, 1997, 1998–1999), and Bisht and Asthana (1979).

3 For the earliest information on Chanhu-Daro, see Majumdar (1934). For preliminary reports and notes on the excavation by the American School of Indic and Iranian Studies and Boston Museum of Fine Arts, see Mackay (1935–1936, 1936a, 1936b, 1937a, 1937b), Ghosh (1937), and Brown (1938). For the main report, see Mackay (1943). For the recent analyses of data from Chanhu-Daro, see Shar and Vidale (1985), and Yule (1988). For the seals from Chanhu-Daro, see Newberry (1983b) and F. R. Allchin (1985).

4 One must note, however, that the deep trench laid by Mackay on mound 2 did not reach virgin soil; water prevented further excavations.

5 Despite the ongoing excavation at Dholavira, very little data is available in print. For brief reports by the ASI, see IAR (1984–85:14, 17, 1987–88:15–16, 1989–90:15–20, 1990–1991:10–12, 16, 1991–92:26–35, 1992–93:27–31). For summaries and interpretations, see Bisht (1989a, 1989b, 1991, 1998–1999, 1999). For the analysis of faunal data, see Patel (1997).

6 For the history of research at Harappa, see Kenoyer (1991b:32–38) and Possehl (1991, 1999:87–92, 132).

7 For the earlier excavation, see Sahni (1916–1917, 1920–1922, 1923–24, 1924–25, 1936), Vats (1926–1927, 1927–1928, 1928–1929, 1929–1930, 1930–1934, 1940); Srivastava (1936–1937); and Wheeler (1947, 1962). The excavation conducted by Mughal is unpublished. For the reports on the excavation conducted since 1986, see Dales and Kenoyer (1986b, 1987, 1989, 1990a, 1990b, 1991, 1992a, 1992b), Meadow (1991), Meadow and Kenoyer (1993), Meadow et al. (1994, 1995, 1996, 1997, 1998, 1999, 2001). For additional summaries and interpretations, see Dales (1989, 1992b), Kenoyer (1991b, 1993, 1994a, 1998), Kenoyer and Meadow (2000), and Meadow and Kenoyer (1994, 1997, 2000, 2001a, 2001b). The excavation reports by HARP are provided as a courtesy by Richard H. Meadow.

8 The date of the earliest human occupation at Harappa remains an open question. It is quite possible that mound AB or mound E contains Neolithic deposits.

9 Importantly, this does not exclude other functions. For example, many walls at Harappa served as retaining structures, i.e., protected and stabilized new construction layers.

10 The results of the excavations at Kalibangan have not been fully published. For brief reports by the ASI, see IAR (1960–1961:31–32, 1961–1962:39–44, 1962–1963:20–31, 1963–1964:30–39, 1964–1965:35–39, 1965–1966:38–41, 1966–1967:31–33, 1967–1968:42–45, 1968–1969:28–32). For the report on the Early Harappan period, see Lal et al. (2003). For summaries and interpretations, see Lal (1979; 1984), Lal and Thapar (1967). Newberry (1983a), Nigam (1995–1996), Raikes (1968), A. K. Sharma (1977–1978, 1982, 1999), and B. K. Thapar (1973, 1975, 1977).

11 These numbers are taken from the most recent report published in the *MASI* (Lal et al. 2003:53). An earlier report published in the IAR gives slightly different measurements, i.e., 1.90 m. for the first phase and 3.70–4.10 m for the second phase (IAR 1965–66:40).

12 I purposely avoid here using the terms "citadel" and "the lower town", as they convey preconceived notions of sociopolitical organizations.

13 For the report on the excavation of Kot-Diji, see Khan (1965). The two unpublished reports of Kot Diji (Khan 1959, 1960) were not available to me at the time of research. For an important revision of the Kot Diji sequence, see Mughal (1970). For popular summaries, see Khan (1964, 2002).

14 Since the terms "citadel" and "outer city" are heavily interpretative, I will hereon refer to "area A" and "area B".

15 For the main reports on the excavation at Lothal, see Rao (1979b, 1985). For a comprehensive analytical summary, see Rao (1973). For brief reports by the ASI, see IAR (1954–55:12, 1955–56:6–7, 1956–57:15–16, 1957–58:11–13, 1958–59:13–15, 1959–60:16–18, 1961–62:9–10, 1962–1963:7). For additional reports, summaries, and interpretations, see Lal (1985a), Leshnik (1968), Pandya (1977), Panjwani (1989), Possehl (1975), Raghunath (1984), Rao (1963, 1968, 1969, 1979a, 1979c), Schmokel (1966), and Yule and Rao (1982).

16 For the earlier excavations, see Marshall (1925–1926, 1931), Mackay (1938), Wheeler (1962), Dales (1965a, 1965b, 1982), Alcock (1986), and Dales and Kenoyer (1986a). For the work conducted in the 1970s and 1980s, see Jansen (1983, 1984a, 1984b, 1984c, 1985, 1987, 1989, 1991, 1993a, 1993b, 1994), Jansen, Marshall and Mackay (1997), Jansen, Tosi, and Leonardi (1988), Jansen and Urban (1984, 1985, 1987), Urban and Jansen (1983), Cavagnaro Vanoni and Cucarzi (1990). For other noteworthy publications on Mohenjo-Daro, see Ardeleanu-Jansen, Franke, and Jansen (1983), Ardeleanu-Jansen (1984, 1987, 1992, 1993), Blackman and Vidale (1992), Bondioli and Lazari (1990), Dales (1965a, 1965b, 1982), During Caspers (1992), Kenoyer (1985), Kondo et al. (1997), Miller (1994), Parpola (1992), Pracchia et al. (1985), Raikes (1979), Sarcina (1978–1979, 1979), Wheeler (1962), Winkelmann (1994).

17 For a detailed discussion on the Early Harappan in Mohenjo-Daro, see Franke-Vogt (1994).

18 For the main reports on the excavation of Nausharo, see J.-F. Jarrige (1974–1986, 1987–1988, 1989, 1990). Excavation at Mehrgarh-Nausharo (J.-F. Jarrige

1995–1996) was the last report available to me at the time of the writing of this book (this report is unpublished and is provided as a courtesy by Richard H. Meadow). For the recent summaries of results, see J.-F. Jarrige (1996) and C. Jarrige (1994, 2000). For other summaries, reports, and interpretations, see Barthelemy de Saizieu and Bouquillon (1997), Bouquillon et al. (1995), Costantini (1990), Gouin (1990, 1992), C. Jarrige (1997), J.-F. Jarrige (1987, 1993, 1994, 1997), Jarrige and Meadow (1992), Mery (1994), Quivron (1994, 1997, 2000), and Samzun (1992).

19 One must note that the existing radiocarbon dates are contradictory and the dating of most cultural periods is based on comparative stratigraphy.

20 The original interpretation, according to which the northern mound was abandoned prior to period II, while the southern mound was settled in period II, is no longer valid. Recent excavations have shown that both the northern and southern mounds were flourishing in period II. Consequently, the wall of period ID divided space between different parts of the settlement already in period ID, which likely indicates that period ID saw the initial stages of social segregation and the shaping of authoritative structures.

21 The results of the excavation at Surkotada are well published. For the main report, see J. P. Joshi (1990). For brief reports by the ASI, see IAR (1970–1971:13–15, 1971–1972:13–21). Also, see Bisht (1989a), and J. P. Joshi (1972, 1974).

22 Following the terminology of the early excavators of Harappa and Mohenjo-Daro, Joshi calls these parts the "citadel" and the "lower town". To avoid the interpretative character contained in these terms, I will refer to them as the eastern and western sections.

23 On one occasion J. P. Joshi (1990:51) notes that "At the extreme southwestern corner of the revetted bastion, there is a projecting structure having one course of stones in an area of 3.40 x 1.60 m. These suggest that in period IC there was some habitational activity outside the rampart".

24 For the early reports on the exploration and excavation of Sutkagen-Dor see Mockler (1877) and Stein (1931:36–60, 135–157). For the report on the excavation by Dales, see Dales and Lipo (1992). Also, see Dales (1962a, 1962b, 1964).

25 It is important to remember that despite of the importance that fortifications carry as evidence for social transformations, fortifications *per se* do not necessarily indicate the emergence of authority. In some cases, fortifications are two modest to be indicative of major social transformations.

Chapter 5

1 To my knowledge, no one has yet produced a comprehensive and interdisciplinary concordance of all the theories of civilization. There are nonetheless several thorough reviews dealing solely with the origin and semantics of this term. For a linguistic perspective see Benveniste (1966). For historical and humanistic perspectives, see Febvre (1930), Marrou (1938), Dampierre (1961), Braudel (1969, 1987), and Toynbee (1934–1961:XII.273–279, 282–292). For anthropological perspective, see Kroeber (1953), Kroeber and Kluckhohn (1952), and Redfield (1962).The reviews written by Braudel and Toynbee are, in my view, particularly illuminating: in them, these two outstanding historians reconstruct a step-by-step history of the term "civilization" to promote their own interpretations.

2 It is argued that in the works of these individuals the word civilization appears for the first time in its sociopolitical and ethical meaning. Although Voltaire omits using the word "civilization" directly, the notion of civilization is implied in his treatment of the world history (see discussion on this issue in the beginning of *Grammaire de Civilizations* (Braudel 1987)).

3 The most notable theories of civilization, in my view, include: Lewis Morgan (1877), Friedrich Engels (1884), Oswald Spengler (1918), Arnold Toynbee (1934–1961), Pitirim Sorokin (1948, 1992), Alfred Kroeber (1948, 1953, 1957), V. Gordon Childe (1934, 1939, 1947, 1950, 1951, 1953), R.G. Collingwood (1942), Robert Braidwood (1952, 1963), Philip Bagby (1959), Robert Redfield (1947, 1953a, 1953b, 1962, 1954), Robert Adams (1960, 1966, 1968), Lewis Mumford (1961), Carroll Quigley (1961), Kent Flannery (1972), Colleen Renfrew (1972), Elman Service (1975), Charles Redman (1978), and Fernand Braudel (1949, 1969, 1987).

4 Civilization is a key analytical concept in Toynbee's voluminous treatise *A Study of History*. Justly seen as Toynbee's *opus magnum*, this treatise develops around the story of twenty odd civilizations designed to present human history as a coherent narrative. Amazingly, having spent almost thirty years working on this treatise, Toynbee provides no precise definition of the term civilization until the very last volume, when requested to do so by his colleagues and opponents.

5 Although this definition is not new—Braudel borrows it from the writings of Marcel Mauss (1929)—in Braudel's interpretation it has a novel meaning. Cultural areas are seen by Braudel (1980:203) as confining a great variety of cultural attributes in a territorially bound space. It is these attributes in their totality that determine the form of a given civilization. Intercultural borrowings are traits or goods that being "constantly on the move" travel back and forth from civilization to civilization. Refusals are those cultural traits or goods that either intentionally or unintentionally denied access into the cultural loci of certain civilizations.

6 Toynbee (1934–1961:XII.292) expressed this idea vividly in the last volume of *A Study of History*. For example, he stated that "when the anthropologist or the cultural historian tries to analyse the observable qualities that have been his clues to the diagnosis of a culture, he analyses them... in terms of ideas and values. Invisibility is... as common characteristic of all forces that potent in human affairs. Even in the realm of non-human nature, over which Man has now established his mastery, invisible microbes and protons are more potent than visible lions and flashes of lightning. In the spiritual realm, where Man is not master, he has to cope with an invisible network of relations between elements in his own psyche, and with another invisible network of relations between himself and his fellow human beings. And the most potent of the forces that move human souls is the spirit that blows like the incalculable wind whose passage is audible but invisible". Not adhering to the final part of this statement which has an explicit Christian subtext, I accept the idea of invisibility. This invisibility, in my view, does not make our explanations less meaningful. Regardless of whether the truth exists and whether it is comprehensible, the desire to acquire it is what really matters.

7 To some degree, this point was expressed by Braudel (1993:22) in *Grammaire de Civilisations*. According to Braudel, "in every period, a certain view of the world, a collective mentality, dominates the whole mass of society. Dictating a society's attitudes, guiding its choices, confirming its prejudices and directing its actions, this is very much a fact of civilization. Far more than the accidents or the historical and social circumstances of a period, it derives from the distant past, from ancient beliefs, fears and anxieties which are almost unconscious—an immense contamination whose germs are lost to memory but transmitted from generation to generation. A society's reactions to the events of the day, to the pressure upon it, to the decisions it must face, are less a matter of logic or even self-interest than the response to an unexpressed and often inexpressible compulsion arising from the collective unconscious... These basic values, these psychological structures, are assuredly the features that civilizations can least easily communicate one to another. They are what isolate and differentiate them most sharply. And such habits of mind survive the passage of time. They change little, and change slowly, after a long incubation which itself is largely unconscious too".

8 For an old yet momentous summary of the Yuga Story, see Jacobi (1908). For early studies, see Bentley (1808), Wilford (1794–1808), Roth (1860), Dumont (1935), Guenon (1937), and Mankad (1941–1942, 1942, 1942–1943). For more recent studies, see Brown (1966), Church (1970, 1971, 1974), Chembukar (1974), Mandal (1968), A. S. Gupta (1969), Mitchiner (1976–1977), Balslev (1983), Cardona (1991), and Gonzales Reimann (2001). For a classical comparative and holistic overview, see Eliade (1949, 1957). For historical perspectives, see Pargiter (1922b) and R. Thapar (2000b). For the interpretations of the Kali Yuga, the last of the four cosmic ages, see Fleet (1911), Gable (1920), and Varma (1978–1979).

9 All translations in this chapter are mine (it seemed overburdensome and unnecessary to cite original passages in transliteration).

10 These sections are called bhuvavinyāsa and are found in most of the canonical Mahāpurāṇas.

11 Parallels with other ancient concepts of time and social change—the myth of five ages by Hesiod, etc.—are quite obvious yet their exploration is far beyond the goal of my current enquiry.

12 For example, when Sụta explains to Śamśapāyana how sacrifice was established, he starts with agriculture, sedentism, "When the plants grew and rains poured, when the agriculture, houses, aśramas (hermitages) and cities were established, Indra, the consumer of the world, for the deeds (karma) of this and other worlds, first created the varṇāśrama system and collated the mantras into the samhitas. Then, joined by all the gods, he established yajña (sacrifice) and all its requisites" (VP 1.57.89–90).

13 Childe's (1950) definition included: dense population; full-time specialist craftsmen, transport workers, merchants, officials and priests; tithe or tax to an imaginary deity or a divine king who thus concentrated the surplus; truly monumental public buildings; a ruling class; writing and numerical notation; exact and predictive sciences—arithmetic, geometry and astronomy; full-time artists; regular foreign trade; and a state organization based on residence rather than kinship. Robert Braidwood (1952:2) modified this definition by highlighting the importance of eight traits: fully efficient food production; cities; formal political state; formal laws (a new sense of moral order); formal projects and works; classes and hierarchies; writing; and monumentality in art. In a slightly different way, Robert Adams (1960:271) defined civilization from a functional point of view. The attainment of civilization, according to Adams, was expressed in four parallel processes: "urbanization, militarization, stratification, and bureaucratization". Civilization thus was "a functionally interrelated set of social institutions: class stratification, marked by highly different degrees of ownership or control of the main productive resources; political and religious hierarchies complementing each other in the administration of territorially organized states; a complex division of labor, with full-time craftsmen, servants, soldiers, and officials alongside the great mass of primary peasant producers".

14 To some extent, this model is reminiscent of the idea of "the

Indian Style" proposed by S. C. Malik. As I mentioned in the first chapter, Malik (1968:106–108) argued that from its inception at the Harappan stage, the Indian civilization was characterized by three traits: caste, the genealogical means of the perpetuation of caste by birth, and the importance of orality in the transmission of ritual and other forms of knowledge. The emergence of the ancient Indian civilization thus was dated to the mid-third millennium BC and its ethos was defined through purely ideational institutions. As in the case with the Purāṇic model, none of these institutions required cities, writing, monumental architecture, or any other traits usually included in the archaeological definitions of civilization.

Chapter 6

1 For recent summaries of the South Asian Neolithic, see Agrawal and Kharakwal (2002:157–224), Chakrabarti (1999:117–150, 205–261, 326–328), Dhavalikar (2002), Ghosh (1989:I.43–68), Korisettar et al. (2002), Misra (1999), Possehl (1999:394–553), Possehl and Rissman (1992) Shaffer (1992), Singh (1987; 2002), and B. K. Thapar (1987).

2 It has been repeated from publication to publication, that the comparison of the orally preserved versions of the Ṛgveda from different parts of India shows that this "text" has been preserved in its authentic form since the time of initial canonization (for example, see Narasimhan 1991:178; Staal 1961:1; Witzel 1995a:91). It is important to note that there are quite a few skeptics who question this argument.

3 For example, with regard to the transition from the oral to written form of the royal genealogies, vaṁśa, of the White Yajurveda, R. M. Smith (1966:112) writes the following: "These lists were not made up for fun, or a parlour games to relieve concentration on yoga exercises. They are a guarantee of the genuineness of the doctrine, which is a matter of real importance and interest to the brahmanic schools... When kings lose their ritual significance and become merely enjoyers of Earth, the genealogies too change, and inform us only of the generations in power, not of the origins of the family: so too though oral teaching is always the more important, the end of the vaṁśa should mark a change, and the most natural is the commission of the teaching to writing, we suggest... in the second century B.C., when the tides of heresy and foreign invasion are at their climax".

4 The question whether ancient Indian oral traditions could have been affected by the invention of writing has been previously raised by Goody, who seems to believe that India was not purely an oral culture even at the time of the first Vedas. Goody (1987:122) asserts that even if the Vedas "were not written down at the moment of composition" they " bear the hallmarks of a literate culture" and that both the organization of the Vedas and the "mnemonic devices used by those who teach and learn them" were influenced by writing.

5 The argument of the advocates of this direction is based on the assumption that the right way to conceptualize India is by using Indian concepts (see Marriott 1990; Marriott and Inden 1977).

6 For the linguistic roots of this term, see Corominas (1961) and Covarrubias Horozco (1611).

7 For a good review on the history of this term, see Julian Pitt-Rivers (1971).

8 As far as case-studies are concerned, the concept of caste has been used in the analysis of social structures in South America (Kubler 1952), Mesoamerica (Reed 1964), Sub-Saharan Africa (Ogbu 1981), the Middle East (Jones 1981), and even the contemporary United States (Berremann 1960; Dollard 1949). Generic cross-cultural studies are well-represented in the writings of the anthropologist Gerald D. Berreman (1966, 1973, 1979a, 1981).

9 On a generic interpretative level, Lamberg-Karlovsky (1999:88) states that "social organization may take three distinctive forms that structure and differentiate the rights, obligations, and privileges of its members: egalitarian society, class society, and caste society". In the context of South Asian civilization, Lamberg-Karlovsky seems to rely on the interpretations of caste by Declan Quigley (1993) and Pauline Kolenda (1978).

10 There has been a significant amount of anthropological literature on the jajmani system (Berremann 1962, 1979b; Caldwell 1991; Gould 1964; Harper 1959; Kolenda 1963; Wiser 1936). In one way or another, most of this literature relates jajmani to caste. For example, Berreman (1979b:318), whom Kenoyer (1989b:189) quotes in support of his argument with regard to jajmani, believes that the jajmani system played a role in expressing and reinforcing the kin component of caste.

11 Textually, the concept of the four varṇas is earlier than the Yuga Story. As the frequently quoted hymn from the Ṛgveda tells us, the four varṇas are created from the limbs of Puruṣa, the primeval god-man sacrificed at the time immemorial (RV X.90).

12 More recently, the role of sacrificial and ritual practices in the Neolithic Revolution has been reaffirmed in the writing of Jacques Cauvin (1972, 1994).

13 An important study of Vedic sacrifice is a recent book by J. C. Heesterman (1993), a long-term professor of Indology at the University of Leiden. Also, noteworthy are the treatises on Vedic sacrifice by A. Hillebrandt (1879, 1897), J. Schwab (1886), W. Caland and V. Henry (1906–1907), P. E. Dumont (1879, 1927), and F. Staal (1983).

14 Mention must be made of the following publications; Hubert and Maus (1899), Burkert (1972), Girard (1972),

Hamerton (1987), Ashby (1988), Baumgarten (2002), and most recently Keenan (2005).

15 The discovery of the four bronze objects—a bull chariot, an elephant, a rhino, and a buffalo—from Daimabad, a chalcolithic site in Maharashtra, is particularly noteworthy. Based on the analysis of these objects, Dhavalikar (1978:209) suggests that "the people of the Malwa period at the site... worshipped a "Lord of Beasts" similar to the Paśupati of the historical period". On another occasion, Dhavalikar (1988:57) draws a parallel between a headless figurine from Inamgaon and the goddess Śākambari of the Skanda Purāṇa. Being attached to the figurine of a bull, this figurine, in Dhavalikar's view, is also reminiscent of the later Brahmnanical concept of vahana

16 For recent analytical summaries of ideas on Harappan religion, see Possehl (2002c:141–155), Atre (2002), and Agrawal and Kharakwal (2003:99–110).

17 Attempts at identifying several houses as temples and a few pottery jars and conch-shells trumpets as libation vessels are quite hypothetical and must not be seen, at this point, as indicators of a general pattern (see Jansen 1985).

18 A good example of such an interpretation is a recent article by J. P. Joshi published in the new voluminous study on the rise of Indian civilization (Pande 1999). In this article, Joshi (1999:382) confidently asserts that the Harappan society had three main religious sects; "the Śiva-Śakti worshippers of Punjab and Sindh; the fire worshippers of Kalibangan-Dholavira, Lothal, Nageshwar and Vagad; and the Surkotada-Dholavira people," whose religion was expressed in the ways they buried their dead.

19 This approach seems to be pursued by G. L. Possehl (2002c:153), who, in his recent synthesis of the Harappan archaeology, states that "the proposed historical links between the Indus civilization and later Indian civilization is a difficult, complex, sometimes contentious, even politicized topic".

Critical Editions of the Quoted Sanskrit and Pāli Texts

Aṅguttara-Nikāya, edited by the Rev. Richard Morris and Edmund Hardy. Published for the Pāli Text Society by H. Frowde, London, 1885–1910.

BrahmāṇḍaPurāṇa, edited by Jagdish Lal Shastri. Motilal Banarsidas, Dehli, 1973.

Kauṭilīya Arthaśāstra, edited by R. P. Kange. Bombay University Press, Bombay, 1960.

Lalitāmāhātmya of the BrahmāṇḍaPurāṇa, edited by Jagdish Lal Shastri. Motilal Banarsidas, Delhi, 1973.

Mahābhārata, edited by Vishnu S. Suthankar, with the cooperation of Balasaheb Pant Pratinidhi [and others] and illustrated from ancient models by Balasaheb Pant Pratinidhi. Bhandarkar Oriental Research Institute, Poona, 1927–1966.

Milindapañha, edited by V. Trenckner. Williams and Norgate, London, 1880.

Vālmīki Rāmāyaṇa, edited by C. S. Patel et al. Oriental Institute, Baroda, 1960–1975.

VāyuPurāṇa, edited by pandits of the Ānandāśrama. Apta, Poona, 1905.

References

Aboshi, Y., K. Sonoda, F. Yoneda, and A. Uesugi
1999 Excavations at Saheth Maheth 1986–1996. *East and West* 49:119–174.

Adams, R. M.
1960 Early civilizations, subsistence, and environment. In *City Invincible*, edited by C. H. Kraeling and R. M. Adams, pp. 269–296. The University of Chicago Press, Chicago.

1966 *The Evolution of Urban Society: Early Mesopotamia and Prehistoric Mexico*. Aldine, Chicago.

1972 Patterns of urbanization in early southern Mesopotamia. In *Man, Settlement, and Urbanism*, edited by P. J. Ucko, R. Tringham, and G. W. Dimbleby, pp. 735–749. Duckworth, London.

1981 *Heartland of Cities*. University Press, Chicago.

Agrawal, D. P., and J. S. Kharakwal
2002 *South Asian Prehistory: A Multidisciplinary Study*. Archaeology of South Asia 1. Aryan Books International, New Delhi.

2003 *Bronze and Iron Ages in South Asia*. Archaeology of South Asia 2. Aryan Books International, New Delhi.

Agrawala, V. S.
1947–1978 The terracotta of Ahichchhatra. *Ancient India* 4:104–179.

Ahmad, Q.
1988 *Patna through the Ages: Glimpses of History, Society and Economy*. Patna College Publications Series No. 1. Commonwealth Publishers, New Delhi.

Alcock, L.

1986 A pottery sequence from Mohenjo-Daro: R. E. M. Wheeler's 1950 "Citadel Mound" excavations. In *Excavations at Mohenjo Daro, Pakistan: The Pottery*, edited by G. F. Dales and J. M. Kenoyer, pp. 493–570. University Museum Monograph 53. The University Museum, University of Pennsylvania, Philadelphia.

Allchin, F. R.

1971 Review of Malik's (1968) "Indian civilization, the formative period. A study of archaeology as anthropology". *Antiquity* XLV(177):68–69.

1985 The interpretation of a seal from Chanhu-Daro and its significance for the religion of the Indus civilization. In *South Asian Archaeology 1983* Vol. 1, edited by J. Schotsmans and M. Taddei, pp. 369–384. Instituto Universitario Orientale, Naples.

1989 City and state formation in Early Historic South Asia. *South Asian Studies* 5:1–17.

1990 Patterns of city formation in Early Historic South Asia. *South Asian Studies* 6:163–174.

1995a *The Archaeology of Early Historic South Asia: The Emergence of Cities and States.* Cambridge University Press, Cambridge.

1995b Early cities and states beyond the Ganges Valley. In *The Archaeology of Early Historic South Asia: The Emergence of Cities and States*, edited by F. R. Allchin, pp. 123–151. Cambridge University Press, Cambridge.

1995c The Mauryan architecture and art. In *The Archaeology of Early Historic South Asia: The Emergence of Cites and States*, edited by F. R. Allchin, pp. 222–273. Cambridge University Press, Cambridge.

1995d The Mauryan state and empire. In *The Archaeology of Early Historic South Asia: The Emergence of Cities and States*, edited by F. R. Allchin, pp. 187–221. Cambridge University Press, Cambridge.

Altekar, A. S., and V. Mishra

1959 *Report on Kumrahar Excavations, 1951–1955*. Jayaswal Research Institute, Patna.

Appadurai, A.

1984 Is *Homo Hierarchicus*? *American Ethnologist* 13(4):745–761.

Ardeleanu-Jansen, A.

1984 Stone sculptures from Mohenjo-Daro. In *Interim Report: Reports on Field Work Carried Out at Mohenjo-Daro, Pakistan, 1982–1983 by the IsMEO-Aachen-University Mission* Vol. 1, edited by M. Jansen and G. Urban, pp. 139–158. RWTH, Aachen.

1987 The theriomorphic stone sculpture from Mohenjo-Daro reconsidered. In *Interim Reports: Reports on Field Work Carried Out at Mohenjo-Daro* Vol. 2, edited by M. Jansen and G. Urban, pp. 59–68. German Research Project Mohenjo-Daro, Aachen.

1992 New evidence on the distribution of artifacts: An approach towards a qualitative-quantitative assessment of the terracotta figurines of Mohenjo-Daro. In *South Asian Archaeology 1989*, edited by C. Jarrige, pp. 5–14. Monographs in World Archaeology 14. Prehistory Press, Madison.

1993 Who fell into the well? Digging up a well in Mohenjo-Daro. In *South Asian Archaeology 1991*, edited by A. J. Gail and G. J. R. Mevissen, pp. 1–16. Franz Steiner Verlag, Stuttgart.

Ardeleanu-Jansen, A., U. Franke, and M. Jansen
1983 An approach towards the replacement of artifacts into the architectural context of the Great Bath in Mohenjo-Daro. In *Forschungsprojekt DFG Mohenjo-Daro: Dokumentation in der Archäologie: Techniken, Methoden, Analysen*, edited by G. Urban and M. Jansen, pp. 43–70. [s.n.] Aachen.

Ashby, G. W.
1988 *Sacrifice: Its Nature and Purpose*. SCM, London.

Atre, S.
2002 Harappan religion: Myth and polemics. In *Indian Archaeology in Retrospect* Vol 2. *Protohistory, Archaeology of the Harappan Civilization*, edited by S. Settar and R. Korisettar, pp. 185–204. Indian Council of Historical Research, Manohar, Delhi.

Augustine, Saint, Bishop of Hippo
1993 *The City of God [De Civitate Dei]*. Translated by M. Dods, with an introduction by T. Merton. Modern Library, New York.

Bagby, P.
1959 *Culture and History: Prolegomena to the Comparative Study of Civilization*. University of California Press, Berkeley.

Bajpai, K. D. (editor)
1986 *Ahicchatra through the Ages*. Panchal Research Institute, Kanpur.

Bakhtin, M. M.
1975 *Voprosy Literatury i Estetiki: Issledovaniia Raznykh Let*. Khudozhestvennaia Literatura, Moskva.

1979 *Estetika Slovesnogo Tvorchestva*. Iskusstvo, Moskva.

1986 *Speech Genres and Other Late Essays*. University of Texas Press, Austin.

Balslev, A. N.
1983 *A Study of Time in Indian Philosophy*. Harrassowitz, Wiesbaden.

Barthelemy de Saizieu, B., and A. Bouquillon
1997 Evolution of glazed materials from the Chalcolithic to the Indus Period based on the data of Mehrgarh and Nausharo. In *South Asian Archaeology 1995* Vol. 1, edited by R. Allchin and B. Allchin, pp. 63–76. Science Publishers, New Delhi.

Barua, B., and B. N. Chaudhuri (editors)
1990 *Inscriptions of Asoka*. Translated by B. Barua. Sanskrit College, Calcutta.

Basu, R. N.
1978 A Critical Study of the *Milindapañha*: *A Critique of Buddhist Philosophy*. Firma KLM, Calcutta.

Baumgarten, A. I. (editor)
2002 *Sacrifice in Religious Experience*. E. J. Brill, Leiden.

Bentley, J.
1808 *Remarkes on the Principal Eras and Dates of the Ancient Hindus*. Asiatic Research 5.

Benveniste, E.
1966 Civilisation: Contribution a l'histoire du mot. Gallimard, Paris. In *Eventail de 1'Histoire Vivante, Hommage à Lucien Febvre Offert à l'Occasion de son 75e Anniversaire* Vol. I, pp. 47–54. A. Colin, Paris, 1953.

1971 *Problems in General Linguistics*. Translated by M. E. Meek. Miami Linguistics Series No. 8. University of Miami Press, Coral Cables, Florida.

Berlin, I., Sir
1953 *The Hedgehog and the Fox: An Essay on Tolstoy's View of History*. Weidenfeld & Nicolson, London.

1954 *Historical Inevitability*. Oxford University Press, London.

Berremann, G. D.
1960 Caste in India and the U.S. *American Journal of Sociology* 66:120–127.

1962 Caste and economy in the Himalayas. *Economic Development and Cultural Change* 8:386–394.

1966 Caste in cross-cultural perspective. In *Japan's Invisible Race: Caste in Culture and Personality*, edited by G. DeVos and H. Wagatsuma, pp. 275–324. University of California Press, Berkeley.

1973 *Caste in the Modern World*. General Learning Press, Morristown, New Jersey.

1979a *Caste and Other Inequities: Essays on Inequality*. Manohar, Delhi.

1979b The evolutionary status of caste in peasant India. In *Caste and Other Inequities: Essays on Inequality*, edited by G. D. Berremann, pp. 313–325. Manohar, Delhi.

1981 Social inequality: A cross-cultural analysis. In *Social Inequality: Comparative and Developmental Approaches*, edited by G. D. Berremann, pp. 3–40. Academic Press, New York.

Bhan, K. K., M. Vidale, and J. M. Kenoyer
1994 Harappan technology: Theoretical and methodological issues. *Man and Environment* 19(1–2):141–157.

Binford, L. R.
1983 *In Pursuit of the Past*. Thames and Hudson, New York.

Bisht, R. S.
1976 *Banawali*. Public Relations Department, Government of Haryana, Chandigarh.

1977 *Banawali: A Look Back Into the Pre-Indus and Indus Civilization*. Special Board of Archaeology, Government of Haryana, Chandigarh.

1978 Banawali: A new Harappan site in Haryana. *Man and Environment* 2:86–88.

1982 Excavations in Banawali: 1974–1977. In *Harappan Civilization: A Contemporary Perspective*, edited by G. L. Possehl, pp. 113–124. Oxford and IBH Publishing, New Delhi.

1984 Structural remains and town-planning of Banawali. In *Frontiers of the Indus Civilization*, edited by B. B. Lal and S. P. Gupta, pp. 89–97. Books and Books, Delhi.

1987 Further excavations at Banawali: 1983–1984. In *Archaeology and History: Essays in Memory of Shri A. Ghosh* Vol. 1, edited by B. M. Pande and B. D. Chattopadhyaya, pp. 135–156. Agam Kala Prakashan, Delhi.

1989a The Harappan colonization of Kutch: An ergonomic study with reference to Dholavira and Surkotada. In *History and Art*, edited by K. Deva and L. Gopal, pp. 265–272. Ramanand Vidya Bhavan, Delhi.

1989b A new model of the Harappan town planning as revealed at Dholavira in Kutch: A surface study of its plan and architecture. In *History and Archaeology: Prof. H. D. Sankalia Felicitation Volume*, edited by B. Chatterjee, pp. 397–408. Ramanand Vidya Bhawan, Delhi.

1991 Dholavira: A new horizon of the Indus civilization. *Puratattva* 20:71–82.

1997 Excavations at Banawali: 1974–1977. In *Indian Prehistory: 1980*, edited by V. D. Misra and J. N. Pal. Department of Ancient History, Culture and Archaeology, University of Allahabad, Allahabad.

1998–1999 Dholavira and Banawali: Two different paradigms of the Harappan Urbis Forma. *Puratattva* 29:14–42.

1999 Harappans and the Rigveda: Points of convergence. In *The Dawn of Indian Civilization (up to 600 B.C.)* Vol. 1, Part 1, edited by G. C. Pande, pp. 393–442. History of Science, Philosophy and Culture in Indian Civilization. Centre for Studies in Civilizations, New Delhi.

Bisht, R. S., and S. Asthana
1979 Banawali and some other recently excavated Harappan sites in India. In *South Asian Archaeology 1977* Vol. 1, edited by M. Taddei, pp. 223–240. Instituto Universitario Orientale, Naples.

Blackman, M. J., and M. Vidale
1992 The production and distribution of stoneware bangles at Mohenjo-Daro and Harappa as monitored by chemical characterization studies. In *South Asian Archaeology 1989*, edited by C. Jarrige, pp. 37–44. Monographs in World Archaeology, 14. Prehistory Press, Madison.

Bloch, T.
1904 Excavations at Basarh. *Annual Report of the Archaeological Survey of India* 1903–4:81–122.

1909 Excavation at Lauriya. *Annual Report of the Archaeological Survey of India* 1906–7:119–126.

Bonazzoli, G.
1979 The dynamic canon of the Purana-s. *Purana* 21(2):116–166.

1980 Puranic Parampara. *Purana* 22(1):33–60.

1981 Places of Puranic recitation according to the Puranas. *Purana* 23(1):48–61.

1982 Schemes in the Puranas: A first approach. *Purana* 24(1):146–189.

1983a Composition, transmission and recitation of the Purana-s. *Purana* 25(2):254–280.

1983b Remarks of the nature of the Purana-s. *Purana* 25(1):77–113.

1985 Considerations on a new method of critically editing the Puranas. *Purana* 27(2):381–434.

Bondioli, L., and A. Lazzari
1990 Some aspects of data treatment of the Shahr-i Sokhta, Ra's al-Junayz and Mohenjo-Daro records. In *South Asian Archaeology 1987* Vol. 1, edited by M. Taddei, pp. 377–390. Istituto Italiano per il Medio ed Estremo Oriente, Rome.

Bongard-Levin, G. M.
2000 *Dreveneindiiskaia Tsivilizatsiia: Istoriia, Religiia, Filosofiia, Epos, Literatura, Nauka, Vstrecha Kultur* 3 izd. Kultura Narodov Vostoka. Nauka, Moskva.

2001 *Indiiskii Etnogenezis: Sotsialno-kulturnaia Istoriia Drevnosti*. Rossiiskie Issledovaniia v Gumanitarnykh Naukakh tom 26. The Edwin Mellen Press, Lewiston.

Bongard-Levin, G. M., and G. F. Iliin
1985 *Indiia v Drevnosti*. Izdatelstvo Nauka, Glavnaia Redaktsiia Vostochnoi Literatury, Moskva.

2001 *Indiia v Drevnosti*. Aleteiia, Sankt Peterburg.

Bouquillon, A., B. Barthelemy de Saizieu, and A. Duval
1995 Glazed steatite beads from Mehrgarh and Nausharo. In *Materials Issues in Art and Archaeology* Vol. 4, pp. 527–538. Material Research Society, Pittsburgh, PA.

Braidwood, R. J.
1952 *The Near East and the Foundations for Civilization*. Condon Lectures. Oregon State System of Higher Education, Eugene.

1963 *Prehistoric Men*. Chicago Natural History Museum, Chicago.

Braudel, F.
1949 *La Méditerranée et le Monde Méditerranéen à l'Époque de Philippe II*. A. Colin, Paris.

1969 *Écrits sur l'Histoire*. Flammarion, Paris.

1972–1973 *The Mediterranean and the Mediterranean World in the Age of Philip II*. Translated by S. Reynolds. Collins, London.

1980 *On History*. Translated by S. Matthews. The University of Chicago Press, Chicago.

1987 *Grammaire des Civilisations*. Arthaud Flammarion, Paris.

1993 *A History of Civilizations*. Translated by R. Mayne. Penguin Books, New York.

Brockington, J. L.
1998 *Sanskrit Epics*. Brill, Leiden

Brockington, M. (editor)
2002 Stages and Transitions: Temporal and Historical Frameworks in Epic and Purāṇic Literature. *Proceedings of the Second Dubrovnik International Conference on the Sanskrit Epics and Purāṇas*. Croatian Academy of Sciences and Arts, Zagreb.

Brockington, M., and P. Schreiner (editors)
1999 Composing a Tradition: Concepts, Techniques and Relationships. *Proceedings of the First Dubrovnik International Conference on the Sanskrit Epics and Purāṇas*. Croatian Academy of Sciences and Arts, Zagreb.

Brown, W. N.
1938 The excavations at Chanhu-Daro. *American Journal of Archaeology* 42:127.

1966 *Man in the Universe: Some Continuities in Indian Thought*. University of California Press, Berkeley.

Bryant, E. F., and L. L. Patton (editors)
2005 *The Indo-Aryan Controversy: Evidence and Inference in Indian History*. Routledge, London.

Buitenen, J. A. B., van
1973 *The Mahabharata*. Translated by J. A. B. van Buitenen. University of Chicago Press, Chicago.

Burkert, W.
1972 *Homo Necans: Interpretationen altgriechischer Opferriten und Mythen*. Religionsgeschichtliche Versuche und Vorarbeiten, Bd. 32. De Gruyter, Berlin.

Caland, W., and V. Henry
1906–1907 *L'Agnistoma: Description Complète de la Forme Normale du Sacrifice de Soma dans le Culte Védique*. E. Leroux, Paris.

Caldwell, B.
1991 *The Jajmani System: An Investigation*. Studies in Sociology and Social Anthropology. Hindustan Publishing Corporation, Delhi.

Cardona, G.
1991 A path still taken: Some early Indian arguments concerning time. *Journal of the American Oriental Society* 111(3):445–464.

Carrasco, D.
1990 *Religions of Mesoamerica: Cosmovision and Ceremonial Centers*. Harper and Row, San Francisco.

Cassirer, E.
1946 *The Myth of the State*. Yale University Press, New Haven.

Cauvin, J.
1972 *Religions Néolithiques de Syro-Palestine*. Documents. Publications du Centre de Recherches d'Écologie et de Préhistoire No. 1. J. Maisonneuve, Paris.

1994 *Naissance des Divinités, Naissance de l'Agriculture: La Révolution des Symboles au Néolithique*. Empreintes CNRS, Paris.

Cavagnaro Vanoni, L., and M. Cucarzi (editors)
1990 *Prospezioni Archeologiche Quaderni*. Edizioni ET, Milano.

Chakrabarti, D. K.
1970 Early Urban Centres in India: An Archaeological Perspective, c. 2500 BC–300 AD. Ph.D. Dissertation, University of Calcutta.

1972–1973 Concept of urban revolution and the Indian context. *Puratattva* 6:27–32.

1974 Some theoretical aspects of early Indian urban growth. *Puratattva* 7:87–89.

1985a Iron and urbanization: An examination of the Indian context. *Puratattva* 15:68–74.

1985b Study of the Iron Age in India. In *Archaeological Perspective of India since Independence*, edited by K. N. Dikshit, pp. 81–85. Books and Books, Delhi.

1988a *A History of Indian Archaeology from the Beginning to 1947*. Munshiram Manoharlal Publishers, New Delhi.

1988b The problems of urbanisation and rural-urban differentiation in Indian archaeology. In *Rural Life and Folk Culture in Ancient India: Proceedings of the Seminar Held at Allahabad in 1985*, edited by U. N. Roy, V. D. Misra and J. N. Pandey, pp. 1–11. University of Allahabad, Allahabad.

1988c *Theoretical Issues in Indian Archaeology*. Munshiram Manoharlal Publishers, New Delhi.

1995 *The Archaeology of Ancient Indian Cities*. Oxford University Press, Delhi, New York.

1997 *Colonial Indology: Sociopolitics of the Ancient Indian Past*. Munshiram Manoharlal Publishers, New Delhi.

1999 *India, An Archaeological History: Palaeolithic Beginnings to Early Historic Foundations*. Oxford University Press, New Delhi, New York.

2000 Mahajanapada states of Early Historic India. In *A Comparative Study of Thirty City-State Cultures: An Investigation*, edited by M. H. Hansen, pp. 375–392. Kongelige Danske Videnskabernes Selskab, Copenhagen.

2001 *Archaeological Geography of the Ganga Plain: The Lower and the Middle Ganga*. Permanent Black, New Delhi.

2003 *Archaeology in the Third World: A History of Indian Archaeology Since 1947*. Updating Indian archaeology, No. 3. D. K. Printworld, New Delhi.

Chang, K.-C.
1983 *Art, Myth, and Ritual: The Path to Political Authority in Ancient China*. Harvard University Press, Cambridge, MA.

1989 Ancient China and its anthropological significance. In *Archaeological Thought in America*, edited by C. C. Lamberg-Karlovsky, pp. 155–166. Cambridge University Press, Cambridge.

Chattopadhyaya, B. D.
1989 Mathura from the Sunga to the Kusana period: An historical outline. In *Mathura: The Cultural Heritage*, edited by D. M. Srinivisan, pp. 19–28. American Institute of Indian Studies, New Delhi.

2003 *Studying Early India: Archaeology, Texts, and Historical Issues*. Permanent Black, New Delhi.

Chemburkar, J.
1974 Historical and religious background of the concept of four Yugas in the Mahabharata and the Bhagavata Purana. *Purana* 16(1):67–76.

Childe, V. G.
1934 *New Light on the Most Ancient East: The Oriental Prelude to European Civilization*. Kegan Paul, Trench, Trubner & Co., London.

1939 *The Dawn of European Civilization*. Kegan Paul, Trench, Trubner and Co., London.

1947 *History*. Cobbet Press, London.

1950 The urban revolution. *Town Planning Review* 21(1):3–17.

1951 *Man Makes Himself*. New American Library, New York.

1953 *What is History?* Henry Schuman, New York.

Christaller, W.
1933 *Die zentralen Orte in Süddeutschland: Eine ökonomisch-geographische Untersuchung über die Gesetzmäßigkeit der Verbreitung und Entwicklung der Siedlungen mit städtischen Funktionen*. Gustav Fisher Verlag, Jena.

1966 *Central Places in Southern Germany*. Translated by C. W. Baskin. Prentice-Hall, Inc., Englewood Cliffs, NJ.

Church, C. D.
1970 The Yuga Story: A Myth of the Four Ages of the World as Found in the Puranas. Ph.D. Dissertation. University of Syracuse. Syracuse.

1971 The Puranic myth of the four Yugas. *Purana* 13(2):151–159.

1974 The myth of the four Yugas in the Sanskrit Puranas: A Dimensional Study. *Purana* 16(1):5–25.

Coe, M. D.
1961 Social typology and the tropical forest civilizations. *Comparative Studies in Society and History* 4(1):65–85.

Cohn, B. S.
1980 History and anthropology: The state of play. *Comparative Studies in Society and History* 22(2):199–221.

Collingwood, R. G.
1942 *The New Leviathan; or, Man, Society, Civilization and Barbarism*. The Clarendon Press, Oxford.

1946 *The Idea of History*. Clarendon Press, Oxford.

Corominas, J.
1961 *Breve Diccionario Etimológico de la Lengua Castellana*. Editorial Gredos, Madrid.

Costantini, L.
1990 Harappan agriculture in Pakistan: The evidence of Nausharo. In *South Asian Archaeology 1987* Vol. 1, edited by M. Taddei, pp. 321–332. Istituto Italiano per il Medio ed Estremo Oriente, Rome.

Covarrubias Horozco, S., De
1611 *Tesoro de la Lengua Castellana o Española*, Madrid.

Croce, B.
1917 *Teoria e Storia della Storiografia*. Laterza, Bari.

1919 La Storia Ridotta Sotto il Concetto Generale dell' Arte. In *Primi Saggi*. Laterza, Bari.

1921 *Theory and History of Historiography*. Translated by D. Ainslie. George G. Harrap & Co. Ltd., London.

1954 *La Storia Come Pensiero e Come Azione*. Laterza, Bari.

Cunningham, A.
1871 *The Ancient Geography of India*. Trubner and Co., London.

Dales, G. F.
1962a Harappan Outposts on the Makran Coast. *Antiquity* 36:86–92.

1962b A search for ancient seaports. *Expedition* 4(2):2–10.

1964 The University of Pennsylvania expedition to Makran. *Pakistan Archaeology* 1:36–37.

1965a New investigations at Mohenjo-Daro. *Archaeology* 18:145–150.

1965b Re-opening the Mohenjo-Daro excavations. *Illustrated London News* May 29:25–27.

1982 Mohenjodaro miscellany: Some unpublished, forgotten, or misinterpreted features. In *Harappan Civilization: A Contemporary Perspective*, edited by G. L. Possehl, pp. 107–112. Oxford and IBH Publishing, New Delhi.

1989 Harappa: A new look at the type site of the Indus civilization. In *Old Problems and New Perspectives in the Archaeology of South Asia*, edited by J. M. Kenoyer, pp. 127–131. F. and H. Printing, Madison.

1992a Excavations at Sutkagen Dor. In *Explorations on the Makran Coast, Pakistan: A Search for Paradise*, edited by G. F. Dales and C. P. Lipo, pp. 135–156. University of California, Berkeley.

1992b Recent Excavations at Harappa. *The Eastern Anthropologist* 45(1-2):21–38.

Dales, G. F., and J. M. Kenoyer
1986a *Excavations at Mohenjo-Daro, Pakistan: The Pottery*. University Museum Monograph 53. The University Museum, University of Pennsylvania, Philadelphia.

1986b *Preliminary Report on First Season at Harappa, 1986, University of California at Berkeley*. Manuscript Submitted to the Department of Archaeology and Museums, Government of Pakistan, Karachi.

1987 *Preliminary Report of the University of California at Berkeley's Second Season at Harappa, Pakistan*. Manuscript submitted to the Department of Archaeology and Museums, Government of Pakistan, Karachi.

1989 Excavation at Harappa—1988. *Pakistan Archaeology* 24:68–176.

1990a Excavations at Harappa—1989. *Pakistan Archaeology* 25:241–282.

1990b *Preliminary Report on the Fifth Season at Harappa, Pakistan, January 1–March 31, 1990*. Manuscript Submitted to the Department of Archaeology and Museums, Government of Pakistan, Karachi.

1991 Summaries of five seasons of research at Harappa (District Sahiwal, Punjab, Pakistan) 1986–1990. In *Harappa Excavations: A Multidisciplinary Approach to Third Millennium Urbanism*, edited by R. H. Meadow, pp. 185–262. Prehistory Press, Madison.

1992a Excavations at Harappa. *Pakistan Archaeology* 27:31–88.

1992b Harappa 1989: Summary of the fourth season. In *South Asian Archaeology* 1989, edited by C. Jarrige, pp. 57–68. Monographs in World Archaeology, 14. Prehistory Press, Rome.

Dales, G. F., and C. P. Lipo
1992 *Explorations on the Makran Coast, Pakistan: A Search for Paradise*. Contributions of the Archaeological Research Faculty, University of California 50. University of California, Berkeley.

Dampierre, E. de
1961 Note sur "culture" et "civilisation". *Comparative Studies in Society and History* 3(3):328–340.

Daniel, E. V.
1984 *Fluid Signs: Being a Person the Tamil Way*. University of California Press, Berkeley.

Demieville, P.
1924 Les versions Chinoises du *Milindapañha*. *Bulletin de l'Ecole Francaise d'Extreme Orient* 24:1–264.

Detienne, M.
1989 Culinary practices and the spirit of sacrifice. In *The Cuisine of Sacrifice among the Greeks*, edited by M. Detienne and J.-P. Vernant, translated by P. Wissing, pp. 1–20. University of Chicago Press, Chicago. (*Cuisine du Sacrifice en Pays Grec*, 1979, Gallimard, Paris).

Deva, K., and V. Mishra
1961 *Vaisali Excavations, 1950*. Vaisali Sangh, Vaisali.

Devi, S. M., B. Sahai, and C. R. P. Sinha (editors)
1980 *Pataliputra through the Ages*. Bihar Puravid Parishad, Patna.

Dhavalikar, M. K.
1970 A prehistoric deity of western India. *Man* 5(1):131–132.

1978 Proto-Pasupati in western India. *East and West* 28(1–4):203–211.

1982 Daimabad Bronzes. In *Harappan Civilization, A Contemporary Perspective*, edited by G. L. Possehl, pp. 361–366. Oxford and IBH Publishing, New Delhi.

1987 Sakambari, the headless goddess. *Annals of the Bhandarkar Oriental Research Institute* LXVIII:281–293.

1988 *The First Farmers of the Deccan*. Ravish Publishers, Pune.

2002 Early farming cultures of central India: A recent perspective. In *Indian Archaeology in Retrospect* Vol I. *Prehistory, Archaeology of South Asia*, edited by S. Settar and R. Korisettar, pp. 253–262. Indian Council of Historical Research, Manohar, New Delhi.

Diakonoff, I. M.
1994 *Puti Istorii: Ot Drevneiishego Cheloveka do Nashikh Dnei*. Vostochnaia Literatura, RAN, Moskva.

Dikshit, M. G.
1952 Beads from Ahichchhatra, UP. *Ancient India* 8:33–63.

Dollard, J.
1949 *Caste and Class in a Southern Town*. Harper, New York.

Donnelly, D. F. (editor)
1995a *The City of God: A Collection of Critical Essays*. Peter Lang, New York.

Donnelly, D. F.
1995b Reconsidering the Ideal: The City of God and Utopian Speculation. In *The City of God: A Collection of Critical Essays*, edited by D. F. Donnelly, pp. 199–211. Peter Lang, New York.

Doxiades, K. A.
1968 *Ekistics, an Introduction to the Science of Human Settlements*. Oxford University Press, New York.

Dumezil, G.
1958 *L'Idéologie Tripartie des Indo-Européens*. Latomus, Brussels.

Dumont, L.
1966 *Homo Hierarchicus: Essai sur le Système de Caste et ces Implications*. Editions Gallimard, Paris.

Dumont, P. E.
1879 *L'Agnihotra*. The John Hopkins Press, Baltimore.

1927 *L'Asvamedha, Decription du Sacrifice Solennel du Cheval dans le Culte Védique d'après le Textes du Yajurveda Blanc*. P. Geuthner, Paris.

1935 Primitivism in Indian literature. In *A Documentary History of Primitivism and Related Ideas*, edited by A. O. Lovejoy, pp. 433–443. The John Hopkins Press, Baltimore.

During Caspers, E. C. L.
1992 The "Calendar Stones" from Mohenjo-Daro reconsidered. In *South Asian Archaeology 1989*, edited by C. Jarrige, pp. 83–96. Monographs in World Archaeology, 14. Prehistory Press, Madison.

Dutt, B. B.
1925 *Town Planning in Ancient India*. Thacker, Spink and Co., Calcutta.

Ehrenreich, R. M., C. L. Crumley and J. E. Levy (editors)
1995 *Heterarchy and the Analysis of Complex Societies*. American Anthropological Association, Arlington, VA.

Eliade, M.
1949 *Le Mythe de l'Éternel Retour: Archétypes et Répétition*. Galimard, Paris

1957 Time and eternity in Indian thought. In *Man and Time*, edited by H. Corgin, et al., pp. 173–200. Papers from the Eranos Yearbooks 3, Bollingen Series 30:3. Pantheon, New York.

Elizarenkova, T. Y.
1999 *Slova i Veshchi v Rigvede*. Vostochnaia Literatura, RAN, Moskva.

Engels, F.
1884 *Ursprung der Familie, des Privateigentums und des Staats. Im Anschluß an Lewis Morgans Forschungen*. Schweizerische Genossenschafts-buchdruckerei, Hottingen-Zurich

Erdosy, G.
1984 Settlement Archaeology of the Kausambi Region. *Man and Environment* 9:66–84.

1985 The economic organisation of Early Historic states in the Ganges Valley. In *South Asian Archaeology 1983* Vol. 2, edited by J. Schotsmans and M. Taddei, pp. 509–522. Instituto Universitario Orientale, Naples.

1987 Early historic cities of northern India. *South Asian Studies* 3:1–23.

1988 *Urbanisation in Early Historic India*. BAR International Series 430. BAR, Oxford.

1989 Ethnicity in the Rigveda and its bearing on the question of Indo-European origins. *South Asian Studies* 5:35–47.

1994 The Meaning of Ṛgvedic 'Pur': Notes on the Vedic Landscape. In *From Sumer to Meluhha: Contributions to the Archaeology of South and West Asia in Memory of Georges F. Dales, Jr.*, edited by J. M. Kenoyer, pp. 223–234. Wisconsin Archaeological Reports 3, Madison.

1995a City states to north India and Pakistan at the time of the Buddha. In *The Archaeology of Early Historic South Asia: The Emergence of Cities and States*, edited by F. R. Allchin, pp. 99–122. Cambridge University Press, Cambridge.

1995b Language, material culture and ethnicity: Theoretical perspectives. In *The Indo-Aryans of Ancient South Asia*, edited by G. Erdosy, pp. 1–31. Walter de Gruyter, Berlin.

1995c The prelude to urbanization: Ethnicity and the rise of late Vedic chiefdoms. In *The Archaeology of Early Historic South Asia: The Emergence of Cities and States*, edited by F. R. Allchin, pp. 75–98. Cambridge University Press, Cambridge.

Evans-Pritchard, E. E.

1962 Anthropology and history. In *Social Anthropology and Other Essays*, edited by E. E. Evans-Pritchard, New York.

Fairservis, W. A., Jr.

1961 The Harappan civilization—New evidence and more theory. *American Museum Novitates* 2055:1–35.

1967 The origin, character and decline of an early civilization. *American Museum Novitates* 2302:1–48.

1973 Preliminary report on excavations at Allahdino (first season 1973). *Pakistan Archaeology* 9:95–102.

1975 *The Roots of Ancient India*, Second edition. The University of Chicago Press, Chicago.

1976 *Excavations at the Harappan Site of Allahdino: The Seals and Other Inscribed Material*. Papers of the Allahdino Expedition, No. 1. The Allahdino Expedition, New York.

1977 *The Graffiti: A Model in the Decipherment of the Harappan Script*. Papers of the Allahdino Expedition, No. 3. The Allahdino Expedition, New York.

1982 Allahdino: An excavation of a small Harappan site. In *Harappan Civilization: A Contemporary Perspective*, edited by G. L. Possehl, pp. 107–112. Oxford and IBH Publishing, New Delhi.

1984a Archaeology in Baluchistan and the Harappan problem. In *Frontiers of the Indus Civilization*, edited by B. B. Lal and S. P. Gupta, pp. 277–287. Books and Books, New Delhi.

1984b Harappan Civilization according to its writing. In *South Asian Archaeology* 1981, edited by B. Allchin, pp. 154–161. Cambridge University Press, Cambridge.

1992 *The Harappan Civilization and Its Writing*. Oxford and IBH Publishing, New Delhi.

Febvre, L. P. V

1930 Civilisation, evolution d'un mot et d'une idée. In *Première Semaine Internationale de Synthèse. Deuxième Fascicule. Civilisation, le Mot et l'Idée*. La Renaissance du Livre, Paris.

Filippi, G. G., and B. Marcolongo (editors)
1999 *Kampilya, Quest for a Mahabharata City*. Venetian Academy of Indian Studies, Venice.

Flannery, K. V.
1972 The cultural evolution of civilizations. *Annual Review of Ecology and Systematics* 3:399–426.

Fleet, J. F.
1911 The Kaliyuga Era of B.C. 3102. *Journal of the Royal Asiatic Society of Great Britain and Ireland*, 479–496.

Franke-Vogt, U.
1993 Stratigraphy and cultural process at Mohenjo-Daro. In *South Asian Archaeology 1991*, edited by A. J. Gail and G. J. R. Mevissen, pp. 87–100. Franz Steiner Verlag, Stuttgart.

1994 The "Early Period" at Mohenjo-Daro. In *From Sumer to Meluhha: Contributions to the Archaeology of South and West Asia in Memory of Georges F. Dales, Jr.*, edited by J. M. Kenoyer, pp. 27–50. Wisconsin Archaeological Reports 3, Wisconsin.

Fuller, C. J.
1984 *Servants of the Goddess: The Priests of a South Indian Temple*. Cambridge University Press, Cambridge.

1989 Misconceiving the grain heap: A critique of the concept of the Indian Jajmani system. In *Money and Morality of Exchange*, edited by J. P. Parry and M. Bloch, pp. 33–63. Cambridge University Press, Cambridge.

Fuller, D. Q., and N. Boivin
2002 Beyond description and diffusion: A history of processual theory in the archaeology of South Asia. In *Indian Archaeology in Retrospect*, Vol. 4. *Archaeology and Historiography: History, Theory and Method*, edited by S. Settar and R. Korisettar, pp. 159–190. Indian Council of Historical Research, Manohar, New Delhi.

Fussman, G.
1993 L'Indo-Grec Menandre ou Paul Demieville revisite. *Journal Asiatique* 281:61–138.

Fustel de Coulanges, N. D.
1864 *La Cité Antique*. Hachete, Paris.

Gable, E. A.
1920 *Kali Yuga, Civilization or Barbarism, Which?* Boston.

Gaur, R. C.
1983 *The Excavations at Atranjikhera: Early Civilization of the Upper Ganga Basin*. Motilal Banarsidas, Delhi.

Geiger, W.
1916 *Pali Literatur und Sprache*. K. J. Trübner, Strassburg.

Gellner, E.
1971 Our current sense of history. *European Journal of Sociology* 12:159–179.

Ghosh, A.
1937 American excavations at Chanhu-Daro in Sind. *Science and Culture* 2:347–49.

1951 Rajgir—1950. *Ancient India* 7:66–78.

1958 *Rajgir*. Archaeological Survey of India, Delhi.

1972–1973 Comments on Chakrabarti's Article "Concept of Urban Revolution and the Indian Context". *Puratattva* 6:34–35.

1973 *The City in Early Historical India*. Indian Institute of Advanced Study, Simla.

1989 *An Encylopedia of Indian Archaeology*. Munshiram Manoharlal Publishers, New Delhi.

Ghosh, A., and K. C. Panigrahi
1946 The potteries of Ahichchhatra. *Ancient India* 1:37–59.

Ghosh, N. N.
1935 *Early History of Kausambi: From the Sixth Century B.C. to the Eleventh Century A.D.* Allahabad Archaeological Society, Allahabad.

Ghoshal, U. N.
1959 *A History of Indian Political Ideas: The Ancient Period and the Period of Transition to the Middle Ages*. Oxford University Press, Oxford.

Girard, R.
1972 *La Violence et le Sacré*. B. Grasset, Paris.

Goldman, R. P., and S. J. Sutherland
1985 *The Ramayaṇa of Valmiki: An Epic of Ancient India* Vol. I, *Balakanda*. Princeton University Press, Princeton, NJ.

Gonzalez Reimann, L.
2001 *The Mahabharata and the Yugas: India's Great Epic Poem and the Hindu System of World Ages*. Asian Thought and Culture Vol. 51. Peter Lang, New York.

Goody, J.
1977 *The Domestication of the Savage Mind*. Cambridge University Press, Cambridge.

1986 *The Logic of Writing and the Organization of Society*. Cambridge University Press, Cambridge.

1987 *The Interface between the Written and the Oral*. Cambridge University Press, Cambridge.

2000 *The Power of the Written Tradition*. Smithsonian Series in Ethnographic Inquiry. Smithsonian Institution Press, Washington.

Gordon, D. H.
1957 Review of the excavations at Hastinapura. *Antiquity* 31:108–109.

Gouin, P.
1990 Rapes, jarres et faisselles: La production et l'exportation des produits laitiers dans l'Indus du 3e Millénaire. *Paléorient* 16(2):37–54.

1992 Guillers Harappéennes: Technologie et interprétation. *Paléorient* 18(2):143–149.

Gould, H.
1964 A Jajmani system of North India: Its structure, magnitude, and meaning. *Ethnology* 3(1):12–41.

Gradmann, R.
1913 *Das ländliche Siedlungswesen des Königreichs Württemberg*. J. Engelhorns Nachf., Stuttgart.

Guenon, R.
1937 Some remarks on the doctrine of cosmic cycles. *Journal of the Indian Society of Oriental Art* 5:21–28.

Guizot, F.
1828 *Histoire Générale de la Civilisation en Europe depuis la Chute de l'Empire Romain jusqu'à la Révolution Française*. Pichon et Didier, Paris.

1829–1832 *Histoire de la Civilisation en France depuis la Chute de l'Empire Romain jusqu'à 1789*. Pichon et Didier, Paris.

Gupta, A. S.
1969 The Puranic theory of Yugas and Kalpas: A study. *Purana* 11(2):304–323.

Gupta, P. L.
1968 The coinage of local kings of northern India and the date of Kanishka. In *Papers on the Date of Kanishka*, edited by A. L. Basham, E. J. Brill, Leiden.

1989 Early coins of Mathura region. In *Mathura: The Cultural Heritage*, edited by D. M. Srinivisan, pp. 124–139. American Institute of Indian Studies, New Delhi.

Gupta, S. P.
1974 Two urbanizations in India: A side study in their social structure. *Puratattva* 7:53–60.

1980 *The Roots of Indian Art*. B. R. Publishing Corporation, Delhi.

1996 *The Indus-Saraswati Civilization*. Pratibha Prakashan, Delhi.

1999 The Indus-Saraswati civilization: Beginnings and developments. In *The Dawn of Indian Civilization (up to c. 600 B.C.)* Vol. 1, Part 1, edited by G. C. Pande, pp. 269–375. History of Science, Philosophy and Culture in Indian Civilization. Center for Studies in Civilizations, New Delhi.

Hamerton-Kelly, R. G. (editor)
1987 *Violent Origins: Ritual Killing and Cultural Formation*. Stanford University Press, Stanford, CA.

Harper, E. B.
1959 Two systems of economic exchange in village India. *American Anthropologist* 61:760–78.

Harris, M.
1979 *Cultural Materialism: The Struggle for a Science of Culture*. Random House, New York.

Härtel, H.
1989 Pottery of Mathura. In *Mathura: The Cultural Heritage*, edited by D. M. Srinivisan, pp. 181–192. American Institute of Indian Studies, New Delhi.

1993 *Excavations at Sonkh: 2,500 Years of a Town in Mathura District*. Monographien zur indischen Archäologie, Kunst und Philologie, Bd. 9. D. Reimer, Berlin.

Havelock, E.
1963 *Preface to Plato*. Harvard University Press, Cambridge, Mass.

1976 *Origins of Western Literacy*. Ontario Institute for Studies in Education, Toronto.

Hazra, R. C.
1940 *Studies in the Puranic Records on Hindu Rites and Customs*. Dacca University Bulletin, No. 20. The University, Dacca.

Heesterman, J. C.
1993 *The Broken World of Sacrifice: An Essay in Ancient Indian Ritual*. University of Chicago Press, Chicago.

Hillebrandt, A.
1879 *Das altindische Neu- und Vollmondsopfer in seiner einfachsten Form*. G. Fischer, Jena.

1897 *Ritual-Litteratur, vedische Opfer und Zauber*. K. J. Trubner, Strassburg.

1923 *Altindische Politik: Eine Übersicht auf Grund der Quellen*. Fischer, Jena.

Hinuber, O. von
1996 *A Handbook of Pali Literature*. Indian Philology and South Asian Studies Vol. 2. Walter de Gruyter, Berlin.

Hoey, W.
1892 Set Mahet. *Journal of the Royal Asiatic Society of Bengal* LVI:1–64.

Hoffman, M. A.
1974a *An Analysis of the Chipped and Groundstone Artifacts from Allahdino and Related Surface Sites—1973 Season. Report.* University of Virginia.

1974b *A Preliminary Report on the Occupational Features at Allahdino—1973 Season. Report.* University of Virginia.

Hoffman, M. A., and J. H. Cleland
1977 *Excavations at the Harappan Site of Allahdino. The Lithic Industry of Allahdino: A Metric and Quantitative Analysis of a Harappan Activity System*. Papers of the Allahdino Expedition, No. 2. New York.

Hoffman, M. A., and J. G. Shaffer
1975 The Harappan settlement at Allahdino: Analyzing the sociology of an archaeological site. In *Ecological Backgrounds of South Asian Prehistory*, edited by K. A. R. Kennedy and G. L. Possehl, pp. 94–117. South Asia Program Cornell University, Ithaca, N.Y.

Hubert, H., and M. Mauss
1899 Essai sur la nature et la fonction du sacrifice. *L'Anée Sociologique* II:29–138

Hultzsch, E.
1925 *Inscriptions of Asoka*. Clarendon Press, Oxford.

Inden, R.
1990 *Imagining India*. Basil Blackwell, Oxford.

Isaac, E.
1962 On the domestication of cattle. *Science* (137):195–204.

1963a Myth, cults and livestock breeding. *Diogenes* 41:70–93.

1963b Religious factors in the geography of animal husbandry. *Diogenes* 44:59–80.

1970 *Geography of Domestication*. Prentice-Hall, Englewood Cliffs, N.J.

Jackson, V. H.
1914 Notes on Old Rajagrha. *Annual Report of the Archaeological Survey of India* 1913–1914:265–271.

Jacobi, H.
1908 Ages of the world (Indian). In *Encyclopaedia of Religion and Ethics* Vol. 1, edited by J. Hastings, pp. 200–202. T. & T. Clark, Edinburgh.

Jacobson, J.
1986 The Harappan civilization: An early state. In *Studies in the Archaeology of India and Pakistan*, edited by J. Jacobson, pp. 137–174. Oxford and IBH, New Delhi.

Jansen, M.
1979 Architektur in der Harappakultur: e. krit. *Betrachtung zum umbauten Raum im Industal* d. 3.-2. Jahrtsd. Veröffentlichungen des Seminars für orientalische Kunstgeschichte an der Universität Bonn: Reihe B, Antiquitates Orientales, Bd. 2. Habelt, Bonn.

1983 Preliminary results of three years' documentation in Mohenjo-Daro. In *Forschungsprojekt DFG Mohenjo-Daro: Dokumentation in der Archäologie: Techniken, Methoden, Analysen*, edited by G. Urban and M. Jansen, pp. 21–36. Veröffentlichungen des Geodätischen Instituts der Rheinish-Westfälischen Technischen Hochschule Aachen, Nr. 34. [s.n.], Aachen.

1984a Architectural remains in Mohenjo-Daro. In *Frontiers of the Indus Civilization*, edited by B. B. Lal and S. P. Gupta, pp. 75–88. Books and Books, Delhi.

1984b *The Architecture of Mohenjo-Daro*. Books and Books, New Delhi.

1984c Theoretical aspects of structural analysis for Mohejo-Daro. In *Interim Report: Reports on Field Work Carried out at Mohenjo-Daro, Pakistan, 1982–1983 by the IsMEO-Aachen-University Mission* Vol. 1, edited by M. Jansen and G. Urban, pp. 39–62. RWTH, Aachen.

1985 Mohenjo-Daro HR-A, House I, a temple? Analysis of an architectural structure. In *South Asian Archaeology 1983*, edited by J. Schotsmans and M. Taddei, pp. 157–206. Instituto Universitario Orientale, Naples.

1987 Preliminary results on the "Forma Urbis": Research at Mohenjo-Daro. In *Interim Reports: Reports on Field Work Carried Out at Mohenjo-Daro* Vol. 2, edited by M. Jansen and G. Urban, pp. 9–22. German Research Project Mohenjo-Daro, Aachen.

1989 Some problems regarding the *forma urbis* Mohenjo-Daro. In *South Asian Archaeology 1985*, edited by K. Frifelt and P. Sorensen, pp. 247–254. Curzon Press, London.

1991 Mohenjo-Daro, A City on the Indus. In *Forgotten Cities on the Indus: Early Civilization in Pakistan from the 8th to the 2nd Millennium BC*, edited by M. Jansen, M. Mulloy and G. Urban, pp. 145–165. Verlag Philipp von Labern, Mainz.

1993a *Mohenjo-Daro, Stadt der Brunnen und Kanäle: Wasserluxus vor 4500 Jahren. (Mohenjo-Daro, City of Wells and Drains: Water Splendour 4500 Years Ago.)* Frontinus Society Publications. Supplementary Vol. 2. Frontinus-Gesellschaft, Bergisch Gladbach.

1993b Pre-, proto-, early-, mature-, urban-, late-, post-Harappan: Linearity, multi-linearity: "Babylonian language confusion" or ideological dispute? In *South Asian Archaeology 1991*, edited by A. J. Gail and G. J. R. Mevissen, pp. 135–148. Franz Steiner Verlag, Stuttgart.

1994 Mohenjo-daro, type site of the earliest urbanization process in South Asia: Ten years of research at Mohenjo-Daro, Pakistan, and an attempt at a synopsis. In *South Asian Archaeology 1993* Vol. 1, edited by A. Parpola and P. Koskikallio, pp. 263–280. Suomalainen Tiedeakatemia, Helsinki.

Jansen, M., J. H. Marshall, and E. J. H. Mackay
1997 *Mohenjo-Daro Complete Sind Volumes.* RWTH, Aachen.

Jansen, M., M. Tosi, and G. Leonardi (editors)
1988 *Interim Report: Reports on Field Work Carried Out at Mohenjo-Daro, Pakistan, 1983–1986 by the IsMEO-Aachen-University Mission* Vol 3. RWTH, IsMEO, Aachen, Roma.

Jansen, M., and G. Urban (editors)
1984 *Interim Report: Reports on Field Work Carried out at Mohenjo-Daro, Pakistan, 1982–1983 by the IsMEO-Aachen-University Mission* Vol 1. RWTH, Aachen.

1985 *Mohenjo Daro: Report of the Aachen University Mission, 1979–1985.* E. J. Brill, Leiden.

1987 *Interim Report: Reports on Field Work Carried out at Mohenjo-Daro, Pakistan, 1983–1984 by the IsMEO-Aachen-University Mission* Vol. 2. German Research Project Mohenjo-Daro, Aachen.

Jarrige, C.
1994 The Mature Indus phase at Nausharo as seen from a block of Period III. In *South Asian Archaeology 1993* Vol. 1, edited by A. Parpola and P. Koskikallio, pp. 281–294. Suomalainen Tiedeakatemia, Helsinki.

1997 The figurines from Nausharo Period I and their further developments. In *South Asian Archaeology 1995* Vol. 1, edited by R. Allchin and B. Allchin, pp. 33–44. Science Publishers, New Delhi.

2000 The Mature Indus phase at Nausharo: Elements of urban infrastructure. In *South Asian Archaeology 1997* Vol. 1, edited by M. Taddei and G. D. Marco, pp. 237–258. Istituto Italiano per l'Africa e l'Oriente, Rome.

Jarrige, J.-F.

1974–1986 Excavations at Mehrgarh-Nausharo. *Pakistan Archaeology* 10-22:63–134.

1987 Mission Française au Pakistan. *Histoire et Archeologie* 122:84–85.

1987–1988 Excavation at Nausharo. *Pakistan Archaeology* 23:149–203.

1989 Excavation at Nausharo, 1987–1988. *Pakistan Archaeology* 24:21–67.

1990 Excavations at Nausharo, 1988–1989. *Pakistan Archaeology* 25:163–192.

1993 The question of the beginning of the mature Harappan civilization as seen from Nausharo excavations. In *South Asian Archaeology 1991*, edited by A. J. Gail and G. J. R. Mevissen, pp. 149–164. Franz Steiner Verlag, Stuttgart.

1994 The final phase of the Indus occupation at Nausharo and its connection with the following cultural complex of Mehrgarh VIII. In *South Asian Archaeology 1993* Vol. 1, edited by A. Parpola and P. Koskikallio, pp. 295–314. Suomalainen Tiedeakatemia, Helsinki.

1995–1996 *Excavations at Mehrgarh-Nausharo. Report*. Mission Archeologique Française au Pakistan.

1996 Les fouilles de Nausharo au Balochistan Pakistanais et leur contributions à l'etude de la civilisations de l'Indus. *Académie des Inscriptions et Belles Lettres: Comptes Rendue de Séances de l'Année 1996* III:821–877.

1997 From Nausharo to Pirak: Continuity and change in the Kachi/Bolan region from the Third to the Second Millennium B.C. In *South Asian Archaeology 1995* Vol. 1, edited by R. Allchin and B. Allchin, pp. 11–32. Science Publishers, New Delhi.

Jarrige, J.-F., and R. H. Meadow

1992 Mélanges Fairservis: A discourse on relations between Kachi and Sindh in prehistory. In *South Asian Archaeology Studies*, edited by G. L. Possehl, pp. 163–178. Oxford and IBH Publishing, New Delhi.

Jcnes, S.

1981 Institutionalized inequalities in Nuristan. In *Social Inequality: Comparative and Developmental Approaches*, edited by G. D. Berremann. Academic Press, New York.

Jcshi, J. P.

1972 Exploration in Kutch and excavation at Surkotada and new light on Harappan Migration. *Journal of the Oriental Institute* 22:98–144.

1974 Surkotada: A chronological assessment. *Puratattva* 7:34–38.

1990 *Excavation at Surkotada 1971–1972 and Exploration in Kutch*. Memoirs of the Archaeological Survey of India, 87. Archaeological Survey of India, Delhi.

1999 Religious and burial practices of Harappans: Indian evidence. In *The Dawn of Indian Civilization (up to c. 600 B.C.)* Vol. 1, Part 1, edited by G. C. Pande, pp. 377–391. History of Science, Philosophy and Culture in Indian Civilization. Center for Studies in Civilizations, New Delhi.

2003a Stratigraphy. In *Excavations at Kalibangan: The Early Harappans (1960–1969)*, edited by B. B. Lal, J. P. Joshi, B. K. Thapar and M. Bala, pp. 33–50. Memoirs of the Archaeological Survey of India, No. 98. Archaeological Survey of India, New Delhi.

2003b Structures. In *Excavations at Kalibangan: The Early Harappans (1960–1969)*, edited by B. B. Lal, J. P. Joshi, B. K. Thapar and M. Bala, pp. 51–94. Memoirs of the Archaeological Survey of India, No. 98. Archaeological Survey of India, New Delhi.

Joshi, M. C.

1989 Mathura as an ancient settlement. In *Mathura: The Cultural Legacy*, edited by D. M. Srinivisan, pp. 165–170. American Institute of Indian Studies, New Delhi.

Kalianov, V. I.

1959 *Arthasastra ili Nauka Politiki*. Perevod V. I. Kalianova. Izdatelstvo Akademii Nauk SSSR, Moskva.

Kane, P. V.

1941–1953 *A History of Dharmasastra*. Bhandarkar Oriental Research Institute, Poona.

Kangle, R. P.

1960 *The Kautilya Arthasastra, Part I. A Critical Edition with Glossary*. Bombay University Press, Bombay

1963 *The Kautilya Arthasastra, Part II. An English Translation with Critical and Explanatory Notes*. Bombay University Press, Bombay.

1965 *The Kautilya Arthasastra, Part III*. Bombay University Press, Bombay.

Keenan, D. K.

2005 *The Question of Sacrifice. Studies in Continental Thought*. Indiana University Press, Bloomington.

Kenoyer, J. M.

1985 Shell working at Mohenjo-Daro, Pakistan. In *South Asian Archaeology 1983* Vol. 1, edited by J. Schotsmans and M. Taddei, pp. 297–344. Instituto Universitario Orientale, Naples.

1989a *Old Problems and New Perspectives in the Archaeology of South Asia*. F and H. Printing Company, Wisconsin.

1989b Socio-economic structure of the Indus civilization as reflected in specialized crafts and the question of ritual segregation. In *Old Problems and New Perspectives in the Archaeology of South Asia*, edited by J. M. Kenoyer, pp. 183–192. F. & H. Printing, Madison.

1991a The Indus Valley tradition of Pakistan and western India. *Journal of World Prehistory* 5(4):331–385.

1991b Urban process in the Indus tradition: A preliminary model for Harappa. In *Harappa Excavations 1986–1990: A Multidisciplinary Approach to Third Millennium Urbanism*, edited by R. H. Meadow, pp. 29–60. Prehistory Press, Madison.

1992 Harappan craft specialization and the question of urban segregation and stratification. *The Eastern Anthropologist* 45(1–2):39–54.

1993 Excavations on Mound E, Harappa: A systematic approach to the study of Indus urbanism. In *South Asian Archaeology 1991*, edited by A. J. Gail and G. J. R. Mevissen, pp. 165–194. Franz Steiner Verlag, Stuttgart.

1994a Experimental studies of Indus Valley technology at Harappa. In *South Asian Archaeology 1993* Vol. 1, edited by A. Parpola and P. Koskikallio, pp. 345–362. Suomalainen Tiedeakatemia, Helsinki.

1994b The Harappan state: Was it or wasn't it? In *From Sumer to Meluhha: Contributions to the Archaeology of South and West Asia in Memory of George F. Dales, Jr.*, edited by J. M. Kenoyer, pp. 71–80. Department of Anthropology, Madison.

1995 Interaction systems, specialized crafts and culture change: The Indus valley tradition and the Indo-Gangetic tradition in South Asia. In *The Indo-Aryans of Ancient South Asia: Language, Material Culture and Ethnicity*, edited by G. Erdosy, pp. 213–257. Walter de Gruyter, Berlin.

1997 Early city-states in South Asia: Comparing the Harappan phase and the Early Historic period. In *The Archaeology of City-States: Cross Cultural Approaches*, edited by D. L. Nichols and T. H. Charlton, pp. 51–70. Smithsonian Institution Press, Washington, D.C.

1998 *Ancient Cities of the Indus Valley Civilization*. Oxford University Press, Karachi.

Kenoyer, J. M., and R. H. Meadow

2000 The Ravi phase: A new cultural manifestation at Harappa (Pakistan). In *South Asian Archaeology 1997* Vol. 1, edited by M. Taddei and G. De Marco, pp. 55–76. Istituto Italiano per l'Africa e l'Oriente, Rome.

Khan, F. A.

1959 *Preliminary Report on Kot Diji Excavations, 1957–58*. Department of Archaeology, Government of Pakistan, Karachi.

1960 *Preliminary Report on Koti Diji Excavations, 1957–58*. Department of Archaeology, Government of Pakistan, Karachi.

1964 *Kot Diji*. Department of Archaeology, Government of Pakistan, Karachi.

1965 Excavations at Kot Diji. *Pakistan Archaeology* 2:11–84.

2002 *The Glory that was Kot Diji Culture of Pakistan: An Archaeology Outline*. Department of Archaeology, Faculty of Science, Shah Abdul Latif University, Khairpur.

Khare, R. S.

1984 *The Untouchable as Himself: Ideology, Identity and Pragmatism among the Lucknow Chamars*. Cambridge University Press, Cambridge.

Kirfel, W.

1927 *Das Purana Pancalaksana: Versuch einer Textgeschichte*. K. Schroeder Verlag, Bonn.

Kolenda, P. M.

1963 Towards a model of the Jajmani system. *Human Organization* 22(1):11–31.

1978 *Caste in Contemporary India: Beyond Organic Solidarity*. Benjamin-Cummings, London.

Kondo, R., A. Ichikawa, and T. Morioka

1997 Taking a bath in Mohenjo-Daro. In *South Asian Archaeology 1995* Vol. 1, edited by R. Allchin and B. Allchin, pp. 127–138. Science Publishers, New Delhi.

Korisettar, R., P. C. Venkatasubbaiah, and D. Q. Fuller
2002 Brahmagiri and beyond: The archaeology of the southern Neolithic. In *Indian Archaeology in Retrospect* Vol I, *Prehistory, Archaeology of South Asia*, edited by S. Settar and R. Korisettar, pp. 151–238. Indian Council of Historical Research, Manohar, New Delhi.

Koskikallio, P. (editor)
2005 Epics, Khilas, and Purāṇas: Continuities and ruptures. *Proceedings of the Third Dubrovnik International Conference on the Sanskrit Epics and Purāṇas*. Croatian Academy of Sciences and Arts, Zagreb

Kroeber, A. L.
1948 *Anthropology*. Harcout, Brace and Company, New York.

1953 The delimitation of civilizations. *Journal of the History of Ideas* 14:264–275.

1957 *Style and Civilization*. Cornell University Press, Ithaca.

Kroeber, A. L., and C. Kluckhohn
1952 *Culture: A Critical Review of Concepts and Definitions*. Papers of the Peabody Museum XLVII, No 1. Cambridge, MA.

Kubler, G. A.
1952 *The Indian Caste of Peru, 1795–1940: A Population Study Based upon Tax Record and Census Reports*. Smithsonian Institution, Washington.

Kumar, B.
1987 *Archaeology of Pataliputra and Nalanda*. The Heritage of Ancient India No. 10. Ramanand Vidya Bhawan, Delhi.

Kuraishi, M. H.
1956 *Rajhir* Fourth Edition. Manager of Publication, Delhi.

Kuzmina, E. E.
1995 *Otkuda Prishli Indo-Arii*. Nauka, Moskva.

Lal, B. B.
1954–1955 Excavation at Hastinapura and other explorations in the Upper Ganga and Sutlej basins 1950–1952. *Ancient India* 10-11:5–151.

1979 Kalibangan and the Indus civilization. In *Essays in Indian Protohistory*, edited by D. P. Agrawal and D. K. Chakrabarti, pp. 65–97. B. R. Publishing Company, Delhi.

1979–1980 Are the defences of Kausambi really as old as 1025 BC. *Puratattva* 11:88–95.

1981 The two Indian epics vis-a-vis archaeology. *Antiquity* 55:27–34.

1984 Some reflections on the structural remains at Kalibangan. In *Frontiers of the Indus Civilization*, edited by B. B. Lal and S. P. Gupta, pp. 55–62. Books and Books, New Delhi.

1985a Report on the chemical analysis and examination of metallic and other objects from Lothal. In *Lothal: A Harappan Port Town (1955–62)* Vol. 78, No. 2, edited by S. R. Rao, pp. 651–666. Archaeological Survey of India, New Delhi.

1985b The so-called syenachiti at Kausambi: A fallen brick mass. *Puratattva* 15:94–104.

1985c When did Udayana rule? In the 6th century B.C. or in the 16th century A.D.? An Assessment of the Dating of the Palace Complex at Kausambi. *Puratattva* 15:80–93.

1993 *Excavations at Sringaverapura (1977–1986)*, Vol. I. Memoirs of the Archaeological Survey of India, No. 88. Archaeological Survey of India, New Delhi.

1997 *The Earliest Civilization of South Asia: Rise, Maturity and Decline*. Aryan Books International, New Delhi.

1998a *India, 1947–1997: New Light on the Indus Civilization*. Aryan Books International, New Delhi.

1998b Rigvedic Aryans: The debate must go on. *East and West* 48(3-4):439–448.

2002a Historicity of the Mahabharat and the Ramayaṇa: What has archeology to say in the matter? In *Indian Archaeology in Retrospect*. Vol. 4. *Archaeology and Historiography: History, Theory and Method*, edited by S. Settar and R. Korisettar, pp. 29–70. Indian Council of Historical Research, Manohar, New Delhi.

2002b *Saravati Flows On: The Continuity of Indian Culture*. Aryan Books International, New Delhi.

2002c *Why Perpetuate Myths? A Fresh Look at Ancient Indian History*. National Council of Educational Research and Training, Delhi.

2003a The agricultural field. In *Excavations at Kalibangan: The Early Harappans (1960–1969)*, edited by B. B. Lal, J. P. Joshi, B. K. Thapar and M. Bala, pp. 95–98. Memoirs of the Archaeological Survey of India, No. 98. Archaeological Survey of India, New Delhi.

2003b Chronology of the early Harappan settlement. In *Excavations at Kalibangan: The Early Harappans (1960–1969)*, edited by B. B. Lal, J. P. Joshi, B. K. Thapar and M. Bala, pp. 25–26. Memoirs of the Archaeological Survey of India, No. 98. Archaeological Survey of India, New Delhi.

2003c The early Harappan culture-complex of Kalibangan in its wider setting. In *Excavations at Kalibangan: The Early Harappans (1960–1969)*, edited by B. B. Lal, J. P. Joshi, B. K. Thapar and M. Bala, pp. 27–32. Memoirs of the Archaeological Survey of India, No. 98. Archaeological Survey of India, New Delhi.

Lal, B. B., and K. N. Dikshit

1978–1979 Sringaverapura: A key-site for the protohistory and early history of the central Ganga Valley. *Puratattva* 10:1–7.

Lal, B. B., and B. K. Thapar

1967 Excavation at Kalibangan: New light on the Indus civilization. *Cultural Forum* IX(4):78–88.

Lal, B. B., J. P. Joshi, B. K. Thapar, and M. Bala

2003 *Excavations at Kalibangan: The Early Harappans (1960–1969)*. Memoirs of the Archaeological Survey of India, No. 98. Archaeological Survey of India, New Delhi.

Lal, M.

1984 *Settlement History and Rise of Civilization in Ganga-Yamuna Doab*. B. R. Publishing, Delhi.

1986 Chronology of the protohistoric and Early Historic cultures of the upper Ganga Plains. *East and West* 36(1–3):83–100.

Lamberg-Karlovsky, C. C.

1999 The Indus civilization: The case for caste formation. *Journal of East Asian Archaeology* 1(1–4):87–113.

Law, B. C.

1933 *A History of Pali Literature* Vols. 1–2. K. Paul, Trench, Trubner and Co., London.

1935 *Sravasti in Indian Literature*. Memoirs of the Archaeological Survey of India, No. 5. Archaeological Survey of India, Delhi.

1939 *Kausambi in Ancient Literature*. Manager of Publications, Delhi.

1942 *Pancalas and their Capital Ahichchhatra*. Memoirs of the Archaeological Survey of India, No. 67. Archaeological Survey of India, Delhi.

Leonardi, G.
1988 New problems of surface archaeology: Sampling in HR east area of Moenjodaro (Pakistan). In *Interim Report: Reports on Field Work Carried out at Mohenjo-Daro, Pakistan, 1983–1986 by the IsMEO-Aachen-University Mission* Vol. 3, edited by M. Jansen, M. Tosi and G. Leonardi, pp. 7–92. RWTH, IsMEO, Aachen, Roma.

Leshnik, L. S.
1968 The Harappan "port" at Lothal: Another view. *American Anthropologist* 70:911–922.

Levi-Strauss, C.
1974 *The Savage Mind*. Weidenfeld and Nicolson, London.

Levy, R. I.
1984 *Mesocosm: Hinduism and the Organization of a Traditional Newar City in Nepal*. University of California Press, Berkeley.

Lewis, B.
1975 *History—Remembered, Recovered, Invented*. Princeton University Press, Princeton.

Lukacs, J. R., and S. R. Walimber
1986–1988 *Excavations at Inamgaon*. Deccan College Post Graduate and Research Institute, Pune.

Mackay, E. J. H.
1931 Architecture and masonry. In *Mohenjo-Daro and the Indus Civilization* Vol. 1, edited by J. H. Marshall, pp. 262–286. Arthur Probsthain, London.

1935 *The Indus Civilization*. L. Dickson and Thompson, London.

1935–1936 Excavations at Chanhu-Daro. *Annual Report of the Archaeological Survey of India* 1935–36:38–44.

1936a Excavations at Chanhu-Daro by the American School of Indic and Iranian Studies and the Museum of Fine Arts, Boston: Season 1935–1936. *Bulletin of the Museum of Fine Arts* 34(205):83–92.

1936b Great new discoveries of ancient Indian culture on a virgin prehistoric site in Sind. *Illustrated London News* November 21:860–864; 908-911.

1937a Early Culture at Chanhu-Daro. *Discovery* 1937:286–289.

1937b Excavations at Chanhu-Daro by the American School of Indic and Iranian Studies and the Museum of Fine Arts, Boston, Season 1935–1936. In *Smithsonian Report for 1937*: 469–478.

1938 *Further Excavations at Mohenjo-Daro*. Government of India, Delhi.

1943 *Chanhu-Daro Excavations 1935–1936*. American Oriental Series, Vol. 20. American Oriental Society, New Haven.

1948 *Early Indus Civilization*, Second Edition. Revised by Dorothy Mackay. Luzac and Co., London.

Maisels, C. K.
1999 *Early Civilizations of the Old World: The Formative Histories of Egypt, the Levant, Mesopotamia, India and China*. Routledge, London.

Majumdar, N. G.
1934 *Explorations in Sind: Being a Report of the Exploratory Survey Carried Out During the Years 1927–28, 1929–30 and 1930–31.* Memoirs of the Archaeological Survey of India, 48. Archaeological Survey of India, Delhi.

Malik, S. C.
1968 *Indian Civilization, the Formative Period: A Study of Archaeology as Anthropology.* Indian Institute of Advanced Study, Simla.

1975 *Understanding Indian Civilization: A Framework of Enquiry. Studies in Indian and Asian Civilizations* 1. Indian Institute of Advanced Study, Simla.

1979 Changing perspectives in archaeology and interpreting Harappan society. In *Essays in Indian Prehistory*, edited by D. P. Agrawal and D. K. Chakrabarti, pp. 187–204. B. R. Publishing, Delhi.

Mandal, K. K.
1968 *A Comparative Study of the Concepts of Time and Space in Indian Thought.* Banaras.

Mankad, D. R.
1941–1942 The Yugas. Poona 6(3–4):206–216.

1942 The manvantara. *Indian Historical Quarterly* 18:208–230.

1942–1943 Manvantara-Caturyuga method (as employed in Puranas for chronological computations). *Annals of the Bhandarkar Oriental Research Institute* 23(1–4):271–290.

Margabandhu, C.
1989 Etched beads from Mathura excavations: A note. In *Mathura: The Cultural Heritage*, edited by D. M. Srinivisan, pp. 200–205. American Institute of Indian Studies, New Delhi.

Marriott, M. (editor)
1990 *India through Hindu Categories.* Sage Publications, Newbury Park, Calif.

Marriott, M., and R. Inden
1977 Toward and ethnosociology of South Asian caste system. In *The New Wind: Changing Identities in South Asia*, edited by K. David, pp. 423–438. Mouton, The Hague.

Marrou, H. I.
1938 Culture, civilization, decadence. *Revue de Synthese* XV:133–160.

Marshall, J. H., Sir
1905 Exploration at Lauriya Nandangarh. *Annual Report of the Archaeological Survey of India* 1904–5:38–40.

1909 Rajagrha and its remains. *Annual Report of the Archaeological Survey of India* 1905–6:86–106.

1913 Excavations at Taxila. *Annual Report of the Archaeological Survey of India* 1912–1913:1–52.

1914 Excavations at Saheth-Maheth. *Annual Report of the Archaeological Survey of India* 1910–11:1–24.

1915a Excavations at Bhita. *Annual Report of the Archaeological Survey of India* 1911–1912:29–94.

1915b Excavations at Taxila. *Annual Report of the Archaeological Survey of India* 1914–15:1–35.

1916 Excavations at Taxila. *Annual Report of the Archaeological Survey of India* 1915–16:1–38.

1925–1926 Exploration, Western Circle, Mohenjo-Daro. *Annual Report of the Archaeological Survey of India* 1925–26:72–98.

1927 Excavations at Taxila. *Annual Report of the Archaeological Survey of India* 1926–1927:110–119.

1928 Excavations at Taxila. *Annual Report of the Archaeological Survey of India* 1927–28:54–66.

1929 Excavations at Taxila. *Annual Report of the Archaeological Survey of India* 1928–29:51–67.

1930 Excavations at Taxila. *Annual Report of the Archaeological Survey of India* 1929–1930:55–97.

1931 *Mohenjo-Daro and the Indus Civilization.* Arthur Probsthain, London.

1934 Excavations at Taxila. *Annual Report of the Archaeological Survey of India* 1930–34:149–175.

Marshall, J. H., Sir, and S. Konow
1908 Excavations at Sarnath. *Annual Report of the Archaeological Survey of India* 1907–8:43–80.

1909 Excavations at Sarnath. *Annual Report of the Archaeological Survey of India* 1906–7:68–101.

Marshall, J. H., Sir, and J. P. Vogel
1903 Excavations at Charsadda. *Annual Report of the Archaeological Survey of India* 1902–3:141–184.

Mate, M. S.
1969–1970 Early historic fortifications in the Ganga valley. *Puratattva* 3:58–69.

Mauss, M.
1929 Civilisation, elements et formes. In *In Première Semaine Internationale de Synthèse. Deuxième Fascicule. Civilisation, le Mot et l'Idée*, pp. 81–108. La Renaissance du Livre, Paris.

McCrindle, J. W.
1877 *Ancient India as Described by Megasthenes and Arrian.* Trubner and Co., London.

McLuhan, M.
1962 *The Guttenberg Galaxy: The Making of Typograhic Man.* Toronto University Press, Toronto.

Meadow, R. H. (editor)
1991 *Harappa Excavations 1986–1990: A Multidisciplinary Approach to Third Millennium Urbanism.* Prehistory Press, Madison, Wisconsin.

Meadow, R. H., and J. M. Kenoyer
1993 *Harappa Archaeological Research Project: 1993 Excavations.* Report Submitted to the Director General, the Department of Archaeology and Museums, Government of Pakistan.

1994 Harappa excavations 1993: The city wall and inscribed materials. In *South Asian Archaeology 1993* Vol. 2, edited by A. Parpola and P. Koskikallio, pp. 451–470. Suomalainen Tiedeakatemia, Helsinki.

1997 Excavations at Harappa 1994–1995: New perspectives on the Indus script, craft activities, and city organization. In *South Asian Archaeology 1995* Vol. 1, edited by R. Allchin and B. Allchin, pp. 139–172. Science Publishers, New Delhi.

2000 The "tiny steatite seals" (incised steatite tablets) of Harappa: Some observations on their context and dating. In *South Asian Archaeology 1997*, edited by M. Taddei and G. De Marco. Istituto Italiano per l'Africa e l'Oriente, Rome.

2001a Excavations at Harappa 2000–2001: New insights on chronology and city organization. In *South Asian Archaeology 2001*, edited by C. Jarrige and V. Lefèvre. Editions Recherche sur les Civilisations, Paris.

2001b Harappa excavations 1998–1999: New evidence for the development and manifestation of the Harappan phenomenon. In *South Asian Archaeology 1999*, edited by E. M. Raven and G. L. Possehl. Groningen Indological Studies XV, Leiden.

Meadow, R. H., J. M. Kenoyer, and R. P. Wright

1994 *Harappa Archaeological Research Project: Harappa Excavations 1994*. Report Submitted to the Director General, the Department of Archaeology and Museums, Government of Pakistan.

1995 *Harappa Archaeological Research Project: Harappa Excavations 1995*. Report Submitted to the Director General, the Department of Archaeology and Museums, Government of Pakistan.

1996 *Harappa Archaeological Research Project: Harappa Excavations 1996*. Report Submitted to the Director General, the Department of Archaeology and Museums, Government of Pakistan.

1997 *Harappa Archaeological Research Project: Harappa Excavations 1997*. Report Submitted to the Director General, the Department of Archaeology and Museums, Government of Pakistan.

1998 *Harappa Archaeological Research Project: Harappa Excavations 1998*. Report Submitted to the Director General, the Department of Archaeology and Museums, Government of Pakistan.

1999 *Harappa Archaeological Research Project: Harappa Excavations 1999*. Report Submitted to the Director General, the Department of Archaeology and Museums, Government of Pakistan.

2001 *Harappa Archaeological Research Project. Harappa Excavations 2000 and 2001*. Report Submitted to the Director General, the Department of Archaeology and Museums, Government of Pakistan.

Mery, S.

1994 Excavation of an Indus potter's workshop at Nausharo (Baluchistan), Period II. In *South Asian Archaeology 1993* Vol. 2, edited by A. Parpola and P. Koskikallio, pp. 471–482. Suomalainen Tiedeakatemia, Helsinki.

Miller, D.

1985 Ideology and the Harappan civilization. *Journal of Anthropological Archaeology* 4:34–71.

Miller, H. M.-L.

1994 Metal Processing at Harappa and Mohenjo-Daro: Information from Non-Metal Remains. In *South Asian Archaeology 1993* Vol. 2, edited by A. Parpola and P. Koskikallio, pp. 497–510. Suomalainen Tiedeakatemia, Helsinki.

Mishra, Y., and S. R. Roy

1964 *A Guide to Vaisali and the Vaisali Museum*. Vaisali Sangha, Vaisali.

Misra, V. D.

1999 Agriculture, domestication of animals and other industries in prehistoric India. In *The Dawn of Indian Civilization (up to c. 600 B.C.)*, edited by G. C. Pande, pp. 233–266. History of Science, Philosophy and Culture in Indian Civilization. Center for Studies in Civilizations, New Delhi.

Mitchiner, J. E.
1976–1977 Saptarsi Yuga: Elucidation of a cyclical era. *Journal of Ancient Indian History* 10:52–95.

Mockler, E.
1877 On ruins of Makran. *Journal of the Royal Asiatic Society* 9:120–34.

Morgan, L. H.
1877 *Ancient Society, or Researches in the Lines of Human Progress from Savgery, through Barbarism to Civilization*. C. H. Kerr, Chicago.

Mughal, M. R.
1970 The Early Harappan Period in the Greater Indus Valley and Northern Baluchistan (c. 3000–2400). Ph.D. Dissertation. University of Pennsylvania, Philadelphia.

1990a The Harappan settlement systems and patterns in the greater Indus Valley. *Pakistan Archaeology* 25:1–72.

1990b The protohistoric settlement patterns in the Cholistan Desert. In *South Asian Archaeology 1987* Vol. 1, edited by M. Taddei, pp. 143–156. Istituto Italiano per il Medio ed Estremo Oriente, Rome.

Mukherji, P. C.
1898 *Report on the Excavations on the Ancient Site of Pataliputra (Patna-Bankipur)*. Calcutta.

Mumford, L.
1961 *The City in History: Its Origins, its Transformations, and its Prospects*. Secker & Warburg, London.

Narain, A. K.
1989 Ancient Mathura and the Numismatic material. In *Mathura: The Cultural Heritage*, edited by D. M. Srinivisan, pp. 115–123. American Institute of Indian Studies, New Delhi.

Narain, A. K., and P. K. Agrawala
1978 *Excavations at Rajghat 1957–1958; 1960–1965 Part IV [B: Plates]: Terracotta Human Figurines*. Banaras Hindu University, Varanasi.

Narain, A. K., and T. N. Roy
1976 *Excavations at Rajghat, 1957/58–1960/1965, Part I: The Cuttings, Stratification and Structures*. Banares Hindu University, Varanasi.

1977 *Excavations at Rajghat 1957–58; 1960–65. Part II: Pottery*. Banaras Hindu University, Varanasi.

Narain, A. K., and P. Singh
1977 *Excavation at Rajghat 1957–58; 1960–65. Part III: Small Finds*. Banaras Hindu University, Varanasi.

Narasimhan, R.
1991 Literacy: Its characterization and implications. In *Literacy and Orality*, edited by D. R. Olson and N. Torrance, pp. 177–197. Cambridge University Press, Cambridge.

Narayan, S.
1983 *Sacred Complexes of Deoghar and Rajgir*. Concept Publications, New Delhi.

Newberry, J.
1983a *Indus Seal-Script of Kalibangan*. John Newberry, Victoria, B.C.

1983b *Indus Seal Engraving at Chanhu-Daro*. J. Newberry, Victoria, B.C.

Nigam, J. S.
1995–96 Sothi pottery at Kalibangan: A reapprisal. *Puratattva* 26(7–22).

Nikam, N. A., and R. McKeon
1958 *The Edicts of Asoka*, edited and translated by N. A. Nikam and R. McKeon. Philosophy and World Community. The University of Chicago Press, Chicago.

O'Daly, G.
1999 *Augustine's City of God: A Reader's Guide*. Clarendon Press, Oxford.

Ogbu, J. U.
1981 Education, clientage, and social mobility: Caste and social change in the United States and Nigeria. In *Social Inequality: Comparative and Developmental Approaches*, edited by G. D. Berremann, pp. 277–306. Academic Press, New York.

Oliver, C. F.
1979 Some aspects of literacy in ancient India. *The Quarterly Newsletter of the Laboratory of Comparative Cognition* 1:57–62.

Olson, D. R.
1991 Literacy as metalinguistic activity. In *Literacy and Orality*, edited by D. R. Olson and N. Torrance, pp. 251–270. Cambridge University Press, Cambridge.

Ong, W. J.
2002 *Orality and Literacy: The Technologizing of the Word*. Routledge, London; New York.

Osborne, R.
1987 *Classical Landscape with Figures: The Ancient Greek City and its Countryside*. Sheridan House, London.

Page, J. A.
1927 Excavations at Bulandibagh. *Annual Report of the Archaeological Survey of India* 1926–27:135–140.

Pande, G. C. (editor)
1999 *The Dawn of Indian Civilization (up to c. 600)*. History of Science, Philosophy and Culture in Indian Civilization. Center for Study in Civilizations, New Delhi.

Pandya, S.
1977 Lothal dockyard hypothesis and sea-level changes. In *Ecology and Archaeology of Western India*, edited by D. P. Agrawal and B. M. Pande, pp. 99–104. Concept Pub., Delhi.

Panjwani, P. A.
1989 Petrography of Harappan pottery from Lothal. *Man and Environment* XIII:83–86.

Pargiter, F. E.
1910 Ancient Indian genealogies and chronology. *Journal of the Royal Asiatic Society of Great Britain and Ireland* 1910:1–56.

1912 Note on the age of the Puranas. *Journal of the Royal Asiatic Society of Great Britain and Ireland* 1912:254–255.

1913 *The Purana Text of the Dynasties of the Kali Age: With the Introduction and Notes*. Oxford University Press, London.

1914 Earliest Indian traditional history. *Journal of the Royal Asiatic Society of Great Britain and Ireland* 1914:267–296.

1922a *Ancient Indian Historical Tradition*. Oxford University Press, London.

1922b The four ages, chronology and date of the Bharata battle. In *Ancient Indian Historical Tradition*, edited by F. E. Pargiter, pp. 175–183. Oxford University Press, London.

Paribok, A. V.
1989 *Voprosy Milindy. Milindapankha*. Perevod s Pali, Predislovie, Issledovanie i Kommentarii A. V. Paribka. Nauka, Glavnaia Redaktsiia Vostochnoi Literatury, Moskva.

Parpola, A.
1992 The "Fig Deity Seal" from Mohenjo-Daro: Its iconography and inscription. In *South Asian Archaeology 1989*, edited by C. Jarrige, pp. 227–236. Monographs in World Archaeology, 14. Prehistory Press, Madison.

Patel, A.
1997 The pastoral economy of Dholavira: A First look at animals and urban life in third millennium Kutch. In *South Asian Archaeology 1995* Vol. 1, edited by R. Allchin and B. Allchin, pp. 101–114. Science Publishers, Delhi

Patil, D. R.
1963 *The Antiquarian Remains in Bihar*. Kashi Prasad Jayaswal Research Institute, Patna.

Piggott, S.
1943 Dating the Hissar sequence: The Indian evidence. *Antiquity* 17(68):169–182.

1945 *Some Ancient Cities of India*. Oxford University Press, Oxford.

1950 *Prehistoric India to 1000 B.C.* Pelican Books. Penguin Books, Harmondsworth, Middlesex.

Pike, K. L.
1954 *Language in Relation of a Unified Theory of the Structure of Human Behavior*. Summer Institute of Linguistics, Glendale, Calif.

Pitt-Rivers, J.
1971 On the word "caste". In *The Translation of Culture: Essays to E. E. Evans-Pritchard*, edited by T. O. Beidelman, pp. 231–256. Tavistock Publications, London.

Polignac, F. de
1984 *La Naissance de la Cité Grecque: Culte, Espace et Société VIIIe–VIIe Siècles avant J.-C.* Éditions la Découverte, Paris.

Possehl, G. L.
1975 Lothal: A gateway settlement of the Harappan civilization. In *Ecological Backgrounds of South Asian Prehistory*, edited by K. A. R. Kennedy and G. L. Possehl, pp. 118–131. South Asia Program Cornell University, Ithaca, N.Y.

1990 Revolution in the urban revolution: The emergence of Indus urbanism. *Annual Review of Anthropology* 19:261–282.

1991 A short history of archaeological discovery at Harappa. In *Harappa Excavations: A Multidisciplinary Approach to Third Millennium Urbanism*, edited by R. H. Meadow, pp. 5–12. Prehistory Press, Madison.

1998 Sociocultural complexity without the state: The Indus civilization. In *Archaic States*, edited by G. M. Feinman, pp. 261–291. School of American Research, Santa Fe.

1999 *Indus Age: The Beginnings*. University of Pennsylvania Press, Philadelphia.

2002a Archaeology of the Harappan civilization: An annotated list of excavations and surveys. In *Indian Archaeology in Retrospect* Vol. 2. *Protohistory, Archaeology of the Harappan Civilization*, edited by S. Settar and R. Korisettar, pp. 421–482. Indian Council of Historical Research, Manohar, Delhi.

2002b Fifty years of Harappan archaeology: The study of the Indus civilization since Indian independence. In *Indian Archaeology in Retrospect* Vol. 2. *Protohistory, Archaeology of the Harappan Civilization*, edited by S. Settar and R. Korisettar, pp. 1–46. Indian Council of Historical Research, Manohar, Delhi.

2002c *Indus Civilization: A Contemporary Perspective*. AltaMira Press, Walnut Creek, CA.

Possehl, G. L., and P. Rissman
1992 The chronology of prehistoric India: From earliest times to the Iron Age. In *Chronologies in Old World Archaeology* Vol. 1, edited by R. W. Ehrich, pp. 465–490, 447–473. University of Chicago Press, Chicago.

Pracchia, S., M. Tosi, and E. Vidali
1985 On the type, distribution and extent of craft industries at Mohenjo-Daro. In *South Asian Archaeology 1983* Vol. 1, edited by J. Schotsmans and M. Taddei, pp. 207–248. Instituto Universitario Orientale, Naples.

Puri, B. N.
1966 *Cities of Ancient India*. Meenakshi Prakashan, Bombay.

Quigley, C.
1961 *The Evolution of Civilizations: An Introduction to historical analysis*. Macmillan, New York.

Quigley, D.
1993 *The Interpretation of Caste*. Clarendon Press, Oxford.

Quivron, G.
1994 The pottery sequence from 2700 to 2400 at Nausharo, Baluchistan. In *South Asian Archaeology 1993* Vol. 2, edited by A. Parpola and P. Koskikallio, pp. 629–644. Suomalainen Tiedeakatemia, Helsinki.

1997 Incised and painted marks on the pottery of Mehrgarh and Nausharo-Baluchistan. In *South Asian Archaeology 1995* Vol. 1, edited by R. Allchin and B. Allchin, pp. 45–62. Science Publishers, Cambridge.

2000 Evolution of the mature Indus pottery style in the light of the excavations at Nausharo, Pakistan. *East and West* 50(1–4):147–190.

Raghunath, S. N.
1984 Lothal "dockyard" was a fishing engine. *Quarterly Journal of the Mythic Society* 75:294–300.

Raikes, R. L.
1968 Kalibangan: Death from natural causes. *Antiquity* XLII(168):286–291.

1979 The Mohenjo-Daro floods: The debate continues. In *South Asian Archaeology 1977* Vol. 1, edited by M. Taddei, pp. 561–566. Instituto Universitario Orientale, Naples.

Ramanujan, A. K.
1970 Towards an anthology of city images. In *Urban India: Society, Space, and Image*, edited by R. G. Fox, pp. 224–244. Duke University, Durham, NC.

Rangarajan, L. N.
1992 *The Arthasastra, Edited, Rearranged, Translated and Introduced*. Penguin Books, New Delhi.

Rao, S. R.
1963 A 'Persian Gulf' seal from Lothal. *Antiquity* 37:96–99.

1968 Contacts between Lothal and Susa. In *Proceedings of the Twenty-Sixth International Congress of Orientalists, New Delhi, 4–10 January 1964* Vol. II, pp. 35–37. Bhandarkar Oriental Research Institute, Poona.

1969 Lothal: Le port de l'empire de l'Indus. *Archaeologia* 29:64–73.

1973 *Lothal and the Indus Civilization.* Asia Publishing House, Bombay.

1979a Contacts between Lothal and Susa. In *Ancient Cities of the Indus*, edited by G. L. Possehl, pp. 174–178. Vikas Publishing House PVT LTD, New Delhi.

1979b *Lothal: A Harappan Port Town (1955–62)* Vol. 1. Memoirs of the Archaeological Survey of India 78. Archaeological Survey of India, New Delhi.

1979c A "Persian Gulf" Seal from Lothal. In *Ancient Cities of the Indus* Vol. 37, edited by G. L. Possehl, pp. 148–150. Carolina Academic Press, Durham, N.C.

1985 *Lothal: A Harappan Port Town (1955–62)* Vol. 2. Memoirs of the Archaeological Survey of India 78. Archaeological Survey of India, New Delhi.

Rau, W.

1956 *Stadt und Gesellschaft im alten Indien.* Otto Harrassowitz, Wiesbaden.

1971 *Weben und Flechten im vedischen Indien.* Akademie der Wissenschaften und der Literature. Abhandlungen der geistes—und sozialwissenschafteichen Klasse, Nr. 11. Verlag der Akademie der Wissenschaften und der Literatur, Mainz.

1972 *Töpferei and Tongeschirr im vedischen Indien.* Abhandlungen der geistes—und sozialwissenschaftlichen Klasse, Nr. 10. Verlag der Akademie der Wissenschaften und der Literatur, Mainz.

1974 *Metalle und Metallgeräte im vedischen Indien.* Steiner, Wiesbaden.

1976 *The Meaning of Pur in Vedic literature.* Wihelm Fink Verlag, München.

1983 *Zur Vedischen Altertumskunde.* Abhandlungen der Geistes—und Sozialwissenschaftlichen Klasse, Jahrg. 1983, Nr. 1. Akademie der Wissenschaften und der Literatur, Meinz.

Ray, N.

1978 Rural-urban dichotomy in Indian tradition and history. *Annals of the Bhandarkar Oriental Research Institute* LVIII–LIX:863–892.

Ray, S. C.

1989 Stratigraphic evidence of coins from excavations at Mathura. In *Mathura: The Cultural Heritage*, edited by D. M. Srinivisan, pp. 140–145. American Institute of Indian Studies, New Delhi.

Redfield, R.

1947 The folk society. *American Journal of Sociology* 52(4):293–308.

1953a The natural history of the folk society. *Social Forces* 31(3):224–8.

1953b *The Primitive World and Its Transformations.* Cornell University Press, New York.

1962 Civilizations as things thought about. In *Human Nature and the Study of Society: The Papers of Robert Redfield*, edited by M. P. Redfield, pp. 364–375. University of Chicago Press, Chicago.

Redfield, R., and M. B. Singer

1954 The cultural role of cities. *Economic Development and Cultural Change* 3:53–73.

Redman, C. L.

1978 *The Rise of Civilization.* W. H. Freeman and Company, San Francisco.

Reed, N.
1964 *The Caste War of Yucatan*. Stanford University Press, Stanford.

Renfrew, C.
1972 *The Emergence of Civilization*. Methuen, London.

Rich, J., and A. Wallace-Hadrill (editors)
1997 *City and Country in the Ancient World*. Routledge, London.

Riquetti, V. de, Marquis de Mirabeau
1756 *L'Ami des Hommes, ou, Traite de la Population*. Avignon.

Rocher, L.
1986 *The Puranas*. A History of Indian Literature 2, Vol. 3. Otto Harrassowitz, Wiesbaden.

Roth, R.
1860 *Über den Mythus von den fünf Menschengeschlechtern und die indische Lehre von den vier Weltaltern*. Gedruckt bei L. F. Fues, Tübingen.

Roy, T. N.
1983 *The Ganges Civilization: A Critical Archaeological Study of the Painted Grey Ware and Northern Black Polished Ware Periods of the Ganga Plains of India*. The Heritage of Ancient India No. 2. Ramanand Vidya Bhawan, New Delhi.

1986 *A Study of Northern Black Polished Ware Culture: An Iron Age Culture of India*. Ramanand Vidya Bhawan, New Delhi.

Roy, U. N.
1954 Fortification of cities in ancient India. *Indian Historical Quarterly* 30(3):237–244.

Sahni, D. R.
1916–1917 Harappa, District Mongomery. *Annual Progress Report of the Superintendent, Hindu and Buddhist Monuments, Northern Circle* 1917:7.

1920–1922 Excavations at Harappa. *Annual Progress Report of the Superintendent, Hindu and Buddhist Monuments, Northern Circle* 1921:8–26.

1923–1924 Exploration and research, northern circle, Punjab, Harappa. *Annual Report of the Archaeological Survey of India, Western Circle* 1923–23:52–54.

1924–1925 Explorations, northern circle, Punjab, Harappa. *Annual Report of the Archaeological Survey of India* 1924–1925:73–80.

1936 Excavations at Bairat. *Annual Report of the Archaeological Survey of India* 1935–36:84–87.

Sali, S. A.
1986 *Daimabad 1976–1979*. Memoirs of Archaeological Survey of India 83. Archaeological Survey of India, New Delhi.

Samzun, A.
1992 Observations on the characteristics of the pre-Harappan remains, pottery, and artifacts at Nausharo, Pakistan (2700–2500 B.C.). In *South Asian Archaeology 1989*, edited by C. Jarrige, pp. 245–252. Monographs in World Archaeology, 14. Prehistory Press, Madison.

Sarao, K. T. S.
1990 *Urban Centres and Urbanization as Reflected in the Pali Vinaya and Sutta Pitakas*. Vidyanidhi, Delhi.

Sarcina, A.
1978–1979 A statistical assessment of house patterns at Moenjo-Daro. *Mesopotamia* 13–14:155–199.

1979 The private house at Mohenjo-Daro. In *South Asian Archaeology 1977* Vol. 1, edited by M. Taddei, pp. 433–462. Istituto Universitario Orientale, Naples.

Scharfe, H.
1989 *The State in Indian Tradition*. Handbuch der Orientalistik. Zwiete Abteilung, Indien. E. J. Brill, Leiden.

1993 *Investigations in Kautalya's Manual of Political Science*. Second Revised Edition. Harrassowitz, Wiesbaden (First Edition 1968 Untersuchungen zur Staatsrechtslehre des Kautalya. Harrassowitz, Wiesbaden).

Schlingloff, D.
1969 *Die Altindische Stadt: eine vergleichende Untersuchung*. Abhandlungen der geistes—und socialwissenschaftlichen Klasse 5. L. C. Wittich, Mainz.

Schmokel, V. H.
1966 Zwischen Ur und Lothal: Die Seehandelsroute von Altmesopotamien zur Induskultur. *Forschungen und Fortschritte (Akademie-Verlag, Berlin)* 40(5):143–147.

Schwab, J.
1886 *Das altindische Thieropfer*. A. Deichert, Erlangen.

Sen, A.
1956 *Asoka's Edicts*. The Institute of Indology, Calcutta.

Sen, D. N.
1918 Sites in Rajgir Associated with Buddha and his Disciples. *Journal of the Bihar and Orissa Research Society* 113–135.

Service, E. R.
1975 *Origins of the State and Civilization: The Process of Cultural Evolution*. Norton, New York.

Shaffer, J. G.
1974 *Allahdino and the Mature Harappan: A Preliminary Report on the Cultural Stratigraphy*, Clevelend, Ohio.

1982 Harappan culture: A reconsideration. In *Harappan Civilization: A Contemporary Perspective*, edited by G. L. Possehl, pp. 41–50. Oxford and IBH Publishing, New Delhi.

1989 Mathura: A protohistoric perspective. In *Mathura: The Cultural Heritage*, edited by D. M. Srinivisan, pp. 171–180. American Institute of Indian Studies, New Delhi.

1992 The Indus Valley, Baluchistan and Helmand traditions: Neolithic through Bronze Age. In *Chronologies in Old World Archaeology*, Third Edition, Vols. 1–2, edited by R. W. Ehrich, pp. 441–64, 425–446. University of Chicago Press, Chicago.

1993 Reurbanization: The eastern Punjab and beyond. In *Urban Form and Meaning in South Asian: The Shaping of Cities from Prehistoric to Precolonial Times*, edited by H. Spodek and D. M. Srinivisan, pp. 53–67. National Gallery of Art.

Shaffer, J. G., and D. A. Lichtenstein
1989 Ethnicity and change in the Indus Valley cultural tradition. In *Old Problems and New Perspectives in the Archaeology of South Asia* Vol. 2, edited by J. M. Kenoyer, pp. 117–126. Wisconsin Archaeological Reports, F. and H. Printing Company, Madison.

Shar, G. M., and M. Vidale
1985 Surface evidence of craft activity in Chanhudaro, March, 1984. *Annali dell'Instituto Universitario Orientale* 45:585–98.

Sharma, A. K.
1977–1978 Locating the graves at Kalibangan. *Puratattva* 9:89–91.

1982 The Harappan Cemetery at Kalibangan: A Study. In *Harappan Civilization: A Contemporary Perspective*, pp. 297–299. Oxford and IBH Pub. Co., New Delhi.

1999 *The Departed Harappans of Kalibangan*. Sundeep Prakashan, New Delhi.

Sharma, G. R.

1958 Excavations at Kausambi, 1949–1955. *Annual Bibliography of Indian Archaeology* XVI:XXXVI–XLV.

1960 *The excavations at Kausambi (1957–1959). The Defences and the Syenaciti of the Purusamedha*. Department of Ancient History, Allahabad.

1969 *Excavations at Kausambi, 1949–1950*. Memoirs of the Archaeological Survey of India, No. 74 Archaeological Survey of India, New Delhi.

Sharma, J. P.

1968 *Republics in Ancient India c. 1500 B.C.–500 B. C.* E. J. Brill, Leiden.

Sharma, R. S.

1959 *Aspects of Political Ideas and Institutions in Ancient India*. Motilal Banarsidas, Delhi.

1966 *Light on Early Indian Economy and Society*. Manaktalas, Bombay.

1974 Iron and urbanisation in the Ganga Basin. *The Indian Historical Review* 1:98–103.

1975–1976 The Later Vedic phase and the Painted Grey Ware culture. *Puratattva* 8(1975–1976):63–67.

Sharma, Y. D.

1964 Remains of Early Historical cities. In *Archaeological Remains, Monuments and Museums* Vol. 1, edited by A. Ghosh, pp. 43–85. Archaeological Survey of India, New Delhi.

1973 Value of common painted ceramic designs from different sites as guide to chronology with special reference to pottery from Bara (Punjab). In *Radiocarbon and Indian Archaeology*, edited by D. P. Agrawal and A. Ghosh, pp. 222–230. Tata Institute of Fundamental Research, Bombay.

Shastri, A. M.

1979 *Kausambi Hoard of Maqha Coins: A Study of the Maqha Coinage Based on the Kausambi Hoard*. Nagpur University, Nagpur.

Simha, B.

1987 *Harappa Sabhyata aur Vaidic Sahitya*. Radhakrishna, Nayi Dilli.

1995 *The Vedic Harappans*. Aditya Prakashan, New Delhi.

Singh, G. P.

1994 *Early Indian Historical Tradition and Archaeology: Puranic Kingdoms and Dynasties with Genealogies, Relative Chronology and Date of Mahabharata War*. Reconstructing Indian History and Culture No. 3. D.K. Printworld, New Delhi.

Singh, P.

1987 Neolithic cultures of northern and northwestern India. In *Archaeology and History: Essays in Memory of Shri A. Ghosh* Vol. 1, edited by B. M. Pande and B. D. Chattopadhyaya, pp. 255–264. Agam Kala Prakashan, Delhi.

2002 The Neolithic cultures of northern and eastern India. In *Indian Archaeology in Retrospect* Vol I., *Prehistory, Archaeology of South Asia*, edited by S. Settar and R. Korisettar, pp. 127–150. Indian Council of Historical Research, Manohar, New Delhi.

Singh, S. B.
1979 *Archaeology of Pancala Region*. Adam, Delhi.

Sinha, B. P,. and L. A. Narain
1970 *Pataliputra Excavation, 1955–1956*. Directorate of Archaeology and Museums, Patna.

Sinha, B. P., and S. R. Roy
1969 *Vaisali Excavations, 1958–62*. The Directorate of Archaeology and Museums, Bihar, Patna.

Sinha, B. P., and B. S. Verma
1977 *Sonpur Excavations, 1956 and 1959–62*. Directorate of Archaeology and Museums, Bihar, Patna.

Sinha, K. K.
1967 *Excavations at Sravasti, 1959*. Benares Hindu University, Varanasi.

1973 Stratigraphy and chronology of early Kausambi—A Reappraisal. In *Radiocarbon and Indian Archaeology*, edited by D. P. Agrawal and A. Ghosh, pp. 231–238. Tata Institute of Fundamental Research, Bombay.

Smith, B. K.
1994 *Classifying the Universe: The Ancient Indian Varna System and the Origins of Caste*. Oxford University Press, New York.

Smith, J. Z.
1987a The domestication of sacrifice. In *Violent Origins: Ritual Killing and Cultural Formation*, edited by R. G. Hamerton-Kelly, pp. 191–205. Stanford University Press, Stanford, CA.

1987b Response to Walter Burkert's "The Problem of Ritual Killing". In *Violent Origins: Ritual Killing and Cultural Formation*, edited by R. G. Hamerton-Kelly, pp. 179. Stanford University Press, Stanford, CA.

Smith, M. L.
2003 Early walled cities of the Indian subcontinent as "small worlds". In *The Social Construction of Ancient Cities*, edited by M. L. Smith, pp. 269–289. Smithsonian Institution, Washington.

2006 The archaeology of South Asian cities. *Journal of Archaeological Research* 14:97–142.

Smith, R. M.
1966 On the white Yajurveda Vamsa. *East and West* 16(1–2):112–25.

Somapala, J.
1994 *Handbook of Pāli Literature*. Karunaratna & Sons, Colombo, Sri Lanka.

Sorokin, P. A.
1948 *The Reconstruction of Humanity*. Beacon Press, Boston.

1992 *Chelovek, Tsivilizatsiia, Obshchestvo*. Izdatelstvo Politicheskoi Literatury, Moskva.

Southall, A.W.
1990 *The City in Time and Space*. Cambridge University Press, Cambridge.

Spellman, J. W.
1964 *Political Theory of Ancient India: A Study of Kingship from the Earliest Times to circa A.D. 300*. Clarendon Press, Oxford.

Spengler, O.
1918 *Der Untergang des Abendlandes: Umrisse einer Morphologie der Weltgeschichte*. Wilhelm Braumüller, Wien.

1926 *The Decline of the West*, C. F. Atkinson Translator and Editor. A. A. Knopf, New York.

Spooner, B. D.
1913 Mr. Ratan Tata's Excavations at Pataliputra. *Annual Report of the Archaeological Survey of India* 1912–1913:53–86.

1914 Excavations at Basarh. *Annual Report of the Archaeological Survey of India* 1913–1914: 98–185.

Srinivisan, D. M. (editor)
1989 *Mathura: The Cultural Heritage*. Manohar Publications for American Institute of Indian Studies, New Delhi.

Srivastava, H. L.
1936–1937 *Excavations at Harappa*. Annual Report of the Archaeological Survey of India 1936–1937:39–41.

Staal, F.
1961 Nambudiri, Veda recitation. *Disputationes Rheno-Trajectinae* 5. Mouton, The Hague.

1983 *Agni, the Vedic Ritual of the Fire Altar*. Asian Humanities Press, Berkeley.

Stein, A., Sir
1931 *An Archaeological Tour in Gedrosia*. Memoirs of the Archaeological Survey of India 43. Government of India Central Publication Branch, Calcutta.

Steinkeller, P.
2006 City and countryside in third millennium Babylonia. In *Settlement in Society. Essays Dedicated to Robert McCormick Adams*. Cotsen Institute, UCLA, Los Angeles, CA.

Stietencron, H., von, K. P. Gietz, A. Malinar, A. Kollman, P. Schreiner and M. Brockington (editors)
1992 *Epic and Puranic Bibliography (up to 1985), Annotated and with Indexes*. Otto Harrassowitz, Wiesbaden.

Street, B. V.
1984 *Literacy in Theory and Practice*. Cambridge University Press, Cambridge.

Taylor, W. W.
1948 *A Study of Archaeology*. Southern Illinois University Press, Carbondale.

Thakur, V. K.
1981 *Urbanisation in Ancient India*. Abhinav Publishers, New Delhi.

Thapar, B. K.
1973 New traits of the Indus civilization at Kalibangan: An appraisal. In *South Asian Archaeology*, edited by N. Hammond, pp. 85–104. Noyes Press, Park Ridge.

1975 Kalibangan: A Harappan metropolis beyond the Indus Valley. *Expedition* 17(2):19–32.

1977 Climate during the period of the Indus Civilization: Evidence from Kalibangan. In *Ecology and Archaeology of Western India: Proceedings of a Workshop Held at the Physical Research Laboratory, Ahmedabad, February 23–26, 1976*, edited by D. P. Agrawal and B. M. Pande, pp. 67–74. Concept Publications, Delhi.

1987 Fresh light on the Neolithic cultures of India. In *Archaeology and History: Essays in Memory of Shri A. Ghosh* Vol. 1, edited by B. M. Pande and B. D. Chattopadhyaya, pp. 247–254. Agam Kala Prakashan, Delhi.

Thapar, R.
1976 Puranic Lineages and Archaeological Cultures. *Puratattva* 8:86–98.

1978 *Ancient Indian Social History: Some Interpretations*. Orient Longman New Delhi.

1984 *From Lineage to State: Social Formations in the Mid-First Millennium B.C. in the Ganga Valley*. Oxford University Press, Bombay.

1989 The early history of Mathura: Up to and including the Mauryan period. In *Mathura: The Cultural Heritage*, edited by D. M. Srinivisan, pp. 12–18. American Institute of Indian Studies, New Delhi.

2000a *History and Beyond*. Oxford University Press, New Delhi.

2000b Time as metaphor of history. In *History and Beyond*, edited by R. Thapar. Oxford University Press, New Delhi.

2003 *Early India: From the Origins to AD 1300*. University of California Press, Berkeley.

Toynbee, A. J.
1934–61 *A Study of History*. Oxford University Press, Oxford.

Trautman, T. R.
1971 *Kautilya and the Arthasastra: A Statistical Investigation of the Authorship and Evolution of the Text*. E. J. Brill, Leiden.

Tripathi, V.
1975 *The Painted Grey Ware: An Iron Age Culture of Northern India*. Concept Pub., Delhi.

Urban, G., and M. Jansen
1983 *Forschungsprojekt DFG Mohenjo-Daro: Dokumentation in der Archäologie: Techniken, Methoden, Analysen*. Veröffentlichungen des Geodätischen Instituts der Rheinish-Westfälischen Technischen Hochschule Aachen, Nr. 34. [s.n.], Aachen.

Vansina, J.
1965 *Oral Tradition: A Study in Historical Methodology*. Aldine Pub. Co., Chicago.

Varma, K. C.
1978–1979 The Kaliyuga era and the ignored glimpses of Indian antiquity. *Annals of the Bhandarkar Oriental Research Institute* LVIII–LIX.

Vats, M. S.
1926–1927 Harappa. *Annual Report of the Archaeological Survey of India* 1926–1927:97–108.

1927–1928 Excavations at Harappa. *Annual Report of the Archaeological Survey of India* 1927–1928:83–90.

1928–1929 Excavations at Harappa. *Annual Report of the Archaeological Survey of India* 1928–1929:76–85.

1929–1930 Excavations at Harappa. *Annual Report of the Archaeological Survey of India* 1929–1930:121–131.

1930–1934 Excavations at Harappa. *Annual Report of the Archaeological Survey of India* 1930–31, 1931–32, 1932–33, 1933–34:73–90.

1940 *Excavations at Harappa*. Government of India Press, Delhi.

Venkataramayya, M.
1981 *Sravasti*. Second Edition (First Edition 1956). Archaeological Survey of India, New Delhi.

Vogel, J. P.
1905 Excavations at Kasia. *Annual Report of the Archaeological Survey of India* 1904–5:43–58.

1908 Excavations at Saheth-Maheth. *Annual Report of the Archaeological Survey of India* 1907–8:81–131.

1909a Excavations at Kasia. *Annual Report of the Archaeological Survey of India* 1906–1907:43–67.

1909b Excavations at Kasia. *Annual Report of the Archaeological Survey of India* 1905–6:61–85.

1909c The Mathura school of sculpture. *Annual Report of the Archaeological Survey of India* 1906–7:137–60.

1914 The Mathura school of sculpture. *Annual Report of the Archaeological Survey of India* 1909–10:44–67.

1915 Explorations at Mathura. *Annual Report of the Archaeological Survey of India* 1911–12:120–134.

1994 *Antiquities of Chamba State*. Archaeological Survey of India, New Delhi.

Voltaire (Arouet, F. M.)

1756 *Essay sur l'Histoire Générale et sur les Moeurs et l'Esprit des Nations, depuis Charlemagne jusqu'en nos Jours*. Cramer, Geneve.

1769 *Essai sur les Moeurs et l'Esprit des Nations, et sur les Principaux faits de l'Histoire, depuis Charlemagne jusqu'à Louis XIII*. Geneve.

Waddel, L. A.

1892 *Discovery of the Exact Site of Asoka's Classic Capital of Pataliputra, the Patalibothra of the Greeks, and the Description of the Superficial Remains*. Bengal Secretariat Press, Calcutta.

1903 *Report on the Excavations at Pataliputra (Patna): The Palibothra of the Greeks*. Bengal Secretariat Press, Calcutta.

Weber, M.

1922 *Wirtschaft und Gesellschaft*. Grundriss der Socialökonomik III. Abt., J. C. B. Mohr (P. Siebeck), Tübingen.

1958 *The City*. Translated by D. Martindale and G. Neuwirth. The Free Press, New York.

Wheatley, P.

1971 *The Pivot of the Four Quarters: A Preliminary Enquiry into the Origins and Character of the Ancient Chinese City*. University Press, Edinburgh.

1972 The concept of urbanism. In *Man, Settlement and Urbanism*, edited by P. J. Ucko, R. Tringham and G. W. Dimbleby, pp. 601–637. Duckworth, London.

Wheeler, R. E. M.

1947 Harappa 1946: The defenses and cemetery R-37. *Ancient India* 3:58–130.

1962 *The Indus Civilization*. The Cambridge History of India, Supplementary Volume. Cambridge University Press, Cambridge.

White, H.

1973 *Metahistory: The Historical Imagination in Nineteenth-Century Europe*. John Hopkins University Press, Baltimore.

Wilford, F.

1794–1808 On the chronology of the Hindus. *Asiatic Researches* 2, 5:88–113.

Wilson, J. A.

1951 *The Burden of Egypt: An Interpretation of Ancient Egyptian Culture*. University of Chicago Press, Chicago.

Winkelmann, S.
1994 Intercultural relations between Iran, central Asia and northwestern India in the light of squatting stone sculptures from Mohenjo-Daro. In *South Asian Archaeology 1993* Vol. 2, edited by A. Parpola and P. Koskikallio, pp. 815–832. Suomalainen Tiedeakatemia, Helsinki.

Wiser, W. H.
1936 *The Hindu Jajmani System: A Socio-Economic System Interrelating Members of a Hindu Village Community in Services*. Lucknow Publishing House, Lucknow, UP.

Witzel, M.
1987 On the localisation of Vedic texts and schools. In *India and the Ancient World: History, Trade and Culture before A.D. 650*, edited by G. Pollet, pp. 173–213. Departement Orientalistiek, Leuven.

1989 The realm of the Kurus: Origin and development of the first state in India. In *Nihon Minami Aija Gakkai Zenkoku Taikai, Hokoku Yoshi (Summaries of the Congress of the Japanese Association for South Asian Sudies)*, Kyoto.

1991 On early Indian historical writing: The role of the Vamsavalis. *Journal of the Japanese Association for South Asian Studies* 2:1–57.

1995a Early Indian history: Linguistic and textual parameters. In T*he Indo-Aryans of Ancient South Asia: Language, Material Culture and Ethnicity*, edited by G. Erdosy, pp. 85–125. Walter de Gruyter, Berlin.

1995b Ṛgvedic history: Poets, chieftains and polities. In *The Indo-Aryans of Ancient South Asia: Language, Material Culture and Ethnicity*, edited by G. Erdosy, pp. 307–352. Walter de Gruyter, Berlin.

1997a The development of the Vedic canon and its schools: The social and political milieu. In *Inside the Texts, Beyond the Texts: New Approaches to the Study of the Vedas*, edited by M. Witzel, pp. 257–345. Harvard Oriental Series, Opera Minora, Vol. 2. Department of Sanskrit and Indian Literature, Cambridge.

1997b Early Sanskritization: Origins and development of the Kuru state. In *Recht, Staat und Verwaltung im klassischen Indien: The State, the Law, and Administration in Classical India*, edited by B. Kolver, pp. 27–52. R. Oldenbeourg Verlag Munchen, Munchen.

2001 Autochthonous Aryans? The evidence from old Indian and Iranian texts. *Electronic Journal of Vedic Studies* 7(3):1–115.

Yule, P.
1988 Harappan 'Snarling Iron' from Chanhu-Daro. *Antiquity* 62(234):116–118.

Yule, P., and S. R. Rao
1982 Lothal, Stadt der Harappa-Kultur in Nordwestindien. *Materialien zur Allgemeinen und Vergleichenden Archäologie*, Bd. 9. Beck, München.

Index

agency, xx, xxvi, 4–5, 29, 167, 185, 187

Augustine, Saint, ix, 8, 17–21, 189, 201, 225

Bakhtin, Mikhail M., xxi, xxvi, 2–3, 5, 201

Bonazzoli, Giorgio, 9, 203

Braudel, Fernand, x, 2, 7, 153–156, 193–194, 204

caste, xxi, 11–12, 14, 173–175, 194–195, 202, 208–209, 218–220, 222, 225–227, 229, 233

Central Place Theory, 15, 17, 19, 21

Chakrabarti, D. K., xxxi, 2, 7, 13–14, 31, 168–170, 177, 188, 190, 195, 205, 211, 219, 221

Childe, V. Gordon, x, xvii, 10–13, 15, 153, 156, 164–165, 180, 193–194, 206

Christaller, Walter, xx, 17, 19–20, 23, 189, 206

Civitas Dei (*The City of God,*) 17

Civitas Terrena (*The Earthly City*), 17

Collingwood, R. G., vii, xx, xxiii, 2–3, 5, 9, 22, 92, 150, 193, 206

Croce, Benedetto, xxvi, 206

Cunningham, Alexander, 7, 31, 33,47, 57, 68–69, 77, 83, 115, 190, 206

Doxiades, K. A., ix, 17, 20, 189, 208

Dvāpara Yuga, 159–161, 170, 173

ekistics, 17, 20, 189, 208

Erdosy, George, i, 7, 13–14, 24, 29, 31, 49, 170, 177, 188, 190, 209–210, 218, 236

Fairservis, Walter A., Jr., xviii, xxi, xxiii, 10, 95–96, 98, 169, 191, 210, 216

free will, xxvi, 4

Fustel de Coulanges, N. D., 20, 211

Gupta, S. P., xxx–xxxi, 1, 11, 74, 188, 202, 210, 212, 214, 219

heterarchy / heterarchical, xxi, xxvii, 11–12, 110, 117, 121, 140, 147–148, 163–164, 175–177, 181, 209

hierarchy / hierarchical, xviii–xix, xxi, xxiii, xxviii, 10–12, 15, 21, 32, 90, 110, 117, 121, 140, 147–148, 160, 163–164, 172–177, 181

historical agents, ix, xxi, xxvi–xxvii, 3–7, 9, 11, 13–15, 21–22, 29, 92, 150, 153, 156, 160, 167–169, 175, 180, 183–185, 187

history (definition of, theory of, in the Yuga Story), xxi–xxii, 2–10, 156–161

Indian Style, the concept of, 14, 194, 240

Jarrige, J.-F., 132–136, 147, 192–193, 200, 203, 207, 209, 215–216, 223, 226, 230

Kali Yuga, 157, 159–161, 163, 170, 173, 194, 211

Kenoyer, J. Mark, xviii, xxiii, xxx–xxxi, 10–11, 14–15, 111–112, 115–117, 130, 142–144, 172, 174, 188, 192, 195, 200, 202, 207, 209, 211, 217–218, 223, 231

Kṛta Yuga, 157, 160–161, 181

Lal, B. B., xxx, 1, 7, 11–12, 31, 43–49, 54, 117–119, 121, 126, 169, 174, 188, 190, 192, 197, 202, 210, 214, 216–217, 219–220

Levy, Robert I., 17, 20–21, 220

literacy, xxviii, 170–172, 181, 213, 225, 234

longue durée, xxvi, 4–5, 9, 155, 163, 240

Malik, S. C., 10–11, 14, 174, 167, 194, 200, 221

Marshall, John H., Sir, xi, 10, 31, 38–43, 68, 77, 111, 128, 130, 132, 170, 179, 190–192, 215, 221–222

metahistory, 2, 7–10, 187, 236

mnemonic/s, x, xxviii, 167, 170–173, 181, 195

mythology, 5, 9–10, 157, 175

Neolithic, ii, 14, 38, 165, 167–168, 171, 178, 180, 185, 187, 192, 195, 218, 231–232, 234

orality / oral traditions, x, xxi, xxviii, 9, 23, 167, 170–172, 181, 186, 195, 225

Paleolithic, 3–4, 168, 178

Piggott, Stuart, 10, 30, 101, 188, 226

positivism/positivist, 3, 14–15, 18, 21

Possehl, Gregory L., xxx–xxxi, 10–11, 95, 100–101, 106, 128–129, 140, 168, 172, 192, 195–196, 202, 207–208, 210, 213–214, 216, 223, 227–228

postmodernism / postmodern, 3, 188

Ramanujan, A. K., 13, 188, 228

reflexivity / reflexive, 3

rural lifestyle, x, 168–170, 181, 186

rural roots, 177

sacrifice, xxi, 50, 157–158, 177–178, 194–195, 201, 204, 208–209, 213–214, 217, 233

Schlingloff, Dieter, 13, 29, 188, 230

Simha, Bhagavana, 1, 11–12, 174, 188, 232

Smith, B. K., 173–175, 233

Smith, J. Z., 178, 233

Smith, M. L., 14–15, 171, 173–175, 178, 195, 233

Smith, R. M., 171, 195, 233

Spengler, Oswald, 3, 17–20, 23, 154, 193, 233

state, the, xvii–xxiv, 5–7, 9–12, 15, 18, 22–23, 31–32, 154, 163, 180–181, 184–185, 194, 200, 204, 214, 217, 227, 230–231, 234, 236–237

structures / structuralism (figurative), xx, xxvi–xxviii, 3–5, 8–9, 11, 219–21, 29–30, 92, 150–151, 160–164, 167, 180–181, 185–187, 189, 194

subjective humanism, ix, xxvi, 4–5

text/s (concept of, texts as historical sources), 1–2, 7–8

Thapar, Romila, xxxi, 7, 177, 194, 234

Toynbee, Arnold, 3, 154–156, 193, 234

Tretā Yuga, xxvii–xxviii, 26–27, 157–165, 168, 170, 173, 175–177

Varṇas, a system of, xxviii, 26, 158–159, 161–165, 167, 173, 175–178, 194

Varṇāśrama, a system of, 26, 158–159, 161–165, 167, 173, 175–178, 194

village/s, xviii, xx–xxi, xxix, 13,18, 20, 26–27, 32, 42, 93, 96, 101, 135, 146, 148, 158, 162–163, 168–169, 172, 177, 189–190, 213, 236

Weber, Max, 17, 19–20, 180, 189, 236

Wheeler, R. E. M., 10, 30, 111–114, 128, 130, 192, 200, 236

White, Hayden, xxvi, 4–5, 8–9, 160, 187, 236

writing, xix, xxi–xxii, xxviii, 4, 8, 11, 13–14, 91, 110, 117, 144, 147–148, 154, 165, 170–172, 176, 186, 194–195, 210, 212, 236

Yuga Story, x, xii, xxvii, 8, 156–157, 160, 162–164, 184, 194–195, 206